P9-DZA-931

WATERLOO PUBLIC LIBRARY
3 3420 00033 0796

TRANSLATOR AND EDITOR:
Rabbi Israel V. Berman

MANAGING EDITOR:
Baruch Goldberg

ASSOCIATE TRANSLATORS AND EDITORS:
Dr. Jeffrey M. Green
Rabbi Moshe Sober
Rabbi Eli Touger
Rabbi Avraham Weiss

COPY EDITORS:
Alec Israel
Michael Plotkin

PRODUCTION MANAGER:
Meir Hanegbi

BOOK DESIGNER:
Ben Gasner

GRAPHIC ARTIST:
Michael Etkin

TECHNICAL STAFF:
Moshe Greenvald
Chana Lawrence
Rachel Lichtenstein

SOFTWARE CONSULTANT
Daniel Weissman

Random House Staff

PRODUCTION MANAGER:
Linda Kaye

ART DIRECTOR:
Bernard Klein

CHIEF COPY EDITOR:
Mitchell Ivers

The Talmud

The Steinsaltz Edition

Volume I

Tractate Bava Metzia

Part I

VOLUME I

TRACTATE BAVA METZIA

PART I

RANDOM HOUSE
NEW YORK

THE TALMUD

תלמוד בבלי

THE STEINSALTZ EDITION

Commentary by Rabbi Adin Steinsaltz

 Published in the United States by Random House, Inc., New York, and simultaneously in Canada by Random House of Canada Limited, Toronto.

This is an English translation of *The Steinsaltz Talmud: Volume I: Tractate Bava Metzia: Part I*, originally published in Hebrew by The Israel Institute for Talmudic Publications, Jerusalem, Israel in 1988. Copyright by The Israel Institute for Talmudic Publications.

Library of Congress Cataloging-in-Publication Data

Talmud. English.
The Talmud : the Steinsaltz edition / the Talmud with commentary by
Adin Steinsaltz
p. cm.
ISBN 0-394-57666-7 (v. 1)
ISBN 0-394-57665-9 (a reference guide)
1. Talmud—Commentaries I. Steinsaltz, Adin. II. Title.
BM499.5.E4 1989 296.1'250521—dc20 89-42911

Manufactured in the United States of America
98765432
First American Edition

ספר זה מוקדש ע״י
ר׳ משה וואהל
לזכר הוריו
הרב מרדכי מנחם ב״ר שמואל וואהל זצ״ל
ומרת מרים רחל בת ר׳ משה זילבערנאגעל ז״ל
שכל חייהם התמסרו להאדרת התורה וערכיה הנצחיים

Dedicated by
Mr. Maurice Wohl
in loving memory of his parents,
Rabbi Mordechai Menachem (Max) Wohl
and Miriam Rachel Wohl,
London, England
whose lives were dedicated to the enhancement of the Torah

The Steinsaltz Talmud in English

The English edition of the Steinsaltz Talmud is a translation and adaptation of the Hebrew edition. It includes most of the additions and improvements that characterize the Hebrew version, but it has been adapted and expanded especially for the English reader. This edition has been designed to meet the needs of advanced students capable of studying from standard Talmud editions, as well as of beginners, who know little or no Hebrew and have had no prior training in studying the Talmud.

The overall structure of the page is similar to that of the traditional pages in the standard printed editions. The text is placed in the center of the page, and alongside it are the main auxiliary commentaries. At the bottom of the page and in the margins are additions and supplements.

The original Hebrew-Aramaic text, which is framed in the center of each page, is exactly the same as that in the traditional Talmud (although material that was removed by non-Jewish censors has been restored on the basis of manuscripts and old printed editions). The main innovation is that this Hebrew-Aramaic text has been completely vocalized and punctuated, and all the terms usually abbreviated have been fully spelled out. In order to retain the connection with the page numbers of the standard editions, these are indicated at the head of every page.

We have placed a *Literal Translation* on the right-hand side of the page, and its punctuation has been introduced into the Talmud text, further helping the student to orientate himself. The *Literal Translation* is intended to help the student to learn the meaning of specific Hebrew and Aramaic words. By comparing the original text with this translation, the reader develops an understanding of the Talmudic text and can follow the words and sentences in the original. Occasionally, however, it has not been possible to present an exact literal translation of the original text, because it is so different in structure from English. Therefore we have added certain auxiliary words, which are indicated in square brackets. In other cases it would make no sense to offer a literal translation of a Talmudic idiom, so we have provided a close English equivalent of the original meaning, while a note, marked "lit.," explaining the literal meaning of the words, appears in parentheses. Our purpose in presenting this literal translation was to give the student an appreciation of the terse and enigmatic nature of the Talmud itself, before the arguments are opened up by interpretation.

Nevertheless, no one can study the Talmud without the assistance of commentaries. The main aid to understanding the Talmud provided by this edition is the *Translation and Commentary,* appearing on the left side of the page. This is Rabbi Adin Steinsaltz's highly regarded Hebrew interpretation of the Talmud, translated into English, adapted and expanded.

This commentary is not merely an explanation of difficult passages. It is an integrated exposition of the entire text. It includes a full translation of the Talmud text, combined with explanatory remarks. Where the translation in the commentary reflects the literal translation, it has been set off in bold type. It has also been given the same reference numbers that are found both in the original text and in the literal translation. Moreover, each section of the commentary begins with a few words of the Hebrew-Aramaic text. These reference numbers and paragraph headings allow the reader to move from one part of the page to another with ease.

There are some slight variations between the literal translation and the words in bold face appearing in the *Translation and Commentary.* These variations are meant to enhance understanding, for a juxtaposition of the literal translation and the sometimes freer translation in the commentary will give the reader a firmer grasp of the meaning.

The expanded *Translation and Commentary* in the left-hand column is intended to provide a conceptual understanding of the arguments of the Talmud, their form, content, context, and significance. The commentary also brings out the logic of the questions asked by the Sages and the assumptions they made.

Rashi's traditional commentary has been included in the right-hand column, under the *Literal Translation.* We have left this commentary in the traditional "Rashi script," but all quotations of the Talmud text appear in standard square type, the abbreviated expressions have all been printed in full, and Rashi's commentary is fully punctuated.

Since the *Translation and Commentary* cannot remain cogent and still encompass all the complex issues that arise in the Talmudic discussion, we have included a number of other features, which are also found in Rabbi Steinsaltz's Hebrew edition.

At the bottom of the page, under the *Translation and Commentary,* is the *Notes* section, containing additional material on issues raised in the text. These notes deepen understanding of the Talmud in various ways. Some provide a deeper and more profound analysis of the issues discussed in the text, with regard to individual points and to the development of the entire discussion. Others explain Halakhic concepts and the terms of Talmudic discourse.

The *Notes* contain brief summaries of the opinions of many of the major commentators on the Talmud, from the period after the completion of the Talmud to the present. Frequently the *Notes* offer interpretations different from that presented in the commentary, illustrating the richness and depth of Rabbinic thought.

The *Halakhah* section appears below the *Notes.* This provides references to the authoritative legal decisions reached over the centuries by the Rabbis in their discussions of the matters dealt with in the Talmud. It explains what reasons led to these Halakhic decisions and the close connection between the Halakhah today and the Talmud and its various interpreters. It should be noted that the summary of the Halakhah presented here is not meant to serve as a reference source for actual religious practice but to introduce the reader to Halakhic conclusions drawn from the Talmudic text.

English commentary and expanded translation of the text, making it readable and comprehensible

Hebrew/Aramaic text of the Talmud, fully vocalized, and punctuated

Literal translation of the Talmud text into English

REALIA

קַלְתָּהּ **Her basket.** The source of this word is the Greek κάλαθος, *kalathos*, and it means a basket with a narrow base.

Illustration from a Greek drawing depicting such a basket of fruit.

CONCEPTS

פֵּאָה ***Pe'ah.*** **One of the presents left for the poor** (מַתְּנוֹת עֲנִיִּים). The Torah forbids harvesting "the corners of your field," so that the produce left standing may be harvested and kept by the poor (Leviticus 19:9).

The Torah did not specify a minimum amount of produce to be left as *pe'ah*. But the Sages stipulated that it must be at least one-sixtieth of the crop.

Pe'ah is set aside only from crops that ripen at one time and are harvested at one time. The poor are allowed to use their own initiaitve to reap the *pe'ah* left in the fields. But the owner of an orchard must see to it that each of the poor gets a fixed share of the *pe'ah* from places that are difficult to reach. The poor come to collect *pe'ah* three times a day. The laws of *pe'ah* are discussed in detail in tractate *Pe'ah*.

Marginal notes provide essential background information

TRANSLATION AND COMMENTARY

[1]**and her husband threw her a bill of divorce into her lap or into her basket,** which she was carrying on her head, [2]would you say **here, too,** that **she would not be divorced?** Surely we know that the law is that she *is* divorced in such a case, as the Mishnah (*Gittin* 77a) states explicitly!

אָמַר לֵיהּ [3]Rav Ashi **said** in reply **to** Ravina: The woman's **basket is** considered to be **at rest, and it is she who walks beneath it.** Thus the basket is considered to be a "stationary courtyard," and the woman acquires whatever is thrown into it.

MISHNAH הָיָה רוֹכֵב [4]**If a person was riding on an animal and he saw an ownerless object** lying on the ground, **and he said to another person** standing nearby, **"Give** that object **to me,"** [5]if **the other person took** the ownerless object **and said, "I have acquired it for myself,"** [6]he has **acquired it** by lifting it up, even though he was not the first to see it, and the rider has no claim to it. [7]**But if, after he gave** the object **to** the rider, the person who picked it up **said, "I acquired** the object **first,"** [8]**he** in fact **said nothing.** His words are of no effect, and the rider may keep it. Since the person walking showed no intention of acquiring the object when he originally picked it up, he is not now believed when he claims that he acquired it first. Indeed, even if we maintain that when a person picks up an ownerless object on behalf of someone else, the latter does *not* acquire it automatically, here, by *giving* the object to the rider, he makes a gift of it to the rider.

GEMARA תְּנַן הָתָם [9]**We have learned elsewhere** in a Mishnah in tractate *Pe'ah* (4:9): **"Someone who gathered *pe'ah*** — produce which by Torah law [Leviticus 23:22] is left unharvested in the corner of a field by the owner of the field, to be gleaned by the poor — **and said, 'Behold, this** *pe'ah* which I have gleaned **is intended for so-and-so the poor man,'** [10]**Rabbi Eliezer says:** The person who gathered the *pe'ah* **has acquired it**

בִּרְשׁוּת הָרַבִּים [1]וְזָרַק לָהּ גֵּט לְתוֹךְ חֵיקָהּ אוֹ לְתוֹךְ קַלְתָּהּ — [2]הָכָא נַמִי דְּלָא מְגָרְשָׁה? [3]אֲמַר לֵיהּ: קַלְתָּהּ מֵינָח נַיְיחָא, וְאִיהִי דְּקָא מְסַגְּיָא מְתּוּתָהּ.

משנה [4]הָיָה רוֹכֵב עַל גַּבֵּי בְהֵמָה וְרָאָה אֶת הַמְּצִיאָה, וְאָמַר לַחֲבֵירוֹ "תְּנָה לִי", [5]נְטָלָהּ וְאָמַר, "אֲנִי זָכִיתִי בָּהּ", [6]זָכָה בָּהּ. [7]אִם, מִשֶּׁנְּתָנָהּ לוֹ, אָמַר, "אֲנִי זָכִיתִי בָּהּ תְּחִלָּה", [8]לֹא אָמַר כְּלוּם.

גמרא [9]תְּנַן הָתָם: "מִי שֶׁלִּיקֵּט אֶת הַפֵּאָה וְאָמַר, 'הֲרֵי זוֹ לִפְלוֹנִי עָנִי', [10]רַבִּי אֱלִיעֶזֶר

LITERAL TRANSLATION

in a public thoroughfare [1]and [her husband] threw her a bill of divorce into her lap or into her basket, [2]here, too, would she not be divorced?

[3]He said to him: Her basket is at rest, and it is she who walks beneath it.

MISHNAH [4][If a person] was riding on an animal and he saw a found object, and he said to another person, "Give it to me," [5][and the other person] took it and said, "I have acquired it," [6]he has acquired it. [7]If, after he gave it to him, he said, "I acquired it first," [8]he said nothing.

GEMARA [9]We have learned there: "Someone who gathered *pe'ah* and said, 'Behold this is for so-and-so the poor man,' [10]Rabbi Eliezer

RASHI

קלתה – סל שעל ראשה, שנותנת בה כלי מלאכתה וטווי שלה. הכי נמי דלא הוי גיטא – והאנן תנן במסכת גיטין (עז,א): זרק לה גיטה לתוך חיקה או לתוך קלתה – הרי זו מגורשת!

משנה לא אמר כלום – דאפילו אמרינן המגביה מציאה לחבירו לא קנה חבירו, כיון דיהבה ליה – קנייה ממה נפשך. אי קנייה קמא דלא מתכוין להקנות לחבירו – הא יהבה ניהליה במתנה. ואי לא קנייה קמא משום דלא היה מתכוין לקנות – הויא ליה הפקר עד דמטא לידיה דהאי, וקנייה האי במאי דעקרה מידיה דקמא לשם קנייה.

גמרא מי שליקט את הפאה – אדם בעלמא שאינו בעל שדה. דאי בבעל שדה – לא אמר רבי אליעזר זכה. דליכא למימר "מגו דזכי לנפשיה", דאפילו הוא עני מוזהר הוא שלא ללקט פאה משדה שלו, כדאמר בשחיטת חולין (קלא,ב): "לא תלקט לעני" – להזהיר עני על שלו.

Hebrew commentary of Rashi, the classic explanation that accompanies all editions of the Talmud

NOTES

מִי שֶׁלִּיקֵּט אֶת הַפֵּאָה **If a person gathered *pe'ah*.** According to *Rashi*, the Mishnah must be referring to someone other than the owner of the field. By Torah law the owner of a field is required to separate part of his field as *pe'ah*, even if he himself is poor, and he may not take the *pe'ah* for himself. Therefore the "since" (מגו) argument

HALAKHAH

קַלְתָּהּ **A woman's basket.** "If a man throws a bill of divorce into a container that his wife is holding, she thereby acquires the bill of divorce and the divorce takes effect." (*Shulḥan Arukh, Even HaEzer* 139:10.)

הַמְלַקֵּט פֵּאָה עֲבוּר אַחֵר **A person who gathered *pe'ah* for someone else.** "If a poor person, who is himself entitled to collect *pe'ah*, gathered *pe'ah* for another poor person, and said, 'This *pe'ah* is for X, the poor person,' he acquires the *pe'ah* on behalf of that other poor person. But if the person who collected the *peah* was wealthy, he does not acquire the *pe'ah* on behalf of the poor person. He must give it instead to the first poor person who appears in the field," following the opinion of the Sages, as explained by Rabbi Yehoshua ben Levi. (*Rambam, Sefer Zeraim, Hilkhot Mattenot Aniyyim* 2:19.)

Numbers link the three main sections of the page and allow readers to refer rapidly from one to the another

Notes highlight points of interest in the text and expand the discussion by quoting other classical commentaries

On the outer margin of the page, factual information clarifying the meaning of the Talmudic discussion is presented. Entries under the heading *Language* explain unusual terms, often borrowed from Greek, Latin, or Persian. *Sages* gives brief biographies of the major figures whose opinions are presented in the Talmud. *Terminology* explains the terms used in the Talmudic discussion. *Concepts* gives information about fundamental Halakhic principles. *Background* provides historical, geographical, and other information needed to understand the text. *Realia* explains the artifacts mentioned in the text. These notes are sometimes accompanied by illustrations.

The best way of studying the Talmud is the way in which the Talmud itself evolved - a combination of frontal teaching and continuous interaction between teacher and pupil, and between pupils themselves.

This edition is meant for a broad spectrum of users, from those who have considerable prior background and who know how to study the Talmud from any standard edition to those who have never studied the Talmud and do not even know Hebrew.

The division of the page into various sections is designed to enable students of every kind to derive the greatest possible benefit from it.

For those who know how to study the Talmud, the book is intended to be a written Gemara lesson, so that, either alone, with partners, or in groups, they can have the sense of studying with a teacher who explains the difficult passages and deepens their understanding both of the development of the dialectic and also of the various approaches that have been taken by the Rabbis over the centuries in interpreting the material. A student of this kind can start with the Hebrew-Aramaic text, examine Rashi's commentary, and pass on from there to the expanded commentary. Afterwards the student can turn to the Notes section. Study of the *Halakhah* section will clarify the conclusions reached in the course of establishing the Halakhah, and the other items in the margins will be helpful whenever the need arises to clarify a concept or a word or to understand the background of the discussion.

For those who do not possess sufficient knowledge to be able to use a standard edition of the Talmud, but who know how to read Hebrew, a different method is proposed. Such students can begin by reading the Hebrew-Aramaic text and comparing it immediately to the *Literal Translation*. They can then move over to the *Translation and Commentary*, which refers both to the original text and to the *Literal Translation*. Such students would also do well to read through the *Notes* and choose those that explain matters at greater length. They will benefit, too, from the terms explained in the side margins.

The beginner who does not know Hebrew well enough to grapple with the original can start with the *Translation and Commentary*. The inclusion of a translation within the commentary permits the student to ignore the *Literal Translation*, since the commentary includes both the Talmudic text and an interpretation of it. The beginner can also benefit from the *Notes*, and it is important for him to go over the marginal notes on the concepts to improve his awareness of the juridical background and the methods of study characteristic of this text.

Apart from its use as study material, this book can also be useful to those well versed in the Talmud, as a source of additional knowledge in various areas, both for understanding the historical and archeological background and also for an explanation of words and concepts. The general reader, too, who might not plan to study the book from beginning to end, can find a great deal of interesting material in it regarding both the spiritual world of Judaism, practical Jewish law, and the life and customs of the Jewish people during the thousand years (500 B.C.E.–500 C.E.) of the Talmudic period.

The Talmud

The Steinsaltz Edition

Volume I

Tractate Bava Metzia

Part I

Introduction to Bava Metzia

The tractate *Bava Metzia* (which means "Middle Gate") is in fact one part of a single ancient tractate called *Nezikin* ("Damages"), the subject of which is civil law, and which, because of its size, was divided into three parts. Like the other parts of the ancient tractate, *Bava Metzia* has one important central subject, which branches out into a large number of detailed Halakhic discussions, and following the general pattern of Talmudic discussion occasionally digresses both to related and to distant topics. The central subject of this tractate is business dealings between people, which are defined, delimited, and given a special form by particular laws contained in the Torah. The tractate does not deal with all the laws of commerce and acquisition, but with those aspects of transactions in which the Torah adds regulations, prohibitions, and commandments to the general laws of acquisition and commerce. For this reason, the subjects of this tractate are found mainly in the area common to both civil and religious (ritual) law.

The laws in this tractate relate to the laws mentioned in the Torah regarding the finding of lost objects, the unloading and loading of goods, the misrepresentation of merchandise and monetary fraud, the prohibition of interest, the permission granted to a worker to eat from the produce with which he is working, the laws of the four kinds of bailees, the laws of delayed payment of wages, the prohibition against damaging a deposit, and so on.

In a certain sense, then, *Bava Metzia* expresses a highly characteristic feature of the entire Torah, namely that civil law, the dealings between man and his fellow, are not merely a matter of agreements freely entered into between people or an arbitrary social contract satisfying most of the members of a community. The Torah makes no essential distinction between "matters between a man and his Creator" (דְּבָרִים שֶׁבֵּין אָדָם לַמָּקוֹם) and those "between man and his fellowman" (דְּבָרִים שֶׁבֵּין אָדָם לַחֲבֵרוֹ), because the structure of relationships between human beings is intimately connected to the relationship between man and his Creator. Although the Torah does make certain divisions by topic between the various Halakhot, nevertheless in general — as can be seen in the Torah portion *Mishpatim* (Exodus 21–23), and even more so in *Kedoshim* (Leviticus 19) or in *Ki Tetse* (Deuteronomy 21–25) — the various laws are interrelated and intermingled. Ritual matters are connected with civil disputes; moral instruction is interwoven with laws of ritual purity and impurity, etc. Not only are commercial and social relations connected and defined by general moral principles (such as the prohibitions against robbery and theft and those against fraud and deceit), but there are also a large number of civil regulations which belong to the category of חוּקִים — "*Ḥukkim*" (Statutes) — in the Torah, because they set rules for behavior which extend far beyond the need for social order, and have fundamental religious significance in themselves (for example, the prohibition against interest, or the laws on returning a pledge).

Mercy and charity are not merely personal additions to the directives of the law — the Halakhah itself, in determining the rules of civil law, makes mercy an integral part of the law. The law itself in many respects extends beyond the letter of the law. It is, therefore, understandable why Rabbinic civil law makes a distinction between general laws pertaining to business dealings in any place and with any person, and many laws pertaining specifically to transactions between Jews. General legal principles and definitions essentially belong within the category of דִּין — "the letter of the law" — and apply to all mankind, both to the universal laws governing the "children of Noah," mankind as a whole, and also to Jewish law. But those aspects of Halakhah which are לִפְנִים מִשּׁוּרַת הַדִּין — "beyond the strict letter of the law" — define a special network of relationships within the Jewish community itself, the relationship with one's "brother" (the unique brotherhood of the Jewish people). The laws of returning lost objects or the laws forbidding the taking of interest are not part of a system of fair trade, but are part of the laws of compassion which belong specifically to the internal framework of the Jewish people.

In this respect one may view the Halakhot in *Bava Metzia* as representing four levels of conduct: General laws governing all humanity which derive from the laws of the transfer of ownership in general (among these there is also a distinction between laws laid down in the Torah and Rabbinical ordinances on the subject). The second level includes laws applying specifically to Jews, which are to be seen as exceptions, placing a special emphasis on tempering justice with mercy. Beyond these are laws which do not empower a court to confiscate property but which condemn conduct with which "the spirit of the Sages is not pleased" (such as the curse מִי שֶׁפָּרַע — "whoever has broken his word" — against someone who does not keep an undertaking, even though he is not required to do so by the letter of the law). And, finally, there is an area which is entirely ethical, which specifically obligates meritorious people, "So that you may walk in the way of good men and keep the paths of the righteous" (Proverbs 2:20).

In addition, from the viewpoint of legal theory, there is one subject which is an integral part of all the discussions in *Bava Metzia*, and that is the general question of קִנְיָן — *kinyan*, "acquisition," "ownership." *Kinyan* is the essential *right of ownership* which a person has over an object which is his. In fact the definition of a valid transaction in civil law is the transfer of ownership (*kinyan*), or certain rights associated with ownership, from one person to another.

Kinyan itself is an essential connection between a person and a certain object, and this connection can be severed in only two ways: By the death of the owner, or when the owner transfers (or relinquishes) his right of ownership to others.

Sometimes the object is in the physical possession and use of its owner, but occasionally it may not be in his possession, either voluntarily — when it is rented or lent to others, or when it is on deposit with others, or against the owner's will (when the object is lost or stolen). In all these cases, it must be determined to what degree the object continues to belong to the owner, even when another person is using it, and in what circumstances his right of ownership is cancelled and replaced by an obligation on the part of the person who is in possession of the object (who, in certain cases, has "acquired" it for himself, whether he has paid for it or not).

These distinctions have many practical consequences concerning the degree of responsibility incumbent upon the person who is in possession of an object, concerning damage to it, concerning obligations stemming from possession of the object, and concerning the laws forbidding interest and misrepresentation.

Even in cases where ownership of an object has passed to others, many problems remain regarding the way in which the ownership passes, and the valid modes of acquisition according to law (most of these, however, are discussed in tractate *Bava Batra*), and more crucially, regarding the exact time when the transfer of ownership takes place. The issue of the time of the transfer of ownership determines which of two people who both lay claim to something has the prior claim. It also affects obligations which are incumbent on purchasers from certain dates (such as a mortgage), and also determines whether agreements to transfer property can be cancelled, either by sale or by some other method. All these problems, many of which are somewhat abstract, have real practical consequences both on civil law itself and on issues of ritual law connected with them.

Because of the great variety of issues connected with *kinyan*, it is not clarified in full as a single subject in any one place in the Talmud. Instead, each individual topic receives specific clarification, taking account of its particular aspects. Nevertheless, all these individual topics are bound up with the general issue of the essence of ownership and the ways of transferring it.

The tractate *Bava Metzia* contains ten chapters, each known by the first words of the Mishnah passage which begin it:

1. שְׁנַיִם אוֹחֲזִין — "Two are holding..." — deciding between rival claims to an object.
2. אֵלּוּ מְצִיאוֹת — "These are the found objects..." — general laws of lost and found objects, and laws of assisting in the unloading and loading of goods.
3. הַמַּפְקִיד — "He who deposits..." — keeping something on deposit, the responsibilities of a bailee, and laws regarding misappropriation of an article on deposit.
4. הַזָּהָב — "The gold..." — problems of the exchange of currency, laws of misrepresentation and fraud.
5. אֵיזֶהוּ נֶשֶׁךְ — "What is usury...?" — laws of interest.
6. הַשּׂוֹכֵר אֶת הָאוּמָּנִים — "He who hires artisans..." — the hiring of craftsmen and the degree of their responsibility for their work.
7. הַשּׂוֹכֵר אֶת הַפּוֹעֲלִים — "He who hires workers..." — the work of laborers and their right to eat of the produce they are harvesting.
8. הַשּׁוֹאֵל — "He who borrows..." — laws of bailees, and, in particular, laws of borrowers. Laws of renting houses.
9. הַמְקַבֵּל — "He who leases..." — laws of tenant farmers and contracted agricultural labor. The prohibition against delaying the payment of wages. The prohibition against keeping a pledged garment.
10. הַבַּיִת וְהָעֲלִיָּיה — "The house and the upper storey...." — problems of tenants who occupy different floors of buildings and share gardens.

Introduction to Chapter One

שְׁנַיִם אוֹחֲזִין

The laws of lost and found objects are discussed in depth and clarified in the second chapter ("אֵלּוּ מְצִיאוֹת") of this tractate, whereas the first chapter deals essentially with one detail of these laws: What is the law when two people both claim ownership of the same found object? This topic may seem of secondary importance, and even premature, but in fact this is not the case. For by discussing the rival claims of those who are holding a garment, we are forced to clarify certain fundamental issues connected with the laws of acquisition and the way in which conflicting claims of ownership are to be treated. Another question, concerning the various modes of acquisition, arises incidentally and is discussed in part. The replies to this question concern the formal procedures by means of which ownership may be transferred. But the central issue of the discussion remains the basic question: When several people lay claim to something (or to the right to make a certain use of something), how are the doubts regarding the matter resolved and how are the rights of ownership determined among the various claimants?

In the clarification of this fundamental problem, a number of questions arise, both theoretical and practical: When two people claim ownership of a single object, is one of them necessarily lying? If so, how is a person who knowingly cheats to be treated? Are the means of persuasion and determination available to the court — for example, making a claimant swear that he is telling the truth — significant in a situation where we actually suspect the claimant of lying? A further aspect involved is: If we assume that neither claimant is lying (because a situation is conceivable in which both sides do in fact have certain rights to the same object), by what criteria can we ascertain the degree to which each has a justified claim, in the absence of decisive proof regarding the truth of their conflicting assertions?

Another basic question arising from these discussions concerns the status and rights of third parties, who are connected to the matter to some degree but who are not represented during the court's deliberations. For example, a dispute between a borrower and a lender over the ownership of a promissory note affects not only the two disputants, but also many other people who may have had dealings with each of the two parties during the course of time. An extension of this problem concerns the legal relations between someone who misappropriates a field and the person from whom it is misappropriated, because people who have bought the field in the meantime are also involved — knowingly or unknowingly — in this dispute.

The clarification of these fundamental issues and a large number of secondary problems connected to them is the main subject of this chapter.

TRANSLATION AND COMMENTARY

MISHNAH שְׁנַיִם אוֹחֲזִין בְּטַלִּית [1]**Two** claimants appear before a Bet Din **holding on to a garment.** [2]**One** of them **says: "I found it,"** and the other says: **"I found it." One** of them **says: "The whole** garment **is mine," and the other says: "The whole** garment **is mine."** [3]The Bet Din resolves such conflicting claims in the following way: **One** of the two claimants **must take an oath that no less than half of** the garment **is his, and the other** claimant **must** likewise **take an oath that no less than half of it is his.** [4]**They shall** then **divide** the garment or its value between them.

LITERAL TRANSLATION

MISHNAH [1]Two are holding on to a garment. [2]This one says: "I found it," and this one says: "I found it." This one says: "All of it is mine," and this one says: "All of it is mine." [3]This one shall swear that he does not have in it less than half of it, and this one shall swear that he does not have in it less than half of it, [4]and they shall divide [it].

[1]אוֹחֲזִין בְּטַלִּית. [2]זֶה אוֹמֵר: "אֲנִי מְצָאתִיהָ", וְזֶה אוֹמֵר: "אֲנִי מְצָאתִיהָ". זֶה אוֹמֵר: "כּוּלָּהּ שֶׁלִּי", וְזֶה אוֹמֵר: "כּוּלָּהּ שֶׁלִּי". [3]זֶה יִשָּׁבַע שֶׁאֵין לוֹ בָּהּ פָּחוֹת מֶחֶצְיָהּ, וְזֶה יִשָּׁבַע שֶׁאֵין לוֹ בָּהּ פָּחוֹת מֶחֶצְיָהּ, [4]וְיַחֲלוֹקוּ.

RASHI

משנה שנים אוחזין בטלית — דוקא אוחזין, דשניהם מוחזקים בה ואין לזה כח בה יותר מזה. שאילו היתה ביד אחד לבדו, הוי אידך המוציא מחבירו, ועליו להביא ראיה בעדים שהיא שלו, ואינו נאמן זה ליטול בשבועה. **זה אומר כולה שלי** — בגמרא מפרש למאי תנא תרתי. **זה ישבע** — מפרש בגמרא (ג,א) שבועה זו למה. **שאין לו פחות מחציה** — בגמרא (ה,ב) מפרש אמאי תקון כי האי לישנא בהך שבועה.

BACKGROUND

טַלִּית **Garment.** This is the specific term for the garment worn by men during the Mishnaic and Talmudic periods. This garment was essentially a large, square piece of cloth in which men would wrap themselves, using it as an outer garment. A טַלִּית might be woven in a geometric pattern for decoration, and occasionally decorations made of more expensive materials were added to it. But in general a טַלִּית was a plain piece of cloth, usually with ritual fringes (צִיצִיּוֹת) on the four corners. After the Jews were exiled from Eretz Israel and other countries in the Middle East, the טַלִּית remained as a garment used during prayer and various other religious ceremonies. The Mishnah used the טַלִּית as an example for a number of reasons: Since it was generally worn as an outer garment, and since people used to take it off while they worked, it was quite common to find a lost טַלִּית. In addition, the simple form of the טַלִּית easily permitted its division into two or more pieces of cloth without destroying the value of the garment. In cases where the litigants claim objects that cannot be divided physically, they divide the value of the object between them.

NOTES

The order and internal structure of the tractate. Rishonim raise questions with regard to the place of tractate *Bava Metzia* in the general sequence of tractates in the Talmud (see *Tosafot:* ד"ה שְׁנַיִם). They also question the order of the chapters within the tractate itself: The first chapter, שְׁנַיִם אוֹחֲזִין, would appear to belong to the laws concerning the finding of lost objects. Would it not have been more natural to begin with the fundamental principles underlying these laws (which are found in the second chapter, אֵלּוּ מְצִיאוֹת) and only then to go on to discuss the various details relating to the subject?

Tosafot explain that the tractates *Bava Kamma, Bava Metzia,* and *Bava Batra* are really only divisions of one long tractate called *Nezikin,* comprising thirty chapters. Since the last chapter of *Bava Kamma* deals with the subject of dividing objects between different claimants and the imposition of an oath in such cases, our tractate begins with a discussion of these laws.

Another explanation is given by *Rosh:* In the case presented at the beginning of our tractate we suspect that one of the disputing claimants may have obtained possession of the object illegally. Therefore it was appropriate to present it immediately after similar cases in the last chapter of the previous tractate.

Rashbatz gives a different explanation: The tractate should actually begin with the laws and general principles concerning the finding of lost objects. But the specific case of שְׁנַיִם אוֹחֲזִין, in which there are two equal claims to the ownership of a found object, contains unusual and interesting principles; hence the Mishnah begins with this case. This is, indeed, a common practice in the Mishnah, where an individual case of special interest often precedes a discussion of general principles.

שְׁנַיִם אוֹחֲזִין בְּטַלִּית **Two men are holding on to a garment.** The Mishnah used the word טַלִּית — "a garment" — and not the more general term חֵפֶץ — "an object" — because, as will be explained below, there are various laws which apply specifically to a garment and to the way in which the claimants are holding it which do not apply to other objects (*Torat Ḥayyim* and other Aḥaronim).

זֶה יִשָּׁבַע **This one shall swear.** In Jewish law an oath is not considered absolute proof but rather as corroboration of a certain claim. The prohibition against uttering a false oath written in the Ten Commandments (Exodus 20:7), and the words of the Torah and the Prophets regarding the many divine punishments imposed on someone who perjures himself (see Numbers 5; Zechariah 4-5), made people very fearful about taking oaths in general and about taking false oaths in particular. In general the obligation to take an oath is used as a threat against someone whose claim, we suspect, is not well founded, for it is possible that he has brought a case to court even though he is not entirely certain of the justice of his claim. Therefore it is assumed that a person would be very reluctant to take an oath in support of such a claim.

זֶה יִשָּׁבַע וְזֶה יִשָּׁבַע **This one shall swear... and this one shall swear....** Rishonim (*Rabbenu Ḥananel* and others) ask why we do not apply here, as we sometimes do in other cases of property whose ownership is in doubt, the principle of כָּל דְּאַלִּים גָּבַר — "whoever is the stronger wins" —

HALAKHAH

שְׁנַיִם אוֹחֲזִין בְּטַלִּית **Two claimants are holding on to a garment.** "Where two claimants are holding on to one object (or have possession of one animal), and each claims ownership of the whole object, each of the claimants must take an oath that he has a valid claim to ownership of the object he is claiming, and that he is entitled to no less than half of it. The claimants then divide the object, or its value, equally between them," in accordance with the Mishnah here and the Gemara's elucidation of it. (*Shulḥan Arukh, Ḥoshen Mishpat* 138:1.)

TRANSLATION AND COMMENTARY

זֶה אוֹמֵר [1]Similarly, if **one** of the two claimants **says: "The whole** garment **is mine," and the other** claimant **says: "Half of it is mine,"** since both claimants agree that half of the garment certainly belongs to the one who claims the whole garment and their dispute is only about the other half, their claims are resolved in the following way: [2]The claimant **who says, "The whole** garment **is mine," must take an oath that no less than three-quarters** of the garment **is his; and the** claimant **who says, "Half of it is mine," must take an oath that no less than a quarter of it is his.** [3]**The one** claimant **takes three-quarters** of the garment, **and the other takes a quarter**.

הָיוּ שְׁנַיִם רוֹכְבִין [4]Similarly, if **two** people **were riding on an animal, or** if **one was riding** it, **and the other was driving** it or leading it, holding on to the halter, [5]and if **one said: "The whole** animal **is mine," and the other said: "The whole** animal **is mine,"** their claims are decided on the same basis as in the earlier cases brought

[1]זֶה אוֹמֵר: "כּוּלָּהּ שֶׁלִּי", וְזֶה אוֹמֵר: "חֶצְיָהּ שֶׁלִּי". [2]הָאוֹמֵר "כּוּלָּהּ שֶׁלִּי", יִשָּׁבַע שֶׁאֵין לוֹ בָּהּ פָּחוֹת מִשְּׁלֹשָׁה חֲלָקִים, וְהָאוֹמֵר "חֶצְיָהּ שֶׁלִּי", יִשָּׁבַע שֶׁאֵין לוֹ בָּהּ פָּחוֹת מֵרְבִיעַ. [3]זֶה נוֹטֵל שְׁלֹשָׁה חֲלָקִים, וְזֶה נוֹטֵל רְבִיעַ.

[4]הָיוּ שְׁנַיִם רוֹכְבִין עַל גַּבֵּי בְהֵמָה, אוֹ שֶׁהָיָה אֶחָד רוֹכֵב וְאֶחָד מַנְהִיג. [5]זֶה אוֹמֵר: "כּוּלָּהּ שֶׁלִּי", וְזֶה אוֹמֵר: "כּוּלָּהּ שֶׁלִּי".

LITERAL TRANSLATION

[1]This one says: "All of it is mine," and this one says: "Half of it is mine." [2]The one who says, "All of it is mine," shall swear that he does not have in it less than three-quarters, and the one who says, "Half of it is mine," shall swear that he does not have in it less than a quarter. [3]This one takes three-quarters, and this one takes a quarter.

[4]Two were riding on an animal, or one was riding and one was driving. [5]This one says: "All of it is mine," and this one says: "All of it is mine."

RASHI

וזה אומר חציה שלי — מודה הוא שהחצי של חבירו, ואין דנין אלא על חציה. הלכך, זה האומר כולה שלי ישבע כו' כמשפט הראשון. מה שהן דנין עליו — נשבעין שניהם שאין לכל אחד בו פחות מחציו. ונוטל כל אחד חציו. **היו שנים רוכבין כו'** — לאשמועינן אתא, דרכוב ומנהיג שניהם שוין לקנות בהמה מן ההפקר.

NOTES

and let the more powerful and determined claimant gain possession of the object. *Tosafot* (ד״ה וְיַחֲלוֹקוּ) answer that since in our case the two claimants appear before the court while in (partial) possession of the object, the court is itself a witness to the existing situation and must assume that both claimants have a valid claim to ownership. Several Rishonim do, in fact, lay down the principle that the law of כָּל דְּאַלִּים גָּבַר only applies where neither claimant is in possession of the object in dispute. (See *Rabbenu Hananel, Rashba,* and others.) *Rosh* adds that if we were to apply the law of כָּל דְּאַלִּים גָּבַר here, where both claimants are in possession of the object in dispute, we would not be protecting the rightful owner and we might be sanctioning the use of force by someone (the other claimant) who does not in fact have a valid claim. Since we do not know which of the two is the rightful owner, we have no choice but to impose an oath and divide the object between them.

זֶה אוֹמֵר חֶצְיָהּ שֶׁלִּי This one says, "Half of it is mine." Commentators ask why this claimant should not be believed, on the basis of the principle of מִיגּוֹ — "since." (Where a claimant could have made a claim more advantageous to himself than the one he did make, we believe him with regard to the less advantageous claim.) In our case he could have claimed that the whole garment belonged to him. Why, then, should we not believe him when he claims that only half of the garment belongs to him? Several answers are given to this question: *Tosafot* and others deduce from this Mishnah that the מִיגּוֹ argument is not strong enough to allow a court to take an object out of one person's possession and award it to another (מִיגּוֹ לְהוֹצִיא לָא אָמְרִינַן). *Rid* is of the opinion that in a case where two people bought a garment, the person who claims that half of it is his does not dare to claim that the whole garment belongs to him, because he is afraid that the seller will contradict him. Our case, then, according to *Rid,* is not one of מִיגּוֹ at all, because the more advantageous claim is not available to the claimant.

נוֹטֵל רְבִיעַ He takes a quarter. In the Jerusalem Talmud (and also in the Tosefta) a general principle is established that where there are two claimants to an object, the one claiming the entire object and the other claiming a part of it, the latter must take an oath that his claim is to no less than half of the part he is claiming, and he acquires ownership of that fraction. (For example, a person claiming a third of an object must take an oath with regard to a sixth of the object, and so on.)

HALAKHAH

זֶה אוֹמֵר כּוּלָּהּ שֶׁלִּי וְזֶה אוֹמֵר חֶצְיָהּ שֶׁלִּי This one says: "All of it is mine," and this one says: "Half of it is mine." "If two litigants claim ownership of something, the one claiming that all of it is his, and the other that half of it is his, the one who claims the entire object must take an oath that he has a valid claim to ownership and that he is entitled to no less than three-quarters of it, and the other must take an oath that he has a valid claim to ownership and that he is entitled to no less than a quarter of it. The former takes three-quarters and the latter a quarter," in accordance with the Mishnah and the Gemara. (*Shulḥan Arukh, Ḥoshen Mishpat* 138:2.)

TRANSLATION AND COMMENTARY

in the Mishnah: [1]**One** of the two claimants **must take an oath that no less than half of** the animal **is his, and the other** claimant likewise **must take an oath that no less than half of** the animal **is his,** [2]**and** they then **divide** the value of the animal between them.

בִּזְמַן שֶׁהֵם מוֹדִים [3]If each of the two claimants **admits** the validity of the other's claim, **or if** the two claimants **have witnesses** testifying that they both have a share in the object in dispute, **they divide** it **without** taking **an oath**. An oath is only imposed when the claimants have no other method of proving their claims.

GEMARA לָמָּה לִי לְמִתְנָא [4]The Gemara begins its examination of the Mishnah by discussing its style and asks: **Why does** the Mishnah appear to repeat itself by saying: **The one** claimant **says: "I found it," and the other** claimant **says: "I found it." The one** claimant **says: "All of it is mine," and the other** claimant **says: "All of it is mine"?** The second clause ("all of it is mine...") seems to be an unnecessary repetition of the first ("I found it..."). [5]**Let** the Mishnah **teach** only **one** clause, containing a single claim.

חֲדָא קָתָנֵי [6]The Gemara answers: The Mishnah **does use only one** clause, and the correct way to understand the Mishnah is indeed that one case and one claim was intended. We should rephrase the Mishnah as follows: **The one** claimant **says: "I found** the object **and all of it is mine," and the other** claimant **says: "I found it and all of it is mine."** According to this answer of the Gemara, therefore, the two statements are fused into one.

וְלִיתְנֵי [7]The Gemara now asks a further question: **But let** the Mishnah **teach** only the first clause, where each claimant says **"I found it,"** and that would be sufficient for us to understand that each claimant means that **"all of** the object **is mine"**!

אִי תָּנָא [8]The Gemara answers that, **if** the Mishnah **had** only **taught** the first clause, **"I found it,"** its intention could have been misunderstood. We **might have thought** that, by saying **"I found it,"** the claimant really meant, **"I saw** the object first, before the other claimant." [9]We might then have drawn the incorrect conclusion that **even though** the object had **not reached** the **hand** of the claimant and he had not yet taken physical possession of it, nevertheless **by merely seeing it he** did in fact **acquire** ownership of **it**.

תָּנָא [10]In order to avoid this incorrect conclusion, the Mishnah added the second clause and **taught** that each claimant says: **"All of it is mine."** The strong assertive language suggests that the object is physically in his possession. In this way the Mishnah shows **that one does not acquire** ownership of something merely **by seeing it**!

[1]זֶה יִשָּׁבַע שֶׁאֵין לוֹ בָּהּ פָּחוֹת מֵחֶצְיָהּ, וְזֶה יִשָּׁבַע שֶׁאֵין לוֹ בָּהּ פָּחוֹת מֵחֶצְיָהּ, [2]וְיַחֲלוֹקוּ.

[3]בִּזְמַן שֶׁהֵם מוֹדִים, אוֹ שֶׁיֵּשׁ לָהֶן עֵדִים, חוֹלְקִין בְּלֹא שְׁבוּעָה.

גמרא [4]לָמָּה לִי לְמִתְנָא: "זֶה אוֹמֵר: 'אֲנִי מְצָאתִיהָ', וְזֶה אוֹמֵר: 'אֲנִי מְצָאתִיהָ'. זֶה אוֹמֵר: 'כּוּלָּהּ שֶׁלִּי', וְזֶה אוֹמֵר: 'כּוּלָּהּ שֶׁלִּי'"? [5]לִיתְנֵי חֲדָא!

[6]חֲדָא קָתָנֵי: "זֶה אוֹמֵר: 'אֲנִי מְצָאתִיהָ וְכוּלָּהּ שֶׁלִּי', וְזֶה אוֹמֵר: 'אֲנִי מְצָאתִיהָ וְכוּלָּהּ שֶׁלִּי'".

[7]וְלִיתְנֵי: "אֲנִי מְצָאתִיהָ", וַאֲנָא יָדַעְנָא דְּ"כוּלָּהּ שֶׁלִּי"!

[8]אִי תָּנָא "אֲנִי מְצָאתִיהָ", הֲוָה אָמִינָא: מַאי "מְצָאתִיהָ"? — רְאִיתִיהָ. [9]אַף עַל גַּב דְּלָא אֲתַאי לִידֵיהּ, בִּרְאִיָּה בְּעָלְמָא קָנֵי.

[10]תָּנָא: "כּוּלָּהּ שֶׁלִּי" דְּבִרְאִיָּה לָא קָנֵי.

LITERAL TRANSLATION

[1]This one shall swear that he does not have in it less than half of it, and this one shall swear that he does not have in it less than half of it, [2]and they shall divide [it].

[3]Whenever they admit, or if they have witnesses, they divide without an oath.

GEMARA [4]Why [is it necessary] to teach: This one says: "I found it," and this one says: "I found it." This one says: "All of it is mine," and this one says: "All of it is mine"? [5]Let him teach [only] one!

[6]He does teach [only] one: This one says: "I found it and all of it is mine," and this one says: "I found it and all of it is mine."

[7]But let him teach: "I found it," and I will know that "all of it is mine"!

[8]If he had taught: "I found it," I would have said: What [does] "I found it" [mean]? — "I saw it [first]." [9]Even though it has not reached his hand, by merely seeing [it] he acquires [it].

[10]He [therefore] taught: "All of it is mine" [to show] that [merely] by seeing [it] he does not acquire [it].

RASHI

בזמן שהן מודין – בגמרא (ח,א) מפרש [דבהאי] משמעינן דהמגביה מציאה לחבירו קנה חבירו.

גמרא ראיתיה קודם שהגבהת אותה. **בראיה קני** – מדקתני יחלוקו. **תנא כולה שלי** – בחזקה גמורה. שהגבהתי תחילה, ואתה תפסת מידי משזכיתי בה.

TERMINOLOGY

לָמָּה לִי לְמִתְנָא... לִיתְנֵי... Why does he need to teach...? Let him teach.... When the Gemara objects to the wording of a Mishnah and suggests a clearer or more concise form of words, it frequently begins: "Why does the author of the Mishnah use this expression? He would make his point more clearly or more concisely if he instead said...."

לִיתְנֵי Let him teach. This expression is used by the Gemara to introduce an objection to the language or style of the Mishnah: "Why did the Tanna who taught this Mishnah not teach the Mishnah's contents in another, clearer, way?!"

הֲוָה אָמִינָא I would have said. This expression is used in the Talmud as an introduction to a possible answer that is later found to be incorrect.

TERMINOLOGY

וּמִי מָצֵית אָמְרַתְּ Can you say that...? How can you make the suggestion you just made, when it is in fact totally unacceptable?

TRANSLATION AND COMMENTARY

וּמִי מָצֵית אָמְרַתְּ [1]The Gemara now raises an objection to the answer just given: **Can you,** in fact, **say** that the meaning of the statement מְצָאתִיהָ — "**I found it**" — really means **"I saw it"**? [2]**Surely** there is an authoritative statement by **Rabbenai** (*Bava Kamma* 113b), who **said** in explaining the verse (Deuteronomy 22:3): "And so shall you do with every lost thing of your brother's, which he has lost and you have found," that the expression וּמְצָאתָהּ — "**and you have found it**" — **means that** the object is considered legally to have been found only when its finder **takes actual physical possession of it.** Thus, according to Rabbenai, the use in the Torah of the Hebrew root מצא — "to find" — in connection with the finding of a lost object, always means that the object found is already in the hands of the finder. How, then, could the Gemara above have suggested that we might have been under the mistaken impression that one could acquire ownership of an object by merely seeing it!?

אִין [3]The Gemara now answers this objection by making a distinction between the use of language in the Torah and the use of language in the Mishnah: **Yes,** says the Gemara, the expression וּמְצָאתָהּ — "**and you have found it**" — in the Torah, **in the verse** just quoted, **does** indeed **mean that** the object **has reached** the **hand**, the physical possession, of the finder. [4]**But** if the Mishnah had not used the extra expression, "All of it is mine," we might have thought that **the Tanna** of our Mishnah, when he chose the expression מְצָאתִיהָ — "I found it" — **was** in fact **using a colloquial expression. When a person sees** an object that appears to be lost or ownerless, **he says: "I found it," even though** the object **has not reached his hand**. He imagines **that merely by seeing it he has** in fact **acquired it**. [5]Therefore, the Mishnah adds the seemingly superfluous clause, **"All of it is mine,"** in order to inform us **that merely seeing** a lost or ownerless object **does not** convey ownership of the object.

וְלִיתְנֵי כּוּלָּהּ שֶׁלִּי [6]The Gemara now attacks this explanation and asks: If the Mishnah really intends to show that mere seeing does not convey ownership of a lost or ownerless object, **let it teach** only the second clause, where each claimant says, **"All of it is mine."** For that purpose **it does not need to** teach the first clause, where each claimant says, **"I found it!"** Surely the second clause alone is sufficient!

[1]וּמִי מָצֵית אָמְרַתְּ: מַאי "מְצָאתִיהָ"? — "רְאִיתִיהָ"? [2]וְהָא אֲמַר רַבְּנַאי: "וּמְצָאתָהּ" דַּאֲתַאי לִידֵיהּ מַשְׁמַע! [3]אִין, "וּמְצָאתָהּ" דִּקְרָא דַּאֲתָא לִידֵיהּ מַשְׁמַע. [4]וּמִידּוּ, תַּנָּא לִישָּׁנָא דְעָלְמָא נָקַט, וּמִדְּחָזֵי לֵיהּ אָמַר: "אֲנָא אַשְׁכַּחִית", וְאַף עַל גַּב דְּלָא אֲתַאי לִידֵיהּ, בִּרְאִיָּה בְּעָלְמָא קָנֵי. [5]תָּנֵי: "כּוּלָּהּ שֶׁלִּי", דִּבְרְאִיָּה בְּעָלְמָא לָא קָנֵי לָהּ. [6]וְלִיתְנֵי: "כּוּלָּהּ שֶׁלִּי", וְלָא בָּעֵי: "אֲנִי מְצָאתִיהָ"!

LITERAL TRANSLATION

[1]But how can you say: What [does] "I found it" [mean]? — [It means:] "I saw it"? [2]But surely Rabbenai said: "And you have found it" means that it has reached his hand!

[3]Yes, [the expression] "and you have found it" in the Biblical verse does mean that it has reached his hand. [4]But the Tanna used the language of the [everyday] world, and once [a person] sees it [an object], he says: "I found [it]," and even though it has not reached his hand [he imagines that] merely by seeing [it] he acquires [it]. [5][Therefore he] teaches: "All of it is mine," [to show] that merely by seeing [it] he does not acquire it.

[6]But let him teach: "All of it is mine," and he would not need [to say]: "I found it"!

RASHI

והאמר רבנאי — בבבא קמא ב"הגוזל ומאכיל". **ומצאתה דאתא לידיה משמע** — ואפילו הכי — "אחיך" ולא נכרי. ולא תימא: כי מיעט רחמנא נכרי — היכא דלא אתאי לידיה דישראל לא מיחייב למטרח עלה ולאהדורה. אבל אתא לידיה — מיחייב להחזירה, דאבידתו אסורה. **תנא לישנא דעלמא נקט** — אי לא הדר תנא "כולה שלי" הוה אמינא: מאי "מצאתיה" דקתני תנא — לשון בני אדם אחז במשנתנו, ולא לשון המקרא, והרבה בני אדם קורין לה מציאה משעת ראיה.

NOTES

וְהָא אֲמַר רַבְּנַאי Surely Rabbenai said. The *Shittah Mekubbetzet* points out that it seems unlikely that Rabbenai was himself the author of the statement attributed to him here. It is more likely that the source of the statement was appreciably earlier than his period, because it is cited in other places in the Talmud as the authoritative Halakhah.

HALAKHAH

בִּרְאִיָּה בְּעָלְמָא לָא קָנֵי Merely by seeing it he does not acquire it. "A person does not acquire ownership of a found object until the object is actually in his hand, or in his domain. If he merely sees the found object (even if he lunges towards it in order to take possession of it but does not actually take hold of it) he does not thereby acquire ownership of it, and whoever is the first to take physical possession of it acquires ownership," in accordance with the ruling in the Gemara. (*Shulḥan Arukh, Ḥoshen Mishpat* 268:1.)

TRANSLATION AND COMMENTARY

אִי תָּנֵי כּוּלָּהּ שֶׁלִּי [1]The Gemara answers that **if** the Mishnah **had** only **taught, "All of it is mine," I might** have mistakenly **said that**, as a general rule, **whenever** the Mishnah uses the expression, **"I found it,"** it follows the idiom of colloquial speech, and its intention is to state **that** merely **by seeing** a lost or ownerless object one **does acquire** it. [2]Therefore, to avoid this erroneous conclusion, the Mishnah first **taught, "I found it," and then taught, "All of it is mine."** Thus, **from the** seemingly **superfluous expression**, "I found it," the Mishnah **made known to us** the principle **that** merely by **seeing** an object one **does not acquire** ownership of it.

וּמִי מָצֵית אָמְרַתְּ [3]Up to this point in its analysis of the Mishnah the Gemara has sought to establish that the first two clauses, "I found it," and, "All of it is mine," are two necessary features of a single, integral unit, dealing with one particular case. The Gemara now proceeds to attack this basic assumption and asks: **Can you**, in fact, **say that** the Mishnah in its two opening statements **is teaching one** particular case with one particular claim? **Surely** the wording indicates that the Mishnah is referring not to one but to two separate and distinct cases. Does **it** not **teach, "This one says...,"** implying one case, **and** then teach, **"This one says...,"** implying a different case? Thus: (case 1) **This one says, "I found it," and this one says, "I found it,"** and (case 2) **This one says, "All of it is mine,"** and this one says, "All of it is mine." The implication, says the Gemara, is that there are two separate and distinct claims, and not the same claim repeated in different terms!

אָמַר רַב פַּפָּא [4]**Rav Pappa said, and some say** that it was **Rav Shimi bar Ashi** who made the statement, **and others say** that it was stated **anonymously: The first clause** in the Mishnah, where each of the two claimants says, "I found it," **deals with something** that was **found** and claimed by two people; and **the latter clause**, where each of the two claimants says, "All of it is mine," deals with **buying and selling,** in which each claimant asserts that he is the one who bought the object from the seller and that he is the rightful owner.

וּצְרִיכָא [5]**And it was necessary** for the Mishnah to teach both cases: [2B] [6]**For if** the Tanna **had** only **taught**

[1]אִי תָּנֵי: ״כּוּלָּהּ שֶׁלִּי״, הֲוָה אָמִינָא: בְּעָלְמָא דְּקָתָנֵי ״מְצָאתִיהָ״ בִּרְאִיָּה בְּעָלְמָא קָנֵי. [2]תָּנָא: ״אֲנִי מְצָאתִיהָ״ וַהֲדַר תָּנָא ״כּוּלָּהּ שֶׁלִּי״, דְּמִמִּשְׁנָה יְתֵירָה אַשְׁמַעִינַן דִּרְאִיָּה לָא קָנֵי.

[3]וּמִי מָצֵית אָמְרַתְּ חֲדָא קָתָנֵי? וְהָא ״זֶה״ וְ״זֶה״ קָתָנֵי: ״זֶה אוֹמֵר: ׳אֲנִי מְצָאתִיהָ׳, וְזֶה אוֹמֵר: ׳אֲנִי מְצָאתִיהָ׳, זֶה אוֹמֵר: ׳כּוּלָּהּ שֶׁלִּי׳, וכו׳״!

[4]אָמַר רַב פַּפָּא, וְאִיתֵּימָא רַב שִׁימִי בַּר אַשִׁי, וְאָמְרִי לָהּ כְּדִי: רֵישָׁא בִּמְצִיאָה, וְסֵיפָא בְּמִקָּח וּמִמְכָּר.

[5]וּצְרִיכָא, [2B] [6]דְּאִי תָּנָא

LITERAL TRANSLATION

[1]If he had taught: "All of it is mine," I would have said [that] in general wherever he teaches "I found it" [it means that] merely by seeing [it] he acquires [it]. [2]He [therefore first] taught: "I found it" and again he taught: "All of it is mine," so that from the extra [sentence in the] Mishnah he makes known to us that seeing does not acquire.

[3]But how can you say [that] he teaches one [plea]? But surely he teaches: "This one" and "this one": This one says: "I found it," and this one says: "I found it." This one says: "All of it is mine," etc.!

[4]Rav Pappa said, and some say (lit., "and if you say") [that it was] Rav Shimi bar Ashi, and others say [that] it [was related] anonymously: The first clause [deals] with something found, and the latter clause with buying and selling.

[5]And it is necessary [to teach both cases]. [2B] [6]For if he had taught

TERMINOLOGY

וְאָמְרִי לָהּ Lit., **and they say it.** An expression used to introduce the revision of a previous statement. This revision may differ from the original either in content or in attribution to a different authority.

צְרִיכָא **It is necessary.** A Mishnah or a Baraita often presents two or more seemingly analogous cases (the Torah itself, or an Amora, will occasionally do this, too). When this apparently unnecessary repetition is challenged, the Gemara points out that the statements are both "necessary." The Gemara justifies the inclusion of the various cases either because each case has a unique feature needing to be stated, or because we might have reached erroneous conclusions if one of the statements had been omitted.

RASHI

בעלמא דקתני מצאתיה — בכל מקום ששנינו שהמוצא מציאה קנאה, הוה אמינא דמציאה קני לה משעת ראיה. דלא אשמעינן שום תנא דלא קני לה אלא בהגבהה. להכי אשמעינן הכא ממשנה יתירה. **והא זה וזה קתני** — גבי "מצאתיה" תנא "זה אומר", וגבי "כולה שלי" קתני "זה אומר". ואי חדא הוא, הכי אבעי ליה למתני: זה אומר מצאתיה וכולה שלי. **במקח וממכר** — "קניתיה מיד פלוני". ודוקא מקח וממכר הוא דאמרינן יחלוקו בשבועה, דאיכא למימר שניהם קנאוה ולשניהם נתרצה המוכר. אבל זה אומר "אני ארגתיה" וזה אומר "אני ארגתיה" — לא יחלוקו, דודאי חד מינייהו רמאי הוא, ותהא מונחת עד שיבא אליהו.

NOTES

בְּמִקָּח וּמִמְכָּר **Buying and selling**. *Rashi* emphasizes that the law here only applies in the case of buying and selling, as explained below, where the two litigants each gave money to a seller for a specific object, and each of them claims that the seller intended to sell him the object. But in a case where they advance other claims of ownership, such as where each of them claims that he wove the cloth, it is obvious that one of them is knowingly seeking to defraud. In such a case we do not make them take oaths, but instead we deposit the object with the court until the matter is clarified in some other way.

מְצִיאָה, [1]הֲוָה אָמִינָא: מְצִיאָה הוּא דְּרָמוּ רַבָּנַן שְׁבוּעָה עֲלֵיהּ, [2]מִשּׁוּם דְּמוֹרֵי וְאָמַר: ״חַבְרָאי לָאו מִידֵּי חָסֵר בָּהּ. אֵיזַל אִתְפִּיס וְאִתְפְּלִיג בַּהֲדֵיהּ״. [3]אֲבָל מִקָּח וּמִמְכָּר, דְּלֵיכָּא לְמֵימַר הָכִי, אֵימָא לָא. [4]וְאִי תָּנָא מִקָּח וּמִמְכָּר, הוּא דְּרָמוּ רַבָּנַן שְׁבוּעָה עֲלֵיהּ, [5]מִשּׁוּם דְּמוֹרֵי וְאָמַר: ״חַבְרָאי דָּמֵי קָא יָהֵיב וַאֲנָא דָּמֵי קָא יָהֵיבְנָא. הָשְׁתָּא דִּצְרִיכָא לְדִידִי אֶשְׁקְלֵיהּ אֲנָא, וְחַבְרָאי לֵיזִיל לִטְרַח לִיזְבַּן״. [6]אֲבָל מְצִיאָה,

LITERAL TRANSLATION

[about] a found object, [1]I would have said: A found object is where the Sages imposed an oath upon him, [2]because he may rationalize (lit., "teach") and say [to himself]: "My fellow loses nothing in it. I will go [and] take hold [of it] and divide [it] with him." [3]But [in] buying and selling, where one cannot say this, say [that] no [oath is imposed].

[4]And if he had taught [about] buying and selling, [I would have said:] This is where the Sages imposed an oath upon him, [5]because he may rationalize (lit., "teach") and say [to himself]: "My fellow paid money and I paid money. Now that I need [it] I will take it, and let my fellow go [and] take the trouble [and] buy [another article]." [6]But [in the case of] a found object,

TRANSLATION AND COMMENTARY

the case of **a found object,** [1]**I might** mistakenly **have said** that it is specifically in disputes over **found objects** that **the Sages imposed an oath** on each claimant, [2]**because** a person **may rationalize** his seizing a found object from its rightful finder **and say to himself: "My fellow loses nothing** if I take the object from him, for he too came upon it by chance. **I will go and take hold** of it **and divide it with him."** I might have thought that it was in order to deter such attempts at self-justification that the Sages decided that both parties in a dispute about a found object must take an oath. [3]**But in** the case of **buying and selling, where** such a justification **cannot be** made, because the other claimant paid money to buy the object, I might mistakenly **say** that **no** oath should be imposed. In such a case each claimant may sincerely believe that the seller intended to sell him the object, and the imposition of an oath might have been considered unnecessary. The Mishnah therefore had to bring the case of buying and selling as well.

וְאִי תָּנָא מִקָּח וּמִמְכָּר [4]Conversely, **if** the Tanna of the Mishnah **had** only **taught** the case involving **buying and selling**, we might mistakenly have said: It is specifically **in** a dispute over the ownership of a bought object that **the Sages imposed an oath** on each claimant, [5]**because** in the case of a bought object, where both claimants paid money, a claimant **may rationalize** his seizing the object from its rightful owner **and say to himself: "My fellow paid money** to the seller **and I,** too, **paid money** to the seller. **Now that I need** the object, **I will take it** for myself, and **my fellow** can **go to the trouble** of buying another one." I might perhaps have thought that it was in order to prevent such attempts at self-justification that the Sages decided that both parties in a dispute about a bought article must take an oath. [6]**But in** the case of **a found object,**

RASHI

דמורה ואמר — מורה היתר לעלמו לאחוז בה בלא משפט. **לאו מידי חסר** — אינו מפסיד כלום, בחנם באה לו, ואף בלא טורח. **אבל מקח וממכר דליכא למימר הכי** — ואף על גב שזה גם הוא נתן את המעות למוכר, כדאוקמינן לקמן, דנקט מתרוייהו חד מדעתיה וחד בעל כרחיה, וכשיחלוקו יטול זה חצי מעותיו וזה חצי מעותיו, אפילו הכי חסרון הוא אצלו, דאי לא הוה צריך לה לא הוה מהדר אבתרה למזבנה, וזה שבא לחלוק וליתן חצי דמים — שלא כדין מחסרו. **דמי קא יהיבנא** — דמים אני רוצה ליתן.

NOTES

מִשּׁוּם דְּמוֹרֵי **Because a claimant may rationalize....** The early Rishonim seek to resolve a number of internal contradictions that this passage seems to contain. For example, it appears that the passage is based on the assumption that *neither* of the parties intends to deceive the other (לֵיכָּא וַדַּאי רַמָּאי) and that both are acting in good faith; but the Gemara also makes the apparently contrary assumption that each of the parties may be seeking to rationalize taking something that does not belong to him. In fact, some of the proposed explanations of these contradictions come to the conclusion that certain sections of the passage are entirely superfluous.

Because of this lack of continuity and conceptual unity, a number of the commentators (*Rabbenu Ḥananel* and others) maintain that the present form of the passage is a compilation of unrelated interpretations of the Mishnah and not a single continuous line of argument.

Others (*Otzar HaGeonim*) go further and suggest that the entire passage is not part of the original text of the Gemara as edited by Ravina and Rav Ashi, but was added later by the Savoraim (the Sages who belonged to the generation that lived after the completion of the Babylonian Talmud). According to this explanation, the Savoraim collected all the various Amoraic explanations of the subject matter of the Mishnah and inserted them in unedited form in the text of the Gemara. (A number of examples of such a process can be found elsewhere in the Talmud.)

Nevertheless, many commentators (*Ramban, Rashba,* and *Shittah Mekubbetzet*) reject this approach. They attempt, albeit with a certain amount of difficulty, to resolve the passage's apparent lack of cohesion, and interpret it as one continuous line of thought.

דְּלֵיכָּא לְמֵימַר הָכִי, אֵימָא לָא. [1]צְרִיכָא.

[2]מִקָּח וּמִמְכָּר: וְלֶחֱזֵי זוּזֵי מִמַּאן נָקַט?

[3]לָא, צְרִיכָא דְּנָקַט מִתַּרְוַיְיהוּ, מֵחַד מִדַּעְתֵּיהּ, וּמֵחַד בְּעַל

LITERAL TRANSLATION

where one cannot say this, say [that] no [oath is imposed]. [1][Therefore both cases are] necessary. [2]Regarding buying and selling: Let them see from whom he took the money?

[3]No, it is necessary [in a case] where he took [money] from both of them, from one with his consent, and from one against

TRANSLATION AND COMMENTARY

where such a justification **cannot** be made — the other claimant to a found object cannot be expected to go away and find another similar object, and it will certainly cost him money to replace it — I might mistakenly **say** that **no** oath should be imposed, and we should not suspect either claimant of having seized something to which he had no right. In such a case each claimant may sincerely believe that he found the object first, and the imposition of an oath would be ineffective. [1]Therefore **both cases are necessary** and the Mishnah had to teach them both.

מִקָּח וּמִמְכָּר [2]The Gemara asks: But if the Mishnah is dealing with a case of **buying and selling**, surely the court can investigate and find out from the seller **from which** of the two claimants **he received payment**, and thus solve the question of ownership!

לָא צְרִיכָא [3]The Gemara answers: **No**, the oath **is necessary in a case where** the seller **took** money **from both** claimants. **From one** he accepted the money **willingly** and **from the other unwillingly**

RASHI

אבל מציאה דליכא למימר — סברי ילך וימצא אחרת — זה ודאי מחסרו ממון. **ולחזי זוזי ממאן נקט** — נשאל את המוכר ממי קיבל דמיה. דתניא בקדושין (עג,ב): נאמן בעל המקח לומר "לזה מכרתי ולזה לא מכרתי". ואף על גב דמסיים "במה דברים אמורים שמקחו בידו אבל אין מקחו בידו אינו נאמן", שלא נתן לב לדבר כל כך להיות זכור, מאחר ששניהם חזרו אחריו בפיסוק דמיה — הא אוקימנא התם בדנקט זוזי מתרווייהו, מחד מדעתיה ומחד בעל כרחיה. דכיון דלא עליה רמיא לאסהודי, לא דק כולי האי להיות נזהר, משהלכו מלפניו, הי מדעתיה והי בעל כורחיה. אבל היכא דלא קיבל דמים אלא מחד — מידכר דכיר ליה. **לא צריכא דנקט זוזי מתרווייהו הכי גרסינן:**

NOTES

אֵימָא לָא, צְרִיכָא Say that no oath is imposed... both cases are necessary. When an oath is administered as a means of making someone admit something he has already denied before the court, we assume that the man who is taking the oath is not actually an evil person who would be willing to steal and lie without hesitation. Since an oath would have no effect on such a person, the obligation to take an oath can only be imposed on the assumption that, although the person taking it has strayed from the truth and made a false claim, he nevertheless employed some rationalization to justify his action to himself. Therefore the court makes him take an oath, and, since he is essentially an honest man, he will recoil from taking a false oath and will tell the truth.

The difference in this passage between finding an object and buying it lies in the subtle differences in rationalization used by the different claimants. In the case of a lost object, someone who falsely asserts that he has found something may in fact think that the actual finder has no particular right to what he has found, for the latter has gone to no effort to acquire it. The other claimant is therefore tempted to share in the actual finder's good fortune. In contrast, in the case of a purchase, the rationalization does not derive from the issue of the buyer's right to the object but rather from the consideration that the other claimant loses nothing if he does not receive what he has purchased, since his money will in any case be refunded. Thus no harm is done if the false claimant, who needs the object, takes it. To counter these two specious justifications, both types of cases must be discussed.

וְלֶחֱזֵי זוּזֵי מִמַּאן נָקַט Let them see from whom he took the money. In every case where it is possible to present manifest evidence, this is preferable to proof based on an oath. In the case of a purchase there is the added possibility that witnesses may have been present at the time of the sale, or at least that the seller himself may be able to testify in the matter. See *Tosafot* (ד״ה וְלֶחֱזֵי), which discusses the extent to which the seller's testimony may be relied on. In any event, it seems that the fact that the seller agreed to receive the money is proof that he was willing to sell the object to the owner of that money.

One aspect of the difficulty in clarifying the facts here is related to the laws of acquisition. Since a purchaser does not become the owner of an object merely by the act of payment, but must actually take physical possession of it, being the first to pay does not necessarily confer ownership on the purchaser.

וְלֶחֱזֵי זוּזֵי מִמַּאן נָקַט Let them see from whom he took the money. According to *Rashi*'s explanation (which has been followed in the translation), the Gemara's question is this: In order to determine who bought the garment, we only need to ask the seller who paid him, since we have confidence that the seller will be able to identify the buyer even after the transaction has already been completed. The Gemara answers that the circumstances are such that the seller is *not* believed, because he received money from *both* claimants.

HALAKHAH

מוֹכֵר שֶׁנָּטַל מָעוֹת מִשְּׁנַיִם A seller who took money from two buyers. "If two men bought an article from one man, and the seller received payment from both buyers, from one willingly and from the other unwillingly, and he does not know from whom he received the money willingly and from whom unwillingly, both claimants must take an oath concerning half the article in dispute, and each claimant then receives half of the article and half of the money he paid to the seller," in accordance with the Gemara here. (*Shulḥan Arukh, Ḥoshen Mishpat* 222:1.)

כָּרְחֵיהּ, [1]וְלָא יָדַעֲנָא מִי הוּא מִדַּעְתֵּיהּ וּמִי הוּא בְּעַל כּוֹרְחֵיהּ.

[2]לֵימָא מַתְנִיתִין דְּלָא כְּבֶן נַנָּס? [3]דְּאִי בֶּן נַנָּס, הָאָמַר: ״כֵּיצַד? אֵלּוּ וְאֵלּוּ בָּאִין לִידֵי שְׁבוּעַת שָׁוְא״!

TRANSLATION AND COMMENTARY

[1]**but we do not know** from **whom** he accepted the money **willingly** and from **whom unwillingly**. Therefore the only way to clarify the matter is to impose an oath on both claimants.

לֵימָא מַתְנִיתִין דְּלָא כְּבֶן נַנָּס [2]The Gemara now proceeds to analyze the contents of the Mishnah, to bring out the legal principles upon which it is based, and asks: **Shall we say that our Mishnah is not in accordance with** the view of **Ben Nannas?** [3]**For if** the Mishnah is indeed in accordance with the view of **Ben Nannas, he has surely said** elsewhere that, where two disputants make contradictory claims, the court must not impose oaths upon them, since it is clear that one of them is lying: "**How** can an oath be imposed on both of them? Surely **one or the other will** definitely **utter a false oath**?" Ben Nannas's view is cited in a Mishnah in tractate *Shevuot* (7:5), which discusses the case of an employer who told his employee to go to a certain storekeeper to receive goods to the value of his wages, and who told the storekeeper to give this employee the goods to the value agreed upon, and to charge the sum to the employer's account. Afterwards a dispute arises: The storekeeper claims that he gave the goods to the employee, and the employee claims that he did not receive them. According to the Sages cited in that Mishnah, the storekeeper must swear that he gave the goods to the employee, whereupon the employer must reimburse the storekeeper; and the employee must swear that he did not receive the goods, whereupon the employer must

LITERAL TRANSLATION

his will, [1]and we do not know [from] which one with his consent and [from] which one against his will.

[2]Shall we say that our Mishnah is not in accordance with Ben Nannas? [3]For if [it is in accordance with] Ben Nannas, surely he said: "How [is this ruling possible]? This one or the other one (lit., 'these and these') [will] come to a false oath!"

RASHI

ולא ידעינן מהי מדעתיה ומהי בעל כורחיה ולא גרסינן ״ולא ידע״, דאפילו ידע – בזו אין המוכר נאמן משהלכו, כדמוקי התם. **מתניתין** – דמשבע לתרוייהו וחד משתבע לשיקרא. **דלא כבן ננס** – במסכת שבועות (מה,א) גבי חנוני על פנקסו, אלו ואלו באין לבית דין על מנת לישבע אחד מהם לשוא. אמר בעל הבית לחנוני: ״תן לבני חטים בדינר ועלי לשלם״, או ״לפועלים בסלע מעות שאני חייב בשכרם ועלי ליתן סלע״. הוא אומר ״נתתי״ והוא אומר ״לא נטלתי״, ושניהם תובעין את בעל הבית – שניהם נשבעין ונוטלין מבעל הבית. אמר בן ננס: כילד? אלו ואלו באין לידי שבועת שוא! אלא שניהם נוטלין בלא שבועה.

NOTES

Several commentators reject *Rashi's* interpretation and explain the Gemara's question as follows: Let us ask the seller for information as an ordinary witness, whose testimony has the power to exempt one of the claimants from taking an oath and to impose a more severe oath on the other claimant. The Gemara then replies: The seller himself does not know to whom he sold, because he received money from both claimants *(Tosafot, Ba'al HaMa'or)*.

Talmidei Rabbenu Yonah explain the Gemara's question as meaning: Let us ask the seller, and even if according to the Halakhah he is not believed, the claimant who is lying may be shamed by the seller's presence into admitting the truth, and the imposition of an oath will be avoided.

Rashba and *Ri* in *Tosafot* explain that the Gemara's suggestion is that we ask the *buyers,* rather than the seller, who gave the money. Even though the buyers disagree as to who bought the garment, they are unlikely to lie about a question of fact such as who gave the money.

Ramban explains along similar lines that the subject does not revolve around the evidence of the seller, but rather concerns the question how the claimants can both justify to themselves that they are entitled to claim ownership, when the seller only received money from *one!* He explains that this difficulty forces the Gemara to conclude that both of the claimants paid money and each is able to justify his claim by saying that it was from *him* that the seller accepted money willingly.

לֵימָא מַתְנִיתִין דְּלָא כְּ... **Shall we say that our Mishnah is not in accordance with...?** These inquiries by the Gemara appear to take up a literary-historical question: Who is the author of our Mishnah? (Or, at least, who cannot be its author?) Nonetheless, they have far deeper significance. Our Mishnah, like most Mishnayot, does not set out abstract juridical principles but rather the detailed Halakhah regarding specific instances. But in order to understand the more general meaning of the Mishnah, one must understand the abstract principles behind it, and this is done by comparing it to the viewpoints of other Sages. These comparisons lead the Gemara to more fundamental definitions of the function and significance of the oath imposed by the Sages of the Mishnah, and they also bring out a general conception of how contradictory claims in civil suits are resolved.

אֵלּוּ וְאֵלּוּ בָּאִין לִידֵי שְׁבוּעַת שָׁוְא **This one and the other one will come to a false oath**. The question is raised by the commentators: Why does Ben Nannas maintain, acording to the literal meaning of the text, that they will *both* be uttering a false oath? It is true that the two oaths contradict each other and hence cannot both be true, but there is no need to say that they are *both* false. One of them may be true!

Some commentators (see *Rashi:* ד״ה דְּלָא כְּבֶן נַנָּס) explain Ben Nannas's statement as meaning that, since the matter cannot be resolved, we can be sure that between the two claimants *one or the other* will definitely utter a false oath. (This explanation is reflected in the translation here.)

SAGES

בֶּן נַנָּס **Ben Nannas.** His full name is Rabbi Shimon ben Nannas, one of the Sages of the Mishnah. It appears that he was a colleague of Rabbi Akiva (though younger than him) and of Rabbi Yishmael. The Talmud quotes his rulings on a number of occasions, and his opponent in Halakhic discussions is frequently Rabbi Akiva.

The Talmud makes no mention of his personal history or family background. The only reference we find to Ben Nannas's personality is the superlative praise accorded him by Rabbi Yishmael (*Bava Batra* 10:8): "A person who desires to gain wisdom should occupy himself with civil law... and a person who desires to occupy himself with civil law should study under Shimon ben Nannas."

TERMINOLOGY

לֵימָא מַתְנִיתִין דְּלָא כְּ... **Shall we say that our Mishnah is not in accordance with...?** The Talmud uses this expression to suggest that our Mishnah does not agree with the view of a particular Tanna, a suggestion which is usually rejected later on in the discussion. The answer usually takes the form אֲפִילּוּ תֵּימָא ר׳ פְּלוֹנִי — "You may even say that our Mishnah does agree with the view of Rabbi X," meaning that the case dealt with by the Mishnah is different from the case dealt with by Rabbi X, and thus the rulings are different.

TRANSLATION AND COMMENTARY

pay him the wages he owed him. But Ben Nannas disagrees: How can both the employee and the storekeeper be permitted to swear, when one of them is clearly lying? It is better, says Ben Nannas, for the two claimants, the storekeeper and the employee, to receive what they claim without recourse to an oath, since there is no way we can prove which of them is lying. Similarly, in our Mishnah, one of the claimants must have taken hold of the garment after the other claimant had already picked it up and acquired it. Thus one of the claimants will swear falsely. It would, therefore, be better not to impose an oath on either of the claimants, and let them divide the garment without taking an oath. Accordingly, it seems that our Mishnah, which requires both claimants to swear, is not in accordance with the view of Ben Nannas.

[1]אֲפִילּוּ תֵּימָא בֶּן נַנָּס. [2]הָתָם וַדַּאי אִיכָּא שְׁבוּעַת שָׁוְא, [3]הָכָא אִיכָּא לְמֵימַר דְּלֵיכָּא שְׁבוּעַת שָׁוְא, אֵימוּר דְּתַרְוַיְיהוּ בַּהֲדֵי הֲדָדֵי אַגְבְּהוּהָ! [4]לֵימָא מַתְנִיתִין דְּלָא כְּסוּמָכוֹס? [5]דְּאִי כְּסוּמָכוֹס, הָאָמַר: "מָמוֹן הַמּוּטָּל בְּסָפֵק חוֹלְקִין בְּלֹא שְׁבוּעָה".

LITERAL TRANSLATION

[1]You may even say [that our Mishnah is in accordance with] Ben Nannas. [2]There, there is certainly a false oath, [3][but] here, it is possible to say that there is no false oath, [as one could] say that both of them picked it up together!

[4]Shall we say that our Mishnah is not in accordance with Summakhos? [5]For if [it is in accordance with] Summakhos, surely he said: "Money of doubtful ownership (lit., 'money placed in doubt') we divide without an oath!"

RASHI

אימור בהדי הדדי אגבהוה — למציאה, וכל אחד ואחד סבור: אני הגבהתיה תחילה וכולה שלי, וכי משתבע על חציה — קושטא משתבע. ולענין מקח וממכר נמי, שמא לשניהם נתרצה! **כסומכוס** — בבבא קמא, גבי שור שנגח את הפרה ונמצא עוברה בצדה (מו,א).

אֲפִילּוּ תֵּימָא בֶּן נַנָּס [1]But the Gemara now rejects this line of reasoning: **You may even say** that our Mishnah is in accordance with the view of **Ben Nannas**, and there is a fundamental difference between the two Mishnayot: [2]**There,** in the case of the storekeeper and the employee brought in tractate *Shevuot,* **there is certainly a false oath**, since the two claims are mutually contradictory (for the storekeeper swears that he gave the goods to the employee, whereas the employee swears that he did not receive them); [3]but **here**, in our Mishnah, **it is possible that there is no false oath,** because **one could say** that it is possible **that both** claimants **picked up** the garment **at the same moment**! Thus, even though the two claims ("I found it," and hence "it is all mine") are mutually exclusive, each claimant may believe in good faith that he is the sole rightful owner. Thus the oaths ("No less than half of it is mine") may still be true; for if the two claimants picked up the garment simultaneously, they would each be entitled to half. Similarly, in a case of buying and selling, the seller may have agreed to sell the object to both prospective buyers. In such a case Ben Nannas may well agree that an oath should be imposed on both claimants.

לֵימָא מַתְנִיתִין דְּלָא כְּסוּמָכוֹס [4]The Gemara continues to analyze our Mishnah, and asks: **Shall we say that our Mishnah is not in accordance with** the view of **Summakhos?** [5]**For if** the Mishnah is, indeed, in accordance with the view of **Summakhos, surely he has** laid down elsewhere a general principle that **property the ownership of which cannot be decided** (where two people claim an article but cannot prove their claim), **is divided** between the claimants **without** their taking **an oath**! Since our Mishnah requires both claimants to take an oath, it cannot be in accordance with the view of Summakhos. (See note מָמוֹן הַמּוּטָּל בְּסָפֵק).

SAGES

סוּמָכוֹס **Summakhos.** His full name is Summakhos ben Yosef, and he was one of the fifth and last generation of Tannaim. Summakhos was Rabbi Meir's most distinguished disciple and was responsible for transmitting much of his master's legacy of teachings. Even after Rabbi Meir's death, Summakhos devoted much effort to resolving possible contradictions in those teachings.

Like Rabbi Meir, Summakhos was famous for his חֲרִיפוּת — his acute powers of reasoning. The Talmud (*Eruvin* 13b) praises him as being capable of providing 48 explanations to substantiate every ruling he made in matters of ritual purity.

He was apparently considered one of the leading Sages of his generation, for we even find him recorded as contesting the Halakhic opinions of the greatest of the contemporaries of Rabbi Meir, including Rabbi Yose and Rabbi Eliezer ben Ya'akov. Even the distinguished Sage, Rabbi Natan, sought out Summakhos's opinion.

Summakhos appears to have lived to a great age, for even the Amora, Rav, met him and was taught by him.

LANGUAGE

סוּמָכוֹס **Summakhos.** The source for this name is the Greek word σύμμαχος, Summakhos, which means "ally."

NOTES

Shittah Mekubbetzet explains Ben Nannas's statement more literally: As far as one of the claimants is concerned, the שְׁבוּעַת שָׁוְא — "the vain oath" — is in fact a false oath (because he is lying). As far as the other claimant is concerned, the oath imposed is an *unnecessary* one, which is also called a שְׁבוּעַת שָׁוְא because it is imposed as a result of the false claim of the other litigant. Thus both claimants will ultimately utter a שְׁבוּעַת שָׁוְא.

מָמוֹן הַמּוּטָּל בְּסָפֵק **Property the ownership of which cannot be decided.** Summakhos's principle, that property the ownership of which cannot be decided is divided equally between the claimants to it, is applied by the Talmud to an anonymous Mishnah in tractate *Bava Kamma* (46a). The case discussed there is that of an ox that gored and killed a cow whose newly born calf was then found dead nearby. It was impossible to decide whether the calf had been born

HALAKHAH

מָמוֹן הַמּוּטָּל בְּסָפֵק **Property the ownership of which cannot be decided.** "In a monetary dispute where there is a doubt as to whom the money should be given, and there is no conclusive evidence in support of either the plaintiff or the defendant, even if the plaintiff states that he is **certain** that his claim is correct and the defendant states that he is **uncertain** of the justice of his position, the burden of proof rests upon the person seeking to extract payment," in accordance with the opinion of the Sages here. (*Shulḥan Arukh, Ḥoshen Mishpat* 223:1, 400:1.)

TERMINOLOGY

הַאי מַאי What is this? A term used to express astonishment at the previous statement, often with the significance: "How can you make such a comparison?!"

בִּשְׁלָמָא In peace [i.e., granted that...] This term introduces a question in which the element that is understood and acceptable is placed first and the difficulty is placed second. Its structure here indicates that a Halakhah is understandable according to the viewpoint of one scholar, but is difficult to understand according to the viewpoint of another scholar: "אִי אָמְרַתְּ בִּשְׁלָמָא רַבָּנַן... אֶלָּא אִי אָמְרַתְּ סוּמְכוֹס..." — "If you accept the viewpoint of the Sages it is all right, but if you accept the viewpoint of Summakhos the following difficulty arises...."

TRANSLATION AND COMMENTARY

וְאֶלָּא מַאי [1]The Gemara now attacks the basis of this question, and objects: **Then what** would you **rather say** instead — that the Mishnah follows the view of the **Sages** who disagree with Summakhos?! [2]Surely not, for in a case where ownership of property cannot be decided **they say**: "The **burden of proof rests on whoever seeks to take** money or property **away from someone else.**" Yet in our Mishnah, even though each claimant seeks to take the garment away from the other one, and neither brings proof that he is telling the truth (by bringing witnesses, for example), nevertheless the Mishnah rules that the claimants take oaths and divide the article. Our Mishnah would seem, therefore, to be in accordance neither with Summakhos nor with the Sages! (In this comparison of cases, three rulings have been quoted: [1] Our Mishnah, where the object is divided after the claimants have each taken an oath; [2] the ruling of Summakhos, that in a case of doubt the object is divided between the claimants without recourse to an oath; [3] the ruling of the Sages in that case that the burden of proof rests on the person seeking to exact payment. Since these three rulings seem to be mutually exclusive, we are seemingly forced to the conclusion that our Mishnah is in accordance neither with Summakhos nor with the Sages!)

הַאי מַאי [3]The Gemara now rejects this objection: **What** sort of comparison **is this** that you have just made? [4]There is no problem **if you say** that our Mishnah follows the view of **the Sages**. It is possible to distinguish between the two cases and to justify the different rulings [5]**There,** in the case brought in tractate *Bava Kamma* where the responsibility for the death of the calf is in doubt, the two litigants **are not both holding on to** (in physical possession of) a disputed item. The money demanded in compensation for the damage done to the calf is in the possession of the owner of the ox. Therefore **the Sages say: Whoever seeks to take** property **away from someone else** (in this case the owner of the calf from the owner of the ox), **must bring proof** that the property is his, because, in principle, possession of money or an article does confer a presumptive advantage on its possessor. Therefore the owner of the calf must bring proof that the ox was responsible for the death of the calf. [6]But **here,** in our Mishnah, **where both** claimants **are holding on** to the garment, and neither is in exclusive possession of it, the claimants are not considered to be "extracting" property from each other, and hence **they divide** the garment between them **after taking an oath.**

[1]וְאֶלָּא מַאי, רַבָּנַן?! [2]הָא אָמְרִי: "הַמּוֹצִיא מֵחֲבֵירוֹ עָלָיו הָרְאָיָה"!

[3]הַאי מַאי?! [4]אִי אָמְרַתְּ בִּשְׁלָמָא רַבָּנַן: [5]הָתָם דְּלָא תָּפְסֵי תַּרְוַיְיהוּ, אָמְרוּ רַבָּנַן: "הַמּוֹצִיא מֵחֲבֵירוֹ עָלָיו הָרְאָיָה". [6]הָכָא, דְּתַרְוַיְיהוּ תָּפְסֵי, פָּלְגִי לָהּ בִּשְׁבוּעָה.

LITERAL TRANSLATION

[1]But what [do you say, that our Mishnah follows] the Sages?! [2]Surely they say: "Whoever seeks to take [property] away from his fellow, upon him is the [burden of] proof"!

[3]What [comparison] is this?! [4]It is well if you say [that our Mishnah is in accordance with] the Sages: [5]There, where both of them are not holding on, the Sages say: "Whoever seeks to take [property] away from his fellow, upon him is the [burden of] proof." [6][But] here, where both are holding on [to the garment], they divide it with an oath.

RASHI

עליו הראיה — בעדים, ואי לא — לא גבי מידי, והכא חולקין [בשבועה]. הכי גרסינן: **אי אמרת בשלמא רבנן, התם דלא תפסי תרוייהו אמור רבנן כו׳, הכא דתפסי תרוייהו פלגי בשבועה, אלא אי אמרת סומכוס, ומה התם דלא תפסי תרוייהו אמר סומכוס פלגי בלא שבועה** — הכא דתפסי תרוייהו לא כל שכן. **תרוייהו תפסי** — ואין כאן מוציא מחבירו. **בשבועה פלגי לה** — כיון דמחסר גויינא במה שחבירו תופס, דהאי תפיס בכולה והאי תפיס [בכולה], לא קים להו לרבנן להוציא ממון מחזקתו בכדי, כדאמרינן התם: לרבנן דבעי ראיה הצריכום שבועה.

NOTES

dead before the goring (in which case the owner of the ox could not be held responsible for the loss of the calf) or after the goring (in which case the miscarriage of the calf could be attributed to the goring). The Mishnah requires the owner of the ox to pay half the damages that he would have had to pay for the calf if it had been certain that the ox had caused its death. In discussing this Mishnah the Talmud asserts that the viewpoint expressed in it is that of Summakhos, who maintains that, where the ownership of property or money is in doubt, the property or money is divided equally between the claimants. The majority viewpoint of the Sages is, however, that the burden of proof rests on the person seeking to extract money from another person. In the case discussed in that Mishnah, therefore, the Sages would exempt the owner of the ox from making any payment for the loss of the calf, because the ox cannot be proved to have been responsible for its death.

דְּלָא תָּפְסֵי תַּרְוַיְיהוּ Where both are holding on to the disputed object. Absolute ownership of an object depends on judicial proof that the object belongs to its possessor (through inheritance, purchase, or gift). But there are also presumptions (חֲזָקָה) regarding ownership, which although not absolute proof nevertheless create a situation of apparent proof. One of these presumptions, as in the case of the owner of the bull, is חֶזְקַת מָרָא קַמָּא — prior ownership:

[1] אֶלָּא אִי אָמְרַתְּ סוּמָכוֹס, [2] הָשְׁתָּא וּמָה הָתָם דְּלָא תָּפְסֵי תַּרְוַיְיהוּ, חוֹלְקִין בְּלֹא שְׁבוּעָה, [3] הָכָא דְּתַרְוַיְיהוּ תָּפְסֵי לָהּ, לֹא כָּל שֶׁכֵּן?!
[4] אֲפִילּוּ תֵּימָא סוּמָכוֹס. [5] כִּי אָמַר סוּמָכוֹס, "שֶׁמָּא וְשֶׁמָּא", אֲבָל "בָּרִי וּבָרִי", לֹא אָמַר.
[6] וּלְרַבָּה בַּר רַב הוּנָא, דְּאָמַר: אָמַר סוּמָכוֹס אֲפִילּוּ "בָּרִי וּבָרִי", [7] מַאי אִיכָּא לְמֵימַר?
[8] אֲפִילּוּ תֵּימָא סוּמָכוֹס. [9] כִּי

LITERAL TRANSLATION

[1] But if you say [that our Mishnah is in accordance with] Summakhos, [2] now if there, where both of them are not holding on [to the disputed object], they divide [it] without [taking] an oath, [3] here, where both of them are holding on to it, how much more so!

[4] You may even say [that our Mishnah is in accordance with] Summakhos. [5] When Summakhos stated [his view, it was in a case of] "perhaps and perhaps," but [in a case of] "certain and certain," he did not say [so].

[6] But [according] to Rabbah bar Rav Huna, who said: "Summakhos said [so] even [in a case of] certain and certain," [7] what is there to say?

[8] You may even say [that our Mishnah is in accordance with] Summakhos. [9] When

RASHI

שמא ושמא — כי התם, דקתני: נמצאת עוברה בצדה, ואין ידוע אם עד שלא ילדה נגחה, אם משילדה נגחה ולא מת הולד מחמת הנגיחה אלא מאליו, וכיון דכל חד שמא טעין, ליכא למרמי עלייהו שבועה. **דרבה בר רב הונא** — בפרק "השואל" (בבא מציעא ק,א).

TRANSLATION AND COMMENTARY

[1] **But if you say that our Mishnah is in accordance with** the view of **Summakhos,** it is difficult to reconcile the different rulings in the two cases. [2] For **if there,** in the case brought in tractate *Bava Kamma,* **where the two** claimants **are not both holding on** to the disputed object, but one, the owner of the ox, is in possession, and the owner of the calf is claiming from him, Summakhos nevertheless maintains that **they divide** the disputed object **without taking an oath,** [3] then **here,** in our Mishnah, **where both** claimants **are** indeed **holding on** to the disputed object, **how much more so** should the two claimants be permitted to divide the garment without taking an oath! Thus it would seem that our Mishnah cannot be in accordance with the view of Summakhos.

אֲפִילּוּ תֵּימָא סוּמָכוֹס [4] But the Gemara rejects this line of reasoning and again seeks to argue that our Mishnah can be in agreement with Summakhos: **You may even say** that our Mishnah follows the view of **Summakhos,** [5] but that there is a fundamental difference between our Mishnah and Summakhos's case: **Summakhos stated** that property the ownership of which cannot be decided is divided between the claimants without an oath, **in a case of "perhaps and perhaps,"** where neither claimant was present at the time of the incident and neither maintains with certainty that his claim is correct, but each maintains: "The other claimant cannot bring more convincing proof than I can, and perhaps the item is mine." **But in a case of "certain and certain,"** where both claimants are positive in their claim that the disputed object is theirs, Summakhos **did not state** that the item should be divided without an oath. Thus even Summakhos may agree that in the case discussed in our Mishnah, which is a case of "certain and certain," where both claimants are positive that the garment is theirs, they divide it only after each claimant has sworn that no less than half the garment is his.

וּלְרַבָּה בַּר רַב הוּנָא [6] The Gemara now asks: **But according to Rabbah bar Rav Huna, who said: Summakhos stated** that disputed property is to be divided without an oath **even in a case** where both litigants **claim with certainty** that the disputed object is theirs, [7] **what is there to say**? Must we assume that, according to Rabbah bar Rav Huna, our Mishnah is not in accordance with the view of Summakhos?

אֲפִילּוּ תֵּימָא סוּמָכוֹס [8] The Gemara now rejects this argument and replies: **You may even say** that our Mishnah is in accordance with **Summakhos**, even according to Rabbah bar Rav Huna, [9] and there is a

NOTES

the fact that an object did previously belong absolutely to a certain person gives him an advantage against any claimant who wishes now to deprive him of it. In the case of "two holding a garment," we have no prior ownership, but there is apparently another presumption, that related to actually grasping the object, and this too creates an apparent presumption regarding ownership. Since, in this case, two people are actually grasping the object, there would seem to be no need to use other means, such as an oath, to resolve the doubt regarding its ownership.

דְּרָרָא דְּמָמוֹנָא **A doubt about the money.** Various explanations have been given of this concept by the commentators: *Rashi* explains the concept as meaning "financial loss," a situation that involves a financial loss to one or both of the parties involved. In many situations we hesitate to award the disputed object to one of the parties (or to divide it), in case we thereby cause the other party an unjust loss. But in the case of our Mishnah neither party stands to lose financially.

Ramban questions *Rashi's* opinion based on a passage in *Bava Batra* 35a and offers the interpretation that דְּרָרָא דְּמָמוֹנָא means עִיקַּר תְּבִיעַת מָמוֹן — "a claim based on an undisputed connection to the money." This interpretation is also accepted by *Rabbenu Ḥananel.*

SAGES

Rabbah bar Rav Huna. The son of Rabbi Huna, this Rabbah was a Babylonian Amora of the second and third generation. He was a student of Rav and transmitted teachings in Rav's name. Rabbah bar Rav Huna was, however, the outstanding student of his father, Rav Huna. He was also closely connected with Rav Hisda and was his student and colleague. However, he took part in Halakhic discussions with most of the Sages of his generation. Rabbah bar Rav Huna had close relations with the Exilarch, and we frequently hear of him visiting his house, though he did not regard himself as subject to the Exilarch's authority, and he defended his own independence. Rabbah bar Rav Huna was known for being extremely humble, and he spoke of even the most junior of his colleagues with respect. He died in Babylonia and was buried in Eretz Israel. A liturgical poem recited to eulogize him at his funeral has been preserved. He had a son, Rava, who was one of the Amoraim of the following generation.

TERMINOLOGY

אֲפִילּוּ תֵּימָא ר׳ פְּלוֹנִי **You may even say [that the Mishnah is in accordance with] Rabbi X,** i.e., it is possible to explain the Mishnah even in accordance with the viewpoint of Rabbi X, even though in the previous stage of the discussion it had been suggested that the Mishnah was incompatible with his opinion.

אָמַר סוּמָכוֹס, הֵיכָא דְּאִיכָּא דְּרָרָא דְּמָמוֹנָא, [1]אֲבָל הֵיכָא דְּלֵיכָּא דְּרָרָא דְּמָמוֹנָא, לָא. [2]וְלָאו קַל וָחוֹמֶר הוּא? [3]וּמָה הָתָם, דְּאִיכָּא דְּרָרָא דְּמָמוֹנָא לְמָר, וְאִיכָּא דְּרָרָא דְּמָמוֹנָא לְמָר, [3A] [4]וְאִיכָּא לְמֵימַר כּוּלָּהּ לְמָר, וְאִיכָּא לְמֵימַר כּוּלָּהּ לְמָר, [5]אָמַר סוּמָכוֹס: "מָמוֹן הַמּוּטָּל בְּסָפֵק חוֹלְקִין בְּלֹא שְׁבוּעָה". [6]הָכָא דְּלֵיכָּא דְּרָרָא דְּמָמוֹנָא, דְּאִיכָּא לְמֵימַר דְּתַרְוַיְיהוּ הִיא, לֹא כָּל שֶׁכֵּן?! [7]אֲפִילּוּ תֵּימָא סוּמָכוֹס. שְׁבוּעָה זוֹ מִדְּרַבָּנַן הִיא, כִּדְרַבִּי יוֹחָנָן.

LITERAL TRANSLATION

Summakhos stated [his view], [it was] where there is a doubt about the money, [1]but where there is no doubt about the money, no.

[2]But is it not a *kal vaḥomer*? [3]If there, where there is a doubt about the money for one, and there is a doubt about the money for the other, [3A] [4]and it is possible to say [that] all of it [belongs] to the one, and it is possible to say [that] all of it [belongs] to the other, [5]Summakhos said: "Money of doubtful ownership we divide without an oath," [6]here where there is no [inherent] doubt about the money, since it is possible to say that it belongs to both of them, how much more so!?

[7]You may even say [that our Mishnah is in accordance with] Summakhos. This oath is Rabbinical, as [maintained] by Rabbi Yoḥanan.

TRANSLATION AND COMMENTARY

fundamental difference between the two cases: **Summakhos stated** that property whose ownership cannot be decided is divided between the claimants without an oath only **where the doubt concerning the** ownership of the disputed **property** (דְּרָרָא דְּמָמוֹנָא) is independent of the two litigants' claims. (Liability for the dead calf depends on the actual cause of death, not on any argument advanced by its owner or by the ox's owner.) [1]**But** he did **not** rule this way in a case **where the doubt concerning the** ownership of the **property** was created by the claims of the litigants, as in the case of our Mishnah, where the doubt regarding the ownership of the garment derives from the two conflicting claims to it, and without their conflicting claims the court would have assumed that the garment belonged to both of them. In such a case, Summakhos would accept the argument of the Sages. Thus it would now seem that even Summakhos could agree that the claimants in our Mishnah divide ownership of the disputed garment after both have taken an oath.

וְלָאו קַל וָחוֹמֶר [2]But the Gemara immediately objects to this line of reasoning: **But** can **it not** be proved by a ***kal vaḥomer*** (an *a fortiori* inference), that according to Summakhos the claimants in our Mishnah should not be required to take an oath? [3]The argument is as follows: **If there,** in a case **where there is an** independent **doubt about** the claims of the **one and a** similar **doubt about** the claims of **the other,** [3A] [4]**and it can be said that all of** the disputed property **belongs to the one** claimant, **and it can be said that all of it belongs to the other** claimant, but it cannot possibly belong to both of them — if even in such a case [5]**Summakhos said: "Property whose ownership cannot be decided is divided** between the claimants **without an oath,"** [6]then **here,** in the case of our Mishnah, **where there is no inherent doubt about the property** at stake, **since it is possible that** the garment **belongs to both of them, how much more so** would Summakhos maintain that it should be divided without an oath!

אֲפִילּוּ תֵּימָא סוּמָכוֹס [7]The Gemara now rejects this argument: **You may even say** that our Mishnah is in accordance with the view of **Summakhos,** and there is no contradiction between the two rulings: **This oath,** mentioned in our Mishnah, which the two claimants are required to take, **is** entirely of **Rabbinic** origin, **as**

TERMINOLOGY

קַל וָחוֹמֶר **An *a fortiori* inference.** One of the fundamental principles of Rabbinic exegesis, קַל וָחוֹמֶר is listed in all the standard lists of exegetical rules. In essence, this is a rule of logical argumentation by means of which a comparison is drawn between two cases, one lenient and the other stringent. קַל וָחוֹמֶר asserts that if the law is stringent in a case where we are usually lenient, then it will certainly be stringent in a more serious case; likewise, if the law is lenient in a case where we are usually not lenient, then it will certainly be lenient in a less serious case. *A fortiori* arguments were compiled by the Talmudic Rabbis. For example, "If you have run with the foot-soldiers, and they have wearied you, how can you contend with horses?" (Jeremiah 12:5.) This is one of the most commonly encountered exegetical principles, since *a fortiori* inferences can be drawn even without support from tradition (as opposed to *gezerah shavah*, for example). Sometimes, the Sages referred to *a fortiori* inferences as דִּין — "logical argumentation."

Occasionally, formal restrictions limit the use of *kal vaḥomer* argumentation.

RASHI

דררא דממונא — חסרון ממון. שאם יפרע זה שלא כדין, הוי חסרון ממון. ואם נפטרנו שלא כדין, נמצא זה חסר ולד פרתו. **ומה התם דאיכא דררא דממונא כו׳** — איזה מהן שמפסיד החצי שלא כדין, אתה מחסרו ממון. **איכא למימר כוליה דמר** — ועוד: על כרחך או כוליה דמר או כוליה דמר, אפילו הכי חולקין בלא שבועה. **הכא דליכא דררא דממונא** — ועוד, דאיכא למימר דתרוייהו בהדי הדדי אגבהוה. **לא כל שכן** — דחולקין בלא שבועה?

NOTES

דְּרָרָא דְּמָמוֹנָא (cont.): *Rashba* explains that both interpretations are correct, and each is used by the Gemara, depending on the circumstances. In the present context the term is to be interpreted as *Rashi* does.

Tosafot offers a third interpretation: דְּרָרָא דְּמָמוֹנָא refers to a situation where our doubts about the ownership of the article arise independently of the parties' claims. But in the case of our Mishnah, before the arguments were heard, the court automatically assumed that the garment was owned *jointly* by both parties. (The translation here reflects the interpretation of *Tosafot.*)

Rosh suggests a similar interpretation: דְּרָרָא דְּמָמוֹנָא means a situation in which it is clear to the court that the money belongs to only *one* of the litigants.

[1] דְּאָמַר רַבִּי יוֹחָנָן: שְׁבוּעָה זוֹ תַּקָּנַת חֲכָמִים הִיא, שֶׁלֹּא יְהֵא כָּל אֶחָד וְאֶחָד הוֹלֵךְ וְתוֹקֵף בְּטַלִּיתוֹ שֶׁל חֲבֵירוֹ וְאוֹמֵר "שֶׁלִּי הוּא".

[2] לֵימָא מַתְנִיתִין דְּלָא כְּרַבִּי יוֹסֵי? [3] דְּאִי כְּרַבִּי יוֹסֵי, הָא אָמַר: "אִם כֵּן, מַה הִפְסִיד רַמַּאי? [4] אֶלָּא, הַכֹּל יְהֵא מוּנָּח עַד שֶׁיָּבֹא אֵלִיָּהוּ".

LITERAL TRANSLATION

[1] For Rabbi Yoḥanan said: This oath is an ordinance of the Sages, so that everyone should not go and seize hold of the garment of his fellow and say, "It is mine."

[2] Shall we say [that] our Mishnah is not in accordance with Rabbi Yose? [3] For if it is in accordance with Rabbi Yose, surely he said: "If so, what has the fraudulent person lost? [4] Rather, let the whole [amount] be deposited until Elijah comes."

RASHI

ותוקף = אוחז. דרבי יוסי – לקמן ב"המפקיד" (בבא מציעא לז,א): שנים שהפקידו אצל אחד, זה מנה וזה מאתים, זה אומר מאתים שלי וזה אומר מאתים שלי. וקאמר תנא קמא: נותן לזה מנה ולזה מנה, והשאר יהא מונח עד שיבוא אליהו. אמר רבי יוסי: אם כן מה הפסיד הרמאי, ולמה יודה? הרי קיבל את שלו! אלא הכל יהא מונח, ויפסיד הרמאי. והכא נמי יהא מונח.

TRANSLATION AND COMMENTARY

maintained by Rabbi Yoḥanan. [1]**For Rabbi Yoḥanan said: The oath** in our Mishnah, where two claimants are holding on to a garment, **is a Rabbinic ordinance** instituted **to prevent anyone from going and seizing another person's garment and saying, "It is mine."** Thus even Summakhos may agree that the claimants in our Mishnah should take an oath, for the oath is not needed in this case to clarify the doubt but in order to deter people from seizing articles that do not belong to them.

לֵימָא מַתְנִיתִין דְּלָא כְּרַ׳ יוֹסֵי [2]The Gemara now continues its analysis of our Mishnah and suggests: **Shall we say that our Mishnah is not in accordance with** the opinion of **Rabbi Yose**? Rabbi Yose states in a Mishnah later on in our tractate (37a) that if two people deposit different amounts of money with a third party (for example, if one deposits one maneh [100 dinarim] and the other deposits 200 dinarim), and the depositary forgets who gave him the larger sum, and each depositor claims that he deposited the larger sum, then none of the money may be returned to either depositor. The entire 300 dinarim are set aside and left until the coming of the Prophet Elijah, who will be able by his prophetic powers to reveal the truth (see note under concepts). The Sages, however, maintain that each depositor is entitled to 100 dinarim and that the remainder is left until the coming of Elijah. [3]The Talmud now suggests that our Mishnah cannot agree with Rabbi Yose, **for if** our Mishnah **is,** indeed, **in accordance with** the viewpoint of **Rabbi Yose, surely he has said** in the Mishnah referred to above: **"If so,"** i.e., if one adopts the position of the Sages that each depositor receives 100 dinarim, **"what has the fraudulent** depositor **lost"** by claiming the larger sum? The depositor of the smaller sum has nothing to lose by lying, since in any case he will get 100 dinarim back! [4]**"Rather,"** says Rabbi Yose, **"let the whole amount be left** with the depositary (according to other opinions, with the court) **until** the Prophet **Elijah comes!"** Thus it seems that, according to Rabbi Yose, disputed property is not divided between the claimants, as our Mishnah rules, but rather left with the depositary (or the court) until the conflict is ultimately resolved by Elijah!

NOTES

שֶׁלֹּא יְהֵא תּוֹקֵף **To prevent a person from seizing...** Summakhos agrees that the oath imposed in our Mishnah is a Rabbinic enactment. The point being added here is that the purpose of the oath is not to clarify ownership but rather to deter fraudulent claimants. For this reason it was instituted only in cases such as that of our Mishnah, which easily lend themselves to fraud, but not in cases where fraudulent disputes are uncommon, such as claims for damages (*Talmid Rabbenu Peretz, Rosh, Ritva*).

יְהֵא מוּנָּח **Let it be deposited.** There are differing views among the Rishonim as to when the object in dispute is set aside until Elijah comes: *Rashi* and others say that wherever it is certain that one of the claims is fraudulent and the two claimants are both in possession of the object, it is set aside until the coming of Elijah.

Tosafot and others say that whenever it is impossible that the object is jointly owned by both claimants, and they are both in possession of the object, it is set aside until the coming of Elijah.

Ramban and others say that wherever it is certain that one of the claims is fraudulent, the object is not divided between the claimants. But the object is only set aside until the coming of Elijah if it is already in the possession of a third party. Otherwise the rule is כָּל דְּאַלִּים גָּבַר — "whoever has the greater power wins."

Another problem related to this subject is: With whom must the deposit be left? Some authorities state that it must remain in the possession of the person with whom it was originally deposited (*Rambam* and others). Other authorities say that the person looking after the deposit gives it to the court; for if that were not the case, any deposit holder could lie and claim that he does not remember the details of the deposit, and then the sum which is in doubt would remain in his hands (*Mordekhai*).

HALAKHAH

שְׁבוּעָה זוֹ תַּקָּנַת חֲכָמִים **This oath is a Rabbinic ordinance.** "This oath that must be taken by two claimants who are both holding on to a disputed article is a Rabbinic ordinance. Its purpose is to prevent people from seizing articles belonging to others and taking them without even being required to take an oath." *(Rambam, Sefer Mishpatim, To'en VeNit'an 9:7.)*

CONCEPTS

עַד שֶׁיָּבֹא אֵלִיָּהוּ **Until Elijah comes.** The Prophet Malachi (3:23-24) writes that before the coming of the Messiah, Elijah the Prophet will come and repair what needs to be repaired in the world. The use of the expression, "Until the coming of Elijah," therefore means that only when a true prophet comes, who will be able, through the faculty of prophecy, to see truths that are hidden from us, then doubt will be resolved absolutely. Practically speaking, it means that the decision in the case is postponed for an indefinite period of time.

SAGES

רַבִּי יוֹסֵי **Rabbi Yose.** See article on p. 21

רַבִּי יוֹחָנָן **Rabbi Yoḥanan.** This is Rabbi Yoḥanan bar Nappaḥa, one of the greatest Amoraim, whose teachings are of primary importance both in the Babylonian and the Jerusalem Talmuds. He lived in Tiberias and lived to a great age. Almost nothing is known of his family origins. He became an orphan at an early age, and, although his family apparently had considerable property, he spent most of his wealth in his strong desire to study Torah constantly, so that he actually became poor. He was just old enough to study under Rabbi Yehudah HaNasi, the editor of the Mishnah. But most of his Torah knowledge was derived from Rabbi Yehudah HaNasi's students, from Ḥizkiyah ben Ḥiyya and from Rabbi Oshaya, from Rabbi Ḥanina and from his outstanding teacher, Rabbi Yannai, who greatly praised him. In time he became the head of a yeshivah in Tiberias, marking the beginning of a period during which his fame and influence constantly increased. For a long time Rabbi Yoḥanan was the leading Rabbinical scholar of the entire Jewish world, not only in Eretz Israel but also in Babylonia, whose Sages respected him greatly. Many of them came to Eretz Israel and became his outstanding students. He was a master of both Halakhah and Aggadah. His teachings in both areas are found very widely, and serve as the basis for both of the Talmuds. In recognition of his intellectual and spiritual greatness the Halakhah is decided according to his opinion in almost every case, even when Rav or Shmuel, the great Amoraim of Babylonia (whom he himself regarded as greater than he), disagree with him. Only when he disagrees with his teachers in Eretz Israel (such as Rabbi Yannai and Rabbi Yehoshua ben Levi) does the Halakhah not follow his opinion.

We know little about his life, and only certain details are recorded. Rabbi Yoḥanan was famous for being handsome, and much was said in praise of his comeliness. By nature he was excitable, so that occasionally he was too severe with his friends and students, and immediately afterwards was stricken with remorse. We know that his life was full of suffering. Ten of his sons died in his lifetime, though he also had daughters. There is a Geonic tradition that one of his sons remained alive, Rabbi Matena, who was an Amora of Babylonia. The death of his student, friend, and brother-in-law, Resh Lakish, for which he considered himself responsible, brought his own death closer.

Rabbi Yoḥanan had many students. In fact all the Amoraim of Eretz Israel in succeeding generations were his students and imbibed his teachings — so much so that he is said to be the author of the Jerusalem Talmud. His greatest students were his brother-in-law Resh Lakish, Rabbi Elazar, Rabbi Ḥiyya bar Abba, Rabbi Abbahu, Rabbi Yose bar Ḥanina, Rabbi Ammi, and Rabbi Assi.

TRANSLATION AND COMMENTARY

אֶלָּא מַאי רַבָּנַן [1]But the Gemara now attacks the suggestion that our Mishnah is not in accordance with the opinion of Rabbi Yose and objects: **Then what would you rather say** instead — that our Mishnah is in accordance with **the Sages** who disagree with Rabbi Yose and maintain that each depositor is entitled to 100 dinarim? [2]**Since the Sages say** there that **the remainder** of the deposit, which is not returned to either of the depositors, is left with the third party (or the court) **until Elijah comes**, they would also argue that the garment mentioned in our Mishnah, **too, is like the remainder** of the deposit in that case, **since** there is obviously a **doubt** as to who actually owns the garment! Thus our Mishnah does not appear to conform to the viewpoint of the Sages who disagree with Rabbi Yose; for they too would presumably argue (contrary to the ruling in our Mishnah) that the garment should be left with the court rather than divided between the claimants! We are thus seemingly forced to the conclusion that our Mishnah is in accordance neither with Rabbi Yose nor with the Sages who differ with him!

הַאי מַאי [3]But the Gemara now rejects this objection to the suggestion that our Mishnah is not in accordance with the opinion of Rabbi Yose: **What** sort of comparison **is this** that you have just made? [4]For, as the Gemara now explains, our Mishnah can in fact be understood in accordance with the view of the Sages: **There is no problem if you say** that our Mishnah is in accordance with the view of **the Sages**, and it is possible to justify the difference between the rulings in the two cases: [5]**There**, in the case of the two depositors, **the** disputed **maneh** (100 dinarim) **definitely belongs to** only **one of** the two depositors, and therefore **the Sages say** that **it** should **be left** with the depositary (or the court) **until Elijah comes!** [6]But **here**, in our Mishnah, **where it is possible to say that the garment belongs to both** claimants, since they might have picked up the garment together and hence each may legitimately be entitled to half of it, **the Sages say** that the two claimants **divide** the garment **after taking an oath**. [7]**But if you say** that our Mishnah is in accordance with **Rabbi Yose**, it is difficult to explain the different rulings in the two cases. [8]For **if there**, in the case of the two depositors, **where both** depositors **are certainly entitled to** the sum of **100 dinarim** each, since each deposited at least 100 dinarim with the depositary, [9]**Rabbi Yose** nevertheless **says: "Let** the entire deposit **be left** with the third party (or the court)

LITERAL TRANSLATION

[1]But what [do you say, that our Mishnah follows] the Sages? [2]Since the Sages say: "Let the remainder be deposited until Elijah comes," this too is like the remainder, since it is a doubt!

[3]What [comparison] is this? [4]It is well if you say [that our Mishnah is in accordance with] the Sages: [5]There, where this maneh definitely [belongs] to one of them, the Sages say: "Let it be deposited until Elijah comes." [6][But] here, where it is possible to say that it [belongs] to both of them, the Sages say [that] they divide [it] with an oath. [7]But if you say [that] it is [in accordance with] Rabbi Yose, [8]now if there, where a maneh definitely belongs to one and a maneh [definitely] belongs to the other, [9]Rabbi Yose said: "Let it be deposited until Elijah comes,"

[1]אֶלָּא מַאי, רַבָּנַן? [2]כֵּיוָן דְּאָמְרִי רַבָּנַן: "הַשְּׁאָר יְהֵא מוּנָּח עַד שֶׁיָּבֹא אֵלִיָּהוּ", הָא נַמִי כִּשְׁאָר דָּמֵי, דִּסְפֵיקָא הִיא!

[3]הַאי מַאי?! [4]אִי אָמְרַתְּ בִּשְׁלָמָא רַבָּנַן: [5]הָתָם, דְּוַדַּאי הַאי מָנֶה דְּחַד מִינַּיְיהוּ הוּא, אָמְרִי רַבָּנַן: "יְהֵא מוּנָּח עַד שֶׁיָּבֹא אֵלִיָּהוּ". [6]הָכָא, דְּאִיכָּא לְמֵימַר דְּתַרְוַיְיהוּ הוּא, אָמְרִי רַבָּנַן פָּלְגִי בִּשְׁבוּעָה. [7]אֶלָּא אִי אָמְרַתְּ רַבִּי יוֹסֵי הִיא, [8]הָשְׁתָּא וּמַה הָתָם, דִּבְוַדַּאי אִיכָּא מָנֶה לְמָר וְאִיכָּא מָנֶה לְמָר, [9]אָמַר רַבִּי יוֹסֵי: "יְהֵא מוּנָּח עַד שֶׁיָּבֹא

RASHI

הא נמי כשאר דמיא — דהתם על מנה השני הם דנין, והלו דנין על הטלית כולה. **דחד מינייהו הוא** — ולין לומר יחלוקו.

NOTES

שִׁיטַת רַבִּי יוֹסֵי **Rabbi Yose's point of view.** Up to this point the discussion in the Gemara has dealt with the relations between three different approaches that we have found among the Sages of the Talmud with regard to an object (or sum of money) whose status is in doubt because various people, none of whom has convincing proof, claim ownership of it. At first glance it seems that the approach taken by the Mishnah is that one imposes an oath on both litigants in order *to clarify the doubt*. The approach taken by Summakhos is that in such a case the sum in doubt is divided between the claimants without the imposition of an oath. Finally, Rabbi Yose's approach is that the disputed object is deposited with someone else rather than being given to either claimant ("יְהֵא מוּנָּח עַד שֶׁיָּבֹא אֵלִיָּהוּ"). Since these three views were not expressed as abstract juridical principles but rather as decisions in specific cases, the possibility arises that we may be able to reconcile them, and that the specific and differing decisions in each separate case may in fact depend on its particular conditions. Therefore Rabbi Yose's approach, in which the disputed sum is actually confiscated, is said to apply only where one of the litigants is known to be fraudulent, and where no third party is responsible for compensating the party who suffers loss through the decision.

אֵלִיָּהוּ", [1]הָכָא, דְּאִיכָּא לְמֵימַר דְּחַד מִינַּיְיהוּ הוּא, לֹא כָּל שֶׁכֵּן?!
[2]אֲפִילּוּ תֵּימָא רַבִּי יוֹסֵי. [3]הָתָם, וַדַּאי אִיכָּא רַמַּאי. הָכָא, מִי יֵימַר דְּאִיכָּא רַמַּאי? [4]אֵימָא תַּרְוַיְיהוּ בַּהֲדֵי הֲדָדֵי אַגְבְּהוּהּ.
[5]אִי נַמִי: הָתָם, קָנֵיס לֵיהּ רַבִּי יוֹסֵי לְרַמַּאי כִּי הֵיכִי דְּלוֹדֵי. [6]הָכָא, מַאי פְּסֵידָא אִית לֵיהּ דְּלוֹדֵי?
[7]תֵּינַח מְצִיאָה, מִקָּח וּמִמְכָּר מַאי אִיכָּא לְמֵימַר? [8]אֶלָּא מְחַוַּורְתָּא כִּדְשָׁנִין מֵעִיקָּרָא.

LITERAL TRANSLATION

[1]here, where it is possible to say that it belongs to one of them, how much more so!?

[2]You may even say [that our Mishnah is in accordance with] Rabbi Yose. [3]There, there is definitely a fraudulent person. Here, who will say that there is a fraudulent person? [4]Say [that] both of them picked it up together.

[5]Alternatively (lit., "if also") [you can say]: There, Rabbi Yose penalized the fraudulent person in order that he should confess. [6]Here, what loss does he have that he should confess?

[7]This is plausible (lit., "let it rest") in [the case of] a found object. [But in] buying and selling what is there to say? [8]Rather, it is clear as we answered in the beginning.

TRANSLATION AND COMMENTARY

until Elijah comes," [1]then **here**, in our Mishnah, **where it is possible to say that** the entire garment **belongs to** only **one** of the claimants, and the other one may be lying, **how much more so** should the entire garment be left until Elijah comes! Rabbi Yose would surely not accept our Mishnah's ruling that the garment is divided between the claimants!

אֲפִילּוּ תֵּימָא רַבִּי יוֹסֵי [2]But the Gemara now rejects this line of reasoning and argues that our Mishnah can indeed be interpreted in accordance with Rabbi Yose's view: **You may even say that our Mishnah is in accordance with Rabbi Yose,** because there is a fundamental difference between the two cases: [3]**There**, in the case of the two depositors, one of the two **is definitely a fraudulent person**, for if both claim that they deposited 200 dinarim, one of them is certainly lying. But **here**, in the case of our Mishnah, **who can say that** one of the claimants **is fraudulent**? [4]Perhaps both claimants are telling what they believe to be the truth, as it is possible to **say** that **both** claimants **picked up** the garment **at the same time**! Thus Rabbi Yose could well agree that in the case in our Mishnah the two claimants divide the garment, since it is possible that each one sincerely believes that he is entitled to it, and there is no reason to penalize them both.

אִי נַמִי [5]Or **an alternative answer** may be offered: **There Rabbi Yose penalized the fraudulent person**, who falsely claimed to have deposited 200 dinarim, **in order** to induce him **to admit** that he was lying. For if he loses everything by lying, he might tell the truth to get back what is really his own. [6]But **here**, in the case of a found object, **what loss would be entailed** for the fraudulent claimant to pursuade him **to admit** the truth? For if one of the claimants falsely claims to have picked up the garment, he has nothing to lose if the garment is ultimately left with the court!

תֵּינַח מְצִיאָה [7]But the Gemara now rejects this latter attempt to reconcile the ruling in our Mishnah with the view of Rabbi Yose: **This** interpretation **is plausible** in the case of a dispute about the ownership of a **found object**, which did not cost the fraudulent claimant anything. In such a case, as we have just seen, the threat that the court will impound the disputed object will not induce him to admit the truth. Therefore Rabbi Yose might agree with our Mishnah. But in the case of a dispute about an **item that was bought, what is there to say**, according to Rabbi Yose, to justify the ruling that the item is divided between the claimants? For since both claimants paid for the garment, they would both incur a loss if the garment were left with the court, and the threat of this loss might induce one of the claimants to admit that he paid for the item without the agreement of the seller. [8]**Rather**, the Gemara concludes, the **first answer** we proposed **is more satisfactory**, and the distinction between the two cases is that in our Mishnah it is not certain that one of the claimants is lying. Thus Rabbi Yose might well agree that disputed property is divided in cases where the litigants may both be fundamentally honest, as in the case of our Mishnah.

RASHI

הכא דאיכא למימר דחד מינייהו הוא — ואין לחבירו חלק בה — לא כל שכן דלית ליה יחלוקו? **מאי פסידא אית ליה** למי שאין לו חלק בה אם תהא מונחת? **דלודי** — שאין לו חלק בה, כשיודה מה יטול? **מקח וממכר מאי איכא למימר** — הא אוקימנא דקיבל דמים מתרווייהו, ואי הוה אמרינן יהא הטלית והדמים מונחים — אית ליה פסידא לרמאי, ויודה על האמת קודם שיפסיד!

NOTES

מִי יֵימַר דְּאִיכָּא רַמַּאי **Who can say that one of the claimants is fraudulent?** *Torat Ḥayyim* raises the problem: Even if both claimants picked up the article at the same time, their claims are still not totally honest, since they each claim ownership of the entire article. He answers that even in such a case we do not need to assume dishonesty, because each claimant may sincerely believe that *he* took possession of the article first.

TERMINOLOGY

מַאי אִיכָּא לְמֵימַר **What is there to say?** Sometimes, when analyzing a controversy, the Talmud notes that the viewpoint of one of the scholars cited seems reasonable, while the other viewpoint presents difficulties. Sometimes, too, the viewpoint of an individual scholar is found to be acceptable in certain circumstances but not in others. In such cases, the Talmud may state: "The first authority's view is understandable, but according to the second, what is there to say?" Or: "You may be right about X, but what is there to say about Y?"

אֶלָּא מְחַוַּורְתָּא כִּדְשָׁנִין מֵעִיקָּרָא **Rather it is clear as we answered originally.** Sometimes, after proposing two answers to a question, the Talmud rejects the second one and states: "Rather it is clear as we answered originally" (i.e., only the first answer is correct). This expression is used when the first answer was given anonymously. Where, however, the first answer was ascribed to a specific scholar, the expression used is: אֶלָּא מְחַוַּורְתָּא כְּדְ׳...' — "Rather it is clear as Rabbi X said."

SAGES

רַבִּי יוֹסֵי **Rabbi Yose.** This is Rabbi Yose ben Ḥalafta, one of the greatest of the Tannaim. He lived in the generation before the completion of the Mishnah, and the imprint of his teachings is felt throught Tannaitic literature.

His father, known as Abba Ḥalafta, was also considered one of the Sages of his generation, and his family, according to one tradition, was descended from Yehonadav the son of Rekhav (see II Kings 10:15 ff.).

In addition to studying with his father, Rabbi Yose was also an outstanding student of Rabbi Akiva. He and his contemporaries, the other students of Rabbi Akiva, Rabbi Meir, Rabbi Yehudah, and Rabbi Shimon bar Yoḥai, formed the center of Talmudic creativity of that entire generation. In his Halakhic method, as in his entire way of life, Rabbi Yose was moderate and refrained from taking an extreme position on

Halakhic issues. Because of his moderation and the logic of his teachings, the Halakhah follows him in every instance, against all his colleagues. A well-known principle in the Halakhah is that "Rabbi Yose's views are based on sound reasoning" ("רַבִּי יוֹסֵי נִימוּקוֹ עִמּוֹ"), and therefore the Halakhah is always in accordance with his view.

Just as Rabbi Yose was a great master of the Halakhah, so too was he famous for his piety. The Talmud tells many stories about his modesty, his humility, and his sanctity. It is related that Elijah the Prophet would reveal himself to him every day, and several conversations between him and Elijah are recorded in the Talmud. Rabbi Yose was apparently the main editor of a series of Baraitot on the history of the Jewish people known as *Seder Olam*. For many years he lived in Tzipori (Sepphoris) in Galilee, and earned his living as a leather-worker.

Many of the Sages of the following generation, including Rabbi Yehudah HaNasi, the editor of the Mishnah, were his students. But the students to whom he was closest were his five sons, all of whom were Sages in their generation. The most famous of them were Rabbi Eliezer ben Rabbi Yose, one of the great masters of Aggadah, and Rabbi Yishmael ben Rabbi Yose.

LITERAL TRANSLATION

[1]Both [according] to the Sages and [according] to Rabbi Yose, [2]there, regarding the storekeeper [writing] on his writing tablet, where it teaches: "This one swears and takes [the money] and this one swears and takes [the money]," [3]what is the difference [in that case] that we do not say: Let us take the money from the employer and let it be deposited until Elijah comes, for surely [there] there is definitely a fraudulent person!

[4]They say: There, this is the reason: For the storekeeper says to the employer: [5]"I performed your mission. What do I have [to do] with the

[1]בֵּין לְרַבָּנַן וּבֵין לְרַבִּי יוֹסֵי, [2]הָתָם, גַּבֵּי חֶנְוָנִי עַל פִּנְקָסוֹ, דְּקָתָנֵי: ״זֶה נִשְׁבָּע וְנוֹטֵל וְזֶה נִשְׁבָּע וְנוֹטֵל״, [3]מַאי שְׁנָא דְּלָא אָמְרִינַן נַפְּקֵיהּ לְמָמוֹנָא מִבַּעַל הַבַּיִת, וִיהֵא מוּנָּח עַד שֶׁיָּבֹא אֵלִיָּהוּ, דְּהָא בְּוַדַּאי אִיכָּא רַמַּאי!

[4]אָמְרִי: הָתָם, הַיְינוּ טַעְמָא: דְּאָמַר לֵיהּ חֶנְוָנִי לְבַעַל הַבַּיִת: [5]״אֲנָא שְׁלִיחוּתָא דִּידָךְ קָא עָבְדִינָא. מַאי אִית לִי גַּבֵּי

RASHI

התם היינו טעמא — דשניהם נשבעין ונוטלין, דחנוני אומר לבעל הבית: אנא שליחותא דידך עבדי, ונתתי לפועלך ממון שלויתני. מאי אית לי גבי שכיר — לערער?

TRANSLATION AND COMMENTARY

בֵּין לְרַבָּנַן וּבֵין לְרַבִּי יוֹסֵי [1]The Gemara now turns its attention to the Mishnah in tractate *Shevuot* (45a) cited earlier, and seeks to analyze it in the light of the present discussion: **Both according to the Sages and according to Rabbi Yose,** who agree that a person making a fraudulent claim should not benefit from his dishonesty, how do they reconcile this principle with the ruling of the Mishnah about the storekeeper in tractate *Shevuot*: [2]**There**, in the case of **the storekeeper writing on his writing tablet**, the Mishnah states: The storekeeper **must swear** that he has already given the goods to the employee, as the employer requested, whereupon the storekeeper **must be reimbursed** by the employer, **and** the employee **must swear** that he has not received the goods, whereupon **he must be paid** by the employer the wages owed to him. [3]But, asks the Gemara, **why do we not say** there: **"Let us take the money** for the employee's wages **from the employer, and leave it** with the court **until Elijah comes, because one** of the two claimants **is certainly lying**"? For if the storekeeper did not pay, then he is lying, and if he did pay, then the employee is lying!

אָמְרִי [4]The Gemara now replies to this objection: **They** — the Sages of the Talmud — **say**: **There**, in the case of the storekeeper, **the reason** why both the storekeeper and the employee are entitled to payment, even though one of them is certainly lying, **is that the storekeeper can say to the employer**: [5]**"I carried out your instructions** by giving the goods to the employee. My business is with you. **What do I have** to do

NOTES

נַפְּקֵיהּ לְמָמוֹנָא מִבַּעַל הַבַּיִת **Let us take the money from the employer...** *Shittah Mekubbetzet* raises the problem: The Gemara's suggestion that the employee's wages be set aside until the coming of Elijah was prompted by the ruling in the case of the third maneh mentioned above. If not for that ruling the Gemara would have been satisfied to penalize the employer and to reward the fraudulent claimant by making the employer pay twice. Why, asks the *Shittah Mekubbetzet*, does the Gemara not suggest setting aside the employee's wages simply in the interests of justice?

The answer of the *Shittah Mekubbetzet* is that this element was also included in the Gemara's question, and the Gemara's reply that it was the employer's own behavior that made him liable to pay both parties answers both elements in its question.

אֲנָא שְׁלִיחוּתָא דִּידָךְ קָא עָבְדִינָא **I carried out your instructions**. *Tosafot* (ד״ה וְלָא אָמְרַתְּ) remarks: One of the principles governing the laws of שְׁלִיחוּת (agency) is that the person who charges the agent with a task may hold him responsible if he performs the task improperly.

For example, in tractate *Ketubot* 85a the Talmud relates an incident where one Sage asked a colleague to pay a debt for him. The colleague did so, but paid the money before receiving the Sage's promissory note from his creditor. When he asked for the note, the creditor replied: "The note is still binding, I took the money from you as payment for another loan."

When the agent returned to the Sage, the latter did not admit the other debt and demanded that the agent reimburse him for the money he had paid, using the following argument: "I sent you to improve my situation and not to make it worse!" The Gemara there upholds the claim of the Sage.

HALAKHAH

חֶנְוָנִי עַל פִּנְקָסוֹ **The storekeeper writing on his writing tablet.** "A storekeeper's statements concerning his writing tablet (i.e., his accounts) are accepted. How does this principle work in practice? An employer has told a storekeeper to give his workers goods to a certain value, and the employer admits to making this statement or there are witnesses to it. The storekeeper now claims that he gave the goods to the workers, but the workers deny that they have received them. In such a case, both the storekeeper and the workers must take a Rabbinically imposed oath similar to that required by the Torah. They both then collect their respective claims from the employer." (*Shulḥan Arukh, Ḥoshen Mishpat* 91:1.)

שָׂכִיר? [1]אַף עַל גַּב דְּקָא מִשְׁתַּבַּע לִי, לָא מְהֵימַן לִי בִּשְׁבוּעָה, [2]אַתְּ הֶאֱמַנְתֵּיהּ, דְּלָא אָמְרַתְּ לִי: ׳בְּסַהֲדֵי הַב לֵיהּ׳״. [3]וְשָׂכִיר נַמִי אָמַר לֵיהּ לְבַעַל הַבַּיִת: [4]״אֲנָא עֲבַדִי עֲבִידְתָּא גַּבָּךְ. מַאי אִית לִי גַּבֵּי חֶנְוָנִי? [5]אַף עַל גַּב דְּמִשְׁתַּבַּע לִי, לָא מְהֵימַן לִי״. [6]הִלְכָּךְ תַּרְוַיְיהוּ מִשְׁתַּבְּעִי וְשָׁקְלִי מִבַּעַל הַבַּיִת.

[7]תָּנֵי רַבִּי חִיָּיא: ״מָנֶה לִי בְּיָדְךָ״, וְהַלָּה אוֹמֵר: ״אֵין לְךָ בְּיָדִי כְּלוּם״. [8]וְהָעֵדִים מְעִידִים אוֹתוֹ שֶׁיֵּשׁ לוֹ חֲמִשִּׁים זוּז, נוֹתֵן לוֹ חֲמִשִּׁים זוּז, וְיִשָּׁבַע עַל

LITERAL TRANSLATION

employee? [1]Even if he swears to me, he is not trustworthy to me in an oath. [2]You trusted him, [in] that you did not say to me: 'Give [it] to him in [the presence of] witnesses.'" [3]And the employee too says to the employer: [4]"I did work for you. What do I have [to do] with the storekeeper? [5]Even if he swears to me, he is not trustworthy to me." [6]Therefore both of them swear and take [payment] from the employer.

[7]Rabbi Ḥiyya taught: [If one says to another:] "A maneh of mine is in your possession," and the other says: "Nothing of yours is in my possession." [8]And the witnesses testify [concerning] him that he has 50 zuz, he gives him 50 zuz and he swears regarding

RASHI

לא מהימן לי – איני מאמינו בשבועה. אני אומר שהוא רשע, ואין לי להאמין אדם בשבועה על כרחי, אלא אם כן האמנתיו מתחילה להפקיד אצלו או להתנות עמו. **את הימנתיה** – ואתה הוא שקלקלת, ואין לי להפסיד בקילקולך שיהיו מעותי מונחין עד שיבא אליהו. **וישבע על השאר** – כדין מודה מקצת הטענה, שאמרה תורה ישבע, כדילפינן בשבועות (לט,ב) מ״כי הוא זה״. ואף על גב דזה לא הודה – הרי יש עדים במקצת, ולא תהא הודאת פיו גדולה לחייבו על השאר שבועה, מהעדאת עדים.

TRANSLATION AND COMMENTARY

with the employee? I had no agreement with him at all. [1]**Even if he swears to me** that he received nothing from me, **I do not trust his oath**. I need only accept the oath of a person with whom I voluntarily chose to do business. [2]It was **you** who **trusted him**, in **that you did not tell me**, as you would have done if you had felt that your employee was untrustworthy: **'Give him** the goods **in the presence of witnesses**.' Therefore you must pay me the value of the goods I handed over to your employee, and if you have a grievance, settle it yourself with your employee." [3]Similarly, **the employee can also say to the employer**: [4]"**I did the work for you**. **What do I have** to do **with the storekeeper**? [5]**Even if he swears to me** that he gave me the goods, **I do not believe him**." [6]**Therefore both** the storekeeper and the employee must **take an oath, and they** both then **receive payment from the employer**. Accordingly, even though either the employee or the storekeeper is certainly lying, both are entitled to reimbursement from the employer, and the disputed payment need not be left with the court until Elijah comes. The logic underlying the decision in tractate *Shevuot* does not apply in the case of the two depositors which is the subject of the difference of opinion between Rabbi Yose and the Sages in our tractate.

תָּנֵי רַבִּי חִיָּיא [7]**Rabbi Ḥiyya taught** the following Baraita: In a case where one person claims against another, "**You owe me a maneh** (equal in value to 100 dinarim or zuz), that you borrowed from me and have not repaid," **and the other person says**: "**I owe you nothing**," [8]**and witnesses testify that** the defendant owes the claimant **50 zuz** (half a maneh), **he** must pay the claimant **50 zuz**, in accordance with the testimony of

NOTES

Similarly, in the present case, it seems that the employer should be able to make the same demand from the storekeeper: "Why did you place me in a situation where I would have to pay twice?"

Tosafot makes a distinction between the two cases. With regard to the promissory note, it is obvious that payment of the debt should have been made in the presence of witnesses, as is customary. A storekeeper, however, generally does not have witnesses observe his transactions, and unless the employer *specifically requested* him to pay the workers in the presence of witnesses, there was no need for him to do so.

וְהָעֵדִים מְעִידִים אוֹתוֹ שֶׁיֵּשׁ לוֹ **And witnesses testify that he does owe him**. The Rishonim ask: How can the witnesses be sure that the borrower still owes the money? Even if they witnessed the issuing of the original loan, it is possible that the borrower has already repaid the money.

Among the answers given is the following: The claimant demands the return of a loan of 100 dinarim, the defendant denies ever having borrowed *any* amount from the claimant, and the witnesses testify that a loan of 50 dinarim was given. Because of the defendant's denial, we can be sure that he never repaid the loan. Thus, the testimony of the witnesses makes him liable (*Rashba*).

HALAKHAH

כְּפִירָה בַּכֹּל וְעֵדוּת עַל מִקְצָת **The denial of an entire claim and the testimony of witnesses concerning a part of it**. "With regard to a claim of 100 dinarim, if the defendant denies the entire claim, and witnesses testify that he owes the claimant 50 dinarim, the defendant must pay 50 dinarim and take a Torah oath concerning the remainder," in accordance with Rabbi Ḥiyya's ruling. (Ibid., 75:4.)

SAGES

רַבִּי חִיָּיא **Rabbi Ḥiyya**. Rabbi Ḥiyya was from the town of Kafri in Babylonia. He was one of the last of the Tannaim, and a student and colleague of Rabbi Yehudah HaNasi.

Rabbi Ḥiyya came from a distinguished family that was descended from King David and produced many Sages. While he still lived in Babylonia he was already considered a great Torah scholar, and when he left Babylonia with the members of his family to settle in Eretz Israel, there were those who said, in exaggeration, that the Torah would have been forgotten in Eretz Israel, had he not arrived from Babylonia to reestablish it. Upon his arrival in Eretz Israel he became the student and colleague of Rabbi Yehudah HaNasi. He became a close friend of Rabbi Yehudah HaNasi and more especially of his son, Rabbi Shimon, who was also Rabbi Ḥiyya's business partner. Rabbi Ḥiyya was one of the greatest Sages of his generation. Just as he was a great Torah scholar, he was also very pious, as is related in many places in the Talmud. His great achievement was the editing of collections of Baraitot, as a kind of supplement to the Mishnah edited by Rabbi Yehudah HaNasi. These collections, which he seems to have edited in collaboration with his colleague and student, Rabbi Oshaya, were considered extremely reliable, so much so that it was said that any Baraita not reported by them was not worthy of being cited in the House of Study.

It seems that, upon his arrival in Eretz Israel, he received some financial support from the house of the Nasi, but he mainly earned his living from international trade on a large scale, especially in silk. He had twin daughters, Pazi and Tavi, from whom important families of Sages were descended. He also had twin sons, Yehudah (Rabbi Yannai's son-in-law) and Hizkiyah, who were important scholars during the transitional generation between the Tannaim and the Amoraim. They apparently took their father's place at the head of his private Yeshiva in Tiberias, where he lived. All of Rabbi Yehudah HaNasi's students were Rabbi Ḥiyya's colleagues, and he was also on close terms with the Tanna Rabbi Shimon ben Ḥalafta. Rabbi Yehudah HaNasi's younger students (Rabbi Ḥanina, Rabbi Oshaya, Rabbi Yannai, and others) all studied under Rabbi Ḥiyya as well, and to some degree they were considered his disciples. Rabbi Ḥiyya's nephews, Rabbah bar Ḥanah, and, above all, the great Amora Rav, were his outstanding disciples. He also appears as one of the central figures in the *Zohar*. Rabbi Ḥiyya was buried in Tiberias, and his two sons were later buried at his side.

TERMINOLOGY

וְתַנָּא תּוּנָא And our Tanna taught it. An expression used by the Gemara to introduce a Mishnah in support of an Amora's statement.

הַשְּׁאָר, [1]שֶׁלֹּא תְּהֵא הוֹדָאַת פִּיו גְּדוֹלָה מֵהַעֲדָאַת עֵדִים, [2]מִקַּל וָחוֹמֶר.
[3]וְתַנָּא תּוּנָא: ״שְׁנַיִם אוֹחֲזִין בְּטַלִּית. זֶה אוֹמֵר: ׳אֲנִי מְצָאתִיהָ׳ וכו׳״. [4]וְהָא הָכָא, כֵּיוָן דְּתָפֵיס, אֲנַן סָהֲדֵי דְּמַאי דְּתָפֵיס הַאי דִּידֵיהּ הוּא, וּמַאי דְּתָפֵיס הַאי דִּידֵיהּ הוּא, [5]וְקָתָנֵי יִשָּׁבַע!
[6]מַאי ״שֶׁלֹּא תְּהֵא הוֹדָאַת פִּיו

LITERAL TRANSLATION

the rest, [1]so that his admission (lit., "the admission of his mouth") should not be greater than the testimony of witnesses, [2][as proved] by a *kal vaḥomer*.

[3]And our Tanna taught [similarly]: "Two are holding on to a garment. This one says: 'I found it,' and so on." [4]And surely here, since he is holding on, we are witnesses that what this one is holding is his, and what this one is holding is his, [5]and [yet] it teaches that [each] swears!

[6]What is [the meaning of] "So that his admission should not

TRANSLATION AND COMMENTARY

the witnesses, **and take an oath regarding the rest** of the money, asserting that he did not borrow the other fifty zuzim from the claimant. [1]The premise upon which this ruling is based, is **that** a defendant's own **admission should not be more effective than the testimony of witnesses**, [2]and this ruling can be proved **by a *kal vaḥomer* (a fortiori) inference**. For the law is that if one person claims that another owes him a certain sum of money, and the defendant admits that he owes the plaintiff part of the sum, the defendant must take an oath that he does not owe the plaintiff any more money. If an oath is required in the case of partial admission, then here, in Rabbi Ḥiyya's case, where witnesses testify that the defendant owes the plaintiff part of his claim, there is even more reason that the defendant should be required to take an oath regarding the rest of the claim!

וְתַנָּא תּוּנָא [3]Rabbi Ḥiyya continues by citing our Mishnah in support of his ruling: **The Tanna of our Mishnah taught** along similar lines: **"Two people** appear before a court **holding on to a garment. One** of them **says: 'I found it,' and so on."** [4]**Now here**, in the case of the disputed garment, **since** each of the claimants **is holding on** to part of the garment, it is as if **we are witnesses** (see note) to the fact **that what the one** claimant **is holding is his, and what the other** claimant **is holding is his**. [5]Thus it is as if each of the two claimants has witnesses confirming that his claim is partially correct, **and** the Mishnah **teaches that** the law in such a case is: **"They must swear"**! In other words, in our Mishnah the fact that the two claimants to the garment come before the court, each holding on to part of the garment, makes it self-evident that part of each person's claim is true. The Mishnah then imposes an oath on each claimant with regard to the part of his claim on which there is no adverse testimony — the part he is holding. Thus our Mishnah seems to confirm Rabbi Ḥiyya's ruling that if witnesses testify against a defendant and maintain that he owes the claimant part of his claim, the defendant must take an oath that he does not owe the claimant the remainder of the claim.

מַאי שֶׁלֹּא תְּהֵא הוֹדָאַת פִּיו [6]Up to this point in the discussion the ruling of Rabbi Ḥiyya has been stated and then supported by our Mishnah. The Gemara now proceeds to analyze the reason given by Rabbi Ḥiyya for his ruling: **What is** the meaning of Rabbi Ḥiyya's statement: **"An admission by a defendant should not**

RASHI

מקל וחומר — לקמן מפרש מאי קל וחומר. **ותנא תונא** — ותנא דידן סייעתא לדידי. **זה אומר כו׳** — וקתני: שניהם ישבעו. **אנן סהדי דמה דתפס האי** — היינו פלגא. **דידיה הוא** — שהרי מוחזק הוא בכפנינו. והרי הוא תובע את כולה, וחבירו כופר את כולה, שאומר: כולה שלי ואף מה שאתה תפוס בידך. ואנו מעידין אותו שיש לו בה מקצת, ומחייבים את חבירו שבועה על השאר, דהיינו חצי שעיכב לעצמו. **מאי לא תהא הודאת פיו גדולה מהעדאת עדים** — מהיכי תיתי לן למידק דתיסק אדעתין דתהא הודאת פיו גדולה מהעדאת עדים, דאיצטריך לתנא למילף מקל וחומר דלא תהא הודאת פיו גדולה?

NOTES

וְתַנָּא תּוּנָא שְׁנַיִם וכו׳ And the Tanna of our Mishnah has also taught: "Two claimants..." The comparison between the case of Rabbi Ḥiyya and the case of our Mishnah is clearly not exact. Rabbi Ḥiyya is referring to an oath imposed by the Torah, whereas the oath in our Mishnah is of Rabbinic origin. Oaths required by the Torah are taken to *absolve* a person from payment, whereas the oath required by our Mishnah is taken in order to *receive* a share of the article. This point, however, is not mentioned by the Gemara, because it rejects the comparison in another way (*Rashba*).

אֲנַן סָהֲדֵי We are witnesses. אֲנַן סָהֲדֵי is a technical term indicating that a matter is so self-evidently true that it is as if "we are witnesses" to it. There is an absolute legal presumption that property in a person's possession is his, until proven otherwise. This presumption is so strong that it is considered the equivalent of testimony, until it is refuted by other testimony. Thus, in the case here described, since both claimants are holding the garment, it is as if witnesses have testified that they both own it.

TRANSLATION AND COMMENTARY

have a **greater** effect **than the testimony of witnesses,** and this principle can be **proved by a *kal vaḥomer*** inference." The problem that the Gemara raises is: Why is a formal *kal vaḥomer* needed to prove something that is seemingly self-evident? Why would we imagine that the evidence of witnesses is not as effective in imposing an oath as the partial admission of a defendant?

שֶׁלֹּא תֹאמַר [1]The Gemara now explains: The *kal vaḥomer* argument is needed by Rabbi Ḥiyya **to prevent you from** coming to a mistaken conclusion and **saying** that it is specifically **in the case of a defendant's partial admission** that **an oath is imposed on him by the Torah**, an argument that would be **in accordance with** the explanation of **Rabbah**. [2]**For Rabbah said: Why did the Torah state** that **a person who admits part of a claim** against him **must take an oath** regarding the rest of the claim, which he denies? At first glance it would seem more reasonable to impose an oath on a person who denies all liability than on a person who admits partial liability. [3]Rabbah answers that this law is based on **a presumption** regarding the behavior of the defendant: We presume that **a person would not be so insolent** as to show complete ingratitude to someone who has lent him money, by lying to him to his face. We must, therefore, try to explain the defendant's behavior as follows: [4]The defendant **would have preferred to deny owing** the claimant **anything, but the reason he did not** totally **deny** the claim **is because a person would not be so insolent** as to deny the claim completely. [3B] [5]On the other hand, out of gratitude to the lender for having advanced the loan, **the defendant would have**

גְּדוֹלָה מֵהַעֲדָאַת עֵדִים מִקַּל וָחוֹמֶר?״

[1]שֶׁלֹּא תֹאמַר: הוֹדָאַת פִּיו הוּא דְּרָמְיָא רַחֲמָנָא שְׁבוּעָה עֲלֵיהּ, כִּדְרַבָּה. [2]דְּאָמַר רַבָּה: מִפְּנֵי מָה אָמְרָה תּוֹרָה: ״מוֹדֶה מִקְצָת הַטַּעֲנָה יִשָּׁבַע״? [3]חֲזָקָה אֵין אָדָם מֵעִיז פָּנָיו בִּפְנֵי בַּעַל חוֹבוֹ. [4]וְהַאי בְּכוּלֵּיהּ בָּעֵי דְּנִכְפְּרֵיהּ, וְהָא דְּלָא כָּפְרֵיהּ מִשּׁוּם דְּאֵין אָדָם מֵעִיז פָּנָיו. [3B] [5]וְהַאי בְּכוּלֵּיהּ בָּעֵי דְּלוֹדֵי לֵיהּ,

LITERAL TRANSLATION

be greater than the testimony of witnesses [as proved] by a *kal vaḥomer*"?

[1]That you should not say: It is [in the case of] a defendant's [partial] admission that the Torah (lit., "the Merciful One") imposed an oath on him, as [maintained] by Rabbah. [2]For Rabbah said: Why did the Torah say: "He who admits part of a claim shall swear"? [3][Because] a presumption [exists that] a person is not [so] insolent before his lender. [4]This [person] wanted to deny the whole [claim], and [the reason] that he did not deny it is because a person is not [so] insolent. [3B] [5]And this [person] wanted to admit all of it to him,

RASHI

מפני מה אמרה תורה כו׳ — ולא חשבו כמשיב אבידה לפטרו, שלא כפר בכולו. והאי בכוליה בעי דלודי כו׳ — וכי תימא: מגו דחשיד אממונא חשיד אשבועתא, ולא נרמי עליה שבועתא? לא חשיד אממונא, לפי שברצונו היה מודה בכולו, אלא שאין בידו לפרוע, וסבר: עד דהוי לי [זוזי], ופרענא ליה.

NOTES

אֵין אָדָם מֵעִיז פָּנָיו **A person would not be so insolent**. The assumption here is psychological, based on human behavior and the motivations of normal people. Since every loan discussed in the Talmud is a loan without interest, the very act of making the loan is an act of kindness towards the recipient, and we assume that a person feels grateful towards someone who has done him a kindness and that he would be embarrassed to lie to him and to deny the whole transaction.

אֵין אָדָם מֵעִיז פָּנָיו **A person would not be so insolent**. *Rashi* explains that the Gemara's assumption, "a person would not be so insolent...," is made in order to negate another regulation that might have been applied: A borrower who denies an obligation entirely is *not* required to take an oath. His admission of part of the debt can, therefore, be compared to the action of a man returning a lost object to its owner. But a person who returns a lost object is exempt from taking an oath about his conduct with regard to the object. Hence the borrower should likewise be exempt, were it not for the fact that he feels compelled to admit at least part of the debt.

Tosafot explain that the Gemara's assumption, "a man would not be so insolent...," has a different purpose: One of the most important principles in the laws of evidence is *miggo*, according to which a person's statement is believed on the assumption that, had he wished to lie, he would have chosen a more effective lie. In this instance, we might have thought that, if the borrower had wished to deny his obligation, he could have claimed that he owed no money to the lender, in which case he would not be required to take an oath. Therefore, his statement that he owes part of the debt should be accepted without an oath, were it not for the fact that he feels compelled to admit at least part of the debt.

This difference of approach between *Rashi* and *Tosafot* is the subject of detailed analysis by later commentators.

HALAKHAH

מוֹדֶה מִקְצָת הַטַּעֲנָה יִשָּׁבַע **A person who makes a partial admission of a claim must take an oath**. "If the plaintiff claims: 'You owe me 100 dinarim,' and the defendant replies: 'I only owe you 50,' the defendant must take an oath imposed by the Torah that he only owes him 50 and must pay the 50 that he admits to owing." (*Shuḥlan Arukh, Ḥoshen Mishpat* 752.)

SAGES

רַבָּה **Rabbah.** Rabbah bar Naḥmani the Priest, called Rabbah for short, was one of the greatest Babylonian Amoraim of the third generation. Rabbah studied under Rav Huna, Rav's disciple, and his entire method in the Halakhah followed that of Rav. He also studied Torah with Rav Yehudah and with Rav Naḥman, and he was a student and colleague of Rav Ḥisda. While still a young man he was considered greater than all the others of his generation in his sharpness of mind, and he was called "the uprooter of mountains" (עוֹקֵר הָרִים). After Rav Yehudah's death Rabbah was chosen, though still a young man, to be the head of the Yeshivah of Pumbedita, even though he did not accept the full appointment until close to the time of his death. Rabbah was involved in Halakhic discussions with all the great Sages of his generation, and the famous controversies between him and his colleague, Rav Yosef (in which the Halakhah follows Rabbah in almost every instance), are an important element of the Babylonian Talmud.

Rabbah trained many students, and in fact all the Sages of the following generation were his students, especially his nephew, Abaye, his outstanding student. It is known that his private life was full of suffering, and his sons apparently died in his lifetime. He was also very poor and supported himself with difficulty by agricultural labor. The people of his city also treated him badly. Although Rabbah died relatively young, he established himself as one of the pillars of the Babylonian Talmud. His son, Rava (רָבָא בְּרֵיהּ דְּרַבָּה), was also an important Sage in the following generation.

LITERAL TRANSLATION

[1]and [the reason] that he did not admit is [because] he is putting him off. [2]He thinks: Until I have money, and [then] I will repay him. [3]And the Torah says: Impose an oath on him so that he will admit all of it to him. [4]But [in the case of] the testimony of witnesses, where one cannot say this, say [that] no [oath is imposed on him]. [5][Therefore Rabbi Ḥiyya] teaches us a *kal vaḥomer.*

[6]And what is the *kal vaḥomer?*

[7]If his own mouth, which does not oblige him [to pay] money, obliges him [to take] an oath, [8]witnesses who oblige him [to pay] money, how much more so should they oblige him [to take] an oath.

[9]But does his mouth not oblige him [to pay] money? [10]But surely the admission of a litigant is like a hundred witnesses!

[1]וְהַאי דְּלָא אוֹדֵי, אִשְׁתַּמּוּטֵי הוּא דְּקָא מִישְׁתַּמֵּט מִינֵּיהּ. [2]סָבַר: עַד דְּהָווּ לִי זוּזֵי, וּפָרַעֲנָא לֵיהּ. [3]וְאָמַר רַחֲמָנָא: רְמֵי שְׁבוּעָה עֲלֵיהּ כִּי הֵיכִי דְּלוֹדֵי לֵיהּ בְּכוּלֵּיהּ. [4]אֲבָל הַעֲדָאַת עֵדִים, דְּלֵיכָּא לְמֵימַר הָכִי, אֵימָא לָא. [5]קָא מַשְׁמַע לָן קַל וָחוֹמֶר.

[6]וּמַאי קַל וָחוֹמֶר?

[7]וּמַה פִּיו, שֶׁאֵין מְחַיְּיבוֹ מָמוֹן, מְחַיְּיבוֹ שְׁבוּעָה, [8]עֵדִים שֶׁמְּחַיְּיבִין אוֹתוֹ מָמוֹן, אֵינוֹ דִּין שֶׁמְּחַיְּיבִין אוֹתוֹ שְׁבוּעָה.

[9]וּפִיו אֵין מְחַיְּיבוֹ מָמוֹן? [10]וְהָא הוֹדָאַת בַּעַל דִּין כְּמֵאָה עֵדִים דָּמֵי!

TRANSLATION AND COMMENTARY

preferred to admit the complete claim, [1]**and the reason why he did not admit** the whole claim **is because he is trying to put off the claimant** temporarily, [2]**thinking**: When **I have** the **money I will repay him**. [3]Because it is possible that the partial admission is the result of these conflicting pressures on the defendant, **the Torah says: Impose an oath on him**, to induce him **to make a complete admission** of the claim against him. [4]**But in the case of** the defendant whose total denial of the claim against him is partially contradicted by **witnesses**, he does not appear to be overcome with shame or scruples deriving from gratitude to the lender, but rather he is intent on deceiving the court. **I might have thought that** such a defendant is to be regarded as fraudulent, and therefore **his taking an oath is of no value**. [5]Therefore Rabbi Ḥiyya needs to strengthen his ruling by **a *kal vaḥomer*** argument.

וּמַאי קַל וָחוֹמֶר [6]The Gemara now begins a detailed analysis of this *kal vaḥomer* and asks: **What is the *kal vaḥomer*** argument to which Rabbi Ḥiyya referred?

וּמַה פִּיו שֶׁאֵין מְחַיְּיבוֹ מָמוֹן [7]The Gemara answers that it is to be explained in the following way: **If a person's** partial **admission** of a claim, **which does not oblige him** to pay **money**, nevertheless **obliges him** to take **an oath** regarding the rest of the claim, [8]then **how much more so should** the evidence of **witnesses, which does oblige him** to pay **money** in accordance with their testimony, **oblige him** to take **an oath** regarding the rest of the claim.

וּפִיו אֵין מְחַיְּיבוֹ מָמוֹן [9]The Gemara now challenges the assumption underlying this argument and asks: But **does a person's admission of a claim not oblige him** to pay **money**? How could such a statement be made? [10]**Surely** there is an accepted general principle that "**the admission of a litigant** in monetary matters **is considered** as strong **as** the evidence of **a hundred witnesses.**" Once a litigant has admitted a monetary claim against him, the court relies on his admission and does not probe further. Since this is so, a person's admission surely *does* oblige him to pay money!

CONCEPTS

הוֹדָאַת בַּעַל דִּין **The admission of a litigant.** In monetary matters (דִּינֵי מָמוֹנוֹת), a litigant's admission, in court or before witnesses, that he owes someone money, is considered a definite statement of liability "equal to the testimony of a hundred witnesses," and no further proof is required. With reference to cases involving corporal punishment (מַלְקוֹת) or capital punishment (דִּינֵי נְפָשׁוֹת), a person's admission of guilt is not acceptable, and it is not recognized by the court either as conclusive proof or even as evidence.

RASHI

דליכא למימר הכי — שהרי כפר בכולו, ואימא מגו דחשיד אממונא חשיד אשבועתא. **פיו שאינו מחייבו ממון** — בהודאתו, ולקמיה מפרש לה. **מחייבו שבועה** — על השאר. **עדים שמחייבין [אותו] ממון** — במה שהעידו. **אינו דין שיחייבוהו שבועה** — על השאר? **הודאת בעל דין כמאה עדים** — ברייתא היא בתוספתא דבבא מציעא בפרק ראשון.

NOTES

אִשְׁתַּמּוּטֵי הוּא **He is trying to put off.** One could argue that the defendant who makes a partial admission of a claim should be considered as a liar concerning the part of the claim he denies, and accordingly his words should not be accepted even when supported by an oath. To avoid this argument the Talmud explains that we do not suspect him of outright dishonesty or the intention to steal. On the contrary, his denial is interpreted as being no more than an attempt to avoid immediate payment, and it is assumed that he will tell the truth when confronted with an oath (*Rosh*).

הוֹדָאַת בַּעַל דִּין כְּמֵאָה עֵדִים **The admission of a litigant is considered as strong as the evidence of a hundred witnesses.** The commentators have offered a number of explanations why the admission made by a litigant is

HALAKHAH

עֵדִים שֶׁמְּחַיְּיבִין אוֹתוֹ מָמוֹן **Witnesses who oblige him to pay money.** If two witnesses testify that a person owes another person money, the defendant is obliged to pay. (*Rambam, Sefer Shofetim, Hilkhot Edut* 5:1. In the original text *Rambam* states that *one* witness is not sufficient, implying that the minimum number of witnesses must be two. See also below.)

הוֹדָאַת בַּעַל דִּין כְּמֵאָה עֵדִים **The admission of a litigant is considered as strong as the evidence of a hundred witnesses.** "If a person admits before two witnesses

¹מַאי ״מָמוֹן״? קְנָס. ²וּמַה פִּיו, שֶׁאֵין מְחַיְּיבוֹ קְנָס, מְחַיְּיבוֹ שְׁבוּעָה, ³עֵדִים שֶׁמְּחַיְּיבִין אוֹתוֹ קְנָס, אֵינוֹ דִּין שֶׁמְּחַיְּיבִין אוֹתוֹ שְׁבוּעָה.

⁴מַה לְּפִיו שֶׁכֵּן מְחַיְּיבוֹ קָרְבָּן, ⁵תֹּאמַר בְּעֵדִים, שֶׁאֵין מְחַיְּיבִין אוֹתוֹ קָרְבָּן?!

LITERAL TRANSLATION

¹What is [meant by] "money"? A fine. ²If his own mouth, which does not oblige him [to pay] a fine, obliges him [to take] an oath, ³witnesses who oblige him [to pay] a fine, how much more so should they oblige him [to take] an oath.

⁴What is [special] about his mouth [is that] it obliges him [to bring] a sacrifice. ⁵Will you say [the same] of witnesses, who do not oblige him [to bring] a sacrifice?!

RASHI

פיו אינו מחייבו קנס – דילפינן (בבא קמא עה,א) מקראי דמודה בקנס פטור, ״אשר ירשיעון אלהים״ – פרט למרשיע את עצמו. **פיו מחייבו קרבן** – דכתיב ״והתודה אשר חטא והביא״ (ויקרא ה). **עדים אין מחייבין אותו קרבן** – אם מכחישין אותו, דכתיב (שם ד) ״או הודע אליו״ ולא שיודיעוהו אחרים.

TRANSLATION AND COMMENTARY

מַאי מָמוֹן קְנָס ¹The Gemara now explains: The meaning of the word **"money"** used in the *kal vahomer* argument **is** "the payment of **a fine.**" The point of the statement is that in all cases where the Torah imposes a fine (for example, in the case of rape), if the defendant voluntarily admits his guilt he is not required to pay the fine. ²The *kal vahomer* argument must therefore be understood as follows: **If a person's admission** of a claim, **which does not oblige him** to pay **a fine**, nevertheless **obliges him** to take **an oath** regarding the rest of the claim, then ³**how** much more **so should** the evidence of **witnesses, which can oblige him** to pay **a fine** in accordance with their testimony, **oblige him** in our case to take **an oath** regarding the rest of the claim!

מַה לְּפִיו שֶׁכֵּן מְחַיְּיבוֹ קָרְבָּן ⁴The Gemara now attempts to refute the *kal vahomer* argument by showing that there is an aspect of a person's admission of a claim that is stronger than the evidence of witnesses: **A person's admission** is surely more effective in that it has the power to **oblige him to bring a sacrifice**. For if a person states that he inadvertently committed a transgression, he is obliged to bring a sacrifice as atonement. ⁵**Can you say the same** with regard to the evidence **of witnesses**? Even if they testify that he committed the transgression, they **do not** have the power to **oblige him to bring a sacrifice** if he denies their claim! We see from this that there are aspects of a person's admission that are stronger than the testimony of witnesses, and thus Rabbi Ḥiyya's *kal vahomer* argument is not valid!

LANGUAGE

קְנָס ***(Kenas)* A fine.** According to some scholars, this word is not of Hebrew origin. It appears to be connected with the Latin word *census* or with the function of the *censor*, a high Roman official who was responsible for meting out punishments for undesirable behavior.

NOTES

accepted by the court: *Mahari ben Lev* explains the principle as follows: Since a person has the right to give his property to another person as a gift, he is believed when he admits that he owes another person money, and the admission is an *obligation* to pay the sum admitted.

Ketzot HaHoshen disagrees and offers a different explanation. He maintains that an admission is granted a unique measure of trustworthiness and has the status of testimony. Just as the Torah accepts the statements of two witnesses with regard to a third party, so too the Torah accepts a litigant's own statements about himself. This concept is further developed by *Tzafnat Pa'aneah* and *Imrei Binah*, who explain the discussion here in the Gemara on the basis of these differing viewpoints. They suggest that the Gemara's initial assumption was that a litigant's admission constitutes an independent obligation to pay the sum admitted, and that its conclusion is that the admission has the status of testimony.

קְנָס **A fine.** The expression "fine" (קְנָס) refers to a financial penalty imposed by law that does not correspond exactly to the value of the damage done or the money claimed. The laws governing fines differ from those governing other financial obligations. Among the differences are:

(a) Fines are imposed only on the basis of the testimony of witnesses and not on the basis of a person's own admission of guilt.

(b) Fines can only be imposed by a court whose members have received full Rabbinic ordination (סְמִיכַת זְקֵנִים). This ordination ceased about the middle of the fourth century and from that time onward Rabbinical courts have not, in principle, had the authority to impose most fines.

עֵדִים שֶׁאֵין מְחַיְּיבִין אוֹתוֹ קָרְבָּן **The evidence of witnesses which does not have the power to oblige him to bring a sacrifice.** *Ramban* raises the following question: Although a person is not obliged to bring a sin-offering if he contradicts witnesses who claim that he *is liable to bring*

HALAKHAH

that he owes another [named] person a certain sum of money, he must repay the money he has admitted owing. This applies even if he did not specifically appoint them to act as witnesses." (*Shulhan Arukh, Hoshen Mishpat* 81:8.)

פִּיו שֶׁאֵין מְחַיְּיבוֹ קְנָס **A person's admission which does not oblige him to pay a fine.** "A thief who, of his own volition, admits to having stolen, must repay the principal but is free from making the double payment [כֶּפֶל] which he would have had to pay if found guilty on the evidence of witnesses. This applies to all fines. A person who admits his guilt is not liable." (*Rambam, Sefer Nezikin, Hilkhot Genevah* 1:5.)

עֵדִים שֶׁמְּחַיְּיבִין אוֹתוֹ קְנָס **Witnesses who oblige him to pay a fine.** "The testimony of witnesses against a person who is liable by Torah law to pay a fine, such as a thief who has to repay twice the amount he stole, causes the defendant to pay the fine." (Ibid., 1:4.)

¹הָא לָא קַשְׁיָא. ²רַבִּי חִיָּיא כְּרַבִּי מֵאִיר סְבִירָא לֵיהּ, דְּאָמַר: עֵדִים מְחַיְּיבִין אוֹתוֹ קָרְבָּן, מִקַּל וָחוֹמֶר. ³דִּתְנַן: אָמְרוּ לוֹ שְׁנַיִם: ״אָכַלְתָּ חֵלֶב״, וְהוּא אוֹמֵר: ״לֹא אָכַלְתִּי״, ⁴רַבִּי מֵאִיר מְחַיֵּיב, וַחֲכָמִים פּוֹטְרִים. ⁵אָמַר רַבִּי מֵאִיר: אִם הֱבִיאוּהוּ שְׁנַיִם לִידֵי מִיתָה חֲמוּרָה, לֹא יְבִיאוּהוּ לִידֵי קָרְבָּן הַקַּל? ⁶אָמְרוּ לוֹ: מָה אִם יִרְצֶה לוֹמַר, ״מֵזִיד הָיִיתִי״? יִפָּטֵר!

LITERAL TRANSLATION

[1]This is not a difficulty. [2]Rabbi Ḥiyya holds [the same opinion] as Rabbi Meir, who says: Witnesses oblige him [to bring] a sacrifice, from a *kal vaḥomer*. [3]For we have learned [in a Mishnah]: Two [witnesses] said to him: "You have eaten forbidden fat," and he says: "I have not eaten," [4]Rabbi Meir obliges [him to bring a sacrifice] and the Sages exempt [him]. [5]Said Rabbi Meir: If two [witnesses] bring him to [the] severe [penalty of] death, shall they not bring him to the light [penalty of a] sacrifice? [6]They said to him: What if he would wish to say, "I did it deliberately"? He would be exempt!

TRANSLATION AND COMMENTARY

הָא לָא קַשְׁיָא [1]The Gemara replies: **This** objection does **not** pose **a difficulty.** [2]**Rabbi Ḥiyya holds the same opinion as Rabbi Meir, who said** that **witnesses oblige** a person **to bring** an atonement **sacrifice**, based on a *kal vaḥomer* **argument.** [3]**For we have learned in a Mishnah:** If **two witnesses say to a person:** "You have unwittingly **eaten forbidden fat,** and you are obliged to bring a sacrifice as atonement," **and** the person **replies:** "I **have not eaten,"** [4]**Rabbi Meir obliges him to bring a sacrifice, and the Sages exempt him.** [5]**Rabbi Meir said** in explanation of his ruling: **If two witnesses** have the power by their testimony to **bring a person** into a situation where he may be liable **to the severe penalty of death,** surely **they** have the power by their testimony to **bring him** into a situation where he is liable **to the light penalty of** bringing **a sacrifice**!? We therefore believe them, and even if the defendant denies their evidence he is liable, according to Rabbi Meir, to bring an atonement sacrifice! [6]But the Sages **said to** Rabbi Meir: **What if** the man **wished to say, "I did it deliberately." He would be exempt** from bringing a sacrifice! In most cases a person does not bring a sacrifice as atonement for a transgression committed deliberately. Thus, if the accused replies to the witnesses that he indeed committed the transgression, but did so deliberately, he is exempt from bringing a sacrifice. Since this is so, it is apparent that the testimony of witnesses is not effective in such a case, and even if the accused contradicted the witnesses and said: "I committed no transgression," he is not obliged to bring a sacrifice as a result of the evidence of witnesses, though he would be required to bring a sacrifice as a result of his own admission.

RASHI

אמרו לו שנים אכלת חלב — שוגג. **והוא אומר לא [אכלתי]** — פטור, שהיה יכול לומר 'מזיד הייתי' ויפטר מן הקרבן, אף כשאמר 'לא אכלתי' — פטור, דמה לו לשקר.

NOTES

a sin-offering, he is nevertheless obliged to bring a sin-offering if he remains silent. Thus, witnesses *do* have the power to oblige him to bring an offering.

Rashba resolves this question by explaining that in this case the obligation to bring the offering is based on the principle of שְׁתִיקָה כְּהוֹדָאָה — "silence is considered like admission." If the person does not contradict the witnesses, he is seen as admitting what they say. It is this admission (and not the witnesses' testimony per se) that obliges him to bring a sacrifice.

מֵזִיד הָיִיתִי I did it deliberately. Such a statement would free him from the obligation of bringing a sin-offering, since (with very few exceptions) a sin-offering cannot atone for the deliberate violation of a Torah commandment. Indeed, with the exception of a number of sins for which a guilt-offering is brought, and the very few exceptions in the case of a sin-offering, no sacrifices atone for deliberate sin.

It appears that this concept of מֵזִיד הָיִיתִי is not the Sages' own reason why witnesses cannot oblige a person to bring a sacrifice. Indeed, *Rashi* explains that the viewpoint of the Sages is based on their exegesis of Leviticus 4:28: "Or if his sin, wherein he has sinned, come to his knowledge." It is his own awareness that obliges him to bring a sacrifice, and not the awareness of others. Thus the Sages introduced the argument of מֵזִיד הָיִיתִי only to disprove Rabbi Meir's *kal vaḥomer* argument.

Tosafot and *Tosefot Rid* raise a further question: One of the fundamental principles of testimony is אֵין אָדָם מֵשִׂים עַצְמוֹ רָשָׁע — "a person is not believed to incriminate himself" (*Sanhedrin* 9b). In this instance, if we accept his statement, his own words are self-incriminatory.

Tosafot answers that it is forbidden to offer sin-offerings unnecessarily, and an animal set aside for such an offering remains nonsacred. Therefore, if the person's statement מֵזִיד הָיִיתִי is rejected, he will be forced to commit an additional sin, that of sacrificing a nonsacred animal. Hence, his word

HALAKHAH

עֵדִים מְחַיְּיבִין אוֹתוֹ קָרְבָּן Whether witnesses oblige a person to bring a sacrifice. "If witnesses testify that a person has committed a transgression for which one is liable to bring a fixed sin-offering, and the person himself denies it, he is not liable to bring a sin-offering," in accordance with the viewpoint of the Sages. (*Rambam, Sefer Korbanot, Hilkhot Shegagot* 3:1.)

TERMINOLOGY

הָא לָא קַשְׁיָא This itself is difficult, i.e., there is an internal contradiction in this Tannaitic source (between the two parts of the source).

דִּתְנַן We have learned. A term used to introduce a quotation from a Mishnah, either in support of an argument or as the basis for an objection.

SAGES

רַבִּי מֵאִיר Rabbi Meir. Rabbi Meir was one of the greatest Tannaim of the generation before the completion of the Mishnah. We do not have definite information about Rabbi Meir's parentage, though it is said that he came from a family of converts descended from the imperial family in Rome.

While he was still a very young man, his extraordinary sharpness of mind in Torah studies was noted, and he studied with two of the greatest scholars of the generation, Rabbi Yishmael and Rabbi Akiva. He was also the only student who continued to draw upon traditions taught by Elisha ben Avuyah, despite the latter's abandonment of Judaism. Rabbi Meir was one of the closest disciples of Rabbi Akiva, who ordained him at a very early age. He was ordained again later by Rabbi Yehudah ben Bava.

Rabbi Meir was officially appointed as the "Ḥakham," the third in rank below the Nasi, or president, of the Sanhedrin. The discussions between him and his colleagues, Rabbi Yehudah, Rabbi Yose, Rabbi Shimon, and Rabbi Elazar are among the most important elements of the Mishnah.

Rabbi Meir's greatest achievement was apparently a continuation of the (oral) editing and organization of the Halakhah according to the Oral Law. Rabbi Yehudah HaNasi followed Rabbi Meir in this task, and for that reason we have the principle that all anonymous Mishnayot are to be attributed to Rabbi Meir (סְתָם מִשְׁנָה רַבִּי מֵאִיר).

Because he was involved in the effort to force the resignation of Rabban Shimon ben Gamliel, the head of the Sanhedrin, Rabbi Meir was fined by him, and for a long

LITERAL TRANSLATION

[1] Rather, what is [special] about his mouth [is that] it obliges him [to bring] a guilt-offering!

[2] A guilt-offering is a sacrifice!

[3] Rather, what is [special] about his mouth, [is that] it obliges him [to pay] an [additional] fifth!

[4] This is not a difficulty. Rabbi Ḥiyya holds [the same opinion] as Rabbi Meir. [5] Just as he obliges him [to bring] a sacrifice, from a *kal vaḥomer*, he obliges him [to pay] an [additional] fifth, from a *kal vaḥomer*.

[1] אֶלָּא, מַה לְּפִיו שֶׁכֵּן מְחַיְּיבוֹ אָשָׁם!

[2] אָשָׁם הַיְינוּ קָרְבָּן!

[3] אֶלָּא, מַה לְּפִיו שֶׁכֵּן מְחַיְּיבוֹ חוֹמֶשׁ!

[4] הָא לָא קַשְׁיָא. רַבִּי חִיָּיא כְּרַבִּי מֵאִיר סְבִירָא לֵיהּ. [5] כִּי הֵיכִי דִּמְחַיֵּיב לֵיהּ קָרְבָּן, מִקַּל וָחוֹמֶר, מְחַיֵּיב לֵיהּ חוֹמֶשׁ, מִקַּל וָחוֹמֶר.

RASHI

חומש ואשם — אם נשבע וכפר ממון והודה, כתיב "או מכל אשר ישבע עליו לשקר וגו'" (שם ה).

TRANSLATION AND COMMENTARY

אֶלָּא מַה לְּפִיו [1] The Gemara now withdraws its previous objection and formulates it in a different way: **A person's admission** is surely more effective than the testimony of witnesses in that it has the power to **oblige him to bring a guilt-offering**. This is because, if a person denies a monetary claim against him and takes a false oath to support his denial, and then later admits his guilt, he must bring an אֲשַׁם גְּזֵילוֹת — "a guilt-offering for robbery." But if witnesses testify to his guilt, he is not obliged to bring a guilt-offering! Again we see that there are situations where a person's admission is stronger than the testimony of witnesses, and thus Rabbi Ḥiyya's *kal vaḥomer* argument is not valid!

אָשָׁם הַיְינוּ קָרְבָּן [2] The Gemara at once dismisses this objection: **A guilt-offering is a** type of **sacrifice** and is in itself the subject of the difference of opinion previously mentioned between Rabbi Meir and the Sages. As explained above, Rabbi Ḥiyya follows the viewpoint of Rabbi Meir and would claim that witnesses do have the power to oblige a person to bring a guilt-offering even if the accused denies their evidence.

אֶלָּא מַה לְּפִיו [3] The Gemara now again reformulates its objection to Rabbi Ḥiyya's *kal vaḥomer* argument: **A person's admission** is surely more effective than the testimony of witnesses in that it has the power to **oblige him to pay an additional fifth**. This is because, if a person denies a monetary claim against him and takes a false oath to support his denial, and later admits his guilt, he must repay the money (or restore the deposit), must bring an אֲשַׁם גְּזֵילוֹת (see above), and must also add a fifth to the money he restores and give it to the claimant. But if witnesses testify to his guilt and he refuses to admit it, he is not obliged to pay the extra fifth of the value of the claim. Again we see that there are situations where a person's admission is stronger than the evidence of witnesses and thus Rabbi Ḥiyya's *kal vaḥomer* argument is not valid!

הָא לָא קַשְׁיָא [4] The Gemara replies: **This** objection does **not** pose **a difficulty. Rabbi Ḥiyya holds** the same opinion **as Rabbi Meir** (mentioned above). [5] **Just as** Rabbi Meir **obliges** a person **to bring an atonement offering** on the evidence of witnesses **based on a *kal vaḥomer* argument**, so too **does he oblige** a person **to pay an additional fifth** on the evidence of witnesses, **based on a *kal vaḥomer* argument**. Thus Rabbi Ḥiyya's original *kal vaḥomer* argument still stands.

NOTES

is accepted when he makes the statement מֵזִיד הָיִיתִי as a penitent, in order to avoid that further transgression. *Tosefot Rid* answers that the principle of אֵין אָדָם מֵשִׂים עַצְמוֹ רָשָׁע only applies where the consequence of accepting the admission would be to obligate the individual in some way. But where the acceptance of the admission would lead to the *removal* of a potential obligation, as in our case of מֵזִיד הָיִיתִי, the self-incriminatory admission is accepted.

אָשָׁם הַיְינוּ קָרְבָּן A guilt-offering is a sacrifice. The rules governing guilt-offerings, despite their similarity to sin-offerings, are unique in several respects (see *Tosafot* ד"ה אָשָׁם). Since, regarding the guilt-offering, the Torah says, "He shall confess that he has sinned in that thing" (Leviticus 5:5), it could be argued that all authorities, including Rabbi Meir, would admit that the testimony of witnesses is ineffective in this matter. The Gemara's conclusion here is, however, that there is no distinction between a guilt-offering and other sacrifices, and that with regard to the guilt-offering the same controversy exists, with Rabbi Meir insisting that the testimony of witnesses obliges the accused to bring a sacrifice. There are two possible explanations of his view in this matter: (1) The "guilt-offering for robbery" (אֲשַׁם גְּזֵילוֹת) is one of those sacrifices that a person brings for a sin, irrespective of whether he committed the transgression unwittingly or intentionally. Hence the accused cannot absolve himself of the sacrifice by claiming that he did the act intentionally. (2) Seeing that the accused brings this guilt-offering only after he has repaid the money he owes, since the witnesses can obligate him to pay the money, they can likewise force him to bring the sacrifice.

period his teachings were not cited in his name but rather introduced by the expression, "Others say" (אֲחֵרִים אוֹמְרִים).

His private life was full of suffering. His two sons died during his lifetime, though he is known to have left a daughter; and his wife, Beruriah, famous for her wisdom and piety, died in tragic circumstances. Ultimately he had to go into exile in Asia Minor, where he died. In his will he requested that his body be taken to Eretz Israel, and that it be buried temporarily near the sea, whose waves reach Eretz Israel.

During his lifetime Rabbi Meir was famous not only for his extraordinary sharpness of mind, which exceeded that of all his generation, but also for his virtuous qualities. He was peace-loving and modest. He was known as an outstanding preacher, and it is said that his death marked the end of "the tellers of parables." Some of his animal fables were retold over many generations. He was also known as a miracle-worker; charity boxes in his name, "Rabbi Meir the Miracle Worker" (רַבִּי מֵאִיר בַּעַל הַנֵּס), were a primary source of contributions to Eretz Israel for many years.

CONCEPTS

אָשָׁם Guilt-offering. One of the categories of sacrifices. There are six sub-categories of the אָשָׁם sacrifice. (1) אֲשַׁם גְּזֵילוֹת — a sacrifice brought by a person who denied a debt, swore a false oath that he was not liable, and later admitted that he was liable and that he had sworn falsely. (2) אֲשַׁם מְעִילוֹת — a sacrifice brought as atonement for מְעִילָה, the misuse of sacred articles. (3) אֲשַׁם שִׁפְחָה חֲרוּפָה — a sacrifice brought as atonement for relations with a partially non-Jewish servant woman singled out to be the wife of a Hebrew slave (שִׁפְחָה חֲרוּפָה). (4) אֲשַׁם נָזִיר — a sacrifice brought as part of the purification process of a נָזִיר, a Nazirite, who had become ritually impure. (5) אֲשַׁם מְצוֹרָע — a sacrifice brought as part of the purification process of a מְצוֹרָע, a leper. (6) אָשָׁם תָּלוּי — a sacrifice brought as atone- not he committed a sin which requires the bringing of a חַטָּאת — a sin-offering. An אָשָׁם is one of the קָדְשֵׁי קָדָשִׁים — sacrifices of the most sacred order — and may only be eaten by priests and only on the day it is offered and the following night. The laws of its slaughter (שְׁחִיטָה), the sprinkling of its blood on the altar (זְרִיקָה), and the offering of its fats (הֶקְטֵר חֲלָבִים) are like those governing the שְׁלָמִים — the peace-offering. A ram (אַיִל) is the only animal used for an אָשָׁם.

TRANSLATION AND COMMENTARY

אֶלָּא מַה לְּפִיו [1]The Gemara now withdraws its previous objection and formulates it in a different way, seeking to show that there is another aspect of a person's admission that is stronger than the evidence of witnesses: **A person's admission** is surely more effective than the evidence of witnesses **in that it cannot be contradicted** by witnesses **nor** can witnesses actually **prove it false**. If a person admits a monetary liability, witnesses do not have the power to contradict the admission (הַכְחָשָׁה), nor is their evidence accepted to prove the admission false, on the grounds that the person making the admission was with the witnesses at the time he claims he became liable for the money and could not, therefore, have undertaken the liability he has admitted (הֲזָמָה). [2]**Can you say the same** with regard to the evidence **of witnesses**! Their evidence **can be contradicted** by other witnesses (הַכְחָשָׁה) and it **can be proved to be false** by other witnesses (הֲזָמָה). We see, therefore, that there are aspects of a person's admission that are more effective than the testimony of witnesses, and thus Rabbi Ḥiyya's *kal vaḥomer* argument is not valid!

אֶלָּא אָתְיָא מֵעֵד אֶחָד [3]In response to this objection the Gemara modifies Rabbi Ḥiyya's *kal vaḥomer* argument: Rabbi Ḥiyya's ruling, that where witnesses partially contradict a defendant's total denial of a monetary claim, the defendant must take an oath with regard to that part of the claim about which the witnesses have not contradicted him, **is derived** by a *kal vaḥomer* inference **from** the testimony of **a single witness:** [4]**If** the testimony of **a single witness** giving evidence against a defendant in a monetary case, **which does not oblige** the defendant **to pay money**, because a single witness does not have the power to obligate payment on the basis of his testimony alone, [5]nevertheless **does oblige** the defendant **to take an oath** to rebut the testimony of the single witness, **how much more so should** the testimony of two **witnesses**, which **does oblige him to pay money** in accordance with their testimony, **oblige him to take an oath**!

[1]אֶלָּא, מַה לְּפִיו שֶׁכֵּן אֵינוֹ בְּהַכְחָשָׁה וּבַהֲזָמָה. [2]תֹּאמַר בְּעֵדִים שֶׁיֶּשְׁנָן בְּהַכְחָשָׁה וּבַהֲזָמָה?!

[3]אֶלָּא, אָתְיָא מֵעֵד אֶחָד. [4]וּמָה עֵד אֶחָד, שֶׁאֵין מְחַיְּיבוֹ מָמוֹן, מְחַיְּיבוֹ שְׁבוּעָה, [5]עֵדִים שֶׁמְּחַיְּיבִין אוֹתוֹ מָמוֹן, אֵינוֹ דִּין שֶׁמְּחַיְּיבִין אוֹתוֹ שְׁבוּעָה!

LITERAL TRANSLATION

[1]Rather, what is [special] about his mouth [is that] it is not subject to (lit., "in") contradiction and refutation. [2]Will you say [the same] of witnesses who are subject to contradiction and refutation!

[3]Rather, it comes from a single witness. [4]If a single witness, who does not oblige him [to pay] money, obliges him [to take] an oath, [5][two] witnesses who oblige him [to pay] money, how much more so should they oblige him [to take] an oath!

RASHI

אינו בהכחשה ובהזמה — אם הודה לו במנה, ובאו עדים והכחישוהו, לומר אינך חייב לו כלום — אינו נפטר בכך, דהודאת בעל דין כמאה עדים. **שישנן בהכחשה ובהזמה** — שאם באו שנים עדים והכחישום או הזימום — אין זה משלם ממון על פיהם. **מחייבו שבועה** — טענו חבירו "מנה לי בידך", והוא אומר "אין לך בידי כלום", ועד אחד מעידו שהוא חייב לו — הרי זה נשבע להכחיש את העד, דכתיב (דברים יט) "לא יקום עד אחד באיש וגו׳" לכל עון ולכל חטאת הוא דאינו קם, אבל לשבועה — קם (שבועות מ,א).

NOTES

מַה לְּפִיו שֶׁכֵּן אֵינוֹ בְּהַכְחָשָׁה וּבַהֲזָמָה **His own admission cannot be contradicted by witnesses (הַכְחָשָׁה), nor can it be refuted (הֲזָמָה).** A person who admits taking a loan and not having repaid it is obliged to repay that sum even if witnesses state that they were with him and the lender at the time he claims to have taken the loan and that no such transaction took place (הַכְחָשָׁה), or that they were with him at the time he claims to have taken the loan and they were nowhere near the place where the loan was said to have taken place (הֲזָמָה). The witnesses do not have the power to change or reduce his obligations (*Rabbenu Ḥananel*).

הַכְחָשָׁה Lit., **contradiction.** When a pair of witnesses contradicts testimony given previously by other witnesses, the testimony of both pairs of witnesses is nullified and the evidence of neither pair is accepted. No greater weight is attached to the evidence of several witnesses than to that of two. In contrast to a case of עֵדִים זוֹמְמִים, in a case of הַכְחָשָׁה the later witnesses contradict the earlier witnesses' description of the facts of the case and do not focus on the first pair of witnesses' presence at the scene.

הֲזָמָה **The refutation of witnesses by proving them false.** There are two ways in which the testimony of witnesses can be invalidated: (1) If a second pair of witnesses testifies that a particular event did not transpire as described by the first pair of witnesses (הַכְחָשָׁה). In such a case, the testimony of *neither* pair of witnesses is accepted and the matter is left undecided. (2) If a second pair of witnesses testifies that the first two witnesses were in a different place at the time

HALAKHAH

וּמָה עֵד אֶחָד, שֶׁאֵין מְחַיְּיבוֹ מָמוֹן **If a single witness, who does not oblige him to pay money...** "No case, whether civil or capital, can be determined on the basis of the testimony of a single witness. But the testimony of a single witness does have the power to oblige a litigant to take an oath to rebut such testimony." (*Rambam, Sefer Shofetim, Hilkhot Edut* 5:1.)

[1]מַה לְעֵד אֶחָד, שֶׁכֵּן עַל מַה שֶּׁהוּא מֵעִיד הוּא נִשְׁבָּע. [4A] [2]תֹּאמַר בְּעֵדִים, שֶׁעַל מַה שֶּׁכָּפַר הוּא נִשְׁבָּע! [3]אֶלָּא אֲמַר רַב פַּפָּא: אָתֵי מִגִּלְגּוּל שְׁבוּעָה דְּעֵד אֶחָד. [4]מַה לְגִלְגּוּל שְׁבוּעָה דְּעֵד אֶחָד שֶׁכֵּן שְׁבוּעָה גּוֹרֶרֶת שְׁבוּעָה. [5]תֹּאמַר בְּעֵדִים דְּמָמוֹן קָא מְחַיְּיבֵי!

LITERAL TRANSLATION

[1]As for one witness, he [the defendant] swears about what he [the witness] testifies. [4A] [2]Will you say [the same] of witnesses, where he swears about what he has denied!

[3]Rather, Rav Pappa said: It comes from the addition (lit., "rolling on") of an oath [by the testimony] of a single witness.

[4]What is [special] about the addition of an oath [by the testimony] of a single witness [is that] an oath brings about [another] oath. [5]Will you say [the same] of witnesses, who [only] oblige [the payment of] money!

TRANSLATION AND COMMENTARY

מַה לְעֵד אֶחָד [1]The Gemara now seeks to refute this proof by showing that there is a fundamental difference between the testimony of one witness and the testimony of two or more witnesses with regard to the imposition of an oath upon a defendant: The evidence of **one witness** is in a special category in that it has the power to make **the defendant take an oath** to rebut precisely those claims **about which the witness testifies**, but not any other claims that the plaintiff may make. [4A] [2]**Can you say the same** with regard to the testimony **of** two **witnesses**? There, if we accept Rabbi Ḥiyya's argument, **he takes an oath** not to refute what the witnesses testified but specifically with regard to what the witnesses did not testify. The defendant **is** thus **taking an oath** to support **his own denial** and not to refute the witnesses' testimony. By what authority is such a stringency to be imposed on the defendant?

אֶלָּא אֲמַר רַב פַּפָּא [3]**Rav Pappa** now seeks to reinstate the *kal vaḥomer* inference in a slightly modified form and **says**: Rabbi Ḥiyya's *kal vaḥomer* **is based on the law imposing an additional oath** (גִּלְגּוּל שְׁבוּעָה) as a result of the oath imposed because of the evidence **of a single witness**. If a defendant in a monetary dispute is obliged to take an oath, either because of the evidence of one witness or for any other reason, the plaintiff can say to him: Now that you are obliged to take an oath with regard to this dispute between us, include in your oath a denial of other claims that I have against you. The *kal vaḥomer* argument would run as follows: If the imposition of an oath caused by the testimony of a single witness, which does not oblige the defendant to pay money, nevertheless obliges the defendant to take an oath with regard to aspects of the case not covered by the testimony of the single witness, then how much more so should the testimony of two or more witnesses, which *does* oblige him to pay money in accordance with their testimony, oblige him to take an oath with regard to aspects of the case not covered by their testimony.

מַה לְגִלְגּוּל שְׁבוּעָה [4]The Gemara now refutes this argument by showing that there is a fundamental difference between the imposition of an additional oath and the imposition of an oath caused by the testimony of witnesses: **The imposition of an additional oath** as a result of the testimony **of a single witness** is in a special category, because the **one oath** (to rebut the one witness) **brings** about the **other oath** (with regard to other claims by the plaintiff). The imposition of the additional oath does not stem from the testimony of the single witness but from the special laws of the imposition of oaths. [5]**Can you say the same** with regard to the evidence **of witnesses, which requires** the defendant to pay back a specific sum of **money** and no more? There is no primary oath imposed here that could bring about another additional oath with regard to the rest of the plaintiff's claim! Thus Rabbi Ḥiyya's *kal vaḥomer* argument cannot be made in the form suggested by Rav Pappa.

RASHI

מה לעד אחד – כלומר: היכי ילפת שבועה דשנים משבועה דעד אחד? מה לעד אחד – שכן על מה שהעד מעיד הוא נשבע להכחישו. **תאמר** – בשבועה דעדים, שאינו נשבע על מה שהעידו אלא על מה שלא העידו, ועל כפירתו הוא נשבע ולא אהעדאתן. ומנין לך להחמיר כל כך? **מגלגול שבועה דעד אחד** – אם נתחייב לו שבועה על ידי עד אחד כדאמרינן, והיתה עליו טענה אחרת שלא היתה מוטלת עליו שבועה – מגלגלין אותה עם שבועה זאת, ונשבע על שניהן. דגלגול שבועה דאורייתא היא, דילפינן ליה בקדושין (כז,ב) מ"ואמרה האשה אמן אמן". הרי שעל מה שלא העיד העד הוא משביעו. **שכן שבועה גוררת שבועה** – עד לא חייבו שבועה אלא על מה שהעיד, והשבועה גוררת שבועה. תאמר בעדים הללו, שהחמשים שהעידוהו הם מחייבין אותו לשלם, ואין כאן שבועה לגרור על ידה שבועה על השאר.

CONCEPTS

גִּלְגּוּל שְׁבוּעָה **The rolling on of an oath,** the imposition of an additional oath. When a defendant is obliged to take an oath in order to free himself from liability, the plaintiff has the right to require him to include in his oath an affirmation that he is not liable for other claims that the plaintiff has against him which would not in themselves require the defendant to take an oath.

The law of גִּלְגּוּל שְׁבוּעָה is of Torah authority. The Torah states that a woman suspected of adultery (סוֹטָה) must answer "Amen, Amen," to the oath administered to her by the priest (Numbers 5:22). The Mishnah explains that this reply implies both acceptance of the oath with regard to the man with whom she is suspected of committing adultery and also acceptance of the oath with regard to other men (*Sotah* 2:5).

NOTES

the incident they are testifying about took place, and could not possibly have witnessed the events about which they have testified (הֲזָמָה). In such a case, the Torah gives credence to the statements of the *second pair* of witnesses. The testimony of the first two witnesses is rejected, they are classified as false witnesses, and they are condemned to suffer the punishment they had sought to inflict or pay the money they had conspired to make the defendant lose (see Deuteronomy 19:16–19).

[1] פִּיו יוֹכִיחַ.

[2] מַה לְּפִיו שֶׁכֵּן אֵינוֹ בְּהַכְחָשָׁה.

[3] עֵד אֶחָד יוֹכִיחַ, שֶׁיֶּשְׁנוֹ בְּהַכְחָשָׁה וּמְחַיְּיבוֹ שְׁבוּעָה.

[4] מַה לְּעֵד אֶחָד שֶׁכֵּן עַל מַה שֶּׁמֵּעִיד הוּא נִשְׁבָּע. [5] תֹּאמַר בְּעֵדִים שֶׁעַל מַה שֶּׁכָּפַר הוּא נִשְׁבָּע!

[6] פִּיו יוֹכִיחַ.

[7] וְחָזַר הַדִּין, [8] לֹא רְאִי זֶה כִּרְאִי זֶה, וְלֹא רְאִי זֶה כִּרְאִי זֶה.

[9] הַצַּד הַשָּׁוֶה שֶׁבָּהֶן שֶׁעַל יְדֵי טַעֲנָה וּכְפִירָה הֵן בָּאִין, וְנִשְׁבָּע.

[10] אַף אֲנִי אָבִיא עֵדִים שֶׁעַל יְדֵי טַעֲנָה וּכְפִירָה הֵם בָּאִין, וְנִשְׁבָּע.

[11] מַה לְהַצַּד הַשָּׁוֶה שֶׁבָּהֶן שֶׁכֵּן לֹא הוּחְזַק כַּפְרָן.

LITERAL TRANSLATION

[1] [The case of] his mouth will prove [it].

[2] What is [special] about his mouth [is that] it is not subject to contradiction.

[3] [The case of] one witness will prove [it], for he is subject to contradiction and does oblige him [to take] an oath.

[4] What is [special] about one witness [is that] he [the defendant] swears about what he [the witness] testifies. [5] Will you say [the same] of witnesses, where he swears about what he has denied!

[6] His mouth will prove [it].

[7] And the argument is circular (lit., "returns"). [8] This characteristic is not like that characteristic, and that characteristic is not like this characteristic. [9] The common factor in them is that they come [to court] as a result of a claim and a denial, and he swears. [10] Likewise I will bring [the case of] witnesses who come [to court] as a result of a claim and a denial, and he swears.

[11] What is [special] about the common factor in them [is that] he is not established as a liar.

TRANSLATION AND COMMENTARY

פִּיו יוֹכִיחַ [1] Having failed to establish a successful *kal vaḥomer* argument based on a single case, the Gemara now changes its argument and attempts to establish Rabbi Ḥiyya's ruling by developing a *kal vaḥomer* argument based on a common characteristic found in two cases: **The case of** partial **admission by the defendant**, where the defendant has to take an oath to rebut the rest of the claim against him, **will prove** that the testimony of witnesses, that the defendant owes part of the sum claimed against him, should also be able to force him to take an oath to rebut the rest of the claim against him.

מַה לְּפִיו [2] Now if you argue against this that **a person's admission** is stronger than the evidence of witnesses, **in that witnesses cannot contradict it,** [3] **the case of a single witness, whose evidence can be condicted** by other witnesses but who, nevertheless, **does oblige** the defendant **to take an oath, will prove** that the testimony of witnesses that the defendant owes part of the sum claimed against him should also be able to force him to take an oath to rebut the rest of the claim against him.

עֵד אֶחָד יוֹכִיחַ [4] Now you may argue against this that the testimony of **a single witness** is in a special category **in that** it obliges **the defendant to take an oath** specifically to rebut **the testimony of the witness,** [5] **whereas** the testimony of two **witnesses**, according to Rabbi Ḥiyya, forces the defendant **to take an oath** specifically with regard to the rest of the claim which **he denies** and not with regard to the witnesses' testimony.

פִּיו יוֹכִיחַ [6] If you argue in this way, the case of partial **admission by the defendant**, where the defendant has to take an oath to rebut the rest of the claim against him, **will prove** that the testimony of witnesses that the defendant owes part of the sum claimed against him should also be able to force him to take an oath to rebut the rest of the claim against him.

וְחָזַר הַדִּין [7] Thus we see that **the argument is circular:** [8] **The characteristic of the first** case (partial admission by the defendant) **is not the same as the characteristic of the second** case (one witness) **and the characteristic of the second** case **is not the same as the characteristic of the first** case. [9] Nevertheless the cases share a **common factor in that they arise through claim and denial** and in both cases the defendant has to come to court and **take an oath.** [10] **Likewise I can bring the case of** two **witnesses** partially contradicting the denial of the defendant, **which** also arises through **claim and denial**, and I can argue that the defendant must come to court and **take an oath**. This, then, says the Gemara, is the foundation of the *kal vaḥomer* argument on which Rabbi Ḥiyya bases his ruling.

מַה לְהַצַּד הַשָּׁוֶה שֶׁבָּהֶן [11] The Gemara now seeks to refute this argument by showing that there is a characteristic shared by the other cases that is not shared by witnesses: As far as **the common factor** shared by the case of partial admission and the case of evidence of one witness is concerned, in both cases the defendant **is not established as** being **a** confirmed **liar**, and we are still prepared to believe that he is telling

RASHI

פיו יוכיח – מודה מקצת הטענה, שעל מה שכופר ופיו לא הודה הוא נשבע. **טענה וכפירה** – זה טוען וזה כופר, הן באין לדין. **לא הוחזק כפרן** – על מה שכפר אינו מוחזק כפרן שמא לא כיחש, שהעד אינו נאמן להכחישו ולהחזיקו כפרן.

TERMINOLOGY

לֹא רְאִי זֶה...וְחָזַר הַדִּין... **The argument is circular... the characteristic of the first case....** This pattern of reasoning, sometimes referred to as מַה הַצַּד, is frequently found in Halakhic Midrashim. Indeed, some commentators consider that this argumentation is a form of בִּנְיַן אָב מִשְּׁנֵי כְתוּבִים — "a generalization based on two special cases" which is one of the thirteen rules of Biblical exegesis attributed to Rabbi Yishmael.

The מַה הַצַּד pattern of reasoning is as follows: Though two cases do not totally correspond to each other, they share a certain common factor. Hence, the laws that govern them can be applied to all other cases which share this common factor.

To state the principle in mathematical terms: Though A does not equal B, A and B share a common factor, X, and are governed by the same rule, Z. Therefore, C and any other cases that possess the factor X will be governed by rule Z.

Nevertheless, this is an argument that can easily be refuted. As long as another factor, however unimportant, can be found that is common to the subjects from which the principle was inferred but does **not** apply to the principle to which they are compared, the comparison is invalidated: If A and B possess another common factor, Y, which C does not possess, C is not governed by rule Z.

מַה הַצַּד The common factor. This expression describes a method of argumentation in Tannaitic Halakhic exegesis where a third law is derived from two other laws. This method is used when it would not be possible to derive the third law from either of the other laws alone, because of an unusual stringency which applies uniquely to each of the other laws. Since the stringency is not identical in the two laws, it is possible to put aside the unique feature in each of them and to use the "common factor" they share in order to arrive at the third law.

[1]תֹּאמַר בְּעֵדִים שֶׁכֵּן הוּחְזַק כַּפְרָן!

[2]וּבְעֵדִים מִי הוּחְזַק כַּפְרָן? [3]וְהָאָמַר רַב אִידִי בַּר אָבִין אָמַר רַב חִסְדָּא: הַכּוֹפֵר בְּמִלְוֶה כָּשֵׁר לְעֵדוּת, בְּפִיקָּדוֹן פָּסוּל לְעֵדוּת.

[4]אֶלָּא, פְּרֵיךְ הָכִי: מַה לְּהַצַּד הַשָּׁוֶה שֶׁבָּהֶן שֶׁכֵּן אֵינָן בְּתוֹרַת הֲזָמָה. [5]תֹּאמַר בְּעֵדִים שֶׁיֶּשְׁנָן בְּתוֹרַת הֲזָמָה!

LITERAL TRANSLATION

[1]Will you say [the same] of witnesses, where he is established as a liar!

[2]But in [the case of] witnesses is he established as a liar? [3]Surely Rav Idi bar Avin has said in the name of Rav Ḥisda: He who denies a loan is fit for testimony, [but he who denies] a deposit is unfit for testimony.

[4]Rather, object this way: What is [special] about the common factor in them is that they are not subject to the penalty (lit., "law") for being proved false. [5]Will you say [the same] of witnesses, who are subject to the penalty for being proved false!

TRANSLATION AND COMMENTARY

the truth. [1]**Can you say** the same with regard to the evidence **of** two or more **witnesses, by which he is established as a** confirmed **liar**? Once his total denial of the plaintiff's claim has been refuted by the evidence of witnesses with regard to part of the claim, the defendant is surely established as a proven liar. Why, then, should he be believed if he takes an oath with regard to the remaining part of the claim?

וּבְעֵדִים מִי הוּחְזַק כַּפְרָן [2]This argument is immediately attacked by the Gemara: But **is a person** whose claim is **contradicted by** two **witnesses** in fact **established as** being **a** confirmed **liar**? [3]**Surely Rav Idi bar Avin has stated in the name of Rav Ḥisda**: **A person who denies a loan**, whether partially or entirely, and against whom witnesses testify that he did borrow money from the claimant, **is** still **fit to serve as a witness** in another case, and we do not say that he has been proved to be a liar and therefore unfit to testify. We prefer to assume that the borrower intended to repay the loan later, and his only motive in denying the loan was to delay repaying his debt. **But a person who denies** having received **a deposit** and against whom witnesses testify that he is lying, **is disqualified from being a witness**. Here he has no reason to delay returning the deposit, since he is not allowed to make use of it, and if he has done so he is regarded as a robber. The statement of Rav Ḥisda shows that even where a borrower is contradicted by two witnesses, he is not thereby disqualified as a witness. Thus the *kal vaḥomer* argument of Rabbi Ḥiyya still stands.

אֶלָּא פְּרֵיךְ הָכִי [4]**Rather**, says the Gemara, **raise your objection** to the *kal vaḥomer* argument in the following way: **As far as the common factor** shared by the case of partial admission and the case of evidence of one witness is concerned, in neither case does **the law of retaliation** for being proved false (הֲזָמָה) apply. The law of הֲזָמָה does not apply to a defendant who has made a partial admission, as his admission cannot be refuted by witnesses, and even if witnesses testify that a single witness gave false evidence, that witness is not penalized and forced to pay the amount his evidence would have cost the defendant. [5]**Can** you **say** the same with regard to the evidence **of** two or more **witnesses who,** if proven to have been false witnesses, *are* compelled to make restitution to the defendant to the extent of the loss or damage their evidence would have caused him? Thus, the *kal vaḥomer* argument of Rabbi Ḥiyya would seem to have been refuted.

RASHI

תאמר בעדים – שמאחר שכפר הכל, והם העידו על החמשים – הוחזק כפרן, ולא נאמר נאמינהו על השבועה. **הכופר במלוה** – בין על כולה בין על מקצת, ובאו עדים והעידוהו על שלא נשבע. **כשר לעדות** – ולא אמרינן גזלן הוא, והתורה אמרה (שמות כג) "אל תשת רשע עד". דכיון דמלוה להוצאה נתנה – דלמא צריך להוציאה, וסבר עד דהוא ליה [זוזי] ופרענא ליה. ואי מודינא ליה השתא – יתבעני מיד. אבל הכופר בפקדון, אפילו על מקצת, דמאי הוא ליה גבי פקדון לאשתמוטי נפשיה? ושמא תאמר אבד ממנו ואשתמיט ליה עד דמשכח ליה, לקמן בפירקין (ה,ב) מוקמינן בדאתו סהדי ואמרי ההיא שעתא בידיה נקיט ליה. **בתורת הזמה** – לשלם קנס, דכאשר זמם דעד אחד שהוזם פטור. ופיו גבי הודאה כל שכן דלא שייכא הזמה כלל. **תאמר בעדים** – אם הוזמו בחמשים שהעידו משלמין ממון.

NOTES

אֵינָן בְּתוֹרַת הֲזָמָה **The law of being proven false (הֲזָמָה) does not apply to them.** Even if witnesses testify that a person could not possibly have been at the place where he says he undertook a financial obligation at the time he claims to have undertaken it, his statements are binding. Thus, the principle of הֲזָמָה does not apply to his statements

HALAKHAH

כּוֹפֵר בְּמִלְוֶה וְכוֹפֵר בְּפִיקָּדוֹן **A person who denies a loan... a person who denies having received a deposit**. "When a person demands repayment of a loan from someone and the latter denies having received the loan, even if there are witnesses who contradict him, he is not suspected of willingness to swear falsely (nor is he disqualified from being a witness in another case) as long as he has not taken a false oath to support his denial. By contrast, a person who denies having received a deposit and whose denial is contradicted by witnesses, *is* suspected of willingness to wear falsely (and *is* disqualified from being a witness in another case), even though he has not yet taken an oath to support his denial." (*Shulḥan Arukh, Ḥoshen Mishpat*, 92:4.)

LITERAL TRANSLATION

[1] This is not a difficulty. [2] Rabbi Ḥiyya does not object [on the basis of] the penalty for being proved false! [3] But [with regard to] what he said: "And our Tanna taught [similarly]," is it comparable? [4] There the lender has witnesses, [but] the borrower does not have witnesses that he owes him nothing, [5] for if the borrower did have witnesses that he owed him nothing, Rabbi Ḥiyya would not require him to swear. [6] [But] here, just as we are witnesses about this [half], we are [likewise] witnesses about the other [half], and even so they swear!

[1] הָא לָא קַשְׁיָא. [2] רַבִּי חִיָּיא תּוֹרַת הֲזָמָה לָא פָּרֵיךְ. [3] אֶלָּא דְּקָאָמַר: "וְתַנָּא תּוּנָא", מִי דָּמֵי? [4] הָתָם לְמַלְוֶה אִית לֵיהּ סַהֲדֵי, לְלֹוֶה לֵית לֵיהּ סַהֲדֵי דְּלָא מָסֵיק לֵיהּ וְלָא מִידֵּי, [5] דְּאִי הָווּ לֵיהּ סַהֲדֵי לְלֹוֶה דְּלָא מָסֵיק לֵיהּ וְלָא מִידֵּי, לָא בָּעֵי רַבִּי חִיָּיא לְאִשְׁתַּבּוּעֵי. [6] הָכָא, כִּי הֵיכִי דַּאֲנַן סַהֲדֵי בְּהַאי, אֲנַן סַהֲדֵי בְּהַאי, וַאֲפִילּוּ הָכִי מִשְׁתַּבְּעִי!

TRANSLATION AND COMMENTARY

הָא לָא קַשְׁיָא [1] The Gemara replies: **This** objection does **not** pose **a difficulty**: [2] **Rabbi Ḥiyya does not** accept that **the objection** raised above **based on the law of retaliation** is a valid objection. Rabbi Ḥiyya claims that there is no substantive difference in the laws of הֲזָמָה between the testimony of a single witness and that of two witnesses. The fact that a single witness, if found guilty of perjury, does not suffer the penalty he planned to impose on the defendant, whereas two or more such conspiring witnesses do suffer this penalty, is not, in Rabbi Ḥiyya's opinion, sufficient reason to make a profound distinction between the two cases. What they have in common, that in both cases the testimony of the single witness and that of the two witnesses is cancelled out, is much more important, in Rabbi Ḥiyya's opinion, than the fact that they differ in this small respect. Rabbi Ḥiyya's *kal vaḥomer* argument thus remains intact.

אֶלָּא דְּקָאָמַר וְתַנָּא [3] The Gemara now proceeds to probe the second part of Rabbi Ḥiyya's argument, where he claims that **the Tanna of our Mishnah taught** the same principle. This does pose a difficulty. **Are** the two cases in fact **alike?** [4] **There**, in Rabbi Ḥiyya's case, where the defendant denies owing money to the claimant and witnesses partially support the claimant, **the lender** (the claimant) **has witnesses** that he lent the borrower 50 zuz, **but the borrower** (the defendant) **does not have witnesses that he does not owe** the lender the other 50 zuz. [5] **For if the borrower did have witnesses that he owes nothing** of the other 50 zuz, **Rabbi Ḥiyya would not require him to take an oath** regarding them. If the witnesses testified that the defendant owed 50 zuz but has repaid 50 zuz, Rabbi Ḥiyya would not impose an oath on the defendant. [6] But **here** in our Mishnah, **just as we are witnesses** for the one claimant, **that half the garment is his, we are** likewise **witnesses** for the other claimant **that half the garment is his,** and **even so** both claimants have to **take an oath**! Why did the Sages insist that both parties to the dispute must take an oath? Clearly the imposition of the oath on both parties has nothing to do with their having made a partial admission, as Rabbi Ḥiyya claims, and is not an oath imposed by the Torah, as Rabbi Ḥiyya implies, but is, as we have established (above, 3a), a Rabbinic enactment to prevent people from seizing other people's property and claiming it as theirs. In other words, the two cases are quite different. and the reason for the imposition of an oath is quite different in each case.

RASHI

תורת הזמה לא פריך — אינה חשובה לו פירכא, דכיון דעד אחד ישנו בהזמה — ליבטל עדותו בעדות שני עדים, אם הוא לן למימר בעדים משום דישנן בהזמה לא יחייבוהו שבועה — הוה לן למימר נמי בעד אחד לא יחייבהו שבועה, דהא ישנו בהזמה ליבטל עדותו. ואי משום דאין משלם קנס — אין בזו יפוי כח להאמין עדותו. **אלא דקאמר ותנא תונא** — אם יש לך להשיב על דברי ר׳ חייא — כך יש לך להשיב, דקאמר ותנא תונא והביא ראיה לדבריו ממשנתינו — מי דמי. **התם** — בדר׳ חייא. **למלוה אית ליה סהדי** — דמסיק ביה חמשים. **ללוה לית ליה סהדי** — באותן חמשים שאינו חייב לו עליה. **אי הוה ליה כו׳** — כגון אילו העידו העדים חמשים חייב וחמשים פרע בכהאי גוונא לא הוה אמר ר׳ חייא דצריך לישבע על השאר. **מתניתין כי היכי דאנן סהדי להאי** — דחציה שלו. **אנן סהדי להאי** — דחציה שלו, ולמה הצריכוהו חכמים שבועה? שמע מינה טעמא לאו משום מקצת הטענה הוא כר׳ חייא, ואינה שבועה דאורייתא, אלא תקנת חכמים שלא יהא כל אחד הולך כו׳.

NOTES

at all. With regard to a single witness: If a pair of witnesses testify that this witness could not possibly have been present at the place where the events about which he testifies transpired at the time he claims that they transpired, his testimony is indeed discarded, but he is not penalized for his false testimony; hence the principle of הֲזָמָה does not apply to him fully.

Since the principle of הֲזָמָה does apply to a single witness, the common factor shared by the case of a litigant's admission and the case of a single witness is relatively unimportant — that in neither case does the evidence of witnesses involve them in a penalty, and the reasons for this are different in each case. Nevertheless, a comparison based on a common factor (מָה הַצַּד) is not considered a powerful argument and can be refuted even by pointing out a relatively minor common factor such as this.

תּוֹרַת הֲזָמָה לָא פָּרֵיךְ **Rabbi Ḥiyya does not regard the argument based on** הֲזָמָה **as a refutation.** *Rosh* and *Rabbenu Ḥananel* (in *Shittah Mekubbetzet)* explain that since, as described above, the extent to which the principle

TRANSLATION AND COMMENTARY

אֶלָּא כִּי אִיתְּמַר ״וְתַנָּא תּוּנָא״ [1]As a result of this objection the Gemara now offers a new version of Rabbi Ḥiyya's use of our Mishnah: **Rather**, says the Gemara, **when the statement, "The Tanna of our Mishnah taught** likewise," **was made, it was made** with reference to **another of Rabbi Ḥiyya's** rulings. [2]**For Rabbi Ḥiyya says**: If one man claims against another: **"You owe me a maneh** (100 zuz), **and the other says, "I only owe you 50 zuz, and here it is"** (i.e., I have not spent this money and it is yours wherever it may be), **he is obliged** to take an oath with regard to the rest of the amount claimed. [3]**What is the reason** that he has to take an oath? [4]Because even though he used the expression "here it is," it **is** still **considered like** a **partial admission of the claim**. We might possibly have considered the two parts of the claim separately: The first 50 zuz is not only admitted by the borrower but is at once repaid to the lender, and the second 50 zuz might possibly be considered as a separate claim that is being totally denied by the borrower. However, Rabbi Ḥiyya maintains that we do *not* separate the two parts of the claim. Therefore we do not say that since the borrower is physically giving back to the lender the amount he admits owing, it is as if there is no partial admission by him.

[1]אֶלָּא, כִּי אִיתְּמַר ״וְתַנָּא תּוּנָא״, אַאִידָךְ דְּרַבִּי חִיָּיא אִיתְּמַר. [2]דְּאָמַר רַבִּי חִיָּיא: ״מָנֶה לִי בְּיָדְךָ״, וְהַלָּה אוֹמֵר: ״אֵין לְךָ בְּיָדִי אֶלָּא חֲמִישִּׁים זוּז, וְהֵילָךְ״, חַיָּיב. [3]מַאי טַעְמָא? [4]״הֵילָךְ״ נַמִי כְּמוֹדֶה מִקְצָת הַטַּעֲנָה דָּמֵי.

[5]וְתַנָּא תּוּנָא: שְׁנַיִם אוֹחֲזִין בְּטַלִּית. [6]וְהָא הָכָא, כֵּיוָן דְּתָפֵיס, [אֲנַן סַהֲדֵי דְּמַאי דְּתָפֵיס] ״הֵילָךְ״ הוּא, [7]וְקָתָנֵי יִשָּׁבַע.

LITERAL TRANSLATION

[1]Rather, when [the statement], "Our Tanna taught [similarly]" was said, it was said with regard to another [ruling] of Rabbi Ḥiyya. [2]For Rabbi Ḥiyya says: [If one person says:] "A maneh of mine is in your possession," and the other says: "Only 50 zuz of yours is in my possession and here it is (lit., "behold to you"), he is obliged [to take an oath]. [3]What is the reason? [4]"Here it is" is also like a partial admission of the claim.

[5]And our Tanna taught [similarly]: "Two are holding on to a garment." [6]And surely here, since [each] is holding on, we are witnesses that what [each] is holding on to is [a case of] "here it is," [7]and [yet] it teaches that [each] must swear.

RASHI

והילך – לא הוצאתים, והן שלך בכל מקום שהם. **חייב** – לישבע על השאר, ולא אמרינן הכי דקמודי ליה בגוייהו, הואיל ואיתנהו בעינייהו – כמאן דנקיט להו דמי. אלא כשאר מודה במקצת הוא, וחייב. **ותנא תונא כו׳** – קא סלקא דעתך דלר׳ חייא טעמא דמתניתין משום דאכן סהדי דמאי דתפיס דיליה הוא, והוי כמנה לי בידך והלה אמר אין לך בידי כלום והעידים מעידים אותו שיש לו חמשים. וכי אידך דר׳ חייא דמחייב ליה שבועה דאורייתא. **והא הכא** – דהך העדאת עדים אכן סהדי דמאי דתפיס האי הילך הוא, שהרי בפנינו הוא. **וקתני** – דמחייב שבועה אשארא, והוא הדין להודאה במקצת.

וְתַנָּא תּוּנָא [5]The Gemara suggests that it was to bring support for this second ruling that Rabbi Ḥiyya quoted from our Mishnah: **And the Tanna of our Mishnah taught likewise:** "If **two people** appear before the court **holding** on to **a garment**...." [6]The analogy between the two cases is as follows: **Here**, in our Mishnah, **since** each of the claimants **has** physically **taken possession** of part of the garment, **we are witnesses** to the fact **that what each has seized is** a case of "here it is" as far as the other claimant is concerned. In other words, since the part of the garment that we are about to award to each litigant is already in his possession, it is no longer in fact being claimed, and it is like that part of a debt that is being made available for the lender to take. [7]Nevertheless the Mishnah **teaches that each** claimant **must take an oath**. The implication is that even if a litigant uses the expression "here it is" with reference to part of a claim made against him, he is still liable to take an oath with reference to the part of the claim he denies, in accordance with Rabbi Ḥiyya's ruling.

NOTES

of הֲזָמָה does not apply to a litigant's statements is different from the extent to which it does not apply to the statements of an individual witness, the similarity between the two cases is not considered of sufficient weight to disprove even a relatively fragile comparison based on a common factor (מָה הַצַּד).

Based on *Rashi's* commentary, *Ritva* explains further that, in fact, the principle of הֲזָמָה *does* apply to a single witness, for his testimony is discarded entirely. The reason why he is not penalized in accordance with the penalty he wished to impose upon the defendant is because the maximum he could have caused the defendant to do is to take an oath, and there is no sense in penalizing him by compelling him to take an oath.

HALAKHAH

הֵילָךְ פָּטוּר מִשְּׁבוּעָה **One who says** הֵילָךְ — "here it is" — **is exempt from taking an oath**. "A person who admits part of a claim, states הֵילָךְ, and pays it immediately, is exempt from taking a Torah oath denying the rest of the claim. Nevertheless, he is required to take a Rabbinic oath (שְׁבוּעַת הֶיסֵּת) like a person who *totally* denies a claim made against him." (*Shulḥan Arukh, Ḥoshen Mishpat* 75:6; 87:1.)

TERMINOLOGY

וְאִידָךְ **And the other one?** i.e., what does the other scholar, holding the conflicting opinion, say to this argument? This expression is used to clarify differences of opinion between scholars, with the Gemara asking each in turn how he will answer the argument brought by the other.

SAGES

רַב שֵׁשֶׁת **Rav Sheshet**. He was a famous Babylonian Amora of the second and third generations, a colleague of Rav Naḥman and of Rav Ḥisda. He was outstanding in his knowledge of Mishnayot and Baraitot, which he had acquired through his exceptional diligence. In his controversies with Rabbi Naḥman, the Geonim decided the Halakhah according to him in all matters of ritual law. He was blind. Many of the Amoraim of the third and fourth generations, including Rava, were his students.

[1]וְרַב שֵׁשֶׁת אָמַר: ״הֵילָךְ״ פָּטוּר. [2]מַאי טַעְמָא? [3]כֵּיוָן דְּאָמַר לֵיהּ ״הֵילָךְ״, הָנֵי זוּזֵי דְּקָא מוֹדֵי בְּגַוַּיְיהוּ כְּמַאן דְּנָקֵיט לְהוּ מַלְוֶה דָּמֵי. בְּאִינָךְ חַמְשִׁים הָא לָא מוֹדֵי. [4]הִלְכָּךְ לֵיכָּא הוֹדָאַת מִקְצָת הַטַּעֲנָה.

[5]וּלְרַב שֵׁשֶׁת קַשְׁיָא מַתְנִיתִין! [6]אָמַר לָךְ רַב שֵׁשֶׁת: מַתְנִיתִין תַּקָּנַת חֲכָמִים הִיא.

[7]וְאִידָךְ?

[8]אִין, תַּקָּנַת חֲכָמִים הִיא. [9]וּמִיהוּ, אִי אָמְרַתְּ בִּשְׁלָמָא מִדְּאוֹרַיְיתָא ״הֵילָךְ״ חַיָּיב, מְתַקְּנִי רַבָּנַן שְׁבוּעָה כְּעֵין דְּאוֹרַיְיתָא. [10]אֶלָּא אִי אָמְרַתְּ מִדְּאוֹרַיְיתָא ״הֵילָךְ״ פָּטוּר, מְתַקְּנִי רַבָּנַן שְׁבוּעָה דְּלֵיתָא דִּכְווֹתָהּ בִּדְאוֹרַיְיתָא?

LITERAL TRANSLATION

[1]But Rav Sheshet says: "Here it is" is exempt. [2]What is the reason? [3]Since he said to him, "Here it is," those zuz about which he has admitted are considered as if the lender has [already] taken them. As for the other 50 [zuz], surely he does not admit [to owing them]. [4]Therefore there is no partial admission of the claim.

[5]But according to Rav Sheshet our Mishnah is difficult!

[6]Rav Sheshet can say to you: [The oath in] our Mishnah is a Rabbinic ordinance.

[7]And [what does] the other [say]?

[8]Yes, it is a Rabbinic ordinance. [9]But nevertheless, it is well if you say that by Torah law "here it is" is liable, [since] the Sages enacted an oath similar to that of the Torah. [10]But if you say that by Torah law "here it is" is exempt, would the Sages enact an oath the like of which does not exist in the Torah?

RASHI

תקנת חכמים היא — ולא משום העדאת עדים. וכדפרכינן לעיל: כי היכי דלמן סהדי להאי למן סהדי להאי. אי אמרת בשלמא מדאורייתא חייב — כלומר, גבי שבועה דאורייתא, כגון בהודאה במקצת.

TRANSLATION AND COMMENTARY

וְרַב שֵׁשֶׁת אָמַר [1]**Rav Sheshet**, however, disagrees with Rabbi Ḥiyya and **says**: A litigant who says הילך with reference to part of a claim made against him, admitting part of the claim and offering immediate payment of that part, **is exempt** from taking an oath with regard to the remainder of the claim.

מַאי טַעְמָא [2]The Gemara now asks: **What is the reason** why Rav Sheshet exempts the borrower from taking an oath? [3]The Gemara answers: **Since** the borrower **said "here it is"** with reference to part of the claim made against him, **it is as if that money** (the 50 zuz) **that he admits owing** has already been handed back to **the possession of the lender**, and that part of the dispute is considered as resolved. **The other 50** zuz, which the lender claims, **are not admitted** by the borrower at all. [4]**Therefore**, according to Rav Sheshet, **there is no partial admission of a claim** and no oath is imposed on the borrower.

וּלְרַב שֵׁשֶׁת קַשְׁיָא מַתְנִיתִין [5]**But**, asks the Gemara, **according to Rav Sheshet** surely **our Mishnah poses a difficulty**, in that it imposes an oath in seemingly similar circumstances!? How does Rav Sheshet reconcile his own ruling with our Mishnah?

אָמַר לָךְ רַב שֵׁשֶׁת [6]The Gemara answers: **Rav Sheshet can** reply: The oath imposed in **our Mishnah is a** special **Rabbinic ordinance**, whereas generally cases of "here it is" are exempt from an oath.

וְאִידָךְ [7]The Gemara now asks: **And how does the other** authority, Rabbi Ḥiyya, **reply** to this argument by Rav Sheshet?

אִין [8]**Yes**, says the Gemara, Rabbi Ḥiyya agrees that the imposition of an oath in our Mishnah **is a** special **Rabbinic ordinance.** [9]**Nevertheless, if you say** that in the case of "here it is" **an oath of Torah authority is imposed**, then it is understandable that **the Sages** in our Mishnah **enacted** that **an oath** is obligatory **in similar circumstances**, because its underlying principle is of **Torah** authority. [10]**But if you say** that **in the case of** "here it is" **the Torah does not impose an oath, would the Sages** enact **an oath to which there is no parallel in the Torah**? On the contrary, says Rabbi Ḥiyya, there is definitely a basis in Torah law for the imposition of the oath in the case of "here it is," and it is on this basis that the Sages instituted that an oath be imposed in the case described in our Mishnah.

NOTES

מְתַקְּנֵי שְׁבוּעָה דְּלֵיתָא דִּכְווֹתָהּ בִּדְאוֹרַיְיתָא **Would the Sages enact an oath to which there is no parallel in the Torah?** The commentators ask: Surely we find many oaths instituted by the Sages to which there is no parallel in the Torah? For example, in a situation where the court suspects the defendant of willingness to swear falsely, an oath is imposed instead on the plaintiff, and the taking of this oath gives the plaintiff the right to collect his claim from the defendant. This oath is entirely a Rabbinic ordinance.

However, we can differentiate between the two types of situations: (1) Those in which an obligation to take a Torah oath already exists and the Sages merely modified it in the light of the circumstances. (2) Those in which no obligation to take a Torah oath exists at all and the imposition of an

TRANSLATION AND COMMENTARY

מֵיתִיבֵי [1]The Gemara now examines the difference of opinion between Rabbi Ḥiyya and Rav Sheshet as to whether an oath of Biblical authority is imposed in a case of "here it is," and objections are raised against the viewpoints of both scholars: **An objection is raised** from a Baraita: [4B] If a lender produces in court a promissory note on which it is written that X borrowed **sela'im** (silver coins of considerable value) or **dinarim** (small silver coins) from Y, but the amount of sela'im or dinarim is not specified, and the lender and the borrower do not agree on the amounts involved: [2]**The lender says,** "I lent **five** sela'im," **and the borrower says,** "I borrowed **three.**" [3]**Rabbi Shimon ben Elazar says: Since** the borrower has **admitted part of the claim, he must take an oath** with regard to the rest, as in all cases of partial admission. [4]Whereas **Rabbi Akiva** says: The borrower **is** regarded **merely** as **the restorer of lost property and is exempt** from taking an oath with regard to the rest of the claim. The use of the plural in the document ("sela'im", "dinarim") gives no indication that the loan was for more than two sela'im or dinarim. Thus the lender should have made sure that the document clearly stated the amount lent, if the amount involved was more than two. In effect the borrower, by admitting that the loan was three sela'im or dinarim, is restoring lost property, because of his own accord he is giving more to the lender than he would have received on the basis of the document. The term used to describe a person who voluntarily offers more than can be claimed is "restorer of lost property," and it is an accepted principle that such restoration is not treated like a case of partial admission and is not subject to an oath. Thus, in our case, the borrower should be exempt from taking an oath with regard to the rest of the lender's claim.

[1]מֵיתִיבֵי: [4B] סְלָעִים, דִּינָרִין. [2]מַלְוֶה אוֹמֵר: "חָמֵשׁ", וְלֹוֶה אוֹמֵר: "שָׁלֹשׁ". [3]רַבִּי שִׁמְעוֹן בֶּן אֶלְעָזָר אוֹמֵר: הוֹאִיל וְהוֹדָה מִקְצָת הַטַּעֲנָה יִשָּׁבַע. [4]רַבִּי עֲקִיבָא אוֹמֵר: אֵינוֹ אֶלָּא כְּמֵשִׁיב אֲבֵידָה וּפָטוּר.

LITERAL TRANSLATION

[1]They objected: [4B] Sela'im, Dinarim. [2]The lender says: "Five," and the borrower says: "Three." [3]Rabbi Shimon ben Elazar says: Since he has admitted part of the claim he must swear. [4]Rabbi Akiva says: He is only like the restorer of a lost object and is exempt.

RASHI

סלעים דינרין – שטר שכתוב בו: פלוני לוה מפלוני סלעין, ולא פירש כמה. וכן שטר שכתוב בו דינרין סתם. **אינו אלא כמשיב אבידה** – מדהוה ליה למימר שתים, והשטר מסייעו, דכיון דלא פירש ניכרים הדברים ששנים היו – לכן לא הולרך לפרש. דמיעוט סלעים שנים. וכיון דאמר שלש – משיב אבידה הוא, וחכמים פטרו את משיב אבידה מן השבועה, דתנן: המולא את המליאה לא ישבע וכו' (גיטין מח,ג).

SAGES

רַבִּי שִׁמְעוֹן בֶּן אֶלְעָזָר Rabbi Shimon ben Elazar. One of the Sages of the Mishnah during the last gneration of Tannaim. We know little or nothing of his life or family, and, because he belonged to the generation when the Mishnah was edited, not many of his teachings appear in the Mishnah itself (although they are found in Baraitot and in the Talmud). Rabbi Shimon ben Elazar was a friend of Rabbi Yehudah HaNasi, and controversies between them are mentioned several times. He received most of his knowledge of the Torah from his teacher, Rabbi Meir, to whom he was devoted, and he customarily reports many teachings in Rabbi Meir's name.

He lived in or near Tiberias, and although he did not apparently have an academy of his own, many teachings are cited in his name, both in the Halakhah and in the Aggadah.

NOTES

oath is entirely a Rabbinic ordinance. In the latter situation there still must be a Torah principle underlying the Rabbinic ordinance in order for it to be made. Thus, where the Sages ordained that the *plaintiff* should take an oath, there already existed, according to Torah law, an obligation on the *defendant* to take an oath. However, rather than have the defendant take the oath, because they suspected his honesty, the Sages gave that option to the plaintiff. In our case, there is no obligation for an oath at all according to Torah law, and therefore the Gemara has to justify its institution. But in a case where no similar Torah oath is required, the Sages do not impose an oath *(Rosh).*

סְלָעִים, דִּינָרִין A promissory note that states merely "sela'im" or "dinarim." The question is raised by the commentators: Why does the Tannaitic source give two examples, a case of sela'im and a case of dinarim? Surely one would be sufficient. Among the explanations offered are: (1) Both types of coinage are mentioned, in order to demonstrate clearly the positions of both Sages whose opinions are quoted: The mention of sela'im shows the extent of Rabbi Shimon ben Elazar's position, which maintains that even where the defendant obligates himself to pay three sela'im, where the difference between the amount stated in the document and the amount he commits himself to paying is substantial, he is not considered as a restorer of lost property and is required to take an oath. Conversely, it mentions dinarim to show the strength of Rabbi Akiva's view, which considers the defendant as a restorer of lost property and frees him from taking an oath even when his admission concerns as meager a sum as a dinar *(Shittah Mekubbetzet).* (2) By mentioning both types of coinage, the Tannaitic source precludes a defendant from offering the following argument: If the loan was for five dinarim, it would have been proper to write that the sum lent was a sela (equivalent to four dinarim) and a dinar. By stating both sela'im and dinarim, the text implies that such an argument is untenable because the amount of the loan can be stated in either denomination *(Naḥalat Yisrael).*

רַבִּי עֲקִיבָא אוֹמֵר Rabbi Akiva says. Some commentators suggest a different reading here and substitute the name of Rabbi Ya'akov for Rabbi Akiva. To support this change, they argue: (1) Rabbi Shimon ben Elazar would not be involved in a difference of opinion with Rabbi Akiva, a Sage from a previous generation. (2) The line of argument that follows cannot easily be reconciled with Rabbi Akiva's other known positions. Nevertheless, other commentators do not accept this textual change, arguing that there is not sufficient proof in the source material to justify the emendation *(Rosh, Tosafot).*

כְּמֵשִׁיב אֲבֵידָה He is like the restorer of lost property. On the surface it would seem that the same argument, that he

HALAKHAH

סְלָעִים, דִּינָרִין A promissory note that states merely "sela'im" or "dinarim." "In a case where a promissory note states merely 'sela'im' or merely 'dinarim,' and the lender claims that the loan was for five whereas the borrower

¹קָתָנֵי מִיהַת: ״רַבִּי שִׁמְעוֹן בֶּן אֶלְעָזָר אוֹמֵר: הוֹאִיל וְהוֹדָה מִקְצָת הַטַּעֲנָה יִשָּׁבַע״. ²טַעְמָא דַּאֲמַר ״שָׁלשׁ״. הָא ״שְׁתַּיִם״, פָּטוּר. ³וְהַאי שְׁטָר דְּקָמוֹדֵי בֵּיהּ ״הֵילָךְ״ הוּא. ⁴וּשְׁמַע מִינָּהּ: ״הֵילָךְ״ פָּטוּר!

⁵לָא. לְעוֹלָם אֵימָא לָךְ: ״שְׁתַּיִם״ חַיָּיב, ⁶וְהַאי דְּקָתָנֵי ״שָׁלשׁ״ לְאַפּוּקֵי מִדְּרַבִּי עֲקִיבָא,

LITERAL TRANSLATION

¹At all events it teaches: "Rabbi Shimon ben Elazar says: Since he has admitted part of the claim he must swear." ²The reason is that he said "three." But [if he had said] "two," he would have been exempt. ³And this document to which he admits is [a case of] "here it is." ⁴And conclude from this [that] "here it is" is exempt!

⁵No. In fact I can say to you: (If he says) "two" he is obliged, ⁶and [the reason] that it teaches "three" is to negate (lit., "exclude from") [the opinion] of Rabbi Akiva,

TRANSLATION AND COMMENTARY

קָתָנֵי מִיהַת ¹The Gemara now proceeds to analyze the source just quoted: **At all events the Baraita says** that **Rabbi Shimon ben Elazar says: Since** the borrower has **admitted part of the claim, he must take an oath** with regard to the rest. ²From this we can infer that **the reason** why an oath is imposed **is** that the borrower admitted borrowing **three** sela'im or dinarim. If he had admitted borrowing only **two**, **he would have been exempt** from taking an oath. ³Now **this document**, the validity **of which** the borrower **is admitting, is** itself like a case of **"here it is,"** since the borrower has thereby mortgaged his property towards the repayment of the two sela'im and must repay the lender accordingly. ⁴Thus it would seem that we can **conclude from this** source that in a case of **"here it is"** the defendant **is exempt** from taking an oath with regard to the part of the claim he denies. This conclusion would support the viewpoint of Rav Sheshet, who maintains that "here it is" is exempt from an oath, as against that of Rabbi Ḥiyya.

לָא לְעוֹלָם אֵימָא לָךְ ⁵The Gemara now rejects this argument: **No, in fact I can say to you** that even if the borrower admitted that the loan was for **two** sela'im or dinarim, Rabbi Shimon ben Elazar would say that **he is** also **obliged** to take an oath with regard to the rest of the claim. ⁶**And** the reason why the Baraita presents his opinion in a case where the borrower admits owing **three** sela'im or dinarim has nothing to do with the laws of "here it is," but **is** rather **to stress that he disagrees with** the opinion of **Rabbi Akiva**, who says that in this case the borrower **is** regarded as **the restorer**

TERMINOLOGY

קָתָנֵי מִיהַת At all events it teaches.... When, as part of an objection, a lengthy Mishnah or Baraita is cited by the Talmud, and only one part of it is actually relevant to the objection being raised, the Talmud may first cite this Mishnah or Baraita in its entirety, and then repeat the relevant section, introducing it with this expression.

לְאַפּוּקֵי מִדְּרַבִּי פְּלוֹנִי To exclude from Rabbi X. Sometimes the Talmud explains that a source was worded in a particular way in order "to negate Rabbi X's viewpoint."

RASHI

טעמא דאמר שלש — קא סלקא דעתך השתא דמייתי תיובתא מדנקט פלוגתייהו בשלש וחמש, ולא נקט ולוה אמר שתים. שמע מינה: בשתים לא מחייב ליה ר׳ שמעון בן אלעזר, וכדמפרש ואזיל. דכיון דכל הודאתו בשטר כתובה, דשטר נמי שתים משמע, וכל משמעות השטר דשטר נמי שתים משמע, וכל משמעות השטר הילך הוא — שהרי הקרקעות משועבדים על כך. אבל כי אמר שלש סלעים — שלישי מלוה על פה הוא, דלאו בשטר כתובה, ואין הקרקעות משועבדים, ולאו הילך הוא. הכי גרסינן: **ושטרא דקמודה הילך הוא** ולא גרסינן: **כיון דקמודה ביה** — דבלאו הודאתו נמי כל שטרי הילך הוא. והכי פירושו: ומאי דקמודה ביה — דכתוב בשטר הילך הוא. **לאפוקי מדר׳ עקיבא כו׳** — דאי תנא שתים לא הוה פליג ר׳ עקיבא.

NOTES

could have admitted less than he did, can be advanced in favor of anyone who acknowledges part of a plaintiff's claim (מוֹדֶה בְּמִקְצָת). The consequence of such an argument would be that an oath explicitly stipulated in the Torah would never be imposed. But there is a difference between the two situations: Generally, we suspect that the reason why a person who acknowledges part of a claim does not totally deny the obligation is because he is not so insolent as to do so. In this case, however, the defendant could have dared to deny the amount that he admits, because the promissory note supports such a denial. The fact that he admits more than the promissory note states makes him like a person returning lost property *(Ramban, Pnei Yehoshua)*.

וְהַאי שְׁטָר דְּקָמוֹדֵי בֵּיהּ הֵילָךְ הוּא And this document to which he admits is a case of "here it is." The assumption that a person who admits to a claim and says, "Here it is," is then exempt from any further negotiation is based on the fact that, by his use of that phrase, it is as if he is actually returning the amount claimed; hence there is no further claim. However, a standard promissory note (as explained below) is actually guaranteed by a mortgage, for it is regarded as if it contained a clause guaranteeing it by a lien against the borrower's real estate. Anyone who admits to the validity of a note that he issued is thus automatically giving the lender the right to collect the debt from his real estate, and this real estate, which cannot be spirited away, is tantamount to a case of "here it is," for it is as if the debtor is offering the physical return of the money.

לְאַפּוּקֵי מִדְּרַבִּי עֲקִיבָא To negate the opinion of Rabbi Akiva. The way matters are understood here, the

HALAKHAH

claims that the loan was for two, the borrower is not liable to take a Torah oath. Even if the borrower admits that he owes three, one more than is implied by the text of the promissory note, he is exempt, for he is considered as a restorer of lost property, since he could have stated that the loan was for two."

Furthermore, the *Baḥ* does not require even a Rabbinic oath (שְׁבוּעַת הֶיסֵּת) in such an instance, whereas the *Shakh* and the *Sma* maintain that the case is not completely analogous to the restoring of lost property and impose a Rabbinic oath on the borrower. (*Shulḥan Arukh, Ḥoshen Mishpat* 88:32.)

דְּאָמַר: מֵשִׁיב אֲבֵידָה הָוֵי וּפָטוּר. ¹קָא מַשְׁמַע לָן דְּמוֹדֶה מִקְצָת הַטַּעֲנָה הָוֵי וְחַיָּיב. ²אִי הָכִי, ״רַבִּי שִׁמְעוֹן בֶּן אֶלְעָזָר אוֹמֵר: הוֹאִיל וְהוֹדָה מִקְצָת הַטַּעֲנָה יִשָּׁבַע״? ³״אַף זֶה יִשָּׁבַע״ מִבָּעֵי לֵיהּ! ⁴אֶלָּא לְעוֹלָם ״שְׁתַּיִם״ פָּטוּר, וְ״הֵילָךְ״ חַיָּיב, ⁵וְשָׁאנֵי הָכָא דְּקָא מְסַיֵּיע לֵיהּ שְׁטָרָא. ⁶אִי נַמִי, מִשּׁוּם דַּהֲוָה לֵיהּ

LITERAL TRANSLATION

who says: He is the restorer of a lost object and is exempt. [1]It informs us that he is one who admits part of a claim and is obliged.

[2]If so, "Rabbi Shimon ben Elazar says: Since he has admitted part of the claim he must swear"? [3]"This one too must swear," is what he needed [to say]!

[4]But in fact "two" is exempt, and "here it is" is obliged, [5]but it is different here because the document supports him.

[6]Alternatively, because it is a

TRANSLATION AND COMMENTARY

of lost property and is exempt from taking an oath. [1]The text, therefore, **informs us that** according to Rabbi Shimon ben Elazar the borrower **is** indeed **making a partial admission of a claim and is obliged** to take an oath with regard to the rest of the claim.

אִי הָכִי [2]The Gemara now objects to this explanation: **If so,** if the intention of the Tannaitic text had been as just stated and Rabbi Shimon ben Elazar does in fact maintain that even where the borrower admits to owing two sela'im or dinarim he is liable to take an oath, then there is an imprecision in the statement, **"Rabbi Shimon ben Elazar says: Since** the borrower has **admitted part of the claim, he must take an oath."** [3]The statement should instead read: **"He too must take an oath."** According to the explanation offered above by the Gemara, the borrower has to take an oath with regard to the rest of the claim if he admits to owing two sela'im or dinarim. The text should, therefore, have been worded to the effect that he *also* has to take an oath if he admits to owing *three* sela'im or dinarim!

אֶלָּא לְעוֹלָם שְׁתַּיִם פָּטוּר [4]This objection leads the Gemara to reject the explanation it previously offered and to explain the text in a different way: **In fact,** if the borrower admits to owing **two** sela'im or dinarim he **is exempt** from taking an oath, **and** in a case of **"here it is"** an oath **is** generally **imposed.** [5]But the case **here,** in which the borrower admits to owing two sela'im or dinarim, **is different because the document** presented in court by the lender **supports** the borrower's claim. The witnesses whose signatures appear on the document support his claim that the amount of the loan was no more than two sela'im, and there is therefore no need for him to take an oath regarding the rest of the claim against him.

אִי נַמִי [6]The Gemara goes on to give another reason why the borrower who admits to owing two sela'im or dinarim is exempt from taking an oath: **Alternatively,** it is **because the** lender's **document** has the effect

RASHI

אי הכי — דבשתים נמי חייב, אמאי תנא הואיל והודה מקצת הטענה ישבע? ר׳ שמעון בן אלעזר אומר אף זה ישבע מבעיא ליה! ושמעינן דלא משיב אבידה חשיב ליה. ומדנקט הואיל -- משמע דחיובא משום דגרם לעצמו, שהודה במקצת. דהשתא הוא דהויא הודאה, משום דסלע שלישי לאו הילך הוא. אבל שתים — לא הוה הודאה, משום הילך. **אלא לעולם כו׳** — אלא אי אית לך לתרוצי — תריץ הכי: לעולם כדקאמרת, הא שתים פטור. וטעמא לאו משום הילך, דה הילך בעלמא חייב. **ושאני הכא דקא מסייע ליה שטרא** — העדים החתומים על השטר מעידים כדבריו אלא שלא היו אלא שתים, ולכך לא פירשו מנייכן, הלכך אין צריך שבועה. **אי נמי** — להכי לא הוו שתים הודאה לחייבו שבועה — לפי שהשטר אומר כן, ושטר הוי שעבוד קרקעות. וכשם שאין נשבעין על כפירת קרקעות, כך הודאתן אינה מביאה לידי שבועה. דקרקעות אמעוט מתורת שבועה, במסכת שבועות פרק ״שבועת הדיינין״ (מב,ב). אבל כי אמר מלוה חמש ולוה שלש — אינה כפירה והודאה במה שאין כתוב בשטר.

NOTES

assumption underlying the position of Rabbi Akiva, who exempts the defendant from taking an oath, is that because he admitted to three dinarim, although the wording of the note obligated him to pay only two, his admission of the third dinar is an act of kindness on his part (similar to the returning of a lost object), for he has admitted something that could not otherwise be proved. But if the defendant had only admitted that he owed two dinarim, Rabbi Akiva would not have said that he was like a person returning a lost object. By contrast, Rabbi Shimon ben Elazar (according to our understanding at this stage) does not accept the argument that where the defendant admits to owing the third dinar he is like a person returning a lost object. According to Rabbi Shimon ben Elazar, even if the defendant admits to more than the amount to which the note obligates him, this must be treated like any other dispute regarding someone who admits part of a claim.

אִי נַמִי **Alternatively.** The difference between the two explanations is that, according to the first, it is the style of the words written in the note that provides evidence in support of the defendant who claims that he only owes two dinarim. It is as if his claim is supported by the witnesses who signed the note, whereas the plaintiff has no evidence in his support. On the other hand, according to the second explanation, the very fact that the defendant is relying on the note makes the dispute into the equivalent of a dispute over real estate. According to both explanations, if the defendant admits to a debt of three dinarim, by so doing he admits that he too is not basing his arguments on the note — neither on its style nor on its content. Therefore, the case is like any other one in which a defendant admits part of a claim.

שְׁטַר שִׁעְבּוּד קַרְקָעוֹת, וְאֵין נִשְׁבָּעִין עַל כְּפִירַת שִׁעְבּוּד קַרְקָעוֹת.

[1]אִיכָּא דְּמוֹתִיב מִסֵּיפָא: ״רַבִּי עֲקִיבָא אוֹמֵר: אֵינוֹ אֶלָּא כְּמֵשִׁיב אֲבֵידָה וּפָטוּר״. [2]טַעְמָא דַּאֲמַר ״שָׁלֹשׁ״. הָא ״שְׁתַּיִם״ חַיָּיב. [3]וְהָא שְׁטָר, כֵּיוָן דְּקָא מוֹדֵי בֵּיהּ, כְּ״הֵילָךְ״ דָּמֵי. [4]שְׁמַע מִינָּהּ: ״הֵילָךְ״ חַיָּיב!

[5]לָא. לְעוֹלָם אֵימָא לָךְ: ״שְׁתַּיִם״, נַמִי פָּטוּר, [6]וְהַאי דְּקָתָנֵי ״שָׁלֹשׁ״ לְאַפּוּקֵי מִדְּרַבִּי שִׁמְעוֹן בֶּן אֶלְעָזָר, דְּאָמַר:

LITERAL TRANSLATION

document of mortgage of land, and [people] do not swear on a denial of mortgage of land.

[1]There are some who object from the last clause: "Rabbi Akiva says: He is only like the restorer of a lost object and is exempt." [2]The reason is that he said "three." But [if he had said] "two," [he would have been] obliged. [3]And surely the document, since he admits to it, is like [a case of] "here it is." [4]Conclude from this [that] "here it is" is obliged!

[5]No. In fact I can say to you: [If he says] "two," he is also exempt, [6]and [the reason] that it teaches "three" is to negate [lit., "exclude from"] [the opinion] of Rabbi Shimon ben Elazar, who says:

RASHI

הא שתים — דליכא משיב אבידה. **חייב** — מדלא תנא פטור בשתים, ונימא טעמא משום הילך.

TRANSLATION AND COMMENTARY

of **mortgaging** the borrower's **landed property** to the extent of the value of the loan recorded in it. There is a general principle in Talmudic law that **an oath is not imposed** in a case where the defendant **denies** a claim involving **the mortgage of landed property.** Oaths are only imposed when a dispute involves money or movable property. The lender's document, according to this explanation, shifts the focus of the dispute between the lender and the borrower to the area of real estate, and in a dispute about real estate oaths are not imposed.

אִיכָּא דְּמוֹתִיב מִסֵּיפָא [1]The discussion of the Baraita quoted above raised an objection to the viewpoint of Rabbi Hiyya from the first clause of the text — the statement of Rabbi Shimon ben Elazar. The Gemara now presents another version of the discussion: **There are some** authorities **who quote the objection** as having been raised against the viewpoint of Rav Sheshet **from the last** clause of the text — the statement of Rabbi Akiva: **"Rabbi Akiva says:** When the borrower admits that he owes 'three,' **he is** regarded **merely** as **the restorer of lost property and is exempt** from taking an oath with regard to the rest of the claim." [2]The Gemara now proceeds to analyze this statement: **The reason** why Rabbi Akiva does not impose an oath **is because** the borrower **admitted** borrowing **three** sela'im or dinarim. **But** if he had admitted borrowing only **two**, he would indeed have been **obliged** to take an oath. [3]Now, **since** the borrower **admits** that **the document** is valid, **it is like** a case of **"here it is,"** since the borrower has thereby mortgaged his property towards the repayment of the two sela'im and must repay the lender accordingly. [4]Thus it would seem that we can **conclude from this** source that in a case of **"here it is"** the defendant **is obliged** to take an oath with regard to the part of the claim he denies. This inference would support the viewpoint of Rabbi Ḥiyya as against that of Rav Sheshet.

לָא לְעוֹלָם אֵימָא לָךְ [5]The Gemara now rejects this argument: **No, in fact I can say to you** that if the borrower admitted that the loan was for **two** sela'im or dinarim, Rabbi Akiva would say that the borrower **is also exempt** from taking an oath with regard to the rest of the claim. [6]**And** the reason why the Baraita presents his opinion in a case where the borrower admits owing **three** sela'im or dinarim has nothing to do with the laws of "here it is," but **is** rather **to stress that he disagrees with** the opinion of **Rabbi Shimon ben Elazar, who says**

NOTES

שְׁטַר שִׁעְבּוּד קַרְקָעוֹת A promissory note that has the effect of mortgaging the borrower's landed property. A number of questions have been raised concerning this argument. On the one hand, **Tosafot** notes that it is not tenable according to Rabbi Akiva, since he maintains that oaths *are* imposed in cases involving landed property. By contrast, according to Rabbi Shimon ben Elazar, this explanation is so obvious that it should have been given immediately and not brought as an alternative explanation. *Rashba* suggests that the two explanations offered by the Talmud should not be considered as one continuous line of reasoning. Rather, the first explanation — "the promissory note supports the borrower" — is offered according to the opinion of Rabbi Akiva; while the second explanation — "a promissory note has the effect of mortgaging the borrower's landed property" — is offered according to the opinion of Rabbi Shimon ben Elazar.

שְׁבוּעָה עַל קַרְקָעוֹת An oath is not imposed in cases involving landed property. Exodus 22:9, the Biblical source for the obligation to take oaths, mentions a number of different articles concerning the return of which claims may be made and oaths may be imposed. Based on the exegesis of this verse, *Bava Metzia* 57b explains that an oath is only

HALAKHAH

שְׁבוּעָה עַל כְּפִירָה בְּקַרְקַע An oath in the case of a denial of a claim involving landed property. "The following are matters concerning which the Torah does not require an oath: Landed property.... Nevertheless, a Rabbinic oath (שְׁבוּעַת הֶיסֵּת) must be taken concerning these claims." (*Shulḥan Arukh, Ḥoshen Mishpat* 95:1.)

[1]מוֹדֶה מִקְצָת הַטַּעֲנָה הָוֵי, וְחַיָּיב. [2]קָא מַשְׁמַע לָן דְּמֵשִׁיב אֲבֵידָה הָוֵי וּפָטוּר.

[3]הָכִי נַמִי מִסְתַּבְּרָא: דְּאִי סָלְקָא דַּעְתָּךְ ״שְׁתַּיִם״ חַיָּיב, [4]בְּ״שָׁלֹשׁ״ הֵיכִי פָּטַר לֵיהּ רַבִּי עֲקִיבָא? [5]הַאי אַעֲרוּמֵי קָא מַעֲרִים, סָבַר: אִי אָמֵינָא ״שְׁתַּיִם״, בָּעֵינָא אִשְׁתַּבּוּעֵי. אֵימָא ״שָׁלֹשׁ״ דְּאֶהֱוֵי כְּמֵשִׁיב אֲבֵידָה וְאִיפָּטַר. [6]אֶלָּא, שְׁמַע מִינָּהּ: ״שְׁתַּיִם״ נַמִי פָּטוּר.

[7]אֶלָּא קַשְׁיָא לְרַבִּי חִיָּיא!

[8]שָׁאנֵי הָתָם, דְּקָא מְסַיֵּיעַ לֵיהּ שְׁטָרָא.

LITERAL TRANSLATION

[1]He is one who admits part of a claim, and is obliged. [2]It informs us that he is the restorer of a lost object and is exempt.

[3]So, too, it is reasonable, for if it entered your mind [that if he says] "two" he is obliged, [4]in [the case of] "three" how could Rabbi Akiva exempt him? [5]This [person] is cheating. He thinks: If I say "two," I will need to swear. I will say "three" so that I will be like the restorer of a lost object and I will be exempt. [6]Rather, conclude from this: [If he says] "two," he is also exempt.

[7]But it is difficult for Rabbi Ḥiyya!

[8]It is different there, because the document supports him.

TRANSLATION AND COMMENTARY

that in this case [1]the borrower **is** regarded merely as **one who is making a partial admission of a claim and is** therefore **obliged** to take an oath with regard to the rest of the claim. [2]The Baraita, therefore, **informs us that** according to Rabbi Akiva the borrower **is** considered to be **the restorer of lost property and is exempt** from taking an oath.

הָכִי נַמִי מִסְתַּבְּרָא [3]The Gemara now adds that the explanation just offered **is** in fact **also reasonable** and logical, **for if it entered your mind** to suggest **that** a borrower who admitted to owing **two** sela'im or dinarim **would be obliged** to take an oath, [4]**how could Rabbi Akiva exempt** from an oath a borrower who admitted to owing **three**? [5]**Such a borrower** is suspected, because he **may** be tempted to **cheat**. Knowing that he really owes five sela'im or dinarim, **he may calculate** as follows: **If I say** that I owe *two*, **I will be required to take an oath**. Instead **I will say** that I owe **three**, in which case **I will be** regarded **as the restorer of lost property and I will be exempt** from taking an oath. By admitting to owing three I will not have to perjure myself and I will still keep some of the money I owe. [6]**From this** argument, says the Gemara, we must **conclude** that in a case where the borrower admits to owing **two** sela'im or dinarim, he **is also exempt** from taking an oath!

אֶלָּא קַשְׁיָא לְרַבִּי חִיָּיא [7]**But**, says the Gemara, surely this explanation poses **a difficulty for Rabbi Ḥiyya!** We have just concluded that where the borrower admits to owing two sela'im or dinarim he is exempt from taking an oath with regard to the rest of the claim. But we have also established that the admission by the borrower of what is written in the lender's document is itself a form of "here it is." Thus it would seem that in a case of "here it is" an oath is not imposed, which would contradict the ruling of Rabbi Ḥiyya that in a case of "here it is" an oath *is* imposed!

שָׁאנֵי הָתָם [8]The Gemara answers as it did in the first version of the discussion: **There,** in the case of the loan of an indeterminate number of sela'im or dinarim, the situation **is different**. The reason why an oath is not imposed on the borrower where he admits to owing **two** sela'im or dinarim is **because the document** presented in court by the lender **supports** the borrower's admission, and is not connected with the ruling regarding a case of "here it is."

RASHI

מודה מקצת הוי — ואינו משיב אבידה, דאיערומי קמערים, דלחזקיה בנאמן. **קא משמע לן** — כיון דבשתים נמי פטור — ליכא למימר איערומי מערים, אלא משיב אבידה הוי. **הכי נמי מסתברא** — דבשתים פטור. **ואלא קשיא לר׳ חייא** — דהא איכא למידק מינה דשתים פטור, כדאמרינן דאי סלקא דעתך כו׳. **שאני הכא** — האי דקאמר שתים פטור — טעמא לאו משום הילך, אלא דקא מסייע ליה שטרא.

TERMINOLOGY

הָכִי נַמִי מִסְתַּבְּרָא So, too, it is reasonable. This expression is sometimes used to introduce an argument supplementing an explanation presented in the Gemara. In the Talmudic dialectic, one may reject a proof or objection by showing that it is possible to explain matters otherwise, and that the assumption according to which we had constructed the proof or objection is not a necessary one. The existence of an alternative explanation is enough to deprive an assumption of its decisive power, and this is sufficient to reject it. However, in certain cases the Gemara comments that the alternative explanation is not merely possible but also that it is the most likely one in the context, irrespective of the specific problem under discussion.

NOTES

imposed in cases involving goods that are movable and have an intrinsic fixed value of their own, and not in cases involving landed property or promissory notes that are guaranteed by landed property.

קַשְׁיָא לְרַבִּי חִיָּיא This poses a difficulty for Rabbi Ḥiyya. The Gemara's inference poses a difficulty for Rabbi Ḥiyya because his statement appears to contradict the opinions of Tannaim. But this in itself raises a question: Rabbi Ḥiyya was himself a Tanna, and according to Talmudic principles any Tanna has sufficient authority to dispute the teachings of another. Among the possible resolutions to this difficulty are: Though Rabbi Ḥiyya was a Tanna, he was from the final generation of the Mishnah's Sages, who did not consider themselves of sufficient authority to contradict the opinions of earlier Sages. Alternatively, Rabbi Ḥiyya could indeed disagree with the individual opinion of another Tanna. This Baraita, however, quotes a difference of opinion between two Tannaim, whose views are mutually exclusive. Thus there is no room for Rabbi Ḥiyya to introduce a third opinion not hinted at in the Baraita. (*Rabbi Zvi Ḥayyot.*)

[1]אִי נַמִי, מִשּׁוּם דַּהֲוָה לֵיהּ שְׁטַר שִׁעְבּוּד קַרְקָעוֹת, וְאֵין נִשְׁבָּעִין עַל כְּפִירַת שִׁעְבּוּד קַרְקָעוֹת.

[2]מְתִיב מָר זוּטְרָא בְּרֵיהּ דְּרַב נַחְמָן: [3]טְעָנוֹ כֵּלִים וְקַרְקָעוֹת, הוֹדָה בַּכֵּלִים וְכָפַר בַּקַּרְקָעוֹת, [4]הוֹדָה בַּקַּרְקָעוֹת וְכָפַר בַּכֵּלִים — פָּטוּר. [5]הוֹדָה מִקְצָת קַרְקָעוֹת, פָּטוּר. [6]מִקְצָת כֵּלִים, חַיָּיב.

[7]טַעְמָא דְּכֵלִים וְקַרְקָעוֹת, דְּקַרְקַע לָאו בַּת שְׁבוּעָה הִיא. [8]הָא כֵּלִים וְכֵלִים, דּוּמְיָא דְּכֵלִים וְקַרְקָעוֹת, חַיָּיב. [9]הֵיכִי דָּמֵי? [10]לָאו דְּאָמַר לֵיהּ:

LITERAL TRANSLATION

[1]Alternatively, because it is a document of mortgage of land, and [people] do not swear on a denial of mortgage of land.

[2]Mar Zutra the son of Rav Naḥman objects: [3][If someone] claimed vessels and land [from another person], [and the latter] admitted the vessels and denied the land, [4][or] admitted the land and denied the vessels — he is exempt. [5][If] he admitted part of the land, he is exempt. [6][If he admitted] some of the vessels, he is obliged.

[7]The reason is that vessels and land [are involved], because land is not subject to an oath. [8]But [if the case is] vessels and vessels, like vessels and land, he is obliged. [9]What is it like? [10]Is it not that he said to him:

RASHI

טענו – חבירו בבית דין כלים וקרקעות. **פטור** – דלא כפירתו ולא הודאתו מביאתו לידי שבועה. **חייב** – אף על הקרקעות לישבע, כדאמרינן לקמן: שהנכסים שאין להן אחריות זוקקין את הקרקעות לישבע עליהן, משנתחייב לישבע על המטלטלין זוקקין ומגלגלין עמהם שבועת קרקע. **דומיא דכלים וקרקעות** – שכלים שהודה עליהם מונחים לפנינו, ואמר ליה הילך.

TRANSLATION AND COMMENTARY

אִי נַמִי [1]The Gemara goes on to give another reason why the borrower who admits to owing two sela'im or dinarim is exempt from taking an oath: **Alternatively,** as the Gemara stated above, it is **because the** lender's **document** has the effect of **mortgaging** the borrower's **landed property** to the extent of the value of the loan recorded in it. There is a general principle in Talmudic law that **an oath is not imposed** in a case where the defendant **denies** a claim involving **the mortgage of landed property.** Oaths are only imposed when a dispute involves money or movable property. The lender's document, according to this explanation, shifts the focus of the dispute between the lender and the borrower to the area of real estate, and in a dispute about real estate oaths are not imposed. From this long discussion of the Baraita recording the dispute between Rabbi Shimon ben Elazar and Rabbi Akiva, no conclusive objection has been made against the viewpoints of either Rabbi Ḥiyya or Rav Sheshet on the subject of "here it is."

מְתִיב מָר זוּטְרָא בְּרֵיהּ דְּרַב נַחְמָן [2]**Mar Zutra the son of Rav Naḥman raised an objection** against the point of view of Rav Sheshet (who said that in a case of "here it is" the defendant is exempt from taking an oath) from the following Mishnah (*Shevuot* 38b): [3]"If a man **claims vessels** (movable property) and **landed** property from someone, and the defendant **admits** owing the plaintiff **vessels** but **denies** owing him **land**ed property, [4]or on the contrary if the defendant **admits** owing the plaintiff **land**ed property but **denies** owing him **vessels**, **he is exempt** from taking an oath with regard to the part of the claim he denies. [5]If the defendant **admits** owing the plaintiff **part of the land**ed property claimed, **he is exempt** from taking an oath with regard to those parts of the claim he denies. [6]But if **he admits** owing the plaintiff **some of the vessels** claimed, **he is obliged** to take an oath with regard to the rest of the claim he denies."

טַעְמָא דְּכֵלִים וְקַרְקָעוֹת [7]The Gemara now proceeds to analyze this Mishnah: **The reason** why an oath is not imposed in three out of the four cases mentioned in the Mishnah **is** that the two types of property claimed by the plaintiff are **vessels and land, because land is not subject to an oath**, i.e., oaths are not imposed in cases involving land. [8]Now, says the Gemara, if the case here had been a claim involving two sets of **vessels, like** the Mishnah's combined claim of **vessels and land**, we would have said that the defendant **is obliged** to take an oath. [9]**How do we visualize the case**? [10]**Is** it **not** like a case **where** the defendant **says** to

HALAKHAH

טְעָנוֹ כֵּלִים וְקַרְקָעוֹת **A claim involving vessels and land.** "If a plaintiff claims the return of both vessels and landed property, and the defendant admits his obligation to return all or part of the landed property but denies any obligation to return the vessels, he is exempt from taking a Torah oath. But if he makes a partial admission regarding the vessels, even if he denies any obligation to return the landed property, he is liable to take a Torah oath concerning the vessels he denies owing. As a result he is required to take an oath concerning the landed property as well." (*Shulḥan Arukh, Ḥoshen Mishpat* 95:5.)

TRANSLATION AND COMMENTARY

the plaintiff: **"Here it is"**? All land is essentially a case of "here it is." Thus a case of vessels parallel to a case of land should also be a case of "here it is." If so, may we not **conclude from this that** in a case of **"here it is"** the defendant **is obliged** to take an oath?! This argument, if accepted, would be a refutation of the opinion of Rav Sheshet, who said that in a case of "here it is" the defendant is exempt from taking an oath.

לָא לְעוֹלָם אֵימָא לָךְ [1]The Gemara rejects this argument and says: **No, in fact I can** answer this argument and **say to you that** even if the case involves a claim of **two sets of vessels**, the defendant **is** still **exempt** from taking an oath where he admits the claim with regard to one set of vessels and denies that he owes the other set. [2]**And the reason why the Mishnah brings** the case of a claim for **vessels and landed** property is in order to lay down another legal principle and **to inform us** that **if** the defendant **admits part of the** claim for **vessels** and is obliged to take an oath in denial of the rest of the claim for vessels, **he is also obliged** to take an oath **regarding the landed** property that he denies owing, even though if he had denied owing the landed property alone he would not have been obliged to take an oath.

מַאי קָא מַשְׁמַע לָן [3]The Gemara now asks: **What does** the Mishnah **teach us** by this? That the claim for vessels **binds** to itself the claim for land and enforces an oath on both vessels and land? In other words, is it trying to tell us that even though an oath is not imposed directly in a case where a defendant denies a claim against him for land, nevertheless in a case where the defendant is obliged to take an oath about one aspect of the claim against him, he is also obliged to take an oath about other aspects of the case regarding which he would not normally be required to take an oath? [4]If the purpose of the Mishnah is to teach us this rule, it is surely superfluous, because **we have** already **learned** in another Mishnah *(Kiddushin* 26a): **"Movable property** and **money**, which cannot be mortgaged as security for repayment of a loan, **binds immovable property,** and extends a defendant's obligation **to take an oath** regarding movable property to immovable property as well." Even though oaths are not normally imposed in cases involving land, they can be attached to existing oaths, as explained above. But since this principle is already known to us from the Mishnah in *Kiddushin,* why does it need to be mentioned in the Mishnah in *Shevuot?*

"הֵילָךְ", וּשְׁמַע מִינָּהּ: "הֵילָךְ" חַיָּיב?!

[1]לָא. לְעוֹלָם אֵימָא לָךְ: כֵּלִים וְכֵלִים נַמִי פָּטוּר. [2]וְהָא דְּקָתָנֵי כֵּלִים וְקַרְקָעוֹת — הָא קָא מַשְׁמַע לָן: הוֹדָה בְּמִקְצָת כֵּלִים, חַיָּיב אַף עַל הַקַּרְקָעוֹת. [3]מַאי קָא מַשְׁמַע לָן? זוֹקְקִין? [4]תָּנֵינָא: זוֹקְקִין הַנְּכָסִים שֶׁאֵין לָהֶן אַחֲרָיוּת אֶת הַנְּכָסִים שֶׁיֵּשׁ לָהֶן אַחֲרָיוּת לִישָּׁבַע עֲלֵיהֶם!

LITERAL TRANSLATION

"Here it is," and conclude from this: "Here it is" is obliged?!

[1]No. In fact I can say to you: [In a case of] vessels and vessels he is also exempt. [2]And [the reason] that it teaches vessels and land — this informs us: [If] he has admitted some of the vessels, he is also obliged regarding the land.

[3]What is he teaching us? [The rule of] "binding"? [4]We have [already] learned: Movable property (lit., "property that does not have security") binds immovable property (lit., "property that has security") to swear concerning them!

RASHI

זוקקין — המטלטלין זוקקין הקרקעות לישבע על ידי גלגול. **תנינא** — בקדושין (כו,א) הנכסים שאין להן אחריות זוקקין את הנכסים שיש להן אחריות לישבע עליהם.

TERMINOLOGY

מַאי קָא מַשְׁמַע לָן תָּנֵינָא **What is he teaching us? We have [already] learned [this].** Here the Gemara is questioning a Mishnah, a Baraita, or an Amoraic statement on the grounds that it is superfluous, having already been mentioned in a Mishnah.

CONCEPTS

הַנְּכָסִים שֶׁיֵּשׁ לָהֶן אַחֲרָיוּת **Immovable property (lit., "property that has security").** In many Halakhic contexts a distinction is made between property that can be mortgaged — land and other real estate — and property that cannot be mortgaged. The source of this distinction is found in the Torah itself, but the meaning of the expression is that property connected to land can serve as a guarantee and be subject to a lien, because it cannot be removed and smuggled away. Hence it provides a trustworthy guarantee.

NOTES

וּשְׁמַע מִינָּהּ הֵילָךְ חַיָּיב **And conclude from this: "Here it is" is obliged?** When we seek to equate a claim regarding vessels and land with one regarding vessels and vessels, we already know that land is by its nature a matter of "here it is." Therefore the explanation must be that in the parallel case, in which the defendant admits the claim regarding some of the vessels, he is in fact saying, "Here it is," with regard to those that he admits.

מַאי קָא מַשְׁמַע לָן זוֹקְקִין **What is he teaching us? The rule of "binding"?** A basic Talmudic assumption in interpreting Mishnaic sources is that these sources are extremely brief, and that every phrase in them is meant to teach us something we did not previously know. If we were to interpret the Mishnah as propsed by Mar Zutra, the innovation would be that it teaches us the Halakhah regarding the subject of "here it is." However, according to our present interpretation, this Halakhah (זוקקין) is not a new one, for it is already found in another Mishnah! The explanation given by the Gemara for this seeming repetition is that the Mishnah sometimes repeats an established Halakhah, when it is presented incidentally, and in such circumstances it need not teach something entirely new. In the present case, the Halakhah in tractate *Shevuot* is a summary of Halakhot regarding oaths on various kinds of property, whereas in tractate *Kiddushin* the matter is referred to incidentally without any intended innovation.

HALAKHAH

זוֹקְקִין **The rule of "binding."** "If a plaintiff claims the return of different kinds of property, some of which oblige the defendant denying the claim to take an oath and others of which do not, once he is obliged to take an oath regarding part of the property claimed, the obligation to take an oath is extended to include an oath regarding the rest of the property as well, regarding which he would not normally be obliged to take an oath." (Ibid., 95:5.)

BACKGROUND

בּוֹרוֹת שִׁיחִין וּמְעָרוֹת Pits, ditches and caves. All these terms refer to essentially the same thing: an excavation in the earth for use as a container (generally to hold water). But there are technical differences between these terms (and other terms in the same context): a (pit) בּוֹר is an excavation in the earth with a round opening. A ditch (שִׁיחַ) is long, narrow, and rectangular, while a cave (מְעָרָה) is covered by a sort of roof.

TRANSLATION AND COMMENTARY

הָכָא עִיקָּר [1]The Gemara answers: The Mishnah **here** in tractate *Shevuot,* in its discussion of the laws pertaining to oaths imposed on defendants in cases about vessels and land, **is the main source** for the rule that a claim for the return of movable property can force a defendant to take an oath also with regard to immovable property. [2]Whereas the Mishnah **there** in tractate *Kiddushin* deals with the subject **incidentally,** as part of a general comparison of the various modes of acquisition of different kinds of property. Just as movable property can be "bound" to immovable property for the purposes of acquisition, so too can immovable property be "bound" to movable property for the purposes of oaths. At all events the main source for the rule is found in the Mishnah in tractate *Shevuot* quoted here. It therefore has importance in its own right, and no inferences can be drawn from it with regard to a case of "here it is."

וּלְמַאן דְּאָמַר הֵילָךְ פָּטוּר [5A] [3]The Gemara now asks: But **according** to the authority (Rav Sheshet) **who said** that in all cases of "here it is" the defendant **is exempt** from taking an oath regarding the rest of the claim against him, **why is a** special interpretation of a **verse** in the Torah **needed to exclude real estate from** the imposition of **an oath** in a case where a defendant admits part of a claim against him for land? [4]**Surely all real estate** is a form of **"here it is,"** for obviously land is by definition immovable and is always readily available to its rightful owner. Thus, there is no better example of "here it is" than this. Why then is a special verse needed to exclude real estate from an oath?

אֲמַר לָךְ [5]The Gemara replies: Rav Sheshet **could answer you** as follows — The **verse** (Exodus 22:8) **is needed** for a case **where** the defendant **dug** the land that is now claimed from him and created **pits, ditches and caves.** Such a situation would then no longer be one of "here it is," where the item is returned to the claimant in its original form, because in this case the field has been altered and damaged by his actions.

אִי נַמִי [6]The Gemara now gives an additional reply: **Alternatively,** there is also a need for the verse in a case **where** the plaintiff **claims** that the defendant owes him **vessels** (movable property) **and real estate,** [7]**and** the defendant **admits** owing the **vessels but denies** owing the **real estate.** Such an admission would not be a case of "here it is." The verse teaches us that in such a case the defendant would be exempt from taking an oath because the denial was made with regard to real estate.

[1]הָכָא עִיקָּר. [2]הָתָם אַגַּב גְּרָרָא נַסְבָּהּ.

[5A] [3]וּלְמַאן דַּאֲמַר "הֵילָךְ" פָּטוּר, אַמַּאי אִיצְטְרִיךְ קְרָא לְמַעוּטֵי קַרְקַע מִשְּׁבוּעָה? [4]הָא כָּל קַרְקַע "הֵילָךְ" הוּא!

[5]אֲמַר לָךְ: אִיצְטְרִיךְ קְרָא הֵיכָא דְּחָפַר בָּהּ בּוֹרוֹת, שִׁיחִין וּמְעָרוֹת.

[6]אִי נַמִי: הֵיכָא דִּטְעָנוֹ כֵּלִים וְקַרְקָעוֹת, [7]וְהוֹדָה בַּכֵּלִים וְכָפַר בַּקַּרְקָעוֹת.

LITERAL TRANSLATION

[1]Here is the main [source]. [2]There, he brought it.

[5A] [3]And according to him who says: "Here it is" is exempt, why is a verse needed to exclude land from an oath? [4]Surely all land is "here it is"!

[5]He can say to you: The verse is needed where he dug in it pits, ditches and caves.

[6]Alternatively: Where he claimed vessels and land from him, [7]and he admitted to the vessels but denied the land.

RASHI

הכא עיקר — שמשנה זו שנויה במסכת שבועות (לח,א). **התם** — בקדושין. **אגב גררא נסבה** — דאיירי התם נכסים שאין להן אחריות נקנין עם נכסים שיש להן אחריות בכסף בשטר ובחזקה, ואגב דאיירי דנקנין עמהם תנא בהדה זוקקין אותן לישבע עליהם. **למאי איצטריך קרא למעוטי קרקע משבועה** — דילפינן לה מכלל ופרט בשבועות (מב,ב), ולקמן בפרק "הזהב" (נז,ב). **וחפר בה בורות שיחין ומערות** — דלאו "הילך" הוא, שהרי קלקלה. **אי נמי** — להיכן דהודה בכלים, דלאו "הילך" הוא. ואשמועינן דאינו נשבע אכפירת (שעבוד) קרקעות.

NOTES

לְמַעוּטֵי קַרְקַע מִשְּׁבוּעָה To exclude land from an oath. The laws requiring a person to take an oath to absolve himself from a claim against him are laid down in the Torah in the following terms: "For all manner of trespass, whether it be for ox, for ass, for sheep, for a garment, or for any manner of lost thing, of which one can say, 'This is it,'" (Exodus 22:8). The detailed list (ox, ass, sheep, garment) indicates that the obligation to take an oath applies only with reference to items of the kind mentioned in the verse, i.e., only movable property with intrinsic monetary value. Hence land and real estate are excluded from the obligation to take an oath, as are promissory notes and other documents with no intrinsic monetary value.

חָפַר בָּהּ בּוֹרוֹת He dug pits in it. Some commentators point out that, because of the damage done to the land, the plaintiff's claim also includes a demand for financial reimbursement for the damage done. Hence the claim is both for movable property (money) and for land, and would thus require an oath. (*Shittah Mekubbetzet.*) This matter is the subject of much debate among the commentators and Halakhic authorities. *Rambam* (*Hilkhot To'en VeNit'an* 5:2) rules, based on our Gemara, that no oath is imposed in a case involving land, even where, as in our case, the claim has been transformed into a claim of money. *Ra'avad* and other authorities, however, require an oath in such a case, and explain that in our Gemara there is no monetary claim being made, and the plaintiff is simply demanding that the defendant repair the damage and fill in the pits he dug.

[1] תָּא שְׁמַע דְּתָנֵי רָמִי בַּר חָמָא: אַרְבָּעָה שׁוֹמְרִין צְרִיכִין כְּפִירָה בְּמִקְצָת וְהוֹדָאָה בְּמִקְצָת: [2] שׁוֹמֵר חִנָּם וְהַשּׁוֹאֵל, נוֹשֵׂא שָׂכָר וְהַשּׂוֹכֵר. [3] הֵיכִי דָּמֵי? [4] לָאו דְּאָמַר

TRANSLATION AND COMMENTARY

תָּא שְׁמַע [1] The Gemara continues to probe the dispute between Rabbi Ḥiyya and Rav Sheshet as to whether a defendant is obliged to take an oath in a case of "here it is": **Come** and **hear** the following Baraita transmitted by **Rami bar Ḥama**: "The **four** kinds of **bailee** mentioned in the Torah are all obliged to take an oath if they claim that an article placed in their care was lost under circumstances for which they are not responsible. These bailees must take an oath only if in addition they **deny part** of the claim against them **and admit part** of the claim against them. And these are the four kinds of bailee: (1) [2] **the unpaid bailee**, who receives no payment for looking after the article entrusted to him; (2) **the borrower**, who receives the article to make use of it, but does not pay for its use; (3) **the paid bailee**, who receives payment for looking after the article entrusted to him; and (4) **the hirer**, who pays the owner of the article for the right to make use of it." It is impossible to postulate a case of partial admission and partial denial where the bailee was entrusted with *one* article or *one* animal. The case must be where the owner claims to have entrusted *three* animals to the bailee's care. The bailee denies one entirely, returns the second one to the owner, and claims that the third was lost in circumstances for which he was not responsible.

הֵיכִי דָּמֵי [3] The Gemara now proceeds to analyze this statement: **How do we visualize the case?** How can partial admission and partial denial occur in the case of bailees? [4] **Is** the situation **not** one where the bailee **says to the** owner of the animals, who is demanding the return of all the animals: "One animal never existed. In other words, I only received two animals from you. This one (the second one you claim) I am returning

LITERAL TRANSLATION

[1] Come [and] hear what Rami bar Ḥama taught: Four bailees require a partial denial and a partial admission: [2] the unpaid bailee and the borrower, the paid bailee and the hirer.

[3] What is it like? [4] Is it not where he says

RASHI

ארבעה שומרין – שבועה האמורה בהן. בשומר חנם – שנגנבה הימנו, ושומר שכר – שנאנסה, ובשואל – שמתה מחמת מלאכה. **צריכין כפירה במקצת והודאה במקצת** – כפירה לא הויא אלא בכופר ממש; או "לא היו דברים מעולם", או "החזרתי לך". הודאה לא הויא אלא אם כן הודה ממש שיש לו בידו, שחייב להחזיר לו. נמצא שאין חיוב שבועת השומרים באה אלא אם כן טען שלש פרות; באחת כפר לו, ובאחת הודה לו שישנה בידו, והשלישית אומר לו "נאנסה", או אם שומר חנם הוא – אומר לו בשלישית "נגנבה", דחייב עליה שבועה האמורה בפרשה (שמות כב) שלא שלח ידו במלאכת רעהו. דאילו שבועה דכפירה – אין זו שבועה האמורה בשומרים. ובלאו כפירה נמי לא תחייביה שבועת שומרים, דכתיב בשומר חנם "כי הוא זה" דמינה נפקא לן (שבועות לט,ב) שמודה במקצת וכפר במקצת. ולאפוקי מאן דאמר בבבא קמא ב"הגוזל [קמא]" (קז,א): עירוב פרשיות כתוב כאן, וכי כתיב "כי הוא זה" – לאו אשומר חנם דכתיב גביה קאי, אלא א"אם כסף תלוה". ואשמועינן האי תנא דבשומרים נמי בעינן כפירה והודאה, והשבועה האמורה בפרשה – על פרה שלישית. **היכי דמי** – פרה של הודאה. **לאו** – דקיימא קמן, ואמר ליה: קחנה בכל מקום שהיא, דהיינו "הילך"?

NOTES

שׁוֹמְרִים בִּכְפִירָה וְהוֹדָאָה בְּמִקְצָת **These bailees only take an oath if they deny part of the claim and admit part of it.** Rishonim have raised the following difficulty: According to Rami bar Ḥama's position, why did the Torah specifically obligate *bailees* to take an oath? The Torah could instead have mentioned the obligation to take an oath in the general case where the defendant admits part of the claim (מוֹדֶה בְּמִקְצָת), and then the oaths required in the specific case of a bailee would automatically be imposed on the basis of the principle of גִּלְגּוּל שְׁבוּעָה. *Ramban* explains that even according to Rami bar Ḥama the laws of bailees include many legal principles unconnected with oaths. Moreover, the Torah does not mention in any other context the oath taken by a defendant who admits part of a claim. Thus Rami bar Ḥama can explain that the Torah is simply informing us of the general law as part of the exposition of the many details of the laws of bailees, and that the source of the specific language of the oath taken by bailees is indeed גִּלְגּוּל שְׁבוּעָה. *Ra'avad* explains that even according to Rami bar Ḥama there is a case of an oath taken by bailees which cannot be derived from גִּלְגּוּל שְׁבוּעָה. In the case of the three cows mentioned above, if the plaintiff waived his claim concerning the cow which the watchman denied receiving, there would be no way of imposing an oath on the basis of גִּלְגּוּל שְׁבוּעָה because the only remaining dispute between the parties is with regard to the cow that died as a result of an accident. Nevertheless, the Torah tells us that even in such a situation the bailee *is* required to take an oath.

צְרִיכִין כְּפִירָה וכו׳ **Require a partial denial....** The obligation of bailees to take an oath is mentioned twice in the Torah (Exodus 22,6-14): first, in the case of an unpaid bailee who claims that the bailment was stolen from him ("the master of the house shall be brought to the judges, to swear that he has not put his hand to his neighbor's goods," Exodus 22:8); and second, in the case of a paid bailee who claims that the animal placed in his care has died or been forcibly removed from his possession ("then shall an oath of the Lord be between them both, that he has not put his hand to his neighbor's goods," Exodus 22:10). In the opinion of the Baraita presented by Rami bar Ḥama this obligation to swear does not apply in every case in which the bailee claims that the object is no longer in his possession, but specifically when the bailee admits to part of the liability but denies the rest. As explained below, this can happen only when several animals or objects have been entrusted to the bailee, and he admits to part of the claim against him (regarding a single animal or more) but denies the rest.

LANGUAGE

אַפְּטוֹרִיקִי Aptoriki. This proper noun is derived from the Latin *"patricius,"* meaning "of noble, aristocratic birth."

TRANSLATION AND COMMENTARY

to you and **here it is** (הֵילָךְ). The third one was lost in circumstances outside my responsibility." This interpretation of the Baraita transmitted by Rami bar Ḥama would support Rabbi Ḥiyya's viewpoint that a partial admission using the expression "here it is" or its equivalent does oblige the defendant to take an oath regarding the rest of the claim!

לָא [1]The Gemara now rejects this argument: **No**, the partial admission by a bailee can take place in different circumstances, such as **where** the owner of cattle **says to** an unpaid bailee: **"I** entrusted **three cows** into your care, **and all of them died through** your **negligence**, and you must repay me their value." [2]The bailee **answers him**: "As far as **one** cow is concerned, **it never happened**. In other words, I only received two cows into my care. [3]**One** cow **died as a result of an accident**, and I am exempt from compensating you. **And one** cow **did die as a result of** my **negligence and I must compensate you for it**." [4]In this case, even though the bailee makes a partial admission, **it is not** a case of **"here it is,"** because the bailee is not returning the animal, but only promising to pay for it, and the case has no bearing on our discussion.

תָּא שְׁמַע [5]The Gemara now proceeds to raise an objection to the earlier ruling (above, 3a) of Rabbi Ḥiyya: **Come** and **hear the following Baraita** transmitted **by the father of Rabbi Aptoriki** which contradicts **the first** ruling of **Rabbi Ḥiyya** : [6]"If one person claims from another: **'You owe me a maneh** [100 zuz],' **and the latter says, 'I owe you nothing at all,'** [7]**and witnesses testify that** the defendant **owes** the plaintiff **50 zuz,**

לֵיהּ: ״הֵילָךְ״? [1]לָא, דְּאָמַר לֵיהּ: ״שָׁלֹשׁ פָּרוֹת מָסַרְתִּי לְךָ, וּמֵתוּ כּוּלְּהוּ בִּפְשִׁיעָה״. [2]וְאָמַר לֵיהּ אִיהוּ: ״חֲדָא — לֹא הָיוּ דְּבָרִים מֵעוֹלָם, [3]וַחֲדָא מֵתָה בְּאוֹנֶס, וַחֲדָא מֵתָה בִּפְשִׁיעָה, דְּבָעֵינָא שַׁלּוּמֵי לָךְ״. [4]דְּלָאו ״הֵילָךְ״ הוּא.

[5]תָּא שְׁמַע דְּתָנֵי אֲבוּהּ דְּרַבִּי אַפְּטוֹרִיקִי לִדְרַבִּי חִיָּיא קַמָּיְיתָא: [6]״מָנֶה לִי בְּיָדְךָ״! וְהַלָּה אוֹמֵר: ״אֵין לְךָ בְּיָדִי כְּלוּם״, [7]וְהָעֵדִים מְעִידִים אוֹתוֹ שֶׁיֵּשׁ בְּיָדוֹ חֲמִשִּׁים זוּז.

LITERAL TRANSLATION

to him: "Here it is"?

[1]No, where he says to him: "I handed over three cows to you, and they all died through [your] negligence." [2]And he says to him: "One — it never happened (lit., "there were never such things"), [3]and one died through an accident, and one died through [my] negligence, for which I must compensate you." [4]So that it is not [a case of] "here it is."

[5]Come [and] hear what the father of Rabbi Aptoriki taught, [which is] against the first [ruling] of Rabbi Ḥiyya: [6][If one says to another:] "A maneh of mine is in your possession!" And the other says: "Nothing of yours is in my possession," [7]and the witnesses testify [concerning] him that he has in his possession 50 zuz.

RASHI

אידך מתה לה באונס — ועליה הוא נשבע שבועת שומרין. **וחדא מתה לה בפשיעה** — היא של הודאה, ולאו ״הילך״ הוא. **תא שמע דתני אבוה דרבי אפטוריקי** — תא שמע מינה תיובתא. **לרבי חייא קמייתא** — כלומר: תא שמע לדרבי חייא קמייתא, דאמר לעיל שלא תהא הודאת פיו גדולה מהעדאת עדים כו׳.

NOTES

הֵילָךְ "Here it is." This discussion revolves around two Halakhot laid down by Rabbi Ḥiyya regarding the oath to be taken by a defendant who admits to part of a liability. In both cases Rabbi Ḥiyya attempts to extend the obligation to take an oath, and both Halakhot are connected (or are capable of being connected) to our Mishnah regarding two people who are holding on to a garment. One Halakhah stated by Rabbi Ḥiyya (4a) is that even when the defendant admits to part of the claim and says, "Here it is," he does not free himself of the obligation to take an oath. In Rabbi Ḥiyya's opinion, even the fact that the defendant is willing at once to relinquish the thing for which he admits a liability still leaves untouched both the claim against him and the partial admission. He does not regard the saying of "here it is" as dividing the claim into two parts: admission of one whole claim and denial of a second whole claim. This approach, with which Rav Sheshet disagrees, is discussed at length in our passage, but no final decision is reached, because the Tannaitic sources can be interpreted in support of either approach.

The other Halakhah stated by Rabbi Ḥiyya (3a) is based on the assumption that the admission of part of a claim is in fact a total confirmation of part of the claim. Rabbi Ḥiyya believes that in every case where there is confirmation of part of a claim (when witnesses testify to it), the defendant must take an oath. This approach of Rabbi's Ḥiyya's is based on that of Rabbi Meir, who argues that the testimony of witnesses is the fullest proof of any matter, and when there is such testimony, it is even preferable to the confession of the defendant. However, in the course of this passage we find that the opposing approach (that of the Sages) is also brought out, according to which there are areas in which the testimony of witnesses has less force than a confession. Regarding the matter of someone who admits to part of a claim, there is a psychological consideration (Rabbah's explanation), which distinguishes between a defendant's admission of part of a claim and the determining of facts independent of the defendant's testimony.

TRANSLATION AND COMMENTARY

[1]I might have thought that the defendant should take an oath regarding the other 50 zuz. [2]Therefore the verse (Exodus 22:8, concerning bailees) states: For all manner of trespass, whether it be for ox, for ass, for sheep, for a garment, or for any manner of lost thing, of which one can say, 'This is it,' the cause of both parties shall come before the judges. [3]From this verse we learn that, as a result of the admission of the defendant (indicated by the expression 'of which one can say, "This is it"'), an oath is imposed upon him (indicated by the expression 'before the judges'), [4]but an oath is not imposed upon him as a result of the testimony of witnesses!" By interpreting the Biblical verse in this way, this Baraita directly contradicts the earlier statement of Rabbi Ḥiyya that, where witnesses partially corroborate the plaintiff's claim, the defendant must pay in accordance with the witnesses' evidence and must take an oath regarding the rest of the plaintiff's claim.

[1]יָכוֹל יִשָּׁבַע עַל הַשְּׁאָר.
[2]תַּלְמוּד לוֹמַר: "עַל כָּל אֲבֵידָה
אֲשֶׁר יֹאמַר 'כִּי הוּא זֶה'" —
[3]עַל הוֹדָאַת פִּיו אַתָּה מְחַיְּיבוֹ,
[4]וְאִי אַתָּה מְחַיְּיבוֹ עַל הָעֲדָאַת
עֵדִים!
[5]מַתְנִיתָא קָא רָמֵית עֲלֵיהּ
דְּרַבִּי חִיָּיא?! [6]רַבִּי חִיָּיא תַּנָּא
הוּא, וּפָלֵיג.
[7]וְהָא קְרָא קָאָמַר!
[8]הַהוּא לְמוֹדֶה מִקְצָת הַטַּעֲנָה.
[9]וַאֲבוּהּ דְּרַבִּי אַפְּטוֹרִיקִי?

LITERAL TRANSLATION

[1]I might have thought (lit., "it is possible") that he should swear regarding the rest. [2][Therefore] the verse states: "For any manner of lost thing of which one can say, 'This is it,'" — [3]for the admission of his mouth you oblige him [to take an oath], [4]but you do not oblige him for the testimony of witnesses!

[5]Is it [from] a Baraita that you [seek to] contradict (lit., "cast against") Rabbi Ḥiyya!? [6]Rabbi Ḥiyya is himself a Tanna, and disagrees.

[7]But surely he cited a verse!

[8]That [verse refers] to one who admits part of the claim.

[9]And the father of Rabbi Aptoriki?

RASHI

אשר יאמר וגו' — מודה לו במקצת, מכלל דכופר במקצת. וכתב בההוא לעיל מיניה "ונקרב בעל הבית אל האלהים" ודרשינן (מח,ב): ונקרב לשבועה. **ההוא** — מיבעי ליה להודאת מקצת דמחייבא עליה שבועה, ואתיא העדאת עדים מינה בקל וחומר כדלעיל, דליכא קרא יתירא דתדרוש מינה מיעוטא.

TERMINOLOGY

לֹא הָיוּ דְּבָרִים מֵעוֹלָם It never happened. This phrase, which is sometimes abbreviated as "להד"ם," expresses total denial of a claim or a story. It does not imply the rejection or correction of certain details, but denies the existence of the case itself, claiming that it never took place. In the case of the shepherd, he does not explain his behavior but totally denies what is being claimed, arguing that the animals were never placed in his charge, so that there are no grounds for further claims. A similar case is that of a purported borrower who denies that he ever received a loan.

מַתְנִיתָא קָא רָמֵית עֲלֵיהּ [5]The Gemara now rejects this refutation of Rabbi Ḥiyya's ruling: Are you attempting to point out **a contradiction of Rabbi Ḥiyya's** ruling **from a Baraita?** [6]**Rabbi Ḥiyya is himself a Tanna, and he** is entitled to **disagree** with the Baraita transmitted by the father of Rabbi Aptoriki! Rabbi Ḥiyya lived during the transition period between the period of the Tannaim and that of the Amoraim, and considered himself entitled to disagree with the scholars of the immediately preceding period.

וְהָא קְרָא קָאָמַר [7]The Gemara now raises another objection: **But surely** the Baraita contradicting Rabbi Ḥiyya is based on no less an authority than **a verse** from the Torah! How can Rabbi Ḥiyya argue against this?

הַהוּא לְמוֹדֶה מִקְצָת הַטַּעֲנָה [8]The Gemara answers that Rabbi Ḥiyya uses that verse to derive a different teaching: **That** verse, in which the expression "This is it" is used, comes to teach us another principle, that only **a person who makes a partial admission of a claim** must take an oath regarding the rest of the claim. A person who completely denies a claim is exempt from taking an oath of the Torah.

וַאֲבוּהּ דְּרַבִּי אַפְּטוֹרִיקִי [9]The Gemara now asks: **And** as for **the father of Rabbi Aptoriki**, from where does he learn the principle that a partial admission of a claim requires an oath?

NOTES

אֲשֶׁר יֹאמַר כִּי הוּא זֶה "Of which one can say, 'This is it.'" The Sages deduced from this verse that a defendant takes an oath only when he admits to part of the claim against him. Bible commentators have explained that, according to the Sages, the verse means that the defendant points to a specific thing and says that *it* alone is the object for which he is liable, and that he is liable for nothing else other than that which he admits (see *Ramban* and *Rashi* on the Torah). The obligation to take an oath is deduced not only from a comparison of this verse (Exodus 22:8) with the parallel verse (22:10), where it says, "An oath of the Lord shall be between them," but also from the fact that the language the Bible uses for appearing before judges is "to stand before the Lord," indicating that the matter is to be decided on high by means of the defendant's oath.

HALAKHAH

מוֹדֶה מִמִּין הַטַּעֲנָה A defendant whose admission refers to the same kind of object as that claimed by the plaintiff. "If a plaintiff claimed an amount of wheat and the defendant admitted that he owed him barley, the defendant is free of all obligation, even for the value of the barley," in accordance with the view of the Sages who disagree with Rabban Gamliel. (*Shulḥan Arukh, Ḥoshen Mishpat* 88:12.)

TRANSLATION AND COMMENTARY

אָמַר לָךְ [1]The Gemara answers: **He can answer you** as follows: The phrase כִּי הוּא זֶה — **"this is it"** — in the verse contains two expressions limiting the application of the law: הוּא — **"it"**; and זֶה — **"this."** [2]**One** of them is needed to teach the principle **that** only **a partial admission of a claim** requires an oath, [3]**and the other** is needed to teach the principle **that the testimony of witnesses** corroborating part of a plaintiff's claim **does not oblige** the defendant to take an oath denying the rest.

וְאִידָךְ [4]The Gemara now asks: **And** how does **the other** authority (Rabbi Ḥiyya), explain why *two* limiting expressions are found in the verse?

חַד לְמוֹדֶה מִקְצָת הַטַּעֲנָה [5]The Gemara answers: According to Rabbi Ḥiyya, **one** of them is needed to teach the principle **that only a partial admission of a claim** requires an oath, [6]**and the other** is needed to teach the principle that an oath is only required if the defendant's **admission** refers **to the same kind of object as that claimed** by the plaintiff. If the plaintiff claimed the return of a one kind of merchandise, and the defendant admitted owing a different, cheaper, kind of merchandise, this partial admission does not require the defendant to take an oath.

וְאִידָךְ [7]The Gemara now asks: **And** why does **the other** authority (the father of Rabbi Aptoriki), not explain the verse in the same way as Rabbi Ḥiyya and interpret the two limiting expressions the way that Rabbi Ḥiyya does?

מוֹדֶה מִמִּין הַטַּעֲנָה לֵית לֵיהּ [8]The Gemara answers: **He does not accept the principle that** an oath is only required if the defendant's **admission** refers **to the same kind of object as that claimed** by the plaintiff. [9]**He agrees** on this point **with Rabban Gamliel**, whose opinion **we have learned** in the following Mishnah (*Shevuot* 38b): [10]**"If** the plaintiff **claims**, that the defendant owes him **wheat, and** the defendant **admits** owing him **barley**, even though the price of barley is less than that of wheat and the defendant is making the equivalent of a partial admission, **he is** nevertheless **exempt** from taking an oath, because his admission has no connection with the claim against him. [11]**But** Rabban Gamliel obliges him to take an oath." The father of Rabbi Aptoriki, says the Gemara, is transmitting a Baraita reflecting the viewpoint of Rabban Gamliel. At the end of this discussion the viewpoints of Rabbi Ḥiyya remain unrefuted.

הַהוּא רָעֲיָא [12]The Gemara now relates the following incident that came before the court for decision: There was **a certain shepherd to whom** people **used to hand over animals** for safekeeping **each day in the presence of witnesses.** [13]**One day, they handed over the animals to him without witnesses** who could testify as to the number of animals he had received that day. [14]**Ultimately,** when the owners came to take their animals back, the shepherd **said to them: "It never happened.** I never received the animals that you now claim," and

[1]אָמַר לָךְ: כְּתִיב "הוּא" וּכְתִיב "זֶה". [2]חַד לְמוֹדֶה מִקְצָת הַטַּעֲנָה, [3]וְחַד לְהַעֲדָאַת עֵדִים, דְּפָטוּר.

[4]וְאִידָךְ?

[5]חַד לְמוֹדֶה מִקְצָת הַטַּעֲנָה, [6]וְחַד לְמוֹדֶה מִמִּין הַטַּעֲנָה.

[7]וְאִידָךְ?

[8]מוֹדֶה מִמִּין הַטַּעֲנָה לֵית לֵיהּ, [9]וְסָבַר לֵיהּ כְּרַבָּן גַּמְלִיאֵל, דִּתְנַן: [10]טְעָנוֹ חִטִּין וְהוֹדָה לוֹ בִּשְׂעוֹרִין — פָּטוּר, [11]וְרַבָּן גַּמְלִיאֵל מְחַיֵּיב.

[12]הַהוּא רָעֲיָא דַּהֲווּ מָסְרֵי לֵיהּ כָּל יוֹמָא חֵיוָתָא בְּסַהֲדֵיהּ. [13]יוֹמָא חַד מָסְרוּ לֵיהּ בְּלָא סָהֲדֵי. [14]לְסוֹף אֲמַר לְהוּ: "לֹא הָיוּ דְּבָרִים מֵעוֹלָם".

LITERAL TRANSLATION

[1]He can say to you: [The word] "it" is written and [the word] "this" is written. [2]One [applies] to one who admits part of the claim, [3]and one [applies] to the testimony of witnesses, [teaching] that he is exempt.

[4]And the other?

[5]One [applies] to one who admits part of the claim, [6]and one [applies] to one who admits to the same kind [of object] as the claim.

[7]And the other?

[8]He does not accept (lit., "he does not have") [the principle of] one who admits to the same kind [of object] as the claim, [9]and he agrees with [the opinion of] Rabban Gamliel, as we have learned: [10][If] he claimed wheat from him, and he admitted to him regarding barley — he is exempt, [11]but Rabban Gamliel obliges [him].

[12][There was] a certain shepherd to whom [people] handed over animals each day in [the presence of] witnesses. [13]One day they handed over [the animals] to him without witnesses. [14]Ultimately he said to them: "It never happened (lit., 'there were never such things')."

RASHI

וחד להעדאת עדים — למעוטה. **וחד להודאה ממין הטענה** — דבעינן שתהא הודאה ממין טענת כפירה, שהם טענו סאה של חטים והודה לו בשעורים — פטור.

NOTES

הַהוּא רָעֲיָא וכו׳ There was a certain shepherd.... The commentators point out: On the surface, the details mentioned in the story of the shepherd, that every day the owners would entrust their animals to him in the presence of witnesses, etc., appear unnecessary. Surely all that is relevant is the fact that the owners demanded the return of

LITERAL TRANSLATION

[1] Witnesses came [and] testified against him that he had eaten two of them.

[2] Rav Zera said: If the first [ruling] of Rabbi Ḥiyya is [accepted], [3] he must swear regarding the rest.

[4] Abaye said to him: "If it is [accepted] he must swear"? [5] But surely he is a robber!

[6] He said to him: I [meant to] say his opponent [must swear].

[7] Now also [even if we say] that Rabbi Ḥiyya's [ruling] is not [accepted], [8] we should oblige him [to swear] on the basis of [the ruling of] Rav Naḥman.

[1] אָתוּ סָהֲדֵי אַסְהִידוּ בֵּיהּ דְּאָכַל תַּרְתֵּי מִינַּיְיהוּ.
[2] אָמַר רַב זֵירָא: אִם אִיתָא לְדְרַבִּי חִיָּיא קַמַּיְיתָא, [3] מִשְׁתַּבַּע אַשְּׁאָרָא.
[4] אָמַר לֵיהּ אַבַּיֵי: "אִם אִיתָא מִשְׁתַּבַּע"? [5] וְהָא גַּזְלָן הוּא!
[6] אָמַר לֵיהּ: שֶׁכְּנֶגְדּוֹ קָאָמִינָא.
[7] הַשְׁתָּא נַמִי דְּלֵיתָא לְדְרַבִּי חִיָּיא, [8] נְחַיְּיבֵיהּ מִדְּרַב נַחְמָן.

RASHI

אם איתא לדרבי חייא – אם הלכה כמותו. **אמר ליה אביי ואם איתא לדרבי חייא משתבע האי** – בתמיה. **והא גזלן הוא** – וכי אמר רבי חייא – במלוה, אי נמי, בפקדון שלא שלח בו יד ואבד ממנו, דאיכא למימר אשתמוטי משתמיט. **לשכנגדו קאמינא** – אם שבועה מוטלת עליו – נשבע שכנגדו ונוטל, כדאמרינן בשבועות (מד,ג) שהחשוד על השבועה, תקנו חכמים שכנגדו נשבע. **השתא נמי** – כי ליתא לדרבי חייא, ואין כאן הודאה במקצת. **נחייבה** – שבועת היסת מדרב נחמן, וישבע שכנגדו ויטול.

TRANSLATION AND COMMENTARY

he refused to return them. [1] Then **witnesses came and testified that** the shepherd **had eaten two of** the animals that he had previously denied receiving.

אָמַר רַב זֵירָא [2] **Rav Zera said** regarding this case: "**If Rabbi Ḥiyya's first ruling is accepted,** [3] then in this case the shepherd **must take an oath regarding the remaining** animals, affirming that he never received them; otherwise, he must pay in full not only for the animals about which the witnesses have testified, but also for all the rest claimed by the owners. For Rabbi Ḥiyya ruled (3a) that if witnesses testify that a defendant owes part of a claim, he must pay back the amount concerning which the witnesses testified and swear that he does not owe the plaintiff any more money. Accordingly, says Rav Zera, the same principle should apply in our case: Since witnesses testified against the shepherd with regard to two of the animals, he should be required to swear that he did not receive any more animals than those two.

אָמַר לֵיהּ אַבַּיֵי [4] Rav Zera's argument is now rejected: **Abaye said to** Rav Zera: How can you say: "**If** Rabbi Ḥiyya's first ruling **is accepted,** the shepherd **must swear**"?! [5] **Surely he is a robber**, for witnesses have testified that he disposed of two animals that did not belong to him! According to the Halakhah, a robber is automatically disqualified from taking an oath. So how can Rav Zera maintain that the discredited shepherd be permitted, much less required, to take an oath?

אָמַר לֵיהּ [6] Rav Zera **said to** Abaye: I did not mean that the shepherd should take an oath. **I meant** that **his opponent**, the plaintiff, **must take an oath,** and receive the compensation to which he is entitled. Thus, according to Rav Zera, after the owner of the animals swears that the shepherd still owes him additional livestock, the shepherd must reimburse him for the remainder of his claim, in addition to the value of the two animals about which the witnesses testified.

הַשְׁתָּא נַמִי דְּלֵיתָא לְדְרַבִּי חִיָּיא [7] The Gemara now asks: But **even if** for the sake of argument **we assume that Rabbi Ḥiyya's ruling is not accepted,** [8] **we should** still **require the taking of an oath, on the basis of Rav Naḥman's**

SAGES

רַב זֵירָא Rav Zera. Babylonian Amora of the fourth generation, contemporary of Rava and Abaye. Not to be confused with Rabbi Zera, a third generation Amora who left Babylonia and resettled in Eretz Israel.

NOTES

their animals and the shepherd denied receiving them. *Rashba* explains that the details also contribute valuable information: The fact that the owners would entrust their animals to the shepherd every day only in the presence of witnesses clearly demonstrates that they did not trust him at all; hence it does not seem credible that they entrusted the animals to him on this occasion without witnesses. By mentioning these details the Gemara informs us that, although this argument strengthens the shepherd's position, his word is still not accepted, even concerning the animals not seen by the witnesses, and the owners are given the opportunity of taking an oath and being reimbursed by the shepherd.

גַּזְלָן הוּא He is a robber. An oath as a means of determining facts that are in doubt is only significant when the person taking the oath is fundamentally honest, God-fearing, and would certainly swear only to the truth. But when a person is known to be a criminal, his oath is held to be worthless (in the language of the Sages, מִיגּוֹ דְּחָשִׁיד אַמָּמוֹנָא חָשִׁיד אַשְּׁבוּעֲתָא — since he is suspect in money matters, he is suspect regarding an oath). Moreover, since his oath cannot be trusted, obliging him to swear is not only useless but also prohibited, for it would be causing him to take a false oath. In every case involving the obligation to take an oath it is assumed that the person who has denied a claim without taking an oath is not a criminal but is inaccurate in what he says, or else is attempting to delay payment of a debt.

שֶׁכְּנֶגְדּוֹ His opponent. One of the principles governing the imposition of oaths is that when a defendant is prevented from taking an oath required of him (either because he is suspected of swearing falsely or for some other reason), that obligation is transferred to the plaintiff. He may collect the money he is claiming from the defendant only by taking the oath. If, however, the defendant simply refuses to take the oath, the plaintiff collects his claim without having to take an oath. It is only if the defendant is *prevented* from taking an oath that the plaintiff is obliged to take an oath before he collects.

LITERAL TRANSLATION

[1] For we have learned: [If one claims from another:] "A maneh of mine is in your possession," [2] [and the other replies:] "Nothing of yours is in my possession," he is exempt. [3] And [we know that] Rav Nahman said: We make him swear an "oath of inducement"!

[4] [The ruling] of Rav Naḥman is a Rabbinic ordinance [5B] [5] and we do not add a Rabbinic ordinance to [another] Rabbinic ordinance.

[6] But let him derive it from his being a shepherd, [7] and Rav Yehudah said: An ordinary shepherd is unfit!

[1] דִּתְנַן: ״מָנֶה לִי בְּיָדְךָ״! [2] ״אֵין לְךָ בְּיָדִי״, פָּטוּר. [3] וְאָמַר רַב נַחְמָן: מַשְׁבִּיעִין אוֹתוֹ שְׁבוּעַת הֶיסֵּת!

[4] דְּרַב נַחְמָן תַּקַּנְתָּא הִיא, [5B] [5] וְתַקַּנְתָּא לְתַקַּנְתָּא לָא עָבְדִינַן.

[6] וְתֵיפּוֹק לֵיהּ דַּהֲוָה לֵיהּ רוֹעֶה, [7] וְאָמַר רַב יְהוּדָה: סְתָם רוֹעֶה פָּסוּל!

RASHI

היסת — שבועה שהסיתו חכמים לכך, להסיתו להודות. וטעמא מפרש בשבועות (מ,ב): חזקה אין אדם טוען אלא אם כן יש לו בידו. **דרב נחמן תקנתא היא** — דהא מדאורייתא לא רמי שבועה עליה. **ותקנתא** — דכשנגדו ישבע ויטול, דהויא נמי תקנתא. דמן התורה, מי שעליו לשלם הוא ישבע ויפטר מן התשלומין, ואין נשבע ונוטל מן התורה. ואותן המנויין בשבועות (מד,ב) — תקנת חכמים הן. ולשבועה דאורייתא — עבוד רבנן תקנתא, אבל לתקנתא לא עבדינן. **ותיפוק ליה דהוה ליה רועה** — אדאביי קא מתמה, דקשיא ליה והא גזלן הוא. ותיפוק ליה דבלאו הך גזילה פסול לשבועה. **דאמר רב יהודה סתם רועה** — אפילו לא הועד עליו שגזל. **פסול** לעדות. דסתמיה גזלן הוא, שמרעה בהמותיו בשדות של אחרים.

TRANSLATION AND COMMENTARY

ruling, and we should then transfer the oath to the plaintiff. [1] **For we have learned** in a Mishnah (*Shevuot* 38b): **"If one** person **claims from another, 'You have a maneh of mine,'** [2] **and the other replies, 'I have nothing of yours,'** the defendant **is exempt** from taking an oath." [3] **And we know that Rav Naḥman,** commenting on this Mishnah, **said** (*Shevuot* 40b) that even when the defendant totally denies the claim against him **we make him swear an "oath of inducement"** (שְׁבוּעַת הֶיסֵּת), forcing the defendant to affirm that he does not owe the plaintiff anything. The purpose of this oath, traditionally ascribed to Rav Naḥman, is to *induce* the defendant to admit the truth of the plaintiff's claim, it being assumed that a plaintiff will not make a totally baseless claim. Thus, even though according to Torah law no oath should be necessary in our case, an oath of inducement should be required by Rabbinic law, since the shepherd completely denies the claim made by the owner of the animals. And since the shepherd cannot take an oath, because of the evidence of the witnesses proving him to be a robber, the oath should be transferred to the plaintiff and *he* should swear and be reimbursed by the shepherd.

דְּרַב נַחְמָן תַּקַּנְתָּא הִיא [4] But the Gemara replies: **Rav Naḥman's ruling is a Rabbinic ordinance,** [5] **and we do not add one Rabbinic ordinance to another.** The law that the plaintiff must take an oath instead of the defendant when the latter is suspected of swearing falsely (as in our case, where the shepherd is a robber) is itself a Rabbinic ordinance. We do not superimpose a second Rabbinic ordinance, requiring the plaintiff to take an oath when the defendant is suspected of swearing falsely, on another Rabbinic ordinance, the ruling of Rav Naḥman imposing an oath of inducement on a defendant who completely denies a claim.

וְתֵיפּוֹק לֵיהּ דַּהֲוָה לֵיהּ רוֹעֶה [6] The Gemara now questions the assumption made above, that the reason for disqualifying the shepherd from taking an oath is that he has been proved to be a robber. **Let the ruling** that the shepherd is unfit to give evidence and to take an oath **be derived from the** very **fact that he is a shepherd,** [7] as **Rav Yehudah has said: "An ordinary shepherd is disqualified** from giving evidence," for the typical shepherd grazes his animals in other people's fields, and hence is assumed to be a robber!

BACKGROUND

הָרוֹעֶה **Shepherds.** Shepherds who tended their own herds generally kept them overnight in pens inside the village and took them out to pasture every morning. Normally flocks were grazed on unclaimed, uncultivated land — in semi-desert areas, alongside streams, etc. However, in general, flocks pass by the village fields, and the shepherd, either intentionally or through negligence, does not prevent his flocks from eating what is in those fields. He profits by doing so and saves himself some of the extra food that he has to give his flocks if the pasturage is insufficient. However, a shepherd who grazes other people's flocks derives no profit from what they eat in other people's fields. Moreover, since he grazes flocks belonging to the entire village, he watches the sheep very carefully to prevent them from entering other people's fields.

CONCEPTS

וְתַקַּנְתָּא לְתַקַּנְתָּא לָא עָבְדִינַן **And we do not add a Rabbinic ordinance to another Rabbinic ordinance.** This concept (and the parallel one in Hebrew, אֵין גּוֹזְרִין גְּזֵירָה לִגְזֵירָה) limits the severity of Rabbinical decrees and rulings and differentiates them from Torah law. The Sages do add decrees and rulings to Torah prohibitions in order to construct an additional defense to prevent people from accidentally being drawn into transgressions. But when the source of the Halakhah is a Rabbinical decree, one does not generally add other decrees and stringencies to the ruling. This is the reason why one does not superimpose one decree on another. Nevertheless, there are exceptional cases in which the Sages did decide that "the words of the Sages demanded reinforcement," and they added an additional safeguard. However, as a general rule this distinction between Rabbinical decrees and Torah law remains in force.

NOTES

שְׁבוּעַת הֶיסֵּת **An oath of inducement**. The context and significance of this oath is clear. But the meaning of the word הֶיסֵּת itself is a matter of doubt. In our text, *Rashi* renders it as related to the word הֲסָתָה — "inducement." This oath was instituted to induce and motivate the defendant to admit the truth. In tractate *Shevuot* he interprets it as an "imposition," as in I Samuel 26:19: "If the Lord has imposed upon you." The Sages "imposed upon" the defendant the obligation of taking this oath. *Sefer HaTerumot* offers the interpretation that the word הֶיסֵּת means "consultation," i.e., the Sages instituted this oath after "consultation" among themselves, in order to promote social harmony. This

HALAKHAH

שְׁבוּעַת הֶיסֵּת **An oath of inducement.** "A person who denies a claim entirely is not required to take a Torah oath, but the Rabbis decreed that he must take an oath of inducement," in accordance with the ruling of Rav Naḥman. (*Shulhan Arukh, Ḥoshen Mishpat* 75:7.)

רוֹעֶה פָּסוּל **The disqualification of a shepherd**. "Shepherds who tend their own flocks (whether sheep and goats or cattle) are disqualified from serving as witnesses because of the presumption that they allow their flocks to graze in fields belonging to others." (Ibid., 34:13.)

TRANSLATION AND COMMENTARY

לָא קַשְׁיָא [1]The Gemara replies: This presents **no difficulty**: [2]Rav Yehudah disqualifies the shepherd when the animals are **his own,** because we suspect him of grazing his own animals in other people's fields. But **in our case**, where the animals were entrusted to the shepherd **by others,** he has nothing to gain by grazing the animals in other people's fields, and hence we do not assume that he is a robber. [3]**For if you do not make this distinction**, but assume that shepherds do graze other people's animals for which they are responsible in other people's fields, [4]**how can we hand over animals to shepherds** under any circumstances? [5]**Surely it is written** in the Torah (Leviticus 19:14): "**You shall not put a stumbling block before the blind**." The Sages interpret this verse in a general sense as meaning that it is forbidden to set a *moral* stumbling block before a person by tempting him to commit a sin! If we assume that shepherds do graze the animals that they tend in other people's fields, then we should never entrust our animals to the care of a shepherd, since by doing so we are indirectly causing him to sin! [6]**Rather, the presumption is that a person does not sin if it is not for his own benefit**, and hence there is no reason to assume that a shepherd will graze animals that do not belong to him in other people's pastures.

[1]לָא קַשְׁיָא: [2]הָא דִּידֵיהּ, הָא דְּעָלְמָא. [3]דְּאִי לָא תֵּימָא הָכִי, [4]אֲנַן חֵיוָתָא לְרוֹעֶה הֵיכִי מָסְרִינַן? [5]וְהָא כְּתִיב: "לִפְנֵי עִוֵּר לֹא תִתֵּן מִכְשֹׁל"! [6]אֶלָּא, חֲזָקָה אֵין אָדָם חוֹטֵא וְלֹא לוֹ. [7]"זֶה יִשָּׁבַע שֶׁאֵין לוֹ בָּהּ פָּחוֹת מֵחֶצְיָהּ [וכו׳]". [8]עַל דְּאִית לֵיהּ מִשְׁתַּבַּע [9]אוֹ עַל דְּלֵית לֵיהּ מִשְׁתַּבַּע?

LITERAL TRANSLATION

[1][It is] not difficult: [2]That [case involves] his own [animals], this [case involves animals] of others (lit., "the world"). [3]For if you do not say this, [4]how do we hand over animals to a shepherd? [5]And surely it is written: "You shall not put a stumbling block before the blind"! [6]Rather, there is a presumption [that] a man does not sin if it is not for himself.

[7]"This one shall swear that he does not have in it less than half of it [etc.]." [8]Does he swear regarding what he has [9]or does he swear regarding what he does not have?

RASHI

דידיה — רועה בהמות שלו — פסול, דבשביל הנאתו רועה אותן בשדות אחרות. אבל רועה בהמות העיר בשכר, בשביל הנאת אחרים אינו חוטא להרעות עד שיגיע למרעה המופקר לכל. **דאי לא תימא הכי** — דלא אמרינן על רועה בהמות דעלמא שהוא גזלן — אנן חיותא לרועה היכי מסרינן? **על דאית ליה משתבע או על דלית ליה משתבע** — הכא לישבע וליטול חציה, צריך הוא לישבע שיש לו בה חציה או לישבע שאין לו בה פחות מחציה. שמא אין לו בה כלום, וכי משתבע שאין לו בה פחות מחציה — באמת הוא נשבע, שהרי אין לו כלום. דבשלמא אם היה לו בה שליש או רביע, והוא נשבע שאין לו בה פחות מחציה — נשבע בשקר, שהרי יש לו בה שליש שהוא פחות מחציה, ואין לו בה חציה. אבל כשאין לו בה כלום — נשבע הוא באמת.

זֶה יִשָּׁבַע [7]The Gemara now returns to the explanation of our Mishnah, which states that if two claimants dispute the ownership of a garment, then "**This one must take an oath that no less than half of it is his,**" and the other claimant must do likewise. [8]On this point the Gemara asks: **Does** each claimant **take an oath** worded positively, stating **that he has** a claim to half the garment, [9]**or does** each one **take an oath** worded negatively, as formulated in the Mishnah, stating **that he does not have** a claim to less than half the garment? The problem with the negative formulation used in the Mishnah is that it may be interpreted to mean that the claimant *has no claim at all* to the garment. If the claimant swears, "I do not own less than half of the garment," and he in fact owns a third of it, the oath is false. But if in fact he does not own the garment at all, the oath may be true. How, asks the Gemara, can the ambiguity in the formulation of the oath laid down in the Mishnah be avoided?

NOTES

interpretation is supported by the Targum on Deuteronomy 13:7, which translates the words כִּי יְסִיתְךָ אָחִיךָ — "When your brother will consult." In one of his responsa, *Rambam* interprets it as stemming from an Arabic root meaning "weighing down"; i.e., the oath was instituted as a means of exerting pressure on the defendant. *Rav Hai Gaon* interprets הֵיסֵּת as meaning "casting down" or "causing to fall."

הָא דִּידֵיהּ הָא דְּעָלְמָא That case involves his own animals, this case involves animals of others. This interpretation of the text is based on *Rashi*'s commentary. *Shittah Mekubbetzet* suggests an alternative way of understanding the text, explaining דִּידֵיהּ — "his own" — as referring to a shepherd who arranges to pasture the flocks of others *in his own field.* He gains an obvious benefit if he pastures the flocks in the fields of others. דְּעָלְמָא — "of others" — refers to a shepherd who arranges to pasture the flocks of others in fields which are public domain. Such a shepherd will not stand to benefit from pasturing flocks in fields belonging to other people.

אֵין אָדָם חוֹטֵא וְלֹא לוֹ A man does not sin if it is not for himself. This presumption applies in several areas of the Halakhah. It is based on the premise that a person will not purposely commit a transgression unless he has sufficient need and reason for doing so. Therefore, one may suspect that a person has sinned if he derives benefit by doing so — either financial profit or some other benefit. But he will not commit a sin if he himself derives no benefit from it. Therefore, even someone suspected of transgressing for his own benefit is not suspected of doing so for someone else's benefit.

עַל דְּאִית לֵיהּ מִשְׁתַּבַּע Do the claimants take oaths formulated positively...? The expression used by the

[1]אֲמַר רַב הוּנָא: דְּאָמַר: [2]״שְׁבוּעָה שֶׁיֵּשׁ לִי בָּהּ, [3]וְאֵין לִי בָּהּ פָּחוֹת מֵחֶצְיָהּ״.
[4]וְנֵימָא: ״שְׁבוּעָה שֶׁכּוּלָּהּ שֶׁלִּי״!
[5]וּמִי יָהֲבִינַן לֵיהּ כּוּלָּהּ?
[6]וְנֵימָא: ״שְׁבוּעָה שֶׁחֶצְיָהּ שֶׁלִּי״.

LITERAL TRANSLATION

[1]Rav Huna said: He says: [2]"[I declare under] oath that I have [a share] in it, [3]and [that] I do not have in it less than half of it."
[4]But let him say: "[I declare under] oath that it is all mine!"
[5]But do we give him all of it?
[6]But let him say: "[I declare under] oath that half of it is mine"!

TRANSLATION AND COMMENTARY

אֲמַר רַב הוּנָא [1]**Rav Huna said** in reply that in order to avoid this ambiguity the formula should be as follows: Each claimant **says**: [2]**"I declare under oath that I have a share in** the garment, [3]**and that no less than half of it is mine."** In formulating the oath in this way, Rav Huna maintains the phraseology of the Mishnah but removes its ambiguity.

וְנֵימָא שְׁבוּעָה שֶׁכּוּלָּהּ שֶׁלִּי [4]The Gemara now asks: **But let** each claimant **say: "I declare under oath that all of it is mine,"** as originally claimed. Why must each one take an oath that only part of the garment is his?

וּמִי יָהֲבִינַן לֵיהּ כּוּלָּהּ [5]The Gemara answers this question rhetorically: **But would we give him the entire** garment if he swore that all of it was his? Of course not, because the other claimant is also holding on to it. If each of the claimants were permitted to take an oath that the entire garment was his, the court would ultimately appear in a negative light in awarding half to each claimant.

וְנֵימָא שְׁבוּעָה שֶׁחֶצְיָהּ שֶׁלִּי [6]The Gemara now asks: **Then let** each claimant **say: "I declare under oath that half of it is mine."** Why do we need the complicated formula laid down by Rav Huna ("I swear that part of it is mine, and that no less than half if it is mine")?!

RASHI

שבועה שיש לי בה — ואם תאמרו: שמא שליש או רביע — שבועה שאין לי חלק בה פחות מחציה. מי יהבינן ליה כולה. — הרי חבירו תופס בה, ואם ישביעוהו על כולה — הרי לעז לבית דין, מאחר שכולה שלו והם אמרו: יחלוקו!

SAGES

רַב הוּנָא **Rav Huna**. Rav Huna was one of the greatest Babylonian Amoraim of the second generation, and was most closely associated with his teacher, Rav. Rav Huna was of aristocratic descent, and belonged to the house of the Exilarchs. For many years, however, he lived in great poverty. Later he became wealthy and lived in comfort, distributing his money for the public good.

Rav Huna was the greatest of Rav's students, so much so that Shmuel, Rav's colleague, used to treat him with honor and direct questions to him. After Rav's death Rav Huna became the head of the yeshivah of Sura and occupied that position for about forty years. His eminence in Torah and his loftiness of character helped make the Sura Yeshivah the preeminent center for Torah study in Babylonia for many centuries. Because of his great knowledge of Torah, the Halakhah is almost always decided according to his view against all his colleagues and the members of his generation (except in monetary matters, where Rav Naḥman's views are followed).

Rav Huna had many students, some of whom received their Torah knowledge directly from him; moreover, Rav's younger students continued to study with Rav Huna, his disciple. Rav Huna's son, Rabbah bar Rav Huna, was one of the greatest Sages of the next generation.

NOTES

Mishnah: "This one shall swear that he does not have in it less than half" indicates quite clearly that the oath is formulated in a negative form. Thus, there would seem to be no place for the Talmud's question.

Hokhmat Manoaḥ explains that the Sages required additional clarification, since the formula of the oath used by the Mishnah leaves open the possibility of deception. But they also wished to remain faithful to the text of the Mishnah. The solution offered by Rav Huna takes both considerations into account. It maintains the negative formulation laid down by the Mishnah, and adds an extra clause to preclude the possibility of deception.

עַל דְּלֵית לֵיהּ מִשְׁתַּבַּע **Does he swear regarding what he does not have?** The expression אֵין לִי בָּהּ פָּחוֹת מֵחֶצְיָהּ — "I do not own less than half of it" — is ambiguous. It can be understood to mean that the person taking the oath swears that his claim is not only to some part of the object (a third or a quarter), but rather to at least half of it, and if in fact he does own less than half of it, his oath would be false. However, the phrase is merely negative and advances no positive claim to any part of the object. Therefore, it might permit someone to rationalize the taking of a false oath by saying to himself that he has merely sworn that he has no less than half, secretly meaning: I have no part in this object at all. However, *Tosafot* (ד״ה על) point out that, in the imposition of any oath, the person swearing is warned that he is taking the oath by direction of the court. He cannot rely upon the wording alone. He must also consider the meaning of the words in their context. Nevertheless, it is not a good idea *ab initio* to use wording that could lead a person to swear falsely by rationalizing regarding the literal meaning of the oath.

דְּאָמַר שְׁבוּעָה שֶׁיֵּשׁ לִי כו׳ **Each claimant says: "I swear that part of it is mine...."** *Tosefot Rid* points out that this was not necessarily the precise formula used in taking the oath. Rather, it reflects what is intended to be conveyed by the language of the oath.

וְאֵין לִי בָּהּ פָּחוֹת מֵחֶצְיָהּ **"And no less than half of it is mine."** The Sages did not accept the viewpoint of Ben Nannas (2b), who prohibited imposing oaths that would inevitably lead to one of the parties swearing falsely. Nevertheless, they, too, did their best, wherever possible, to prevent false oaths. Hence, they were prepared to use somewhat ambiguous phraseology in this instance in order to make a false oath less likely (*Agudah*).

וְנֵימָא שְׁבוּעָה שֶׁכּוּלָּהּ שֶׁלִּי **Let each claimant say: "I swear that all of it is mine."** On the surface, this would require one of the litigants to take a false oath. The Sages surely would not institute an oath which would have such an effect! *Rosh* resolves this difficulty by explaining that, when the claimant takes the oath, he does so with his original claim — that the entire garment belongs to him — in mind. Hence, says the Gemara, he may as well state this claim explicitly.

וּמִי יָהֲבִינַן לֵיהּ כּוּלָּהּ **But do we give him all of it?** Generally speaking, the oath of a litigant in any doubtful case is sufficient proof, and, in the absence of decisive proof to the contrary, the court accepts the content of the liltigant's oath

HALAKHAH

שְׁבוּעָה שֶׁיֵּשׁ לִי בָּהּ **"I declare under oath that I have a share in it."** "If two people are holding on to a garment, each claiming ownership, each of them must take an oath that part of the article belongs to him and that no less than half of it is his," in accordance with the formula of Rav Huna, by means of which several possible misleading interpretations of the oath are removed. (*Shulḥan Arukh, Ḥoshen Mishpat*, 138:1).

TRANSLATION AND COMMENTARY

מְרַע לֵיהּ לְדִיבּוּרֵיהּ [1]The Gemara answers: By swearing that he is entitled to half the garment, the claimant **damages his** original **statement**. Such an oath contradicts his initial claim that the entire garment belongs to him!

הַשְׁתָּא נַמִּי [2]But the Gemara objects: **Now, too,** if he takes an oath using the terminology suggested by Rav Huna, **he** still **damages his** original **statement**. For each of the claimants originally maintained that the entire garment was his, whereas now they both take an oath with regard to only half of it!

דְּאָמַר כּוּלָּהּ שֶׁלִּי [3]But the Gemara answers: Each claimant **says** to the court: "The garment **is** in fact **all mine, but according to you**, since you do not believe me about the whole garment, and you intend to award me only half of it, [4]**I declare under oath that I have a share in it, and that no less than half of it is mine.**"

וְכִי מֵאַחַר שֶׁזֶּה תָּפוּס [5]The Gemara now challenges the Mishnah's basic assumption, asking why an oath is necessary at all in our case: **Since the one claimant is standing holding on** to half of the garment, **and the other claimant is** also **standing holding on** to half of the garment, and since in the end each one will receive whatever part of the garment he is holding, [6]**why is this oath necessary** at all? It would surely be better to divide the garment between the claimants without requiring them to take any oaths in support of their claims!

אָמַר רַבִּי יוֹחָנָן [7]The Gemara replies: **Rabbi Yohanan said: This oath is an ordinance of the Sages.** [8]They require each of the litigants to swear that he is telling the truth, in order **to deter a person from going and seizing hold of another person's garment and saying: "It is mine."** The result of such a claim would be that the owner of the garment would be forced to divide it with his assailant. The Sages therefore decreed that an oath be imposed upon both claimants in order to deter people from seizing hold of other people's property and claiming it as their own.

וְנֵימָא [9]The Gemara now raises an objection to the viewpoint of Rabbi Yoḥanan, who says that the oath in our Mishnah is imposed to deter people from seizing other people's property and claiming it as their own: **Let us say: Since** each claimant **is suspected of dishonesty in money matters**, as each one is suspected of seizing the other's garment and of lying when he claims that the entire garment is his, [10]**he should also be suspected of taking false oaths**! Why, then, should we believe the claimants when they take oaths in support of their respective claims?

[1]מְרַע לֵיהּ לְדִיבּוּרֵיהּ.
[2]הַשְׁתָּא נַמִּי מְרַע לֵיהּ לְדִיבּוּרֵיהּ!
[3]דְּאָמַר: "כּוּלָּהּ שֶׁלִּי. וּלְדִבְרֵיכֶם, [4]שְׁבוּעָה שֶׁיֵּשׁ לִי בָּהּ, וְאֵין לִי בָּהּ פָּחוֹת מֵחֶצְיָהּ".
[5]וְכִי מֵאַחַר שֶׁזֶּה תָּפוּס וְעוֹמֵד, וְזֶה תָּפוּס וְעוֹמֵד, [6]שְׁבוּעָה זוֹ לָמָּה?
[7]אָמַר רַבִּי יוֹחָנָן: שְׁבוּעָה זוֹ תַּקָּנַת חֲכָמִים הִיא, [8]שֶׁלֹּא יְהֵא כָּל אֶחָד וְאֶחָד הוֹלֵךְ וְתוֹקֵף בְּטַלִּיתוֹ שֶׁל חֲבֵירוֹ, וְאוֹמֵר: "שֶׁלִּי הוּא".
[9]וְנֵימָא: מִיגּוֹ דַּחֲשִׁיד אַמָּמוֹנָא, [10]חֲשִׁיד נַמִּי אַשְּׁבוּעֲתָא!

LITERAL TRANSLATION

[1]He damages his statement.
[2]Now, too, he damages his statement!
[3]He says: "It is all mine. But according to your words, [4][I declare under] oath that I have [a share] in it, and [that] I do not have in it less than half of it."
[5]But since this [claimant] stands holding [the garment], and this [claimant also] stands holding [the garment], [6]why is this oath [necessary]?
[7]Rabbi Yoḥanan said: This oath is an ordinance of the Sages, [8]so that everyone should not go and seize his fellow's garment, and say: "It is mine."
[9]But let us say: Since he is suspected [of dishonesty] in money [matters], [10]he is also suspected of [taking false] oaths!

RASHI

מרע ליה לדיבוריה — דאמר ברישא "כולה שלי", והשתא אמר בהדיא "חציה שלי". **דאמר כולה שלי** — תירוצא הוא. **ולדבריכם** — שאין אתם מאמינים לי בכולה — שבועה שיש לי בה, ואין לי בה פחות מחציה. **ונימא מגו דחשיד אממונא חשיד כו'** — אדרבי יוחנן פריך, דאמר: אשדוהו רבנן שמא ילך ותוקף בטליתו של חבירו, ואומר "שלי הוא". אם חשוד הוא בכך — חשוד הוא נמי לישבע!

TERMINOLOGY

וּלְדִבְרֵיכֶם But according to your words. This expression, in various forms, means: "I am not changing my opinion or retracting my first argument, but I am prepared to continue the discussion even on the basis of an assumption different from my first one." This form of expression is used frequently, both in Talmudic discussions and in actual litigation in every system of jurisprudence. In our case, the positive declaration (or oath) of the claimant who argues that half of the object belongs to him constitutes a retreat from his first position. But the oath formulated negatively does not deny the first assertion. Instead it advances an alternative claim: "At the very least I have a right to half of it."

NOTES

as fact. However, in the present case, if both litigants swear that the entire object is theirs, the court will not rely on their oaths, and will only grant half the disputed object to each of them. Therefore, even if perjury was not intentionally committed in this case, for each claimant may believe in good faith that he was the first to pick up the object, in any event the court has caused both litigants to take an oath unnecessarily, since even after swearing they do not receive what they claim, and this is a blow to the reputation of the court.

מִיגּוֹ דַּחֲשִׁיד אַמָּמוֹנָא חֲשִׁיד אַשְּׁבוּעֲתָא Since he is suspected of dishonesty in money matters, he is also suspected of

HALAKHAH

מִיגּוֹ דַּחֲשִׁיד אַמָּמוֹנָא... Someone who is suspected of dishonesty in money matters.... "Anyone who is suspected of taking someone else's money is suspected of dishonesty in the taking of oaths. This only applies if witnesses have

TERMINOLOGY

תֵּדַע Know that this is so. This expression is used to strengthen an argument raised previously by presenting additional evidence permitting it to be proved even more clearly.

TRANSLATION AND COMMENTARY

לָא אָמְרִינַן [1]The Gemara answers: **We do not say that since someone is suspected of dishonesty in money matters, he is also** automatically **suspected of taking false oaths.** A person may be suspected of dishonesty in money matters, but he will not lie if he has to take an oath, because of the severity of the prohibition against swearing falsely. [2]**For if you do not say this**, but instead assume that a person who is dishonest about money matters will also swear falsely, [3]**then** a difficulty arises in connection with **another law of the Torah**, which **states: A person who admits part of a claim** against him **must take an oath** regarding the rest of the claim, which he denies. [4]**Let us say** that there, too, **since** the defendant **is suspected of dishonesty in money matters,** [5]**he should also be suspected of taking false oaths!** Since, however, the Torah does impose an oath on a person who is suspected of withholding part of the money he owes, this surely refutes the argument that a person suspected of monetary impropriety should also be suspected of swearing falsely.

הָתָם אִשְׁתַּמּוּטֵי קָא מִשְׁתַּמֵּיט לֵיהּ [6]The Gemara rejects this proof: **There**, in the case of a partial admission of a claim, the defendant **may** simply **be trying to put off** the claimant **temporarily, as explained by Rabbah.** For Rabbah explained (above, 3a) that in cases of partial admission we assume that the debtor ultimately intends to pay the claim in full, but he does not admit to owing the entire sum because he wants to defer payment to a later date, when he will have the necessary funds. Therefore, according to Rabbah, a person who makes a partial admission of a claim is not considered suspect about monetary matters at all.

תֵּדַע [7]The Gemara now adds: **Know that this is so, for Rav Idi bar Avin said in the name of Rav Ḥisda:** [8]**A person who denies taking a loan** and against whom witnesses testify that he did borrow money from

[1]לָא אָמְרִינַן: מִיגּוֹ דַּחֲשִׁיד אַמָּמוֹנָא, חֲשִׁיד אַשְּׁבוּעֲתָא. [2]דְּאִי לָא תֵּימָא הָכִי, [3]הַאי דְּאָמַר רַחֲמָנָא, מוֹדֶה מִקְצָת הַטַּעֲנָה יִשָּׁבַע, [4]נֵימָא: מִיגּוֹ דַּחֲשִׁיד אַמָּמוֹנָא, [5]חֲשִׁיד אַשְּׁבוּעֲתָא!

[6]הָתָם, אִשְׁתַּמּוּטֵי קָא מִשְׁתַּמֵּיט לֵיהּ, כִּדְרַבָּה.

[7]תֵּדַע, דְּאָמַר רַב אִידִי בַּר אָבִין אָמַר רַב חִסְדָּא: [8]הַכּוֹפֵר

LITERAL TRANSLATION

[1]We do not say: Since he is suspected [of dishonesty] in money [matters], he is suspected of [taking false] oaths. [2]For if you do not say this, [3][concerning] this [law] that the Torah (lit., "the Merciful One") states, [namely that] one who admits part of a claim shall swear, [4]let us say: Since he is suspected [of dishonesty] in money [matters], [5]he is suspected of [taking false] oaths!

[6]There, he is trying to put him off [temporarily], as [explained by] Rabbah.

[7]Know [that this is so], for Rav Idi bar Avin said in the name of Rav Ḥisda: [8]He who denies

RASHI

לא אמרינן כו׳ – דחמיר הוא לאינשי איסור שבועה מאיסור גזילה. **אשתמוטי משתמיט ליה** – ולא חשיד אממונא. **כדרבה** – דאמר לעיל: מפני מה אמרה תורה כו׳. **תדע** – דלאו בגזלן חשדינן ליה אלא באשתמוטי בעלמא. **דאמר רב אידי בר אבין הכופר במלוה** – שבאו עדים והחזיקוהו בכפרן, שהעידוהו שהוא חייב לו.

NOTES

dishonesty in taking oaths. This concept requires explanation. There is an important Halakhic principle which states that, even if a person is known willfully to commit a specific sin (מוּמָר לַעֲבֵירָה אַחַת), it is not taken for granted that he will commit other sins. Thus, in our context, even if a person is proven to be a robber, why should we suspect that he will also be willing to take a false oath? *Rashba* resolves this difficulty by explaining that these transgressions share a common motive — financial gain. Once a person is known to have committed a sin for financial gain, he is suspect with regard to all other sins in which this motive could play a part. The commentators also ask: "According to the view that a person who is suspect in money matters is not suspected of swearing falsely, why are robbers not allowed to take oaths in court [as above, 5a]?" Among the resolutions offered to this difficulty are: (1) Even though there is no certainty that a robber will be willing to perjure himself, there is sufficient doubt about his veracity to justify denying him the opportunity of being able to take an oath (*Tosefot Rid*). (2) The fact that he is a confirmed robber increases our suspicion that transgression has become habitual to him, and he is therefore disqualified from taking an oath (*Ramban*). (3) Since there is no reason to believe that he is going to restore the property he stole in the past to its rightful owner, we believe that he will also not restore stolen property in the future (*Rosh and Rabbenu Tam*). (4) A person who is *definitely known* to have robbed is indeed disqualified from taking an oath. But in our case he is only *suspected* of having robbed, and by taking an oath he removes that suspicion (*Meiri*).

HALAKHAH

actually seen him take the other person's money. But if there are no witnesses that he is a robber (for instance, in a case where a defendant denies having received a loan), he is not suspected of swearing falsely." (*Shulḥan Arukh, Ḥoshen Mishpat* 92:3.)

כּוֹפֵר בְּמִלְוֶה וּבְפִיקָּדוֹן A person who denies a loan... a person who denies having received a deposit. When a person demands repayment of a loan from someone else

TRANSLATION AND COMMENTARY

the claimant, **is** still considered **fit to testify** in other cases. He is not regarded as having been proved to be a robber and thus disqualified from giving evidence in any court case. [1]But **a person who denies** having received **a deposit** and against whom witnesses testify that he is lying, **is** considered **unfit to testify**. The reason for this ruling is that, since a loan is intended to be spent, we assume that the borrower did in fact spend it. If he now denies having received the loan, he may be trying to put off the lender temporarily because he wants more time to repay him. A bailee, on the other hand, is not permitted to use the object entrusted to his care. If, therefore, he denies having received the deposit, and witnesses contradict his denial, we may assume that he was trying to misappropriate it, and hence he is considered a robber and unfit to serve as a witness. Thus we may infer from Rav Idi bar Avin's statement that a person who falsely denies owing someone else money did not in fact intend to keep the money permanently, and is not therefore disqualified as a witness in another case; nor is he considered unfit to take an oath.

אֶלָּא הָא דְּתָנֵי רָמִי בַּר חָמָא [2]The Gemara now asks: **But what about the Baraita that Rami bar Ḥama taught** (above, 5a): [3]"**The four** kinds of **bailees** mentioned in the Torah **are required to** take an oath only if they **deny part** of the claim against them **and admit part** of the claim against them: [4]**the unpaid bailee, the borrower, the paid bailee and the hirer**." According to the Baraita, bailees are required to take an oath only if they make a partial admission, i.e., return part of the bailment entrusted to them, and a partial denial — in other words, deny ever having received part of the bailment entrusted to them. But we have just established that a person who falsely denies having received a deposit is considered a robber! Therefore, the Gemara now argues: [5]**Let us say: Since** the bailee **is suspected of dishonesty in money matters** — for if he did not steal the bailment, he has no reason to try to put off returning it — [6]**he should also be suspected of taking false oaths**! The fact that the bailee is nonetheless required to take an oath would seem to prove that we do not say that a person suspected of dishonesty in money matters is also suspected of swearing falsely!

הָתָם נַמִי [7]The Gemara replies: **There, too,** in the case of the four bailees, it is possible that the bailee **may** simply **be trying to put off** returning the article, and we need not assume that he is a thief. [8]It is quite possible that the article has been stolen or lost, and the bailee **thinks**: "If I am granted more time **I will find the thief** who stole the article from me **and catch him**, and I will take the article back from him, and restore it to its owner," [9]**or alternatively: "I will find** the animal **in the marshland** where it was lost **and bring it** back to its owner." Therefore we do not initially suspect the bailee of stealing, but rather of trying to put off returning the bailment.

LITERAL TRANSLATION

a loan is fit for testimony, [1][but he who denies] a deposit is unfit for testimony.

[2]But [what about] that [Baraita] that Rami bar Ḥama taught: [3]Four bailees require a partial denial and a partial admission: [4]the unpaid bailee and the borrower, the paid bailee and the hirer. [5]Let us say: Since he is suspected [of dishonesty] in money [matters], [6]he is suspected of [taking false] oaths!

[7]There, too, he is trying to put [him] off. [8]He thinks: "I will find the thief and catch him." [9]Or alternatively: "I will find it in the marshland and I will bring it to him."

בְּמִלְוֶה כָּשֵׁר לְעֵדוּת, [1]בְּפִיקָּדוֹן פָּסוּל לְעֵדוּת.

[2]אֶלָּא הָא דְּתָנֵי רָמִי בַּר חָמָא: [3]אַרְבָּעָה שׁוֹמְרִין צְרִיכִין כְּפִירָה בְּמִקְצָת וְהוֹדָאָה בְּמִקְצָת: [4]שׁוֹמֵר חִנָּם וְהַשּׁוֹאֵל, נוֹשֵׂא שָׂכָר וְהַשּׂוֹכֵר. [5]נֵימָא: מִיגּוֹ דַּחֲשִׁיד אַמָּמוֹנָא, [6]חֲשִׁיד אַשְׁבוּעֲתָא! [7]הָתָם נַמִי, אִשְׁתַּמּוּטֵי קָא מִשְׁתַּמֵּיט. [8]סָבַר: "מַשְׁכַּחְנָא לַגַּנָּב וְתָפֵיסְנָא לֵיהּ". [9]אִי נַמִי: "מַשְׁכַּחְנָא לֵיהּ בְּאֲגַם וּמַיְיתִינָא לֵיהּ".

RASHI

כשר לעדות — אלמא: לאו דעתיה למגזליה, דנימא "אל תשת עד חמס", אלא לאשתמוטי עביד. **בפקדון פסול לעדות** — דמאי אשתמוטי איכא? הרי לא ניתן להוצאה, ובעין הוא. ואם אבד — יטעון שאבד ויפטר. **ולימא מגו דחשיד אממונא** — דההוא דאמר "לא היו דברים מעולם" — כופר בפקדון הוא, וליכא למימר משתמיט. **חשיד נמי אשבועה דידה** — דבשלמא אשבועת שומרין, דההוא דקטעין "נאנסה", דחייביה רחמנא שבועה — איכא למימר דלא חשיד אממונא, אלא שמא פשע בשמירתה וחייב לשלם אונסיה, וסבר: עד דהוי לי זוזי ופרענא ליה. אלא ההיא דכפירה — הא ודאי כופר בפקדון הוא, ומשקר, והיכי משבעינן ליה עלה? **התם נמי אשתמוטי משתמיט** — שאבדה ממנו, וסבר משכחנא לגנב כו'.

LANGUAGE

אֲגַם Marshland. Although the word אֲגַם means "lake" in modern Hebrew, the meaning of the word here, as in most passages of the Talmud and in certain places in the Bible (cf. Jeremiah 51:32), is a marshy pasture or meadow. Apparently an אֲגַם was a marshy area of ownerless pastureland next to a water source.

HALAKHAH

and the latter denies having received the loan, even if there are witnesses who contradict him, he is not suspected of willingness to swear falsely until he has actually taken an oath to support his denial. By contrast, a person who denies having received a deposit *is* suspected of willingness to swear falsely even though he has not yet taken an oath to support his denial. However, this applies only if witnesses testify that they actually saw the article in his possession at the time he made his denial." (*Shulḥan Arukh, Ḥoshen Mishpat* 92:4.)

TRANSLATION AND COMMENTARY

אִי הָכִי [1]The Gemara now objects: But **if** this is **so, why is a person who** falsely **denies** having received **a deposit unfit to testify**, as we learned earlier? [2]**Let us say** that there, too, **he is** simply **trying to put off** returning the article, [3]for **he thinks**: "If I am given more time, **I will search** for the lost deposit **and find it!**"

כִּי אָמְרִינַן [4]The Gemara replies that in fact a person who falsely denies having received a deposit is ordinarily *not* disqualified as a witness: **When do we say that a person who** falsely **denies** having received **a deposit is unfit to testify**? [5]**When witnesses came and testified against him,** [6]asserting **that at the very moment** when he denied having received the deposit, **the deposit was in his house and he knew** that it was there, [7]**or alternatively, if he was** actually **holding the deposit in his hand** when he denied having received it. In these cases, it is clear that he is a thief, and is not just attempting to delay returning the deposit. Hence he is disqualified from being able to serve as a witness.

אֶלָּא הָא דְּאָמַר רַב הוּנָא [8]The Gemara continues to ask: **But what about the statement made by Rav Huna** (below, 34b), that if a bailee does not return to its owner an article entrusted to him, and says that he is willing to repay the owner the value of the article, **we** nevertheless **require him to take an oath that it is not in his possession?** [9]Surely, argues the Gemara, in such a case **we should say: Since** the bailee **is suspected of dishonesty in money matters,** [10]**he should** also **be suspected of taking false oaths!** He claims that the article has been lost or stolen, but we suspect that he himself may have misappropriated it. We nevertheless impose an oath upon him, indicating that we believe that he will swear truly!

הָתָם נַמִי [11]The Gemara rejects this argument: **There, too,** in Rav Huna's case, **the bailee may be rationalizing, saying: "I am willing to give the owner of the article money** to the value of the original deposit. Although I have taken the article for myself, since I am reimbursing the owner for the value of the article, I have not done anything wrong." The bailee is, therefore, not suspected of dishonesty in money matters, because he believes that he is doing no wrong, and in his own estimation he is an honest person. Therefore an oath may be imposed on him, and what he says under oath may be believed.

אֲמַר לֵיהּ רַב אַחָא מְדִּיפְתִּי [12]**Rav Aha of Difti said to Ravina: But surely** the bailee **has violated the prohibition of "You shall not covet"** (Exodus 20:14) by not returning the deposit, even if he pays for it. For this

[1]אִי הָכִי, הַכּוֹפֵר בְּפִקָּדוֹן, אַמַּאי פָּסוּל לְעֵדוּת? [2]נֵימָא: אִשְׁתַּמּוֹטֵי קָא מִשְׁתַּמֵּיט. [3]סָבַר: "עַד דְּבָחֲשְׁנָא וּמַשְׁכַּחְנָא לֵיהּ"!

[4]כִּי אָמְרִינַן הַכּוֹפֵר בְּפִקָּדוֹן פָּסוּל לְעֵדוּת, [5]כְּגוֹן דְּאָתוּ סָהֲדֵי וְאַסְהִידוּ בֵּיהּ [6]דְּהַהִיא שַׁעְתָּא אִיתֵיהּ לְפִקָּדוֹן בְּבֵיתֵיהּ וַהֲוָה יָדַע. [7]אִי נַמִי, דַּהֲוָה נְקִיט לֵיהּ בִּידֵיהּ.

[8]אֶלָּא הָא דְּאָמַר רַב הוּנָא: מַשְׁבִּיעִין אוֹתוֹ שְׁבוּעָה שֶׁאֵינָהּ בִּרְשׁוּתוֹ. [9]נֵימָא: מִיגּוֹ דַּחֲשִׁיד אַמָּמוֹנָא, [10]חֲשִׁיד אַשְּׁבוּעֲתָא!

[11]הָתָם נַמִי מוֹרֶה וְאָמַר: "דָּמֵי קָא יָהֲבְנָא לֵיהּ".

[12]אֲמַר לֵיהּ רַב אַחָא מִדִּיפְתִּי לְרָבִינָא: וְהָא קָא עָבַר עַל לָאו דְּ"לֹא תַחְמֹד"!

LITERAL TRANSLATION

[1]If so, one who denies a deposit, why is he unfit for testimony? [2]Let us say: He is trying to put [him] off. [3]He thinks: "[I will put him off] until I search [for it] and find it"!

[4]When we say [that] one who denies a deposit is unfit for testimony, [5][it is], for example, where witnesses came and testified against him [6]that at that [very] hour the deposit was in his house and he knew [about it]. [7]Alternatively, where he was holding it in his hand.

[8]But [what about] that which Rav Huna said: We make him swear an oath that it is not in his possession. [9]Let us say: Since he is suspected [of dishonesty] in money [matters], [10]he is suspected of [taking false] oaths!

[11]There, too, he rationalizes (lit., "teaches") and says: "I am giving him money."

[12]Rav Aha of Difti said to Ravina: But surely he has transgressed the prohibition of "You shall not covet"!

RASHI

אי הכי — בפקדון איכא למימר משתמיט! **דבחשנא** = אחפש. **הכי גרסינן:** דהסיא שעתא איתא בביתיה והוה גביה. ולא גרס: ההיא שעתא דאשתבע. **דאמר רב הונא** — לקמן ב"המפקיד" גבי שילם ולא רצה לישבע. אמר רב הונא: אם בא לשלם — **משביעין אותו שבועה שאינה ברשותו**, חיישינן שמא עיניו נתן בה. **התם** — לא חשיד אממונא, דמורי היתירא למימר: דמי בעינא למיתב. **הא קא עבר בלא תחמוד** — מה לי חשוד על "לא תחמוד", מה לי חשוד על "לא תגזול"? נימא: מיגו דחשיד עליה, חשיד אשבועתא!

BACKGROUND

לֹא תַחְמֹד "You shall not covet." According to Rabbinic tradition, the commandment, "You shall not covet" is not meant to prohibit a person's inner desire to own something belonging to his fellow (though this, too, is forbidden, in that it violates the parallel prohibition, "Neither shall you desire," in the version of the Ten Commandments appearing in Deuteronomy 5:18). לֹא תַחְמֹד only applies when a person performs an action to fulfill this desire, when he coerces or defrauds his fellow to expropriate something that belongs to him. As explained in the Gemara, this prohibition applies to any act of removing things from someone else's possession without his full consent, and, with regard to this prohibition, there is no difference between robbery or some other method. Even if the act is formally legal, it nevertheless violates this prohibition.

SAGES

רַב אַחָא מְדִּיפְתִּי Rav Aha of Difti. An Amora of the sixth and seventh generation of Babylonian Amoraim, whose statements appear in several passages of the Talmud. Rav Aha of Difti was the outstanding pupil of Ravina, and he frequently raises objections to Ravina's teachings. He is mentioned as a colleague of Mar bar Rav Ashi, and he was the preferred candidate to become the head of the great Yeshiva of Sura.

He is named after his place of birth, to distinguish him from many other Sages who were named Rav Aha. Difti was apparently a large city on the Euphrates in the district of Sura.

NOTES

לֹא תַחְמֹד "You shall not covet." *Rosh* makes a distinction between two categories of חַמְסָנִים — "takers by force" — even when money is given for the article taken: (1) One who forces another person to agree to a sale. Despite his lack of

TRANSLATION AND COMMENTARY

commandment is understood by the Gemara to mean that it is forbidden to take property away from another person, whether by force or by guile, even if the original owner of the property is reimbursed for his loss. Since the bailee is surely guilty of violating this prohibition, why do we not suspect that he will swear falsely?

לֹא תַחְמֹד לֶאֱינָשֵׁי [1]The Gemara replies: In fact, the bailee's honesty is not called into question at all. The reason for this is that **people think that "You shall not covet"** applies only if the offender seeks to take the object he covets **without paying money** for it. Accordingly, although the prohibition "You shall not covet" is violated by a person who takes someone else's property even if he pays for it, nevertheless people are not aware that this is forbidden, and they assume that the prohibition only applies if the offender takes possession of the object he covets without paying. Thus, applying this principle to our case, we may conclude that the bailee thought that he was doing nothing wrong when he took the article for himself, since he was ready to pay the owner back. Hence there is no reason to suspect that he will give false evidence or swear falsely.

וְאֶלָּא הָא דְּאָמַר רַב נַחְמָן [6A] [2]The Gemara now asks a series of three questions: (1) **But what about the statement of Rav Naḥman**, that if a person totally denies that he owes any money to the plaintiff (above, 5a), so that it cannot be argued that he is trying to put off repaying the debt, we nevertheless **make him take an oath of inducement? [3]Why do we not say that, since he is suspected of dishonesty in money matters, he should also be suspected of taking false oaths?!**

וְתוּ [4]**And furthermore,** (2) **what about the Baraita that Rabbi Ḥiyya taught,** that in the case of the storekeeper and the employee (above 3a), **both must take oaths, and they both receive payment from the employer?** [5]There, too, **why do we not say: "Since one of them is** definitely **suspected of dishonesty in money matters,** because in this case one of the two claimants is definitely lying, **they should also be suspected of taking false oaths** and neither should take an oath"?

[1]״לֹא תַחְמֹד״ לֶאֱינָשֵׁי בְּלָא דָּמֵי מַשְׁמַע לְהוּ.

[6A] [2]וְאֶלָּא הָא דְּאָמַר רַב נַחְמָן: מַשְׁבִּיעִין אוֹתוֹ שְׁבוּעַת הֶיסֵּת. [3]נֵימָא: מִיגּוֹ דַּחֲשִׁיד אַמָּמוֹנָא, חֲשִׁיד אַשְּׁבוּעֲתָא!

[4]וְתוּ, הָא דְּתָנֵי רַבִּי חִיָּיא: שְׁנֵיהֶם נִשְׁבָּעִין וְנוֹטְלִין מִבַּעַל הַבַּיִת. [5]נֵימָא: מִיגּוֹ דַּחֲשִׁיד אַמָּמוֹנָא, חֲשִׁיד אַשְּׁבוּעֲתָא!

LITERAL TRANSLATION

[1]"You shall not covet" is understood by people [as coveting] without [paying] money.

[6A] [2]But [what about] that which Rav Naḥman said: We make him swear an oath of inducement. [3]Let us say: Since he is suspected [of dishonesty] in money [matters], he is suspected of [taking false] oaths!

[4]And furthermore, [what about] that which Rabbi Ḥiyya taught: Both [claimants] swear and take [payment] from the employer. [5]Let us say: Since he is suspected [of dishonesty] in money [matters], he is suspected of [taking false] oaths!

RASHI

משביעין אותו — לשאינו מודה במקצת, **נימא מיגו** — דמעיז פניו לכפור הכל — לאו לאשתמוטי בעי, וחשוד אשבועה! **שניהם נשבעים** — גבי חנוני על פנקסו. וקשה לי: אמאי שבקה למתניתין דשבועות ומייתי לה מברייתא? **נימא מיגו** — כיון דחד מינייהו ודאי חשיד אממונא!

NOTES

propriety in so doing, this action does not come under the category of robbery. (2) One who takes an article against its owner's will and leaves him money, even though the latter has not agreed to part with his property. In this instance, there *is* an element of robbery involved.

הָא דְּתָנֵי רַבִּי חִיָּיא **What about the Baraita that Rabbi Ḥiyya taught.** *Rashi* raises the question: The law quoted is explicitly mentioned in the Mishnah (*Shevuot* 45a). Why, then, does the Talmud quote the ruling from a Baraita in the name of Rabbi Ḥiyya?

Tosafot suggest that the Talmud based its choice on *Shevuot* 47b, which states that it was Rabbi Ḥiyya who explained the meaning of the Mishnah to Rabbi Yehudah HaNasi. *Ritva* points out that all the questions asked by the Gemara on this theme are based on the teachings of Amoraim. This ruling, therefore, is also quoted from a non-Mishnaic source.

שְׁנֵיהֶם נִשְׁבָּעִין **Both must take an oath**. The question is raised: Why does the Talmud cite this particular law? There are many other cases where a person is required to take an oath even though we have reason to suspect that he has misappropriated money.

HALAKHAH

לֹא תַחְמֹד לֶאֱינָשֵׁי בְּלָא דָּמֵי מַשְׁמַע לְהוּ **People think that "You shall not covet" applies only if the offender seeks to take the object he covets without paying money.** "If the person to whom a deposit has been entrusted is found to have misappropriated it, and he seeks to compensate the owner for its value, he is not disqualified from taking an oath, despite the fact that his actions violate the prohibition 'You shall not covet.'" (Ibid., 92:4 in the additional note of the *Rema*.) This observation by the *Rema* emphasizes that a person who willfully commits a sin is not thereby disqualified from taking an oath unless most people realize that such a deed is forbidden.

TRANSLATION AND COMMENTARY

וְתוּ [1]**And furthermore,** (3) **what about the ruling of Rav Sheshet,** that if an unpaid bailee claims that the bailment was stolen from him, **we require him to take three oaths:** [2](a) **"I swear that I was not negligent** when caring for the bailment," (b) **"I swear that I did not make use of it** for my own personal needs," **and** (c) **"I swear that the bailment is not** now **in my possession"**? The third oath, that the bailment is not now in his possession, was clearly instituted because the bailee may be retaining the bailment unlawfully. But if we suspect the bailee of dishonesty, [3]**why do we not say** that, **since** the bailee **is suspected of dishonesty in money matters, he should also be suspected of taking false oaths?!**

אֶלָּא [4]**Rather,** concludes the Gemara, on the basis of all the objections just raised, **we do not say that, since a person is suspected of dishonesty in money matters, he is also suspected of taking false oaths,** and the assumption made and challenged throughout the previous discussion is now rejected.

אַבַּיֵי אָמַר [5]Abaye, however, rejects this line of reasoning. He **says** that no proof can be brought from the cases cited above, that a person suspected of monetary impropriety is believed if he takes an oath. These cases are special because in each of them **we are concerned that the defendant** (or the claimant of the garment in our Mishnah) **is owed a previous loan** by the plaintiff that he has been unable to collect until now. The defendant (or the claimant of the garment in our Mishnah) may simply be retaining the deposit (or debt or lost article) as compensation for the money that the plaintiff owes him. If this is the case, we in no way suspect the defendant of attempting to rob the plaintiff, and there is no reason for us to disbelieve him if he takes an oath to rebut the claim of the plaintiff. But if we did suspect him of dishonesty about money, we would suspect his veracity if he took an oath.

[1]וְתוּ, הָא דְּאָמַר רַב שֵׁשֶׁת: שָׁלֹשׁ שְׁבוּעוֹת מַשְׁבִּיעִין אוֹתוֹ:
[2]״שְׁבוּעָה שֶׁלֹּא פָּשַׁעְתִּי בָּהּ״. ״שְׁבוּעָה שֶׁלֹּא שָׁלַחְתִּי בָּהּ יָד״. ״שְׁבוּעָה שֶׁאֵינָהּ בִּרְשׁוּתִי״.
[3]נֵימָא: מִיגּוֹ דַּחֲשִׁיד אַמָּמוֹנָא, חֲשִׁיד אַשְּׁבוּעֲתָא!
[4]אֶלָּא, לָא אָמְרִינַן: מִיגּוֹ דַּחֲשִׁיד אַמָּמוֹנָא, חֲשִׁיד אַשְּׁבוּעֲתָא.
[5]אַבַּיֵי אָמַר: חָיְישִׁינַן שֶׁמָּא מִלְוֶה יְשָׁנָה יֵשׁ לוֹ עָלָיו.

LITERAL TRANSLATION

[1]And furthermore, [what about] that which Rav Sheshet said: We make him swear three oaths: [2]"[I declare under] oath that I was not negligent in [guarding] it." "[I declare under] oath that I did not make use of it (lit., 'I did not stretch out a hand onto it')." "[I declare under] oath that it is not in my possession." [3]Let us say: Since he is suspected [of dishonesty] in money [matters], he is suspected of [taking false] oaths!

[4]Rather, we do not say: Since he is suspected [of dishonesty] in money [matters], he is suspected of [taking false] oaths.

[5]Abaye said: We are concerned in case he is owed a previous loan by him (lit., "he has an old loan on him").

RASHI

שלוש שבועות משביעין אותו — לשומר חנם שטוען נגנבה. **שלא שלחתי בה יד** — לעשות מלאכתי. דאי שלח בה יד הוי גזלן עליה, ומיחייב באונסיה. ואפילו נאנסה — ברשותיה היא קיימא, ודידיה היא. **נימא** — גבי שבועה "שאינה ברשותי": מיגו דחשיד אממונא, שמא ברשותיה הוא וכופר בה — חשיד נמי אשבועתא! **אביי אמר** — טעמא דמתניתין לאו כדרבי יוחנן. דאי הוה חשיד לן אהולך ותוקף בטלית חבירו חנם — הוה לן חשוד אשבועה. אלא, חיישינן שמא מלוה ישנה יש לו עליו על זה, ומכיר בו שכחה, ויכפור בו. והולך ותוקף בטליתו, ונשבע שיש לו בה דמי חליה, וטלית זו שלו — דהא אפילו גלימא דעל כתפיה שעביד ליה.

CONCEPTS

מִלְוֶה יְשָׁנָה This refers to a debt or loan made prior to the transaction currently at issue, and from the way it is presented here in the Gemara we infer that it is an obligation not corroborated by any written documentation or clear testimony. If a borrower does not wish to pay such a debt, the lender has no means of forcing him to do so. But if the lender is holding some of the borrower's property, then when the borrower wishes to recover it, the lender can claim the old debt. In this situation the burden of proof falls on the borrower, for in this case he is the one seeking to extract property from his fellow, and *he* must prove his case.

NOTES

MaHaram Shiff explains that this instance is noteworthy because in this case one of the people taking the oath is certainly lying and stealing from the employer. Nevertheless, an oath is required from both.

שְׁבוּעָה שֶׁאֵינָהּ בִּרְשׁוּתִי "I declare under oath that it is not in my possession." Some commentators understand this to be a separate oath, distinct from the usual oath taken by a bailee that the object was lost or destroyed in circumstances under which the bailee is absolved from liability. *Rosh*, however, interprets it as a general term for the various forms of the bailee oath. The situations under which a borrower, a paid bailee, or an unpaid bailee are absolved from liability differ, and each one swears that the object "is not in his possession" in the form appropriate for his case.

שֶׁמָּא מִלְוֶה יְשָׁנָה In case the defendant is owed a previous loan. The commentary follows that of most of the Rishonim, who maintain that Abaye disagrees fundamentally with the conclusion of the Gemara here and maintains that in fact a person suspected of dishonesty in money matters is also suspected of dishonesty in taking oaths. Accordingly, he

HALAKHAH

שְׁבוּעַת שׁוֹמְרִים The oath taken by bailees. Every bailee who takes the oath imposed upon bailees must include three elements in his oath: (1) That he looked after the bailment in accordance with reasonable practice, and that the loss occurred outside the area of his responsibility (e.g., the bailment was stolen from the care of an unpaid bailee,

LITERAL TRANSLATION

[1]If so, let him take [it] without an oath! [2]Rather, we are concerned in case he [thinks he] may be owed a previous loan by him (lit., "he has a doubtful old loan on him")].

[3]But do we not say [that one who] seizes property out of doubt will also swear [falsely] out of doubt?!

[1]אִי הָכִי, נִשְׁקוֹל בְּלָא שְׁבוּעָה! [2]אֶלָּא, חָיְישִׁינַן שֶׁמָּא סְפֵק מִלְוָה יְשָׁנָה יֵשׁ לוֹ עָלָיו. [3]וְלָא אָמְרִינַן תָּפֵיס מָמוֹנָא מִסְּפֵיקָא מִשְׁתַּבַּע נַמִי מִסָּפֵק!

RASHI

אי הכי – אמאי רמו עליה שבועה, כיון דאי לא הוי עליה – לא הוי תפיס **כהז נשקלה בלא שבועה** – לגבות מלוה שלו!

TRANSLATION AND COMMENTARY

אִי הָכִי [1]The Gemara now asks: **If** we really have in mind the possibility that the plaintiff owes the defendant a previous loan, **let the defendant keep the disputed property without** having to take **an oath!** For he may declare under oath that the object in dispute is his, since as far as he is concerned it constitutes the repayment of the money owed him by the plaintiff. Thus, requiring the defendant to take an oath in support of his claim will not necessarily clarify the facts in the dispute!

אֶלָּא [2]**Rather**, answers the Gemara, what Abaye meant was: **We are concerned in case** the defendant may be lying because **he thinks that he may be owed a previous loan by the plaintiff.** In other words, Abaye meant that the defendant is not certain as to whether or not the plaintiff in fact owes him money in repayment of a previous loan. Therefore, the defendant may have decided to retain the plaintiff's deposit for the time being, in case it becomes clear at a later date that the plaintiff does indeed owe him money which he has not yet repaid. In order to deter such behavior, we impose an oath on him.

לָא אָמְרִינַן [3]The Gemara now objects to this interpretation of Abaye's remarks: **But do we not say that if he** is prepared to **seize property when he is not certain** whether or not it belongs to him, **he may also** be prepared to **take an oath** that may not be strictly truthful in support of his doubtful claim, **even if he is not certain** whether or not his claim is true? Why should we believe his oath if we suspect him of taking illegal possession of property to which he may only have, at best, a doubtful claim?

NOTES

maintains that in all the cases mentioned here the oath is imposed because of the possibility that the defendant is owed money by the claimant from a previous transaction between them.

Ramban, however, suggests that it is possible to explain Abaye's viewpoint here as not disagreeing fundamentally with the Gemara. Abaye agrees that oaths are often imposed on people who are suspected of dishonesty in money matters. But his purpose here is to express his disagreement with the viewpoint of Rabbi Yoḥanan in explaining the Mishnah. Abaye maintains that the oath imposed in the Mishnah was *not* instituted in order to prevent people from seizing other people's property and claiming it as theirs, but rather in order to prevent a person from seizing another person's property in payment for a possible claim that he may have against the owner of the article.

סְפֵק מִלְוָה וכו׳ **The defendant thinks that he may be owed a previous loan.** Several of the Rishonim raise the following question: If seizing another person's property because of the possibility of a previous loan does not disqualify a person from taking an oath, why is a bailee who denies receiving a deposit, or even a robber, disqualified? Perhaps he, too, is seizing the property because of the possibility that the plaintiff owes him money from a previous transaction.

Ri Migash answers that there is a difference between the two cases. When two people come to court holding an object, we have no proof as yet that one has misappropriated the other's property. Hence, we can use the argument of "a previous loan" to justify the oath that is imposed. By contrast, if a bailee is proved to have falsely denied receiving a deposit, even if he has done so in order to reclaim a possible previous loan from the plaintiff, he has committed an act of robbery. Therefore we suspect that he may also take a false oath.

תָּפֵיס מָמוֹנָא מִסְּפֵיקָא כו׳ **One who seizes property out of doubt....** When a person knows that his fellow owes him money, and he takes an article from his debtor as repayment of the loan, he has at worst done something which raises certain legal problems (these are discussed at length in the Gemara in clarifying the question of whether a person is permitted to take the law into his own hands). But in certain instances everyone agrees that it is permissible, when there is no other way to recover a debt which the debtor is unwilling to repay.

It is a different matter when someone seizes property to ensure payment of a doubtful debt. This is so even if, as *Tosafot* (ד״ה מָמוֹן) argue the person seizing the object does so with the intention of returning it, if it becomes clear to

HALAKHAH

or an unavoidable accident destroyed the bailment while it was in the care of a paid bailee). (2) That the bailment is not now in his possession. (3) That he did not make use of the bailment for his own purposes before the event that freed him from responsibility for its safekeeping occurred. (*Shulḥan Arukh, Ḥoshen Mishpat* 295:2, in accordance with the ruling of Rav Sheshet.)

סְפֵק מִלְוָה יְשָׁנָה **The possibility of there being an outstanding loan.** "The reason why a person who falsely denies having received a loan is not suspected of taking a false oath is that we consider the possibility that the plaintiff still owes him money from a previous loan, and that the defendant is now seeking to retain the money he owes the plaintiff in lieu of that previous loan. Thus the defendant did not intend to rob the plaintiff of money rightfully his." (Ibid., 92:3.)

[1]אֲמַר רַב שֵׁשֶׁת בְּרֵיהּ דְּרַב אִידִי: פָּרְשִׁי אֱינָשֵׁי מִסְּפֵק שְׁבוּעָה, וְלָא פָּרְשִׁי מִסְּפֵק מָמוֹנָא. [2]מַאי טַעֲמָא? [3]מָמוֹן אִיתֵיהּ בַּהֲדָרָה, שְׁבוּעָה לֵיתֵיהּ בַּהֲדָרָה.

[4]בָּעֵי רַבִּי זֵירָא: תְּקָפָהּ אֶחָד בְּפָנֵינוּ, מַהוּ?

[5]הֵיכִי דָּמֵי? [6]אִי דְּשָׁתֵיק, אוֹדוּיֵי אוֹדֵי לֵיהּ, וְאִי דְּקָא צוֹוֵחַ, מַאי הֲוָה לֵיהּ לְמֶעְבַּד? [7]לָא! צְרִיכָא, דְּשָׁתֵיק מֵעִיקָּרָא, וַהֲדַר צוֹוֵחַ. מַאי? [8]מִדְּאִשְׁתִּיק, אוֹדוּיֵי אוֹדֵי לֵיהּ, [9]אוֹ דִּלְמָא: כֵּיוָן דְּקָא צוֹוֵחַ הָשְׁתָּא, אִיגְּלַאי מִילְּתָא דְּהַאי דְּשָׁתֵיק מֵעִיקָּרָא [10]סָבַר: "הָא קָא חֲזוּ לֵיהּ רַבָּנַן!"

LITERAL TRANSLATION

[1]Rav Sheshet, the son of Rav Idi, said: People refrain from [taking] a doubtful oath, but do not refrain from [keeping] doubtful property. [2]What is the reason? [3]Money is returnable, an oath is not returnable.

[4]Rabbi Zera asked: [If] one seized it in our presence, what [is the law]?

[5]What is it like? [6]If he is silent, he is admitting to him, and if he cries out, what [more] could he have done?

[7]No! [This question] is necessary, where he was silent at first, but afterwards cried out. What [is the law]? [8]Since he was silent, he admitted to him, [9]or perhaps: since he is crying out now, it is apparent that the reason that he was silent at first [10][was because] he thought: "Surely the Rabbis have seen him!"

TRANSLATION AND COMMENTARY

אֲמַר רַב שֵׁשֶׁת [1]**Rav Sheshet, the son of Rav Idi, said** in reply: **People refrain from taking "doubtful oaths,"** and swear only if they are convinced that their claim is justified, **but they do not refrain from retaining "doubtful property"** which they are not certain is theirs. [2]**What is the reason** for this distinction? [3]**It is that property can be returned** to its rightful owner if it is discovered later that a mistake was made, but an **oath cannot be taken back** after a person has already sworn. People are therefore more careful about taking an oath than about retaining property which may not really belong to them.

בָּעֵי ר׳ זֵירָא [4]**Rabbi Zera** raised the following problem and **asked: If** two people holding on to a garment came before the court, and **one** of them used force and **seized** the whole garment from the other **in our** [the court's] **presence, what is the law?**

הֵיכִי דָּמֵי [5]The Talmud now proceeds to clarify this question in order to show that a situation such as that postulated by Rabbi Zera could never occur in real life: **How do we visualize the case?** [6]There would seem to be two clear-cut possibilities: **If** the person from whom the article was seized remains **silent,** we may interpret his silence as an **admission** of the validity of the other person's claim to the whole garment! And **if he cries out** in protest, **what more could he have done?** Surely the fact that he was not strong enough to prevent the other person from seizing the article should not affect the court's decision, and the case should be treated like any other where two people holding the same garment appear before a court and claim ownership of the garment.

לָא צְרִיכָא [7]The Talmud answers: **No! It was necessary** for Rabbi Zera to pose his problem in a case **where** the person from whom the article was seized **was silent at first but afterwards cried out** in protest. **What is the law** in such a case? [8]The Talmud now suggests two possible interpretations of the claimant's original silence: (1) Perhaps, **since he was silent at first, he** thereby **admitted** the legitimacy of the other person's claim, and he only decided to protest later, after changing his mind. If that is the case, the person now holding the garment should be permitted to keep it. (2) [9]**Or perhaps, since he is crying out** in protest **now, it is apparent that he was silent at first** [10]only **because he thought** it was unnecessary to protest, **since** surely **the Rabbis** of the court **had** themselves **seen** what happened. Since the members of the court themselves witnessed the seizure of the article, his original silence should not be interpreted as the relinquishing of his rights to the garment.

RASHI

ולא פרשי מספק ממונא — אבל מודאי דממונא — פרשי, ומאן דלא פריש — חשיד נמי אשבועתא. **תקפה אחד** — הוציאה מיד חבירו בחזקה, והרי כולה בידו קודם שנשבעו.

SAGES

רַבִּי זֵירָא Rabbi Zera. Rabbi Zera was one of the greatest of the third genertion of Palestinian Amoraim. Born in Babylonia, he belonged essentially to the Babylonian tradition, and he studied mainly with the disciples of Rav and Shmuel. After some time he emigrated to Eretz Israel, where he was able to study Torah from Rabbi Yoḥanan, and he was a colleague of Rabbi Yoḥanan's greatest disciples.

When Rabbi Zera reached Eretz Israel he was extremely impressed with the method of learning used there and decided to accept it in full, so much so that he took upon himself a hundred fasts in order to forget the Babylonian system of study.

It is related that he also fasted so that the fire of Gehinom should not hold sway over him, and on one occasion he so exposed himself to fire that his legs were burned. Because of his event he was known as the "short man with the scorched legs."

Rabbi Zera was famous for his great piety, for his modesty, and for being affable and accommodating, and the members of his generation greatly loved and honored him.

He had many disciples throughout Eretz Israel, and the quotations of his teachings are plentiful in both the Jerusalem and the Babylonian Talmuds.

He had a son who was also a Sage, Rabbi Ahavah.

NOTES

him that he cannot be certain of the truth of his claim, and he will not wait in returning the article until there iss decisive proof that he has no valid claim at all. In any event, the person has acted wrongly and may even be guilty of robbery. For this reason there are grounds for suspicion that, since he has not refrained from a doubtful act of robbery, he would not refrain from swearing a false oath.

מָמוֹן אִיתֵיהּ בַּהֲדָרָה Money is returnable. Taking property illegally is not only a crime against one's fellow but also against God. Nevertheless, restitution can be made by

HALAKHAH

תְּקָפָהּ אֶחָד בְּפָנֵינוּ One seized it in our presence. "If two people were holding on to an object to which both laid claim, and one then seized it from the other before the court or in the presence of witnesses, the object is left in the possession of the person who seized it, provided that the other person was initially silent (even if he protested later).

TRANSLATION AND COMMENTARY

אָמַר רַב נַחְמָן [1]**Rav Naḥman said, Come and hear** a resolution of Rabbi Zera's problem from the following Baraita: **"When does the law** in our Mishnah, requiring two people contesting ownership of a garment to take an oath and to divide it between them, **apply? When both** claimants **are holding on to** the garment. [2]**But if the garment is in the possession of** only **one of them** when they appear in court, there is no reason to order that the garment be divided between them, and the law follows the principle: '**The burden of proof rests upon the plaintiff.**'" In such a case the person at present holding the garment may keep it unless the other claimant produces witnesses in support of his claim.

הֵיכִי דָּמֵי [3]Now, says Rav Naḥman, **how do we visualize the case** dealt with by this Baraita? [4]**If we say that the case was as stated**, and we interpret the Baraita literally, i.e., they arrived in court with the garment already entirely in the possession of one of the claimants, **it is surely self-evident** that if someone claims that an object which is in someone else's possession actually belongs to him, the claimant must prove his claim! **Rather,** says Rav Naḥman, the Baraita must be discussing a case **where** the two claimants were both holding the garment when they arrived in court, but **one** of them **seized** the garment from the other **in our presence** and the latter cried out in protest after an initial period of silence, which is precisely the case raised by Rabbi Zera. We may, therefore, infer from the ruling given by this Baraita that in such a case the burden of proof rests upon that litigant who has lost possession of the garment, and that in the absence of such proof the other litigant may keep the garment. This would seem to resolve Rabbi Zera's question.

לָא [5]The Talmud now rejects Rav Naḥman's interpretation of the Baraita he quoted: **No!** says the Gemara. This Baraita may be interpreted differently, in a way that has no bearing on Rabbi Zera's question: **With what are we dealing here** in the Baraita? With a case, **for example, where** the two claimants **came before us while both were holding on to** the garment, **and we** [the court] **told them, "Go and divide it."** [6]**They left** together, **and later,** when **they came back**, only **one of them was holding it.** [7]The two litigants now present opposing claims: The one holding the garment **says,** "The other claimant **admitted to me** that the garment is mine." **But the other** litigant **says, "I rented** my share of the garment to the other claimant **for money,** and his possession of the garment has no bearing on my claim. I still claim that the whole garment is mine."

[1]אֲמַר רַב נַחְמָן: תָּא שְׁמַע: "בַּמֶּה דְּבָרִים אֲמוּרִים? שֶׁשְּׁנֵיהֶם אֲדוּקִין בָּהּ. [2]אֲבָל הָיְתָה טַלִּית יוֹצֵאת מִתַּחַת יָדוֹ שֶׁל אֶחָד מֵהֶן, "הַמּוֹצִיא מֵחֲבֵירוֹ עָלָיו הָרְאָיָה"". [3]הֵיכִי דָּמֵי? [4]אִי נֵימָא כִּדְקָתָנֵי, פְּשִׁיטָא! אֶלָּא, שֶׁתְּקָפָהּ אֶחָד בְּפָנֵינוּ. [5]לָא! הָכָא בְּמַאי עָסְקִינַן? כְּגוֹן דְּאָתוּ לְקַמָּן כִּדְתְפִיסוּ לָהּ תַּרְוַיְיהוּ, וְאָמְרִינַן לְהוּ: "זִילוּ פַּלוֹגוּ". [6]וּנְפַקוּ, וַהֲדַר אָתוּ כִּי תָּפֵיס לָהּ חַד מִינַּיְיהוּ. [7]הַאי אָמַר: "אוֹדוּיֵי אוֹדֵי לִי", וְהַאי אָמַר: "בִּדְמֵי אָגַרְתִּיהּ נִיהֲלֵיהּ".

LITERAL TRANSLATION

[1]Rav Naḥman said: Come [and] hear: In what [case] are these words said? When both are holding on to it. [2]But if the garment was in the possession of (lit., "going out from beneath the hand of") one of them, "whoever seeks to take [something] away from his fellow, upon him is the [burden of] proof."

[3]What is it like? [4]If we say as it was stated, it is self-evident! Rather, [it is] where one seized it in our presence.

[5]No! With what are we dealing here? For example, where they came before us while both of them were holding on to it, and we told them: "Go divide [it]." [6]And they left, and later they came [back] when one of them was holding on to it. [7]This one says: "He admitted to me," and this one says: "I rented [it] to him for money."

RASHI

יוצאה מתחת ידו של אחד מהם — יוצאה (לבדו) לפני בית דין מתחת יד האחד, שהוא לבדו אוחז בה, ולא חבירו. **הראיה** — בעדים. **כדקתני** — שזה לבדו אוחז בה וכו׳. **אלא לאו כו׳** — וכדאוקמינן, דשתיק ולבסוף צווח.

SAGES

רַב נַחְמָן **Rav Naḥman.** This is Rav Naḥman bar Ya'akov, a Babylonian Amora of the second and third generations. Rav Naḥman's father was a scribe at the court associated with the Amora Shmuel. Rav Naḥman studied with Shmuel, whose rulings he frequently cites, and with Rabbah bar Avuha, one of Rav's disciples and a member of the Exilarch's family (according to some opinions he was himself the Exilarch).

Rav Naḥman married Rabbah bar Avuha's daughter, Yalta, a learned and firm-willed woman. By his marriage Rav Naḥman became connected with the House of the Exilarch, and after some time he was appointed judge of the House of the Exilarch in Neharde'a. Because of his status in the House of the Exilarch, and because of his profound knowledge of monetary law, Rav Naḥman was considered a greater authority than his colleagues in this field.

Rav Naḥman discusses Halakhic problems with a great many Sages, in particular Rav Huna, Rav Yehudah, Rav Sheshet, and Rav Ḥisda.

Although Rav Naḥman did not serve as an official head of a yeshivah, many members of his generation studied with him; the great Amora Rava was his outstanding disciple.

Rav Naḥman seems to have been wealthy all his life, and was regarded as the greatest Sage of his generation and the authoritative teacher of Torah in his city. Several of Rav Naḥman's sons were scholars.

NOTES

returning the property that was wrongfully taken. In contrast, there can be no restitution for perjury. As noted in the Gemara, a person is liable to be punished by Heaven for taking a false oath even if he did not intend to commit an act of fraud, and the event took place unintentionally.

בִּדְמֵי אָגַרְתִּי **I rented....** The Talmud mentions this possibility to teach us that, even though the garment may be an article of the kind ordinarily rented out, we still do not accept such

HALAKHAH

Since that other person was silent initially, he is assumed to have acquiesced in the first person's claim." (*Shulḥan Arukh, Ḥoshen Mishpat* 138:6.)

שְׁנֵיהֶם אֲדוּקִין בָּהּ **Two people holding.** "If two people are firmly grasping a garment (and claiming ownership of it) and the court rules that they must divide it, and then the litigants

LANGUAGE

סִרְכָא Hanging on. The root סרך is close in meaning to שרך, "to twist or wind together," and also to one of the senses of סרח, "to overhang." It means something that has been drawn out and stuck to something else, as does the noun סִרְכָא, a membrane or thread stuck to a certain limb. The meaning of the verb here is to grasp the end or edge of something but not the thing itself.

TERMINOLOGY

אִם תִּמְצֵי לוֹמַר If you say... This expression occasionally means, "If you say," or "If you assume." But its precise meaning is: "If you follow this through to the end," i.e., "if you pursue this line of thought and try to draw all the conclusions that follow from it regarding aspects that are not mentioned in connection with the basic Halakhah, but which derive from it." Occasionally, by proceeding in this manner, the Gemara clarifies the subject at hand by adducing additional sources.

TRANSLATION AND COMMENTARY

[1]**The Baraita teaches that** in such a case **we** [the court] **say to** the claimant who is not holding on to the garment that his claim is untenable: "**Until now you considered** the other claimant to be **a robber,** and claimed that he had seized a garment that you had found. **Now,** suddenly, **you** are willing to **rent** the article **to him without witnesses!**" Such a claim is obviously untenable, and hence the law is that the garment remains in the possession of the person at present holding it.

וְאִיבָּעֵית אֵימָא [2]Alternatively, says the Gemara, **if you prefer** to interpret the Baraita differently, you can **say:** The Baraita may indeed be interpreted literally **as stated,** as referring to a case **where** the two litigants **came before us, one of them** firmly **holding** on to the garment itself, **and the other one hanging on to it by its edges.** [3]The Baraita informs us that **even** if one accepts the view of **Summakhos,** who ordinarily **says** that "**property of doubtful ownership is divided** between the claimants **without an oath,**" here even **Summakhos would admit that** mere **hanging on** to the edge of an article **is** Halakhically **insignificant,** and the object is held to belong beyond all reasonable doubt to the person holding it. According to this second explanation, too, the Baraita cited by Rav Naḥman has no bearing on Rabbi Zera's original question, and this question is left unresolved.

אִם תִּמְצֵי לוֹמַר [4]Although the Talmud has left Rabbi Zera's question unresolved, it now proceeds to use it as the basis for raising a new issue: **On the assumption that** in a case where **one person seizes** an object from another person **in our presence, we** [the court] **take it away from him,** it is obvious that **if** either of the two claimants **were to dedicate** the whole object to the Temple without seizing it, **it would not be** considered **dedicated,** since it was not at the time in the possession of the person who dedicated it, and the act of dedicating the object is no more effective than the act of seizing it. [5]But **on the assumption that,** in a case where **one person seizes** an object from another person **in our presence, we** [the court] **do not take it away from him,** and we interpret the other claimant's initial silence as acquiesence, **what is the law if** one of the claimants **dedicated** the garment to the Temple **without seizing it?** Although he has not physically seized the garment, if his act of dedication is deemed valid he will have effectively removed the object from the possession of the other claimant!

[1]דְּאָמְרִינַן לֵיהּ: "עַד הָשְׁתָּא חֲשַׁדְתְּ לֵיהּ בְּגַזְלָן, וְהָשְׁתָּא מוֹגַרְתְּ לֵיהּ בְּלָא סָהֲדֵי?" [2]וְאִיבָּעֵית אֵימָא, כִּדְקָתָנֵי, דְּאָתוּ לְקַמָּן כִּי תָּפֵיס לָהּ חַד מִינַּיְיהוּ, וְאִידָךְ מִסְרַךְ בָּהּ סְרוּכֵי. [3]וַאֲפִילּוּ לְסוּמָכוֹס, דְּאָמַר: "מָמוֹן הַמּוּטָּל בְּסָפֵק חוֹלְקִין בְּלֹא שְׁבוּעָה", מוֹדֶה סוּמָכוֹס דְּסִרְכָא לָאו כְּלוּם הִיא. [4]אִם תִּמְצֵי לוֹמַר תְּקָפָהּ אֶחָד בְּפָנֵינוּ מוֹצִיאִין אוֹתָהּ מִיָּדוֹ, הִקְדִּישָׁהּ, אֵינָהּ מְקוּדֶּשֶׁת. [5]אִם תִּמְצֵי לוֹמַר תְּקָפָהּ אֶחָד בְּפָנֵינוּ, אֵין מוֹצִיאִין אוֹתָהּ מִיָּדוֹ, הִקְדִּישָׁהּ בְּלֹא תְּקָפָהּ מַהוּ?

LITERAL TRANSLATION

[1][The Baraita tells us] that we say to him: "Until now you suspected him of [being] a robber, and now you rent to him without witnesses!"

[2]And if you wish, say as it was stated, that they came before us while one of them was holding it, and the other one was hanging on to [the edge of] it. [3]And even [according] to Summakhos, who says: "Money of doubtful ownership (lit., 'money placed in doubt') is divided without an oath," Summakhos admits that hanging on is insignificant.

[4]If you say [that if] one seized it in our presence we take it away from him, [if] he dedicated it, it is not dedicated. [5][But] if you say [that if] one seized it in our presence, we do not take it away from him, what if he dedicated it without seizing it?

RASHI

אפילו דסומכוס כו' — כלומר: ואליבא דסומכוס דמיקל בחלוקה ולא מצריך אפילו שבועה, איצטריך לאשמועינן דבכהאי גוונא מודי סומכוס דאפילו בשבועה לא שקיל, דהא לאו ממון המוטל בספק הוא. **דסרבא לאו כלום היא** — ואין שור שחוט לפניך, ולא דמי לנמצא עוברה בצדה (בבא קמא מו,א). **ואם תמצא לומר** — בשאילתנו, לפשוט דמוציאין אותה מידו, ויחלוקו. **הקדישה** — בלא תקפה. **אינה מקודשת** — דלא אלים הקדישה מתקפה.

NOTES

a claim in the particular circumstances described by the Gemara, though at first sight it would seem plausible to do so (*Ritva*).

Where the first claimant returns to the court holding the object and the second claimant maintains that it was forcibly taken from him by the first, the Rishonim disagree: *Rambam* and others maintain that such a claim is untenable, while *Ramban* and *Rashba* accept it as valid.

HALAKHAH

leave and return later with only one of them holding it, the law is as follows: If the person now holding the garment states that the other person conceded his claim, and the other litigant maintains that he rented the garment to the first person, then 'the burden of proof rests upon the claimant' not holding the garment, and the claimant holding the garment may keep it." (According to the conclusion reached by the Gemara.) (*Shulḥan Arukh, Ḥoshen Mishpat* 138:8.)

TRANSLATION AND COMMENTARY

כֵּיוָן דְּאָמַר [1]Two rulings are possible here: (1) There is an authoritative anonymous statement by **one of the Sages** in a Mishnah (*Kiddushin* 28b) who **said, "One's declaration to the Most High,** i.e., the verbal dedication of an item to the Temple, **is considered like delivering an object to an ordinary person** in a secular transaction." In other words, verbal dedication automatically effects a valid transfer of property to the Temple in the same way that the physical transfer of an object is effective in secular transactions. Thus, from the moment the verbal dedication has been made, the object is immediately considered to belong to the Temple. In our case, where one of the claimants to the garment dedicated it, do we say that he **is considered as if he has** physically **seized** the article, and hence we validate his act of dedication? [2]**Or** (2) do we **perhaps** say: **Now, at any rate, he has not** yet **seized it,** and the garment is not yet sufficiently in his possession to enable him to dedicate it. [3]This latter argument is strengthened by what **is written** in Leviticus 27:14: **"And when a man shall sanctify his house to be dedicated...,"** from which the Sages deduced: **Just as his house is in his possession, so too everything** that he wishes to dedicate **must be in his possession** for the dedication to be effective. [4]This would **exclude the present case, where** the garment that he wishes to dedicate **is not in his possession,** as it has not yet been seized; and thus dedication performed prior to seizure would not be valid.

תָּא שְׁמַע [5]To resolve this question, the Talmud now proposes: **Come and hear** about an incident that has a bearing on this question: **There was a certain** [6B] **bathhouse over whose ownership two people were quarrelling.** [6]**One said: "It is mine," and the other said: "It is mine."** Then **one of** the disputants **arose and dedicated** the bathhouse to the Temple. [7]**Rav Ḥananyah, Rav Oshaya, and all the Sages stopped using it,** since they were

[1]כֵּיוָן דְּאָמַר מָר: "אֲמִירָתוֹ לַגָּבוֹהַּ כִּמְסִירָתוֹ לְהֶדְיוֹט דָּמֵי", כְּמַאן דִּתְקָפָה דָּמֵי. [2]אוֹ דִּלְמָא הָשְׁתָּא מִיהָא הָא לָא תְּקָפָה, [3]וּכְתִיב: "וְאִישׁ כִּי יַקְדִּישׁ אֶת בֵּיתוֹ קֹדֶשׁ וגו׳". מָה בֵּיתוֹ בִּרְשׁוּתוֹ, אַף כֹּל בִּרְשׁוּתוֹ, [4]לְאַפּוּקֵי הַאי, דְּלָא בִּרְשׁוּתוֹ. [5]תָּא שְׁמַע: דְּהַהִיא [6B] מַסּוּתָא דַּהֲווֹ מִנְצוּ עֲלָהּ בֵּי תְרֵי. [6]הַאי אָמַר: "דִּידִי הוּא", וְהַאי אָמַר: "דִּידִי הוּא". קָם חַד מִינַּיְיהוּ אַקְדְּשָׁהּ. [7]פָּרְשִׁי מִינָּהּ רַב חֲנַנְיָה וְרַב אוֹשַׁעְיָא וְכוּלְּהוּ רַבָּנַן.

LITERAL TRANSLATION

[1]Since the master said, "His declaration to the Most High is equivalent to his handing over to an ordinary person," he is like one who has seized it. [2]Or perhaps now, at any rate, he has not seized it, [3]and it is written: "And when a man shall sanctify his house to be dedicated...." Just as his house is in his possession, so too everything [must be] in his possession, [4]to exclude this [case], where [the object dedicated] is not in his possession.

[5]Come [and] hear: That [there was] a certain [6B] bathhouse over which two people were quarrelling. [6]One said: "It is mine," and the other said: "It is mine." One of them arose and dedicated it. [7]Rav Ḥananyah, Rav Oshaya, and all the Sages stopped using it.

RASHI

הא לא תקפה — ואין יכול להקדישה. **מסותא** = מרחץ. **פרשי מינה** — מלרחוץ בה. ואמר ליה רב אושעיא לרבה גרסינן.

NOTES

פָּרְשִׁי מִינָּהּ רַבָּנַן The Sages stopped using it. In various cases the Sages suspected that a certain action might be forbidden, but this suspicion was not so grave as to make them forbid it to everyone. But the Sages themselves were extremely scrupulous, and refrained not only from things that were clearly forbidden but also from things that were in doubt or suspected of being forbidden. Not only did the Sages have to possess great knowledge of the Torah, they also had to set an example by their behavior. Many of the Sages were strict with themselves but lenient regarding others.

פָּרְשִׁי מִינָּהּ רַבָּנַן The Sages stopped using it. Some commentators ask: Perhaps the Sages stopped using the bathhouse because the person who dedicated it was entitled to at least half of it in any event, and since it was impossible to determine precisely which half belonged to him, the entire bathhouse had to be treated as if it had been dedicated! Their answer: Since it is not clear which part of the bathhouse belongs to each of the litigants, we automatically assume that whenever someone enters it, he is benefiting from that part of it that has *not* been dedicated. Thus, if the act of dedication did not apply to both halves of the bathhouse, the Sages would not have had any reason to

HALAKHAH

אֲמִירָתוֹ לַגָּבוֹהַּ כִּמְסִירָתוֹ לְהֶדְיוֹט One's declaration to the Most High.... "If someone says, I hereby dedicate this object to the Temple [or to charity], he cannot retract his word, even though the object has not physically left his possession. For 'one's verbal declaration to the Most High has the same effect as the physical handing over of an object to an ordinary person.'" (*Rambam, Sefer Kinyan, Hilkhot Mekhirah* 9:1; *Shulḥan Arukh, Yoreh De'ah* 258:13.)

הַקְדָּשַׁת דָּבָר שֶׁאֵינוֹ בִּרְשׁוּתוֹ The dedication of something that is not in one's possession. "A person cannot dedicate an object that is not in his possession." (Even the owner of an item cannot dedicate it while it is in the possession of another person.) (Ibid., 4.)

[1]וַאֲמַר לֵיהּ רַב אוֹשַׁעְיָא לְרַבָּה: ״כִּי אָזְלַתְּ קַמֵּיהּ דְּרַב חִסְדָּא לְכַפְרִי, בְּעֵי מִינֵּיהּ. [2]כִּי אֲתָא לְסוּרָא, אֲמַר לֵיהּ רַב הַמְנוּנָא: מַתְנִיתִין הִיא: [3]״סְפֵק בְּכוֹרוֹת, אֶחָד בְּכוֹר אָדָם וְאֶחָד בְּכוֹר בְּהֵמָה, בֵּין טְהוֹרִים בֵּין טְמֵאִים, הַמּוֹצִיא מֵחֲבֵירוֹ עָלָיו הָרְאָיָה״. [4]וְתָנֵי עֲלָהּ: ״אֲסוּרִים בְּגִיזָּה וּבַעֲבוֹדָה״.

LITERAL TRANSLATION

[1]Then Rav Oshaya said to Rabbah: "When you go to Rav Ḥisda to Kafri, pose the problem to him." [2]When he came to Sura, Rav Hamnuna said to him: It is a Mishnah: [3]"Doubtful firstborn, whether it is (lit., 'one') a human firstborn or a whether it is (lit., 'one') a firstborn animal, whether clean or unclean, whoever seeks to take [property] away from his fellow, upon him is the [burden of] proof." [4]And it was taught concerning this: "They are forbidden to be sheared or worked."

RASHI

לכפרי — שם מקום. **כי אתא לסורא** — כשהיה עובר דרך סורא לילך לכפרי. **ספק בבורות** — כגון בהמה שילדה, ואין ידוע אם בכרה כבר אם לא. **אחד בכור אדם** — כגון שהפילה אמו לפניו ספק דבר הפוטר בבכורה, ספק רוח הפילה, והבא אחריו בכור. **בין טמאין** — כגון פטר חמור. **המוציא מחבירו כו׳** — קא סלקא דעתך: אם ביד ישראל הן — הוי כהן מוציא מחבירו עליו הראיה. ואם תקפה כהן, ושתיק ישראל והדר צווח — הוי ישראל מוציא מחבירו. **אסורין בגיזה ועבודה** — מספק, שמא קדשים הם.

TRANSLATION AND COMMENTARY

not sure whether the act of dedication was valid, and it is prohibited to derive benefit from an object dedicated to the Temple.

וַאֲמַר לֵיהּ [1]**Rav Oshaya then said to Rabbah: "When you go to** study with **Rav Ḥisda in** the town of **Kafri, pose the problem to him."** [2]**When** Rabbah **arrived in Sura** on his way to Kafri and recounted this incident, **Rav Hamnuna said to him,** "The answer to your question may be found in a **Mishnah**. For the Mishnah (*Teharot* 4:12) says as follows: [3]If **there is a doubt whether something** or someone **is a firstborn,** regardless of **whether it is a human firstborn or a firstborn animal, whether** the animal **is a clean,** kosher animal (e.g., a cow) **or an unclean**, non-kosher animal (e.g., a donkey), the law is that **whoever wants to take property away from someone else, must prove his claim.**" Rav Hamnuna understands this Mishnah as meaning that the burden of proof rests upon the claimant, whoever he is, whether he is an Israelite or a priest. Hence, if an animal about which there exists a doubt as to whether it is a firstborn or not is owned by an ordinary Jew (not a priest), it may not be taken away from him by a priest without proof that it is in fact a firstborn (according to Biblical law, a firstborn animal is given to a priest; see notes). But if the priest has taken possession of the animal by force, and its owner was silent at the time the priest seized it but later cried out in protest, the owner must bring proof that the animal is not a firstborn in order to take it back from the priest. [4]**And it was taught** in a Baraita **concerning** this very Mishnah: "These animals of doubtful firstborn status **may not be sheared or used for work**," like all firstborn animals, regardless of who possesses them.

NOTES

stop using it. The fact that the Sages did in fact stop using it would, therefore, imply that they thought that the dedication might have been effective for the entire bathhouse. (*Shittah Mekubbetzet*.)

סְפֵק בְּכוֹרוֹת **Animals of doubtful firstborn status**. The commentaries have noted a fundamental difficulty with the comparison offered by Rav Hamnuna between the bathhouse and firstborn animals. A bathhouse is landed property and a firstborn animal is movable property. Different rules apply to these two types of possessions.

Among the resolutions they offer are: (1) The case of the bathhouse differs from most disputes involving landed property since neither litigant has proof of title. Hence, the principle כָּל דְּאַלִּים גָּבַר — "Whoever is strong enough to take it into his possession prevails" — applies. But why compare a bathhouse to an animal that may possibly be a firstborn? Surely in the latter instance, the animal's owner should be awarded undisputed possession unless a priest can prove that the animal was, in fact, a firstborn! In reply to this it may be claimed that, since the sanctity of the firstborn is

HALAKHAH

סְפֵק בְּכוֹר אָדָם **If it is not certain whether someone was a firstborn**. "If it is not certain (because of a possible previous miscarriage) that a child is a firstborn, his father is not obliged to redeem him; for whenever someone (in this case, the priest) seeks to take something from someone else, the burden of proof rests on him." (*Shulḥan Arukh, Yoreh De'ah* 305:13.)

סְפֵק בְּכוֹר בְּהֵמָה טְהוֹרָה **A doubtful firstborn of a clean (kosher) animal**. "If it is not certain whether a kosher animal is a firstborn, its owner need not give it to a priest. Instead, he may keep it until it becomes blemished and hence unfit for sacrifice, and then he may eat it. Nevertheless, it may not be sheared or used for work." (Ibid., 315:1.)

סְפֵק פֶּטֶר חֲמוֹר **A doubtful firstborn of an ass**. "If it is not certain whether an ass is a firstborn, the owner sets aside a lamb in order to redeem it (as if the ass were definitely a firstborn). But the owner may keep the lamb, since the law is that, whenever someone (in this case, the priest) seeks to take something away from someone else, the burden of proof rests on him." (Ibid., 321:13.)

BACKGROUND

כַּפְרִי *Kafri*. A town in Babylonia approximately 10 miles south of Sura. Apparently, this town had a Jewish community from an early period, as the exilarchs (the leaders of Babylonian Jewry) resided there for a certain period of time. Rav's family (which was of distinguished pedigree) came from Kafri, and it seems that Rav Hisda, too, grew up in this town.

The incident relating to the bathhouse in our passage probably took place in Pumbedita, where Rabbah lived, and so, on his way to Kafri from Pumbedita, he passed through Sura.

CONCEPTS

בְּכוֹרוֹת **A firstborn animal**. The Torah states (Numbers 18:7-18) that male firstborn cattle, sheep and goats belonging to a Jew must be given to a priest and, if unblemished, sacrificed on the altar in the Temple. The remaining meat (apart from those portions of the sacrifice that are burned on the altar) may then be eaten by the priest and the members of his household. If a firstborn animal becomes blemished, it is thereby disqualified as a sacrifice. Nevertheless, it still retains some sanctity and it must still be given to a priest. These laws do not apply to the firstborn of non-kosher animals. However, a firstborn ass must be redeemed with a lamb, and the lamb is then given to a priest who may use it as his private (secular) property. If the ass is not redeemed it must be killed; there is also a prohibition against benefiting from its flesh (see Exodus 13:13).

TERMINOLOGY

תָּנֵי עֲלָהּ. Lit., **it was taught concerning it,** i.e., the following Baraita was taught in reference to the Mishnah. A term used to introduce a Baraita which explains the Mishnah under discussion and in effect forms an integral part of it.

TRANSLATION AND COMMENTARY

וְהָא הָכָא [1]Basing himself on these statements, Rav Hamnuna now argues: **Surely here** it would seem that the Mishnah **is indicating that if a priest seizes** a doubtful firstling, **we do not take it away from him, for the Mishnah says: "Whoever wants to take property away from someone else,** whether priest or Israelite, **must prove his claim."** This shows, says Rav Hamnuna, that the Israelite may not take the animal back from the priest without proof that the animal is not a firstling. [2]And yet, from the Baraita taught in connection with this Mishnah, we learn that even **if** the priest **has not seized** the animal, "it **may not be sheared or used for work."** Thus it seems that anything which would be considered holy if seized by the priest, is already considered holy (at least to a certain extent) even before it has been seized. The same rule, says Rav Hamnuna, should also apply to the case of the bathhouse, and hence it would follow that the dedication of the bathhouse was valid.

אֲמַר לֵיהּ רַבָּה [3]**Rabbah said** in reply **to** Rav Hamnuna: This proof is not valid, because the two cases are not comparable. **You are speaking about the sanctity of a firstborn animal,** which is a special case. [4]**In fact I can say to you** that **if a priest seizes** an animal on the grounds that it may be a firstborn, **we do take it away from him** even if the original owner fails to protest immediately, because the priest's seizing of the animal cannot dispel our doubts as to its ownership. [5]**Even so,** an animal of doubtful firstborn status **may not be sheared or used for work** even before the priest's intervention, while it is still in the possession of the Israelite, **because sanctity that comes about by itself is different.** The sanctity of a firstling is inherent and independent of any act of consecration, and is unconnected to ownership of the animal. Since firstborn animals are not sanctified by a human act of dedication but automatically become holy when they are born, their sanctity is not a function of ownership. Thus, since we do not know whether or not this particular animal was a firstborn, it is forbidden to shear it or work with it so long as there remains a possibility that it is holy. The sanctity of the bathhouse, however, is strictly a function of ownership. Nothing, therefore, can be proved about the case of the bathhouse from this Mishnah.

[1]וְהָא הָכָא, דְּאָמַר: "תְּקָפוֹ כֹּהֵן", אֵין מוֹצִיאִין אוֹתוֹ מִיָּדוֹ, דְּקָתָנֵי: "הַמּוֹצִיא מֵחֲבֵירוֹ עָלָיו הָרְאָיָה", [2]וְכִי לֹא תְקָפוֹ "אֲסוּרִין בְּגִיזָּה וּבַעֲבוֹדָה". [3]אֲמַר לֵיהּ רַבָּה: קְדוּשַּׁת בְּכוֹר קָאָמְרַתְּ. [4]לְעוֹלָם אֵימָא לָךְ, תְּקָפוֹ כֹּהֵן, מוֹצִיאִין אוֹתוֹ מִיָּדוֹ, [5]וַאֲפִילּוּ הָכִי, אֲסוּרִים בְּגִיזָּה וּבַעֲבוֹדָה, דִּקְדוּשָּׁה הַבָּאָה מֵאֵלֶיהָ שָׁאנֵי.

LITERAL TRANSLATION

[1]Now surely here, where it states: "If a priest seized it," we do not take it away from him, for it teaches: "Whoever seeks to take [property] away from his fellow, upon him is the [burden of proof]," [2]and [even] if he has not seized it, "they are forbidden to be sheared or worked."

[3]Rabbah said to him: You are speaking about the sanctity of a firstborn [animal]. [4]In fact I can say to you, if a priest seized it, we do take it away from him, [5][but] even so, they are forbidden to be sheared or worked, because sanctity that comes about by itself is different.

RASHI

דקתני המוציא — משמע, בין כהן בין ישראל. **וכי לא תקפו** — חמור כח הקדש לאוסרן בגיזה ועבודה. שמע מינה: דאם תמצי לומר תקפו אין מוציאין אותו מידו — הקדישה מקודשת. **לעולם אימא לך** — גבי בכור, דאפילו תקפו כהן מוציאין אותו מידו — מסתמא בחזקת ישראל הן, ולעולם הכהן קרוי מוציא מחבירו. וטעמא דגיזה ועבודה — לאו משום דיהא לכהן שום כח בהן, דתפשוט מינה להיכא דאי תקפו אין מוציאין מידו — הקדישה הוי הקדש. אלא הכא משום איסור ספק גיזת קדשים. וקדושה הבאה מאליה שאני, שאם בכור הוא — מאליו קדוש, ואיכא לספוקי בהכי. אבל גבי מסותא, דאין קדושה באה אלא על פיו של זה — אימא לך דאפילו אם תמצי לומר תקפה אין מוציאין, הקדישה בלא תקפה — לא הוי הקדש, דאין יכול להקדיש דבר שאינו ברשותו.

CONCEPTS

אֲסוּרִים בְּגִיזָּה וּבַעֲבוֹדָה They are forbidden to be sheared or worked. Animals that have been consecrated may not be used for any purpose, and their use for secular purposes may even be considered misappropriation of consecrated property (מְעִילָה). Furthermore, animals that had at one time been consecrated and were then rejected because of a blemish (פְּסוּלֵי הַמּוּקְדָּשִׁין) are still subject to certain prohibitions: one may not derive benefit from them while they are alive by shearing their wool or by working them, although their meat may be eaten after they are slaughtered. This prohibition against shearing such animals and working them also applies to animals whose consecrated status is doubtful.

NOTES

independent of human activity, and there is a possibility that this animal is a firstling, the animal may be considered as if it is already in the possession of a priest, thus making it comparable to the case of the bathhouse (*Rashba*). (2) The Talmud had no intention of making an exact comparison between the two instances. Rather, it is asking a question of a different nature: Is the power of *hekdesh* (dedication) only equal to that of the person who wishes to dedicate the article? If so, just as the person himself does not acquire ownership of the article until he takes it into his physical possession, he cannot dedicate it until then either. Or is the power of *hekdesh* greater than that of the person himself? In which case the article may become dedicated, even though the person dedicating it does not possess it. The case of the firstborn animal appears to support the second view. In this case, even though the priest does not possess the animal, it is considered holy and cannot be sheared or used for work (*Rosh*).

קְדוּשָּׁה הַבָּאָה מֵאֵלֶיהָ שָׁאנֵי Inherent sanctity is different. Rav Hamnuna, too, appreciates that sanctity that comes

HALAKHAH

תְּקָפוֹ כֹּהֵן A kosher animal of doubtful firstborn status that was seized by a priest is not taken away from him, in accordance with the ruling of Rav Hamnuna (*Rambam*). Even though Rabbah seems to refute Rav Hamnuna's proof,

1 אֲמַר לֵיהּ רַב חֲנַנְיָה לְרַבָּה: תַּנְיָא דִּמְסַיֵּיעַ לָךְ: הַסְּפֵיקוֹת נִכְנָסִין לַדִּיר לְהִתְעַשֵּׂר. 2 וְאִי סָלְקָא דַּעְתָּךְ תְּקָפוֹ כֹּהֵן, אֵין מוֹצִיאִין אוֹתוֹ מִיָּדוֹ, אַמַּאי נִכְנָסִין לַדִּיר? 3 נִמְצָא זֶה פּוֹטֵר מָמוֹנוֹ בְּמָמוֹנוֹ שֶׁל כֹּהֵן! 4 אֲמַר לֵיהּ אַבַּיֵי: אִי מִשּׁוּם הָא, לֹא תְּסַיְּיעֵיהּ לְמָר. הָכָא בְּמַאי עָסְקִינַן? כְּגוֹן דְּלֵית לֵיהּ אֶלָּא תִּשְׁעָה וְהוּא, 5 דְּמַה

LITERAL TRANSLATION

1 Rav Ḥananyah said to Rabbah: [A Baraita] was taught that supports you: "[Animals] of doubtful status enter the stall to be tithed." 2 And if you assume [that if] a priest seized it, we do not take it away from him, why do they enter the stall? 3 It turns out that this [man] is exempting his money with the money of the priest!

4 Abaye said to him: If [you argue] on the basis of this, you will not support my teacher (lit., "the master"). With what are we dealing here? For instance, where he only has nine [other animals] and this one. 5 For

TRANSLATION AND COMMENTARY

אֲמַר לֵיהּ רַב חֲנַנְיָה לְרַבָּה 1 **Rav Ḥananyah said to Rabbah: There is a Baraita** (see *Bekhorot* 9a and 11a) **that supports your** viewpoint that Rav Hamnuna's inference is wrong and if a priest seizes an animal of doubtful firstborn status, he is not permitted to keep it: "**Animals of doubtful** firstborn **status enter the stall to be tithed**" together with the other animals to be tithed. The newly born animals in a herd (cattle and sheep) are counted at certain fixed times of the year, and every tenth animal is designated "animal tithe" (מַעְשַׂר בְּהֵמָה). These tithed animals, if unblemished, are sacrificed in the Temple, and their meat is eaten by their owners. Now, if an animal was definitely a firstborn and due to be given to the priest, it could not be included in the owner's flock for the purpose of tithing. But the Baraita tells us that animals of doubtful firstborn status are treated exactly like the owner's other animals and *are* tithed.

וְאִי סָלְקָא דַּעְתָּךְ 2 Rav Ḥananyah tries to prove from this Tannaitic statement about animals of doubtful status that if a priest seizes such an animal, the seizure has no legal effect and the animal is returned to its owner: Now, **if you assume that** the law is that **if a priest has seized** an animal that is of doubtful firstborn status, **we do not take it away from him,** because he has partial title to it, **why** does the Baraita just quoted stipulate that animals of doubtful firstborn status **enter the stall** to be tithed? 3 Surely if these animals are tithed together with the others, it may **turn out** that the owner has **exempted his** own **property** from the obligation of animal tithe **by using the property of the priest!** It is possible that this animal is in fact a firstborn and by right belongs to the priest. If the Israelite sets it aside as tithe, he will have freed himself from the obligation of tithing by using an animal belonging to the priest. Such tithing is invalid, and the animals must be tithed again. Rav Ḥananyah concludes from this Tannaitic statement that, since such tithing is permitted, a priest in fact has no legal rights to an animal of doubtful status; and therefore, if he seizes it, we take it away from him.

אֲמַר לֵיהּ אַבַּיֵי 4 **Abaye said to** Rav Ḥananyah: **If** you wish to argue **on the basis of this** Tannaitic statement, **you will not be supporting** my **teacher**, the scholar Rabbah, as your reasoning is invalid: **With what are we dealing here** in the Tannaitic statement? With a case, **for instance, where** the owner of the animals being tithed has only **nine** other animals **and this one,** the lamb of doubtful status, in the stall. 5 In that case,

TERMINOLOGY

תַּנְיָא דִּמְסַיֵּיעַ לָךְ **[What was] taught supports you.** A term used by one Amora to introduce a Baraita which supports the view of another Amora.

אִי מִשּׁוּם הָא, לֹא תְּסַיְּיעֵיהּ **If on the basis of that, you will not support my teacher.** This expression is used to introduce the rejection of a quotation introduced in support of an argument, and it means, "If you want to introduce proof from this source, it is unacceptable. Your supposed proof is unconvincing, because it raises a difficulty or because it can easily be rejected."

RASHI

דמסייע לך — דגבי ספק בכורות, אם תקפה כהן — מוציאין מידו. **הספיקות** — לקמן מפרש: בספק פדיון פטר חמור, דמפריש עליו טלה לאפקועי איסורא, והוא לעצמו — שאין צריך ליתנו לכהן, שהמוציא מחבירו עליו הראיה. ופדיון פטר חמור בר עשורי הוא; אם יש לכהן עשרה פטרי חמורים שנפלו לו מבית אבי אמו ישראל — מפריש עליהם עשרה שיין, ומעשרן, והן שלו. הלכך, ספק פדיון פטר חמור ביד ישראל — נכנס לדיר עם שאר טלאים שלו להתעשר, ואי נפקא בעשירי — ליפוק. **ואי סלקא דעתך** — יש לכהן צד זכייה בו — נמצא זה, אם יצא בעשירי, פוטר ממונו בממונו של כהן. **למר** — רבה, שהוא רבו.

NOTES

about through man's activity (e.g., the dedication of the bathhouse) differs from sanctity brought about by God (the sanctity of the firstborn). However, he maintains that unless *hekdesh* had greater power than an individual's right of ownership, the firstborn would not be considered sacred. Its status would instead be decided according to the majority, and most animals are not firstborn. It is only because the priest has seized the animal, and it is at present in his possession, that we even consider the possibility of allowing him to keep it (*Pnei Yehoshua, Tummim*).

HALAKHAH

this refutation is not considered conclusive (*Rashba* explaining *Rambam*'s ruling). However, *Rema* (followed by *Shakh)* rules that the animal is taken away from the priest in such a case, in accordance with the view of most of the Rishonim (*Tosafot, Ra'avad, Rosh*). (*Shulḥan Arukh, Yoreh De'ah* 315:1.)

נַפְשָׁךְ: [1]אִי בַּר חִיּוּבָא הוּא, שַׁפִּיר קָא מְעַשֵּׂר; אִי לָאו בַּר חִיּוּבָא הוּא, תִּשְׁעָה לָאו בַּר עִשּׂוּרֵי נִינְהוּ! [2]הֲדַר אָמַר אַבָּיֵי: לָאו מִילְּתָא הִיא דַּאֲמַרִי, דִּסְפֵיקָא לָאו בַּר עִשּׂוּרֵי הִיא, דִּתְנַן: [3]"קָפַץ אֶחָד מִן הַמְּנוּיִין לְתוֹכָן, כּוּלָּן פְּטוּרִין"! [4]וְאִי סָלְקָא דַּעְתָּךְ סְפֵיקָא בָּעֵי עִשּׂוּרֵי, לְעַשֵּׂר

LITERAL TRANSLATION

either way: [1]If he is subject to the obligation [of tithing], he tithes correctly; if he is not subject to the obligation [of tithing], nine are not subject to tithing! [2]Abaye reconsidered [and] said: What I said has no merit (lit., "it is nothing, what I said"), for a doubtful [animal] is not subject to tithing, for we have learned: [3]"[If] one of the counted [animals] jumped [back] among [the other animals], they are all exempt!" [4]And if you assume that a doubtful [animal] must be tithed, he should tithe

TRANSLATION AND COMMENTARY

whichever way you look at it, the owner's action was justified: (1) [1]**If**, on the one hand, the animal of doubtful status **is subject to the obligation of tithing,** because it is in fact not a firstborn, then the owner has ten animals to tithe, and in giving this animal as animal tithe **he is tithing** his flock **correctly**, for this animal does not belong to the priest. (2) **If**, on the other hand, this animal **is not subject to the obligation of tithing,** because it really is a firstborn, it does not belong to the Israelite. Hence he owns only nine animals, and his tithing is without significance, since **nine** animals **do not need to be tithed!** For the obligation to give animal tithe applies only if there are at least ten untithed animals in the stall. Here the tenth animal belongs not to the owner but to the priest, so that the other nine need not be tithed. In this case, by designating the tenth animal as animal tithe, the owner gains no benefit from property not his own.

הֲדַר אָמַר אַבָּיֵי [2]**Abaye reconsidered and said: What I said** previously **has no merit.** We cannot explain the Baraita as dealing only with the special case of nine animals plus the one animal of doubtful firstborn status. **For** we know that, in general, **an animal of doubtful status is not subject to** animal **tithe** at all, **as it says in the** following **Mishnah** (*Bekhorot* 58b): [3]"**If** a person was counting his lambs in order to tithe them, and had not yet counted off ten when **a lamb that had** already **been counted jumped back** into the stall and became mixed up **among the others**, which had not yet been tithed, **all** the lambs, both those inside the stall and those outside it that have already been counted, **are exempt** from being tithed. Since each lamb still in the stall could be the one that had been counted previously (and would then be exempt from the obligation of animal tithe), all the animals are considered of doubtful status and exempted.

וְאִי סָלְקָא דַּעְתָּךְ [4]**Now if you assume that an animal of doubtful status must be tithed,** as Abaye had previously claimed, then we can also argue in this case that, **whichever way** you look at it, the owner **should tithe** the

RASHI

אם בר חיובא הוא — אי האי גברא בר חיובא הוא לעשורי, שפדיון זה לאו פדיון פטר חמור שלו הוא — הרי יש לו עשרה טלאים, וחייב לעשרן — שפיר קמעשר. **אי לאו בר חיובא הוא** — שפדיון זה של כהן לא פטר ליה מידי, דתשעה לאו בני עשורי נינהו. **לאו מילתא היא דאמרי** — דודאי סייעתא היא למר. דאי הוה לד זכייה לכהן ביה מספק, ואשתכח דכל הני טלאים ספק חייבים במעשר ספק אין חייבים — מספיקא לא הוי צריך לעשורינהו, כדקאמרת לעשורי ממה נפשך, דכל ספק חייב ספק פטור — לאו בני עשורי נינהו, ואפילו היכא דאיכא למימר ממה נפשך. **קפץ אחד מן המנויין בו'** — היה מעשר טלאים והתחיל למנות כשהיו יוצאים בפתח הדיר, ועד שלא הגיע לעשרה קפץ אחד מן המנויין לתוך הדיר, ואינו מכירו. **כולן פטורין** — בין אותן שיצאו, בין אותן שבתוך הדיר, ואפילו הן אלף שיצאו פטורין, (שהם) מנין הראוי, שכשמנאן היה המנין ראוי להשלים ולבא לכלל מעשר. ואמרינן בבכורות והכי מייתינן לה: מנין הראוי פוטר. ואותן שבתוך הדיר פטורין משום זה המעורב, ד"כל אשר יעבור תחת השבט" אמר רחמנא, ולא שעבר כבר. וכל חד מינייהו ספק כבר עבר הוא. **ואי סלקא דעתך ספיקא** — דאיכא למימר ממה נפשך בעי לעשורי, שמא יעשה כתורה וכמצוה — נעשרינהו להנך דבתוך הדיר ממה נפשך: כל עשרה שיוצאין, אם מעשר שלהן בר חיוב וכראוי הוא, כגון שלא יצא אותו הקופץ לתוכן — שפיר קא מעשר.

TERMINOLOGY

מִמָּה נַפְשָׁךְ **In either case, no matter what...** (lit., "from whatever you desire"). An expression used by the Gemara to indicate an unacceptable dilemma: "No matter which side you take or possibility you favor, the same unacceptable conclusion follows."

BACKGROUND

מַעֲשַׂר בְּהֵמָה **Animal tithe.** This tithe had to be separated from the newborn cattle, sheep and goats born every year. The animals were herded into a stall and then released one by one and counted. Every tenth animal was marked with red paint, and dedicated to the Temple. If the animal was unblemished, it was brought to Jerusalem, where it was offered in the Temple and its meat was eaten by its owner. If, after tithing, a number of animals were left over (e.g., if someone had fifteen sheep, the last five would be left over), these had to be tithed in the following "tithing season," together with the new animals being tithed then. (Every year, there were three such tithing seasons.)

NOTES

קָפַץ אֶחָד... כּוּלָּן פְּטוּרִין **If one jumps back in, all are exempted**. *Tosafot* asks: Why is the animal that has already been counted not "nullified" by the animals that have not yet been counted (following the Halakhic principle of בִּיטּוּל בְּרוֹב — "nullification by majority")? Thus, *all* the animals remaining in the stall should need to be tithed, including the one that had been counted previously! *Rosh* answers that the tithing of animals has a special characteristic: Since the Torah (Leviticus 27:32) speaks of "the *tenth* animal," only an animal that was definitely the tenth to be counted may

HALAKHAH

קָפַץ אֶחָד הַמְּנוּיִין **If one of the animals that had already been counted jumped back in.** "If someone was tithing his animals and counting them one by one as they left the stall, and one of the animals that had already been counted jumped back in among the others that had not yet been counted, all the animals, both those already counted and those still in the stall, are exempt from the obligation of animal tithe," in accordance with the statement of the Mishnah cited here. (*Rambam, Sefer Korbanot, Hilkhot Bekhorot* 8:14.)

מִמַּה נַפְשָׁךְ; [1]דְּאִי בַּר חִיּוּבָא הוּא, שַׁפִּיר מְעַשֵּׂר, [2]וְאִי לָאו בַּר חִיּוּבָא הוּא, נִפְטַר ״בְּמִנְיָן הָרָאוּי״. [3]דְּאָמַר רָבָא: ״מִנְיָן הָרָאוּי״ פּוֹטֵר.

[7A] [4]אֶלָּא מַאי אִית לָךְ לְמֵימַר? [5]עֲשִׂירִי וַדַּאי אָמַר רַחֲמָנָא, וְלֹא עֲשִׂירִי סָפֵק. [6]הָכָא נַמִי עֲשִׂירִי וַדַּאי אָמַר רַחֲמָנָא, וְלֹא עֲשִׂירִי סָפֵק.

LITERAL TRANSLATION

[the group of remaining animals] either way; [1]for if it is subject to obligation, he tithes it justifiably, [2]and if it is not subject to obligation, [the animals] are exempted through a "count properly begun," [3]for Rava said: "A count properly begun" exempts.

[7A] [4]But what can you say? [5]The Torah said: A definite tenth [animal], and not a tenth [animal] of doubtful status. [6]Here too the Torah said: A definite tenth [animal], and not a tenth [animal] of doubtful status.

TRANSLATION AND COMMENTARY

animals remaining in the stall. [1]The argument should be as follows: (1) **If**, on the one hand, a particular group of ten animals **is subject to the obligation** of being tithed, because the previously counted animal is not among them, then the owner who sets aside the tenth animal **as tithe does so justifiably!** (2) [2]**If**, on the other hand, a group of ten animals **is not subject to the obligation** of being tithed, because it contains the animal that has already been counted, **the** nine other **animals should be exempted because** they were part of **"a count properly begun"!** The principle of "a count properly begun" (מִנְיָן הָרָאוּי) states that, if some of a group of ten animals being tithed have already left the stall and been counted, and then one of the other animals still in the stall waiting to be counted dies, so that the group now comprises only nine animals, those animals that have already left the stall and been counted need not be counted again and are exempt from being tithed. Even though no animal has been designated to serve as animal tithe for them, they need not be tithed at a later date, because at the time that they were counted there were sufficient animals in the stall subject to tithe, and they are, therefore, considered to have correctly completed the tithing process. Those animals, however, that are still in the stall and have not yet been counted must be counted again at the next session later in the year. [3]**For Rava said, "A counting properly begun" exempts** those animals that have been counted from being tithed again, and they need not be counted again at the next tithing session.

אֶלָּא מַאי אִית לָךְ לְמֵימַר [7A] [4]Rather, Abaye continues, **what can you say** to explain why all the animals in the stall are not tithed here in any case? [5]The answer, says Abaye, is because **the Torah said** (Leviticus 27:32) that only **an animal** that was **definitely "the tenth"** must be tithed, **and not a tenth animal of doubtful status.** In the case in the Mishnah cited by Abaye of an already tithed animal jumping back into the stall, a doubt exists with regard to each of the animals in the stall that it is the animal that jumped back in. Thus all of them are now of doubtful status and none of them can be tithed. [6]**Here too,** in Rav Ḥananyah's Tannaitic statement, since we see that an animal of doubtful firstborn status is permitted to enter the stall to be tithed together with the other animals, the reason has to be because it is considered the owner's indisputable property. If the priest had any right to such an animal, it would never be permitted to enter the stall to be tithed, because its status would then be doubtful, and the principle stated above would surely be applied, namely that **the Torah said: A definite tenth animal** is subject to tithe **and not a tenth animal of doubtful status.** Thus it is clear that Rav Ḥananyah's support of Rabbah is justified, that a priest who seized a doubtful firstborn has no right to keep it, and that any sanctity possessed by firstlings of doubtul status is not connected with any right of seizure.

RASHI

ואי לאו בר חיובא — כגון אותן עשרה שיצא זה לתוכן, ואין עשירי שלהן מעשר. **נפטרו** — מן המעשר. **במנין הראוי** — שכשמנה ״אחד״ ״שנים״ ״שלשה״ היו בדיר טלאים הרבה שהיו ראוין להשלים, ופוטרים מניינו. **דאמר רבא** — בבכורות (נט,א). **מנין הראוי פוטר** — היה לו עשרה טלאים ומנה חמש, ומת אחד מן שאינן מנוין — המנוין פטורין, ושאינן מנוין מצטרפין לגורן אחר, שיולדו לו טלאים עד שיגיע זמן הגורן ויצטרפם עם אלו. אבל המנוין פטורין במנין הראוי. ויליף לה מ״אשר יעבור״ ולא שכבר עבר, דמשעבר תחת השבט ולא עלה בידו לעשר — שוב אינו מעבירו פעם אחרת כשיולדו לו טלאים לצרף עמהם. **אלא מאי אית לך למימר** — למה לא חייבוהו לעשר ממה נפשך. **עשירי ודאי** — הצריך הכתוב לעשר, ולא הצריך לעשר את הספק. וכל עשירי שבכאן ספק הן, שאפילו יצא הפטור בחמישי — שוב אין העשירי קרוי עשירי אלא תשיעי, שהפטור אינו מן המנין.

NOTES

be given as animal tithe. Since there is now a doubt about each individual animal remaining in the stall, as to whether it may be the animal already counted and exempted, none of these animals can now be tithed.

HALAKHAH

מִנְיָן הָרָאוּי פּוֹטֵר "A count properly begun" exempts. "If someone is tithing his sheep, and one of the sheep inside the stall dies, the sheep that have already been counted are exempt from the obligation of animal tithe, for 'a count properly begun' exempts. However, the sheep inside the stall waiting to be counted must be tithed later, when the next tithing season arrives." (*Rambam, Sefer Korbanot, Hilkhot Bekhorot* 8:10)

[1]אֲמַר לֵיהּ רַב אַחָא מִדִּפְתִּי לְרָבִינָא: מַאי ״סְפֵיקוֹת״? [2]אִילֵימָא סְפֵק בְּכוֹרוֹת, ״יִהְיֶה קֹדֶשׁ״ אָמַר רַחֲמָנָא, וְלֹא שֶׁכְּבָר קָדוֹשׁ.

[3]אֶלָּא, סְפֵק פִּדְיוֹן פֶּטֶר חֲמוֹר, [4]וְכִדְרַב נַחְמָן, דְּאָמַר רַב נַחְמָן אָמַר רַבָּה בַּר אֲבוּהּ: [5]יִשְׂרָאֵל שֶׁיֵּשׁ לוֹ עֲשָׂרָה סְפֵק פִּטְרֵי חֲמוֹר בְּתוֹךְ בֵּיתוֹ מַפְרִישׁ עֲלֵיהֶן עֲשָׂרָה שֵׂיִין וּמְעַשְּׂרָן, וְהֵן שֶׁלּוֹ.

[6]מַאי הָוֵי עֲלָהּ דְּמַסּוּתָא? [7]תָּא שְׁמַע, דְּאָמַר רַבִּי חִיָּיא בַּר אָבִין: [8]הֲוָה עוּבְדָא בֵּי רַב חִסְדָּא, וְרַב חִסְדָּא בֵּי רַב הוּנָא,

LITERAL TRANSLATION

[1]Rav Aḥa of Difti said to Ravina: What are "animals of doubtful status"? [2]If you say: Doubtful firstborn, the Torah says [that the animal given as animal tithe] "shall be holy," and not what is already holy!

[3]Rather, [the statement is referring to lambs used for] redeeming asses of doubtful firstborn status, [4]in accordance with Rav Naḥman, for Rav Naḥman said in the name of Rabbah bar Avuha: [5]An Israelite who has ten asses of doubtful firstborn status in his house separates ten lambs for them and tithes them, and they are his.

[6]What happened with regard to the [case of the] bathhouse? [7]Come [and] hear, for Rav Ḥiyya bar Avin said: [8][A similar] incident came before Rav Ḥisda, and Rav Ḥisda [brought it] before Rav Huna,

RASHI

מאי ספיקות – דאמרן לעיל ״הספקות נכנסין לדיר להתעשר״? **ספק פדיון פטר חמור** – טלה שהופרש על ספק פטר חמור, שאפילו הוא פטר חמור ודאי, אין בטלה זה של פדיון משום קדושה. **עשרה שיין** – לאפקועי איסורייהו למשרי להו בעבודה. **עובדא הוה בי רב חסדא ורב חסדא בי רב הונא** – מעשה היה ובא לפני רב חסדא, ורב חסדא הביאו לפני רב הונא.

TRANSLATION AND COMMENTARY

אֲמַר לֵיהּ רַב אַחָא [1]The Gemara now returns to consider the Tannaitic statement cited previously by Rav Ḥananyah: **Rav Aḥa of Difti said to Ravina: What is** the meaning of the expression "**animals of doubtful status**" used in the Baraita ("animals of doubtful status enter the stall to be tithed")? [2]**If you say** that the Baraita refers to kosher **animals whose firstborn status is in doubt**, such as lambs or calves that may or may not be the firstborn of their mothers, such an explanation is impossible, because a firstborn animal is automatically exempt from the requirement of being tithed, as **the Torah says** (Leviticus 27:32): "And concerning the tithe of the herd, or of the flock, of whatever passes under the rod, the tenth **shall be holy,**" and this last expression is understood as **not** including **what is already holy.** Now, since firstborn kosher animals are already considered to be holy, they cannot receive the sanctity of animal tithe and cannot be offered as animal tithe! But the Tannaitic statement quoted by Rav Ḥananyah was concerned only with the rightful ownership of the doubtful firstling, not with the possibility that it might be exempt from tithing because it is already holy!

אֶלָּא [3]**Rather,** we must say that **the statement is referring to lambs used for redeeming asses of doubtful firstborn status.** For, unlike kosher animals, firstborn asses are not holy, and the lambs used to redeem them have no sanctity, and the priest has nothing other than a monetary interest in them. Nevertheless, even if it is not certain whether a newborn ass was a firstling, it must be redeemed with a lamb as though it were definitely a firstling (see Exodus 13:13), though the lamb need not be given to the priest. [4]This is **in accordance with** the view of **Rav Naḥman, for Rav Naḥman said in the name of Rabbah bar Avuha:** [5]**An Israelite** (i.e., a non-priest) **who has ten asses of doubtful firstborn status in his house separates ten lambs for them** to redeem them, in case all were firstborn. The owner then **tithes** the lambs and designates one of them as animal tithe. **And** all the lambs **are his.** The lambs are not holy, and since the priest cannot prove that any of the lambs belong to him, the owner may keep all of them (the burden of proof rests upon the priest, since it is he who seeks to take property away from the owner of the lambs). Thus, Rav Naḥman's statement shows that sheep that have been designated to redeem asses that were not definitely firstborn are indeed subject to animal tithe.

מַאי הָוֵי [6]After these digressions the Talmud now returns to the earlier question about the bathhouse: **What happened with regard to the case of the bathhouse?** What is the law in this case? For the Talmud's discussion has yet to reach a definite conclusion about the matter!

תָּא שְׁמַע [7]The Gemara answers: **Come and hear what Rav Ḥiyya bar Avin said:** [8]**A similar incident came before Rav Ḥisda, and Rav Ḥisda brought it before Rav Huna, and he solved it on the basis of** the following

CONCEPTS

פִּדְיוֹן פֶּטֶר חֲמוֹר Redemption of a firstborn ass. The Torah states that a firstborn male ass must either be redeemed with a lamb, and the lamb given to the priest, or be destroyed (see Exodus 13:13). If the owner redeems the ass with a lamb, the lamb becomes the personal property of the priest and has no sanctity whatsoever. However, if it is not certain whether an ass was firstborn (for example, if the mother gave birth to twins, one male and the other female, and it is not known which one was born first), the owner need only designate a lamb to redeem the ass. He is then permitted to keep the lamb, as the burden of proof falls on the priest who seeks to claim the lamb as his own.

HALAKHAH

סְפֵק פִּדְיוֹן פֶּטֶר חֲמוֹר לְמַעֲשֵׂר An animal used to redeem an ass which may or may not be firstborn. "If someone has ten lambs, all of which have been designated to redeem asses which may or may not have been firstborn, these lambs are deemed *ḥullin* [secular, non-sacred property] in all respects; one of them is designated to serve as animal tithe, and the owner may keep the rest for himself." (*Rambam, Sefer Zeraim, Hilkhot Bikkurim* 12:23.)

BACKGROUND

מְסוּתָא מְטַּלְטְלִין A movable bathhouse. A bathhouse could be constructed of portable parts, such as benches, cupboards, and even washbasins. However, in antiquity there were also bathhouses, especially the large ones serving entire cities, which were completely permanent structures, with stone basins and benches, and the like.

TRANSLATION AND COMMENTARY

statement of **Rav Naḥman**: [1]"**All property that** a claimant **cannot take away from** the person at present in possession of it **by a decision of judges, if** the claimant **dedicates it** to the Temple, the dedication has no effect and the property **does not become holy.**" This would imply that, in the case of the bathhouse, the dedication is invalid since the person who dedicated it cannot prove that it belongs to him and cannot gain legal possession of it through appeal to the courts.

הָא יָכוֹל [2]However, a new problem now arises: Rav Naḥman's statement implies that, **if** the claimant **can** legally **take** the property **away** from the person at present in possession of it **by a decision of judges, and** [3]**if** the claimant **dedicated** such property to the Temple, the dedication *is* effective and the property **does become holy, even though** the claimant **has not** yet **gained possession** of it through legal process. [4]**But surely** this implication contradicts what **Rabbi Yoḥanan said: If someone has robbed another person of an article, and the** rightful **owner has not given up hope of recovering it,** [5]**neither** the robber nor the owner **may dedicate it:** [6]the robber, **because it is not his, and** the owner, **because it is not in his possession!** Now a stolen article clearly comes into the category of "property that a claimant can take away by appeal to Rabbinical judges," and yet from Rabbi Yoḥanan's statement it seems that only property that is actually in the physical possession of its rightful owner can be dedicated! Two things are required: ownership and possession.

מִי סָבְרַתְּ [7]The Talmud now resolves this apparent difficulty: **Do you think that we are dealing with a**

וּפְשָׁטָהּ מֵהָא דְּאָמַר רַב נַחְמָן: [1]כָּל מָמוֹן שֶׁאֵין יָכוֹל לְהוֹצִיאוֹ בְּדַיָּינִין, הִקְדִּישׁוֹ, אֵינוֹ קָדוֹשׁ. [2]הָא יָכוֹל לְהוֹצִיאוֹ בְּדַיָּינִין, [3]הִקְדִּישׁוֹ, קָדוֹשׁ, אַף עַל גַּב דְּלָא אַפְּקֵיהּ? [4]וְהָאָמַר רַבִּי יוֹחָנָן: גָּזַל, וְלֹא נִתְיָיאֲשׁוּ הַבְּעָלִים, [5]שְׁנֵיהֶם אֵינָם יְכוֹלִין לְהַקְדִּישׁוֹ, [6]זֶה לְפִי שֶׁאֵינָהּ שֶׁלּוֹ, וְזֶה לְפִי שֶׁאֵינָהּ בִּרְשׁוּתוֹ. [7]מִי סָבְרַתְּ בְּמַסּוּתָא מִטַּלְטְלִין

LITERAL TRANSLATION

and he solved it from this that Rav Naḥman said: [1]All money that one cannot take away [from someone else] by [a decision of] judges, if one dedicated it, it is not holy.

[2]But if he *can* take it away by [a decision of] judges, [3]if he dedicated it, would it be holy, even if he had not [yet] taken it away? [4]But surely Rabbi Yoḥanan said: If someone has robbed [another person of an article], and the owner has not given up hope [of recovering it], [5]the two of them cannot dedicate it, [6]this one because it is not his, and this one because it is not in his possession! [7]Do you think we are dealing with a movable bathhouse?

RASHI

שאינו יכול להוציאו כו׳ — והאי נמי דחזינן ליה דאין יכול להוציאו בדיינין, שאין לו ראיה בדבר — אין הקדישו קדוש. **הא יכול להוציאו כו׳** — בתמיה. **שאינו ברשותו** — והא סתם גזילה יכולין להוציאו בדיינין הוא! **במסותא מטלטלין** — כגון גיגית.

NOTES

שֶׁיָּכוֹל לְהוֹצִיאוֹ בְּדַיָּינִין If he can take it away by a decision of judges. Regarding movable property there is a distinction between things that are in a person's possession and those that are not. But regarding land and things attached to the land, which cannot be moved (the presence of a stranger on someone's property is not evidence that the property no longer belongs to its owner), a distinction must be made between property that belongs to a person so thoroughly that if someone else takes possession of it, the owner is capable of recovering it through the court, and between property that is his, but which, for various reasons (such as lack of proof or the inability of the court to impose its decision in the case) he cannot at present recover from the person now holding it.

לֹא נִתְיָיאֲשׁוּ הַבְּעָלִים The owner has not given up hope of recovering it. The fact that the owner of lost property has given up hope of finding it is an essential element in the transfer of ownership to the person who now possesses the object (whether or not he initially gained possession of it legally). As long as the owner believes he has some hope of recovering his property, his ownership of it is not annulled, even though the property is no longer in his possession. When the owner abandons hope, this is a form of relinquishing ownership (הֶפְקֵר), since he has decided that he has lost any possibility of recovering the object.

Some authorities hold that, for transfer of ownership of an object, it is enough if the owner has given up hope, whereas other authorities hold that a change in the object must have taken place, such as its removal to another domain, an alteration in its appearance, etc. From that moment the object becomes the property of the person who possesses it, even if it came into his possession illegally (for example, through theft). Although the person who now possesses the object becomes its owner, this does not relieve him of the obligation of compensating the original owner for the value of the object.

HALAKHAH

הֶקְדֵּשׁ דָּבָר שֶׁנִּגְזַל Consecrating stolen property. "If something has been stolen or robbed from its rightful owner, and the owner has not given up hope of recovering it, neither he nor the thief or robber may dedicate it." (*Shulḥan Arukh, Ḥoshen Mishpat* 354:6.)

TRANSLATION AND COMMENTARY

bathhouse that is **movable property?** [1]No. **We are** in fact **dealing with a bathhouse that is landed property.** [2]A movable bathhouse cannot be dedicated unless it is in the possesion of its rightful owner. But a bathhouse building is landed property; and in cases of landed property, **wherever** the rightful owner **can gain** legal **possession** of it **by a decision of judges,** there is no need for him to regain physical possession of the property, as **it is already** considered to be **in his possession.** For landed property is invariably considered to be in the possession of its rightful owner, no matter who happens to be using it at present.

תָּנֵי רַב תַּחֲלִיפָא [3]**Rav Taḥlifa from the West** (Eretz Israel) **taught** the following Baraita **before Rabbi Abbahu:** [4]**"If two people are firmly holding on to a garment**, each claiming ownership, **one takes up to where his hand reaches, and the other takes up to where his hand reaches, and** both claimants then **divide the remainder** of the garment **equally."** [5]On hearing this Baraita **Rabbi Abbahu gestured** upwards with his hand **to** Rav Taḥlifa, to indicate that the garment is **only** divided **after an oath** has been taken by both of the claimants.

אֶלָּא מַתְנִיתִין [6]The Gemara now asks: **But** then **our Mishnah, which states that** the claimants **divide the whole garment between them, and which does not state** that each claimant takes **"up to where his hand reaches..."** — [7]**under what circumstances** can we visualize it as **applying?**

עָסְקִינַן? [1]בְּמַסּוּתָא מְקַרְקְעֵי עָסְקִינַן, [2]דְּכִי יָכוֹל לְהוֹצִיאָהּ בְּדַיָּינִין, בִּרְשׁוּתֵיהּ קַיְּימָא.
[3]תָּנֵי רַב תַּחְלִיפָא בַּר מַעַרְבָא קַמֵּיהּ דְּרַבִּי אַבָּהוּ: [4]"שְׁנַיִם אֲדוּקִים בְּטַלִּית, זֶה נוֹטֵל עַד מָקוֹם שֶׁיָּדוֹ מַגַּעַת, וְזֶה נוֹטֵל עַד מָקוֹם שֶׁיָּדוֹ מַגַּעַת, וְהַשְּׁאָר חוֹלְקִין בְּשָׁוֶה". [5]מַחֲוֵי לֵיהּ רַבִּי אַבָּהוּ: וּבִשְׁבוּעָה.
[6]אֶלָּא מַתְנִיתִין, דְּקָתָנֵי דְּפָלְגִי בַּהֲדָדֵי, וְלָא קָתָנֵי "זֶה נוֹטֵל עַד מָקוֹם שֶׁיָּדוֹ מַגַּעַת", [7]הֵיכִי מַשְׁכַּחַת לָהּ?

LITERAL TRANSLATION

[1]We are dealing with a bathhouse that is landed property, [2]so that when he can take it away by [a decision of] judges, it is [already] in his possession!

[3]Rav Taḥlifa from the West taught before Rabbi Abbahu: [4]"[If] two people are firmly holding on to a garment, this one takes up to the place where his hand reaches, and this one takes up to the place where his hand reaches, and the remainder they divide equally." [5]Rabbi Abbahu gestured to him: And [only] with an oath.

[6]But our Mishnah, which teaches that they divide [the whole garment] between them, and which does not state "this one takes up to the place where his hand reaches," [7]under what circumstances does it apply (lit., "how can you find it")?

RASHI

מקרקעי — דכל היכא דאיתיה — ברשות מריה קיימא, דקרקע אינה נגזלת. ושפיר פשיטנא מהא, דאי הוה ליה ראיה עלה, הקדישו הקדש. בר מערבא = מארץ ישראל. מחוי ליה — מראה באצבעותיו כלפי מעלה.

TERMINOLOGY

מַעַרְבָא **The West**. Corresponding to the Hebrew מַעֲרָב "west" — this is the normal term for Eretz Israel used by the Sages of Babylonia. Geographically Eretz Israel is indeed to the west (to be precise, westsouthwest) of Babylonia. But there may be an additional reason for the use of this term: In the Temple the west side was the consecrated side, where the Divine Presence dwelt in the Sanctuary, and for that reason the Jews of Babylonia called Eretz Israel by that name.

NOTES

שְׁנַיִם אֲדוּקִים בְּטַלִּית... בִּשְׁבוּעָה **If two people are holding on to a garment... with an oath**. The commentators disagree over the interpretation of this passage (based on their different readings in the Gemara here, see *Tosafot* ד"ה מַחֲוֵי). According to some authorities, each claimant must take an oath about both the part he is holding and the part that he will be awarded after the garment is divided. Since the whole point of the Rabbinic decree requiring the oath is to prevent people from seizing other people's property, this reasoning applies to any part of the garment a claimant receives (*Tosafot, Rashba, Ra'avad* and others). Other authorities read the text as וְהַשְּׁאָר בִּשְׁבוּעָה — "and the rest of the garment is divided with an oath." Accordingly, the oath taken by the claimants only relates to that part of the garment that is *not* already in their possession (*Halakhot Gedolot, Rambam, Mordekhai*). However, even according to this view, it is still possible to impose an oath with regard to the part of the garment already in the claimant's possession, by means of גלגול שבועה — "an oath superimposed on another" (*Rambam, Meiri*).

הֵיכִי מַשְׁכַּחַת לָהּ... **Under what circumstances does it apply?** At first sight, there would seem to be an obvious

HALAKHAH

מַסּוּתָא מְקַרְקְעֵי **A bathhouse which is landed property**. "Ordinarily, a person cannot dedicate something that is not in his possession. However, if a person has been robbed of landed property, the rightful owner, even before gaining restitution in the courts, may dedicate it, even though it is at present in the possession of the robber," following the conclusion of the Gemara. (Ibid., *Yoreh De'ah* 258:7.)

שְׁנַיִם אֲדוּקִים בְּטַלִּית **Two people firmly holding on to a garment**. Two people holding on to a garment and claiming ownership of it divide it equally only if each one is holding on to its edges, and neither is holding on to an area of three by three fingerbreadths of the garment itself. But if the claimants are actually holding on to parts of the garment, each one may keep whatever part of the garment he is holding, and the remainder is divided equally between the claimants after they have each taken an oath, in accordance with the conclusion of the Gemara here. (Based on *Shulḥan Arukh, Ḥoshen Mishpat* 138:3.)

LANGUAGE

כַּרְכַּשְׁתָּא Fringes, tassels. This expression seems to be an Aramaic adaptation of the Greek κροκύς, *krokus,* meaning "fringes, woolen strands extending from a garment."

CONCEPTS

שָׁלֹשׁ עַל שָׁלֹשׁ Three by three fingerbreadths. Usually, a "transfer by symbolic barter" (קִנְיַן סוּדָר) is effected by the buyer having the seller take hold of part of a garment owned by the buyer. The seller must take hold of a portion of the garment at least three by three fingerbreadths in area, because a portion of garment smaller than this is not deemed a "utensil" (כְּלִי) with regard to the laws of ritual impurity, and the Halakhah stipulates that only a "utensil" may be used to effect a "transfer by barter."

TRANSLATION AND COMMENTARY

אֲמַר רַב פַּפָּא [1]**Rav Pappa answered:** The Mishnah refers to a case **where** the two claimants are not holding on to the garment itself but **are holding on to the fringes** of the garment. In such a case they must take an oath and divide the whole garment between them, because neither claimant is holding on to the garment itself.

אֲמַר רַב מְשַׁרְשִׁיָּא [2]**Rav Mesharshiya said:** We may **infer from this** Baraita, cited by Rav Taḥlifa, **that the kerchief** that a buyer gives to a seller, in order to effect by symbolic barter the transfer of ownership of the goods sold from the seller to the buyer, need not pass totally into the possession of the seller. **Once** the seller **has taken hold of** a portion of the kerchief at least **three by three fingerbreadths** in size, which is the minimum size to have Halakhic significance here, this portion becomes the seller's property. [3]**We apply** to such a case **the verse** (Ruth 4:7): "Now this was the custom in former time in Israel... to confirm all manner of transactions; a man pulled off his shoe **and gave it to his neighbor.**" This verse was understood by the Sages as referring to the mode of acquisition known as קִנְיַן סוּדָר — "symbolic barter" — in which property is transferred from seller to buyer by having the buyer give another object, usually an article of clothing such as a kerchief, to the seller. By the transfer of the kerchief from the buyer to the seller, the ownership of the goods being sold passes from the seller to the buyer. From Rav Taḥlifa's Baraita we see that it is possible to gain title to part of an article (such title is necessary in order for the act of exchange to be valid), even though the remainder of that article still belongs to someone else. [4]The part of the kerchief now held by the seller **is** thus **considered as if it has been detached** from the rest of the kerchief, even though the other part of the kerchief is still in the possession of the buyer. Thus the moment the seller takes hold of the portion of the kerchief, **the buyer acquires his purchase** from the seller.

[1]אֲמַר רַב פַּפָּא: דְּתְפִיסִי בְּכַרְכַּשְׁתָּא.
[2]אֲמַר רַב מְשָׁרְשִׁיָּא: שְׁמַע מִינָּהּ הַאי סוּדָרָא, כֵּיוָן דְּתָפֵיס בֵּיהּ שָׁלֹשׁ עַל שָׁלֹשׁ, [3]קָרֵינַן בֵּיהּ "וְנָתַן לְרֵעֵהוּ", [4]דִּכְמַאן דִּפְסִיק דָּמֵי; וְקָנֵי.

LITERAL TRANSLATION

[1]Rav Pappa said: Where they are holding on to the fringes.

[2]Rav Mesharshiya said: Infer from this [that regarding] this kerchief, once one has taken hold of three by three [fingerbreadths] of it, [3]we apply to it [the verse] "And gave it to his neighbor," [4]for it is considered as if it has been detached; and [the buyer] acquires [his purchase].

RASHI

בברכשתא — בגדין שבשני ראשין, שקורין ברניי״ש. **שמע מינה** — מדקתני עד מקום שידו מגעת קנוי לו. **האי סודרא** — של קונה, שקונין בו קנין. **כיון דתפיס ביה** — מקנה שלש על שלש, קרינא ביה ״ושלף איש נעלו ונתן לרעהו״. **דכמאן דפסיק דמי** — וקנייה מקנה, והמכר נקנה בו ללוקח. ודוקא נקט שלש על שלש, דכלי בעינן, דכתיב (רות ד) ״נעלו״, ובציר משלש אצבעות לאו בגד הוא, כדאשכחן גבי טומאה.

NOTES

answer to this question: The Mishnah is referring to a case where each claimant is holding on to exactly half of the garment! Accordingly, some commentators explain that the possibility of both claimants holding on to equal parts of the garment is so remote that it is not plausible to explain the Mishnah in this way (*Shittah Mekubbetzet*).

שָׁלֹשׁ עַל שָׁלֹשׁ Three by three fingerbreadths. This is the smallest piece of cloth (6 x 6 cm., or, at most, 7.5 x 7.5 cm.) that has Halakhic significance. As *Rashi* comments, this measure also applies in the laws of ritual purity as the smallest piece of cloth that can become ritually impure. Since it is important in one respect, it also has importance with regard to being grasped.

כְּמַאן דִּפְסִיק דָּמֵי It is considered as if it has been detached. This juridical assumption is found in many areas of the Halakhah, when we view a possible situation as though it actually existed. Hence, if the necessary action (in the present instance, cutting the piece of cloth off the garment) is technically feasible, although it has not actually been done, one treats the situation as though the action has already been taken. As explained below in this passage, one does not rely upon this assumption in every instance, generally because there may be a specific Biblical injunction or Rabbinical ordinance stipulating that the action must actually be performed.

HALAKHAH

דֶּרֶךְ קְנִיָּה בְּקִנְיַן סוּדָר Transfer of ownership through symbolic barter. "The transfer of ownership through symbolic barter is effective even though the seller has not taken possession of the entire article given to him by the buyer. Even if the seller has grasped only part of the article, and part of it still remains in the hand of the buyer, the transfer is effective, provided that the seller has taken possession of a minimum of three fingerbreadths square. If the seller has grasped less than this minimum amount, he must be holding on to the article firmly enough to enable him to detach it entirely from the possession of the buyer should he wish to do so (*Rambam*). Others say that a valid transfer is only effected if the article is at least three fingerbreadths square (*Rema*)." (*Shulḥan Arukh Ḥoshen Mishpat* 195:4.)

TRANSLATION AND COMMENTARY

וּמַאי שְׁנָא [1]However, a question now arises: **How is this** case **different from** the one discussed elsewhere by **Rav Ḥisda?** [2]**For Rav Ḥisda said** (*Gittin* 78b): **If a bill of divorce** which has been delivered by the husband to the wife **is in** the wife's **hand, and the string** with which the bill of divorce was tied and which is attached to it **is** still **in** the husband's **hand,** [3]**if** the husband by pulling the string **is able to pull** the bill of divorce **away** from his wife **and bring it back into his** possession, the wife **is not divorced;** [4]**but if** the husband **cannot** pull the bill of divorce back into his possession by pulling the string, because the string is not strong enough, the wife **is divorced!** From Rav Ḥisda's ruling it would seem that, as long as part of the bill of divorce remains in the husband's hands, it is not considered as having been given to the wife. Hence the divorce does not take effect, even though she is holding on to the significant part of the bill of divorce! This ruling would seem to contradict Rav Mesharshiya's conclusion that it is possible to acquire part of an object by holding it, even though the other part is still in the original owner's hand.

הָתָם [5]The Gemara answers that there is a fundamental difference between the act of handing over a bill of divorce and the transfer of ownership of property. **There,** in the case of a bill of divorce, **we require** the total **separation** of the couple, **and** as long as the husband is still holding on to any part of the bill of divorce, **this** separation has **not** taken place; [6]but **here,** in the case of the kerchief, **we require** an act of **giving,** the transferring of possession, **and there is** a valid transfer of that part of the kerchief now being held by the seller. Hence the transfer of ownership of the property from the seller to the buyer is effective.

אָמַר רָבָא [7]**Rava,** commenting on the Baraita cited by Rav Taḥlifa, **said:** Even **if it was a garment overlaid with gold,** the claimants **divide it.**

פְּשִׁיטָא [8]The Gemara expresses astonishment at Rava's statement: Surely **this is obvious!** Why should we have imagined the law being otherwise?

לָא צְרִיכָא [9]The Gemara answers: **No,** Rava's statement **was** indeed **necessary,** for he was referring **to a case where the gold was located in the middle** of the garment, and neither claimant was holding it!

הָא נַמִי פְּשִׁיטָא [10]But the Gemara also objects to this interpretation of Rava's statement: Surely **this, too, is obvious,** for we have already established that that portion of the garment that is not held by either claimant should be divided between the two claimants!

[1]וּמַאי שְׁנָא מִדְּרַב חִסְדָּא? [2]דְּאָמַר רַב חִסְדָּא: גֵּט בְּיָדָהּ וּמְשִׁיחָה בְּיָדוֹ, [3]אִם יָכוֹל לְנַתְּקוֹ וּלְהָבִיאוֹ אֶצְלוֹ, אֵינָהּ מְגוֹרֶשֶׁת, [4]וְאִם לָאו, מְגוֹרֶשֶׁת! [5]הָתָם, כְּרִיתוּת בָּעֵינַן, וְלֵיכָּא. [6]הָכָא, נְתִינָה בָּעֵינַן, וְהָא אִיכָּא! [7]אָמַר רָבָא: אִם הָיְתָה טַלִּית מוּזְהֶבֶת, חוֹלְקִין. [8]פְּשִׁיטָא! [9]לָא, צְרִיכָא דְּקָאֵי דַּהֲבָא בֵּי מְצָעֵי. [10]הָא נַמִי פְּשִׁיטָא!

LITERAL TRANSLATION

[1]And how is this different from that of Rav Ḥisda? [2]For Rav Ḥisda said: [If] a bill of divorce is in her hand and a string is in his hand, [3]if he is able to pull it away and bring it [back] to him, she is not divorced, [4]and if not, she is divorced!

[5]There, we require "separation," and there is none. [6]Here, we require "giving," and there is!

[7]Rava said: If it was a garment overlaid with gold, they divide [it].

[8]This is obvious!

[9]No, it is necessary [in the case] where the gold was located in the middle.

[10]This, too, is obvious!

RASHI

גט בידה – שנתנו לה. **ומשיחה** שקשור בה בידו; אם יש כח בחוט שיכול לנתקו לגט מידה ולהביאו אללו. **אינה מגורשת** – אלמא לאו נתינה היא. **כריתות** – הבדלה, שיהיו מובדלים זה מזה, והרי אגודים הם בחוט זה. **אם היתה טלית מוזהבת** – כלומר, אפילו היא מוזהבת – חולקים.

HALAKHAH

גֵּט בְּיָדָהּ וּמְשִׁיחָה בְּיָדוֹ **A bill of divorce in the wife's hand and the string in the husband's hand.** "If the husband gave a bill of divorce to his wife, and part of it, even a string attached to it, was still in his hand, and the connection was strong enough to enable the husband to pull the bill of divorce back into his possession, the handing over of the bill of divorce is not valid," in accordance with the ruling of Rav Ḥisda. (*Shulḥan Arukh, Even HaEzer* 138:2.)

חֲלוּקַת טַלִּית מוּזְהֶבֶת **Division of a garment overlaid with gold.** "If two claimants are holding on to the edges of a garment overlaid with gold, and the gold is closer to one of them than to the other, they nevertheless divide the garment equally, and we do not say that the garment should be divided in such a way that the person whose hand is closer to the gold is permitted to keep it," in accordance with the ruling of Rava. (Ibid., *Ḥoshen Mishpat* 138:3.)

TRANSLATION AND COMMENTARY

לָא צְרִיכָא [1]The Gemara answers: **No,** Rava's statement **was necessary**, for he was referring **to a case where** the gold **is closer to one of the claimants,** although he is not holding it. [2]**You might have thought that** the claimant whose hand is closer to the gold **could claim:** "**Divide** the garment **this way,** breadthwise." In this way he would be able to obtain all the gold! [3]**Hence** Rava **teaches us that** the claimant whose hand is further away from the gold **can say:** "**Why** should we **divide it that way** — breadthwise, as you suggest? **Divide it this way** — lengthwise, so that we both receive an equal share of the gold!"

תָּנוּ רַבָּנַן [4]**Our Sages taught** the following Baraita: **Two people**, a borrower and a lender, appear before the court **firmly holding on to a** promissory **note, and the lender says**: "The note **is mine,** as I have not yet been repaid. **It fell** out of my pocket, **and I found it** again." [5]**And the borrower says: "It** is true that the note **was yours, but I have** already **paid you** what I owed you. You then returned the note to me. I dropped it and then found it again." [6]The law in such a case is as follows: **The note must be authenticated by those who signed it**. These are **the words of Rabbi** (Rabbi Yehudah HaNasi). Rabbi's point of view seems to be that if the witnesses whose signatures appear on the document confirm that their signatures are genuine, the lender may use the promissory note to collect his debt. [7]**Rabban Shimon ben Gamliel says**: The lender and the borrower **divide** the amount of money stipulated in the note. The lender is only entitled to half of his claim, since we do not know which of the two claimants is telling the truth. [8]The Baraita continues: **If** such a promissory note **fell into the hands of a judge, neither** of the claimants **may ever extract it** from the judge's possession, and they must wait until positive proof as to its ownership is established. **Rabbi Yose says**: The promissory note **retains its status of being** legally **valid**, and the lender may use it to collect his debt.

אָמַר מָר [9]The Gemara now proceeds to analyze this Baraita: **It was said above** in the Baraita (lit., the Master said — a formula often used by the Talmud to introduce a quotation from a passage cited previously): "**The** promissory **note must be authenticated by those who signed it.**" [10]The Gemara asks: Does Rabbi mean that, if

[1]לָא, צְרִיכָא דְּמִיקָּרַב לְגַבֵּי דְּחַד. [2]מַהוּ דְּתֵימָא דְּאָמַר לֵיהּ: "פְּלוֹג הָכִי". [3]קָא מַשְׁמַע לָן דְּאָמַר לֵיהּ: "מַאי חָזֵית דְּפָלְגַתְּ הָכִי? פְּלוֹג הָכִי".

[4]תָּנוּ רַבָּנַן: "שְׁנַיִם אֲדוּקִין בִּשְׁטָר, מַלְוֶה אוֹמֵר: 'שֶׁלִּי הוּא, וְנָפַל מִמֶּנִּי, וּמְצָאתִיו'. [5]וְלֹוֶה אָמַר: 'שֶׁלְּךָ הוּא, וּפְרַעְתִּיו לְךָ'. [6]יִתְקַיֵּים הַשְּׁטָר בְּחוֹתְמָיו. דִּבְרֵי רַבִּי. [7]רַבָּן שִׁמְעוֹן בֶּן גַּמְלִיאֵל אוֹמֵר: יַחֲלוֹקוּ. [8]נָפַל לְיַד דַּיָּין, לֹא יוֹצִיאוּ עוֹלָמִית. רַבִּי יוֹסֵי אוֹמֵר: הֲרֵי הוּא בְּחֶזְקָתוֹ".

[9]אָמַר מָר: "יִתְקַיֵּים הַשְּׁטָר בְּחוֹתְמָיו". [10]וְגָבֵי לֵיהּ מַלְוֶה

LITERAL TRANSLATION

[1]No, it is necessary [in the case] where it is closer to one [of the claimants]. [2]You might have said (lit., "what would you have said?") that [one of the claimants] could say to [the other]: "Divide [it] this way." [3][Hence] he teaches us that [the other one] can say to him: "Why divide it (lit., "what did you see that you divided it") that way? Divide it this way!"

[4]Our Sages taught: "Two people are firmly holding on to a note, [and] the lender says: 'It is mine, and it fell from me, and I found it,' [5]and the borrower says: 'It is yours, but I have paid you. [6]he note must be authenticated by those who signed it. [These are] the words of Rabbi [Yehudah HaNasi]. [7]Rabban Shimon ben Gamliel says: They shall divide [it]. [8][If] it fell into the hand of a judge, they cannot extract [it] ever. Rabbi Yose says: It [remains] under its presumption [of validity]."

[9]It was said above (lit., "the master said"): "The note must be authenticated by those who signed it." [10]And shall

RASHI

פלוג הכי – לרוחבה, ויהא הזהב לאחד מהם. **קא משמע לן דאמר ליה כו' פלוג** – לאורכה. **שנים אדוקים בשטר** – המלוה והלוה. **שלך הוא ופרעתיו לך** – והחזרת לי, וממני נפל. **יתקיים השטר בחותמיו** – קא סלקא דעתך דהכי קאמר: אם השטר כשר – שיקיימוהו חותמיו, לומר "כתב ידינו הוא" – הרי הוא בחזקתו. **נפל השטר ליד הדיין** – משמע דהכי קאמר: אם מצאו דיין – לא יוציאו אותו עולמית מיד דיין. ולקמן פריך: מאי שנא דיין מאינשי דעלמא? **וגבי ליה מלוה כוליה** – בתמיה.

NOTES

שֶׁלְּךָ הוּא וּפְרַעְתִּיו **It was yours, but I have paid it.** The commentators ask why the Talmud assumes that the borrower's claim is that he has repaid the loan, rather than some other claim that would exempt him from payment (e.g., that the document was a forgery, or that he had not yet used it to take a loan). *Ritva* answers that the claim of repayment is one that applies to all documents, even predated deeds of sale (see below, 13a). Furthermore, a borrower will not ordinarily claim that a promissory note was forged, since witnesses are liable to appear who will affirm that the document is genuine, thereby proving that the borrower is a liar. Claims of payment, by contrast, cannot easily be rebutted (*Shittah Mekubbetzet*).

כּוּלֵּיהּ?! [1]וְלֵית לֵיהּ מַתְנִיתִין "שְׁנַיִם אוֹחֲזִין כו'"?
[2]אָמַר רָבָא אָמַר רַב נַחְמָן: בִּמְקוּיָּם, דִּבְרֵי הַכֹּל יַחֲלוֹקוּ. [3]כִּי פְּלִיגִי בְּשֶׁאֵינוֹ מְקוּיָּם. [4]רַבִּי סָבַר: מוֹדֶה בִּשְׁטָר שֶׁכְּתָבוֹ, צָרִיךְ לְקַיְּימוֹ, [5]וְאִי מְקַיֵּים לֵיהּ, פָּלֵיג, וְאִי לָא מְקַיֵּים לֵיהּ, לָא פָּלֵיג. [6]מַאי טַעְמָא? חַסְפָּא בְּעָלְמָא הוּא! [7]מַאן קָא מְשַׁוֵּי לֵיהּ לְהַאי שְׁטָרָא? לֹוֶה. הָא קָאָמַר דִּפְרִיעַ?!
[8]וְרַבָּן שִׁמְעוֹן בֶּן גַּמְלִיאֵל סָבַר: מוֹדֶה בִּשְׁטָר שֶׁכְּתָבוֹ, אֵין צָרִיךְ

LITERAL TRANSLATION

the lender collect all of it? [1]But does he not accept our Mishnah: "Two are holding on [to a garment], etc."? [2]Rava said in the name of Rav Nahman: Where [it has been] authenticated, all agree that they divide. [3]Where they disagree is where it has not been authenticated. [4]Rabbi maintains [that even if a borrower] admits concerning a note that he wrote it, [the lender] must authenticate it, [5]and if he authenticates it, he divides [payment], but if he does not authenticate it, he does not divide [payment]. [6]What is the reason? It is a mere potsherd! [7]Who makes this into a [valid] document? The borrower. [But] surely he said that it has been paid!? [8]But Rabban Shimon ben Gamliel maintains: [If a borrower] admits concerning a note that he wrote it, [the lender] does not have

TRANSLATION AND COMMENTARY

the document is proved to be genuine, **the lender is permitted to collect all of** the debt? How can this be? [1]**Does** Rabbi **not accept our Mishnah**, which states that "if **two** people **are holding on to a garment**" they divide it equally!? Just as in the case of the garment neither claimant receives more than half his claim, so here, too, the lender should only be permitted to collect half of the debt!

אָמַר רָבָא [2]The Gemara answers: **Rava said in the name of Rav Nahman:** When Rabbi said that the document must be authenticated, he was not permitting the lender to collect the entire debt, but only the half permitted by our Mishnah. Thus, **where** the promissory note **has** already **been** officially **authenticated** by the court, and the judges have determined and recorded on the document that the signatures on it are genuine, and that it can be used by the lender to collect his debt, **both** Rabbi and Rabban Shimon ben Gamliel **agree that** the borrower and lender should **divide** payment, and the lender is only permitted to collect half of his claim. [3]**Where** Rabbi and Rabban Shimon ben Gamliel **disagree is** in a case **where** the promissory note **has not** yet **been authenticated,** as the Gemara now proceeds to explain. [4]**Rabbi maintains that even if a borrower admits that he wrote a** promissory **note, the lender** still **has to authenticate it** by having the court confirm that the signatures on it are genuine; otherwise, the lender cannot use it to collect his debt. [5]Thus, in the case discussed in the Baraita, **if** the lender **can authenticate** the note in the court, **he divides payment** with the borrower, collecting half of his claim. **But if** the lender **cannot authenticate it, he does not divide payment** with the borrower. According to Rabbi, the lender does not receive anything at all, despite the fact that the borrower admits to having written the promissory note, until the validity of the note is confirmed in court. [6]**What is** Rabbi's **reason**? According to Rabbi, a document that lacks the necessary authentication **is a mere** valueless **potsherd!** [7]**Who** is it who **makes this** scrap of paper **into a valid document? The borrower. But surely he** himself **said that it has been paid!** Thus, while it is the borrower who has rendered the promissory note effective by admitting that he wrote it, the borrower himself has removed its effectiveness by stating that he has already paid back the debt. Thus the document has no value until it has been authenticated by the court.

וְרַבָּן שִׁמְעוֹן בֶּן גַּמְלִיאֵל [8]On the other hand, **Rabban Shimon ben Gamliel maintains: If a borrower admits that he wrote a** promissory **note, the lender does not have to authenticate it,** and the borrower's claim that he has

RASHI

במקוים — שכתוב בו הנפק, שיצא כבר בבית דין והעידו עדים על חתימת ידן, וכותבין הדיינין בו: שטרא דנן נפק קדמנא ואסהידו פלוני ופלוני על חתימת ידייהו, ואשרנוהו וקיימנוהו כדחזי. **כולי עלמא לא פליגי דיחלוקו** — דכי אמרינן דיתקיים השטר בחותמיו — לא למגבי מלוה כולו קאמר, אלא למגבי פלגיה. ופלוגתייהו כשאינו מקוים; רבי סבר: אף על פי שהלוה מודה ליה שכתב שטר זה ולוה לו מעות — צריך המלוה לקיימו בחותמיו. ואפילו השטר בידו — נאמן הלוה לומר "פרעתיך", דכל זמן שאינו מקוים מאן קמשוי ליה שטרא — לוה שמודה לו שכתבו, הא אמר דפריע. אבל משהשטר מוחזק על פי עדיו — אין הלוה נאמן לומר "פרעתי". הלכך, זה ששניהם מוחזקים, אי מקיים ליה מלוה בעדות ומשוי ליה שטר מעליא — אין הלוה נאמן באמירתו אלא על ידי חזקה זו שאדוק בו, והרי הוא כשאר מציאה, ופליג. **ואי לא לא פליג** — שאפילו כולו ביד המלוה — נאמן הלוה לומר "פרעתי".

CONCEPTS

שְׁטָר מְקוּיָּם **An authenticated document.** A promissory note properly written and signed may still be challenged if the borrower claims that it is forged. To prevent such suspicion (or to remove it after such a claim has been advanced) the owner of the note brings it to court. The court examines the signatures of the witnesses and certifies them either by the testimony of the signatories themselves, who declare that these are their signatures, or by having other people testify that these are the true signatures of the witnesses. When a note has been certified, the judges write a הֶנְפֵּק — "endorsement" — on it, declaring that the note has been brought before them and found to be genuine, and the judges sign the endorsement. Henceforth this note may serve as absolute proof for the purpose of collecting a debt or seizing property in payment of it.

HALAKHAH

מוֹדֶה בִּשְׁטָר שֶׁכְּתָבוֹ **A borrower who admits that he wrote a promissory note.** "If a borrower admits that a promissory note that has not been authenticated by the court was in fact written by him, but claims that he has already repaid it, he is believed. Thus the lender must first arrange to have the court authenticate the document, and then he can present his claim to be repaid." (*Shulhan Arukh, Hoshen Mishpat* 82:1.)

לְקַיְּימוֹ, [1]וְאַף עַל גַּב דְּלָא מְקַיֵּים לֵיהּ, יַחֲלוֹקוּ.
[2]״נָפַל לְיַד דַּיָּין, לֹא יוֹצִיאוּ עוֹלָמִית.
[7B] [3]מַאי שְׁנָא לְיַד דַּיָּין?
[4]אָמַר רָבָא: הָכִי קָאָמַר: וְאַחֵר שֶׁמָּצָא שְׁטָר שֶׁנָּפַל לְיַד דַּיָּין, [5]וְהֵיכִי דָּמֵי? דִּכְתַב בֵּיהּ הֶנְפֵּק, לֹא יוֹצִיאוּ עוֹלָמִית.
[6]וְלָא מִיבָּעֲיָא לָא כְּתַב בֵּיהּ הֶנְפֵּק, [7]דְּאִיכָּא לְמֵימַר כְּתַב לִלְוֹת וְלֹא לָוָה. [8]אֶלָּא אֲפִילוּ כְּתַב בֵּיהּ הֶנְפֵּק, דִּמְקוּיָּם, לֹא יַחֲזִיר, [9]דְּחָיְישִׁינַן לְפֵירָעוֹן.
[10]וְרַבִּי יוֹסֵי אוֹמֵר: הֲרֵי הוּא בְּחֶזְקָתוֹ, [11]וְלָא חָיְישִׁינַן לְפֵירָעוֹן.

LITERAL TRANSLATION

to authenticate it, [1]and even though he does not authenticate it, they divide [payment].
[2]"[If] it fell into the hand of a judge, they cannot extract [it] ever."
[7B] [3]What is the difference [if it falls] into the hand of a judge? [4]Rava said: This is what [the Baraita] says: And someone else who found a promissory note that had fallen into the hand of a judge, [5]and how is it to be understood (lit., "what is it like")? Where [the court's] endorsement is written on it, [then] they may never extract [it].
[6]And there is no need [to say this where the court's] endorsement has not been written on it, [7]where it is [possible] to say [that the borrower] wrote in order to borrow but did not borrow. [8]But even [where the court's] endorsement *has* been written on it, when it is authenticated, he must not return it, [9]because we are concerned about [the possibility of] payment. [10]But Rabbi Yose says: It remains under its presumption [of validity], [11]and we are not concerned about [the possibility of] payment.

TRANSLATION AND COMMENTARY

repaid the loan is not accepted. [1]Thus, in the case discussed in the Baraita, **even though** the lender **does not authenticate** the promissory note, the claimants **divide** the amount of the debt, and the borrower is obliged to pay half to the lender.

נָפַל לְיַד דַּיָּין [2]The Gemara now proceeds to analyze the next statement in this Baraita: "If the promissory note **fell into the hands of a judge, neither** of the claimants **may ever extract it** from his possession."

מַאי שְׁנָא לְיַד דַּיָּין [7B] [3]The line of the Baraita just quoted appears to distinguish between an ordinary person who finds a lost document and a judge. Hence the Gemara asks: **What is the difference** whether or not the document happened to **fall into the hands of a judge**? Whoever found it should be subject to the same law!

אָמַר רָבָא [4]**Rava answered: This is what the Baraita is** really **saying: "If someone else**, neither the lender nor the borrower, **found a promissory note that had** previously **fallen into the hands of a judge** — [5]**how is** the expression, 'it had fallen into the hands of a judge' **to be understood? Where the court's endorsement is written on** the note, confirming that the signatures on it are genuine, and thus validating it for collection — **neither** the borrower nor the lender **may ever extract it**, and the finder must keep it indefinitely until witnesses testify from whose hand the document fell."

וְלָא מִיבָּעֲיָא [6]The Gemara clarifies further: The Baraita applies this rule not only to unendorsed documents but even to endorsed documents. Whenever a third party finds a lost document he should not return it. **It goes without saying** that a found promissory note should not be returned **where the court's endorsement has not been written on** it, [7]**where it is possible that the borrower wrote** the note **in order to borrow money, but** in fact **never borrowed** it. [8]**But even where** this consideration does not apply, where **the court's endorsement** authenticating the note **has been written on** it, **in which case** it **is considered valid**, the finder still **must not return** the note to the lender, [9]**because we are concerned about the possibility that payment** has already been made by the borrower to the lender. It is possible that the borrower may have already repaid the debt, received the note back, and then lost it before having had time to destroy it, and not even a court endorsement can allay this doubt. [10]**But Rabbi Yose says**: A court-endorsed promissory note **retains its status of being** legally **valid**, [11]**and we are not concerned about the possibility of payment**; for the borrower would certainly have destroyed the original note if he had already paid his debt, and he would not have allowed the note to be lost. Hence, since we are certain that a loan was made and that the note is genuine, the lender is entitled to payment.

RASHI

מאי שנא ליד דיין — מאיש אחר? **הכי קאמר ואחר** — שאינו לא לוה ולא מלוה. **שמצא שטר שנפל** — כבר ליד הדיין, ומאי ניהו הך נפילה — דכתיב ביה הנפק. **לא יוציאוהו מידו** — לא לוה ולא מלוה, עד שיבא אליהו, או עדים שראו מיד מי נפל. **לפירעון** — שמא אמת טוען הלוה שפרעו. **ורבי יוסי לא חייש לפירעון** — דמאן דמהדרי ליה שטר פרוע — לאלתר זהיר ביה לקורעו, ולא משהי ליה?

NOTES

לָא דְּחָיְישִׁינַן לְפֵירָעוֹן **We are not concerned about the possibility of payment**. The Rishonim ask: Why does the Talmud not raise the possibility of קְנוּנְיָא — a conspiracy between the husband and the wife to defraud others (see

CONCEPTS

הֶנְפֵּק **Endorsement**. A document containing a הֶנְפֵּק, a legal endorsement, is a document that has been produced in court, examined, and found to be authentic. The הֶנְפֵּק confirms that the document may be used as a valid legal instrument.

LANGUAGE

הֶנְפֵּק **Endorsement**. This is the Aramaic term for a certificate endorsing a promissory note. The meaning of the word is "taking out," meaning that from the time when the certificate is written, it is possible to use the note to take money out of the hands of the borrower or to seize his property.

[1]וְלָא חָיֵישׁ רַבִּי יוֹסֵי לְפֵירָעוֹן? [2]וְהָתַנְיָא: "מָצָא שְׁטַר כְּתוּבָּה בַּשּׁוּק, [3]בִּזְמַן שֶׁהַבַּעַל מוֹדֶה, יַחֲזִיר לָאִשָּׁה; [4]אֵין הַבַּעַל מוֹדֶה, לֹא יַחֲזִיר, לֹא לָזֶה וְלֹא לָזֶה. [5]רַבִּי יוֹסֵי אוֹמֵר: עוֹדָהּ תַּחַת בַּעְלָהּ, יַחֲזִיר לָאִשָּׁה; [6]נִתְאַרְמְלָה אוֹ נִתְגָּרְשָׁה, לֹא יַחֲזִיר, לֹא לָזֶה וְלֹא לָזֶה"! [7]אֵיפּוּךְ: "נָפַל לְיַד דַּיָּין, לֹא יוֹצִיאוּ עוֹלָמִית — דִּבְרֵי רַבִּי יוֹסֵי. [8]וַחֲכָמִים אוֹמְרִים: הֲרֵי הוּא בְּחֶזְקָתוֹ". [9]אִי הָכִי, קַשְׁיָא דְּרַבָּנַן אַדְּרַבָּנַן!

LITERAL TRANSLATION

[1]But is Rabbi Yose not concerned about [the possibility of] payment? [2]Surely it was taught: "[If someone] found a ketubah document (marriage settlement) in the marketplace, [3]at the time when the husband admits, he shall return [it] to the wife; [4][when] the husband does not admit, he shall not return [it], not to this [one] and not to this [one]. [5]Rabbi Yose says: [If] she is still with her husband, he shall return [it] to the wife; [6][if] she was widowed or divorced, he shall not return it, not to this [one] and not to this [one]!"
[7]Reverse it: "[If] it fell into the hands of a judge, they may never extract [it] — [these are] the words of Rabbi Yose. [8]But the Sages say: It remains under its presumption [of validity]."
[9]If this is so, there is a contradiction between the Sages and the Sages!

RASHI

שהבעל מודה — שלא נתן לה כתובתה. אין הבעל מודה — שאמר "פרעתי, ומידי נפל". עודה תחת בעלה — שלא גרשה. יחזיר לאשה — דלא עביד איניש ליתן כתובה קודם גירושין.

TRANSLATION AND COMMENTARY

וְלָא חָיֵישׁ רַבִּי יוֹסֵי [1]The Gemara now objects: But why **is Rabbi Yose** really **not concerned about the possibility** that the debt contained in the note **may have been paid** but that the borrower lost the note after it was returned to him? [2]**Surely there is a Baraita that states: "If someone finds a ketubah document** (marriage settlement) **in the marketplace,** [3]in a case **where the husband admits** that he has not yet paid his wife the money stipulated in her ketubah, the finder **must return** the document **to her;** [4]but if **the husband does not admit** that he owes his wife the money stipulated in her ketubah, but claims instead that he has already paid her and received the ketubah from her in return, and subsequently lost it, the finder **must return** the ketubah **neither to** the husband **nor to** the wife. [5]**Rabbi Yose says:** We must make the following distinction: **If** the wife **is still** married to **her husband**, the finder **must return** the ketubah **to the wife,** even if the husband objects, for the husband is presumed not to have paid his wife the money of her ketubah as long as they are still married. [6]But **if she is widowed or divorced**, the finder **must return** the ketubah **neither to** the husband or his heirs **nor to** the wife. For in such a case it is possible that the wife has already received the money stipulated in her ketubah and returned the ketubah to her ex-husband or his heirs, who subsequently lost it! Thus we see that even Rabbi Yose is afraid that a debt may have been repaid and the note returned, but that the former debtor may have lost the note (in this case — the ketubah) before having the opportunity to destroy it!

אֵיפּוּךְ [7]The Gemara resolves the contradiction between Rabbi Yose's two statements by suggesting: **Reverse** the text of the first Baraita, and amend it as follows: "**If** a promissory note **fell into the hands of a judge**, i.e., if it was authenticated, neither of the claimants **may ever extract it from** the finder's **possession**" — **these are the words of Rabbi Yose.** [8]**But the Sages say:** The promissory note **retains its status of being valid**.

אִי הָכִי קַשְׁיָא [9]But, observes the Gemara, **if** we reverse the text of the first Baraita, **we create a contradiction between the** views of the **Sages** found in the two Baraitot: According to the new reading of the first

NOTES

below, 13a) — in this case? Many other legal documents are disqualified because of the suspicion of such behavior.

Rashba maintains that the Tanna whose opinion is under discussion does not, in fact, consider the possibility of קְנוּנְיָא in other instances as well.

Ramban explains that this passage is specifically discussing a ketubah that does not include a lien on the husband's landed property. Hence there is no possibility of קְנוּנְיָא.

HALAKHAH

מָצָא שְׁטָר שֶׁנָּפַל לִידֵי דַּיָּין **And if someone found a promissory note that had fallen into the hands of a judge**. "If someone finds a promissory note, even if it contains an official endorsement by the court (הֶנְפֵּק), he must not restore it to its owner, for we are concerned that it may already have been repaid and that some conspiracy to defraud is taking place," in accordance with the ruling of Rava. (*Shulhan Arukh, Hoshen Mishpat* 65:6.)

מָצָא כְּתוּבָּה **If someone finds a ketubah.** "If someone finds a ketubah, even if both the husband and the wife agree that it has not yet been paid, he must not return it to the wife, for we suspect that some conspiracy to defraud is taking place." (*Rambam, Sefer Nezikin, Hilkhot Gezelah* 18:12.)

LITERAL TRANSLATION

[1]The entire [Baraita about the] ketubah document is [the view of] Rabbi Yose, [2]but [some of the text] is missing, and it [should] be taught as follows: [3]"If the husband does not admit, he shall not return [it], not to this [one] and not to this [one]. [4]In what [situation] are these words said? When [the wife] was widowed or divorced; [5]but [if] she is still with her husband, he shall return [it] to the wife, [6]for Rabbi Yose says: [7][If] she is still with her husband, he shall return [it] to the wife; if she was widowed or divorced, he shall not return it, not to this [one] and not to this [one]."

[8]Rav Pappa said: In fact, do not reverse! [9]Rabbi Yose was speaking to them [according] to the words of the Sages: [10]"According to me, even if she was widowed or divorced, we are also not concerned about [the possibility of] payment; [11]according to you — admit to me at least that as long as she is still with her husband, he shall return it to the wife, for it is not [yet] subject to payment."

[1]שְׁטַר כְּתוּבָּה כּוּלָּהּ רַבִּי יוֹסֵי, [2]וְחַסּוּרֵי מִחַסְּרָא, וְהָכִי קָתָנֵי: [3]"אֵין הַבַּעַל מוֹדֶה, לֹא יַחֲזִיר, לֹא לָזֶה וְלֹא לָזֶה. [4]בַּמֶּה דְּבָרִים אֲמוּרִים? שֶׁנִּתְאַרְמְלָה אוֹ שֶׁנִּתְגָּרְשָׁה; [5]אֲבָל עוֹדָהּ תַּחַת בַּעְלָהּ, יַחֲזִיר לָאִשָּׁה, [6]שֶׁרַבִּי יוֹסֵי אוֹמֵר: עוֹדָהּ תַּחַת בַּעְלָהּ, יַחֲזִיר לָאִשָּׁה; [7]נִתְאַרְמְלָה אוֹ שֶׁנִּתְגָּרְשָׁה, לֹא יַחֲזִיר, לֹא לָזֶה וְלֹא לָזֶה".

[8]רַב פַּפָּא אָמַר: לְעוֹלָם לָא תֵּיפּוֹךְ, [9]רַבִּי יוֹסֵי לְדִבְרֵיהֶם דְּרַבָּנַן קָאָמַר לְהוּ: [10]"לְדִידִי, אֲפִילּוּ נִתְאַרְמְלָה אוֹ נִתְגָּרְשָׁה נַמִי לָא חָיְישִׁינַן לְפֵירָעוֹן; [11]לְדִידְכוּ — אוֹדוּ לִי מִיהַת בְּעוֹדָהּ תַּחַת בַּעְלָהּ, דְּיַחֲזִיר לָאִשָּׁה, דְּלָאו בַּת פֵּירָעוֹן הִיא".

TRANSLATION AND COMMENTARY

Baraita, a promissory note that has fallen into the hands of a judge (i.e., a legally endorsed note) is deemed valid by the Sages, and thus it would seem that the Sages are not concerned by the possibility that the debt may have been repaid. On the other hand the Sages' view concerning a lost ketubah is that it must not be returned to the wife without the husband's express permission, even where she is still married, because the ketubah money may already have been paid! Thus from here it would seem that the Sages *do* take the possibility of repayment into consideration.

שְׁטַר כְּתוּבָּה כּוּלָּהּ רַבִּי יוֹסֵי [1]The Gemara now presents three possible solutions to this contradiction. The first is to retain the emendation of the first Baraita and to amend the second, as follows: **The** entire Baraita about the **ketubah document** reflects only the view of **Rabbi Yose**; and the views of the Sages, known to us from the first Baraita, do not appear in it at all. [2]In order to read the second Baraita as reflecting the view of Rabbi Yose alone, we must presume that **some of the text** of the Baraita **is missing, and it** should be emended to **read as follows:** [3]**"If the husband does not admit** that he owes his wife the money stipulated in her ketubah, the finder **must return** the ketubah **neither to** the husband **nor to** the wife. [4]**When does this ruling apply**? Only **when the wife was widowed or divorced;** [5]**but if she is still** married to **her husband**, the finder **must return** the ketubah to the wife, [6]**for Rabbi Yose says: If she is still** married to **her husband**, the finder **must return** the ketubah **to the wife**. [7]But **if she was widowed or divorced**, the finder **must return** the ketubah **neither to** the husband **nor to** the wife."

רַב פַּפָּא אָמַר [8]**Rav Pappa said** that there is another way of resolving the contradiction between the two statements of the Sages and between the two statements of Rabbi Yose in the two Baraitot: **In fact, do not reverse** the text of the original Baraita, but leave the text in its original form. Rav Pappa's explanation is that in the Baraita dealing with the laws governing a found ketubah [9]**Rabbi Yose was speaking in accordance with the words of the Sages**, and was arguing with the Sages based on their own line of reasoning, that it is possible for a borrower to have lost a document after repayment, although he himself was not concerned about that possibility.

Rabbi Yose's argument would then be as follows: [10]**"According to my view**, expressed in the first Baraita, **even if** the wife **was widowed or divorced, we should also not be concerned about the possibility** that the money stipulated in the ketubah has already been paid, for a lost document is ordinarily assumed not to have been paid. Thus, in my opinion, it should always be permitted to return the lost ketubah to the wife. [11]But even **according to you**, the Sages, who are concerned that lost documents may already have been repaid, **at least admit to me that**, in the case of a ketubah, **if** the wife **is** still living **with her husband**, the finder is allowed to **return** the ketubah **to the wife. For** a ketubah of a married woman **is not yet subject to payment**, and there is no reason to suspect that it has already been paid, returned to the husband, and then lost."

TRANSLATION AND COMMENTARY

[1]**But the Sages said to** Rabbi Yose: "Here, too, while the woman is still married, there is reason to suspect payment: Consider the possibility **that** a husband may have **deposited bundles of money with** his wife, to serve as payment for the ketubah in the event of his death. Such an arrangement would spare her possible harassment by the heirs to her husband's estate. In exchange for this money she has returned the ketubah to him. Now, if the finder returns the ketubah to the wife, she may decide to keep the bundles of money and subsequently use the ketubah to collect a second time!

רָבִינָא אָמַר [2]**Ravina said** that another solution to the contradiction between Rabbi Yose's two statements may be proposed: **In fact, reverse the first** Baraita, as originally suggested. Hence it is the Sages who are not concerned about the possibility of payment, because a borrower normally destroys the promissory note immediately after he has repaid the debt. [3]The resulting apparent contradiction between the two statements of the Sages in the two Baraitot can be explained as follows: **The reasoning of the Sages here** in the case of a lost ketubah **is** not that we are concerned that the ketubah may have been paid, because normally when a person has repaid what he owes he gets back the promissory note (in this case the ketubah) and destroys it at once! **We are**, in fact, **concerned** that the husband may have written **two ketubot** for his wife, the second one as a replacement for this one, after it was lost. Now, if the finder returns the ketubah to the wife without her husband's permission, she may already have a replacement ketubah, and thus she will be able to collect twice! [4]**But Rabbi Yose is not concerned about the possibility** that the husband may have written **two ketubot,** since it is very rare for people to do so.

[1]וְאָמְרוּ לֵיהּ רַבָּנַן: "אֵימוּר צְרָרֵי אַתְפָּסַהּ". [2]רָבִינָא אָמַר: לְעוֹלָם אֵיפוּךְ קַמַּיְיתָא, [3]וְטַעֲמָא דְּרַבָּנַן הָכָא מִשּׁוּם דְּחָיְישִׁינַן לְשְׁתֵּי כְתוּבּוֹת. [4]וְרַבִּי יוֹסֵי לִשְׁתֵּי כְתוּבּוֹת לֹא חָיֵישׁ.

LITERAL TRANSLATION

[1]But the Sages said to him: "Say that he deposited bundles [of money] with her."

[2]Ravina said: In fact, reverse the first [Baraita], [3]and the reason of the Sages here is because we are concerned about [the possibility of] two ketubot. [4]But Rabbi Yose is not concerned about [the possibility of] two ketubot.

RASHI

צררי אתפסה – מעות צרורות או כספים מסר לה ליחוד כתובתה כשנשאה או לאחר מכאן, שלא יטריחוה יורשים אם תתאלמן. לעולם איפוך קמייתא – ודקשיא לך דרבנן אדרבנן – לא תיקשי, דטעמייהו דרבנן בכתובה – לאו משום דחיישינן לפירעון, דמאן דפרע ואהדר ליה שטרא – לאלתר קרע ליה. אלא משום דחיישינן לשתי כתובות, שמא חזר וכתב לה כתובה אחרת שניה לאחר שנפלה זאת מידה. ו"אין הבעל מודה" דקתני – לאו באומר "פרעתי", אלא באומר "אל תחזרו לה, שיש בידה אחרת, ותוציא על יורשי שטר אחר שטר".

NOTES

צְרָרֵי אַתְפָּסַהּ **He deposited bundles of money with her.** Some commentators (see *Rashi*) explain the text as referring to a situation where the husband gave money to his wife to save her from having to appear before a court after his death and become involved in a lawsuit to extract the money from his estate.

Other Rishonim discuss whether this explanation applies under all circumstances, from the time of the marriage and at any time thereafter, or whether it is limited to specific situations. Some commentators maintain that we must consider the possibility that the husband has deposited money with his wife only in a situation where the original ketubah has been lost and the husband has given her money to replace the lost ketubah (*Rashba, Ritva*).

אֵיפוּךְ קַמַּיְיתָא **Reverse the first Baraita.** It has been pointed out that, according to the viewpoint of Ravina, it would also have been possible to reconcile the contradictions between the two Baraitot by reversing the *second* Baraita. Some commentators explain that Ravina prefers to reverse the first Baraita because he holds that we are not concerned about the possibility of payment, and wishes to establish this viewpoint as that of the majority (*Shittah Mekubbetzet*).

חָיְישִׁינַן לִשְׁתֵּי כְתוּבּוֹת **We are concerned about the possibility of two ketubot.** This concern is unique to ketubot and does not apply to other documents, because a husband is forbidden by law from living with his wife if she does not have her ketubah in her possession. Thus if it happened that the ketubah was lost, he would have to write her a new one, and she might then come to possess two ketubot if the first were found.

שְׁתֵּי כְתוּבּוֹת **Two ketubot**. The Halakhah envisages the possibility that a man may have written two marriage contracts for his wife. For example, while they are married he may wish to write her an additional marriage contract, to increase the settlement guaranteed by the original marriage contract. However, in such a case there is no difficulty in having the woman collect both settlements.

Here in the Talmud we have a case in which the first marriage contract was lost and the husband wrote a second one in place of it. In fact, however, it is the practice to write a special version of the marriage contract in such instances, stipulating that the second is to replace the earlier one. Nevertheless, even this cannot entirely prevent a woman from misusing a marriage contract if she illegally possesses two. She can go to a second court, which does not know that she has already received her marriage settlement on the basis of the second ketubah, and sue to collect it again by means of the first.

LANGUAGE

טוֹפֶס ***Tofes.*** The source of this word is the Greek τύπος, *tupos,* which has many meanings connected to the underlying meaning of the word as used here: an imprint, the creation of an impression. The Sages made frequent use of this Greek word, creating a Hebrew root close to דפס — "to print." The word טוֹפֶס, based on one of the meanings of the Greek word, refers to a pattern or standard formula for promissory notes and the like. Occasionally, standard forms were written in advance, like today's printed contracts and applications, leaving blank spaces for the particular details of the specific transaction.

תּוֹרֶף ***Toref.*** The origin of this word is not certain, and the connection between its various meanings is not clear. In the juridical sense, this word is the opposite of טוֹפֶס, the standard form. The תּוֹרֶף is the part of the note containing the details identifying the particular document (names, dates, signatures, amounts), in contrast to the טוֹפֶס, which was standard for documents of a given type. The difference of opinion presented here in the notes regarding the meaning of טוֹפֶס and תּוֹרֶף emerges because in this case the תּוֹרֶף was written on a separate part of the note.

TRANSLATION AND COMMENTARY

אָמַר רַבִּי אֶלְעָזָר [1]**Rabbi Elazar said:** The ruling by Rabban Shimon ben Gamliel in the case of two claimants holding on to a promissory note (above, 7a), that **they divide** the document between them, **applies** only **when both of** the claimants **are holding on to the *tofes,*** the part of the promissory note that contains the standard, fixed text of the document, **or** when **both of them are holding on to the *toref,*** the part that contains the names of the borrower and the lender, the date of the loan, and the amount of money borrowed. [2]**But if one** of the claimants **is holding on to the *tofes* and the other is holding on to the *toref,*** the **one** holding on to the ***tofes* takes the *tofes* and the other one takes the *toref.*** In this case each claimant is permitted to keep whichever part of the promissory note he is holding. (The Gemara later explains precisely how much each claimant is entitled to retain.)

וְרַבִּי יוֹחָנָן אָמַר [3]**But Rabbi Yohanan said:** The claimants **always divide** the entire document.

וַאֲפִילּוּ אֶחָד אָדוּק בַּטּוֹפֶס [4]The Gemara now objects: May we assume that, according to Rabbi Yohanan, the claimants divide the document equally between them **even if one is holding on to the *tofes* and the other is holding on to the *toref?*** [5]**Surely it was taught** in a Baraita (above, 7a): "**This** claimant **may keep up to where his hand reaches,** and the other one may keep up to where his hand reaches"! Thus, from the Baraita just quoted, we see that the two claimants do not always divide the disputed object equally!

[1]אָמַר רַבִּי אֶלְעָזָר: מַחֲלוֹקֶת בְּשֶׁשְּׁנֵיהֶם אֲדוּקִים בַּטּוֹפֶס, וּשְׁנֵיהֶם בַּתּוֹרֶף. [2]אֲבָל אֶחָד אָדוּק בַּטּוֹפֶס וְאֶחָד אָדוּק בַּתּוֹרֶף, זֶה נוֹטֵל טוֹפֶס וְזֶה נוֹטֵל תּוֹרֶף.

[3]וְרַבִּי יוֹחָנָן אָמַר: לְעוֹלָם חוֹלְקִין.

[4]וַאֲפִילּוּ אֶחָד אָדוּק בַּטּוֹפֶס וְאֶחָד בַּתּוֹרֶף? [5]וְהָתַנְיָא: "זֶה נוֹטֵל עַד מָקוֹם שֶׁיָּדוֹ מַגַּעַת"!

LITERAL TRANSLATION

[1]Rabbi Elazar said: The dividing [of the document applies] in [a case] where both of them are holding on to the *tofes,* or both of them [are holding] on to the *toref,* [2]but if one is holding on to the *tofes* and one is holding on to the *toref,* this [one] takes the *tofes* and this [one] takes the *toref.*

[3]But Rabbi Yohanan said: They always divide.

[4]And even if one is holding on to the *tofes* and one [is holding] on to the *toref?* [5]Surely it was taught: "This [claimant] takes up to the place where his hand reaches...!"

RASHI

מחלוקת — האי "יחלוקו" דקאמר רבן שמעון [בן גמליאל] דמשמע: חולקין בשוה. כך שמעתי משום רבי יצחק בן רבי מנחם, ונראה בעיני. **ושניהם אדוקים בתורף** — כלומר, או שניהם אדוקים בתורף. **ותורף** — גילוי של שטר, מקום הלוה והמלוה והמעות והזמן. **טופס** — שאר כל לשון השטר. **זה נוטל כו׳** — דמאי דתפיס דידיה הוא, כדקתני לעיל: זה נוטל עד מקום שידו מגעת כו׳. ולקמן מפרש למאי מיבעי ליה. **ואפילו אחד אדוק כו׳** — בתמיה. **והא תניא עד מקום שידו מגעת** — שלו!

NOTES

מַחֲלוֹקֶת בְּשֶׁשְּׁנֵיהֶם אֲדוּקִים The ruling that they divide the document between them applies when both of them are holding on to.... *Rashi* (whom this translation follows) and most other commentators interpret the expression מַחֲלוֹקֶת here in the sense of "division" (i.e., division of the promissory note), rather than in its usual meaning of "dispute, controversy." Although this interpretation is somewhat forced, it was adopted by most of the commentators, because there seems to be no necessary connection between Rabbi Elazar's statement ("if one was holding on to the *tofes,*" etc.) and the original dispute between Rabbi and Rabban Shimon ben Gamliel. Indeed, it would appear that Rabbi Elazar's ruling is possible according to either or both of these Tannaim (see the commentaries, where this matter is discussed in greater detail). However, *Levush Mordekhai* interprets מַחֲלוֹקֶת in its usual sense ("dispute"), and attributes this interpretation to *Rambam* and the commentators on *Rambam.*

טוֹפֶס וְתוֹרֶף *Tofes* and *toref.* Numerous explanations of these terms have been offered, but all present certain difficulties. Some commentators (e.g. *Ramban*) maintain that the entire passage beginning דְּאָמַר הָכִי (below, p. 82) is a late addition to the Talmudic text, which should be disregarded.

Rashi explains that the *toref* is the first part of the promissory note, which includes such details as the names of the borrower and the lender, the amount of money loaned, and the date and place of the loan, while the *tofes* is the rest of the document.

Others explain that the *toref* is that part of the promissory note that contains the witnesses' signatures (as well as a brief summary of the contents of the document), while the *tofes* is the first part of the note, without the witnesses' signatures (see *Ramban, Rashba,* and *Rosh,* who go into detail on this point).

HALAKHAH

שְׁנַיִם אוֹחֲזִין בִּשְׁטָר If two people are holding on to a promissory note. "If a borrower and a lender are holding on to a promissory note, and each one claims that he dropped it, they divide the amount of the debt between them after taking an oath (so *Rif* and *Rambam,* who apparently followed R. Yohanan's opinion [these authorities may also have had a different reading in the text of the Talmud here — *Maggid Mishneh*]). Others maintain that if one of the claimants was holding on to the *toref* and the other was holding on to the *tofes,* the claimant holding on

TRANSLATION AND COMMENTARY

לָא צְרִיכָא [1]The Gemara answers: **No,** Rabbi Yoḥanan's statement **is necessary** in a case **where the *toref* is located in the middle** of the promissory note, so that neither of the claimants' hands reach it. Only in such a case does Rabbi Yoḥanan maintain that the claimants divide the disputed note equally, and he is not, in fact, disagreeing with Rabbi Elazar at all!

אִי הָכִי מַאי לְמֵימְרָא [2]But now the Gemara objects: **If this is so, what is the point of** Rabbi Yoḥanan's **statement**? Surely, where the *toref* was located in the middle of the document, it goes without saying that the claimants divide the document equally!

לָא צְרִיכָא [3]The Gemara answers: **No,** Rabbi Yoḥanan's statement **is necessary** in a case **where the** *toref* **is closer to one** of the claimants than to the other, although neither of them is actually holding it. [4]**You might have said** that the **claimant** whose hands are closer to the *toref* **can say to the other** claimant, "**Divide** the document **this way** — down the middle." In this way he would be able to obtain the entire *toref*! [5]To prevent us from drawing this mistaken conclusion, Rabbi Yoḥanan had to **inform us that the other** claimant **may say to** the first, "**What** reason **do you see to divide** the note **that way** — in such a way as to give yourself the entire *toref*? **Divide it this way,** so that both of us may share the *toref* equally!"

אֲמַר לֵיהּ רַב אַחָא מִדִּפְתִּי [6]**Rav Aḥa of Difti said to Ravina: According to Rabbi Elazar, who said that one** claimant **takes the *tofes* and** the other **takes the *toref*,** [7]**for what purpose does** each claimant holding on to one part of the document wish to retain it? What use can he make of it? Since pieces of the document cannot be used by themselves for collection of the debt, surely they have no value. [8]**Does** the claimant holding it **need it** as paper **to stop up his bottle**?

אֲמַר לֵיהּ [9]Ravina **said to** R. Aḥa of Difti: Rabbi Elazar's statement does not mean that the document is to be divided physically between the claimants and that each claimant will receive a piece of the paper on which the promissory note was written. Rabbi Elazar is referring **to the value** of the content of the document. A valuation must be made of the various parts of the document, and according to this valuation one claimant will receive more than the other.

[1]לָא, צְרִיכָא, דְּקָאֵי תּוֹרֶף בֵּי מִצְעֵי.

[2]אִי הָכִי, מַאי לְמֵימְרָא?

[3]לָא, צְרִיכָא, דְּמִקָּרַב לְגַבֵּי דְּחַד. [4]מַהוּ דְּתֵימָא: אָמַר לֵיהּ: "פְּלוּג הָכִי". [5]קָא מַשְׁמַע לַן דַּאֲמַר לֵיהּ: "מַאי חָזֵית דְּפָלְגַתְּ הָכִי? פְּלוּג הָכִי".

[6]אֲמַר לֵיהּ רַב אַחָא מִדִּפְתִּי לְרָבִינָא: לְרַבִּי אֶלְעָזָר, דְּאָמַר זֶה נוֹטֵל טוֹפֶס וְזֶה נוֹטֵל תּוֹרֶף, [7]לְמָה לֵיהּ? [8]וְכִי לָצוּר עַל פִּי צְלוֹחִיתוֹ הוּא צָרִיךְ?

[9]אֲמַר לֵיהּ: לְדָמֵי.

LITERAL TRANSLATION

[1]No, it is necessary, where the *toref* is located in the middle [of the document].

[2]If this is so, what is the point of the statement (lit., "what is there to say")?

[3]No, it is necessary, where it is closer to one. [4]You might have said (lit., "what would you have said?"): [One claimant] could say to [the other]: "Divide [it] this way." [5][Hence] he teaches us that [the other one] can say to him: "Why divide it (lit., "what did you see that you divided it") that way? Divide it this way!"

[6]Rav Aḥa of Difti said to Ravina: According to Rabbi Elazar, who said that this [one] takes the *tofes* and this [one] takes the *toref,* [7]for what [purpose] does he [do so]? [8]Does he need it to stop up his bottle?

[9]He said to him: For its value.

RASHI

דקאי תורף בי מצעי – ומר אמר הדא, ומר אמר הדא, ולא פליגי. **לדמי** – מעלין בדמים כמה תורף יפה מן הטופס.

NOTES

וְכִי לָצוּר עַל פִּי צְלוֹחִיתוֹ Does he need it to stop up his bottle? Even though the Talmud elsewhere assumes that people might indeed go to court over a dispute concerning paper to stop up a container, this possibility is ruled out here. For if the litigants are merely disputing who is entitled to keep the paper on which the note was written, it should make no difference whether one is holding on to the *toref* or the *tofes* (*Ramban* and others).

HALAKHAH

to the *toref* keeps the difference between the value of the *toref* and the value of the *tofes* (as explained by the Gemara), and the remainder of the debt is divided between the two parties after they have taken an oath (*Rosh,* following Rabbi Elazar, since that Sage's opinion serves as the basis of the subsequent discussion in the Gemara [*Bet Yosef*])."

Some later authorities maintain that there is no dispute between Rabbi Elazar and Rabbi Yoḥanan, and thus the Halakhah is in accordance with the views of both these scholars. Thus, if both litigants are holding on to equal portions of the promissory note, they divide it; otherwise, the claimant holding on to the *toref* receives the difference between the values of the *toref* and the *tofes* (as explained in the Gemara; see *Shakh*). (*Shulḥan Arukh, Ḥoshen Mishpat* 65:15.)

TRANSLATION AND COMMENTARY

דְּאָמַר הָכִי [1]The Gemara proceeds to explain how the extra value of the *toref* over the *tofes* is determined. Clearly, both the *tofes* and the *toref* are essential parts of the document, and can only be treated as of equal value. However, the *toref* contains one additional element that is not essential for the document to be valid, but which increases its value — the date. Therefore **one estimates as follows: How much is a dated promissory note worth?** (The date being part of the *toref*.) **And how much is an undated promissory note worth?** [2]The difference between these two figures, explains the Gemara, is that, **in the case of a dated promissory note**, if the borrower has no resources to repay the loan when it becomes due, the lender **can collect** his debt **from mortgaged property** that the borrower sold to another person after the loan was made (a dated promissory note places a lien on all property in the borrower's possession at the time of the loan). [3]**But in the other case**, where there is no date recorded in the note, **the** lender **cannot collect from** the borrower's **mortgaged property** that has been sold to a third party. He can only collect from property that is at present in the borrower's possession. [4]**Therefore, the claimant** who is now holding on to the *tofes* **gives the other** claimant **the difference between** the two figures mentioned above, and they divide the rest of the document's value equally. This differential is the value of the *toref*.

וְיַחֲלוֹקוּ נַמִי דַּאֲמָרַן [5]**And** similarly, notes the Gemara, the expression **"they shall divide" that we have used**, and that is used in the Mishnah and in other sources dealing with disputes over ownership, **also refers to dividing the value of the** disputed **article** between the claimants, rather than to the actual physical division of the article. [6]**For if you do not say** that the division is a division of value, but instead assume that a disputed object must be physically divided between the claimants, **would you really suggest that "two people holding on to a garment" also** physically **divide** it into two pieces? [7]Surely by doing so **they would destroy** it, and render it useless to them!

הָא לָא קַשְׁיָא [8]But the Gemara rejects this line of reasoning: **This** objection poses **no difficulty**, and it is possible to understand the words of the Mishnah literally,

[1]דַּאֲמַר הָכִי: שְׁטָרָא דְּאִית בֵּיהּ זְמַן כַּמָּה שָׁוֵי, וּדְלֵית בֵּיהּ זְמַן כַּמָּה שָׁוֵי? [2]בִּשְׁטָרָא דְּאִית בֵּיהּ זְמַן, גָּבֵי מִמְּשַׁעְבְּדֵי, [3]וְאִידָךְ לָא גָּבֵי מִמְּשַׁעְבְּדֵי. [4]יָהֵיב לֵיהּ הֵיאָךְ דְּבֵינֵי בֵּינֵי.

[5]וְ"יַחֲלוֹקוּ" נַמִי דַּאֲמָרַן לְדָמֵי. [6]דְּאִי לָא תֵּימָא הָכִי, "שְׁנַיִם אוֹחֲזִין בְּטַלִּית" הָכִי נַמִי דְּפָלְגִי? [7]הָא אַפְסְדוּהּ!

[8]הָא לָא קַשְׁיָא,

LITERAL TRANSLATION

[1]For one says as follows: How much is a dated promissory note worth, and how much is an undated promissory note worth? [2]In [the case of] a dated promissory note, he collects from mortgaged property, [3]and [in] the other [case] he does not collect from mortgaged property. [4][Therefore] this [claimant] gives [the other one] that which is in between.

[5]And also [the expression] "they shall divide" that we have used (lit., "said") also [refers] to [dividing the] value [of the article]. [6]For if you do not say so, [would you really suggest] that "two people holding on to a garment" here also [physically] divide [it]? [7]Surely they would destroy it!

[8]This is no difficulty,

RASHI

שטרא דאית ביה זמן כמה שוה — דתורף עדיף מטופס, דאית ביה מקום הזמן. דאילו שם המלוה והלוה והמעות כתובין אף בטופס, שצריך לחזור מענינו של שטר בשיטה אחרונה, והוא עיקר, כדתנן (בבא בתרא קסה,ב): כתוב בו [מלמעלה מנה ולמטה מאתים], מלמעלה מאתים ולמטה מנה — הכל הולך אחר התחתון. אבל זמן לא מיהדר. ואי משום חתימת עדים דהוא תחת הטופס — הא אית ליה לרבן שמעון בן גמליאל מודה בשטר שכתבו — אין צריך לקיימו, והאי מודה שכתבו הוא.

NOTES

שְׁטָרָא דְּאִית בֵּיהּ זְמַן A dated promissory note. As has been explained, by Rabbinical decree all promissory notes are guaranteed by the borrower's property, whether or not this is explicitly stated in the document. In other words, the borrower's property is automatically regarded as mortgaged against repayment of the debt. This mortgage is in force from the moment the financial obligation is undertaken, which we assume to be the date written on the promissory note, and earlier dates take precedence over later ones for the purpose of enforcing payment. Thus, if a person sells his property, even if he guarantees the transaction in the bill of sale, a creditor whose promissory note predates the sale of the property may seize (לִטְרוֹף) the property from the buyer for the payment of his prior debt. Conversely, an undated promissory note may not be used to seize property that has already been sold to a third party, for the buyer can argue that the lien resulting from the promissory note was created after the sale of the property. Therefore, the creditor may only seize property which is still owned by the debtor, בְּנֵי חוֹרִין — "free property." Since an undated promissory note offers a weaker basis for seizing mortgaged property, it is less valuable than a dated note.

TRANSLATION AND COMMENTARY

[8A] **for** a garment that has been cut in half **is fit for children** to wear, and each half does retain a certain value.

וְהָא דְּאָמַר רָבָא [1]The Gemara continues to ask: **But what about** the statement of **Rava**, who **said: "If it was a garment overlaid with gold, the** claimants **divide it"?** [2]**Would you** really **suggest that here, too, they physically divide it** into two pieces? **Surely** by dividing it in that way **they would destroy it!**

הָא לָא קַשְׁיָא [3]Again the Gemara rejects this reasoning: **This** objection poses **no difficulty, for** a garment overlaid with gold that has been cut in half **is fit for the children of kings** and other wealthy people to wear.

וְהָא דִּתְנַן [4]Once again the Gemara asks: **But what about what we learned** in the Mishnah: **"If two people were riding on an animal** and they contest its ownership, the animal must be divided between them." [5]Would you really suggest that **here, too,** it means that the claimants **physically divide it** into two pieces? **Surely** by doing so **they would destroy it!** [6]**Granted, if it is a clean** (kosher) **animal** that may be used for food, a physical division of the animal into two halves is possible, as the flesh **is fit to be used for meat**, and each claimant would keep half of the meat. **But** if it is **an unclean** (non-kosher) **animal**, **surely** by cutting it in half **they would destroy it!**

אֶלָּא לְדָמֵי [7]**Rather**, the Gemara replies, we must conclude that the intention of the Mishnah is that **the value** of the disputed animal **is divided**. Similarly **here, too** — in all those other cases (such as the case of the promissory note) where it is stated that a disputed object is divided — the meaning is that **its value is divided** between the claimants.

אָמַר רָמִי בַּר חָמָא [8]**Rami bar Hama**, introducing a new subject, **said:** The Mishnah at the beginning of our chapter **implies** the general principle that if **someone picks up a found object on behalf of another person,**

[8A] דְּחַזְיָא לִקְטַנִּים.
[1]וְהָא דְּאָמַר רָבָא: "אִם הָיְתָה טַלִּית מוּזְהֶבֶת חוֹלְקִין", [2]הָכִי נַמִי דְּפָלְגִי לָהּ? הָא אַפְסְדוּהָ!
[3]הָא לָא קַשְׁיָא, דְּחַזְיָא לִבְנֵי מְלָכִים.
[4]וְהָא דִּתְנַן: "הָיוּ שְׁנַיִם רוֹכְבִין עַל גַּבֵּי בְהֵמָה וכו'", [5]הָכִי נַמִי דְּפָלְגִי לָהּ? הָא אַפְסְדוּהָ!
[6]בִּשְׁלָמָא טְהוֹרָה, חַזְיָא לְבָשָׂר, אֶלָּא טְמֵאָה — הָא אַפְסְדוּהָ!
[7]אֶלָּא, לְדָמֵי; הָכָא נַמִי, לְדָמֵי.
[8]אָמַר רָמִי בַּר חָמָא: זֹאת אוֹמֶרֶת: הַמַּגְבִּיהַּ מְצִיאָה

LITERAL TRANSLATION

[8A] for it is fit for children.

[1]But [what about] that which Rava said: "If it was a garment overlaid with gold, they divide [it]." [2][Would you suggest] that here, too, they [physically] divide it? Surely they would destroy it!

[3]This is no difficulty, for it is fit for the children of kings.

[4]But what [about what] we learned: "[If] two people were riding on an animal," etc., [5]here, too, do they [physically] divide it? Surely they would destroy it!

[6]Granted [if it is] a clean [animal], it is fit [to be used] for meat, but an unclean [animal] — surely they would destroy it!

[7]Rather, [we divide it] for its value; here, too, [we divide it] for its value.

[8]Rami bar Hama said: This implies (lit., "says") [that] someone who picks up a found object

RASHI

דחזיא לבני מלכים — לבנים קטנים. **זאת אומרת** — מתניתין דקתני שנים שהגביהו מציאה קנאוה ויחלוקו, וכשמגביה מגביה לדעת שיקנה בה חבירו עמיה, שמע מינה: המגביה מציאה כו'. ולקמיה פריך: דיוקא דרמי בר חמא מהיכא, מאיזו בבא ממשנתנו הוא למד כן?

BACKGROUND

לִקְטַנִּים For it is fit for children. The garment in question is a טַלִּית — a blanket-like garment, consisting of a rectangular length of cloth, which one wrapped around oneself and wore over other clothing. The question is raised because cutting the garment in two would obviously leave both pieces too small to be used by an adult. This also explains the answer: each of the two pieces of cloth could serve as an outer garment for children.

SAGES

רָמִי בַּר חָמָא Rami bar Ḥama. Rami (Rabbi Ami) bar Ḥama was one of the most important Babylonian Amoraim of the fourth generation. As a boy he was the outstanding student of Rav Ḥisda, and afterwards he married Rav Ḥisda's daughter. Rami bar Ḥama learned Torah from Rav Naḥman and Rav Sheshet and also discussed Halakhic issues with them. He was famous for his sharpness of mind and brilliance, but some of his contemporaries observed that because of his great intelligence and creativity, he did not always submit the problems that came before him to precise analysis. Rami bar Ḥama was closely connected with his younger colleague, Rava, and after his death Rava married his widow, Rav Ḥisda's daughter. Rami bar Ḥama's wife's daughter was the mother of the Amora Amemar.

NOTES

אֶלָּא לְדָמֵי Rather, for its value. The Gemara's proof here is based on the argument that it is unreasonable to assume that the animal should be destroyed with no benefit to either claimant. Why, however, in the case of the promissory note does the Gemara resort to analogy in order to prove that division of a promissory note refers to division of its value, when it could simply have stated that physical division of the promissory note would render it useless? *Rashba* answers that, in the case of a promissory note, physical division would not render it totally useless as the borrower, who would thereby be exempted from payment, would in fact benefit from the physical division of the note. But in the case of a disputed animal, physical division would result in the total loss of the animal, with no resulting benefit for either claimant.

הַמַּגְבִּיהַּ מְצִיאָה לַחֲבֵירוֹ וכו' Someone who picks up a found object for his fellow. The Halakhic problem with regard to picking up a found object for another person, which both Rami bar Ḥama and Rava try to solve in different ways, is related to a number of broader principles. Although a person's agent may perform certain acts of acquisition for him, this normally applies when the person sending the agent has some prior claim to the property (having paid for it or the like). In such cases the agent acts as an extension of the buyer's legal personality. This, however, is not the case with a found object. Since the agent has no prior claim to

HALAKHAH

לְדָמֵי For value. "If the physical division of a disputed object would destroy it (or decrease its value — *Sma*), then the object is sold and the proceeds are divided, rather than the object itself (in accordance with the conclusion of the Gemara)." (*Shulḥan Arukh, Ḥoshen Mishpat* 138:4.)

TRANSLATION AND COMMENTARY

the other person acquires it. Lifting (הַגְבָּהָה) is the normal method of acquiring ownerless objects. In general, in commercial transactions, it is possible for one person to perform an act of acquisition on behalf of another person. Rami bar Hama seeks to prove that the same principle applies with regard to ownerless objects, so that if one person picks up an ownerless object on behalf of someone else, the latter acquires it.

דְּאִי סָלְקָא דַּעְתָּךְ [1]In order to prove his contention, Rami bar Ḥama argues that each of the claimants to the garment mentioned in our Mishnah must be taking possession of the disputed garment, not only on his own behalf, with regard to the half he ultimately receives, but also on behalf of the other claimant, with regard to the other half (see further in the notes). **For if you assume that** whenever someone finds and picks up an object on behalf of another person his act of acquisition is ineffective and **the other person does not acquire it**, then in our case, when two people pick up the garment together, the garment should remain ownerless. Neither party is assisting the other. In fact, they are interfering with each other. Neither party picks up more than half the garment, and [2]thus, **that part** of the garment which the first claimant is holding **should be considered as if it is** still **resting on the ground** as far as the second claimant is concerned, **and the other** part of the garment should be considered **as if it is** still **resting on the ground** as far as the first claimant is concerned. But "lifting" (הַגְבָּהָה) is effective only if the entire object is lifted! [3]Accordingly, **neither the one** claimant **nor the other should acquire** the garment, and a third person may intervene and seize it from them and acquire it. [4]Hence Rami bar Ḥama concludes: **May we not infer from this** that, in all cases, **if someone lifts a found object for another person, the other person acquires** it; and therefore, in our case, the two claimants are considered to be assisting each other to acquire the garment jointly.

לַחֲבֵירוֹ, קָנָה חֲבֵירוֹ.
[1]דְּאִי סָלְקָא דַּעְתָּךְ לֹא קָנָה חֲבֵירוֹ, [2]תֵּיעָשֶׂה זוֹ כְּמִי שֶׁמּוּנַּחַת עַל גַּבֵּי קַרְקַע, וְזוֹ כְּמִי שֶׁמּוּנַּחַת עַל גַּבֵּי קַרְקַע, [3]וְלֹא יִקְנֶה לֹא זֶה וְלֹא זֶה. [4]אֶלָּא לָאו שְׁמַע מִינָּהּ: הַמַּגְבִּיהַּ מְצִיאָה לַחֲבֵירוֹ, קָנָה חֲבֵירוֹ.

LITERAL TRANSLATION

for his fellow, his fellow acquires [it].

[1]For if you assume [that] his fellow does not acquire [it], [2]this [part] should be considered as if it is resting on the ground, and the other [part] as if it is resting on the ground, [3]and neither this one nor that one should acquire [it]. [4]Rather, should we not conclude from here: Someone who picks up a found object for his fellow, his fellow acquires [it]?

RASHI

ולא יקנה לו זה ולא זה — וכל הרוצה יחטפנה מידם.

NOTES

the object, it cannot be argued that the agent has been empowered and authorized to act by the person who sent him. In the case of picking up a found object, two juridical explanations of the situation that is created may be offered: (1) The person who picks up the object acquires it for himself, but in some way he transfers that acquisition to another person (this is the main basis of Rava's explanation below). Or else (2) the person who picks up the object, since he reveals that he did not intend to acquire it for himself, does not acquire any right of ownership of it by picking it up. In contrast to these two assumptions, Rami bar Ḥama seeks to argue that this is a special instance of acquisition, in which a person may acquire something for someone else. See below, 9b and 10a, for a thorough discussion of this question of acquiring for another person.

הַמַּגְבִּיהַּ מְצִיאָה לַחֲבֵירוֹ **Someone who picks up a found object for his fellow**. *Rashi* explains Rami bar Ḥama's statement as meaning that each claimant picked up the object with the intention that the other claimant should acquire half of it. Later commentators find it difficult to understand this reasoning, as each claimant seems to be lifting the object only on behalf of himself! Among the solutions suggested: Since neither claimant can receive a share except if they act together, we assume that they would prefer assisting each other to losing altogether. (*Ritva*.) Others maintain that *Rashi* bases himself here on the conclusion of the discussion in the Gemara, and is referring only to the last clause in our Mishnah, which states: "If the claimants agree, they divide without taking an oath." In this case it is reasonable to assume that each claimant intended that his own lifting up of the object should enable the other claimant to acquire half. (*Pnei Yehoshua*.)

HALAKHAH

הַמַּגְבִּיהַּ מְצִיאָה לַחֲבֵירוֹ **Someone who lifts a found object on behalf of another person**. "If someone lifts a found object on behalf of another person, the other person acquires it." According to some authorities, this applies only if the person who lifted the object stated explicitly while doing so that he was lifting it for the other person; otherwise, he may retract and keep the object for himself (*Sema, Ketzot HaHoshen*). Other authorities, however, maintain that even if the person who lifted the object did not explicitly state at the time that he was doing so for another person, but later admitted that such had been his intention, he may not retract, and the other person has acquired the object (*Tosefot Yom Tov, Shakh, Netivot*). (*Shulḥan Arukh, Ḥoshen Mishpat* 269:1.)

[1] אֲמַר רָבָא, לְעוֹלָם אֵימָא לָךְ: הַמַּגְבִּיהַּ מְצִיאָה לַחֲבֵירוֹ, לֹא קָנָה חֲבֵירוֹ, [2] וְהָכָא הַיְינוּ טַעְמָא: מִגּוֹ דְּזָכֵי לְנַפְשֵׁיהּ, זָכֵי נַמִי לְחַבְרֵיהּ.

[3] תֵּדַע, שֶׁאִילּוּ אָמַר לִשְׁלוּחוֹ, "צֵא וּגְנוֹב לִי", וְגָנַב, פָּטוּר, [4] וְשׁוּתָּפִין שֶׁגָּנְבוּ חַיָּיבִין. [5] מַאי טַעְמָא? [6] לָאו מִשּׁוּם דְּאָמְרִינַן מִגּוֹ דְּזָכֵי לְנַפְשֵׁיהּ, זָכֵי נַמִי לְחַבְרֵיהּ? [7] שְׁמַע מִינָּהּ.

LITERAL TRANSLATION

[1] Rava said: In fact I can say to you: Someone who picks up a found object for his fellow, his fellow does not acquire [it], [2] but here the reason is: Since [each] one acquires for himself, he also acquires for his fellow.

[3] Know [that this is so], for if [a person] said to his agent, "Go out and steal for me," and [the agent] stole, [the person who sent him] is exempt, [4] but partners who stole are [both] liable. [5] What is the reason? [6] Is it not because we say that, since [a person] acquires for himself, he also acquires for his fellow? [7] Conclude [accordingly] from here.

TRANSLATION AND COMMENTARY

אֲמַר רָבָא [1] **Rava**, however, **said** that Rami bar Hama's initial contention, that it is always possible for one person to pick up an ownerless object on behalf of another person, is not conclusive. For **in fact I can say to you** that, in general, if **someone lifts a found object for another person** without intending to acquire part of it for himself, **the other person does not acquire** the object. [2] **But here** in our Mishnah, **the reason** why each claimant is able to assist the other to keep the garment **is: Since** each one actually **acquires** part of the found object **for himself, he** is **also** able to **acquire** part of it **for the other person**.

תֵּדַע [3] Rava now seeks to provide proof for his opinion: **Know that this is so. For if a person said to his agent, "Go out and steal for me," and the agent stole**, as he had been directed, **the person who sent him** to steal **is exempt** from punishment, since he himself did not commit the theft. (His exemption from punishment is based on the established Halakhic principle that אֵין שָׁלִיחַ לִדְבַר עֲבֵירָה — "there is no agency for sin" — and the person who commits a sin, not the instigator, bears the full responsibility.) [4] **But partners who stole** — i.e., who committed a theft together — **are** both **liable**, even if only one of them actually picked up the stolen object. [5] **What is the reason** that both partners are liable in this latter case? [6] **Is it not because we say that since a person acquires for himself, he also acquires for another person**, and thus both partners are considered thieves, even though technically only one of them actually committed the act of theft? [7] Accordingly, concludes the Gemara, we may **conclude from here** that even in a case where a person cannot act on another's behalf, he can still assist that other person to perform the act. Hence, Rami bar Hama's contention is unwarranted, and while it is true that in the case in our Mishnah each claimant is in fact assisting the other to acquire the ownerless garment, it does not follow that in general a finder can pick up an ownerless object on behalf of someone else.

RASHI

לעולם אימא לך לא קנה חבירו — היכא דמגביה לא נתכוין לקנות בה כלום. וטעמא אמר לקמן (י,א), דהוי תופס לבעל חוב במקום כו'. **והבא** — דקתני במתניתין שניס שהגביהו מציאה קנו — **מגו דזכי לנפשיה זכי נמי לחבריה. תדע** — דאפילו אמר לא קנה חבירו היכא דהגביה כולה לדעת חבירו, הכא דהגביה לעצמו ולחבירו — קני משום מגו. **פטור** — המשלח פטור מלשלם כפל, דקיימא לן: אין שליח לדבר עבירה להתחייב שולחו, אלא שליח. דדברי הרב ודברי התלמיד — דברי מי שומעין? **ואילו שותפין שגנבו** — והאחד הוציאה מרשות בעלים לדעתו ולדעת חבירו, אמרינן בבבא קמא (עח,ב) דחייבין.

NOTES

שׁוּתָּפִים שֶׁגָּנְבוּ **Partners who stole**. *Rashi* explains that this refers to a case where only one of the partners committed the actual theft, but his intention was to share the stolen property with his partner. *Tosafot, Ramban, Rashba,* and many other commentaries do not accept that position.

They note that the text of the Gemara in *Bava Kamma* 78b appears to support *Rashi*'s view. But they explain that that text deals with a unique instance, the obligation to reimburse an owner four or five times the value of a sheep or an ox that was stolen and afterwards slaughtered or sold (טְבִיחָה וּמְכִירָה). This case is an exception to the rule אֵין שָׁלִיחַ לִדְבַר עֲבֵירָה — "there is no agency for transgression" — and a thief who asks someone else to do the slaughtering is personally subject to the penalty of reimbursing the owner four or five times the value of the animal. However, in general, taking an article for someone else does not implicate the latter. Therefore, they interpret our case as one in which both partners were physically involved in the actual theft.

מִגּוֹ דְּזָכֵי לְנַפְשֵׁיהּ **Since each one acquires for himself**. Rava's basic assumption is that acquisition cannot take place unless the person who performs the action wishes to acquire the object for himself: an act of acquisition is only valid when performed by someone who intends to acquire

HALAKHAH

שׁוּתָּפִים שֶׁגָּנְבוּ **Partners who stole**. "Two partners who together stole an object must repay the rightful owner double the value of the stolen object. If the stolen object was a lamb or an ox, and one of the partners slaughtered it or sold it with the other's knowledge, they must both pay the rightful owner four times the value of the lamb and five times the value of the ox." (*Rambam, Sefer Nezikin, Hilkhot Genevah* 2:14.)

TRANSLATION AND COMMENTARY

אָמַר רָבָא [1]Continuing his previous line of reasoning, **Rava said: Now that you accept that we say: "Since** a person is actually acquiring part of an object for himself, he can at the same time acquire the other part for someone else," we can draw another conclusion: By Torah law, a deaf-mute is considered mentally incompetent and incapable of performing a legal act of acquisition. But the Sages instituted that he should be treated as if he were able to acquire for himself, to avoid needless strife. This arrangement, however, does not extend to acquiring on behalf of someone else. Now, according to Rava's reasoning, [2]if **a deaf-mute and a normal person were to lift up a found object** together, [3]**since the deaf-mute acquires** part of the object for himself, **the normal person should** also **acquire** his part of it.

בִּשְׁלָמָא חֵרֵשׁ קָנָה [4]The Gemara raises an objection and asks: **Granted**, following Rava's reasoning, that **the deaf-mute should acquire his part, for a normal person lifted** the other half of the object **for him.** Since the normal person ostensibly acquires part of the object for himself, he can acquire the rest of it for the deaf-mute. [5]**But with what does the normal person acquire his** share of the item? The Sages did not give the deaf-mute real power of acquisition. They merely prevented other, normal, people from interfering with his attempts to acquire an object. Hence, from the point of view of the normal person, the deaf-mute cannot even acquire for himself, let alone assist a normal person to acquire anything. So how does the normal person acquire his share of the article in such a case? From his point of view, the half of the article in the deaf-mute's hands is as if it is still lying on the ground!

[1]אֲמַר רָבָא: הָשְׁתָּא דְּאָמְרַתְּ אָמְרִינַן מִגּוֹ, [2]חֵרֵשׁ וּפִקֵּחַ שֶׁהִגְבִּיהוּ מְצִיאָה, [3]מִתּוֹךְ שֶׁקָּנָה חֵרֵשׁ, קָנָה הַפִּקֵּחַ.

[4]בִּשְׁלָמָא חֵרֵשׁ קָנָה, דְּקָא מַגְבַּהּ לֵיהּ בֶּן דַּעַת, [5]אֶלָּא פִּקֵּחַ — בְּמַאי קָנָה?

LITERAL TRANSLATION

[1]Rava said: Now that you say [that] we say "since...," [2][if] a deaf-mute and a normal person picked up a found object, [3]since the deaf-mute acquires, the normal person acquires.

[4]Granted [that] the deaf-mute acquires, for a normal person picked up [the object] for him, [5]but the normal person — with what does he acquire?

RASHI

השתא דאמרת מגו — דזכי לנפשיה כו׳, **חרש ופקח שהגביהו מציאה** — קנאוה. אף על פי שהגבהה של חרש אינה הגבהה לקנות אלא מפני דרכי שלום, כדתנן (גיטין נט,ב): חרש שוטה וקטן יש בהן גזל מפני דרכי שלום, אפילו הכי אמר: מגו דזכי לנפשיה כו׳. **בשלמא חרש קני דקא מגבה לה בן דעת** — לראשה השני לצורך שניהם, וראשו של צד חרש לגבי חרש מיהא הויא הגבהה כדתקון ליה מפני דרכי שלום. אלא פקח במאי קני? לגבי פקח הוי ראשה שהגביה החרש כמונח על גבי קרקע, דהגבהה דחרש לא קניא אלא מדרכי שלום בעלמא!

NOTES

the object for himself and is capable of so doing. The fact that a second person may also acquire the object does not derive from the finder's conferring a right of ownership that is not his own, but rather, on the contrary, it results from the finder's acquiring full ownership of the object, so that he can then transfer it to someone else. In a certain sense two people who find a single object become partners, whether or not they wish to do so, and the acquisition by one partner also makes acquisition by the other one possible. The idea behind this מִגּוֹ is as follows: Since a valid acquisition has taken place (זָכֵי לְנַפְשֵׁיהּ), this acquisition may also pass to others, by transfer (intentional or unintentional) of the right of ownership.

הָשְׁתָּא דְּאָמְרַתְּ אָמְרִינַן מִגּוֹ Now that you say that we say.... The wording of this statement poses problems, since it was *Rava himself* who said that "since one acquires for himself," etc. Accordingly, some commentaries cite different readings here (see *Shittah Mekubbetzet*). *Ritva* explains that in fact all the Sages accepted Rava's principle of "since one acquires for himself...," and thus it was possible for Rava to use the expression "Now that *you* say that *we* say."

חֵרֵשׁ A deaf-mute. In Talmudic literature, this expression refers to a person who can neither hear nor speak; such a person is assumed to be mentally deficient (in modern Hebrew, by contrast, חֵרֵשׁ means "a deaf person," and this term refers even to deaf people who are able to speak and are mentally normal). A deaf-mute has essentially the same Halakhic status as a minor (קָטָן) or an imbecile (שׁוֹטֶה). Nevertheless, since a deaf-mute is not altogether mentally deficient, the Sages instituted a number of special regulations concerning deaf-mutes (e.g., as we see in the Gemara's discussion here, they were granted partial rights of acquisition). However, by Torah law, no one considered to be mentally deficient (including a deaf-mute) is able to sell or acquire property; similarly, such a person is exempt from fulfilling mitzvot.

HALAKHAH

חֵרֵשׁ וּפִקֵּחַ שֶׁהִגְבִּיהוּ כְּאֶחָד A deaf-mute and a normal person who lifted a found object together. "If a deaf-mute and a normal person lifted a found object together, neither one acquires it; since the normal person does not acquire the object, neither does the deaf-mute. Thus, if someone else seized the object from them, it belongs to him. However, if a single deaf-mute lifted a found object, or if two deaf-mutes lifted a found object together, they do acquire it, by Rabbinic decree (this decree having been enacted to prevent disputes)." (*Shulḥan Arukh, Ḥoshen Mishpat* 269:4.)

TRANSLATION AND COMMENTARY

אֶלָּא אֵימָא [1]The Gemara seeks to resolve this objection by amending Rava's statement: **Rather, say: The deaf-mute acquires** his part of the found object, but **the normal person does not acquire** any part of the found object.

וּמַאי מִגּוֹ [2]**And what is** the place of **the "since" argument** in this ruling, as this is not a case of two people acquiring an object together, and Rava based his statement on the premise that "now that you say 'since'," etc.?!

מִגּוֹ דִּשְׁנֵי חֵרְשִׁין [3]The Gemara answers: **Since two deaf-mutes** who lift up a found object together do **ordinarily acquire** the object, **this** deaf-mute in our case **also acquires** his share in the found object (see also notes).

הַאי מַאי [4]But the Gemara objects: **What** sort of reasoning **is this?** [5]**Even if you say that** if **someone lifts a found object on behalf of someone else**, then **the other person acquires** it even where the finder is not also acquiring a part of the object for himself, as Rami bar Hama argued, [6]**this would only apply where the first person lifted** the object **with the intention that the other person** should acquire it. [7]But here in our case, where a deaf-mute and a normal person lifted the object together, **the normal person lifted** the object **with the intention of acquiring it for himself!** He may be considered to have had the intention of assisting the deaf-mute to acquire his portion, as Rami bar Hama reasoned, but he certainly has no intention of enabling the deaf-mute to acquire the entire object. [8]Now, since in fact **he does not acquire** for himself, as we have just established, how **can he acquire for others?**

אֶלָּא אֵימָא [9]**Rather**, says the Gemara, it is necessary to amend Rava's statement again and to **say** that it should read as follows: **Since the normal person does not acquire** any part of the lost object, **the deaf-mute does not acquire** it either, as Rava's position is that an ownerless object can be acquired on behalf of someone else only if the finder himself also acquires part of it.

וְכִי תֵּימָא [10]The Gemara now anticipates a possible objection and proceeds to rebut it: **And if you say: What difference is there between this case**, where we say that neither the normal person nor the deaf-mute acquires ownership, **and the general case** previously mentioned **of two deaf-mutes**, where we say that both deaf-mutes acquire ownership? [11]The answer is: **There the Sages instituted** that both deaf-mutes should have **the power of acquisition so that they should not come to quarrel** with other people. This decree was instituted to prevent other people from trying to take unfair advantage of deaf-mutes, by taking away objects that they found.

[1]אֶלָּא אֵימָא: חֵרֵשׁ קָנָה, פִּקֵּחַ לֹא קָנָה.
[2]וּמַאי מִגּוֹ?
[3]מִגּוֹ דִּשְׁנֵי חֵרְשִׁין בְּעָלְמָא קָנוּ, הַאי נַמִי קָנֵי.
[4]הַאי מַאי?! [5]אִם תִּמְצָא לוֹמַר הַמַּגְבִּיהַּ מְצִיאָה לַחֲבֵירוֹ קָנָה חֲבֵירוֹ, [6]הָנֵי מִילֵּי הֵיכָא דְּקָא מַגְבַּהּ לֵיהּ אַדַּעְתָּא דְּחַבְרֵיהּ. [7]הַאי אַדַּעְתָּא דִּידֵיהּ קָא מַגְבַּהּ לֵיהּ. [8]אִיהוּ לָא קָנֵי. לְאַחֲרִינֵי מַקְנֵי?!
[9]אֶלָּא אֵימָא: מִתּוֹךְ שֶׁלֹּא קָנָה פִּקֵּחַ, לֹא קָנָה חֵרֵשׁ.
[10]וְכִי תֵּימָא: מַאי שְׁנָא מִשְּׁנֵי חֵרְשִׁין דְּעָלְמָא? [11]הָתָם, תַּקִּינוּ לְהוּ רַבָּנַן דְּלָא אָתֵי לְאִנְצוּיֵי,

LITERAL TRANSLATION

[1]Rather, say: The deaf-mute acquires, [but] the normal person does not acquire.

[2]And what is the "since" [argument]?

[3]Since two deaf-mutes ordinarily acquire, this one also acquires.

[4]What [sort of reasoning] is this? [5][Even] if you say [that] someone who picks up a found object for his fellow, his fellow acquires [it], [6]this [only] applies (lit., "these words") where [the first person] picks it up with the intention that his fellow [should acquire it]. [7][But here] this [normal] person picks it up with the intention of himself [acquiring it]. [8]He does not acquire. Can he acquire for others?

[9]Rather, say: Since the normal person does not acquire, the deaf-mute does not acquire.

[10]And if you say: What difference is there [between this case and] the general [case] of two deaf-mutes? [11]There, the Sages instituted for them [that they should acquire] so that they should not come to quarrel.

RASHI

ומאי מגו – היכא למימר הכא, דקאמר: השתא דאמרת מגו – אמרינן מגו, וחרש אמאי קני? הא לא זכי פקח לנפשיה, דנימא דזכי נמי לחבריה, ולא הויא הגבהה דפקח הגבהה! **אם תמצא לומר** – כלומר, אפילו אם תמצא לומר המגביה מציאה לחבירו כו'. **הכא אדעתא דידיה קא מגבה ליה** – האי פיקח. **דלא ליתי לאינצויי** – עם החוטפים מהם. **מהיכא** – מאיזו בבא ממשנתנו קא דייק לומר "זאת אומרת"?

NOTES

מִגּוֹ דִּשְׁנֵי חֵרְשִׁים **Since two deaf-mutes**. Since two deaf-mutes who pick up a found object together acquire it, even though a deaf-mute is ordinarily not capable of acquiring property (except by Rabbinic decree), the Sages also ordained that if a deaf-mute and a normal person lift up a found object together, the deaf-mute acquires ownership of the part he is holding, even though the normal person does not acquire the object at all (*Ritva*).

TERMINOLOGY

אֶלָּא מִמִּשְׁנָה יְתֵירָה Rather, from the additional clause. A proof based on the principle of מִשְׁנָה יְתֵירָה — (an additional, apparently superfluous, expression in the Mishnah) — parallels a form of proof used in Halakhic Midrashim based on apparently superfluous expressions in the Bible. In other words, although the content of the text offers no direct proof, one may nevertheless claim that the "superfluous" wording is meant to teach something additional about the subject and to expand the Halakhah to an area that was not explicitly mentioned but is in fact logically connected to it.

TRANSLATION AND COMMENTARY

[1]But **here**, where a deaf-mute and a normal person pick up the found object together, **the deaf-mute says** to himself: **"The normal person does not acquire** the found object. How, then, **should I acquire** it?" Therefore, if other people intervene and take the found object away from them both, the deaf-mute will not quarrel with them.

This concludes the discussion of the difference of opinion between Rami bar Ḥama and Rava as to the implications of Rami bar Ḥama's inference from our Mishnah regarding the general case of a person picking up an ownerless object on behalf of someone else. The Gemara now proceeds to analyze from which particular part of our Mishnah Rami bar Ḥama draws his inference.

אֲמַר לֵיהּ [2]**Rav Aḥa the son of Rav Adda said to Rav Ashi: From where** in our Mishnah **is Rami bar Ḥama's inference drawn?** [3]**If we say:** It is derived **from the first clause** of the Mishnah, which states: **"Two people are holding on to a garment,"** [4]**surely there** the Mishnah is dealing with a case where **the first** claimant **says,** "The found object **is all mine, and I lifted all of it,"** [5]**and the other one says,** "The found object **is all mine, and I lifted all of it."** It is possible that both of them picked up the garment together, but it is also possible that one of them is telling the truth and the entire garment belongs to him. Hence how can any conclusions be drawn from this part of the Mishnah regarding acquisition on behalf of another person?

אֶלָּא מֵהָא דְּקָתָנֵי [6]**Rather,** suggests the Gemara, Rami bar Ḥama's inference was drawn **from what** the Mishnah **teaches** in the **next** clause: **"One says, 'It is all mine,' and the other says, 'It is all mine.'"** [7]**Why do we need** the further elaboration contained in **this** clause? Surely the Mishnah has already stated that each claimant maintains that it was he who found the lost garment! [8]**Rather, from this additional,** seemingly superfluous, **clause of the Mishnah, infer** that the Mishnah meant to teach us that [9]**if someone lifts up a found object for another person, the other person acquires it.**

וְהָא אוֹקִימְנָא רֵישָׁא [10]The Gemara now objects: **But surely we established** earlier in our analysis of the Mishnah (above, 2a) that **the first clause** of the Mishnah ("I found it") **refers to a dispute** about a **found object, and the second clause** ("It is all mine") **refers to a dispute about buying and selling!** Thus neither clause is superfluous, and we still have not found the source of Rami bar Ḥama's inference!

אֶלָּא מִסֵּיפָא [11]Accordingly, a new source for this ruling is now suggested: **Rather,** suggests the Gemara, Rami bar Ḥama derived his inference **from a later clause** of the Mishnah: **"One says, 'It is all mine,' and the other one says, 'Half of it is mine.'" Why do we need this** clause as well? It seems to be merely

[1]הָכָא, מֵימַר אָמַר: ״פִּקֵּחַ לָא קָנֵי, אֲנָא אַקְנֵי?״

[2]אֲמַר לֵיהּ רַב אַחָא בְּרֵיהּ דְּרַב אַדָּא לְרַב אַשִׁי: דִּיּוּקֵיהּ דְּרָמִי בַּר חָמָא מֵהֵיכָא? [3]אִי נֵימָא: מֵרֵישָׁא, ״שְׁנַיִם אוֹחֲזִין בְּטַלִּית״, [4]הָתָם הַאי קָאָמַר ״כּוּלָּהּ שֶׁלִּי, וַאֲנָא אַגְבַּהְתָּהּ כּוּלָּהּ״, [5]וְהַאי אָמַר ״כּוּלָּהּ שֶׁלִּי, וַאֲנָא אַגְבַּהְתָּהּ כּוּלָּהּ״.

[6]אֶלָּא, מֵהָא דְּקָתָנֵי: ״זֶה אוֹמֵר ׳כּוּלָּהּ שֶׁלִּי׳, וְזֶה אוֹמֵר ׳כּוּלָּהּ שֶׁלִּי׳״. [7]הָא תּוּ לָמָּה לִי? [8]אֶלָּא, מִמִּשְׁנָה יְתֵירָה שְׁמַע מִינָּהּ: [9]הַמַּגְבִּיהַּ מְצִיאָה לַחֲבֵירוֹ, קָנָה חֲבֵירוֹ.

[10]וְהָא אוֹקִימְנָא רֵישָׁא בִּמְצִיאָה וְסֵיפָא בְּמִקָּח וּמִמְכָּר!

[11]אֶלָּא, מִסֵּיפָא: ״זֶה אוֹמֵר ׳כּוּלָּהּ שֶׁלִּי׳ וְזֶה אוֹמֵר ׳חֶצְיָהּ שֶׁלִּי׳״. הָא

LITERAL TRANSLATION

[1]Here, [the deaf-mute] says: "The normal person does not acquire. Shall I acquire?

[2]Rav Aha the son of Rav Adda said to Rav Ashi: From where is Rami bar Ḥama's inference [drawn]? [3]If we say: From the first clause, "Two people are holding on to a garment," [4][surely] there this one says, "It is *all* mine, and I lifted *all* of it," [5]and the other one says, "It is *all* mine, and I lifted *all* of it."

[6]Rather, [it is drawn] from what [the Mishnah] teaches [next]: "This one says, 'It is all mine,' and this one says 'It is all mine.'" [7]Why do I also need this? [8]Rather, from the additional [clause in the] Mishnah infer: [9]Someone who picks up a found object for his fellow, his fellow acquires it.

[10]But surely we established the first clause [as referring] to a found object and the later clause [as referring] to [a dispute about] buying and selling!

[11]Rather, from a later clause [of the Mishnah]: "This one says, 'It is all mine,' and this one says, 'Half of it is mine.'" Why

RASHI

הא קאמר כולה שלי ואנא אגבהתיה — והיאך נאמר: לא יקנה לא זה ולא זה, ויבא אחר ויטלנה. והלא כל אחד טוען "אני הגבהתיה", ואין כאן מגביה מציאה לחבירו, ומה יש לו להשיב? בשלמא האי שכנגדו המוחזק בה כמוהו — אמר "לא הגבהת אתה כי אם אני", אבל אחר מן השוק מה יטעון? **ממשנה יתירה** — אמרינן דהגביה מציאה כו׳. ומשום הכי אמרינן יחלוקו; דאמרינן שניהם הגביהוה, והוה ליה כל אחד מגביה מציאה לו ולחבירו וקני. דאי משום דלא ידעינן הי מינייהו משקר, והוה ליה ממון המוטל בספק, וחולקין בשבועה משום שלא יהא כל אחד ואחד הולך ותוקף, כדאמרינן לעיל (ג,א) — הא שמעינא ליה מרישא!

TRANSLATION AND COMMENTARY

an application of the principle previously established in our Mishnah. [1]**Rather, from this additional**, seemingly superfluous, **clause in the Mishnah infer** that, **if someone lifts up a found object for someone else, the other person acquires it**.

וּמִמַּאי דִּבְמְצִיאָה [2]But the Gemara objects: **On what basis do you assume that** this clause in the Mishnah **is dealing with a dispute over a found object? Perhaps it is dealing with a dispute about buying and selling**, in which case Rami bar Ḥama's interpretation would not apply! [3]And **should you say** that **if** this clause of the Mishnah is merely dealing **with a dispute about buying and selling, what** need is **there** for the Mishnah **to state it** at all? [4]I can answer, says the Gemara, that even if this statement is dealing with buying and selling, **it is still necessary** for its own sake. **You might have imagined that you should say:** Since the claimant **who says "half of it is mine"** could have claimed that the entire object was his, but did not do so, he **should be considered like someone who returns a lost object** (in this case, the other half of the garment) to its rightful owner. **He should** thus **be exempt from taking an oath**. [5]The Mishnah, therefore, **informs us that** we do not employ this argument but rather suspect that **this** claimant **may be trying to deceive the court** when he says that only half of the object belongs to him. [6]**He may be thinking: "If I say** that **all of it is mine, I will have to take an oath**. [7]**I will say instead** that only half of the object is mine, **so that I will be** considered **like someone who returns a lost object, and I will be exempt from taking an oath**." Thus, even if this clause of the Mishnah is dealing with a dispute about buying and selling, it is still not superfluous, and therefore it cannot serve as the source for Rami bar Ḥama's inference.

אֶלָּא מֵהָא [8]**Rather**, suggests the Gemara, Rami bar Ḥama's inference **was derived from a later clause in the Mishnah: "If two people were riding on an animal,** and each one claims that the whole animal is his, they divide it." [9]**Why do we need this** clause as well? It seemingly teaches us nothing new. [10]**Rather, from this additional,** apparently superfluous, **clause of the Mishnah, infer** that, **if someone lifts up a found object for another person, the other person acquires it.**

וְדִלְמָא הָא קָמַשְׁמַע לַן [11]But again the Gemara objects: **Perhaps** this clause in the Mishnah is needed to **inform us of the following** law: **That** a person can **also acquire** an animal **by riding it**, despite the fact

תּוּ לָמָּה לִי? [1]אֶלָּא, מִמִּשְׁנָה יְתֵירָה שְׁמַע מִינָּהּ: הַמַּגְבִּיהַּ מְצִיאָה לַחֲבֵירוֹ, קָנָה חֲבֵירוֹ.
[2]וּמִמַּאי דִּבְמְצִיאָה? דִּלְמָא בְּמִקָּח וּמִמְכָּר! [3]וְכִי תֵּימָא: אִי בְּמִקָּח וּמִמְכָּר, מַאי לְמֵימְרָא? [4]אִיצְטְרִיךְ, סָלְקָא דַּעְתָּךְ אָמֵינָא: הַאי דְּקָאָמַר "חֶצְיָהּ שֶׁלִּי" לֶהֱוֵי כְּמֵשִׁיב אֲבֵידָה, וְלִיפָּטַר, [5]קָמַשְׁמַע לַן דְּהַאי אִיעֲרוּמֵי קָא מַעֲרִים. [6]סָבַר: "אִי אָמֵינָא 'כּוּלָּהּ שֶׁלִּי', בָּעֵינָא אִשְׁתַּבּוּעֵי. [7]אֵימָא הָכִי, דְּאֶהֱוֵי כְּמֵשִׁיב אֲבֵידָה, וְאִיפָּטַר".
[8]אֶלָּא מֵהָא: "הָיוּ שְׁנַיִם רוֹכְבִין עַל גַּבֵּי בְהֵמָה". [9]הָא תּוּ לָמָּה לִי? [10]אֶלָּא מִמִּשְׁנָה יְתֵירָה שְׁמַע מִינָּהּ: הַמַּגְבִּיהַּ מְצִיאָה לַחֲבֵירוֹ, קָנָה חֲבֵירוֹ.
[11]וְדִלְמָא הָא קָמַשְׁמַע לַן: דְּרוֹכֵב נַמִּי קָנֵי!

LITERAL TRANSLATION

do I also need this? [1]Rather, from the additional [clause in the] Mishnah infer: Someone who picks up a found object for his fellow, his fellow acquires [it].

[2]But from what [do you infer] that [we are dealing] with [a dispute about] a found object? Perhaps [we are dealing] with [a dispute about] buying and selling? [3]And should you say: If [we are dealing] with [a dispute about] buying and selling, what [need] is there to say [it]? [4]It is [still] necessary, [because] you might have thought [that you] should say: This one who says, "Half of it is mine," should be [considered] like someone who returns a lost object, and he should be exempt [from taking an oath], [5][therefore] it informs us that this one [may be trying] to deceive [the court]. [6][For] he thinks: "If I say, 'All of it is mine,' I will have to take an oath. [7]I will say this [instead], so that I will be like someone who returns a lost object, and [I] will be exempt [from taking an oath].

[8]Rather, [it is derived] from this [later clause in the Mishnah]: "If two [people] were riding on an animal." [9]Why do I also need this? [10]Rather, from the additional [clause in the] Mishnah infer: Someone who picks up a found object for his fellow, his fellow acquires [it].

[11]But perhaps it is informing us of the following: that the rider also acquires it!

RASHI

דאהוי כמשיב אבידה – מדהוה מצי למימר "כולה שלי", ואמר "חציה שלי". **וליפטר** – משבועה. **ממשנה יתירה כו׳** – כדפרישית. **דרוכב קני** – ואף על גב דלא משיכה היא, שאינה זזה ממקומה, שאין מנהיגה ברגליו.

TERMINOLOGY

צְרִיכָא לְמֵימַר Is it necessary to say this? Since a similar matter has already been discussed, surely this is self-evident!

TRANSLATION AND COMMENTARY

that riding is not the normal mode of acquisition of an animal! Thus this clause, too, is not superfluous, and cannot serve as the basis for Rami bar Ḥama's inference!

אֶלָּא מְסֵיפָא [1]**Rather**, suggests the Gemara, Rami bar Ḥama drew his inference **from the** very **last clause of** our **Mishnah: "When** the claimants **admit or they have witnesses, they divide the object without an oath."** [2]The Gemara now proceeds to explain how this passage serves as Rami bar Ḥama's proof-text: **With what is this clause of the Mishnah dealing?** [3]**If it is dealing with buying and selling, is it necessary to state** that the claimants divide the object when they are in agreement? Surely this is obvious! [4]**Rather, is it not** obvious that this clause of the Mishnah is **dealing with a found object**, and since the claimants admit that they picked up the garment together they clearly create the situation described by Rami bar Ḥama. [5]We may therefore **infer from here** that **if someone picks up a found object for another person, the other person acquires it**, and a third party has no right to take it away from them.

וְרָבָא [6]**But**, asks the Gemara, what about **Rava**, who disagrees with the application of Rami bar Ḥama's principle to the general case where only one person picks up the object?

אָמַר לָךְ [7]The Gemara answers: Rava **can say to you**, as he said earlier, that this proof from our Mishnah is not conclusive, for it is possible to explain the ruling in the Mishnah on the basis of the general principle that, **since** the one claimant **acquires** part of the found object **for himself, he also acquires** part of it **for the other** claimant. In a situation where a person seeks to acquire an object for someone else without acquiring any part of the object for himself, Rava maintains that the act of acquisition for the other person is ineffective.

הָיוּ שְׁנַיִם רוֹכְבִין [8]The Mishnah stated: **"If two people were riding** an animal, or if one was riding and the other was holding on to the reins and driving it, the animal is divided between the two claimants." With reference to this Mishnah **Rav Yosef said: Rav Yehudah said to me:** [8B] [9]**I heard two** Halakhic rulings **from Mar Shmuel** regarding a **person** who **was riding an animal and a person** who **was driving** an animal. (Throughout the next discussion, the term "driving" will mean walking behind the animal and directing it, or leading it and pulling it along, unless the Gemara indicates otherwise.) [10]In **one** of these two cases the person **acquires** the animal

[1]אֶלָּא, מְסֵיפָא: ״בִּזְמַן שֶׁהֵן מוֹדִין אוֹ שֶׁיֵּשׁ לָהֶן עֵדִים, חוֹלְקִין בְּלֹא שְׁבוּעָה״. [2]בְּמַאי? [3]אִי בְּמִקָּח וּמִמְכָּר, צְרִיכָא לְמֵימַר?! [4]אֶלָּא לָאו, בִּמְצִיאָה? [5]וּשְׁמַע מִינָּהּ: הַמַּגְבִּיהַּ מְצִיאָה לַחֲבֵירוֹ, קָנָה חֲבֵירוֹ.

[6]וְרָבָא?

[7]אָמַר לָךְ: מִגּוֹ דְּזָכֵי לְנַפְשֵׁיהּ, זָכֵי נַמִי לְחַבְרֵיהּ.

[8]״הָיוּ שְׁנַיִם רוֹכְבִין״. אָמַר רַב יוֹסֵף: אָמַר לִי רַב יְהוּדָה: [8B] [9]שְׁמָעִית מִינֵּיהּ דְּמָר שְׁמוּאֵל תַּרְתֵּי: רָכוּב וּמַנְהִיג, [10]חַד קָנֵי

LITERAL TRANSLATION

[1]Rather, from the last clause [of the Mishnah]: "When they admit or they have witnesses, they divide [the object] without an oath." [2]With what [is this clause of the Mishnah dealing]? [3]If [it is dealing] with buying and selling, is it necessary to say [this]? [4]Rather, is it not [dealing] with a found object? [5]And infer from here: Someone who picks up a found object for his fellow, his fellow acquires [it].

[6]And Rava?

[7]He can say to you: Since he acquires for himself, he also acquires for his fellow.

[8]"If two [people] were riding." Rav Yosef said: Rav Yehudah said to me: [8B] [9]I heard two [things] from Mar Shmuel: [If a person was] riding [an animal] and [a person was] driving [it], [10]one acquires

RASHI

צריכה למימר — דהיכא דלקוחה בין שניהם שיחלקוה בלא שבועה? **אלא לאו במציאה** — ואיצטריך לאשמועינן שאין אחר יכול לחוטפה, דמגביה מציאה לחבירו קנה חבירו. **ורבא אמר לך** — בעלמא היכא דלא נתכוין המגביה לזכות בה — לא קנה חבירו. ומשנה יתירה דמתניתין אשמועינן המגביה מציאה לו ולחבירו — קנה אף חבירו, דמגו דזכי לנפשיה זכי נמי לחבריה. **שמעית מיניה דמר שמואל תרתי** — שמעתי ממנו שני דברים: דין רכוב ודין מנהיג. בחד אמר לי קני: ובחד אמר לי: לא קני, ולא ידענא כו׳.

NOTES

שְׁמָעִית מִינֵּיהּ דְּמָר שְׁמוּאֵל I heard from Mar Shmuel. Some commentators explain that Rav Yehudah did not actually hear *two separate rulings* from Shmuel. In fact Shmuel had issued a ruling concerning a case that came before him where one person was riding an animal and another was driving it. Rav Yehudah remembered that Shmuel had decided in favor of one of the two parties, but did not remember what that decision had been (cf. especially the conclusion of the Gemara). (*Rosh.*)

וְחַד לָא קָנֵי, [1]וְלָא יָדַעֲנָא הֵי מִינַּיְיהוּ.

[2]הֵיכִי דָּמֵי? [3]אִילֵימָא רָכוּב לְחוּדֵיהּ וּמַנְהִיג לְחוּדֵיהּ, [4]מַנְהִיג לְחוּדֵיהּ, מִי אִיכָּא מַאן דְּאָמַר לָא קָנֵי? [5]אֶלָּא, אִי אִיכָּא לְמֵימַר דְּלָא קָנֵי, רָכוּב הוּא דְּאִיכָּא לְמֵימַר.

[6]אֶלָּא, רָכוּב בִּמְקוֹם מַנְהִיג אִיבַּעֲיָא לֵיהּ, [7]מַאי? [8]רָכוּב עָדִיף, דְּהָא תָּפֵיס בָּהּ, [9]אוֹ דִּלְמָא מַנְהִיג עָדִיף, דְּאָזְלָא מֵחֲמָתֵיהּ?

LITERAL TRANSLATION

and one does not acquire, [1]and I do not know which of them [acquires].

[2]How do we visualize the case? (Lit., "how is it like?") [3]If we say [that the person] riding is by himself and [the person] driving is by himself, [4][if a person] driving is by himself, is there anyone who says that he does not acquire? [5]Rather, if it is [possible] to say that [one] does not acquire, it is [only possible] to say [this concerning] the one riding.

[6]Rather, he was in doubt concerning [one person] riding while [another] was driving. [7]What [is the law]? [8]Does [the person] riding have a better [claim], since he is holding on to [the animal], [9]or perhaps does [the person] driving have a better [claim], since [the animal] walks because of him?

TRANSLATION AND COMMENTARY

through the act of riding or of driving **and in the other** he **does not acquire,** [1]**but I do not remember** in **which of the** cases he said that the person **acquires**.

הֵיכִי דָּמֵי [2]The Gemara now attempts to clarify the issue under discussion: **How do we visualize the case?** [3]**If we say** that Shmuel was referring to two separate cases, one where **the person riding is by himself, and** the other where **the person driving is by himself**, and in each of these two cases another person appears and physically dispossesses the rider or the driver of the animal, and Shmuel justified the action of the second person in one of the cases, but Rav Yosef is unsure which one, then a problem arises. [4]If **the person driving** the animal **was by himself, is there anyone who would say that he does not acquire?** The normal way of acquiring an animal is to pull it until it moves its feet (מְשִׁיכָה), and driving achieves precisely this! [5]**Rather,** says the Gemara, **if it is possible to say that one** of the parties **does not acquire** the animal, **it is only possible to say this concerning the person riding** the animal. If, therefore, there were two separate cases referring to a single person riding or driving an animal, what doubt could Rav Yehudah have had about Shmuel's rulings? Shmuel must have been referring to riding an animal when he said that the act of acquisition was not effective and the animal remains ownerless!

אֶלָּא [6]**Rather**, another interpretation of Shmuel's ruling is now suggested: Driving an ownerless animal is definitely a valid mode of acquisition, and riding it may also be effective. Indeed, Rav Yehudah must have assumed that riding is just as effective as driving. But Rav Yehudah **was in doubt** as to what the law is in a case where two people are involved, **one riding** an animal, **while another was driving** it. [7]**What is the law** in such a case? [8]Do we say that **the person riding** the animal has a **better** claim to it, **since he is holding on to the animal** itself, and the law that an animal is acquired by pulling or driving only appies when there is no one riding it? [9]**Or** do we **perhaps** say that **the person driving** the animal has a **better** claim to it, **since** he is pulling or driving the animal and **it walks because of him**, and this, after all, is the normal way of acquiring an animal. Hence, even if riding is also effective, this can only be the case where no one is driving.

RASHI

אי נימא רכוב לחודיה — שאין אחר מנהיג עמו, ובא אחד מן השוק וחוטפו ממנו בפניו ומושכה לקנותה. וכן מנהיג ואין רכוב עמו ובא אחד וחוטפו ממנו בפניו לקנותה. וקאמר שמואל בחד מינייהו דלא קני, ומאן דחטף — שפיר חטף. ומבעיא ליה לרב יהודה בהי מינייהו. **מנהיג לחודיה מי איכא למאן דאמר דלא קני** — הא משיכה היא זו, ובהמה נקנית במשיכה, ומאי תיבעי ליה לרב יהודה? אי ודאי אמר שמואל בחד מינייהו דלא קני — ברכוב הוא דקאמר, דקסבר משיכה בעינן, שתעקור יד ורגל, כדאמרינן בקדושין (כב,ב). **אלא רכוב במקום מנהיג** — שניהם באים לפנינו זה רכוב וזה מנהיג, זה אומר "כולה שלי" וזה אומר "כולה שלי", אמר שמואל: חד קני. ומבעיא ליה לרב יהודה היכא דאיתנהו לתרוייהו, הי עדיף? רכוב עדיף — דהא תפיס בה, וכי אמרינן משיכה קני — היכא דליכא רכוב, אבל במקום רכוב — לא. **או דלמא מנהיג עדיף דקאזלא מחמתיה** — והיא הגדולה בקנין. **"למאן אי לרבי מאיר" כו' עד "לרבנן"** — לא גרס.

NOTES

רָכוּב וּמַנְהִיג One person riding the animal and another driving it. The Mishnah explicitly states that, if one person was riding a found animal and the other was driving it, each one may keep half. How, then, could Shmuel have maintained that only one person acquires the animal (either the rider or the person driving it)? Likewise, how could Rav Yehudah have been uncertain as to which party may keep the animal? Rabbi Yosef of Jerusalem answered that the rider referred to by Shmuel may not be the same sort of rider mentioned by the Mishnah. Shmuel's rider may have been spurring the animal on with his feet; since he rode the animal *actively*, he acquires it. By contrast, the rider mentioned in the Mishnah may have been passive, and hence he keeps only half of the animal. Alternatively, the

[1]אֲמַר רַב יוֹסֵף: אֲמַר לִי רַב יְהוּדָה: נֶחֱזֵי אֲנַן. [2]דִּתְנַן: ״הַמַּנְהִיג סוֹפֵג אֶת הָאַרְבָּעִים, וְהַיּוֹשֵׁב בַּקָּרוֹן סוֹפֵג אֶת הָאַרְבָּעִים. [3]רַבִּי מֵאִיר פּוֹטֵר אֶת הַיּוֹשֵׁב בַּקָּרוֹן״. [4]וּמִדְּאַפֵּיךְ שְׁמוּאֵל וְתָנֵי: וַחֲכָמִים פּוֹטְרִין אֶת הַיּוֹשֵׁב בַּקָּרוֹן, [5]שְׁמַע מִינָּהּ: רָכוּב לְחוּדֵיהּ לָא קָנֵי, [6]וְכָל שֶׁכֵּן רָכוּב בִּמְקוֹם מַנְהִיג.

LITERAL TRANSLATION

[1]Rav Yosef said: Rav Yehudah said to me: Let us see. [2]For we have learnt: "The person driving [the animals] receives the forty [lashes], and the person sitting in the wagon receives the forty [lashes]. [3]Rabbi Meir exempts the person sitting in the wagon." [4]And since Shmuel reversed [the Mishnah] and taught: "And the Sages exempt the person sitting in the wagon," [5]infer from here: [a person] riding [on an animal] by himself does not acquire, [6]and how much more so [a person] riding where [another person] is driving [does not acquire].

TRANSLATION AND COMMENTARY

אֲמַר רַב יוֹסֵף [1]**Rav Yosef** continued and **said: Rav Yehudah** did not remember exactly what Shmuel said, so he **said to me: Let us see** if we can solve the problem by ourselves, and work out what the two rulings of Shmuel were, and in which case he said that the act of acquisition was not effective. [2]**For we have learnt** in a Mishnah (*Kilayim* 8:3): "**A person who drives** an ox and an ass, or any other two animals of different species that are pulling a wagon, is punished by **receiving forty lashes**, since he violates the Torah's commandment (Deuteronomy 22:10): 'You shall not plow with an ox and an ass together,' since the Sages interpreted this verse as prohibiting all work done with mixed teams of animals, not just plowing. **And the person sitting in the wagon** is also punished by **receiving forty lashes**. [3]**Rabbi Meir**, however, **exempts the person sitting in the wagon** from punishment, because he performed no action that caused the animals to work." [4]Now, from the fact that **Shmuel reversed** the attributions in **the Mishnah**, attributing Rabbi Meir's opinion to the Sages, **and read** it as follows: "**The Sages exempt** from punishment **the person sitting in the wagon**," it is obvious that this is the viewpoint accepted by Shmuel, since the only reason he could have had for making such an emendation was in order to attribute the accepted view to the majority opinion of the Sages. [5]We may, therefore, **infer from here** that the act of sitting in a wagon drawn by animals, and presumably also riding the animal itself, is not considered Halakhically significant. Hence it follows that even **a person riding on an animal by himself**, with no driver present, **cannot** thereby **acquire** it without a formal act of acquisition. If that is true of a person riding an animal when no one is driving it, [6]**how much more so** is it the case that **a person riding** an animal cannot possibly acquire any share in it **where** someone else is **driving** the animal at the same time.

TERMINOLOGY

נֶחֱזֵי אֲנַן Let us see. When the scholars of the Talmud propose to clarify an issue on the basis of their own, independent, reasoning, they may use this expression.

LANGUAGE

קָרוֹן Wagon. This word is derived from the Greek κάρρον, *karron,* which means "wagon," "coach," or occasionally "chariot."

RASHI

נחזי אנן – אית לן למפשט משמעתא דמר שמואל בהי מינייהו אמר. **המנהיג** – בשור וחמור. **פוטר** – קסבר: לאו מידי עביד. **ומדאפיך שמואל כו׳** – שמע מינה: סבירא לשמואל רכוב לאו מידי מעשה עביד, ומשום דיחיד ורבים הלכה כרבים – אפכה למתניתין לאוקמא פטורא כרבנן. הכי גרסינן: שמע מינה סבירא ליה לשמואל רכוב לחודיה לא קני, ולא גרס: לרבנן.

NOTES

rider mentioned by Shmuel may have been passive, and therefore he does not acquire the animal at all, while the Mishnah may have been referring to an active rider, who was spurring the animal on; hence, he may keep half of it (cited by *Tosafot Rabbenu Peretz*). Others point out that the rider in our Mishnah does not claim to have acquired the animal together with the driver. Rather, he acquired the animal by himself, by riding it, and then the other claimant came along and seized the reins. From the Mishnah we can prove only that riding an animal is a way of demonstrating ownership, even when someone else is driving it; and even if riding is not a valid method of joint acquisition, so long as it is valid when done alone, it remains a demonstration of ownership (*Tosafot, Ran*).

הַמַּנְהִיג סוֹפֵג אֶת הָאַרְבָּעִים The person driving receives forty lashes. Two prohibitions apply regarding the mixing of different species of animals (e.g., an ox and an ass). (1) It is prohibited to breed them with each other (Leviticus 19:19). (2) It is prohibited to plow with them together, or to do any other work with them together (Deuteronomy 22:10).

הַיּוֹשֵׁב בַּקָּרוֹן One who sits in the wagon. At first glance, it would seem that the person sitting in the wagon is completely passive. Why, then, is he held liable for working with animals of diverse species (כִּלְאַיִם)? *Rashba* explains that, in fact, the animals begin to move as soon as they sense that someone is sitting in the wagon, and therefore he is the active cause of their moving. The same reasoning applies to a person riding an animal: even though he may be completely passive, not spurring the animal to move, it begins to move as soon as it feels the weight of the rider.

HALAKHAH

נְהִיגָה בְּכִלְאַיִם Driving a wagon drawn by animals of diverse species. "It is forbidden to sit in a wagon drawn by animals of diverse species (e.g., an ox and an ass), and it goes without saying that it is forbidden to drive such a wagon. Likewise, it is forbidden for one person to sit in the wagon and the other to drive it." (*Shulḥan Arukh, Yoreh De'ah* 297:12.)

Rambam (*Sefer Zeraim, Hilkhot Kelayim 9:9*), *Rif,* and *Rosh* maintain that not only the person driving the wagon, but also the person sitting in it, receives forty lashes, in

TRANSLATION AND COMMENTARY

אֲמַר לֵיהּ אַבַּיֵי לְרַב יוֹסֵף [1]**Abaye said to Rav Yosef:** On many occasions in teaching this law **you** have used the expression **to us, "Let us see** what the law is in this case," [2]**and you never quoted this expression in the name of Rav Yehudah!** Abaye often had to remind Rav Yosef about previous statements of his, because Rav Yosef had once fallen ill and his memory had been impaired. Abaye, therefore, thought that perhaps Rav Yehudah had never made the comment attributed to him by Rav Yosef!

אֲמַר לֵיהּ [3]But Rav Yosef **said to** Abaye: **Rav Yehudah indeed said this, and** to show you that I remember what happened, **I also remember that I said to** Rav Yehudah at the time, "While you have certainly proved that sitting in a wagon is not significant Halakhically, you have merely assumed that the same applies to a rider. [4]**How can you, Sir, derive the law** in the case **of a rider from** the law in **the case of a person sitting in a wagon**? [5]Surely **the person sitting** in the wagon **is not holding on to the reins, while the rider** of an animal **is holding on to the reins?!**" And, as the Gemara explains below, holding on to the reins may itself be a valid mode of acquisition! Thus, even though someone sitting in a wagon led by animals of mixed species may not violate any prohibition and may not acquire the animals, this does not mean that someone *riding* an animal does not acquire it! [6]But in response to this observation of mine Rav Yehudah **said to me: "Both Rav and Shmuel said:** [7]'Merely **holding on to the reins does not acquire** an ownerless animal.'" To acquire an ownerless animal, one must make the animal move. Passively holding the reins is not sufficient. Accordingly, the same laws apply whether a person is riding an animal or sitting in a wagon.

אִיכָּא דְּאָמְרִי [8]**There are some who say** that a slightly different exchange took place between Abaye and Rav Yosef, and Rav Yosef did not speak in the name of Rav Yehudah but gave his own opinion: **Abaye said**

[1]אֲמַר לֵיהּ אַבַּיֵי לְרַב יוֹסֵף: הָא זִמְנִין סַגִּיאִין אֲמַרְתְּ לָן "נֶחֱזֵי אֲנַן", [2]וְלָא אֲמַרְתְּ לָן מִשְּׁמֵיהּ דְּרַב יְהוּדָה!

[3]אֲמַר לֵיהּ: אִבְרָא, וּדְכַרְנַן נַמִי דַּאֲמַרִי לֵיהּ: [4]"הֵיכִי פָּשֵׁיט מָר רָכוּב מִיּוֹשֵׁב? [5]יוֹשֵׁב לָא תָּפֵיס בְּמוֹסֵירָה, רָכוּב תָּפֵיס בְּמוֹסֵירָה". [6]וַאֲמַר לִי: "רַב וּשְׁמוּאֵל דְּאָמְרִי תַּרְוַיְיהוּ: [7]מוֹסֵירָה לָא קָנֵי".

[8]אִיכָּא דְּאָמְרִי: אֲמַר לֵיהּ אַבַּיֵי לְרַב יוֹסֵף: הֵיכִי פָּשֵׁיט מָר

LITERAL TRANSLATION

[1]Abaye said to Rav Yosef: Surely many times you have said to us "Let us see," [2]and you did not say [this] to us in the name of Rav Yehudah.

[3]He said to him: [Rav Yehudah] indeed [said this], and I also remember that I said to him, [4]"How can you, Sir, derive [the law of a person] riding from [the case of a person] sitting [in a wagon]? [5][The person] sitting [in the wagon] is not holding on to the reins, [while the person] riding is holding on to the reins." [6]He said to me: "Both Rav and Shmuel said: [7][Holding on to the] reins does not acquire [an ownerless] animal."

[8][There are] some [who] say: Abaye said to Rav Yosef: How can you, Sir, derive

RASHI

והא זמנין סגיאין אמרת – להא שמעתין "נחזי אנן". **ולא אמרת לן** – אלא מסמך למפסט ספיקו דרב יהודה! **אברא** = אמת. הוא אמר לי "נחזי אנן", וזכור אני שאמרתי לו "היכי תפשוט מר רכוב מיושב בקרון"? **מוסירה** = קבישטר"א. **מוסירה אינה קונה** – במליאה, עד שיוליכנה ותעקור יד ורגל. ואף על גב דבמכירה קני, כדתנן (קדושין כה,ב): בהמה גסה נקנית במסירה, לגבי מליאה לא קני, כדאמרינן טעמא לקמן בשמעתין. **איבא דאמרי** – רב יוסף משמיה דנפשיה קאמר "נחזי אנן", ואמר ליה אביי "היכי תפשוט רכוב כו'".

LANGUAGE

אִבְרָא **Indeed, it is true.** Some scholars maintain that this word is derived from the Persian *avar*, which means "truth," or "in truth," while others suggest that it is derived from Middle Persian *evar*, with the same meaning.

NOTES

מוֹסֵירָה לָא קָנֵי **Holding on to the reins does not acquire.** The mere fact of touching or holding an object does not in itself confer ownership of it. Some action must be performed which affects the object, or it must be moved in an appropriate manner (pulling, lifting, transferring from one domain to another). Merely holding the reins of an animal, even though one may lift up the reins themselves, does not cause the animal to move, and therefore it may be claimed that it does not confer ownership of the animal. Moreover, the acquisition of an animal by receiving the reins from its former owner is not the same as acquisition by pulling, but is an expression of the transfer of possession from one person to another (similar to the transfer of a key in the sale of a dwelling). In order for this form of acquisition to be valid, one person must confer the object upon another. In such cases דַּעַת אַחֶרֶת מַקְנָה — "another person consciously conveys ownership" — and the act of acquisition is Halakhically effective.

מוֹסֵירָה לָא קָנֵי **Holding on to the reins does not acquire.** The Gemara refers here to a case where the person holding on to the reins *did not pull* on them, and thus did not perform the valid act of acquisition called קִנְיַן מְשִׁיכָה — "acquisition by pulling." Thus, if the rider merely holds on to the reins without pulling them, he can only acquire the animal by the valid act of acquisition called מְסִירָה — "transfer" — if someone actively transfers it to him, whether by handing him the reins or by telling him to take possession of the animal.

HALAKHAH

accordance with the Sages' opinion here. Shmuel's emendation of the Mishnah is not accepted, because his view involves many difficulties (see the continuation of the discussion below). (*Rosh*.)

TRANSLATION AND COMMENTARY

to Rav Yosef: How can you, Sir, derive the law in the case **of a rider from** the law in **the case of a person sitting in a wagon?** [1]Surely **the person sitting in the wagon is not holding on to the reins, while the rider** of an animal **is holding on to the reins!**

אֲמַר לֵיהּ [2]Rav Yosef **said** in reply **to** Abaye, **Idi taught** a Baraita **as follows:** Merely **holding on to the reins does not acquire** an ownerless animal. [3]And not only was this view reported by Idi as a Baraita, but **it was also stated** in the following Amoraic dictum: **Rav Ḥelbo said in the name of Rav Huna**, In buying and selling, merely by **taking over the reins** of an animal a buyer **acquires** an animal **from another person.** [4]But he **cannot** use this method to **acquire a found object or the property of a proselyte** who died without leaving any heirs, since in such cases the animal has no owner.

מַאי לְשׁוֹן מוֹסֵירָה [5]The Gemara now explains that the reasoning behind this ruling is linguistic: **What is the meaning of the word** מוֹסֵירָה — "reins"?

אֲמַר רָבָא [6]**Rava said: Idi explained it to me:** The word מוֹסֵירָה is derived from the Hebrew root מסר — "to hand over, to transfer" — as in "**a person who hands over** (מוֹסֵר) **something to someone else.**" [7]Thus, the reins are designed to be handed by one person to another, as a way of transferring ownership of an animal. Hence I will **grant** you **that** a buyer **can acquire** an animal **from another person by taking hold of the reins,** [8]**because the other person is handing over the reins** of the animal **to him.** [9]**But in the case of a found object or the property of a proselyte** who died without heirs, [10]**who** was there to **hand over the reins** of the animal **to him to enable him to acquire it**? Certainly, merely holding on to the reins without being handed them is of no Halakhic significance.

רָכוּב מִיּוֹשֵׁב? [1]יוֹשֵׁב לָא תָּפֵיס בְּמוֹסֵירָה, רָכוּב תָּפֵיס בְּמוֹסֵירָה!

[2]אֲמַר לֵיהּ: הָכִי תָּנָא אִידִי: מוֹסֵירָה לָא קָנֵי.

[3]אִתְּמַר נַמִי: אָמַר רַבִּי חֶלְבּוֹ אָמַר רַב הוּנָא: מוֹסֵירָה מֵחֲבֵירוֹ קָנָה, [4]בִּמְצִיאָה וּבְנִכְסֵי הַגֵּר לָא קָנֵי.

[5]מַאי לְשׁוֹן מוֹסֵירָה?

[6]אֲמַר רָבָא: אִידִי אַסְבְּרָא לִי: כְּ״אָדָם הַמּוֹסֵר דָּבָר לַחֲבֵירוֹ״. [7]בִּשְׁלָמָא מֵחֲבֵירוֹ קָנֵי, [8]דְּקָא מָסַר לֵיהּ חַבְרֵיהּ. [9]אֶלָּא בִּמְצִיאָה וּבְנִכְסֵי הַגֵּר, [10]מַאן קָא מָסַר לֵיהּ דְּלִיקְנֵי?

LITERAL TRANSLATION

[the law of a person] riding from [the case of a person] sitting [in a wagon]? [1][The person] sitting [in the wagon] is not holding on to the reins, [while the person] riding is holding on to the reins!

[2]He said to him: Idi taught as follows: [Holding on to the] reins does not acquire [an ownerless animal].

[3]It was also said: Rav Ḥelbo said in the name of Rav Huna: [A person taking over the] reins acquires from another person, [4][but] does not acquire [in this way] a found object or the property of a proselyte.

[5]What is [the meaning of] the word מוֹסֵירָה — "reins"?

[6]Rava said: Idi explained it to me: As [in] "a person who hands over (מוֹסֵר) something to another person." [7]Granted that he acquires from another person [by taking hold of the reins], [8]for the other person hands over [the reins] to him. [9]But in [the case of] a found object or the property of a proselyte, [10]who handed over [the reins] to him that he might acquire?

RASHI

אידי — שם חכם. **מחבירו** — מקח וממכר. **בנכסי הגר** — שמת ואין לו יורשין, וכל הקודם בנכסיו זכה בהן. **ומהו לשון מוסירה** — שמוסרין אותו בו ללוקח.

TERMINOLOGY

אִתְּמַר נַמִי It was also said. An expression used to introduce an Amoraic tradition (usually attributed to one of the early Amoraim) in support of a statement (usually by one of the later Amoraim).

SAGES

אִידִי Idi. This could be Rav Idi bar Avin Nagara, an Amora of the third generation, who was a student of Rav Ḥisda and also studied under Rav's other disciples. In Rava's time he was already one of the most important Sages of his generation, and Rava presents his explanations in several instances. Generally these explanations are proofs deriving from linguistic usage in the Bible or based on grammar. Idi apparently lived in the city of Shekanzib, and important Sages such as Rav Pappa and Rav Huna the son of Rav Yehoshua were his students. Two of his sons were also Sages.

CONCEPTS

נִכְסֵי הַגֵּר The property of a proselyte. A proselyte who dies childless leaves his property without heirs, because by converting he has joined the Jewish people, and his legal connections with his non-Jewish family are no longer taken into consideration. In contrast, if a Jew dies, even if he has no children or other known close relatives, since he is a Jew by birth he certainly has some relative, even if only a distant one, who can inherit the property. In such cases, while it may be difficult to locate the heirs, from a legal point of view they do exist, and the property belongs to them, wherever they may be. On the other hand, a proselyte who dies childless has no heirs, and his property is therefore regarded as ownerless, and whoever takes possession of it first acquires it. Because of this, the term נִכְסֵי הַגֵּר — "the property of a proselyte" — is regarded as a classic example of ownerless property.

HALAKHAH

קִנְיָן בְּמוֹסֵירָה מֵחֲבֵירוֹ Acquisition from another person by holding on to the reins. "An animal cannot be acquired by the buyer merely holding on to the reins, but only by being pulled by the buyer (מְשִׁיכָה; *Bet Yosef*). Others maintain that transfer (מְסִירָה — as, for example, by taking hold of the reins) is a valid mode of acquisition of animals, but only for large cattle (*Haggahot Maimoniyyot*). Still other authorities maintain that transfer is a valid means of acquisition even for smaller animals (e.g., sheep and goats), if performed in the presence of the seller (*Tur*, based on *Rashi* and *Rabbenu Tam*; followed also by *Sma*)." There is a difference of opinion among those who follow this view as to precisely what type of transfer is necessary here; some argue that the seller must physically transfer the animal from his possession to that of the buyer, while others maintain that it is sufficient for the buyer to take hold of the animal after having been instructed to do so by the seller (see also *Arukh HaShulḥan*). (*Shulḥan Arukh, Ḥoshen Mishpat* 197:1.)

מוֹסֵירָה בִּמְצִיאָה וּבְנִכְסֵי הַגֵּר Holding on to the reins in order to acquire a found animal or the property of a proselyte. "If a person took hold of the reins of a found animal (or an animal that had previously been owned by a proselyte who died without leaving any heirs), he does not thereby acquire it. Hence, if someone else pulls the animal or drives it, he acquires it, and the person holding on to the reins acquires only the reins (Gemara below)." (*Shulḥan Arukh, Ḥoshen Mishpat* 271:2.)

TRANSLATION AND COMMENTARY

מֵיתִיבֵי [1]**An objection** based on our Mishnah **was raised** against Rav Yehudah's opinion that a person does not acquire an animal by riding it in the same way as he does not acquire it by sitting in a wagon: Our Mishnah states: "If **two people were riding an animal**, and they both claim to have found it, they divide ownership of the animal between them." This surely implies that riding is a valid mode of acquisition!

מַנִּי [2]The Gemara clarifies the objection: **Whose view is** our Mishnah reflecting? [3]**If we say** that it represents the minority opinion of **Rabbi Meir,** who stated previously, in the Mishnah in *Kilayim* (according to Shmuel's emendation), that even the person sitting in the wagon drawn by animals of diverse species is punished by receiving forty lashes, [4]**now**, according to Rabbi Meir, even **a person sitting in a wagon** can **acquire** a found animal, since in his view sitting is considered a Halakhically significant act both with regard to the laws of כִּלְאַיִם — "diverse species" — and with regard to the laws of acquisition. If this is so, **can there be any doubt that a person riding** an ownerless animal acquires it? Thus, if our Mishnah follows the view of Rabbi Meir, there was no need for it to teach us that riding is considered a Halakhically significant act! [5]**Rather**, must we **not** say that our Mishnah follows the view of **the Sages**, who maintain that someone sitting in a wagon drawn by animals of diverse species is exempt from punishment, and by implication cannot acquire. Hence the Mishnah needs to inform us that riding on an animal and holding its reins is not equivalent to sitting in a wagon. [6]**And we may infer from here** that, according to the Sages, **a person riding a found animal acquires** it against Rav Yehudah's view equating "riding" with "sitting in a wagon"!

הָכָא בְּמַאי עָסְקִינַן [7]But the Gemara replies: The Mishnah does indeed reflect the view of the Sages, and it certainly does prove that "riding" as defined in the Mishnah is not equivalent to sitting in a wagon. However, **with what** circumstances **are we dealing here** in our Mishnah? [8]**With** a rider who is not sitting passively on the animal, but who is **driving the animal with his feet** by spurring it on or kicking it. Since this rider causes the animal to move, even the Sages would agree that he acquires the animal, not because he is holding the reins, but because he is also driving the animal.

אִי הָכִי [9]The Gemara now objects: **If** we assume that our Mishnah is referring only to a rider who actively causes the animal to move, the case of a "rider" discussed by our Mishnah **is** essentially **the same as** that of **a person driving** the animal in the regular way while himself walking next to it! Why, then, did our Mishnah distinguish between "one person riding and the other person driving," as if these were two separate legal categories?

[1]מֵיתִיבֵי: ״הָיוּ שְׁנַיִם רוֹכְבִין עַל גַּבֵּי בְהֵמָה וכו׳״.
[2]מַנִּי? [3]אִילֵימָא: רַבִּי מֵאִיר, [4]הָשְׁתָּא יוֹשֵׁב קָנֵי, רָכוּב מִיבָּעֲיָ?! [5]אֶלָּא לָאו רַבָּנַן, [6]וּשְׁמַע מִינָּהּ: רָכוּב קָנֵי! [7]הָכָא בְּמַאי עָסְקִינַן? [8]בְּמַנְהִיג בְּרַגְלָיו.
[9]אִי הָכִי, הַיְינוּ מַנְהִיג!

LITERAL TRANSLATION

[1]An objection was raised: "[If] two [people] were riding on an animal..."
[2]Who[se view] is this? [3]If we say: Rabbi Meir's, [4]now [if a person] sitting [in a wagon] acquires, is there a question [about a person] riding?! [5]Rather, is it not the Sages, [6]and infer from here: [a person] riding acquires [a found animal]!
[7]With what [circumstances] are we dealing here? [8]With someone driving [the animal] with his feet.
[9]If so, it is the same as a person driving!

RASHI

אי נימא רבי מאיר — דאמר היושב בקרון סופג את הארבעים. ומתניתין יחידאה היא, ולית הלכתא כוותיה. **השתא לרבי מאיר יושב קני** — דקאמר: היושב בקרון סופג את הארבעים, **רכוב מיבעיא** — ולמה לי לאשמועינן בתרתי?! **אלא לאו רבנן** — ואשמועינן דיושב הוא דפטור, אבל רכוב — לא, ותיובתא לרב יהודה דפשט רוכב מיושב. **במנהיג ברגליו** — דקנייה במשיכה, שבועט בה ברגליו והולכת מחמתו, כדרך רוכבי סוסים. **היינו מנהיג** — והוה ליה למיתני: או שהיו שניהם מנהיגים!

HALAKHAH

קָנְיַן בִּרְכִיבָה **Acquiring an animal by riding it**. "An animal is acquired by riding. According to *Rif* and *Rambam*, passive riding is a valid mode of acquisition (these authorities reject Shmuel's view, because the difficulties that it entails can only be resolved through forced explanations — *Gra*). According to *Bet Yosef*, however, *Rambam* agrees that riding an animal is a valid mode of acquisition only if the animal moves because of the rider (the same view is expressed by the *Shulḥan Arukh*). According to *Rosh* and *Tur*, the rider acquires the animal only if he drives it while he is riding it." (*Shulḥan Arukh, Ḥoshen Mishpat*, 138:1, 197:5, 271:3.)

LANGUAGE

גַּוְונֵי Types, categories. The primary source of this word is the Persian *"gun,"* meaning color. This word was adopted by Hebrew in antiquity and is mainly used in that primary sense. In modern Hebrew the word has come to mean the shade of a color, but in Mishnaic Hebrew it apparently meant simply "color," as opposed to צֶבַע, which meant "dye." The word was also widely used by extension to refer to "a kind of thing," and here תְּרֵי גַּוְונֵי means two colors, something that appears in two colors, two aspects of something that is actually a single thing.

TRANSLATION AND COMMENTARY

תְּרֵי גַּוְונֵי מַנְהִיג [1]The Gemara answers: In fact, **there are two types of "driving"** being discussed by the Mishnah, one called "riding" and the other called "driving." [2]Legally, they are equivalent, but the reason why the Mishnah had to mention both of them was that **you might** mistakenly **have thought** that **the rider** mentioned in this Mishnah **has a better claim** than someone who merely drives the animal without riding it, **since he both drives the animal and** physically **holds on to it.** [3]**The Mishnah, therefore, informs us** that this is not so and that there is no difference between such a rider and someone who drives the animal without touching it.

תָּא שְׁמַע [4]The Gemara now returns to the earlier question, whether or not riding is a valid mode of acquisition: **Come, and hear** a proof from a Tosefta: If **two people were** together **pulling a camel or driving an ass,** [5]**or** if **one was pulling and the other was driving, [9A] they** each **acquire** a share in the animal **in this manner.** [6]**Rabbi Yehudah says: In fact, no one acquires a camel unless he pulls it, and no one acquires an ass unless he drives it,"** since these are the normal ways of making these animals move.

קָתָנֵי מִיהַת [7]The Gemara now proceeds to analyze the Tosefta: **At all events, the Tosefta stated: "Or one was pulling and one was driving."** [8]From the Tosefta's use of these terms we may infer: **Pulling and driving** are **indeed** valid modes of acquisition, **but riding** is not!

הוּא הַדִּין [9]However, the Gemara rejects this proof: **The same applies even to riding**, as riding is also a valid mode of acquisition, and the Tosefta is not attempting to present an exhaustive list of all the valid methods of acquiring camels and asses. [10]**But the reason why** the Tosefta **mentioned** only **pulling and driving was to exclude Rabbi Yehudah's view** as being incorrect. **For Rabbi Yehudah said**: [11]No one acquires **a camel unless he pulls it, and** no one acquires **an ass unless he drives it.** [12]**Hence**, the first opinion in the Tosefta was designed to **inform us that even the opposite way** - driving the camel and pulling the ass — is **also** a valid way to **acquire** the animals.

[1]תְּרֵי גַּוְונֵי מַנְהִיג. [2]מַהוּ דְּתֵימָא: רָכוּב עָדִיף, דְּהָא מַנְהִיג וְתָפֵיס בָּהּ; [3]קָא מַשְׁמַע לָן.

[4]תָּא שְׁמַע: "שְׁנַיִם שֶׁהָיוּ מוֹשְׁכִין בְּגָמָל וּמַנְהִיגִין בַּחֲמוֹר, [5]אוֹ שֶׁהָיָה אֶחָד מוֹשֵׁךְ וְאֶחָד מַנְהִיג, [9A] בְּמִדָּה זֹאת קָנוּ. [6]רַבִּי יְהוּדָה אוֹמֵר: לְעוֹלָם לֹא קָנָה עַד שֶׁתְּהֵא מְשִׁיכָה בְּגָמָל וְהַנְהָגָה בַּחֲמוֹר".

[7]קָתָנֵי מִיהַת: "אוֹ שֶׁהָיָה אֶחָד מוֹשֵׁךְ וְאֶחָד מַנְהִיג". [8]מוֹשֵׁךְ וּמַנְהִיג — אִין; אֲבָל רָכוּב — לָא!

[9]הוּא הַדִּין דַּאֲפִילּוּ רָכוּב, [10]וְהָא דְּקָתָנֵי מוֹשֵׁךְ וּמַנְהִיג לְאַפּוּקֵי מִדְּרַבִּי יְהוּדָה, דְּאָמַר: [11]"עַד שֶׁתְּהֵא מְשִׁיכָה בְּגָמָל וְהַנְהָגָה בַּחֲמוֹר". [12]קָמַשְׁמַע לָן דַּאֲפִילּוּ אִיפְּכָא נָמֵי קָנֵי.

LITERAL TRANSLATION

[1]There are two types of driving. [2]What you might have said is: The rider [has a] better [claim], since he is [both] driving [the animal] and holding on to it; [3][therefore] the [Mishnah] informs us [that this is not so].

[4]Come and hear: "Two [people] who were pulling a camel or driving an ass, [5]or where one was pulling and one was driving, [9A] they acquire in this manner. [6]Rabbi Yehudah says: In fact, no [one] acquires unless there is pulling of the camel and driving of the ass."

[7]At all events, [the Tosefta] stated: "Or one was pulling and one was driving." [8]Pulling and driving — yes; but riding — no! [9]The same applies (lit., "it is the argument") even to riding, [10]and the [reason] why [the Tosefta] mentioned pulling and driving was to exclude [the view of] Rabbi Yehudah, who said: [11]"Unless there is pulling of the camel and driving of the ass." [12][Therefore] it informs us that even the opposite [way] also acquires.

RASHI

תרי גווני מנהיג — דאי אשמועינן בשני מנהיגים דיחלוקו — לא היינו יודעים להאי. **מהו דתימא כו׳** — חמור דרכו בהנהגה, וגמל — דרכו במשיכה. **במדה זו** — לקמיה מפרש למעוטי מאי.

NOTES

תְּרֵי גַּוְונֵי מַנְהִיג Two types of driving. According to *Rashba*, the statement beginning מַהוּ דְּתֵימָא — "what you might have said is" — is not a continuation of the Gemara's original answer (i.e., "there are two types of driving"), but rather a separate, independent answer. According to this view, the Gemara's first answer must be interpreted as meaning that

HALAKHAH

מְשִׁיכָה בְּגָמָל וְהַנְהָגָה בַּחֲמוֹר Pulling and driving camels and asses. "If two people saw a lost ass and both drove it or pulled it, or if one pulled it and the other drove it, both acquire it. If two people found a lost camel and both pulled it or drove it, they both acquire it. But if one pulled the animal and the other drove it, only the person who pulled

[1]אִי הָכִי, לִיעָרְבִינְהוּ וְלִתְנִינְהוּ: [2]"שְׁנַיִם שֶׁהָיוּ מוֹשְׁכִין וּמַנְהִיגִין בֵּין בְּגָמָל בֵּין בַּחֲמוֹר"! [3]אִיכָּא חַד צַד דְּלָא קָנֵי. [4]אִיכָּא דְּאָמְרִי, מְשִׁיכָה בַּחֲמוֹר, [5]וְאִיכָּא דְּאָמְרִי, הַנְהָגָה בְּגָמָל. [6]וְאִית דְּמוֹתִיב מִסֵּיפָא: "בְּמִדָּה זוֹ קָנָה". [7]"בְּמִדָּה זוֹ" לְמַעוּטֵי מַאי? [8]לָאו לְמַעוּטֵי רָכוּב? [9]לָא, לְמַעוּטֵי אִיפְּכָא.

LITERAL TRANSLATION

[1]If so, let [the Tosefta] combine [the two parts of the sentence] and teach them: [2]"Two [people] who were pulling and driving either a camel or an ass"! [3]There is one method (lit., "side") that does not acquire. [4]Some say, pulling [in the case] of an ass, [5]and some say, driving [in the case] of a camel.
[6]And some raise the objection from the latter clause [of the Tosefta]: "They acquire in this manner." [7]"In this manner" excludes what? [8]Does it not exclude riding?
[9]No, it excludes the opposite.

TRANSLATION AND COMMENTARY

אִי הָכִי [1]The Gemara objects: **If so** — if the only reason why pulling and driving were mentioned in our Tosefta was to teach us that there is no difference between pulling a camel and driving an ass, and vice versa — **let the Tosefta combine the two parts of the** first **sentence and teach them** as follows: [2]"If **two people were pulling and driving either a camel or an ass**...." But since the Baraita was not phrased in this way, it is clearly intended to be understood as excluding some other action as not being effective as a mode of acquisition. Hence it seems reasonable to infer that "riding" was indeed omitted in order to teach us that this is not a valid mode of acquisition!

אִיכָּא חַד צַד [3]But the Gemara replies that it was not possible to combine the two parts of the first sentence of the Baraita for another reason, whose purpose was to exclude one type of action as an effective mode of acquisition: **There is one way** of moving a camel or an ass, among those mentioned in the Tosefta, **whereby** the person moving it **does not acquire** it. However, it is not clear which it is. In fact, a difference of opinion exists as to which way of moving which animal is invalid. [4]**Some say** that **pulling** is not a valid mode of acquisition **in the case of an ass**, since this is not the normal way to make it move, [5]**and some say** that **driving** is not a valid mode of acquisition **in the case of a camel**, since this is not the normal way to make it move. Thus, according to both opinions one of the animals can be acquired by both methods (by pulling and by driving) and the other animal can only be acquired by one. In dispute is which of the animals is restricted in this way. The Tanna of the Tosefta first specified the normal way used in the acquisition of each animal, and then indicated that *one* of the animals could be acquired by both methods. At all events, according to this explanation, nothing can be learnt from this Tosefta as to whether *riding* is an effective mode of acquisition or not.

וְאִית דְּמוֹתִיב מִסֵּיפָא [6]The Gemara now reports another version of the previous discussion: **And some raise the objection**, that riding is not an effective mode of acquisition, **from the latter clause of the Tosefta: "They acquire** the animal **in this manner."** [7]**What** are the words **"In this manner"** — i.e., *only* in this manner — intended to **exclude?** [8]**Are they not** intended specifically to **exclude riding?** According to this interpretation of the Baraita it would seem that riding is not a valid mode of acquisition!

לָא [9]But the Gemara rejects this interpretation and replies: **No**, the expression, "In this manner," **excludes** causing the animals to move by using **the opposite** method — driving the camel and pulling the ass, these being ineffective modes of acquisition.

RASHI

אי הכי — דלתנא קמא איפכא קני, אמאי קתני משיכה בגמל והנהגה בחמור? **ליערבינהו וכו׳ מושכין ומנהיגין! איכא חד צד דלא קני** — להכי לא מצי למתני בתרוייהו משיכה והנהגה. ותנא הכי: מושכין בגמל ומנהיגין בחמור, או שהיה אחד מושך ואחד מנהיג באחד מהן, אותו שדרכו בשניהם. **במדה הזאת** — קא סלקא דעתך במשיכה או בהנהגה, בין בגמל בין בחמור.

TERMINOLOGY

לִיעָרְבִינְהוּ וְלִתְנִינְהוּ Let him combine them and teach them! When a Mishnah (or a Baraita) discusses several cases in separate clauses, and the same law applies in each of the cases, the Talmud may ask why the Tanna did not formulate his statement more concisely. "Let him [=the Tanna] combine them [=the different cases] and teach them as one general principle!"

BACKGROUND

גָּמָל וַחֲמוֹר Camels and asses. Camels are not acquired in the same way as asses, because these animals are ordinarily directed and made to move in different ways. An ass is normally "driven," because it walks in front of its driver, who directs it from behind with a stick. This is not possible with a camel, whose driver usually walks in front of his animal and "pulls" it by the reins. This difference between camels and asses also finds expression in the Talmudic idiom חַמָּר-גַּמָּל — "ass driver-camel driver" — which the Sages used to describe an irreconcilable conflict caused by two forces pulling in opposite directions (see, e.g., Mishnah *Eruvin* 3:4).

NOTES

a rider who directs the animal with his feet has as great a power to acquire as a driver of the animal with his hands. The second answer is that a rider who holds the animal as well as drives it is no better than an ordinary driver.

וְאִית דְּמוֹתִיב מִסֵּיפָא Some raise the objection from the latter clause. Some commentators interpret the word מוֹתִיב (ordinarily used in the sense of "raises an objection") in our passage as meaning "brings a proof" (i.e., brings support for Shmuel's view that riding is not a valid mode of acquisition). (*Rivan* cited in the *Tosefot Rabbenu Peretz*.)

HALAKHAH

the animal acquires it." This ruling, which follows *Rambam*'s view, is based on the last clause of the second explanation of the Baraita, that there are circumstances when driving is not an effective mode of acquiring a camel. (*Maggid Mishneh*.) (*Shulḥan Arukh, Ḥoshen Mishpat* 271:1.)

BACKGROUND

איכא בינייהו צד אחד There is a difference of opinion between them regarding one method. Four possibilities (צדדים, lit., "sides") are mentioned here: pulling an ass, pulling a camel, driving an ass, and driving a camel. We assert that one of these possibilities is the subject of a difference of opinion, but we cannot determine which possibility is the one in dispute merely from the style or wording of the text.

[1]אִי הָכִי, הַיְינוּ רַבִּי יְהוּדָה! [2]אִיכָּא בֵּינַיְיהוּ צַד אֶחָד דְּלָא קָנָה. [3]אִית דְּאָמְרִי, מְשִׁיכָה בַּחֲמוֹר, [4]וְאִיכָּא דְּאָמְרִי, הַנְהָגָה בְּגָמָל. [5]תָּא שְׁמַע: ״אֶחָד רָכוּב חֲמוֹר וְאֶחָד תָּפוּס בְּמוֹסֵירָה, [6]זֶה קָנָה חֲמוֹר וְזֶה קָנָה מוֹסֵירָה״. [7]שְׁמַע מִינָּהּ: רָכוּב קָנֵי! [8]הָכָא נַמִי בְּמַנְהִיג בְּרַגְלָיו. [9]אִי הָכִי, נִקְנֵי נַמִי רָכוּב בְּמוֹסֵירָה!

LITERAL TRANSLATION

[1]If so, it is the same as [the view of] Rabbi Yehudah! [2]There is [a difference of opinion] between them [regarding] one method that does not acquire. [3]Some say, pulling [in the case] of an ass, [4]and some say, driving [in the case] of a camel.

[5]Come and hear: "[If] one was riding an ass and one was holding the reins, [6]this one acquires the ass and this one acquires the reins." [7]Infer from this [that] the rider [of an animal] acquires!

[8]Here, too, [the Baraita refers] to someone driving [the animal] with his feet.

[9]If so, the rider should also acquire the reins!

RASHI

אחד תפוס במוסירה — ואינו מנהיג.

שמע מינה רכוב קני — שלא במקום מנהיג. וכיון דשלא במקום מנהיג קני כוליה — במקום מנהיג פלגי. **נקני נמי רכוב במוסירה** — שבראש החמור, שהוא תכשיט החמור, וכחמור דמי!

TRANSLATION AND COMMENTARY

אִי הָכִי [1]The Gemara now objects to this explanation: **If** the Tosefta is understood in the way that has just been suggested, the first Tanna's view **is the same as the view of Rabbi Yehudah**. Both Tannaim agree that the only way to acquire these animals is by pulling the camel and driving the ass!

אִיכָּא בֵּינַיְיהוּ [2]The Gemara answers: **There is a difference between** the views of the first Tanna and Rabbi Yehudah **regarding one of the** two doubtful **methods** of causing the camel or the ass to move, **in which** the person causing it to move **does not acquire** it. According to the first Tanna, one of the two modes of acquisition, pulling and driving, is not always effective, although the other is; Rabbi Yehudah, by contrast, maintains that an ass and a camel can only be acquired if they are moved in the prescribed fashion, pulling for a camel and driving for an ass. [3]Thus, **some say** that, according to the first Tanna, it is **pulling** that is not a valid mode of acquisition **in the case of an ass**, [4]**and some say** that it is **driving** that is not a valid mode of acquisition **in the case of a camel** according to this Tanna. At all events, according to this second explanation of the Tosefta as well, nothing can be inferred from here as to whether riding is a valid mode of acquisition.

תָּא שְׁמַע [5]The Gemara now examines another Baraita, in order to determine whether riding is a valid mode of acquisition: **Come and hear**: "If **one** person **was riding an ass and** the other **was holding the reins** but not driving the animal, [6]the rider **acquires the ass, and** the person holding the reins **acquires the reins.**" [7]On the basis of this Baraita, the Gemara suggests: **Infer from this that the rider of an animal** indeed **acquires** the animal if no one else is driving it. And infer further that, since the rider acquires the whole animal in a case where there is no other person driving it, he should also acquire half of it in a case where another person *is* driving it.

הָכָא נַמִי [8]But the Gemara rejects this proof: **Here, too, the Baraita refers** not to a person passively seated upon the animal but **to** a rider who is actively **driving the animal with his feet**, and we have already established that such "active" riding is acknowledged by all authorities to be a valid mode of acquisition.

אִי הָכִי [9]The Gemara now objects: **If so**, if the riding mentioned in this Baraita is a fully valid mode of acquisition, **the rider should also acquire the reins** with the animal! Since the reins are attached to the animal, they should be considered as if they are an integral part of it, and the rider should acquire the reins together with the animal! But since, according to the Baraita, the rider does not acquire the reins, there must be something lacking in his acquisition of the animal as well!

NOTES

רָכוּב קָנֵי The rider acquires. Some commentators disagree with *Rashi* (whose explanation of the passage is included in the commentary) and explain that this inference was drawn in order to refute Rav Yehudah's ruling, in connection with the person sitting in the carriage (above, 8b), that one who rides an animal does not acquire it, even if no one else is driving it. (*Rashba, Ran.*)

HALAKHAH

אֶחָד רָכוּב חֲמוֹר וְאֶחָד תָּפוּס בְּמוֹסֵירָה One person was riding an ass and the other was holding the reins. "If two people wanted to acquire an ownerless animal, and one rode it while the other held on to the reins, the rider acquires the animal and the reins attached to the animal's head, while the person holding on to the reins acquires that portion of the reins which is in his hands," following the opinion of Rav Ashi. (*Shulḥan Arukh, Ḥoshen Mishpat* 271:3.)

[1]אֵימָא: ״זֶה קָנָה חֲמוֹר וַחֲצִי מוֹסֵירָה, [2]וְזֶה קָנָה חֲצִי מוֹסֵירָה״.

[3]בִּשְׁלָמָא רָכוּב קָנֵי, [4]דְּקָמַגְבַּהּ לֵיהּ בֶּן דַּעַת. [5]אֶלָּא תָּפוּס בְּמוֹסֵירָה — בְּמַאי קָנֵי?

[6]אֵימָא: ״זֶה קָנָה חֲמוֹר וְכוּלֵּיהּ מוֹסֵירָה, [7]וְזֶה קָנֵי מַה שֶּׁתָּפוּס בְּיָדוֹ״.

[8]הָאי מַאי?! [9]אִם תִּימְצֵי לוֹמַר הַמַּגְבִּיהַּ מְצִיאָה לַחֲבֵירוֹ, קָנָה חֲבֵירוֹ, [10]הָנֵי מִילֵּי הֵיכָא דְּקָא מַגְבַּהּ לֵיהּ אַדַּעְתָּא דְּחַבְרֵיהּ. [11]הָאי, אַדַּעְתָּא דִּידֵיהּ קָא מַגְבַּהּ לֵיהּ. [12]אִיהוּ לָא קָנֵי, לַאֲחֵרִינֵי מַקְנֵי?!

[13]אָמַר רַב אַשִׁי: זֶה קָנָה חֲמוֹר וּבֵית פַּגֶּיהָ, וְזֶה קָנָה מַה שֶּׁתָּפוּס בְּיָדוֹ, [14]וְהַשְּׁאָר לֹא קָנָה לֹא זֶה וְלֹא זֶה.

[15]רַבִּי אַבָּהוּ אָמַר: לְעוֹלָם

LITERAL TRANSLATION

[1]Say: "This one acquires the ass and half the reins, [2]and this one acquires half the reins."

[3]Granted that the rider acquires [half the reins], [4]because a mentally competent person lifted it up for him. [5]But the one holding the reins — with what does he acquire?

[6]Say: "This one acquires the ass and all of the reins, [7]and this one acquires what he is holding in his hands."

[8]What [sort of argument] is this? [9][Even] if you say [that] someone who picks up a found object for his fellow, his fellow acquires [it], [10]this [only] applies (lit., "these words") where he picks it up with the intention that his fellow [should acquire it]. [11][But] this one picks it up with the intention of [acquiring it] himself. [12][Now, if] he does not acquire [it, how can he] transfer it to another person?

[13]Rav Ashi said: This one acquires the ass and its halter, and this one acquires what he is holding in his hands, [14]but the remainder [of the reins] he does not acquire, neither this one nor this one.

[15]Rabbi Abbahu said: In fact,

TRANSLATION AND COMMENTARY

אֵימָא [1]The Gemara answers: It is necessary to amend the text of the Baraita and to say: "The rider **acquires the ass and half the reins,** [2]**and** the person holding the reins **acquires half the reins.**"

בִּשְׁלָמָא [3]But once again the Gemara objects: **Granted that the rider acquires half the reins,** [4]**because a mentally competent person** legally capable of making an act of acquisition, namely the person holding the reins, **lifted up** his part of the reins **for the rider.** The Gemara has already established (above, 8a) that when two people pick up an object together, each is considered to be performing the act of acquisition both for himself and for the other person. [5]**But** what about **the one holding the reins, with what does he acquire** even half of the reins, since the other half of the reins is resting on the ass? In order to acquire ownerless property by lifting, it is necessary to lift all of it!

אֵימָא [6]Accordingly, the Gemara amends the text of the Baraita once more and suggests: **Say:** "The rider **acquires the ass and all** [or, more precisely, almost all] **of the reins,** [7]**and** the person holding the reins **acquires whatever he is** actually **holding in his hands.**"

הָאי מַאי [8]Again the Gemara objects: **What sort of an argument is this?** How is such an explanation possible? [9]**Even if you say that** the law is that if **someone picks up a found object on behalf of someone** else, then **the other person acquires** it, [10]**this only applies where** the first person **picks up** the object **with the intention that the other person should acquire it.** [11]**But** here, in our case, **the** person holding the reins **picked** them **up with the intention of acquiring** them **for himself.** He has no intention of enabling the rider to acquire the reins! [12]**Now, if** the person holding the reins **does not** himself **acquire** the reins, as explained above, **how can he transfer** ownership of the reins **to someone else** (the rider)?

אָמַר רַב אַשִׁי [13]**Rav Ashi said** in reply that the Baraita must be amended as follows: "The rider **acquires the ass and its halter, and** the person holding the reins **acquires what he is holding in his hands.** [14]**But the remainder of the reins,** which neither the one nor the other is holding, **is not acquired by either** of them," since neither of them performed a valid act of acquisition for this part of the reins.

רַבִּי אַבָּהוּ אָמַר [15]**Rabbi Abbahu** gave a different explanation and **said: In fact, the Baraita** should be understood

RASHI

בשלמא רכוב — מצית למימר דקנה בהגבהת חבירו שהגביה ראשו השני מן הקרקע, דקא מגבה לה בן דעת, **אלא תפוס במוסירה במאי קני** — פלגא? והלא ראשה השני מונח במקומו, והגבהת הפקר לא קניא עד דעקר לכוליה! **האי מאי** — דקא אמרת הגבהת תופס במוסירה לא הויא הגבהה לדידיה, והויא הגבהה לאחריני. **אפילו אם תימצי לומר כו'. ובית פגיה** — קיבצי"ל בלעז, מה שבראש החמור, וכחמור דמי. **מה שתפוס בידו** — דמה שבתוך ידו הוי מגביה לגמרי. **לא זה ולא זה** — והבא לחוטפו יחטוף.

TERMINOLOGY

הָאי מַאי What is this? A term used to express astonishment at the previous statement, often with the significance: "How can you make such a comparison?!"

LANGUAGE

בֵּית פַּגֶּיהָ Its halter. The source of the term is apparently Arabic, meaning "cheek". בֵּית פַּגֶּיהָ is therefore the part of the harness which fits the animal's cheek. Some scholars have attributed the origin of the word to the Greek παγίς, *pagis*, some of the meanings of which are: ornamental pin, anchor, something that will grasp. In this view, בֵּית פַּגֶּיהָ is the part of the harness to which the reins are attached.

כִּדְקָתָנֵי, [1]הוֹאִיל וְיָכוֹל לְנַתְּקָהּ וּלְהָבִיאָהּ אֶצְלוֹ.
[2]וְהָא דְּרַבִּי אַבָּהוּ בָּרוּתָא הִיא.
[3]דְּאִי לָא תֵּימָא הָכִי, [4]טַלִּית, שֶׁהִיא מוּנַּחַת חֶצְיָהּ עַל גַּבֵּי קַרְקַע וְחֶצְיָהּ עַל גַּבֵּי עַמּוּד, [5]וּבָא אֶחָד וְהִגְבִּיהַּ חֶצְיָהּ מֵעַל גַּבֵּי קַרְקַע, [6]וּבָא אֶחָד וְהִגְבִּיהַּ חֶצְיָהּ מֵעַל גַּבֵּי עַמּוּד, [7]הָכִי נַמִי דְּקַמָּא קָנֵי וּבַתְרָא לָא קָנֵי, [8]הוֹאִיל וְיָכוֹל לְנַתֵּק וּלְהָבִיא אֶצְלוֹ! [9]אֶלָּא, הָא דְּרַבִּי אַבָּהוּ בָּרוּתָא הִיא.

LITERAL TRANSLATION

[the Baraita is] as taught [originally], [1]because [the person holding on to the reins] can detach [them] and bring [them] to himself.

[2]But this [statement] of Rabbi Abbahu is baseless.

[3]For if you do not say so, [4][if there is] a garment, half of which is resting on the ground and half of it on a pillar, [5]and one [person] comes and picks up half of it from the ground, [6]and another [person] comes and lifts [the other] half of it from the pillar, [7]so too the first person should acquire [it all] and the last person should not acquire [it at all], [8]because [the first person] can detach [the whole garment] and bring [it] to himself! [9]Rather, this [statement] of Rabbi Abbahu is baseless.

TRANSLATION AND COMMENTARY

as it was **originally transmitted,** without any emendation. Thus the person riding the ass acquires the ass, and the person holding the reins acquires the reins and the halter. [1]The reason for this ruling is **because the person holding on to the reins can** easily **detach** the reins and the halter **and bring them** over **to himself** without any help on the part of the rider. Since this person is potentially capable of pulling all the reins over to himself, he does not actually need to pick up the entire reins, and he acquires even that part of the reins which is at present resting on the ass.

וְהָא דְּרַבִּי אַבָּהוּ בָּרוּתָא הִיא [2]On this, however, the Gemara notes: **But this statement by Rabbi Abbahu is baseless**, and cannot be used as the basis for a discussion in the Academy. [3]**For if you do not say** that Rabbi Abbahu's statement is mistaken, [4]you will arrive at the false conclusion that where **half a garment is resting on the ground and half** is resting **on a pillar,** [5]**and one person comes and picks up** the one **half of it from the ground,** [6]**and another person comes and picks up the other half of it from the pillar** — [7]here, **too, the first person**, who picked up half of the garment from the ground, **should acquire** the entire garment, **and the second person should not acquire it at all,** [8]**because the first person could have detached the whole garment and brought it to himself!** But such a distinction between acquisition of a garment found on level ground and acquisition of a garment found partly on the ground and partly resting on an object above the ground is unknown. [9]**Rather,** concludes the Gemara, **this statement by Rabbi Abbahu is baseless**. Hence, if we wish to explain the Baraita as referring to "active driving," we must amend it along the lines suggested by Rav Ashi. In any case, we have still not solved the question whether riding is a valid mode of acquisition or not.

RASHI

כדקתני — זה קנה חמור וזה קנה מוסירה, אפילו בית פגיה של חמור. **הואיל ויכול** — התפוס במוסירה למושכו בכח, וינתק מראש החמור ויביאנו אצלו. דהואיל וראש החמור גבוה נוח להביאה אצלו בנתיקה אחת. **ברותא היא** — דאף על גב דיכול לנתק — לאו הגבהה היא. **חציה על גב העמוד** — דכיון דבמקום גבוה הוא, האוחזה בראשה השני נוח לו לנתק ולהביאה אצלו, דלא מחסר הגבהה. **הכי נמי דקמא קני** — דמכי אגבהה קניא כולה משום דיכול לנתקה — אם כן יש חילוק בשנים שהגביהו מציאה, זה מכאן וזה מכאן, בין מקום גבוה למקום נמוך. דהיכא דשני ראשיה מונחים בקרקע — אין הגבהת של ראשון קונה כולה, שאין יכול לנתקו ולהביאו אצלו. מתוך שהוא ארוך ומונח בקרקע כל מה שהוא נותקו ומושכו אחריו נגרר הוא על גבי קרקע. והיכא דאחד מראשיה גבוה, כגון בראש החמור או על גבי עמוד — המגביה תחלה ראש שעל גבי קרקע קונה כולה, ואנן לא אשכחן תנא דמפליג.

SAGES

רַבִּי אַבָּהוּ Rabbi Abbahu. A Palestinian Amora of the third generation, Rabbi Abbahu was the most important of Rabbi Yoḥanan's disciples. He was the head of a yeshivah and a judge in Caesarea as well as the representative of the Jewish people to the Romans. He also transmits teachings in the name of Resh Lakish, Rabbi Elazar, Rabbi Yose bar Ḥanina, and others. Rabbi Zera was a student and colleague of his. His colleagues were: Rabbi Ḥiyya bar Abba, and Rabbi Ami and Rabbi Assi, the heads of the Tiberias Yeshivah. Among his students were: Rabbi Yonah, Rabbi Yose, and Rabbi Yirmeyah. Sages gathered around him, becoming known as the Rabbis of Caesarea. He was prolific in Aggadah and an excellent preacher. He spoke Greek well, and taught that language to his daughter. His father-in-law was Rabbi Taḥlifa of Caesarea, and his sons were the Sages Ḥanina, Avimi, and Zera.

NOTES

בָּרוּתָא הִיא It is baseless. בָּרוּתָא means literally "something external, outside," i.e., a viewpoint which is "foreign," and not worthy of serious consideration in the Academy. Others read בְּרוּתָא — "fiction"; according to this reading, the Gemara is saying that it is simply not true that Rabbi Abbahu ever made the remark attributed to him. This expression is at all events a polite way of rejecting the Sage's opinion.

טַלִּית שֶׁהִיא מוּנַּחַת A garment partly resting on the ground. *Tosafot* asks: On what basis does the Gemara assume that Rabbi Abbahu would agree that where parts of a found garment are lying at different heights both litigants have equal claim to the garment? Perhaps Rabbi Abbahu has a different opinion! *Ritva* explains that, since such cases were encountered every day, it was common knowledge that all the Sages agreed that both litigants have equal claim to the garment. Alternatively, since our Mishnah does not distinguish between cases where the ends of a contested garment may or may not be lying on the ground, we may infer that in any case the claimants divide the garment, and thus both have equal claim to it (*Ra'avad*).

חֶצְיָהּ עַל גַּבֵּי עַמּוּד Half of it on a pillar. The explanation offered by Rabbi Abbahu, "because the person holding the

HALAKHAH

טַלִּית חֶצְיָהּ עַל קַרְקַע וְחֶצְיָהּ עַל עַמּוּד A garment, half of which was lying on the ground, and half on a pillar. "If half a garment was lying on a pillar (which was at least three handbreadths high) and the other half was lying on

LITERAL TRANSLATION

[1]Come and hear: "Rabbi Eliezer says: One who rides [an animal] in the field or drives [it] in the city acquires [it]."

[2]Here too [we are dealing] with someone driving [the animal] with his feet.

[3][But] if so, it is the same as [a person] driving!

[4]There are two types of driving.

[5]If so, what is the reason [that] someone riding in a city does not acquire?

[6]Rav Kahana said: Because it is not usual for people to ride in a city.

[1]תָּא שְׁמַע: "רַבִּי אֱלִיעֶזֶר אוֹמֵר: רָכוּב בַּשָּׂדֶה וּמַנְהִיג בָּעִיר קָנָה".

[2]הָכָא נַמִי מַנְהִיג בְּרַגְלָיו.

[3]אִי הָכִי, הַיְינוּ מַנְהִיג!

[4]תְּרֵי גַּוְונֵי מַנְהִיג.

[5]אִי הָכִי, רָכוּב בָּעִיר מַאי טַעְמָא לָא קָנֵי?

[6]אָמַר רַב כָּהֲנָא: לְפִי שֶׁאֵין דַּרְכָּן שֶׁל בְּנֵי אָדָם לִרְכּוֹב בָּעִיר.

RASHI

רכוב בשדה — בהמה של מציאה קונה, אבל לא בעיר. וטעמא מפרש לקמיה. ומנהיג אף בעיר קנה, וכל שכן בשדה. שמע מינה: רכוב לחודיה קני כו'. **אין דרכן** — משום לניעותא.

TRANSLATION AND COMMENTARY

תָּא שְׁמַע [1]The Gemara now cites another Baraita in its continuing effort to determine whether or not riding is a valid mode of acquisition: **Come and hear: "Rabbi Eliezer says: One who rides an animal in the field or drives** it **in the city acquires it."** From this statement it seems clear that riding *is* considered a valid mode of acquisition!

הָכָא נַמִי [2]But the Gemara rejects this proof: **Here, too,** we are dealing **with** a rider who is **driving the animal with his feet.**

אִי הָכִי [3]But **if so,** objects the Gemara, the rider mentioned in this Baraita **is** legally **the same as the person driving** the animal! Why, then, did the Baraita speak of "riding" and "driving" as if these were two different methods of acquisition?

תְּרֵי גַּוְונֵי מַנְהִיג [4]The Gemara answers: **There are two types of "driving"** discussed by the Baraita — one is "riding," and the other is "driving," and the reason why the Baraita distinguishes between them is because one is effective only in the fields and the other is effective in the city.

אִי הָכִי [5]But, asks the Gemara, **If** the rider is at the same time driving the animal with his feet, **what is the reason that someone riding** in that manner **in a city does not acquire** the animal? We have established that "active riding" is an eminently acceptable mode of acquisition, yet the Baraita seems to indicate that an "active rider" can acquire an animal only in the field!

אָמַר רַב כָּהֲנָא [6]**Rav Kahana said** in reply: **Because it is not usual for people to ride in a city.** Since it is crowded in the city and people generally drive their animals through the city on foot, it is considered immodest to ride an animal there. For this reason riding is not a valid mode of acquisition there.

BACKGROUND

רָכוּב בָּעִיר **Riding in a city** Cities, and especially walled cities, were very densely built in ancient times, and the public domain was often little more than a maze of narrow alleys. Moreover, the crowding of the cities was such that the streets were crammed with people and occasionally with wagons full of goods. In general, there were no sidewalks for pedestrians. Therefore, riding in a city was neither practical nor common, except in the main streets (the public domain, רְשׁוּת הָרַבִּים). Moreover, since one generally could not make more rapid progress in a city by riding than by walking, riding was considered a demonstration of arrogance. Only the most important people (who did not wish to be pressed among the throng) and women or sick people used to ride inside cities (see also below, 9b).

TERMINOLOGY

תְּרֵי גַּוְונֵי **Two types, two categories** (lit., "two colors"). Sometimes a seemingly superfluous repetition in a Mishnah is explained by suggesting that the clause (or statement) deals with "two similar but different categories" of the item under discussion.

NOTES

reins can detach them," can be generalized in the following way: A person who holds part of an object in such a way that he could take it all without difficulty is regarded as though he were holding the entire object. A difficulty is raised by the Gemara concerning this generalization in the case of an object that is lying partially on the ground and partially on a pillar. Clearly it is more difficult to lean over and pick an object up from the ground than to take it from a pillar, and in that case the part that is on the pillar is moved as well. Therefore, according to Rabbi Abbahu's approach, if someone raises the part of an object that is lying on the ground, he is regarded as if he had picked up the entire object.

מַנְהִיג בָּעִיר **Driving an animal in the city.** *Rashi* maintains that, since driving is considered a valid mode of acquisition in the city, it is certainly valid in the field. *Rashba,* however, maintains that riding is a valid mode of acquisition only in the city, since an animal driven in the field is liable to run away.

רָכוּב בָּעִיר **Riding in the city.** *Tosafot* explains that riding is a valid mode of acquisition in the field, because there the animal moves in response to the rider's weight; but in the city, since there are usually many people in the way, the animal will not move merely in response to the rider's weight. Therefore riding in the city is not a valid mode of acquisition. *Ritzbash* disagrees, and explains that riding the animal in a field is a valid mode of acquisition even if the animal does not move, since animals are normally used this way (e.g., by people who want to survey their fields from a distance). But people do not ordinarily use their animals in this fashion in the city, so riding is not a valid mode of acquisition there.

אֵין דַּרְכָּן שֶׁל בְּנֵי אָדָם וכו' **It is not usual for people to ride in a city.** As Rav Ashi comments below, Rav Kahana has

HALAKHAH

the ground, and someone came and picked up the half that was lying on the ground, thereby causing the other half to move, he acquires the garment. But if the other half did not move, the person who lifted the garment does not acquire it," against the viewpoint attributed to Rabbi Abbahu. (*Shulḥan Arukh, Ḥoshen Mishpat* 269:5.)

רָכוּב בַּשָּׂדֶה וּמַנְהִיג בָּעִיר **Riding an animal in a field and driving it in the city.** "If someone sells an animal and says to the buyer: 'Acquire this animal the way people ordinarily do,' the animal may be acquired either by pulling it or lifting it. If the buyer rode the animal in a field, he acquires it, but not in the city, since most people do not ride animals in the

[1]אֲמַר לֵיהּ רַב אַשִׁי לְרַב כָּהֲנָא: אֶלָּא מֵעַתָּה, הִגְבִּיהַּ אַרְנָקִי בְּשַׁבָּת, [2]שֶׁאֵין דַּרְכָּן שֶׁל בְּנֵי אָדָם לְהַגְבִּיהַּ אַרְנָקִי בְּשַׁבָּת, הָכִי נַמִי דְּלָא קָנֵי?! [3]אֶלָּא, מַאי דַּעֲבַד עֲבַד, וְקָנֵי. [4]הָכָא נַמִי, מַאי דַּעֲבַד עֲבַד, וְקָנֵי.

[5]אֶלָּא, בְּמִקָּח וּמִמְכָּר עָסְקִינַן, דַּאֲמַר לֵיהּ: [6]"קְנֵי כְּדֶרֶךְ שֶׁבְּנֵי אָדָם קוֹנִין". [9B] [7]וְאִי רְשׁוּת הָרַבִּים הוּא, קָנֵי. [8]וְאִי אָדָם

LITERAL TRANSLATION

[1]Rav Ashi said to Rav Kahana: According to you (lit., "but from now"), [if] someone picked up a moneybag on the Sabbath, [2]as it is not usual for people to pick up a moneybag on the Sabbath, so too he should not acquire [it]!? [3]Rather, whatever he did, he did, and he acquires [it]. [4]Here, too, whatever he did, he did, and he acquires [it].

[5]Rather, we are dealing with buying and selling, where [the seller] says to [the buyer]: [6]"Acquire the way people [usually] acquire." [9B] [7]And if it is a public thoroughfare, he acquires [it]. [8]And if he is an

RASHI

ואי רשות הרבים הוא קני — בעיר, דדרך לרכוב שם ולא להנהיג, פן יפסקו עוברי דרכים בינו לבין בהמתו.

TRANSLATION AND COMMENTARY

אֲמַר לֵיהּ רַב אַשִׁי [1]**Rav Ashi said to Rav Kahana: According to you,** who claim that an act of acquisition is invalidated if performed in an abnormal manner, if **someone picked up an** ownerless **moneybag on the Sabbath** with the intention of acquiring it, would you say that here, **too, he should not acquire** it?! Even though lifting is a valid way of acquiring ownerless objects, would you invalidate his act of acquisition merely [2]**because it is not usual for people to pick up a moneybag on the Sabbath**, since the Halakhah forbids the handling of money on the Sabbath? Surely you would not say so! [3]**Rather** you would say: **Whatever he did, he did**, albeit in violation of the Sabbath, **and he acquires** the moneybag. [4]**Here, too,** where a person was riding an ownerless animal in the city and driving it with his feet, **whatever he did, he did**, albeit in violation of local etiquette, **and he acquires** the animal!

אֶלָּא בְּמִקָּח וּמִמְכָּר [5]Having rejected Rav Kahana's explanation, the Gemara is left with the following question: Since the "riding" mentioned in the Baraita is "active riding," why is it not effective in the city? The Gemara answers: The Baraita is not dealing with a case of an ownerless animal, as we previously assumed. There, both modes of acquisition would be effective even in the city. **Rather we are dealing with buying and selling, where the seller said to the buyer:** [6]"**Acquire** this animal **the way people usually acquire.**" Since the seller's consent is needed to effect the transaction, it cannot be performed in a manner that he considers abnormal. Hence, riding the animal does not serve as a valid mode of acquisition in this case, even if it is "active riding," since people do not ordinarily ride animals in the city. [9B] [7]Therefore **if** the transaction takes place **in a public thoroughfare,** the buyer **acquires** the animal there by riding it, because it is customary to ride animals in a public thoroughfare in a city. [8]**And if** the person buying the animal **is an important person**, who is accustomed

NOTES

introduced a new element into the laws of acquisition. Until now the various methods of acquisition were regarded as a list of technical instructions describing the proper way of acquiring objects of different kinds. The differences in the methods of acquisition derived in part from the practical possibilities of moving a particular kind of object (lifting or pulling, etc.), and the controversy regarding the driving of an ass or a camel was also connected with the practical question of how it was possible to drive or lead such animals. But Rav Kahana introduced a new element, דַּרְכָּן שֶׁל בְּנֵי אָדָם — ("common practice among men") — which is not connected to practical problems but is of a social nature. In other words, if, technically speaking, something can be done, but is not commonly done (for cultural or religious or other reasons), it would not be a proper means of acquisition. Rav Ashi is not prepared to accept this element, because by so doing he would deprive the formal laws of acquisition of their meaning, making them subject to considerations beyond the fixed structure of the Halakhah.

מַאי דַּעֲבַד עֲבַד וְקָנֵי Whatever he did, he did, and he acquires the moneybag. The commentators ask: Why should this person acquire the moneybag? Ordinarily, an action taken in violation of Torah law is considered null and void! Some commentators answer that here no Torah law was violated, since handling a moneybag on the Sabbath is only forbidden by Rabbinic injunction (*Ḥavvat Da'at, Netivot HaMishpat,* and others).

HALAKHAH

city. But if the buyer was an important person, who ordinarily rides an animal in the city, or a person who is not concerned about his appearance, or a woman, or a person in the public domain, which is very crowded, in such a case the buyer does acquire the animal if he rides it in the city," following the Gemara. *Rema*, however, apparently follows the view of *Rosh* (see *Gra*), who seems to have had a slightly different reading here in the Gemara. *Rema* rules that generally no one can acquire an animal by riding it in the city (not even an important person). Only in a public domain or an alley can one acquire an animal by riding it (and anyone can acquire the animal under such circumstances). See also *Sma*, who distinguishes between different types of public domain, and *Arukh HaShulḥan*. (*Shulḥan Arukh, Ḥoshen Mishpat* 197:5.)

TRANSLATION AND COMMENTARY

to riding an animal in the city, even in a side street, **he acquires** the animal in the city by riding it. [1]**And if** the person buying the animal **is a woman**, who does not have the strength to drive or pull an animal, **she acquires** the animal in the city by riding it. [2]**And if the person** buying the animal **is undignified**, and has no inhibitions about riding an animal even in places where more dignified people would not do so, **he**, too, **acquires** the animal in the city by riding it.

בָּעֵי רַבִּי אֶלְעָזָר [3]**Rabbi Elazar** posed the following problem and **asked:** If **someone says to another person, "Pull this animal in order to acquire the utensils that are on it" — what is the law?** The problem posed by Rabbi Elazar refers to a business transaction in which the seller wishes to transfer ownership of objects resting upon an animal, but not the animal itself.

לִקְנוֹת [4]The Gemara is puzzled by the way this question was framed: How could Rabbi Elazar ask about a case where the seller told the buyer to "pull the animal **in order to acquire** goods"? [5]**Did** the seller **tell** the buyer: "**Acquire** the goods"? In general, if a seller does not explicitly indicate that he wants a purchaser to acquire the goods, the buyer cannot acquire them!

אֶלָּא [6]**Rather**, says the Gemara, Rabbi Elazar must have posed the problem in a more precise way: If a seller tells a buyer: **"Pull this animal and acquire the utensils that are on it**, but not the animal itself" — **what is the law?** [7]The Gemara now explains that the basic issue involved here is as follows: **Is pulling an animal** an **effective** way to transfer **ownership of utensils** resting on it, **or not?**

חָשׁוּב הוּא, קָנֵי. [1]וְאִי אִשָּׁה הִיא, קָנְיָא. [2]וְאִי אִינִישׁ זִילָא הוּא, קָנֵי.

[3]בָּעֵי רַבִּי אֶלְעָזָר: הָאוֹמֵר לַחֲבֵירוֹ: "מְשׁוֹךְ בְּהֵמָה זוֹ לִקְנוֹת כֵּלִים שֶׁעָלֶיהָ" — מַהוּ? [4]לִקְנוֹת?! [5]מִי אֲמַר לֵיהּ: "קְנֵי"?!

[6]אֶלָּא: "מְשׁוֹךְ בְּהֵמָה זוֹ וּקְנֵי כֵּלִים שֶׁעָלֶיהָ" — מַהוּ? [7]מִי מְהַנְּיָא מְשִׁיכָה דִּבְהֵמָה לְאַקְנוּיֵי כֵּלִים, אוֹ לָא?

LITERAL TRANSLATION

important person, he acquires [it]. [1]And if [the buyer is] a woman, she acquires [it]. [2]And if he is an undignified (lit., "cheap") person, he acquires [it].

[3]Rabbi Elazar asked: Someone who says to his fellow: "Pull this animal to acquire the utensils that are on it" — what is [the law]?

[4]"To acquire"? [5]Did he tell him: "Acquire [them]"?

[6]Rather: "Pull this animal and acquire the utensils that are on it" — what is [the law]? [7]Is pulling an animal effective to transfer ownership of utensils, or not?

RASHI

ואי אדם חשוב הוא – אין דרכו להנהיג בהמה ברגליו, ודרך כבוד לרכוב עליה אף בסמטא שאין בני אדם שם. וכן אשה שאין בה כח לאחוז הבהמה פן תינתק הימנה. **ואי איניש זילא הוא קני** – שדרכו לרכוב לפני כל, אף בלא דוחק, לפי שאינו צנוע. אבל אדם בינוני, כגון שאינו חשוב בעושר ואינו בוש להוליך בהמה ברגליו – אין דרכו לרכוב בסמטא בעיר, משום צניעות. **משוך בהמה זו על מנת לקנות כלים שעליה** – במקח וממכר, ומוכר לו את הכלים ולא את הבהמה. **לקנות מי קאמר ליה קני** – לקנות משמע: אתה התכוין לקנות, אני איני מקנה לך.

SAGES

רַבִּי אֶלְעָזָר **Rabbi Elazar**. In the Talmud, citations of Rabbi Elazar with no patronymic refer to Rabbi Elazar ben Pedat, an Amora of the second generation. He was born in Babylonia and immigrated to Eretz Israel and came to inherit the position of Rabbi Yoḥanan as head of the Tiberias Yeshivah. In Babylonia he was a student of both Rav and Shmuel. His teacher in Eretz Israel was Rabbi Ḥanina bar Ḥama. He also studied with Rabbi Oshaya, but his main teacher was Rabbi Yoḥanan, and in time he came to be considered his colleague. He was given the honorific title of מרא — "master" — of Eretz Israel. Many Sages transmit teachings in his name, especially Rabbi Abbahu. He did not live long after Rabbi Yoḥanan. We know that he was a priest and that he had sons who died during his lifetime. The only one to survive was Rabbi Pedat, who was the "Amora" (translator) in Rabbi Assi's yeshivah.

NOTES

אִי אִינִישׁ זִילָא **If he is an undignified person**. As explained above, the assumption here is that acquisition is conditional on the way people generally acquire things, and for that reason it is dependent upon patterns of human behavior. An ordinary person, someone with self-respect, would not ride an animal inside a city except in particular places. However, people who do not behave politely and who lack self-respect would ride animals within a city too. If we define acquisition as the way in which people actually acquire, we must take exceptions into account, exceptionally important people and exceptionally common people. Since this is their normal way of behaving, for them this is a legitimate mode of acquisition.

בָּעֵי רַבִּי אֶלְעָזָר **Rabbi Elazar asked**. The commentators ask why Rabbi Elazar's question appears in our tractate and in the present context. It would seem more appropriate to include it in tractate *Bava Batra*, where the laws of the various modes of acquisition are discussed. Some commentators answer that the question is even more relevant where the objects on the animal are ownerless. In the case of a business transaction, it may be argued that the objects should remain in the seller's ownership. But in the case of ownerless (found) objects, on a bound animal, you might have thought that the act of pulling is effective. Therefore the case is brought here to teach us that if someone else intervenes, and takes the objects on the animal after the finder has pulled the animal, the latter's act of pulling is not effective. (*Shittah Mekubbetzet.*)

מְשׁוֹךְ בְּהֵמָה זוֹ וּקְנֵי כֵּלִים **Pull this animal and acquire the utensils that are on it.** The commentators all have difficulty

HALAKHAH

מִי אֲמַר לֵיהּ קְנֵי **Did he say to him, "Acquire"?** "If one person tells another, 'Pull this and you will acquire it,' or 'Take possession of this and you will acquire it,' the second person does not acquire it. Only if the first person says: 'Pull this *and acquire* it,' or 'Take possession of this *and acquire* it,' does the second person acquire it." This follows the ruling of *Rambam* (*Sefer Kinyan, Hilkhot Mekhirah* 2:8) on the basis of the discussion in the Gemara here (see also *Ra'avad* and *Maggid Mishneh*). (*Shulḥan Arukh, Ḥoshen Mishpat* 197:6.)

קִנְיַן בְּהֵמָה וְכֵלִים שֶׁעָלֶיהָ **The acquisition of an animal and the objects that are on it**. "If a person sells an animal

TRANSLATION AND COMMENTARY

אֲמַר רָבָא [1]By raising a problem as to whether it is possible to acquire utensils resting on an animal while not acquiring the animal itself, the Gemara implies that it is obvious that one *could* certainly acquire the utensils if one were acquiring the animal itself. **Rava**, objecting to this implication, **said**: If the seller had **told** the buyer, **"Acquire the animal and acquire the utensils** together with the animal," **would he** in fact **have acquired the utensils?** [2]Surely in such a case **the animal is** considered **a "walking courtyard,"** and even if the buyer acquires the animal by pulling it, and the animal is now as much his property as is his courtyard, nevertheless even then he does not acquire the utensils on the animal's back, because **a "walking courtyard" does not acquire the objects in it!** Ordinarily, a person may acquire objects through the fact that they have entered his domain (this mode of acquisition is known in Hebrew as קִנְיַן חָצֵר — "courtyard-acquisition"). But here the animal is moving, and the Halakhah is that one cannot acquire the objects located in a "moving courtyard"! [3]**And** even

[1]אֲמַר רָבָא: אִי אֲמַר לֵיהּ: ״קְנֵי בְּהֵמָה וּקְנֵי כֵּלִים״, מִי קָנֵי כֵּלִים? [2]חָצֵר מְהַלֶּכֶת הִיא, וְחָצֵר מְהַלֶּכֶת לֹא קָנְה. [3]וְכִי

LITERAL TRANSLATION

[1]Rava said: If he told him: "Acquire the animal and acquire the utensils," would he have acquired the utensils? [2][The animal] is a "walking courtyard," and a "walking courtyard" does not acquire [the objects in it]. [3]And if

RASHI

מי קני כלים — במשיכה דבהמה עם הבהמה? דמדקא מבעיא לך במוכר כלים בלא בהמה — מכלל דבמוכר שניהם פשיטא לך דמדקני בהמה — קני כלים, משום תורת חצר, דקיימא לן חצרו של אדם קונה לו, ובהמתו כחצרו. והא חצר מהלכת היא, וחצר מהלכת לא שמעינן דתקני. דכי אתרבאי (גיטין עז,א) מ״אם המצא תמצא בידו״ — גגו חצרו וקרפיפו אתרבאי, דלא נייד, והוי משתמר.

NOTES

with this passage. They agree that, if the animal were to be replaced by an inanimate object, like a table or a box, then pulling it would be an effective way of acquiring the objects on (or in) it. *Tosafot* and *Ran* (and apparently *Rashi*) explain that pulling an animal is essentially different from pulling an inanimate object, since the actual movement is performed by the animal itself, not by the puller. Such pulling is an effective way of acquiring the animal itself, but Rabbi Elazar was unsure whether or not it applies to the objects on the animal as well.

Ramban takes this idea further. He says that it was clear to Rabbi Elazar that pulling an animal is not an effective way of acquiring objects on it, and his question revolved around courtyard-acquisition: Is it possible to acquire utensils by performing an act of acquisition in a courtyard, if there is no intention of acquiring the courtyard as well?

Rashba and *Ritva* take the opposite approach to *Ramban*: It is clear that pulling an animal is an effective way of acquiring objects on it. But for some reason the purchaser wishes to acquire these objects only through courtyard-acquisition. Hence, the question is: Can an animal be used for courtyard-acquisition, and under what circumstances, bearing in mind that pulling an animal is normally done with a walking animal, and courtyard-acquisition requires a stationary courtyard?

חָצֵר מְהַלֶּכֶת A walking courtyard. The particular mode of acquisition by means of a courtyard is discussed at length below (10b ff.). Acquisition' by means of a courtyard is not self-evident, because it does not refer to a person's ownership of land, which, according to the Halakhah, extends downward to the center of the earth and upward to the sky. Hence everything beneath the earth belongs to the owner of the land. However, in this case we are referring to the ability of a courtyard to acquire things that are not part of the ground itself, but come from elsewhere. It seems that in Rava's opinion this type of power of acquisition must be restricted to things that are truly courtyards, or at least to things that are essentially similar to them. Thus, a "walking courtyard," since it is not like a real courtyard, should not have a courtyard's power of acquisition. Some commentators maintain that Rava's rule was not universally accepted, and that some authorities are of the opinion that a courtyard can acquire in all circumstances.

חָצֵר מְהַלֶּכֶת לֹא קָנְה A "walking courtyard" does not acquire. *Rashba* asks: The Gemara explains later that a "courtyard" can acquire property for its owner either because it is considered an extension of *his hand* (יָד מִטַּעַם חָצֵר), or because it is considered *his agent* (חָצֵר מִטַּעַם שְׁלִיחוּת). Now, just as a human agent can acquire property while walking, so too a "walking courtyard" should be able to acquire property for its owner! *Rosh* (on *Gittin* 78a) answers that courtyard-acquisition is primarily based on the "hand" principle, and the "agent" principle is only secondary. Therefore, just as a person's hand is essentially stationary, moving only at the behest of its owner, so too a courtyard must not move of its own accord.

Ritva expands this idea further: Even if we were to view the courtyard as an agent, the argument would still apply.

HALAKHAH

together with the goods it is carrying, even if the purchaser pulls the animal, thereby acquiring it, he does not acquire the goods (unless he pulls or lifts them separately). Even if the seller explicitly told the buyer to pull the animal and acquire the objects on it, he does not acquire them, for such an animal is deemed a "moving courtyard," and a moving courtyard does not acquire the property on it. But if the animal was bound, so that it was unable to move, the buyer acquires whatever goods it is carrying." According to *Rosh*, a person who acquires a found animal also acquires the objects it is carrying. Since unresolved questions in the Gemara about ownership are usually decided by leaving the disputed object in the possession of its previous owner, and in this case there is no previous owner (the found object is considered ownerless), the finder may keep it (*Sma*). (*Shulḥan Arukh, Hoshen Mishpat* 202:13.)

TRANSLATION AND COMMENTARY

if you say that Rabbi Elazar was referring to a case **where** the animal was first pulled by the buyer and acquired by him, and then **it stood** in its place and acted as a "stationary courtyard" to enable the buyer to acquire the objects it was carrying, this too would have been ineffective. [1]For **whatever** type of courtyard **would not acquire if it were walking** — in our case, the animal — **does not acquire** while **standing or sitting** either, since it can walk away at any time! Under what circumstances, then, can an animal act as a stationary courtyard?

וְהִלְכְתָא [2]The Gemara concludes: **But the Halakhah is** that there is a way whereby an animal can cause its owner to acquire the objects it is carrying: **When** the animal **is bound** and therefore incapable of moving. In other words, if the buyer acquired the animal by pulling it, and then tied it up, it could then act as his courtyard and enable him to acquire the objects it was carrying.

אָמְרוּ לֵיהּ [3]**Rav Pappa and Rav Huna the son of Rav Yehoshua said to Rava:** [4]**But according to your** argument that a moving courtyard cannot acquire property on behalf of its owner, then **if someone was travelling on** his own **boat, and fish jumped and fell into the boat,** [5]would you say that the boat, **too, should be** considered **a "walking courtyard,"** with the result that its owner **would not acquire** the fish!?

אֲמַר לֵיהּ [6]Rava **said** in reply **to** Rav Pappa and Rav Huna: **The boat** itself **is at rest, and it is the water that moves it;** hence a boat is not considered to be a moving courtyard and its owner *does* acquire the fish.

אֲמַר לֵיהּ רָבִינָא לְרַב אַשִׁי [7]**Ravina said to Rav Ashi: But according to your** argument that a moving courtyard cannot acquire property on behalf of its owner, then **if a married woman were walking in a public thoroughfare**

תֵּימָא, כְּשֶׁעָמְדָה — [1]וְהָא כָּל שֶׁאִילּוּ מְהַלֵּךְ לֹא קָנָה, עוֹמֵד וְיוֹשֵׁב לֹא קָנָה!
[2]וְהִלְכְתָא: בִּכְפוּתָה.
[3]אָמְרוּ לֵיהּ רַב פַּפָּא וְרַב הוּנָא בְּרֵיהּ דְּרַב יְהוֹשֻׁעַ לְרָבָא: [4]אֶלָּא מֵעַתָּה, הָיָה מְהַלֵּךְ בִּסְפִינָה וְקָפְצוּ דָּגִים וְנָפְלוּ לְתוֹךְ הַסְּפִינָה — [5]הָכִי נַמִי דְּחָצֵר מְהַלֶּכֶת הִיא וְלָא קָנֵי?
[6]אֲמַר לֵיהּ: סְפִינָה מֵינָח נַיְיחָא, וּמַיָּא הוּא דְּקָא מְמַטוּ לַהּ.
[7]אֲמַר לֵיהּ רָבִינָא לְרַב אַשִׁי: אֶלָּא מֵעַתָּה, הָיְתָה מְהַלֶּכֶת

LITERAL TRANSLATION

you say, when it stood — [1]but surely whatever would not acquire if it were walking, does not acquire standing or sitting!

[2]But the Halakhah is: When it is bound.

[3]Rav Pappa and Rav Huna the son of Rav Yehoshua said to Rava: [4]But according to you (lit., "from now"), [if] someone was travelling on a boat and fish jumped and fell into the boat — [5]so, too, would it be a "walking courtyard" and would it not acquire [them]?

[6]He said to them: The boat is at rest, and it is the water that moves it.

[7]Ravina said to Rav Ashi: But according to you, if [a married woman] were walking

RASHI

וכי תימא כשעמדה — לאחר שעקרה ידה ורגלה, ונקנית לו הבהמה במשיכה — עמדה ולא הלכה, ונקנו כליס בעמידתה, דקנה לו חלרו. **כל שאילו מהלך לו קנה כו׳** — כלומר: כיון דרלויה היא לילך — לאו דומיא דחלר היא, ואין קונה בתורת חלר. **והלכתא** — האי דפשיטא ליה דכי אמר ליה "קני בהמה וקני כליס" קני. **בכפותה** — היא דפשיטא ליה, דדומיא דחלר הוא קני. וכל היכא דאמרינן בגמרא: והאמר רבא כל שאילו מהלך לא קני כו׳ — מהכא קאמרי ליה.

NOTES

By definition, an agent is one who moves at the behest of the person who appointed him. Therefore, a courtyard that moves of its own accord cannot even be an agent.

סְפִינָה מֵינָח נַיְיחָא **The boat is at rest.** *Tosafot* (ד״ה סְפִינָה) comments that the assumption that a ship is to be regarded as a stationary object, and that the water moves beneath it and makes it move, is not applicable in every area of the Halakhah. In fact we find basic discussions of the definition of motion in various places in the Talmud, and to some extent they foreshadow the essential problem of the theory of the relativity of motion, where the question (though formulated entirely differently) is: What is the structure of coordinates by which motion is determined? In certain contexts the issue is whether one adopts the point of view of the observer, who is standing elsewhere and is stationary in relation to the moving object, or that of the object itself, which can be said to be in a state of rest.

Tosafot's conclusion is itself relative: There is no absolute definition of motion and rest (except in the case of an object that moves under its own power, such as a person or an animal). Regarding solutions to Halakhic problems, the conclusion will be specific to the state of motion and rest in a particular Halakhic context, which is not identical to all others.

HALAKHAH

קִנְיָן בִּסְפִינָה **Acquiring objects on a boat.** "Fish (and other ownerless items) that fall into a boat become the property of the boat's owner. Since the ship does not move on its own, it is not considered a 'moving courtyard' and is governed by the rules of acquisition applying to a regular courtyard," in accordance with the Gemara here. (*Shulḥan Arukh, Ḥoshen Mishpat* 273:15.)

בִּרְשׁוּת הָרַבִּים [1]וְזָרַק לָהּ גֵּט לְתוֹךְ חֵיקָהּ אוֹ לְתוֹךְ קַלְתָּהּ — [2]הָכָא נַמִי דְּלָא מְגָרְשָׁה? [3]אֲמַר לֵיהּ: קַלְתָּהּ מֵינָח נַיְיחָא, וְאִיהִי דְּקָא מְסַגְּיָא מִתּוּתָהּ.

מִשְׁנָה [4]הָיָה רוֹכֵב עַל גַּבֵּי בְהֵמָה וְרָאָה אֶת הַמְּצִיאָה, וְאָמַר לַחֲבֵירוֹ "תְּנָה לִי", [5]נְטָלָהּ וְאָמַר, "אֲנִי זָכִיתִי בָּהּ", [6]זָכָה בָּהּ. [7]אִם, מִשֶּׁנְּתָנָהּ לוֹ, אָמַר, "אֲנִי זָכִיתִי בָּהּ תְּחִלָּה", [8]לֹא אָמַר כְּלוּם.

גְּמָרָא [9]תְּנַן הָתָם: "מִי שֶׁלִּיקֵּט אֶת הַפֵּאָה וְאָמַר, 'הֲרֵי זוֹ לִפְלוֹנִי עָנִי', [10]רַבִּי אֱלִיעֶזֶר

TRANSLATION AND COMMENTARY

[1]**and her husband threw her a bill of divorce into her lap or into her basket**, which she was carrying on her head, [2]would you say **here, too,** that **she would not be divorced**? Surely we know that the law is that she *is* divorced in such a case, as the Mishnah (*Gittin* 77a) states explicitly!

אֲמַר לֵיהּ [3]Rav Ashi **said** in reply **to** Ravina: The woman's **basket is** considered to be **at rest, and it is she who walks beneath it.** Thus the basket is considered to be a "stationary courtyard," and the woman acquires whatever is thrown into it.

MISHNAH הָיָה רוֹכֵב [4]**If a person was riding on an animal and he saw an ownerless object** lying on the ground, **and he said to another person** standing nearby, **"Give** that object **to me,"** [5]if **the other person took** the ownerless object **and said, "I have acquired it** for myself," [6]he has **acquired it** by lifting it up, even though he was not the first to see it, and the rider has no claim to it. [7]But **if, after he gave** the object **to** the rider, the person who picked it up **said, "I acquired** the object **first,"** [8]**he** in fact **said nothing**. His words are of no effect, and the rider may keep it. Since the person walking showed no intention of acquiring the object when he originally picked it up, he is not now believed when he claims that he acquired it first. Indeed, even if we maintain that when a person picks up an ownerless object on behalf of someone else, the latter does *not* acquire it automatically, here, by *giving* the object to the rider, he makes a gift of it to the rider.

GEMARA תְּנַן הָתָם [9]**We have learned elsewhere** in a Mishnah in tractate *Pe'ah* (4:9): **"Someone who gathered** ***pe'ah.*** — produce which by Torah law [Leviticus 23:22] is left unharvested in the corner of a field by the owner of the field, to be gleaned by the poor — **and said, 'Behold, this** *pe'ah* which I have gleaned **is** intended **for so-and-so the poor man,'** [10]**Rabbi Eliezer says:** The person who gathered the *pe'ah* **has acquired it**

LITERAL TRANSLATION

in a public thoroughfare [1]and [her husband] threw her a bill of divorce into her lap or into her basket, [2]here, too, would she not be divorced?

[3]He said to him: Her basket is at rest, and it is she who walks beneath it.

MISHNAH [4][If a person] was riding on an animal and he saw a found object, and he said to another person, "Give it to me," [5][and the other person] took it and said, "I have acquired it," [6]he has acquired it. [7]If, after he gave it to him, he said, "I acquired it first," [8]he said nothing.

GEMARA [9]We have learned there: "Someone who gathered *pe'ah* and said, 'Behold this is for so-and-so the poor man,' [10]Rabbi Eliezer

RASHI

קלתה — סל שעל ראשה, שנותנת בה כלי מלאכתה וטווי שלה. הכי נמי דלא הוי גיטא — והאנן תנן במסכת גיטין (עז,א): זרק לה גיטה לתוך חיקה או לתוך קלתה — הרי זו מגורשת!

משנה **לא אמר כלום** — דאפילו אמרינן המגביה מציאה לחבירו לא קנה חבירו, כיון דיהבה ליה — קנייה ממה נפשך. אי קנייה קמא דלא מתכוין להקנות לחבירו — הא יהבה ניהליה במתנה. ואי לא קנייה קמא משום דלא היה מתכוין לקנות — הויא ליה הפקר עד דמטא לידיה דהאי, וקנייה האי במאי דעקרה מידיה דקמא לשם קנייה.

גמרא **מי שליקט את הפאה** — אדם בעלמא שאינו בעל שדה. דאי בבעל שדה — לא אמר רבי אליעזר זכה. דליכא למימר "מגו דזכי לנפשיה", דאפילו הוא עני מוזהר הוא שלא ללקט פאה משדה שלו, כדאמר בשחיטת חולין (קלא,ב): "לא תלקט לעני" — להזהיר עני על שלו.

REALIA

קַלְתָּהּ **Her basket.** The source of this word is the Greek κάλαθος, *kalathos*, and it means a basket with a narrow base.

Illustration from a Greek drawing depicting such a basket of fruit.

CONCEPTS

פֵּאָה ***Pe'ah.*** **One of the presents left for the poor** (מַתְּנוֹת עֲנִיִּים). The Torah forbids harvesting "the corners of your field," so that the produce left standing may be harvested and kept by the poor (Leviticus 19:9).

The Torah did not specify a minimum amount of produce to be left as *pe'ah*. But the Sages stipulated that it must be at least one-sixtieth of the crop.

Pe'ah is set aside only from crops that ripen at one time and are harvested at one time. The poor are allowed to use their own initiaitve to reap the *pe'ah* left in the fields. But the owner of an orchard must see to it that each of the poor gets a fixed share of the *pe'ah* from places that are difficult to reach. The poor come to collect *pe'ah* three times a day. The laws of *pe'ah* are discussed in detail in tractate *Pe'ah*.

NOTES

מִי שֶׁלִּיקֵּט אֶת הַפֵּאָה **If a person gathered** ***pe'ah.*** According to *Rashi*, the Mishnah must be referring to someone other than the owner of the field. By Torah law the owner of a field is required to separate part of his field as *pe'ah*, even if he himself is poor, and he may not take the *pe'ah* for himself. Therefore the "since" (מגו) argument

HALAKHAH

קַלְתָּהּ **A woman's basket.** "If a man throws a bill of divorce into a container that his wife is holding, she thereby acquires the bill of divorce and the divorce takes effect." (*Shulḥan Arukh, Even HaEzer* 139:10.)

הַמְלַקֵּט פֵּאָה עֲבוּר אַחֵר **A person who gathered** ***pe'ah*** **for someone else.** "If a poor person, who is himself entitled to collect *pe'ah*, gathered *pe'ah* for another poor person, and said, 'This *pe'ah* is for X, the poor person,' he acquires the *pe'ah* on behalf of that other poor person. But if the person who collected the *peah* was wealthy, he does not acquire the *pe'ah* on behalf of the poor person. He must give it instead to the first poor person who appears in the field," following the opinion of the Sages, as explained by Rabbi Yehoshua ben Levi. (*Rambam, Sefer Zeraim, Hilkhot Mattenot Aniyyim* 2:19.)

LITERAL TRANSLATION

He has acquired it for him. [1]But the Sages say: He must give it to the first poor person who comes."

[2]Ulla said in the name of Rabbi Yehoshua ben Levi: [3]The difference of opinion is [when the *pe'ah* comes] from a wealthy person for a poor person, [4]for Rabbi Eliezer maintains: Since, if he had wished, he [could have] declared his property ownerless and become a poor person, and [the *pe'ah*] would have been fit for him, [5]now too it is fit for him. [6]And since he can acquire for himself, he can also acquire for someone else. [7]But the Sages maintain: One "since" [argument] we may say, two "since" [arguments] we do not say. [8]But [when the *pe'ah* comes] from a poor person for a poor person, [9]all agree (lit., "the words of all") [that the first person] acquires [the *pe'ah*] for [the second person], [10]for since he can acquire [the *pe'ah*] for himself, he can also acquire [it] for someone else.

[11]Rav Naḥman said to Ulla: But you, Sir, should say, [that] the difference of opinion is from a poor person for a poor person.

אוֹמֵר: זָכָה לוֹ. [1]וַחֲכָמִים אוֹמְרִים: יִתְּנֶנָּה לֶעָנִי הַנִּמְצָא רִאשׁוֹן".

[2]אָמַר עוּלָּא אָמַר רַבִּי יְהוֹשֻׁעַ בֶּן לֵוִי: [3]מַחֲלוֹקֶת מֵעָשִׁיר לֶעָנִי, [4]דְּרַבִּי אֱלִיעֶזֶר סָבַר: מִגּוֹ דְּאִי בָּעֵי מַפְקַר נִכְסֵיהּ וְהָוֵי עָנִי, וְחָזֵי לֵיהּ, [5]הָשְׁתָּא נַמִי חָזֵי לֵיהּ. [6]וּמִגּוֹ דְּזָכֵי לְנַפְשֵׁיהּ, זָכֵי נַמִי לְחַבְרֵיהּ. [7]וְרַבָּנַן סָבְרִי: חַד "מִגּוֹ" אָמְרִינַן, תְּרֵי "מִגּוֹ" לָא אָמְרִינַן. [8]אֲבָל מֵעָנִי לֶעָנִי, [9]דִּבְרֵי הַכֹּל זָכָה לוֹ, [10]דְּמִגּוֹ דְּזָכֵי לְנַפְשֵׁיהּ, זָכֵי נַמִי לְחַבְרֵיהּ. [11]אָמַר לֵיהּ רַב נַחְמָן לְעוּלָּא: וְלֵימָא מָר, מֵעָנִי לֶעָנִי מַחֲלוֹקֶת.

TRANSLATION AND COMMENTARY

for the poor man. [1]**But the Sages say** that the poor man has not acquired the produce, and the person who gathered it **must give it to the first poor person who comes."** Any poor person who takes possession of this *pe'ah* acquires it.

אָמַר עוּלָּא [2]Interpreting this Mishnah, **Ulla said in the name of Rabbi Yehoshua ben Levi:** [3]**This difference of opinion** between Rabbi Eliezer and the Sages applies in a case **where the pe'ah** was gleaned by **a wealthy person**, who is not entitled to keep it for himself, **on behalf of a poor person.** [4]**For Rabbi Eliezer maintains** that (1) **since** the wealthy person, **if he had wished, could have declared his property ownerless** and would thereby have **become a poor person, and the pe'ah would thus have been fit for him,** since he would have been as entitled to it as anyone else, [5]**now, too,** the *pe'ah* **is** considered in a sense **fit for him,** even though at present he is wealthy and not entitled to keep it. [6]**And** (2) **since,** if he had wanted to, **he could have acquired** the *pe'ah* **for himself, he can also acquire** it **for someone else.** [7]**But the Sages maintain: We may use one "since" argument**, but **we may not use two "since" arguments.** The Sages, unlike Rabbi Eliezer, maintain that this principle of מִגּוֹ — "since," i.e., since something could have happened in theory, we act as if it has already happened — can only be invoked once. [8]**But** if **the pe'ah** was gleaned **by** one **poor person on behalf of** another **poor person,** [9]**all agree** — both Rabbi Eliezer and the Sages — **that** the pauper who gleaned the *pe'ah* **has acquired** the *pe'ah* **on behalf of the second** poor person, [10]**for** in this case the principle of "since" is only invoked once — **since he can acquire the *pe'ah* for himself, he can also acquire it for someone else.**

אָמַר לֵיהּ רַב נַחְמָן לְעוּלָּא [11]The Gemara now brings an objection to the previous interpretation of the difference of opinion between Rabbi Eliezer and the Sages: **Rav Naḥman said to Ulla,** Instead of limiting the difference of opinion between Rabbi Eliezer and the Sages to the case of a rich person gleaning *pe'ah* for a poor person, **you, Sir, should say** instead that **the difference of opinion** in this Mishnah applies even where the *pe'ah* is gleaned **by** one **poor person for** another **poor person**.

RASHI

מעשיר לעני — שעשיר הוא שליקטה לצורך העני. **מגו דזכי לנפשיה** — דאי בעי הוה זכי לנפשיה אם הגביה לעצמו. **חד מגו** — מעני לעני. **ולימא מר דאפילו מעני לעני** — אמרי רבנן דלא זכה לו.

NOTES

would not apply. But most commentators maintain that the Mishnah could just as well be referring to the owner of the field (see *Rash, Rosh, Ran,* and the Jerusalem Talmud). If, as Rabbi Eliezer maintains, the principle of "since" (מִגּוֹ) can be invoked twice, then the owner of the field could always declare all his property, including this field, ownerless. He would then be permitted to keep the *pe'ah*, since it would no longer be his field (*Ritva, Meiri*).

דְּאִי בָּעֵי מַפְקַר נִכְסֵיהּ **If he had wished, he could have declared his property ownerless**. According to this explanation, Rabbi Eliezer distinguishes between a situation where a person lacks a right because of some intrinsic flaw (such as being mentally incompetent) and one where some external condition is lacking. Wealth is not intrinsic to a person (the proof of this is that one may abandon all one's property and be left without any possessions at all), and would not therefore be a condition preventing one from acquiring things for a poor person. Those who disagree with Rabbi Eliezer maintain that, since a wealthy person is not entitled to glean at that time, he is denied the right to glean both for himself and for others.

[1]דְּהָא מְצִיאָה הַכֹּל עֲנִיִּים אֶצְלָהּ, [2]וּתְנַן: ״הָיָה רוֹכֵב עַל גַּבֵּי בְהֵמָה וְרָאָה אֶת הַמְּצִיאָה, וְאָמַר לַחֲבֵירוֹ, ׳תְּנָהּ לִי׳, [3]נְטָלָהּ וְאָמַר, ׳אֲנִי זָכִיתִי בָּהּ׳, זָכָה בָּהּ.

[4]אִי אָמְרַתְּ בִּשְׁלָמָא מֵעָנִי לְעָנִי מַחֲלוֹקֶת, [10A] [5]מַתְנִיתִין מַנִּי? רַבָּנַן הִיא. [6]אֶלָּא אִי אָמְרַתְּ בְּעָשִׁיר וְעָנִי מַחֲלוֹקֶת, [7]אֲבָל מֵעָנִי לְעָנִי דִּבְרֵי הַכֹּל זָכָה לוֹ, [8]הָא מַנִּי? לָא רַבָּנַן וְלָא רַבִּי אֱלִיעֶזֶר!

LITERAL TRANSLATION

[1]For surely everyone is [considered like] a poor person with regard to a found object, [2]and we have learned: "[If a person] was riding on an animal and he saw a found object, and he said to another person, 'Give it to me,' [3][and the other person] took it and said, 'I have acquired it,' he has acquired it."

[4]It is well if you say [that] the difference of opinion [applies] from a poor person for a poor person. [10A] [5]Whose [viewpoint does] our Mishnah [follow]? It is [that of] the Sages.

[6]But if you say [that] the difference of opinion [applies] in [the case of] a wealthy person and a poor person, [7]but [that] from a poor person to a poor person all agree [that] he acquires for him, [8]whose [viewpoint does] this [Mishnah follow]? Neither the Sages nor Rabbi Eliezer!

TRANSLATION AND COMMENTARY

[1]Rav Naḥman now supports his objection by considering the case brought in our Mishnah: **For surely everyone**, whether rich or poor, **is** considered **with regard to** the procedure for acquiring **a found object, like a poor person** with regard to *pe'ah*, since anyone can acquire it, and no one has any special claim to it. [2]**And we have learned** in our Mishnah: **"If a person was riding on an animal and he saw an ownerless object, and he said to another person, 'Give it to me,'** [3]**and the other person took it and said, 'I have acquired it** for myself,' the second person **acquires it** for himself." Rav Naḥman understands our Mishnah as meaning that even if the other person originally picked the object up with the intention of giving it to the rider, he can change his mind, as the rider has not yet acquired it. Now, according to Ulla's argument, once the other person could have acquired the object for himself by picking it up, he should also have been able to acquire it for the rider by picking it up! But from our Mishnah it would seem that one person *cannot* acquire an ownerless object on behalf of another person, for the person walking does not acquire the ownerless object on behalf of the rider!

אִי אָמְרַתְּ בִּשְׁלָמָא [4]**Now there is no problem if you say that the difference of opinion** between Rabbi Eliezer and the Sages **applies** even where the *pe'ah* is acquired **by** one **poor person for** another poor **person**, and Rabbi Eliezer accepts the "since" argument (at least once), whereas the Sages reject it entirely. [10A] [5]We could then say: **Whose viewpoint does our Mishnah** follow? **That of the Sages!** For our present assumption is that the Sages maintain that nobody can acquire *pe'ah* for another, even though he could have acquired it for himself, because they do not accept the "since" argument ("since he could have acquired it for himself, he can also acquire it for someone else"). Similarly, one person cannot acquire a found article on behalf of another person, and this explains why the rider in our Mishnah has no claim to the object that the other person picked up for him. [6]**But if you say that the difference of opinion** between Rabbi Eliezer and the Sages **applies** specifically **in the case of a wealthy person and a poor person**, as Ulla suggested, [7]**but that** in the case of **a poor person** gleaning *pe'ah* **for** another **poor person** both Rabbi Eliezer and the Sages **agree that the one can acquire** the *pe'ah* **for the other,** [8]**whose viewpoint does our Mishnah follow? Neither** that of **the Sages** nor that **of Rabbi Eliezer**! Our Mishnah seems to reject the possibility that one person can acquire an object on behalf of another, even if the finder could have acquired it for himself, and to insist that the rider only acquires ownership of the found object when it is placed in his hand.

RASHI

דהא מציאה הכל עניים אצלה — כלומר, הכל כשרים לזכות בה כעניים בפאה. **ותנן** — המגביה מציאה לחבירו לא קנה חבירו, ולא אמרינן: מגו דאי הוה בעי הוה זכי לנפשיה — זכי נמי לחבריה, כי מגבה לה כולה לשם חבירו. דתנן: היה רוכב כו׳. **ואמר אני זכיתי בה** — קא סלקא דעתך: אני רוצה לזכות בה עכשיו קאמר. ומודה הוא שמתחילה הגביה לשם חבירו, וקתני: זכה בה — אלמא לא קנה חבירו. **אי אמרת בשלמא מעני לעני מחלוקת** — דאמרי רבנן: לא אמרינן ״מגו דזכי לנפשיה זכי נמי לחבריה״ אלא היכא דהגביה לדעת שניהם, כגון שנים שהגביהו מציאה, דאמר בה לעיל (ח,א) גבי בזמן שהם מודים — חולקים בלא שבועה, דטעמא משום מגו דזכי בהגבהה זו לנפשיה זכי נמי לחבריה, אבל מגו דאי בעי הוה זכי לנפשיה זכי לחבריה — לא אמרינן. **מתניתין רבנן היא** — ואשמועינן רישא, דהיכא דזכי ביה איהו — אמרינן מגו. וסיפא אשמועינן דהיכא דלא זכי ביה איהו, מגו דאי בעי זכי — לא אמרינן. **הא** — מתניתין דהכא — מני?

[1]אֲמַר לֵיהּ: מַתְנִיתִין דַּאֲמַר "תְּחִילָּה".
[2]הָכִי נַמִי מִסְתַּבְּרָא, דְּקָתָנֵי סֵיפָא: [3]"אִם, מִשֶּׁנְּתָנָהּ לוֹ, אָמַר: 'אֲנִי זָכִיתִי בָּהּ תְּחִילָּה', לֹא אָמַר כְּלוּם". [4]"תְּחִילָּה" בְּסֵיפָא לָמָּה לִי? [5]פְּשִׁיטָא אַף עַל גַּב דְּלָא אֲמַר "תְּחִילָּה", "תְּחִילָּה" קָאָמַר! [6]אֶלָּא לָאו, הָא קָא מַשְׁמַע לָן: רֵישָׁא דַּאֲמַר "תְּחִילָּה".
[7]וְאִידָךְ?
[8]תָּנָא סֵיפָא לְגַלּוּיֵי רֵישָׁא:

LITERAL TRANSLATION

[1]He said to him: Our Mishnah [applies] where he said, "[I acquired it] first."
[2]So, too, it is also reasonable, for the last clause teaches: [3]"If, after he gave it to him, he said: 'I acquired it first,' he said nothing." [4]For what do I [need] "first" in the last clause? [5]It is obvious [that] even if he did not say "first," he meant "first"! [6]Rather, is it not [that] it informs us of this: The first [clause also refers to] where he said "first."
[7]And the other?
[8][The author of the Mishnah] taught the last [clause] to shed light [on] (lit., "reveal") the first [clause]:

RASHI

דאמר תחילה — האי "אני זכיתי בה" דקאמר — "תחילה" קאמר ליה: מתחילה הגבהתיה לצורכי ולא לצרכך. ולעולם המגביה מציאה לחבירו קנה חבירו, דומיא דמעני לעני. **הכי נמי מסתברא** — ד"זכיתי תחילה משעת הגבהה" קאמר מתניתין. **מדקתני סיפא כו'** — ואי "תחילה" דסיפא לאו משעת הגבהה קאמר, אלא "אני זכיתי תחילה" — קודם שנתתי לך נתכוונתי לזכות בה. **למה לי** — למיתנא בה "תחילה"? פשיטא דאפילו לא אמר "תחילה" בפירוש מסתמא תחילה קאמר. דמי מצי למימר אני זוכה בה עכשיו? והלא אינה בידו! **אלא לאו הא קא משמע לן** — דרישא דמתניתין דקתני זכה בה — בדאמר "תחילה". ואשמועינן סיפא דאם משנתנה לו טען לו אותה טענה, ואמר "אני הגבהתיה מתחילה לצורכי" — לא אמר כלום, דגלי דעתיה כשנתנה לו דאדעתיה דהאי הגבהה. **ואידך** — רב נחמן אמר לך דתנא סיפא "תחילה". **לגלויי רישא** — למימר: דוקא קתני. מדסיפא תחילה קתני ורישא לא תנא — דוקא הוא.

TRANSLATION AND COMMENTARY

אֲמַר לֵיהּ [1]Ulla, contesting Rav Naḥman's interpretation of our Mishnah, **said to** Rav Naḥman: **Our Mishnah**, which gives the rider no claim at all, only applies **where** the person who picked up the lost object **said**, "I acquired it **first**." In other words, the person who picked up the lost object did not change his mind about giving it to the rider, because from the very outset he had intended to acquire it for himself. This is the reason why he acquires it for himself and not for the rider. But if he had picked up the object with the intention that the rider should acquire it, the latter would have acquired it, just as one poor man can glean *pe'ah* on behalf of another.

הָכִי נַמִי מִסְתַּבְּרָא [2]The Gemara now provides additional support for this interpretation of the Mishnah from the wording of the Mishnah itself and says: **This** interpretation **is also reasonable, for the last clause** of the Mishnah **teaches:** [3]**"If, after he gave** the object **to** the rider, the person who picked it up **said: 'I acquired it first,' his words are of no effect."** [4]**What need is there** for the word **"first" in the latter clause** of the Mishnah? [5]Surely, in the case described, where the finder makes his claim only after he has given the object to the rider, **it is obvious that even if** the finder **did not** specifically **say** that he acquired the object **first, he** must have **meant** that he acquired it **first**. The person who picked up the found object obviously cannot acquire it now when it is no longer in his hand! He must mean that he intended to acquire the article at the moment he picked it up! [6]**Rather, is it not the case that** the word "first" in the latter clause of the Mishnah does not add to our understanding of the latter clause itself, but was included to **inform us** that **the first clause** of the Mishnah **also refers to** a case **where** the finder **said** "I acquired the found object **first**." According to Ulla's argument the claim of the finder in both clauses of the Mishnah is the same: "I acquired the object first — at the moment I picked it up." Hence, according to this interpretation, the reason why the finder's claim in the second clause of the Mishnah is not accepted is because he has shown by his action in handing over the object to the rider that his original intention when he picked it up was to acquire it on behalf of the rider and not on his own behalf. Therefore we do not believe his statement. But where, as in the first clause of the Mishnah, the finder's claim is credible, it is believed. Ulla claims that the assumption underlying the whole Mishnah is that a person who picks up an ownerless object for someone else does acquire it for that person.

וְאִידָךְ [7]The Gemara now asks: **But** how does **the other** Amora, Rav Naḥman, explain this expression in the Mishnah?

תָּנָא סֵיפָא לְגַלּוּיֵי רֵישָׁא [8]The Gemara answers that Rav Naḥman maintains that the author of the Mishnah **taught the latter clause in order to shed light on the first clause** and to bring out the contrast between the two

TERMINOLOGY

תָּנָא סֵיפָא לְגַלּוּיֵי רֵישָׁא **He taught the last clause to shed light in (lit., "reveal") the first clause**. Sometimes the Talmud rejects inferences drawn from the last clause of a Mishnah by suggesting: "The Tanna taught the last clause to shed light on the first clause [and thus the latter part of the Mishnah was never intended to teach us anything new]."

NOTES

וְאִידָךְ תָּנָא סֵיפָא כו' **And the other? The author of the Mishnah taught the last clause to throw light on the first clause**. Usually, after the Gemara has used the expression: "[The view of X] is also reasonable" (הָכִי נַמִי מִסְתַּבְּרָא), it does not afterwards go on to explain the opposing viewpoint. But in this case, since Ulla's explanation seems exceptionally convincing, the Talmud felt it necessary to explain and justify Rav Naḥman's position (*Ḥokhmat Manoaḥ*).

תָּנָא סֵיפָא לְגַלּוּיֵי רֵישָׁא **He taught the last clause to shed light on the first clause**. Both Ulla and Rav Naḥman agree

LITERAL TRANSLATION

[1]The last [clause applies] where he said "first," the first [clause applies] where he did not say "first."
[2]Rav Naḥman and Rav Ḥisda both say: Someone who picks up a found object for his fellow, his fellow does not acquire it. [3]What is the reason? [4]He is seizing [property] for a creditor in a situation where he causes loss to others, [5]and one who seizes [property] for a creditor in a situation where he causes loss to others does not acquire [it].

[1]סֵיפָא דְּאֲמַר "תְּחִילָּה", רֵישָׁא דְּלָא אֲמַר "תְּחִילָּה".
[2]רַב נַחְמָן וְרַב חִסְדָּא דְּאָמְרִי תַּרְוַיְיהוּ: הַמַּגְבִּיהַּ מְצִיאָה לַחֲבֵירוֹ, לֹא קָנָה חֲבֵירוֹ. [3]מַאי טַעְמָא? [4]הָוֵי תּוֹפֵס לְבַעַל חוֹב בְּמָקוֹם שֶׁחָב לַאֲחֵרִים, [5]וְהַתּוֹפֵס לְבַעַל חוֹב בְּמָקוֹם שֶׁחָב לַאֲחֵרִים לֹא קָנָה.

TERMINOLOGY

דְּאָמְרִי תַּרְוַיְיהוּ [X and Y who] both say. This expression is used to introduce a joint statement by two Amoraim, stressing that they agree about the matter under discussion, though in other matters they usually disagree with each other, e.g., "Rav and Shmuel, who both say..." or "Abaye and Rava who both say...."

TRANSLATION AND COMMENTARY

cases: [1]**The** ruling in the **latter clause applies** specifically **where** the finder **said**, "I acquired the lost object **first**," whereas the ruling in **the first clause applies** even **where** the finder **did not say**, "I acquired it **first**." In other words, Rav Naḥman maintains that the exclusion of the word "first" in the first statement of the Mishnah and its inclusion in the second statement is deliberate. According to Rav Naḥman, the first statement of the Mishnah shows that the only way the rider can acquire the found object is for the finder to put it into the rider's hand. In that case, the finder does not need to say that he acquired the object first, because, according to Rav Naḥman, he cannot acquire the object on behalf of the rider merely by picking it up. He has to hand it over to the rider. Only then does the rider acquire it.

רַב נַחְמָן וְרַב חִסְדָּא [2]The Gemara continues its analysis of our Mishnah and cites the following statement made jointly by two Sages: **Rav Naḥman and Rav Ḥisda both say: If someone picks up a found object for another person, that other person does not** thereby **acquire it.** Normally, an act of acquisition performed by one person on behalf of another is effective. Indeed, if the act of acquisition is to the other person's benefit, it can be performed without his consent or even his awareness. But Rav Naḥman and Rav Ḥisda are of the opinion that the acquisition of ownerless objects is different from other acts of acquisition. [3]**What is the reason** for this distinction? [4]The Gemara explains that the finder of an ownerless object is considered like someone who **seizes** a debtor's **property on behalf of a creditor in a situation where he causes a loss to other** creditors of the same debtor, [5]**and one who seizes property on behalf of a creditor in a situation where he causes a loss to other** creditors **does not acquire it**. Ordinarily, a creditor is permitted to keep property that he seizes from the debtor in payment of his own debt, even if there are other creditors to whom this debtor owes money. But a third party is not permitted to seize the debtor's property on behalf of a particular creditor. If a third party were allowed to intervene in this way, he would effectively be preventing other creditors from seizing this property. It is true that he is benefiting one creditor, but he is causing a loss to all the others, and the principle that a person is permitted to perform an act of acquisition on behalf of someone else does not apply in such situations. Similarly, say Rav Naḥman and Rav Ḥisda, if a person seizes a found object, which is potentially everybody's property, on behalf of a particular person, he is thereby denying all other potential finders the opportunity to acquire that object for themselves.

RASHI

סיפא — דלא אפשר בלא "תחילה", אמר "אני זכיתי תחילה קודם שנתתיה לך" — לא אמר כלום, דגלי דעתיה כשנתנה לו דלדעתא דהאי אגבהה. **ורישא** — דלא אמר "תחילה", ואפילו הכי זכה בה. **הוי תופס לבעל חוב במקום שחב לאחרים** — כאדם הבא מאליו ותופס ממון חבירו בשביל חוב שיש לאחר עליו, ובא לקדם עד שלא יתפסנו בעל חוב אחר, ונמצא תופס זה חב בתפיסתו זאת את הנושים האחרים. **חב לאחרים** — מפסיד את האחרים. כמו "אין חבין לאדם" (כתובות יא,א). **לא קנה** — כדאמר בכתובות, דלאו כל כמיניה להיות קופץ מאליו וחב לאלו, מאחר שלא עשאו אותו הנושה שליח לתפוס.

NOTES

that the word תְּחִילָּה which appears in the second section of the Mishnah is not necessary in its context. But they understand the connection between the first and second sections of the Mishnah differently. According to Ulla, the first and second sections are fully parallel, so that the expression תְּחִילָּה refers to the entire Mishnah. Rabbi Nahman, on the other hand, sees the emphasis on the word תְּחִילָּה in the second part as an expression of contrast, emphasizing that the previous passage deals with a situation in which he did not say תְּחִילָּה.

הָוֵי תּוֹפֵס לְבַעַל חוֹב He is seizing property for a creditor. *Shittah Mekubbetzet* writes that in fact these two cases are not exactly the same, for when someone seizes something from a debtor in the name of a creditor, the other creditors suffer a loss, whereas here someone who does not receive a found object, although he is indeed denied a certain profit, incurs no loss. Moreover, there is no certainty that others will actually receive the found object, for they may not see it, or the owner may return in the meantime and find it himself.

תּוֹפֵס לְבַעַל חוֹב One who seizes property for a creditor. A person's capacity to acquire something for someone else

HALAKHAH

תּוֹפֵס לְבַעַל חוֹב בְּמָקוֹם שֶׁחָב לַאֲחֵרִים Someone who seizes property for a creditor in a situation where he causes loss to other creditors. "If a person owes money to a number of people, but does not have the means to repay all

TRANSLATION AND COMMENTARY

אֵיתִיבֵיהּ רָבָא לְרַב נַחְמָן [1]Rava raised an objection against Rav Naḥman's opinion from a statement in a Baraita: "Whatever is found by a worker belongs to him, and not to the employer for whom he is working at the time. [2]When, and under what circumstances, does this ruling apply? [3]When the employer said to the worker: 'Perform a specific type of work for me.' For example, 'Weed for me today,' or 'Hoe for me today.' In such a case an object found by the worker during the time he is employed by the employer belongs to the worker. [4]But if the employer said to the worker: 'Work for me today,' without specifying what particular type of work was involved, [5]whatever he finds belongs to the employer," since the worker's acquisition of the found object is considered part of his work for the employer. At all events, says Rava, we see from this Baraita that a worker can acquire a found object on his employer's behalf. Thus the general principle must be that if a person lifts up a found object for another person, that other person *does thereby acquire it!*

אֲמַר לֵיהּ [6]Rav Naḥman **said** in reply **to** Rava: You cannot raise an objection from this case, because **a worker is different, for his hand is like the hand** of his employer. By hiring himself out, a worker subordinates his independent legal status to his employer and he becomes a kind of extension of the legal personality of the employer. On the other hand, says Rav Naḥman, an ordinary person does not acquire lost property for someone else.

[1]אֵיתִיבֵיהּ רָבָא לְרַב נַחְמָן: "מְצִיאַת פּוֹעֵל לְעַצְמוֹ. [2]בַּמֶּה דְּבָרִים אֲמוּרִים? [3]בִּזְמַן שֶׁאָמַר לוֹ בַּעַל הַבַּיִת: 'נַכֵּשׁ עִמִּי הַיּוֹם', 'עֲדוֹר עִמִּי הַיּוֹם'. [4]אֲבָל אָמַר לוֹ: 'עֲשֵׂה עִמִּי מְלָאכָה הַיּוֹם', [5]מְצִיאָתוֹ שֶׁל בַּעַל הַבַּיִת הוּא".

[6]אֲמַר לֵיהּ: שָׁאנֵי פּוֹעֵל, דְּיָדוֹ כְּיַד בַּעַל הַבַּיִת הוּא.

LITERAL TRANSLATION

[1]Rava raised an objection against Rav Nahman: "Whatever is found by a worker is his. [2]When do these words apply? [3]When the employer said to him: 'Weed for me today,' [or:] 'Hoe for me today.' [4]But if he said to him: 'Work for me today,' [5]whatever he finds [belongs] to the employer."

[6]He said to him: A worker is different, for his hand is like the hand of the employer.

RASHI

נכש עמי היום — דלא נשכר עמו אלא לניכוש ועידור, וכשהגביה המציאה אין זו ממלאכת בעל הבית, וקנאה פועל. והוא ינכה לו משכרו שכר פעולת ניכוש ועידור כל שעת הגבהה. **אמר לו עשה עמי מלאכה היום** — כל מלאכה שהוא עושה — מלאכת בעל הבית היא, וקנה בעל הבית. אלמא: המגביה מציאה לחבירו קנה חבירו.

NOTES

apparently depends upon his having become his agent, even if he has not been officially appointed. As an agent, he acquires the object for the other person as if he were doing so for himself. But, in a situation where there are many creditors, the agent must be specifically appointed by one of them; for, while an undefined appointment as an agent does indeed benefit one creditor, it also involves loss for others, and it is forbidden to bring about a loss for another person without the latter's knowledge. According to *Rashi*, if the person who seizes money or property from the debtor is the appointed agent of the person he is benefiting, his status is identical to that of his sender, and he takes possession exactly like him. Just as the creditor could have acted without an agent and taken compensation for himself (even though the debtor owed money to other people), the agent can do the same. Even those (*Tosafot, Rid, Rashba*) who disagree with *Rashi* and believe that an agent does not have this right, do, however, concede that if the agent has been given explicit authorization to do so, he may receive what is due, even if debts are owed to others. In that case he has certainly not volunteered to do someone a favor and receive something for him, but his mission is clearly defined, and his status is identical to that of the creditor.

אֵיתִיבֵיהּ רָבָא לְרַב נַחְמָן Rava raised an objection against Rav Naḥman. In this discussion Rava seems to be of the opinion that it *is* possible to acquire ownerless property on behalf of another person. But earlier in the Gemara (above, 8a), in a difference of opinion with Rami bar Ḥama, Rava pursued the line of argument that if someone lifts up an ownerless object for another person, the other person does *not* acquire it unless he too receives a share! Some commentators resolve this seeming contradiction by suggesting that Rava retracted his previous position after hearing Rav Naḥman's answer in the present discussion in the Gemara (*Tosafot*). Others explain that Rava did not reveal his true opinion in either passage, and his objections in both discussions were made for the sake of theoretical analysis of the issues under consideration (*Rosh*).

HALAKHAH

of them, and someone else comes and seizes some of the debtor's movable property on behalf of one of the creditors, he does not thereby acquire it. Rather, all the creditors are entitled to their share of this property, as if it were still in the borrower's possession." (*Shulḥan Arukh, Ḥoshen Mishpat* 105:1.)

מְצִיאַת פּוֹעֵל לְעַצְמוֹ A lost object found by a worker is his. "Ownerless objects found by a worker belong to him, even if his employer did not engage him to perform a specific type of work. But if the worker was employed specifically to look for and to pick up lost objects, whatever he finds belongs to his employer," in accordance with the Baraita here as interpreted by Rav Pappa (see below, 12b). (*Shulḥan Arukh, ibid.,* 270:3.)

TRANSLATION AND COMMENTARY

וְהָאָמַר רַב [1]The Gemara (Rava) now objects: **But surely Rav said, A worker** (unlike a slave) **can** change his mind and **go back** on his commitment to work for his employer **even in the middle of** a work **day!** From this we see that even while he is employed the worker still retains his independent legal status. How, then, can he be considered a mere extension of his employer?

אָמַר לֵיהּ [2]Rav Naḥman **said to** Rava in reply: **As long as** the worker **has not retracted** and continues to work for the employer, **his hand is like the employer's hand** and what he acquires, he acquires for his employer. [3]But **when he** does **retract, there is another reason why his act** of cancelling his commitment **is effective.** [4]**For it is written** (Leviticus 25:55): **"For to Me the children of Israel are servants;** they are My servants whom I brought forth out of the land of Egypt." [5]From this verse the Gemara deduces: **They are My servants, and not the servants of servants.** Therefore, no agreement can bind a Jew to continue to work against his will. The obligations of an employee, unlike those of a slave, are limited to the wages he receives. Accordingly, a worker can cancel his contract of employment whenever he wants. Nevertheless, as long as the worker is employed by someone else, he is considered to be an extension of his employer, and what he acquires, he acquires for his employer. But, says Rav Naḥman, I still maintain that an ordinary person who picks up an ownerless object for someone else, *does not* acquire it for him.

אָמַר רַבִּי חִיָּיא בַּר אַבָּא [6]A contrary view was expressed by **Rabbi Ḥiyya bar Abba,** who **said in the**

[1]וְהָאָמַר רַב: פּוֹעֵל יָכוֹל לַחֲזוֹר בּוֹ אֲפִילּוּ בַּחֲצִי הַיּוֹם! [2]אָמַר לֵיהּ: כָּל כַּמָּה דְּלָא הֲדַר בֵּיהּ, כְּיַד בַּעַל הַבַּיִת הוּא. [3]כִּי הֲדַר בֵּיהּ, טַעְמָא אַחֲרִינָא הוּא, [4]דִּכְתִיב: "כִּי לִי בְנֵי יִשְׂרָאֵל עֲבָדִים". [5]עֲבָדַי הֵם, וְלֹא עֲבָדִים לַעֲבָדִים. [6]אָמַר רַבִּי חִיָּיא בַּר אַבָּא אָמַר

LITERAL TRANSLATION

[1]But surely Rav said: A worker may retract even in the middle of the day!

[2]He said to him: As long as he has not retracted, [his hand] is like the employer's hand. [3]When he retracts, there is another reason [why his act is effective], [4]for it is written: "For to Me the children of Israel are servants." [5]They are My servants, and not the servants of servants.

[6]Rabbi Ḥiyya bar Abba said in the name of

RASHI

כי הדר ביה טעמא אחרינא הוא – הא דאמר דכי הדר ביה הרשות בידו – לאו משום דעד השתא לאו כיד בעל הבית הוא. אלא טעמא אחרינא הוא! שאינו שלו כעבד. שאם בא לעזוב לו שכרו מכאן ואילך ולחזור בו – יחזור בו.

NOTES

וְהָאָמַר רַב פּוֹעֵל יָכוֹל לַחֲזוֹר But surely Rav said: A worker may retract.... *Tosafot* points out that (below, 77a), where the Gemara deals with this question at length, there is no dispute that a worker may retract at any time. However, there is a question whether the worker has any obligations to the employer if by unexpectedly leaving him he causes him financial loss. Therefore, the Gemara here quotes Rav, who rules in accordance with the opinion that the worker is under no obligation in this regard. Accordingly, Rava feels that the worker also has the right to take time off at any point to pick up an object he finds, and then return to his work, with merely a small deduction from his wages for the lost time. But Rav Naḥman replies that the worker may indeed retract, but that until he does so his time is his employer's and may not be misused.

כִּי לִי בְנֵי יִשְׂרָאֵל עֲבָדִים "For to Me the children of Israel are servants." Nevertheless a Jew is permitted to hire himself out to work for another person; for our verse only prohibits actual slavery, whereby a person is considered in certain respects his master's property (*Rosh,* and see *Tosafot*). Indeed, Aḥronim ask how the Gemara knows that an employer acquires property found by his employees, since a worker is not considered his master's property (see *Kehillot Ya'akov* and others).

כִּי לִי בְנֵי יִשְׂרָאֵל עֲבָדִים "For to Me the children of Israel are servants." *Tosafot* (ד״ה כי) comments that one must not conclude from this verse that a Jew may not hire himself out as a laborer, because the emphasis in the verse is clearly on actual slavery, and does not refer to any other kind of obligation. In fact, some commentators interpret the verse as a warning, prohibiting a Jew from submitting himself to bondage. Indeed, this is Rav's main argument regarding the laborer's work. He explains that any absolute obligation to work for other people is in reality a situation of slavery, even if it only lasts for a short time. For that reason the worker has the right to stop working any time, and this is an expression of his status as a free man, bound only by his obligations to God.

HALAKHAH

פּוֹעֵל יָכוֹל לַחֲזוֹר בּוֹ A worker can retract even in the middle of the day. "Even if a worker has begun working and has already received his wages, he is entitled to retract, even in the middle of the workday, and the money he received over and above his wages for the hours he actually worked is a debt that he must repay to his employer," following Rav's ruling. (*Shulḥan Arukh, Ḥoshen Mishpat* 333:3.)

רַבִּי יוֹחָנָן: [1]הַמַּגְבִּיהַּ מְצִיאָה לַחֲבֵירוֹ, קָנָה חֲבֵירוֹ. [2]וְאִם תֹּאמַר מִשְׁנָתֵינוּ, [3]דְּאָמַר: "תְּנָהּ לִי", וְלֹא אָמַר: "זְכֵה לִי".

משנה [4]רָאָה אֶת הַמְּצִיאָה וְנָפַל עָלֶיהָ, וּבָא אַחֵר וְהֶחֱזִיק בָּהּ, [5]זֶה שֶׁהֶחֱזִיק בָּהּ זָכָה בָּהּ.

TRANSLATION AND COMMENTARY

name of Rabbi Yoḥanan: [1]If **someone picks up a found object for another person, that other person acquires it.** [2]**And if you say that** the first clause of **our Mishnah** seems to contradict this view, as explained above, [3]I can answer that the Mishnah is specifically dealing with a case **where** the rider **said**: **"Give** the object **to me," and he did not say: "Acquire it for me."** If he had said, "Acquire it for me," he would have acquired the object as soon as the finder picked it up, since a person who picks up an ownerless object on someone else's behalf does acquire it for that person. But since the rider used the word "give" rather than "acquire," he indicated that he did not expect to acquire the object until it actually reached his possession. Hence the finder was entitled to change his mind until the moment he delivered the object into the rider's possession.

MISHNAH רָאָה אֶת הַמְּצִיאָה [4]If a person **saw a lost object and threw himself on it** with the intention of acquiring it, but did not perform a formal act of acquisition, he did not acquire it. Therefore, if **another person came and seized it,** [5]**the person who seized it acquired it**, because the object was still considered ownerless and the second person's action was a valid mode of acquisition.

LITERAL TRANSLATION

Rabbi Yoḥanan: [1]Someone who picks up a found object for his fellow, his fellow acquires [it]. [2]And if you say [that] our Mishnah [disagrees], [3][it applies] where he said: "Give it to me," and he did not say: "Acquire [it] for me."

MISHNAH [4][If a person] saw the found object and fell on it, and another person came and seized it, [5]the one who seized it has acquired it.

RASHI

ואם תאמר משנתינו — דקתני: אני זכיתי בה — זכה בה, ומשמע לן: אני זוכה בה עכשיו זכה בה, ואף על פי שהגביה לצורך חבירו — היינו טעמא משום דקתני: ואמר לחבירו "תנה לי" ולא אמר "זכה אתה לי בהגבהתך" נמצא שלא עשאו שליח להקנות בהגבהתה עד שעת נתינה, והרי קודם נתינה הדר בו זה משליחותו.

NOTES

אָמַר ר׳ יוֹחָנָן הַמַּגְבִּיהַּ וכו׳ Rabbi Yoḥanan said: Someone who picks up a found object for his fellow, his fellow acquires it. The Rishonim ask: Following the Gemara's reasoning, since Rabbi Yoḥanan maintains that one can acquire an ownerless object on behalf of someone else, he must also maintain that it is possible to seize a debtor's property on behalf of one creditor at the expense of other creditors. But in fact Rabbi Yoḥanan maintains elsewhere that someone who seizes property on behalf of a creditor at the expense of others *does not* acquire it! (See, for example, *Ketubot* 84b and *Gittin* 11b.) Moreover, the Halakhah follows Rabbi Yoḥanan in both rulings! Some commentators answer that, since a person can acquire an ownerless object for himself, he can also acquire it on behalf of another person, even though a non-creditor cannot seize property for one creditor at the expense of other creditors (*Rid, Rabbenu Tam*). Others suggest that one who picks up a found object does not do so at the expense of others, since the found object does not yet belong to anyone before it has been picked up (*Ramban*).

דְּאָמַר תְּנָהּ לִי Where he said: "Give it to me." Many of the Rishonim discuss the meaning of Rabbi Yoḥanan's statement, for in various Halakhot we do, in fact, say that the word תֵּן — "give" — is equivalent to זְכֵה — "acquire."

Rabbenu Tam and *Talmid Rabbenu Peretz* say that the word תֵּן is only to be interpreted as זְכֵה in certain cases, and these cases do not include gifts and loans.

Rosh maintains that in the present case the rider intentionally said תֵּן and not זְכֵה, because he did not want the person who lifted the object up to know that it was a found object (for then the person who lifted it up would acquire it for himself). He used the expression תֵּן because he wanted the person who lifted up the object to think that it was his and that he had dropped it.

Ramban explains that the phrase דְּאָמַר תְּנָהּ לִי is said by the person who picked up the object, arguing against the person riding, and claiming that he had not told him from the start that he had intended to acquire the object, but merely to give it to him, and therefore he had not become his agent to acquire it for him at all. This argument is similar to that of Ulla, who emphasized the word תְּחִילָּה — "first." (See *Shittah Mekubbetzet.*)

HALAKHAH

הַמַּעֲבִיר מְצִיאָה לַחֲבֵירוֹ Transferring a found object to another person. "If one person instructs another: 'Acquire this found object for me,' the first person acquires it as soon as the other person picks it up. But if the first person said: 'Give it to me,' the person who picked it up may keep it for himself, as long as he decides to do so while the object is still in his hands," following Rabbi Yoḥanan's view. (*Shulḥan Arukh,* ibid., 269:6.)

הַנּוֹפֵל עַל הַמְּצִיאָה One who falls upon a lost object. "If a person noticed a lost object and fell upon it, and then another person seized the lost object, the person who seized it acquired it." *Rema,* however, maintains that if the lost object was located in a place where "four cubits" is a valid mode of acquisition (e.g., a side street), the person who initially fell upon the lost object acquired it (*Tur* and *Baḥ* in the name of *Rif* and *Rosh*), in accordance with the second answer (the opinions of Rav Pappa and Rav Sheshet on 10b) in the Gemara (*Sma*). (*Shulḥan Arukh,* ibid., 268:1.)

SAGES

אַבָּא כֹּהֵן בַּרְדְּלָא **Abba Kohen Bardela.** A Sage who was active during the last generations of the Tannaitic period. Only a few of his statements are found in the Talmud. It is not clear whether "Bardela" is the name of a person or a place. Perhaps this word should actually be read בַּר דְּלָיָה — "Bar Dlayah" — following an alternative reading in the Gemara, and accordingly it would mean "a member of the priestly watch called "Dlayah."

TRANSLATION AND COMMENTARY

GEMARA אָמַר רֵישׁ לָקִישׁ [1]**Resh Lakish said in the name of Abba Kohen Bardela:** [2]**A person's four cubits acquire** ownerless property **for him everywhere.** A person acquires any ownerless property that is within a four cubit radius of him, because this area is considered as if it were his private "courtyard," and it acquires ownerless property on his behalf as his own courtyard would.

מַאי טַעְמָא [3]On this the Gemara asks: **What is the reason** that a person's four cubits are effective in acquiring property on his behalf, even though they are not, in fact, his courtyard?

תַּקִּינוּ רַבָּנַן [4]The Gemara answers that **the Sages instituted this** law concerning a person's four cubits so **that people should not come to quarrel** over the ownership of property they find.

אָמַר אַבַּיֵי [5]**Abaye said: Rabbi Ḥiyya bar Yosef raised an objection** against this ruling of Resh Lakish from a Mishnah in tractate ***Pe'ah.*** **Rava said:** [6]**Rabbi Ya'akov bar Idi raised an objection** against this ruling of Resh Lakish **from** our Mishnah which is part of the **tractate** called ***Nezikin*** ("Damages").

אָמַר אַבַּיֵי [7]The Gemara now explains these objections in detail: **Abaye said: Rabbi Ḥiyya bar Yosef raised an objection** from the following Mishnah in tractate ***Pe'ah:*** [8]"**If** a poor **person took part of the *pe'ah*** [produce in the corner of a field, which is left unharvested so that it may be gleaned by the poor] that he had gathered for himself, **and threw it over the rest** of the *pe'ah* in order to acquire it by this action, **none of it is his.**

גמרא [1]אָמַר רֵישׁ לָקִישׁ מִשּׁוּם אַבָּא כֹּהֵן בַּרְדְּלָא: [2]אַרְבַּע אַמּוֹת שֶׁל אָדָם קוֹנוֹת לוֹ בְּכָל מָקוֹם.
[3]מַאי טַעְמָא? [4]תַּקִּינוּ רַבָּנַן דְּלָא אָתֵי לְאִנְצוּיֵי.
[5]אָמַר אַבַּיֵי: מוֹתִיב רַבִּי חִיָּיא בַּר יוֹסֵף פֵּיאָה. [6]אָמַר רָבָא: מוֹתִיב רַבִּי יַעֲקֹב בַּר אִידִי נְזִיקִין.
[7]אָמַר אַבַּיֵי: מוֹתִיב רַבִּי חִיָּיא בַּר יוֹסֵף פֵּיאָה: [8]"נָטַל מִקְצָת פֵּיאָה וְזָרַק עַל הַשְּׁאָר, אֵין לוֹ

LITERAL TRANSLATION

GEMARA [1]Resh Lakish said in the name of Abba Kohen Bardela: [2]A person's four cubits acquire for him everywhere.

[3]What is the reason?

[4]The Sages instituted [this] so that [people] should not come to quarrel.

[5]Abaye said: Rabbi Ḥiyya bar Yosef raised an objection [from tractate] *Pe'ah.* [6]Rava said: Rabbi Ya'akov bar Idi raised an objection [from tractate] *Nezikin.*

[7]Abaye said: Rabbi Ḥiyya bar Yosef raised an objection [from tractate] *Pe'ah:* [8]"[If a person] took part of the *pe'ah* and threw it over the rest, none of

RASHI

קונות לו — אם יש סביבותיו דבר הפקר — אין אחר רשאי לתופסו. **אמר אביי מותיב רבי חייא** — עלה מיובתא ממתניתין דמסכת פיאה. **ואמר רבא מותיב רבי יעקב** — עלה ממתניתין דסדר נזיקין. **נטל** — אחד מן העניים. **מקצת פיאה** — שליקט ככר. **וזרק (לה) על השאר** — כדי לקנות.

NOTES

אַרְבַּע אַמּוֹת שֶׁל אָדָם **A person's four cubits.** The measurement of a person's four cubits is found in various areas of the Halakhah, and it is defined as the immediate area of which a person disposes. It is the area in which a person can lie down comfortably and which he can reach without taking a lot of trouble when bending over. Abba Kohen Bardela's innovation lies in his stating that this area should not only be regarded as a person's private area as a definition of space (as in matters of Sabbath boundaries), but should also be significant in matters of acquisition.

אַרְבַּע אַמּוֹת קוֹנוֹת **Four cubits acquire.** Most Rishonim maintain that only ownerless objects can be acquired through "four cubits," and that this is not a valid mode of acquisition for purchases or gifts (see *Meiri*). From the Jerusalem Talmud, however, it would appear that there are differences of opinion as to whether or not gifts and purchases can be acquired through "four cubits," (see *Ramban*). Some commentators explain that the Jerusalem Talmud distinguishes between cases where the buyer entered the area of "four cubits" before the object being transferred entered it, in which case the "four cubits" acts as his courtyard and is thus a valid mode of acquisition, and cases where the object being transferred entered this area before the buyer entered it, in which case "four cubits" is *not* a valid mode of acquisition (*Nimmukei Yosef, Ran*).

The commentators ask: Since it was the Sages who ordained "four cubits" as a mode of acquisition, how can a person divorce his wife by placing a *get* (bill of divorce) within her four cubit radius? Surely a divorce is only valid if the woman acquires her *get* by a mode of acquisition that is valid according to *Torah law!* Some answer that the Sages are authorized by Torah law to transfer property rights as they see fit (הֶפְקֵר בֵּית דִּין הֶפְקֵר), and they transferred the four cubits near a person to him for the sole purpose of courtyard acquisition. Accordingly, "four cubits" is effective as a mode of acquisition even according to the Torah (*Talmid Rabbenu Peretz*).

מוֹתִיב נְזִיקִין **Rabbi Ya'akov bar Idi raised an objection**

HALAKHAH

נָטַל מִקְצָת פֵּיאָה וְזָרַק עַל הַשְּׁאָר **One who took part of the *pe'ah* and threw it over the rest.** "If a poor person took some *pe'ah* and threw it over the rest of the *pe'ah,* or if he fell on it or spread his garment over it, he is penalized by having all the *pe'ah,* including what he has already collected, taken away from him" (*Rambam, Hilkhot Mattenot Aniyyim* 2:18.)

LITERAL TRANSLATION

it is his. [1] [If he] fell upon it, [or] spread his garment over it, we remove him from it. [2] And similarly with a forgotten sheaf." [3] But if you say [that] a person's four cubits acquire for him everywhere, [4] let his four cubits acquire [it] for him!

[5] With what are we dealing here? [6] Where he did not say: "I will acquire [it]."

[7] But if the Sages instituted [this], [8] when he did not say ["I will acquire it"], what [difference] is there?

[9] Since he fell, he revealed his intention [10] that he wished to acquire by falling, [and] he did not wish to acquire with [his] four cubits.

[10B] [11] Rav Pappa said: When the Sages enacted

TALMUD

1 נָפַל לוֹ עָלֶיהָ, פָּרַס טַלִּיתוֹ עָלֶיהָ, מַעֲבִירִין אוֹתוֹ הֵימֶנָּה. 2 בְּעוֹמֶר שִׁכְחָה". 3 וְאִי אָמְרַתְּ אַרְבַּע אַמּוֹת שֶׁל אָדָם קוֹנוֹת לוֹ בְּכָל מָקוֹם, 4 נִקְנוּ לֵיהּ אַרְבַּע אַמּוֹת דִּידֵיהּ!

5 הָכָא בְּמַאי עָסְקִינַן? 6 דְּלָא אֲמַר: "אִקְנֵי".

7 וְאִי תַּקּוּן רַבָּנַן, 8 כִּי לָא אֲמַר, מַאי הָוֵי?

9 כֵּיוָן דְּנָפַל, גַּלֵּי דַּעְתֵּיהּ 10 דִּבְנְפִילָה נִיחָא לֵיהּ דְּנִקְנֵי, בְּאַרְבַּע אַמּוֹת לָא נִיחָא לֵיהּ דְּנִקְנֵי.

[10B] 11 רַב פַּפָּא אֲמַר: כִּי תַּקִּינוּ לֵיהּ רַבָּנַן

RASHI

ליקנו ליה — גבי נפל לו עליה ארבע אמות דתקון ליה רבנן. בנפילה ניחא ליה דנקני — לא נתכוין לקנות בתורת תקנת חכמים, כסבור שנפילתו יפה לו.

TRANSLATION AND COMMENTARY

[1] Moreover, even **if** the poor person **threw himself upon** the *pe'ah,* **or spread his garment over it, we remove him from it**, for he did not perform a valid act of acquisition. [2] **And similarly with a forgotten sheaf** (שִׁכְחָה)," which a poor person is also entitled to keep (Deuteronomy 24:19), if the poor person throws himself upon it or spreads his garment over it, etc., he does not thereby acquire it. [3] **But if you say that a person's four cubits acquire for him everywhere**, then if a person threw himself upon the *pe'ah,* [4] **let his four cubits acquire it for him**, since the *pe'ah* lies within his four cubit radius! Thus we see from this Mishnah in tractate *Pe'ah* that Resh Lakish's ruling that a person's four cubits acquire for him is incorrect!

הָכָא בְּמַאי עָסְקִינַן [5] The Gemara answers: **With what are we dealing here?** [6] With a case **where** the poor person **did not** specifically **say**: **I intend to acquire** it. Hence, his intentions are determined purely on the basis of his actions, and we cannot assume that he wished to acquire the *pe'ah* by means of his four cubits.

וְאִי תַּקּוּן רַבָּנַן [7] The Gemara now asks: **But if the Sages instituted** the law that a person can acquire by means of his "four cubits," [8] even **if he did not say, "I intend to acquire it," what difference does it make?** Since the four cubits belong by Rabbinic decree to the finder, why should he be required to state explicitly that he intends to acquire the *pe'ah* by this means?

כֵּיוָן דְּנָפַל [9] The Gemara answers that the situation here is different: **Since** the poor person **threw himself** upon the *pe'ah* without saying anything, **he** thereby **revealed his intention** [10] **that he wished to acquire** the *pe'ah* **by throwing himself** upon it, **and** that **he did not wish to acquire** it by means of his **four cubits**. Thus, since he waived his right to acquire the *pe'ah* by the Rabbinic enactment of the "four cubits," and since his act of throwing himself upon the *pe'ah* is not itself a valid mode of acquisition, he does not acquire the *pe'ah*.

רַב פַּפָּא אֲמַר [10B] [11] Rav Pappa now offers a different explanation of why the poor person cannot acquire the *pe'ah* with his "four cubits" in the circumstances described above in the Mishnah from tractate *Pe'ah:* **Rav**

NOTES

from *Nezikin*. According to *Rashi,* נְזִיקִין — "damages" — here refers to the fourth of the six orders of the Mishnah, which is known as "Damages" (נְזִיקִין). Others explain that the word *Nezikin* here refers specifically to our tractate. Even though this tractate is divided into three parts (*Bava Kamma, Bava Metzia,* and *Bava Batra*), these three *Bavot* are actually all one tractate called *Nezikin* (*Torat Ḥayyim, Rashash*).

אֵין לוֹ בָּהּ כְּלוּם If a person took part of the *pe'ah* and threw it over the rest, none of it is his. *Rambam* and *Rash,* following the Tosefta and the Jerusalem Talmud, explain that the poor person is penalized here by not being permitted to keep *any* of the *pe'ah,* not even what he had previously acquired legitimately (for the Mishnah states: "*none* of it is his"). This fine is a Rabbinic enactment, presumably ordained in order to prevent potentially dangerous quarreling (*Rashba*).

מַעֲבִירִין אוֹתוֹ הֵימֶנָּה We remove him from it. The Rishonim disagree as to the precise sense of these words. Some believe that the meaning is that other poor people can take away what he has received in this manner (*Tosafot* and others), while other authorities maintain that the court fines him and that it also expropriates what he has already gleaned, because he acted illegally (*Rambam* and others).

HALAKHAH

אַרְבַּע אַמּוֹת קוֹנוֹת Four cubits acquire. "The four cubits around a person acquire property for him. Thus, if a lost object entered a person's four cubits, he acquires it. This law applies to a side street, the sides of a public thoroughfare, or an ownerless field. But in a public thoroughfare, or in a field belonging to another person, a person's four cubits do

״אַרְבַּע אַמּוֹת״, בְּעָלְמָא. [1]בְּשָׂדֶה דְּבַעַל הַבַּיִת, לָא תַּקִּינוּ לֵיהּ רַבָּנַן. [2]וְאַף עַל גַּב דְּזָכָה לֵיהּ רַחֲמָנָא בְּגַוָּהּ, [3]כִּי זָכָה לֵיהּ רַחֲמָנָא, לְהַלּוּכֵי בָּהּ וּלְנַקּוּטֵי פֵּיאָה; [4]לְמֶיהֱוֵי חֲצֵירוֹ, לָא זָכָה לֵיהּ רַחֲמָנָא.

[5]אָמַר רָבָא: מוֹתִיב רַבִּי יַעֲקֹב בַּר אִידִי נְזִיקִין: [6]״רָאָה אֶת הַמְּצִיאָה וְנָפַל לוֹ עָלֶיהָ, וּבָא אַחֵר וְהֶחֱזִיק בָּהּ, [7]זֶה שֶׁהֶחֱזִיק בָּהּ זָכָה בָּהּ״. [8]וְאִי אָמְרַתְּ אַרְבַּע אַמּוֹת שֶׁל אָדָם קוֹנוֹת לוֹ בְּכָל מָקוֹם, [9]נִקְנוּ לֵיהּ אַרְבַּע אַמּוֹת דִּידֵיהּ!

[10]הָכָא בְּמַאי עָסְקִינַן? דְּלָא אֲמַר: ״אִקְנֵי״.

[11]וְאִי תַּקּוּן רַבָּנַן, [12]כִּי לָא אֲמַר, מַאי הָוֵי?

LITERAL TRANSLATION

[that] "four cubits" [should be effective] for him, [they meant] in general [in a public place]. [1][But] in the field of a private person, the Sages did not enact [that four cubits should be effective] for him. [2]And even though the Torah (lit., "the Merciful One") granted [rights] to [a poor person] in the [field], [3]when the Torah granted [these rights] to him, [it was] to walk in it and to collect *pe'ah;* [4][but for it] to become his courtyard, the Torah did not grant him.

[5]Rava said: Rabbi Ya'akov bar Idi raised an objection [from the tractate] *Nezikin*: [6]"[If a person] saw the found object and fell upon it, and another person came and seized it, [7]the one who seized it has acquired it." [8]But if you say [that] a person's four cubits acquire for him everywhere, [9]let his four cubits acquire [it] for him [here]!

[10]With what are we dealing here? Where he did not say: "I will acquire [it]."

[11]But if the Sages instituted [this], [12]when he did not say ["I will acquire it"], what [difference] is there?

TRANSLATION AND COMMENTARY

Rav Pappa said: When the Sages enacted that "four cubits" was an **effective** mode of acquisition, **they meant** it to apply **in general,** i.e., to public land. [1]**But the Sages did not enact that** acquisition by "**four cubits" should be effective in a private person's field**, in which the poor man has no exclusive rights. [2]**And even though the Torah did grant the poor person** limited **rights in** such **a field** at the time of harvesting the corner of the field, [3]**the** rights that **the Torah granted him** were restricted **to walking** in the field **and collecting** ***pe'ah*** [4]**but the Torah did not grant the poor man** the right to acquire objects in the field **as if it had become his** own personal **courtyard**. Thus the statement of Resh Lakish that a person's "four cubits acquire property for him" has not been refuted by the argument brought from the case of *pe'ah*.

אָמַר רָבָא [5]The Gemara now turns to the other objection to Resh Lakish's ruling that was mentioned earlier: **Rava said: Rabbi Ya'akov bar Idi raised an objection from** our Mishnah which is part of **the tractate** called ***Nezikin***: [6]**"If a person saw a lost object and threw himself upon it, and another person came and seized it,** [7]**the person who seized it has acquired it."** [8]**Now, if you say that a person's four cubits acquire** an ownerless object **for him everywhere,** [9]**let the four cubits** of the person who threw himself upon the lost object **acquire it for him here!**

הָכָא בְּמַאי עָסְקִינַן [10]The Gemara answers in the same way as it did to the objection (based on *pe'ah*) above: **With what are we dealing here**? With a case **where** the finder **did not** specifically **say: "I intend to acquire** the lost object." Here, too, as in the case of *pe'ah* above, his intentions are determined purely on the basis of his actions, and we cannot assume that he wished to acquire the lost object by means of his four cubits.

וְאִי תַּקּוּן רַבָּנַן [11]The Gemara now asks: **But if the Sages instituted** the law of acquisition through four cubits, [12]**even if** the finder **did not say,** "I intend to acquire," **what difference does it make?** Since the four cubits belong to the finder by Rabbinic decree, why should he be required to state explicitly that he intends to acquire the lost object by this means?

RASHI

הכי גרסינן: כי תקון ליה רבנן בעלמא – כגון בסמטא שהוא רשות לכל אדם, או ברשות הרבים, או בצידי רשות הרבים, והיא הפקר לרבים למשוך לתוכה הצריכין לצאת מן הדחק. **לא תקון ליה רבנן** – שהרי אין לאדם שם ארבע אמות מיוחדות, שהרבה חברים יש לו בתוכה עומדים אצלו.

NOTES

בְּעָלְמָא Lit., In general. Our reading here follows Rashi. But the Ge'onim and others read here: בְּשָׂדֶה דְּעָלְמָא, i.e., "in an ownerless field" (*Rambam*), not a public thoroughfare and not private land.

HALAKHAH

not acquire for him," following the views of Rav Pappa and Rav Sheshet here. *Shakh* questions whether "four cubits" is a valid mode of acquisition for gifts; *Gra*, however, maintains that gifts can be acquired in this way. (*Shulḥan Arukh, Ḥoshen Mishpat* 268:2.)

[1]כֵּיוָן דְּנָפַל עָלֶיהָ, גַּלֵּי דַּעְתֵּיהּ דְּבִנְפִילָה נִיחָא לֵיהּ דְּנִקְנֵי, [2]בְּאַרְבַּע אַמּוֹת לָא נִיחָא לֵיהּ דְּנִקְנֵי.

[3]רַב שֵׁשֶׁת אֲמַר: כִּי תַּקִּינוּ רַבָּנַן, בְּסִמְטָא, דְּלָא דָּחֲקִי רַבִּים; [4]בִּרְשׁוּת הָרַבִּים, דְּקָא דָּחֲקִי רַבִּים, לָא תַּקִּינוּ רַבָּנַן.

[5]וְהָא ״בְּכָל מָקוֹם״ קָאָמַר!

[6]״כָּל מָקוֹם״ לְאַתּוּיֵי צִידֵּי רְשׁוּת הָרַבִּים.

[7]וְאָמַר רֵישׁ לָקִישׁ מִשּׁוּם אַבָּא כֹּהֵן בַּרְדְּלָא: קְטַנָּה אֵין לָהּ חָצֵר, וְאֵין לָהּ אַרְבַּע אַמּוֹת. [8]וְרַבִּי יוֹחָנָן מִשּׁוּם רַבִּי יַנַּאי אָמַר: יֵשׁ לָהּ חָצֵר וְיֵשׁ לָהּ אַרְבַּע אַמּוֹת.

LITERAL TRANSLATION

[1]Since he fell on it, he revealed his intention that he wished to acquire by falling, [2][and] he did not wish to acquire with [his] four cubits.

[3]Rav Sheshet said: When the Sages enacted [that four cubits should be effective, they meant] in a side street, where there are not many people pushing; [4]in a public thoroughfare, where many people are pushing, the Sages did not institute [four cubits].

[5]But surely [Resh Lakish] said "everywhere"!

[6]"Everywhere" is to include the sides of a public thoroughfare.

[7]Resh Lakish further said in the name of Abba Kohen Bardela: A girl who is a minor does not have a courtyard, and she does not have four cubits. [8]But Rabbi Yoḥanan said in the name of Rabbi Yannai: She has a courtyard and she has four cubits.

TRANSLATION AND COMMENTARY

כֵּיוָן דְּנָפַל עָלֶיהָ [1]The Gemara answers: **Since he threw himself upon** the lost object, **he** thereby **revealed his** true **intention**, that **he wished to acquire** the lost object **by throwing himself** upon it, [2]and that **he did not wish to acquire** it **by means of his four cubits**. Thus, since he waived his right to acquire the lost object by means of the Rabbinic enactment of the "four cubits," and since his act of throwing himself upon the object is not itself a valid mode of acquisition, he does not acquire it.

רַב שֵׁשֶׁת אֲמַר [3]**Rav Sheshet** offered a different solution to Rabbi Ya'akov bar Idi's objection and **said: When the Sages enacted that four cubits was** an **effective** mode of acquisition, **they meant** that it should be effective **in a** place like a **side street, where there are not crowds of people pushing** their way. In a side street a person's "four cubits" can be treated as if the space provided actually belongs to him for the moment and can acquire things for him. [4]But **in a public thoroughfare, which may be crowded with many people pushing** their way, **the Sages did not institute** that **four cubits** should be a valid mode of acquisition. In such crowded conditions, where everybody has equal right of way, it would prove impossible to demarcate each person's radius of four cubits.

וְהָא בְּכָל מָקוֹם קָאָמַר [5]The Gemara objects: **But surely Resh Lakish said** that "four cubits acquire **everywhere**," and the ruling presumably applies even to a public thoroughfare!

כָּל מָקוֹם לְאַתּוּיֵי [6]The Gemara answers that Resh Lakish's use of the word "everywhere" was not meant to be interpreted literally: The word **"everywhere"** was intended **to include the sides of a public thoroughfare,** but not the main highway itself. Even people standing at the side of a public thoroughfare can acquire objects which enter their four cubits, because unlike the public thoroughfare itself the sides of a public thoroughfare are not so crowded.

וְאָמַר רֵישׁ לָקִישׁ [7]The Gemara now introduces another ruling involving the principle of "four cubits": **Resh Lakish further said in the name of Abba Kohen Bardela: A girl** under the age of twelve, **who is** legally **a minor, does not** acquire property by means of her **"courtyard,"** and she **does not** acquire property by means of her **"four cubits."** In contrast to adults, she does not acquire an object placed within her courtyard, nor does she acquire an object that comes within a radius of four cubits of her. [8]But **Rabbi Yoḥanan said in the name of Rabbi Yannai**: A girl who is a minor **does** acquire property by means of her **courtyard and** by means of her **four cubits**.

RASHI

קטנה אין לה חצר — אם זרק לה בעלה גט תוך חצרה — לא קנתה לה חצרה להתגרש בו. וכן אם היתה עומדת ברשות הרבים וזרקו לה גט בארבע אמותיה. ואף על גב דגדולה מיגרשה, כדתנן (גיטין עח,א): הזורק גט לאשתו בתוך ביתה כו׳, היתה עומדת ברשות הרבים וזרקו לה, קרוב לה — מגורשת כו׳.

CONCEPTS

צִידֵּי רְשׁוּת הָרַבִּים The sides of a public thoroughfare. The public domain (in the sense we are discussing in the context of this Halakhah) is a street or a space between private houses and courtyards. Not only does the public domain belong to the public, it is also a place where many people are always present. Adjoining the public domain itself there were places slightly separate from it, such as **חִיפּוּפֵי רְשׁוּת הָרַבִּים** — areas where border stones were placed alongside the public thoroughfare, by private home-owners to prevent people from rubbing against their walls. There were also bends and corners off the main thoroughfare, into which large numbers of people did not ordinarily enter. There are differences of opinion as to the Halakhic definition of the sides of the public domain; nor is this definition identical in every area of the Halakhah.

LANGUAGE

סִימְטָא A side street, an alley. This word is probably derived from the Latin *semita*, meaning "path, narrow road."

HALAKHAH

חָצֵר וְאַרְבַּע אַמּוֹת לִקְטַנָּה The "courtyard" and "four cubits" of a girl who is a minor. "A girl below the age of twelve acquires property that enters her courtyard or four cubits (this law is derived from Biblical verses). But a boy who is a minor cannot acquire property in this way." *Rema* maintains that a girl who is a minor can only acquire property by means of her courtyard if her father is no longer alive. But *Shakh* maintains that even a girl who is a minor and whose father is alive can acquire property by means of her courtyard. (*Shulḥan Arukh, Ḥoshen Mishpat* 243:23; 268:5.)

CONCEPT

קַרְפֵּף **Enclosure**. The exact origin of this word is unclear. It may be connected to the root קפף or גפף, in the sense of making a partition. At all events, a קַרְפֵּף is a courtyard surrounded by a partition, which one cannot enter without the right key. Some authorities hold that a קַרְפֵּף was situated outside the city, and others say that a קַרְפֵּף is actually a back courtyard, adjacent to a house, which is not used all the time but rather serves as a storage area.

TRANSLATION AND COMMENTARY

בְּמַאי קָמִיפַּלְגִי [1]The Gemara asks: **About what** legal principle do Rabbi Yoḥanan and Resh Lakish **disagree**?

מָר סָבַר [2]The Gemara now seeks to explain the basis of their difference of opinion: **One** Sage (Rabbi Yoḥanan) **maintains**: The legal power of a person's **courtyard** to acquire on his behalf **is an extension of** the legal power of a person's **hand** to acquire on his behalf. [3]**Just as** a girl below the age of twelve **has** the legal capacity to acquire objects by means of **her hand** (for example, a bill of divorce from her husband takes effect if it is placed in her hands), **she** is **also** able to acquire objects by means of **her courtyard**, since her courtyard is considered to be an *extension* of her hand. [4]**But the other** Sage, Resh Lakish, **maintains** that the legal power of **a** person's **courtyard** to acquire on his behalf **is an extension of the principle of agency**, the courtyard being considered the agent. [5]**And just as a girl who is a minor does not have** the power of **agency**, since a minor does not have the legal capacity to appoint an agent, **she** is **also unable** to acquire objects by means of her **courtyard**, since the principle of acquisition by a courtyard is considered to be an extension of the principle of agency.

מִי אִיכָּא מַאן דְּאָמַר [6]The Gemara now questions this analysis of the difference of opinion between the Sages: **Is there** in fact **anyone who maintains that** the power of acquisition by **a courtyard is an extension of the principle of agency**? [7]**Surely** the following statement **was taught** in a Baraita (see below, 56b) with regard to Exodus 22:3 ("If the theft be certainly found in his [the thief's] hand... he shall restore double"): "The verse uses the expression '**In his hand**.' **From this** expression **I know only** that the thief is liable if the stolen object is found physically in **his hand**. [8]But **from where do we derive** that he is liable if it was found on **his roof**, or in **his courtyard**, or in **his enclosure**? [9]Therefore **the verse teaches** us this additional law by using the emphatic expression, '**If the theft be certainly found**,' and from the extra emphasis ('*certainly* found') we learn that **in all cases** where the stolen object is found in the thief's possession, including when it is found in his courtyard, the thief is liable."

[1]בְּמַאי קָמִיפַּלְגִי? [2]מָר סָבַר: חָצֵר מִשּׁוּם יָדָהּ אִיתְרַבַּאי. [3]כִּי הֵיכִי דְּאִית לָהּ יָד, חָצֵר נַמִי אִית לָהּ. [4]וּמָר סָבַר: חָצֵר מִשּׁוּם שְׁלִיחוּת אִיתְרַבַּאי. [5]וְכִי הֵיכִי דִּשְׁלִיחוּת לֵית לָהּ, חָצֵר נַמִי לֵית לָהּ.

[6]מִי אִיכָּא מַאן דְּאָמַר חָצֵר מִשּׁוּם שְׁלִיחוּת אִיתְרַבַּאי? [7]וְהָתַנְיָא: "'בְּיָדוֹ'. אֵין לִי אֶלָּא יָדוֹ. [8]גַּגּוֹ, חֲצֵירוֹ, וְקַרְפֵּיפוֹ, מִנַּיִן? [9]תַּלְמוּד לוֹמַר: 'הִמָּצֵא תִמָּצֵא' — מִכָּל מָקוֹם".

LITERAL TRANSLATION

[1]About what do they disagree?

[2]One maintains: A courtyard is an extension of the principle of her hand. [3]Just as she has a hand, she also has a courtyard. [4]And the other maintains: A courtyard is an extension of the principle of agency. [5]And just as [a girl who is a minor] does not have agency, she also does not have a courtyard.

[6]Is there anyone who maintains that a courtyard is an extension of the principle of agency? [7]Surely it was taught: "'In his hand.' [From this] I know (lit., 'have') nothing except his hand. [8]His roof, his courtyard, his enclosure, from where [are they derived]? [9]The verse teaches: '[If the theft] be certainly found' — in all cases (lit., 'anyhow')."

RASHI

משום ידה אתרבאי — דכתיב "ונתן בידה", ו"ידה" — רשותה משמע, כדכתיב (במדבר כא) "ויקח את כל ארצו מידו". **כי היכי דאית לה יד** — דמשיודעת לשמור את גיטה מגורשת. דלא מיעט רחמנא אלא שוטה, דמשלחה והיא חוזרת. **משום שליחות איתרבאי** — מדרבי רחמנא שליחות לאדם, כדתניא (קידושין מא,א) "ושלח" — מלמד שהאיש עושה שליח, "ושלחה" — מלמד שהאשה עושה שליח, איתרבאי נמי חצרה, דהויא לה כשלוחה. **וכי היכי דשליחות לית לה** — דתנן שאין הקטן עושה שליח, דכי כתיב שליחות בין בגיטין בין בפסח — "איש" כתיב בענין. **ידו** — "אם המצא תמצא בידו". **גגו חצרו וקרפיפו מנין** — שאם נכנסה שם ונעל בפניה לגונבה, שהוא חייב?

NOTES

יָד חָצֵר וּשְׁלִיחוּת **Hand, courtyard, and agency**. The basic difference between acquisition by "hand" and acquisition through "agency" may be summarized as follows: If the laws of courtyard-acquisition are derived from hand-acquisition, the courtyard is deemed an extension of the personality of its owner; thus, whatever the owner acquires if it enters his hand can be acquired by him by its entry into his courtyard. Agency, by contrast, is a valid mode of acquisition because the agent was appointed by another person; hence, the effectiveness of agency is limited by such factors as the intentions and desires of the agent and of the person who appointed him.

גַּגּוֹ חֲצֵירוֹ וכו׳ **His roof, his courtyard, etc.** *Rashi* wishes to emphasize how a courtyard or something like it becomes an "agent." Therefore he explains that if a stray animal wanders into a person's courtyard, and the landlord then locks the gate, one can say that the theft was performed by the courtyard itself, and that the landlord was merely an accessory to that theft.

¹וְאִי סָלְקָא דַּעְתָּךְ חָצֵר מִשּׁוּם שְׁלִיחוּת אִיתְרַבַּאי, אִם כֵּן, מָצִינוּ שָׁלִיחַ לִדְבַר עֲבֵירָה, ²וְקַיְימָא לָן: אֵין שָׁלִיחַ לִדְבַר עֲבֵירָה!

³אֲמַר רָבִינָא: הֵיכָא אָמְרִינַן דְּ״אֵין שָׁלִיחַ לִדְבַר עֲבֵירָה״? ⁴הֵיכָא דְּשָׁלִיח בַּר חִיּוּבָא הוּא. ⁵אֲבָל בְּחָצֵר, דְּלָאו בַּר חִיּוּבָא הוּא, מִיחַיַּיב שׁוֹלְחוֹ.

LITERAL TRANSLATION

¹But if you assume [that] a courtyard is an extension of the principle of agency, if so, we find an agent for a matter of transgression, ²and it is accepted by us [that] there is no agent for a matter of transgression!

³Ravina said: Where do we say that "there is no agent for a matter of transgression"? ⁴Where the agent is subject to liability. ⁵But in [the case of] a courtyard, which is not subject to liability, the one who appoints it is liable.

TRANSLATION AND COMMENTARY

וְאִי סָלְקָא דַּעְתָּךְ ¹The Gemara proceeds to explain the difficulty posed by this Baraita to the analysis offered above: If courtyard-acquisition is an extension of hand-acquisition, the Baraita poses no problem. Just as a thief is liable for objets found in his hand, so too is he liable for objects found in his courtyard. **But if you assume that** the power of acquisition by **a courtyard is an extension of the principle of agency, then we find** a contradiction to an accepted Halakhic principle. We find that the courtyard of the thief has served as an **agent for transgression**, in that it has enabled the thief to acquire the stolen object, and in so doing it has caused him to be guilty of a crime. In other words, the thief is held responsible for the transgression committed by his agent, the courtyard! This surely cannot be correct, ²for **there is** an **accepted** Halakhic principle that **there is no agent for transgression**! For if a person instructs his agent to commit a transgression on his behalf, it is the agent who is fully responsible for the transgression and not the person who sent him. In fact, as soon as an agent is sent to perform the transgression, he ceases to be the sender's agent and acts on his own behalf alone. Yet in our case the responsibility is transferred to the person who gave the instructions (the thief) himself.

אֲמַר רָבִינָא ³In answer to this objection **Ravina said**: This is not a valid objection: **Where do we say that "there is no agent for transgression,"** and that the agent is himself responsible for the transgression and cannot pass on any responsibility to the person who instructed him to transgress? ⁴**Where the agent is** himself **subject to liability** for transgressing the law. In such a case the responsibility falls on the agent and not on the person who instructed him. ⁵**But in the case of a** thief's **courtyard, which is not subject to liability** for transgressing the laws of theft, **the person who**, as it were, **appointed it** as his agent — i.e., the thief — **is liable.**

RASHI

אם כן מצינו תורת שליחות לדבר עבירה — לומר: שלוחו כמותו, וחייב השולח במעשה השליח. **וקיימא לן** — בקידושין בפרק שני (מב,ב). **בר חיובא הוא** — שאף הוא מוזהר על הדבר — התם פטור השולח, דאמרינן ליה: דברי הרב ודברי התלמיד דברי מי שומעין, ולא היה לו לעשות. **דלאו בני חיובא נינהו** — לשלם, כדתנן: הם שחבלו באחרים — פטורין (בבא קמא פז,א).

NOTES

אֵין שָׁלִיחַ לִדְבַר עֲבֵירָה There is no agent for transgression. From a discussion elsewhere in the Gemara (*Kiddushin* 42b), it would appear that there is a logical rationale behind this ruling, namely, "If the agent has a choice between obeying the words of the Master [here, the Torah], or obeying the words of the disciple [here, the person who instructed the agent], whose words should be obeyed?" (דִּבְרֵי הָרַב וְדִבְרֵי הַתַּלְמִיד, דִּבְרֵי מִי שׁוֹמְעִין?) Since it is obviously the Torah's words that must be obeyed, the agent is not considered to be acting at the behest of the person who instructed him in a case where he was told to violate Torah laws. This has two important effects: (1) The transgression is ascribed to the agent, and not to the principal. It is the agent who suffers the consequences of his actions; the principal's orders, while clearly morally reprehensible, are exempt from all penalties. (2) Any illegal transaction, such as a forbidden marriage or an illegal purchase, undertaken by the agent at the principal's behest, is considered null and void. The Gemara's rationale is clearly insufficient to explain all the ramifications of this principle. A number of explanations of this principle have been suggested, and the commentators disagree as to whether they are complementary or mutually exclusive.

(1) Some authorities suggest that a person who instructs an agent to commit a transgression does not expect that

HALAKHAH

אֵין שָׁלִיחַ לִדְבַר עֲבֵירָה There is no agent for transgression. "Even though an agent ordinarily has the same Halakhic status as the person who appointed him, a person cannot be an agent in committing a transgression. Therefore, if an agent commits a sin at the behest of another person, that person bears no responsibility for the transgression committed by the agent. This holds true only if the agent is himself forbidden to perform the action; otherwise, the person who appointed him is liable," following Ravina (*Rema*). Other authorities maintain that the person who appointed the agent is liable only if the agent is incapable of free choice; but if the agent *is* capable of free choice, the person who appointed him is not responsible for the agent's actions (following Rav Sama; *Shakh*, based on *Rosh* and *Remah*). (*Rema's* gloss on *Shulḥan Arukh, Ḥoshen Mishpat* 182:1; ibid., 410:8.)

TRANSLATION AND COMMENTARY

אֶלָּא מֵעַתָּה [1]The Gemara now objects to Ravina's reasoning: **But** according to your argument, **if a person says to a woman or a slave, who is not subject to liability** for transgressing the laws of theft, **Go out and steal for me,** [2]**here too** you would say that **the person who instructed them** to steal **should be liable!** A woman and a slave are not required to pay for property they may steal, since they do not have means of their own with which to reimburse the person whose property they have stolen. Why, then, according to Ravina, is the person who instructed them to steal not held accountable for their actions rather than they themselves?

אָמְרַתְּ [3]The Gemara answers: **You may say: A woman and a slave are** in fact legally **subject to liability** if they transgress the laws of theft. [4]**But now, at all events, they do not have the means to pay.** The wife's property is not controlled by her but by her husband, and the slave has no property of his own. But even though it is not possible to collect from them at present, it is clear that they are nevertheless legally liable for their actions.

דִּתְנַן [5]The Gemara now proceeds to prove this point: **For we have learned** in a Mishnah *(Bava Kamma* 8:4): "If **the woman** who caused damage while she was married **was divorced,** so that she now has her own money (while she was married, her property was under the control of her husband), **or** if **the slave** who caused damage while in slavery **was freed,** so that he now has his own money, **they must pay** for the damage they caused or the thefts they committed." Thus, women and slaves *are* held legally liable for thefts they commit, even though they may be temporarily incapable of reimbursing the victims.

רַב סַמָּא אָמַר [6]Another, slightly different, distinction is now suggested between a thief, acting through an agent, who is exempt, and a thief, acting through a courtyard-agent, who is liable: **Rav Sama said: Where do we say that "there is no agent for transgression,"** and that the agent is himself fully responsible for the transgression and cannot pass on any responsibility to the person who instructed him to transgress? [7]In a case **where, if** the agent **wishes, he acts** as he was instructed and commits the transgression, **and if he wishes, he does not act** as he was instructed and does not commit the transgression. [8]**But in the case of a courtyard, in which** stolen **articles are placed without its agreement**, since the courtyard obviously has no power of choice, in such a situation **the person who "appoints" it** — i.e., the thief — **is liable.**

[1]אֶלָּא מֵעַתָּה, הָאוֹמֵר לְאִשָּׁה וְעֶבֶד: "צְאוּ גִּנְבוּ לִי", דְּלָאו בְּנֵי חִיּוּבָא נִינְהוּ, [2]הָכִי נַמִי דְּמִיחַיֵּיב שׁוֹלְחָן?!
[3]אָמְרַתְּ: אִשָּׁה וְעֶבֶד בְּנֵי חִיּוּבָא נִינְהוּ, [4]וְהָשְׁתָּא, מִיהָא, לֵית לְהוּ לְשַׁלּוּמֵי.
[5]דִּתְנַן: "נִתְגָּרְשָׁה הָאִשָּׁה, נִשְׁתַּחְרֵר הָעֶבֶד, חַיָּיבִין לְשַׁלֵּם".
[6]רַב סַמָּא אָמַר: הֵיכָא אָמְרִינַן: "אֵין שָׁלִיחַ לִדְבַר עֲבֵירָה"? [7]הֵיכָא דְּאִי בָּעֵי, עָבֵיד, וְאִי בָּעֵי, לָא עָבֵיד. [8]אֲבָל חָצֵר, דִּבְעַל כָּרְחֵיהּ מוּתִיב בָּהּ, מִיחַיֵּיב שׁוֹלְחוֹ.

LITERAL TRANSLATION

[1]But if so (lit., "from now"), [a person] who says to a woman or a slave, who are not subject to liability: "Go out [and] steal for me," [2]so too the one who appoints them should be liable?!

[3]You may say: A woman and a slave are subject to liability, [4]but now, at all events, they do not have [the means] to pay. [5]For we have learned: "[If] the woman was divorced, [or] the slave freed, they must pay." [6]Rav Sama said: Where do we say [that] "there is no agent for a matter of transgression"? [7]Where if he wishes, he acts, and if he wishes, he does not act. [8]But [in the case of] a courtyard, in which [articles] are placed without its will, the one who "appoints" it is liable.

RASHI

דאי בעי עביד — את השליחות.

BACKGROUND

רְכוּשׁ אִשָּׁה A wife's property. A wife did not usually have property of her own when she married. Although she was given various objects from her father's house, which she brought into her husband's house, they were known as נִכְסֵי צֹאן בַּרְזֶל and were entirely the property of the husband as long as the couple remained married. The marriage contract written by the husband for his wife is also only an obligation on his part to pay her a settlement when their marriage is dissolved by his death or their divorce. There were, however, women who brought property of their own into their marriage (נִכְסֵי מְלוֹג). Such property belonged entirely to the wife, though during the marriage it was administered by the husband, and he was entitled to the income from it. See the Halakhah section regarding special agreements by which women reserved the right to use their personal property while they were married.

NOTES

the agent will follow his instructions, and thus he does not commission the agent wholeheartedly in the first place (*Tosefot Sens*; alluded to by other Rishonim as well).

(2) Others explain that it is the Torah which confers the special status of "agent" on a person instructed by another person to act on his behalf; accordingly, there can be no agency where the agent acts in violation of Torah law (*Pnei Yehoshua*, *Rabbi Akiva Eger*).

(3) From *Tosafot*, however, it would appear that this principle is derived by specific exegesis from Biblical verses (גְּזֵירַת הַכָּתוּב).

HALAKHAH

נִתְגָּרְשָׁה הָאִשָּׁה נִשְׁתַּחְרֵר הָעֶבֶד If a woman was divorced or a slave freed. "If a slave or a married woman injured another person, or damaged another person's property, he or she is exempt from compensation, because he/she has no property. But if the woman is later divorced or the slave freed, they must then pay for the damage they caused." *Rema* adds that if the woman owned property of her own while she was married, she must pay damages even while she is still married (*Shulḥan Arukh, Ḥoshen Mishpat* 424:9).

גֵּט לִקְטַנָּה Divorcing a female minor. "A female minor,

TRANSLATION AND COMMENTARY

מַאי בֵּינַיְיהוּ [1]The Gemara now asks: **What is** the practical **difference between** Ravina's answer and Rav Sama's in relation to the principle, "there is no agent for transgression"?

אִיכָּא בֵּינַיְיהוּ [2]The Gemara answers: **There is a** practical **difference between** these views: (1) There is **the case of a priest**, who is forbidden to marry a divorcee, **who says to an Israelite** (a non-priest), who is permitted to marry a divorcee, **"Go and betroth a divorcee for me."** [3]**Or alternatively** (2) There is **the case of a man who says to a woman, "Cut off the earlocks of a minor** for me" (a man is forbidden to shave off his earlocks [see Leviticus 19:27], but a woman is not, and it is accepted that people who are forbidden to shave themselves are equally forbidden to shave others). [4]Now, **according to that version** (of Rav Sama) **which states** that **wherever** the agent **acts** as instructed **if he wishes** to do so, **and does not act** as instructed **if he does not wish** to do so, in such a situation **the person who appoints** the agent **is not liable** and the agent *is* liable

[1]מַאי בֵּינַיְיהוּ? [2]אִיכָּא בֵּינַיְיהוּ כֹּהֵן דַּאֲמַר לֵיהּ לְיִשְׂרָאֵל, "צֵא וְקַדֵּשׁ לִי אִשָּׁה גְּרוּשָׁה", [3]אִי נַמִי אִישׁ דַּאֲמַר לָהּ לְאִשָּׁה, "אַקְּפִי לִי קָטָן". [4]לְהַךְ לִישָּׁנָא דַּאֲמַר: "כָּל הֵיכָא דְּאִי בָּעֵי, עָבֵיד, אִי בָּעֵי לָא עָבֵיד, לָא מִיחַיַּיב שׁוֹלְחוֹ",

LITERAL TRANSLATION

[1]What is [the difference] between [the two opinions]?

[2]There is [a difference] between them: [The case of] a priest who says to an Israelite, "Go out and betroth a divorced woman for me," [3]or alternatively [the case of] a man who says to a woman, "Cut off [the earlocks] of a minor for me."

[4]According to that version (lit., "language") which states: "Where if he wishes, he acts, [and] if he wishes, he does not act, the one who appoints him is not liable,"

RASHI

וקדש לי אשה גרושה – ומשעת קידושין עובר משום "לא יקחו". אשה אינה באזהרת "לא תקיפו" לפי שאינה ב"בל תשחית פאת זקנך", כדאמר בקדושין (לה,ב). והמקיף את הקטן חייב, שהמקיף באזהרה כניקף, דכתיב "לא תקיפו" – אחד הניקף ואחד המקיף במשמע, במסכת [נזיר] (כז,ב). ו"קטן" דנקט, משום דסתמא גדול לא שביק לאקופי נפשיה.

CONCEPTS

הַקָּפַת הָרֹאשׁ Shaving the sides of the head. This prohibition is written in the Torah without any explanation, but, in the opinion of *Rambam*, it was forbidden because such shaving was practiced by non-Jews, and this was one of the commandments given to the Jews to set them apart. Some authorities believe that the reason for the prohibition is that pagan priests used to cut their hair in this way. According to this explanation it is clear why this commandment applies only to men.

The main prohibition is against having one's hair cut all around the head in such a way that no hair remains on the temples. The Halakhah gives precise definitions of the amount of hair that must be left on the temples so as not to violate this prohibition. For this reason some Jews let their sidelocks grow, in order to emphasize their strict compliance with this commandment.

NOTES

כֹּהֵן שֶׁאָמַר לְקַדֵּשׁ גְּרוּשָׁה A priest who told an Israelite, "Go and betroth a divorcee for me." A priest is forbidden to marry a divorcee (Leviticus 21:7). In tractate *Kiddushin* (78a) the Gemara records a difference of opinion over whether a priest is also forbidden to betroth a divorcee (the opinion of Abaye), or whether he is technically forbidden only to consummate such a marriage (the opinion of Rava, also followed by the Halakhah). A priest may serve as an agent to betroth a divorcee to an Israelite. But an Israelite serving as an agent to betroth a divorcee to a priest is clearly behaving improperly. Accordingly, the Rishonim find our Gemara puzzling: Why should there be less of a problem if a priest betroths a divorcee by the agency of an Israelite, than if he does so by the agency of another priest? *Ritva* and others suggest that there is indeed no difference, and the language of the Gemara is not to be taken literally, whereas *Tosafot* and others defend the literal meaning of the text.

The Rishonim are disturbed by an additional problem: The agent can do no more than perform the betrothal. How then is our Gemara to be understood in the light of Rava's authoritative view, cited above, that only consummation, not betrothal, is forbidden? Some authorities answer that our passage indeed follows the view of Abaye, and is not in accordance with the Halakhah (*Ramban*). Other commentators reinterpret Rava's view to correspond to our Gemara. Alternatively, they suggest that the issue here is not whether the priest is subject to punishment, but whether the agent's actions are effective and the betrothal is valid. Normally, the marriage of a priest and a divorcee is valid, even though it is illegal. But since there can be no agent to perform a transgression, such a betrothal should not take effect if performed by an agent. Hence the question in our Gemara is relevant even according to Rava (*Tosafot* and others).

אַקְּפִי לִי קָטָן Cut off the earlocks of a minor for me. *Rashi* and *Ramban* explain that the Gemara speaks of a minor here, because an adult could not be shaven against his will. Thus, one who shaved an adult would be acting on behalf of the adult, rather than on behalf of the person who had appointed him as his agent.

אַקְּפִי לִי קָטָן Cut off the earlocks of a minor for me. The prohibition against cutting off the hair of one's temples is one of the negative prohibitions from which women are exempted. Nevertheless, in the Halakhah it is understood that the prohibition applies both to the person who actually performs the act and also to the person who willingly has the act done to him. In the passage where the primary statement of this Halakhah is set out (*Nazir* 57b) there is a discussion as to whether this prohibition in no way affects women (i.e., they are not only permitted to cut their own hair but are also permitted to cut the hair of men) or whether they are only permitted to cut the hair off their own temples, but must not cut the hair off the temples of men.

HALAKHAH

whose betrothal was arranged by her father who subsequently died, can accept her bill of divorce on her own behalf while she is still a minor, if she is sufficiently mature to distinguish between her bill of divorce and another object. The bill of divorce may be given directly into her hand or it may be placed in her courtyard or her four cubits," following the Gemara. (*Shulan Arukh, Even HaEzer* 141:6-7.)

[1]הָכָא נַמִי, אִי בָּעֵי, עָבֵיד, אִי בָּעֵי, לָא עָבֵיד; [2]לָא מִיחַיַּיב שׁוֹלְחָן. [3]לְהַךְ לִישָּׁנָא, דְּאָמְרַתְּ: כָּל הֵיכָא דְּשָׁלִיחַ לָאו בַּר חִיּוּבָא, מִיחַיַּיב שׁוֹלְחוֹ, [4]הָנֵי נַמִי, כֵּיוָן דְּלָאו בְּנֵי חִיּוּבָא נִינְהוּ, מִיחַיַּיב שׁוֹלְחָן.

[5]וּמִי אִיכָּא לְמַאן דַּאֲמַר חָצֵר לָאו מִשּׁוּם יָדָהּ אִיתְרַבַּאי? [6]וְהָתַנְיָא: "'יָדָהּ'. אֵין לִי אֶלָּא יָדָהּ. [7]גַּגָּהּ, חֲצֵירָהּ, וְקַרְפֵּיפָהּ, מִנַּיִן? [8]תַּלְמוּד לוֹמַר: 'וְנָתַן' — מִכָּל מָקוֹם".

[9]לְעִנְיַן גֵּט, כּוּלֵּי עָלְמָא לָא פְּלִיגִי דְּחָצֵר מִשּׁוּם יָדָהּ אִיתְרַבַּאי. [10]כִּי פְּלִיגִי? לְעִנְיַן מְצִיאָה. [11]מָר סָבַר: [11A] יָלְפִינַן מְצִיאָה מִגֵּט, [12]וּמָר סָבַר:

LITERAL TRANSLATION

[1]here too, if [the agent] wishes, he acts, [and] if he wishes, he does not act; [2][hence] the one who appoints him is not liable.

[3]According to that version, that you say: Where the agent is not subject to liability, the one who appointed him is liable, [4]in these [cases] too, since they are not subject to liability, the one who appointed them is liable.

[5]But is there anyone who says that a courtyard is not an extension of the principle of her hand? [6]Surely it was taught: "'Her hand.' [From this] I know nothing except her hand. [7]Her roof, her courtyard, her enclosure, from where [are these derived]? [8]The verse teaches: 'He shall give' — in all cases (lit., 'anyhow')."

[9]With regard to a bill of divorce, everyone does not dispute that a courtyard is an extension of the principle of her hand. [10]When do they disagree? With regard to a found object. [11]One maintains: [11A] We derive [the law of] a found object from [the law of] a bill of divorce, [12]and the other maintains:

TRANSLATION AND COMMENTARY

[1]**here too, if** the Israelite in the first case or the woman in the second case **wishes** do so **he** (or she) **acts** as instructed, and **if he wishes** to do so **he does not act** as instructed. [2]Hence, **the person who appointed** the agent **is not liable.**

[3]But **according to the** other **version** (that of Ravina), **that you say: Wherever the agent is not subject to liability, the person who appointed him is liable** [4]in **these cases too, since the** Israelite and the woman **are not subject to liability** for committing the acts which they were instructed to perform, **the person who appointed them is liable.**

וּמִי אִיכָּא לְמַאן דַּאֲמַר [5]The Gemara returns to its original question regarding the principle of acquisition by means of a courtyard and asks: **But is there anyone who says that** acquisition by means of a **courtyard is not an extension of the principle** of acquisition by means of a person's **hand**? [6]**Surely it was taught** in a Baraita (below, 56b) explaining the meaning of the verse in Deuteronomy 24:1 ("And he shall write her a bill of divorce and he shall give it *in her hand*"): "The verse uses the expression, '**Her hand'. From this** expression **I know only** that the bill of divorce is effective if it is placed physically in **her hand.** [7]But **from where do we derive** that the bill of divorce is effective if it is placed on **her roof,** or in **her courtyard,** or in **her enclosure**? [8]**The verse teaches** us this additional law by using the expression, '**He shall give**,' implying that the divorce is effective **in all cases** where he delivers the bill of divorce into her possession or into her property. It seems quite clear from this Baraita that acquisition by means of a courtyard is an extension of acquisition by means of a person's hand!

לְעִנְיַן גֵּט [9]The Gemara gives three answers to this objection: (1) It is true that, **with regard to a bill of divorce**, there is no difference of opinion and **all** authorities **agree that** acquisition by means of **a courtyard is an extension of the principle of** acquisition by means of a person's **hand.** [10]**When do** Rabbi Yoḥanan) anan and Resh Lakish **disagree? With regard to** the acquisition of **a found object** by a girl who is a minor. [11]**One** Sage (Rabbi Yoḥanan) **maintains** [11A] that **we derive the law** regarding the acquisition **of a found object from the law** regarding the acquisition **of a bill of divorce**. Just as a girl who is a minor acquires her bill of divorce when it enters her courtyard, so too a found object is acquired by her when it enters her courtyard.[12]**And the other**

RASHI

תלמוד לומר ונתן מכל מקום — מדלא כתיב "ובידה יתנהו" — דרוש "ונתן" א"וכתב לה ונתן". אלמא משום ידה אתרבאי. דאי משום שליחות — הא כבר כתיבא הכא, כדתניא (ושלח) [ושלחה] — מלמד שהאשה עושה שליח, בקדושין בפרק שני (מא,א). **ילפינן מציאה מגט** — כי היכי דגבי גט אית לה חצר לקטנה. גבי מציאה נמי אית לה.

NOTES

וְנָתַן בְּיָדָהּ **"He shall give it in her hand."** *Rashi* explains that the Gemara's proof that a woman's courtyard is a valid means of acquiring a bill of divorce on her behalf is based on the wording of this phrase, and the proof that the courtyard works as a "hand," rather than as an "agent," is based on a logical argument. *Ramban* suggests that the proof of the courtyard's effectiveness is the repetition of the entire phrase (Deuteronomy 24:1,3). *Rashba* adds that the proof that the courtyard is a "hand" is the repetition of the expression "in her hand" in the two verses.

TRANSLATION AND COMMENTARY

Sage (Resh Lakish) **maintains** that **we do not derive the law** regarding the acquisition **of a found object from the law** regarding the acquisition **of a bill of divorce**. Hence a girl who is a minor does not acquire found objects by means of her courtyard.

וְאִיבָּעֵית אֵימָא [1]The Gemara now offers an alternative answer to this question: (2) **And if you wish**, you can **say**: **With regard to a girl who is a minor**, there is no difference of opinion and **all agree that we derive the law** regarding the acquisition **of a found object from the law** regarding the acquisition **of a bill of divorce**. Thus, just as a girl who is a minor can acquire her bill of divorce by means of her courtyard, by an extension of the principle that she can acquire it by means of her hand, so too she can acquire found objects by means of her courtyard. [2]**But here** Rabbi Yoḥanan and Resh Lakish **disagree about** the laws of acquisition by **a boy who is a minor**. [3]**One** (Rabbi Yoḥanan) **maintains** that **we derive the law of a male minor from the law of a female minor**, because there is seemingly no Halakhic difference between them. Accordingly, a male minor can acquire property that enters his courtyard in the same way as a female minor can. [4]**But the other** Sage (Resh Lakish) **maintains** that **we do not derive the law of a male minor from the law of a female minor**. Since the Torah gave a female minor the right to acquire her bill of divorce by means of her courtyard, she is also given that right with regard to a found object. But this right is not given to a male minor.

וְאִיבָּעֵית אֵימָא [5]A third answer is now suggested by the Gemara which eliminates completely the difference of opinion between Rabbi Yoḥanan and Resh Lakish: (3) **And if you wish**, you can **say: One** Sage **was explaining one case and the other was explaining** another, different, **case, and they do not** really **disagree** on a point of law. Resh Lakish, who said that a female minor does not acquire by means of her courtyard, meant that a female minor cannot acquire *found objects* by means of her courtyard, whereas Rabbi Yoḥanan, who said that a female minor does acquire by means of her courtyard, meant that a female minor does acquire her *bill of divorce* by means of her courtyard. Thus there is really no dispute between these two scholars.

MISHNAH רָאָה אוֹתָן רָצִין [6]**If** the owner of a field **saw people** in his field **running after an ownerless object,**

לָא יָלְפִינַן מְצִיאָה מִגֵּט.

[1]וְאִיבָּעֵית אֵימָא: בִּקְטַנָּה, כּוּלֵּי עָלְמָא לָא פְּלִיגִי דְּיָלְפִינַן מְצִיאָה מִגֵּט. [2]וְהָכָא בְּקָטָן קָא מִיפַּלְגִי. [3]מָר סָבַר: יָלְפִינַן קָטָן מִקְּטַנָּה, [4]וּמָר סָבַר: לָא יָלְפִינַן קָטָן מִקְּטַנָּה.

[5]וְאִיבָּעֵית אֵימָא: מָר אֲמַר חֲדָא, וּמָר אֲמַר חֲדָא, וְלָא פְּלִיגִי.

מִשְׁנָה [6]רָאָה אוֹתָן רָצִין אַחַר מְצִיאָה, אַחַר צְבִי שָׁבוּר,

LITERAL TRANSLATION

We do not derive [the law of] a found object from [the law of] a bill of divorce.

[1]And if you wish, say: With regard to a female minor, everyone agrees (lit., "the whole world does not dispute") that we derive [the law of] a found object from [the law of] a bill of divorce. [2]But here they disagree about a male minor. [3]One maintains: We derive [the law of] a male minor from [the law of] a female minor, [4]and the other maintains: We do not derive [the law of] a male minor from [the law of] a female minor.

[5]And if you wish, say: One [Sage] said one [case], and the other said one [case], and they do not disagree.

MISHNAH [6][If] one saw [people] running after a found object, after a lame (lit., "broken") gazelle,

RASHI

ומר סבר לא ילפינן — ממונא מאיסורא. וגבי ממונא חצר מ"אם המצא" אתרבאי. ואיכא למימר דשליחות הוא. ומשום דאין שליח לדבר עבירה אצטריך למכתב התם. **והכא בקטן פליגי** — דלא אשכחן דרבי ביה חצר. **מר אמר חדא כו'** — רבי שמעון בן לקיש אמר לענין מציאה. ורבי יוחנן לענין גט. אי נמי: מר אמר קטן. ומר אמר קטנה.

משנה אחר צבי שבור — דהוא דומיא דמציאה שאינו יכול לרוץ, ומשתמר בתוך השדה. אם לא יטלוהו אחרים.

TERMINOLOGY

מָר אֲמַר חֲדָא, וּמָר אֲמַר חֲדָא, וְלָא פְּלִיגִי One scholar said one, and the other scholar said another, and they do not disagree. Sometimes, when seemingly contradictory statements are made by two scholars, the Talmud explains that there was in fact no dispute between them, since each scholar was discussing a different case.

NOTES

לָא יָלְפִינַן מְצִיאָה מִגֵּט We do not derive the law of a found object from the law of a bill of divorce. *Rashi* explains that the two subjects come under two different categories of Torah law. A found object comes under the category of מָמוֹנָא — monetary law — while a bill of divorce comes under the category of אִיסּוּרָא — ritual law. Frequently, the Talmud explains that comparisons cannot be made between laws in these two categories.

Other commentators make a further differentiation. A bill of divorce can be given against a woman's will, whereas a found object must be consciously acquired.

Some authorities explain that the view that compares acquisition of found objects to acquisition of a bill of divorce, and grants a female minor the power to acquire found objects that enter her courtyard, grants her this power by Torah law. Others, however, maintain that a female minor acquires the found objects that enter her courtyard only by Rabbinic decree (*Tosefot Sens* and others).

מָר אֲמַר חֲדָא, וּמָר אֲמַר חֲדָא One said one case and the other said another case. In other words, the two Sages cited were actually discussing different topics (*Geonim*). This expression is commonly employed by the Talmud to counter a previous assumption that statements made by different Sages contradict each other. In fact, says the Gemara, their statements concern separate and unrelated issues.

TRANSLATION AND COMMENTARY

for example, **after a lame gazelle**, which could not run quickly, [1]or **after young pigeons that had not yet** learned to **fly**, and which could be caught easily, **and he said: "My field has acquired** ownership of **these** objects **for me,"** his field **has acquired** the ownerless objects **for him** and the people chasing after them have no claim on them. [2]But **if the gazelle was running normally, or if the young pigeons were flying, and** the owner of the field **said: "My field has acquired** ownership of these objects **for me," his words are of no effect**, and the objects may be taken by anyone, because his courtyard can only acquire on his behalf if the ownerless objects in the courtyard will stay there if left undisturbed.

[1]אַחַר גּוֹזָלוֹת שֶׁלֹּא פָּרְחוּ, וְאָמַר: ״זָכְתָה לִי שָׂדִי״, זָכְתָה לוֹ. [2]הָיָה צְבִי רָץ כְּדַרְכּוֹ, אוֹ שֶׁהָיוּ גּוֹזָלוֹת מַפְרִיחִין, וְאָמַר: ״זָכְתָה לִי שָׂדִי״, לֹא אָמַר כְּלוּם.

גמרא [3]אָמַר רַב יְהוּדָה אָמַר שְׁמוּאֵל: וְהוּא שֶׁעוֹמֵד בְּצַד שָׂדֵהוּ.

[4]וְתִקְנֵי לֵיהּ שָׂדֵהוּ, דְּאָמַר רַבִּי יוֹסֵי בְּרַבִּי חֲנִינָא: [5]חֲצֵרוֹ שֶׁל אָדָם קוֹנָה לוֹ שֶׁלֹּא מִדַּעְתּוֹ!

LITERAL TRANSLATION

[1]after young pigeons that had not [yet] flown, and he said: "My field has acquired [these] for me," it has acquired [them] for him. [2][If] the gazelle was running normally, or where the young pigeons were flying, and he said: "My field has acquired for me," he has not said anything.

GEMARA [3]Rav Yehudah said in the name of Shmuel: And this [applies only] when he is standing by the side of his field.

[4]But let his field acquire for him, for Rabbi Yose, the son of Rabbi Ḥanina, said: [5]A person's courtyard acquires for him without his knowledge!

GEMARA אָמַר רַב יְהוּדָה [3]**Rav Yehudah said in the name of Shmuel**: The Mishnah's ruling, that a field acquires on behalf of its owner the ownerless objects that enter it, **applies** only **when** the owner of the field **is** actually **standing by the side of his field**.

וְתִקְנֵי לֵיהּ שָׂדֵהוּ [4]The Gemara now objects: **But let his field acquire for him** even if he is not present, **for Rabbi Yose, the son of Rabbi Ḥanina, said:** [5]**A person's courtyard acquires for him** even **without his knowledge**!

BACKGROUND

הָיָה צְבִי רָץ כְּדַרְכּוֹ **If the gazelle was running normally**. As noted in *Tosafot*, the issue is not whether the gazelle is healthy, but a practical question: Can the owner of the field catch it? This case was merely presented as an example, because the gazelle is one of the fleetest of animals (its speed was proverbial, see II Samuel 2:18), and a man cannot catch a gazelle if it is running normally.

NOTES

זָכְתָה לִי שָׂדִי **My field has acquired for me**. There is a difference of opinion among the commentators as to whether the owner of the field has to make this verbal declaration. According to some commentators the owner of the field acquires ownerless objects in the circumstances described in the first clause of the Mishnah *even if he does not say*, "My field has acquired for me." According to this interpretation, it was unnecessary for the Mishnah to state that the owner of the field said "My field has acquired for me" in the first clause. The phraseology of this clause was apparently influenced by the parallel formulation in the last clause, which states that if the ownerless objects were moving normally and quickly, the owner of the field does not acquire them even if he does say, "My field has acquired for me" (*Tosafot*).

Others explain that the verbal declaration in the first clause has been included because the owner of the field will normally say, "My field has acquired for me," and it is necessary to warn the other people who are running after the object that it has already been acquired (*Rosh*). Still others make a distinction between acquisition by "courtyard" and acquisition by "four cubits." They maintain that the owner of a field does not acquire ownerless objects which enter it unless he says, "My field has acquired for me." But it is not necessary for him to say this in order to acquire property that enters his "four cubits." Here the Rabbis ordained that the finder should automatically acquire the ownerless object, in order to prevent strife and quarreling (*Maggid Mishneh*). Still other explanations are suggested by the Aḥaronim (see also the next note).

וְהוּא שֶׁעוֹמֵד בְּצַד שָׂדֵהוּ **Only if the owner is standing by the side of his field**. Shmuel's interpretation of the Mishnah, according to which the owner of the field must be standing next to it in order to acquire the ownerless objects, seems somewhat forced. If only a guarded field can be used to acquire ownerless objects, why not assume that the field in the Mishnah was surrounded by a fence? One commentator observes that, according to the Mishnah, the owner of the field must say "My field has acquired for me," in order to acquire ownerless objects. We may infer from this that the field is considered "guarded" only because its owner is present; for if the field were surrounded by a fence, the owner would surely automatically acquire whatever is there without having to say anything (*Melo HaRo'im*).

HALAKHAH

זְכִיָּה בִּצְבִי רָץ בְּשָׂדֵהוּ **Acquiring a running gazelle**. "If an ownerless gazelle that has been injured, or ownerless young pigeons that are unable to fly, enter a field, and the owner of the field says, 'My field has acquired these for me,' he acquires them, provided they were moving sufficiently slowly for him to be able to overtake them if he were to run after them. But if the owner of the field is unable to catch them, they are treated as though they were running (or flying) normally, and hence the owner does not acquire them," following the Mishnah. (*Shulḥan Arukh, Ḥoshen Mishpat* 268:4.)

חֲצֵרוֹ קוֹנָה לוֹ שֶׁלֹּא מִדַּעְתּוֹ **A person's courtyard acquires for him without his knowledge**. "The owner of a guarded courtyard (i.e., a private house, or fenced-in courtyard or field, where property may be kept safely) acquires ownerless objects that enter the courtyard, even if he is unaware of their presence." (Ibid., 268:3.)

עוֹמֵד בְּצַד שָׂדֵהוּ **If the owner is standing by the side of**

TRANSLATION AND COMMENTARY

הָנֵי מִילֵּי [1]The Gemara answers: **This** ruling of Rabbi Yose, the son of Rabbi Ḥanina, **applies** only **in a guarded courtyard**, where property can be kept safely without special supervision, for example a fenced-in field or a private home. [2]**But in an unguarded courtyard**, only **if** the owner **is standing by the side of his field** does he acquire the ownerless objects found there by means of his courtyard, because his physical presence makes the courtyard secure. [3]**But if** he is **not** standing there, he does **not** acquire ownerless objects in the field by means of his courtyard.

וּמְנָא תֵּימְרָא [4]The Gemara now provides proof of this distinction between a guarded and an unguarded courtyard: **And from what** source **do you infer that in the case of an unguarded courtyard**, only **if** the owner **is** actually **standing by the side of his field** does he acquire ownerless objects found there, **but** that **if** he is **not** standing there, he does **not** acquire them? [5]**From what has been taught** in the following Baraita: "**If** the owner of a field **was standing in the city and he said: 'I know that a** particular **sheaf belonging to me in my field** outside the city **has been forgotten by my workers** there; they have forgotten it but I am aware of it, and it is my wish that **it not become *shikhḥah***, a forgotten sheaf!' Normally, a sheaf forgotten in the field by its owner during the harvesting must be left for the poor (such a sheaf is called *shikhḥah*). But here, where the owner remembers that the sheaf is in the field but is afraid that the workers may have forgotten it, [6]**I might think that it is possible that** the sheaf **is not** considered ***shikhḥah*** if the owner were to forget it subsequently! [7]**Therefore the verse teaches** (Deuteronomy 24:19): 'When you cut down your harvest in your field, **and you forget a sheaf in the field,** you shall not go again to take it; it shall be for the stranger, for the fatherless and for the widow.' From here the Baraita infers: Only **if you forget** the sheaf while you are still **in the field, but not** when you are already **in the city.**"

[1]הָנֵי מִילֵּי בְּחָצֵר הַמִּשְׁתַּמֶּרֶת, [2]אֲבָל חָצֵר שֶׁאֵינָהּ מִשְׁתַּמֶּרֶת, אִי עוֹמֵד בְּצַד שָׂדֵהוּ, [3]אִין, אִי לָא, לָא.

[4]וּמְנָא תֵּימְרָא דְּחָצֵר שֶׁאֵינָהּ מִשְׁתַּמֶּרֶת, אִי עוֹמֵד בְּצַד שָׂדֵהוּ, אִין, אִי לָא, לָא? [5]דְּתַנְיָא: ״הָיָה עוֹמֵד בָּעִיר וְאוֹמֵר: ׳יוֹדֵעַ אֲנִי שֶׁעוֹמֶר שֶׁיֵּשׁ לִי בַּשָּׂדֶה פּוֹעֲלִים שְׁכֵחוּהוּ — לֹא יְהֵא שִׁכְחָה׳! [6]יָכוֹל לֹא יְהֵא שִׁכְחָה; [7]תַּלְמוּד לוֹמַר: ׳וְשָׁכַחְתָּ עֹמֶר בַּשָּׂדֶה׳ — בַּשָּׂדֶה וְשָׁכַחְתָּ, וְלֹא בָּעִיר״.

LITERAL TRANSLATION

[1]This applies (lit., "these words") [in] a guarded courtyard, [2]but [in] an unguarded courtyard, if he is standing by the side of his field, yes, [3][but] if not, no. [4]And from where do you say that [in the case of] an unguarded courtyard, if he stands by the side of his field, yes, [but] if not, no? [5]As it has been taught: "[If] someone was standing in the city and he said: 'I know that a sheaf that I have in the field has been forgotten by the workers — let it not be *shikhḥah*,' [6][I might think that] it is possible [that] it is not *shikhḥah*; [7][therefore] the verse teaches: 'And you forget a sheaf in the field' — if you forget [it] in the field, but not in the city."

RASHI

גמרא אי עומד בצד שדהו אין — דעכשיו היא משתמרת על ידו. **עומר שיש לי בשדה** — שהנחתיו שם מדעתי, וסמכתי על הפועלים שיביאוהו ופועלים שכחוהו. **לא יהא שכחה** — אם חזר ושכחו. **בשדה ושכחת** — אם שכחתו בצאתך מן השדה — הוי שכחה, ולא ששכחתו משנכנסת לעיר.

TERMINOLOGY

יָכוֹל... תַּלְמוּד לוֹמַר... I might have thought X, therefore the Torah states.... An expression found in Halakhic Midrashim. Sometimes the Midrash introduces the possibility of a mistaken interpretation of a Biblical verse (...יָכוֹל — "I might have thought"), before setting forth the correct explanation of the verse, which is based on careful scrutiny of the Biblical text.

NOTES

שִׁכְחָה ***Shikhḥah***. The primary source in the Torah for the laws of *shikhḥah* is Deuteronomy 24:19, and a detailed treatment of these laws is set forth in tractate *Pe'ah*. The basic principle of this commandment is that the owner of a field is forbidden to take as his own a sheaf that was forgotten in his field in the course of harvesting. He must leave such a sheaf for the poor. It should be noted that certain categories of forgotten sheaves are not considered *shikhḥah*, e.g., sheaves that are unusual in appearance and therefore readily distinguishable from others, or sheaves that though initially forgotten can be picked up easily, without any special effort being involved in going back to get them.

HALAKHAH

his field. "An unguarded courtyard (and similarly an unfenced field) only acquires ownerless objects on behalf of its owner if he is standing by the side of the courtyard or field and specifically declares that it is his intention that his courtyard should acquire for him." (Ibid.)

שִׁכְחַת עִיר וְשָׂדֶה ***Shikhḥah* in the field and in the city**. "A sheaf is considered *shikhḥah* only if it was forgotten by all, both by the owner of the field and by the workers. Indeed, even if both the owner and the workers had forgotten a sheaf, if uninvolved bystanders noticed that a particular sheaf had not been picked up, it is not considered *shikhḥah*. If the owner was standing by his field, and he remarked that he was aware of certain sheaves that the workers had forgotten, those sheaves are not considered *shikhḥah*. But if the owner said this while he was in the city, the sheaves are considered *shikhḥah*." (*Rambam, Sefer Zeraim, Hilkhot Mattenot Aniyyim* 5:1-2.)

¹הָא גּוּפָא קַשְׁיָא: ²אָמַרְתָּ "יָכוֹל לֹא יְהֵא שִׁכְחָה" — אַלְמָא הָוֵי שִׁכְחָה. ³וּנְסֵיב לָהּ תַּלְמוּדָא: "בַּשָּׂדֶה וְשָׁכַחְתָּ", וְלֹא בָּעִיר — אַלְמָא לָא הָוֵי שִׁכְחָה!

⁴אֶלָּא לָאו הָכִי קָאָמַר: בַּשָּׂדֶה, שָׁכוּחַ מֵעִיקָּרוֹ הָוֵי שִׁכְחָה; ⁵זָכוּר וּלְבַסּוֹף שָׁכוּחַ, אֵין שִׁכְחָה. ⁶מַאי טַעְמָא? ⁷דְּכֵיוָן דְּקָאֵי גַּבָּהּ, הָוְיָא לֵיהּ חֲצֵרוֹ, וְזָכְתָה לֵיהּ. ⁸אֲבָל בָּעִיר, אֲפִילּוּ זָכוּר וּלְבַסּוֹף שָׁכוּחַ, הָוְיָא שִׁכְחָה. ⁹מַאי טַעְמָא? ¹⁰דְּלֵיתֵיהּ גַּבֵּיהּ דְּלִזְכֵּי לֵיהּ.

¹¹מִמַּאי? ¹²דִּלְמָא גְּזֵירַת הַכָּתוּב

LITERAL TRANSLATION

[1]This itself is difficult: [2]You say, "[I might think that] it is possible [that] it is not *shikhhah*" — implying [that] it is *shikhhah*. [3]And [then the Baraita] brings the argument: "If you forget in the field," but not in the city — implying [that] it is not *shikhhah*!

[4]Rather, is it not [the case that] it is [really] saying as follows: In the field, [a sheaf that was] forgotten from the outset is *shikhhah*; [5][one that was] remembered and later forgotten is not *shikhhah*. [6]What is the reason? [7]Since he is standing nearby [next to the field], it is considered his courtyard, and it acquires for him. [8]But in the city, even if [the sheaf] was remembered and later forgotten, it is *shikhhah*. [9]What is the reason? [10]Because he is not nearby that it should acquire for him.

[11]How can you be sure that this is the correct interpretation (lit., "from what")? [12]Perhaps it is a decree of the Torah

TRANSLATION AND COMMENTARY

הָא גּוּפָא קַשְׁיָא [1]Before indicating how this Baraita can serve as a proof-text, the Gemara begins by analyzing its language and meaning: Surely **this** Baraita **is itself difficult**, as it contains a self-contradiction! [2]First of all **you say, "I might think that it is possible that** the sheaf **is not** considered ***shikhhah***" — thereby **implying that** the author of the Baraita is seeking to prove that the forgotten sheaf **is** in fact considered ***shikhhah***. [3]**But then the Baraita brings** as proof **the argument** from the Biblical text, explaining it as meaning: "The sheaf is *shikhhah* only **if you forget** it while you are still **in the field," but not** when you are already **in the city** — thereby **implying that** such a sheaf **is not** considered ***shikhhah***!

אֶלָּא לָאו הָכִי קָאָמַר [4]The Gemara resolves this apparent contradiction by suggesting a new interpretation of the Baraita: **Rather, is it not the case that** the Baraita **really** meant to point out **the following** distinction: If the incident occurred while the owner of the field was present **in the field**, a **sheaf that was forgotten from the outset** both by the owner of the field and by the workers **is** considered *shikhhah*; [5]but a sheaf **that was** originally **remembered** by the owner **and** only **later forgotten** by the workers **is not** considered ***shikhhah***. [6]**What is the reason** for this difference? [7]**Since** the owner **is standing nearby, the field is considered his courtyard, and it acquires** the sheaf **for him** before the workers' error can have any effect. [8]**But** once the owner of the field has entered **the city, even if** the sheaf **was** at first **remembered** by the owner when he reached the city **and** was **later forgotten** by the workers in the field, **it is** considered ***shikhhah***. [9]**What is the reason**? [10]Presumably, **because** the owner **is not** there, **nearby**, close enough to the sheaf in the field to enable the field to **acquire** the sheaf **for him**. The reinterpreted Baraita is thus a source for the principle that an unguarded courtyard (in this case an unfenced field) cannot acquire property for its owner unless he is standing nearby.

מִמַּאי [11]The Gemara now objects: **How can you be sure that this is the correct interpretation** of the verse and the correct understanding of the Baraita? [12]**Perhaps** the Baraita can be explained, with a much smaller

CONCEPTS

גְּזֵירַת הַכָּתוּב **A decree of the Torah.** The term גְּזֵירָה — "decree" — has various meanings. גְּזֵירַת חֲכָמִים are ordinances (usually prohibitions or stringencies) introduced by the Sages, principally because of fear lest people accidentally commit a transgression, either because a certain action might lead to transgression or because there is a similarity between the permitted action and a forbidden one. In contrast, the expression גְּזֵירַת הַכָּתוּב means a ruling laid down in the Torah without explanation, which must be obeyed even though we do not know the reason for it. For this reason general Halakhic principles may not be deduced from it.

RASHI

אלא לאו הכי קאמר בשדה שכוח מעיקרו כו' — בעוד האיש בשדה, עומר השכוח מעיקרו, ששכחו הוא תחילה לפועל — הוי שכחה, אבל זכור שהניחו שם מדעתו ולבסוף שכחו על ידי פועלים — לא הוי שכחה. **אבל בעיר** — משנכנס לעיר, אפילו זכור ולבסוף שכח — הוי שכחה, דליתיה גביה כו'. והכי קא נסיב ליה תנא לתלמודיה: יכול לא יהא שכחה — תלמוד לומר "בשדה ושכחת" — בעודך בשדה הוא דבעינן דשכחתיה אתה, ולא בעיר — לא בעינן "ושכחת". שאף שכחת פועלים עושה אותה שכחה. **וממאי** — דקרא הכי מתרץ, ומתניתין הכי אמרה. **דלמא גזירת הכתוב היא** — דמשמע דבשדה יהא שכחה, אבל משבא בעל הבית לעיר — אין שכחתו ושכחת פועלים כלום, והכי קאמר: יכול יהא שכחה תלמוד לומר כו'.

NOTES

זָכוּר וּלְבַסּוֹף שָׁכוּחַ אֵין שִׁכְחָה **A sheaf that was originally remembered and later forgotten is not considered *shikhhah*.** Most commentaries (see *Ramban, Tosafot*, etc.) explain that the Gemara refers here to a case where the owner of the field declares his continued awareness of the sheaf after the workers have already forgotten it. Accordingly, even if the owner subsequently forgets this sheaf, it is not considered *shikhhah*, as his field has already acquired it for him. But such a declaration by the owner made before the workers have forgotten the sheaf is of no effect. Otherwise, the owner could exempt himself from *shikhhah* by simply declaring his awareness of all his sheaves before the workers begin harvesting, thus enabling his field to acquire them for him.

דִּלְמָא גְּזֵירַת הַכָּתוּב **Perhaps it is a decree of the Torah.** According to *Rashi* (whose interpretation is followed in the

TRANSLATION AND COMMENTARY

emendation, as follows: "I might have thought that it is possible that the sheaf forgotten in the city *is indeed* (rather than 'is not') considered *shikhḥah*. Therefore the verse teaches, 'in the field,' implying 'not in the city.'" If this reading is correct, the Baraita is simply informing us that **it is a decree of the Torah that whatever** the owner **forgets** while he is still **in the field is** considered ***shikhḥah*, and whatever** he or his workers **forget** once he reaches **the city is not** considered ***shikhḥah***! If this explanation is correct, the decision as to whether a sheaf is *shikhḥah* or not, as laid down in the Baraita, is in no way connected with the laws of acquisition!

אֲמַר קְרָא [1]The Gemara answers: **The verse** which **says: "You shall not go back to take it"** (Deuteronomy 24:19) comes **to include** in the category of ***shikhḥah*** a sheaf forgotten by its owner once he has reached **the city**. The seemingly superfluous expression in the verse thus comes to teach us that our previous suggested interpretation of the verse is incorrect, and even if the owner forgets the sheaf when he is in the city, the sheaf still falls under the category of *shikhḥah*. Since a forgotten sheaf is considered *shikhḥah* no matter where the owner is, our suggested emendation of the Baraita is untenable. We are forced to return to the earlier amended reading and to conclude that the Baraita is teaching us that the laws of *shikhḥah* are affected by the laws of acquisition only if the owner is in or near his field.

הַאי מִיבָּעֵי לֵיהּ לְלָאו [2]The Gemara now rejects this suggested explanation of the superfluous expression, "You shall not go again to take it": **But** surely **this** part of the **verse is needed** to teach us that going back to take *shikhḥah* is a violation of **a negative commandment**, in addition to being a violation of the positive commandment to leave a forgotten sheaf for the poor.

אִם כֵּן, נֵימָא קְרָא [3]The Gemara replies: **If** this was all that the verse intended to teach us, it should have used the expression: **"You shall not take it"**. [4]**Why was it necessary** to include the seemingly superfluous phrase: **"You shall not go back"**? This expression must have been included in order **to include** in the category of ***shikhḥah*** a sheaf forgotten by its owner once he has reached **the city**!

וְאַכַּתִּי מִיבָּעֵי לֵיהּ [5]Once again the Gemara objects: **But** surely **this expression**, "You shall not go back," **is still needed** in order to teach us another law of ***shikhḥah* which we have learned** in the following Mishnah (*Pe'ah* 6:4): "Sheaves **in front of** the person harvesting a field **cannot become *shikhḥah***. Since the reaper has not reached these sheaves yet, they are not considered *shikhḥah* (even if he has forgotten them).

הִיא דִּבְשָׂדֶה נֶהֱוֵי שִׁכְחָה וּבְעִיר לָא נֶהֱוֵי שִׁכְחָה! [1]אֲמַר קְרָא "לֹא תָשׁוּב לְקַחְתּוֹ" — לְרַבּוֹת שִׁכְחַת הָעִיר. [2]הַאי מִיבָּעֵי לֵיהּ לְלָאו! [3]אִם כֵּן, נֵימָא קְרָא "לֹא תִקָּחֶנּוּ"; [4]מַאי "לֹא תָשׁוּב"? לְרַבּוֹת שִׁכְחַת הָעִיר! [5]וְאַכַּתִּי מִיבָּעֵי לֵיהּ לִכְדִתְנַן: "שֶׁלְּפָנָיו אֵין שִׁכְחָה.

LITERAL TRANSLATION

that [what is forgotten] in the field should be *shikhḥah* and [what is forgotten] in the city should not be *shikhḥah*!

[1]The verse says: "You shall not go back to take it" — [this is] to include *shikhḥah* in the city.

[2][But] this [verse] is needed as a negative commandment!

[3]If so, let the verse say, "You shall not take it"; [4]what is [the need for] "You shall not go back"? To include *shikhḥah* in the city!

[5]But [this expression] is still needed for what we have learned: "What is in front of him is not *shikhḥah*.

RASHI

שלפניו אין שכחה — בשכחת הקוצר קאי. יחיד שהתחיל לקצור מראש השורה, ושכח לפניו ולאחריו, שלאחריו הוי שכחה, שלפניו לא הוי שכחה.

NOTES

commentary), the Gemara's objection should be understood as follows: Perhaps the Torah decreed that the laws of *shikhḥah* should apply only when the owner is in the field. But if the owner is in the city, the sheaves should not be considered *shikhḥah*, even if the owner forgets them! According to this view, the Gemara seems to be suggesting that the Baraita should be emended to read: "I might think that such a sheaf *is* considered *shikhḥah*."

Most commentaries, however (see *Tosafot, Ramban, Rashba*, etc.), understand the Gemara's objection as being aimed at the Baraita itself rather than at the Gemara's previous interpretation of it. Granted that the Baraita's intention was to teach us about the laws of acquisition by means of one's courtyard, how did the Baraita itself derive this information from the verse? Perhaps, says the Gemara, the verse was simply excluding sheaves forgotten in the city from the laws of *shikhḥah*.

HALAKHAH

שִׁכְחָה לְפָנָיו וְאַחֲרָיו *Shikhḥah* in front of the reapers and behind them. "If the reapers, or the people binding the grain into sheaves, forget sheaves in front of them, in an area they will later pass in the course of their work, the sheaves are not considered *shikhḥah*. But if they forget sheaves behind them, so that picking them up would necessitate a special return journey, such sheaves are considered *shikhḥah*." (*Rambam, Sefer Zeraim, Hilkhot Mattenot Aniyyim* 5:10.)

[1]שֶׁלְּאַחֲרָיו יֵשׁ שִׁכְחָה, שֶׁהוּא בְּ׳בַל תָּשׁוּב׳. [2]זֶה הַכְּלָל: כָּל שֶׁהוּא בְּ׳בַל תָּשׁוּב׳ שִׁכְחָה; [3]כָּל שֶׁאֵינוֹ בְּ׳בַל תָּשׁוּב׳ אֵינוֹ שִׁכְחָה״!

[4]אֲמַר רַב אַשִׁי: אֲמַר קְרָא: ״יִהְיֶה״ — לְרַבּוֹת שִׁכְחַת הָעִיר.

[5]וְכֵן אָמַר עוּלָּא: וְהוּא שֶׁעוֹמֵד בְּצַד שָׂדֵהוּ. [6]וְכֵן אָמַר רַבָּה בַּר בַּר חָנָה: וְהוּא שֶׁעוֹמֵד בְּצַד שָׂדֵהוּ.

[7]אֵיתִיבֵיהּ רַבִּי אַבָּא לְעוּלָּא: ״מַעֲשֶׂה בְּרַבָּן גַּמְלִיאֵל וּזְקֵנִים שֶׁהָיוּ בָּאִים בִּסְפִינָה. [8]אָמַר רַבָּן גַּמְלִיאֵל: ׳עִישּׂוּר שֶׁאֲנִי עָתִיד לָמוֹד נָתוּן לִיהוֹשֻׁעַ, [11B] וּמְקוֹמוֹ מוּשְׂכָּר לוֹ.

LITERAL TRANSLATION

[1]What is behind him is *shikhḥah*, because it is [included] in 'You shall not go back.' [2]This is the rule: Whatever is [included] in 'You shall not go back' is *shikhḥah*; [3]whatever is not [included] in 'You shall not go back' is not *shikhḥah*!"

[4]Rav Ashi said: The verse said: "It shall be" — to include *shikhḥah* in the city.

[5]And similarly Ulla said: And this [applies] when he is standing by the side of his field. [6]And similarly Rabbah bar Bar Ḥanah said: And this [applies] when he is standing by the side of his field.

[7]Rabbi Abba raised an objection to Ulla: "It happened that Rabban Gamliel and the elders were traveling on a ship. [8]Rabban Gamliel said: 'One-tenth which I will measure out [later] is given [now] to Yehoshua, [11B] and its place is leased to him.

RASHI

יהיה – ״לגר ליתום ולאלמנה יהיה״. **עישור שאני עתיד למוד** – נזכר שלא עישר מעשרותיו והוקשה לו, ומיהר לעשרן באשר הוא שם. **נתון ליהושע** – לרבי יהושע בר חנניא שהיה עמו בספינה, והוא לוי, ונוטל מעשר ראשון. כדאמרינן בערכין (יא,ב) מעשה ברבי יהושע שהלך לסייע את רבי יוחנן בן גודגדא בהגפת דלתות, אמר לו: חזור בך, שאתה מן המשוררים ואני מן המשוערים, ומשורר שסיער במיתה. **ומקומו מושכר לו** – וקבל ממנו שם שכר המקום. דהכי קתני סיפא: נתקבלו זה מזה שכר. וכל כך למה – כדי לקנות מעשר, שתהא חצרו קונה לו. לפי שהמטלטלין אין קונין אלא או במשיכה, או חצרו תקנה לו.

TRANSLATION AND COMMENTARY

[1]But sheaves **behind** the person harvesting the field **can become *shikhḥah* because they are included in** the prohibition **'You shall not go back.'** [2]**This is the** general **rule: Whatever can be included in** the prohibition **'You shall not go back,'** because the person harvesting the field must *go back* specially in order to get it, **is** subject to the law of ***shikhḥah;*** [3]**whatever cannot be included in** the prohibition **You shall not go back,'** because it will be reached later in the course of harvesting, **is not** subject to the law of ***shikhḥah***!" Thus the expression 'You shall not go back' teaches us only that sheaves still in front of the person harvesting the field are not subject to the law of *shikhḥah*, but it does not teach us anything about *shikhḥah* in the city!

אֲמַר רַב אַשִׁי [4]**Rav Ashi said** in reply: **The verse** uses the expression, **"It shall be"** (*"It shall be* for the stranger, for the fatherless and for the widow") so as **to include** in the category of ***shikhḥah*** a sheaf forgotten by its owner once he has reached **the city**. Thus we see that we must accept the earlier, amended reading of the Baraita and conclude that the laws of acquisition affect the laws of *shikhḥah* only if the owner is in or near his field. This concludes the Gemara's proof of Shmuel's statement that courtyard-acquisition is effective only if the owner is in or near his courtyard.

וְכֵן אָמַר עוּלָּא [5]The Gemara now provides support for Shmuel's interpretation of the Mishnah (cited at the beginning of the passage), by quoting the remarks of the other Amoraim who agree with him: **And similarly Ulla said:** The Mishnah's ruling, that a field acquires on behalf of its owner the ownerless objects that enter it, **applies** only **when** the owner **is** actually **standing by the side of his field.** [6]**And similarly Rabbah bar Bar Ḥanah said: This** ruling of the Mishnah **applies** only **when** the owner **is standing by the side of his field**.

אֵיתִיבֵיהּ רַבִּי אַבָּא לְעוּלָּא [7]**Rabbi Abba raised an objection to Ulla** from the following Mishnah (*Ma'aser Sheni* 5:9): **"It happened that Rabban Gamliel and the elders were travelling on a ship.** [8]**Rabban Gamliel said: 'One-tenth** of the produce of my fields [the first tithe] **which I will measure out** for him **later is given** by me **now to Yehoshua** ben Ḥananyah, who, as a Levite, is entitled to first tithe. [11B] **And** the **place** where that tithe is at present located **is** hereby **leased to him** by me." Thus, once Rabbi Yehoshua pays a nominal sum to lease the land, he is automatically able to acquire the first tithe that Rabban Gamliel has designated for him. The assumption at this point in the discussion is that Rabbi Yehoshua can acquire Rabban Gamliel's tithe either by physically moving it (קִנְיַן מְשִׁיכָה) or by means of his courtyard (i.e., the field where the produce is). Since they are both on board ship far away from the produce to be tithed, the second method is apparently being used. The

NOTES

מַעֲשֶׂה בְּרַבָּן גַּמְלִיאֵל וּזְקֵנִים **It happened that Rabban Gamliel and the elders were traveling....** The commentators differ concerning the particulars of this incident, but most of them agree that Rabban Gamliel had separated

TRANSLATION AND COMMENTARY

Mishnah in *Ma'aser Sheni* continues: [1]"**Another tenth** of the produce of my fields **that I will measure out later is** hereby **given** by me **now to Akiva ben Yosef, so that he may acquire it for the poor, and its place is** hereby **leased to him** by me." In the third and sixth years of the seven-year Sabbatical cycle (שְׁמִיטָּה) a second tithe, in addition to the first tithe given to the Levite, had to be removed from agricultural produce and distributed to the poor. This tithe was called מַעְשַׂר עָנִי — "poor man's tithe." Rabbi Akiva happened at that time to be the community official responsible for distributing charity to the poor.

וְכִי רַבִּי יְהוֹשֻׁעַ [2]On the basis of this Mishnah we may ask: **Now, were Rabbi Yehoshua and Rabbi Akiva standing** at that moment **next to Rabban Gamliel's field**, where the tithes were located? Of course not! They were all together on the ship! Thus, from this Mishnah it seems that the owner (or renter) of a field *can* acquire property located there even if he is not standing nearby!

אָמַר לֵיהּ [3]Ulla rejected this argument of Rabbi Abba and **said to him: This Rabbi** — Rabbi Abba — **is like a person who has not been trained in Halakhah!** In Ulla's opinion, Rabbi Abba's question was not even worthy of consideration!

כִּי אֲתָא לְסוּרָא [4]**When Rabbi Abba came to Sura, he said to** the local scholars: **This is what Ulla said, and this is the objection that I raised to his view.**

[1]וְעִישּׂוּר אַחֵר שֶׁאֲנִי עָתִיד לָמוֹד נָתוּן לַעֲקִיבָא בֶּן יוֹסֵף, כְּדֵי שֶׁיִּזְכֶּה בּוֹ לַעֲנִיִּים, וּמְקוֹמוֹ מוּשְׂכָּר לוֹ״.
[2]וְכִי רַבִּי יְהוֹשֻׁעַ וְרַבִּי עֲקִיבָא בְּצַד שָׂדֵהוּ שֶׁל רַבָּן גַּמְלִיאֵל הָיוּ עוֹמְדִין?
[3]אֲמַר לֵיהּ: דָּמֵי הַאי מֵרַבָּנַן כִּדְלָא גְּמִרִי אֱינָשֵׁי שְׁמַעְתָּא.
[4]כִּי אֲתָא לְסוּרָא, אֲמַר לְהוּ: הָכִי אֲמַר עוּלָּא, וְהָכִי אוֹתְבִיתֵיהּ.

LITERAL TRANSLATION

[1]Another tenth that I will measure out [later] is given [now] to Akiva ben Yosef, so that he may acquire it for the poor, and its place is leased to him!"

[2]Now, were Rabbi Yehoshua and Rabbi Akiva standing next to the field of Rabban Gamliel?

[3]He said to him: This one of our Rabbis is like a person who has not been trained in Halakhah.

[4]When [Rabbi Abba] came to Sura, he said to them: Ulla said thus, and I objected to him thus.

RASHI

נתון לעקיבא — גבאי היה, ואותה שנה שנת מעשר עני היתה. **כי אתא** — רבי אבא לסורא אמר להו כו׳.

NOTES

terumah (lit., "heave-offering," which must be given directly to a priest) from his produce while he was still at home. Apparently, however, he had been unable to separate the other tithes before setting out on his journey. The incident is quoted from a Mishnah (*Ma'aser Sheni* 5:9) dealing with the laws of tithes appertaining to Pesaḥ of the fourth and seventh years of the seven-year Sabbatical cycle, when all tithes owing from the previous three years must be distributed immediately to their designated recipients. The Mishnah quotes this story to illustrate the procedure to be followed if one finds oneself, like Rabban Gamliel did, away from home at the critical time.

שֶׁאֲנִי עָתִיד לָמוֹד **That I will measure out**. Ordinarily, a person separating tithes must indicate exactly where they are located in relation to the pile of produce being tithed (e.g., "on the northern side," "on the southern side," etc). Why did Rabban Gamliel not do this? Some commentators answer that Rabban Gamliel did indeed indicate where the tithes were situated, but this was not reported here, since it is not directly relevant to the Gemara's discussion.

Ordinarily, tithes may not be separated at a distance (שֶׁלֹּא מִן הַמּוּקָף). Why, then, did Rabban Gamliel apparently violate this regulation? The commentators explain the regulation as meaning that the tithes themselves must be near the produce from which they are being separated; but the person separating the tithes need not be near the produce. Rabban Gamliel's behavior was, therefore, perfectly correct (*Meiri, Ritva*).

נָתוּן לַעֲקִיבָא בֶּן יוֹסֵף **Is given to Akiva ben Yosef**. In the Jerusalem Talmud the Sages discuss whether Rabbi Akiva received the tithe for the poor because he was himself poor, and since he was entitled to some of it, he was entitled to acquire all of it and to transfer ownership of it to others (cf. the difference of opinion regarding פֵּאָה — the corners of the field — above). Ultimately they conclude, as *Rashi* points out, that Rabbi Akiva received the tithe because he was a פַּרְנַס עֲנִיִּים (administrator for the poor), and, since he was responsible for the distribution of charity, he had great power of acquisition (his hand was regarded as that of the poor themselves).

דָּמֵי הַאי מֵרַבָּנַן וכו׳ **This Rabbi is like a person who has not been trained in Halakhah**. Ulla apparently considered Rabbi Abba's question baseless, because the incident involving Rabban Gamliel is not dealing with ownerless property but rather with a case where one person (Rabban Gamliel) is *actively* transferring property to another (Rabbi Yehoshua and Rabbi Akiva). By contrast, in cases of ownerless property, the finder has to acquire the property without the assistance of another party. This answer to Rabbi Abba's objection is, indeed, given by the Gemara later in the discussion (*Shittah Mekubbetzet*).

TRANSLATION AND COMMENTARY

אָמַר לֵיהּ [1]One of the Rabbis of Sura said to Rabbi Abba: **Rabban Gamliel transferred movable property to** Rabbi Yehoshua and Rabbi Akiva **along with land**, and did not transfer ownership of the tithes by means of the principle of acquisition by courtyard. One of the methods of transferring ownership of movable property is *kinyan aggav*, whereby the recipient of the movable property acquires it together with a piece of land not necessarily connected in any way with the movable property. When movable property is acquired in this way, and not through courtyard-acquisition, the transfer of ownership is valid even if the owner of the land is not standing near it. Thus, the transfer performed by Rabban Gamliel as described in the Mishnah from *Ma'aser Sheni* can be interpreted as being "transfer together with land," and the Mishnah does not necessarily support Rabbi Abba's view.

רַבִּי זֵירָא [2]The Gemara remarks that **Rabbi Zera accepted** this answer, whereas **Rabbi Abba did not accept it.**

אָמַר רָבָא [3]**Rava said:** Rabbi Abba **did well in not accepting it**; for if Rabban Gamliel had merely wanted to give Rabbi Yehoshua and Rabbi Akiva the tithes, is it possible that **they did not have a kerchief to acquire the tithes from him through *ḥalifin*** (symbolic barter)? In addition to the other methods of acquisition mentioned above (*meshikhah, kinyan aggav* and courtyard), movable property can also be acquired by having the buyer transfer a kerchief (or similar object) to the seller; such a symbolic act validates the transaction, and is known as *ḥalifin* or *kinyan suddar*. Now, if Rabban Gamliel merely wanted the other Sages to acquire the produce, why did he resort to the more complicated procedure of transferring it along with land? Why did he not simply transfer the produce to them by performing *ḥalifin?* Instead, Rabban Gamliel's conduct must be explained differently. The tithes were not really the property of Rabban Gamliel. Since tithes must be given to another person, Rabban Gamliel's ownership of the produce was limited to a discretionary power (טוֹבַת הֲנָאָה) that he had over it, namely, the right to give the tithes to whomever he wished. [4]**But discretionary power,** while possessing a certain market value, is not true ownership, as it **is not considered** a true **monetary** interest that can be **acquired from another person through *ḥalifin*.** [5]**Here, too,** in our case, Rabban Gamliel's **discretionary power** over the allocation of the tithes **is not considered** something that has **money** value, that can be **acquired from him along with** a plot of **land.** Thus Rabban Gamliel could not transfer the tithes to the others together with the land, not because of regulations pertaining to the laws of acquisition, but because of the nature of tithes. In fact, the owner of the tithes does not need to involve

[1]אֲמַר לֵיהּ הַהוּא מֵרַבָּנַן: רַבָּן גַּמְלִיאֵל מְטַלְטְלֵי אַגַּב מְקַרְקְעֵי הִקְנָה לָהֶם.

[2]רַבִּי זֵירָא קִבְּלָהּ, רַבִּי אַבָּא לֹא קִבְּלָהּ.

[3]אֲמַר רָבָא: שַׁפִּיר עָבֵיד דְּלָא קִבְּלָהּ, וְכִי לֹא הָיָה לָהֶם סוּדָר לִקְנוֹת מִמֶּנּוּ בַּחֲלִיפִין? [4]אֶלָּא, טוֹבַת הֲנָאָה אֵינָהּ מָמוֹן לִקְנוֹת מִמֶּנּוּ בַּחֲלִיפִין. [5]הָכָא נַמִי, טוֹבַת הֲנָאָה אֵינָהּ מָמוֹן

LITERAL TRANSLATION

[1]One of the Rabbis said to him: Rabban Gamliel transferred movable property to them along with land. [2]Rabbi Zera accepted it. Rabbi Abba did not accept it.

[3]Rava said: He did well in not accepting it. Did they not have a kerchief to acquire [the tithes] from him through *ḥalifin* (barter)? [4]Rather, discretionary power (lit., "the benefit of pleasure") is not [considered] money to be acquired from [a person] through *ḥalifin.* [5]Here, too, discretionary power is not

RASHI

מטלטלי אגב מקרקעי הקנה להם — ולאו משום דתקני להם מקומם בתורת חצר. שאפילו הקנה להן חצר אחרת שאינן בתוכה — קנוי נמי, כדתנן (קדושין כו, א): נכסים שאין להן אחריות נקנין עם נכסים שיש להן אחריות בכסף, משנתן כסף בשביל הקרקע והמטלטלין, או אפילו קרקע במכר ומטלטלין במתנה — נקנין המטלטלין בקנין הקרקע בלא משיכה, כדילפינן בקדושין (שם) מ״ויתן להם אביהם מתנות רבות לכסף ולזהב עם ערים בצורות אשר ביהודה״. **קבלה** — להאי תירוצא. **וכי לא היה להן סודר כו׳** — למה לו לקבל מהן מעות? **אלא** — סודר מאי טעמא לא — דטובת הנאה שהיתה לו לרבן גמליאל במעשרות הללו. **אינה חשובה ממון** — דתהא נקנית בחליפין, דליכא למימר כי קנה ליה רבן גמליאל להאי סודר אקנייה חליפין דידיה בכל מקום שהן, דכיון דאין לו בהן אלא טובת הנאה שבידו לתתו לכל מי שירצה אין זו חשובה ממון לחול עליו קנין חליפין. **הכא נמי** — גבי קנין קרקע. **אינה ממון לקנות על גבי קרקע** — בקנין שהקרקע נקנה בו, אלא אפקורי בעלמא אפקר גבייהו. **וכי אוגר להו מקום** — קנתה לו חצרו בתורת חצר, כשאר הפקר.

CONCEPTS

חֲלִיפִין **Exchange.** A legal act of acquisition formalizing the transfer of ownership of an article. Once two parties agree on the barter of one article for another, the acquisition by one party of one of the articles through a recognized mode of acquisition (for example, by מְשִׁיכָה) automatically causes the second article to become the legal property of the other party. This principle is also the basis for the transfer of ownership by means of קִנְיַן סוּדָר, a symbolic form of barter that extends the principle of חֲלִיפִין to many formal legal acts of acquisition. There are differing views in the Talmud as to whether money and other things can be acquired by means of חֲלִיפִין.

NOTES

טוֹבַת הֲנָאָה **Discretionary power.** Discretionary power (טוֹבַת הֲנָאָה) means the power to give an object to whomever one pleases (for example, the power to give terumah to any priest one wishes), even though the object itself does not really belong to the giver. (He cannot keep it for himself, sell it, or do anything other than give it away.) Although discretionary power clearly has a market value, the question here is whether or not this market value amounts to an intrinsic monetary interest in the object itself.

טוֹבַת הֲנָאָה אֵינָהּ מָמוֹן **Discretionary power is not considered something that has a true money value.** The question of the status of discretionary power is discussed in

לִקְנוֹת עַל גַּבֵּי קַרְקַע.
[1]וְלֹא הִיא. מַתְּנוֹת כְּהוּנָּה נְתִינָה כְּתִיבָא בְּהוּ. [2]חֲלִיפִין דֶּרֶךְ מִקָּח וּמִמְכָּר הוּא. מִטַּלְטְלִין אַגַּב מְקַרְקַע נְתִינָה אַלִּימְתָּא הִיא.
[3]רַב פַּפָּא אָמַר: דַּעַת אַחֶרֶת מַקְנָה אוֹתָן שָׁאנֵי.

LITERAL TRANSLATION

[considered] money to be acquired from [a person] along with land.

[1]But this is not so. [The word] "giving" is stated with regard to the gifts of priesthood. [2]*Ḥalifin* is a form of buying and selling. [The transfer of] movable property along with land is a most powerful [method of] giving.

[3]Rav Pappa said: The will of another party transferring ownership of them is different.

RASHI

ולא היא — מהאי, דכי לא היה להן סודר — לאו ראיה היא למילף מינה דאין טובת הנאה נקנית בחליפין, ועל גבי קרקע, דשפיר איכא למימר מטלטלי אגב קרקעי הקנה להן. ודקשיא לך לקנינהו בחליפין. **מתנות** — של כהונה ולויה ומעשר עני. **נתינת כתיבא בהו** — כדכתיב (דברים כו) "ונתתה ללוי" — זה מעשר ראשון, "לגר ליתום ולאלמנה" — זה מעשר שני. לפיכך אסור להקנותן בסודר, דדרך מקח הוא, שזה נותן לו כליו תחתיהן, ונראה זה כמוכרן לו. **נתינה אלימתא** — מותר להקנות מתנות כהונה על גבי קרקע. **רב פפא אמר** — לעולם בתורת חצר קנאו, ואפילו הכי לא תקשי לעולא. דהא דלא בעינן הכא עומד בצד השדה — משום דדעת אחרת מקנה אותן, שרבן גמליאל הקנה להן מטלטלין שהיו לו בחצר שלהן, ולא מהפקירא קנו, ונוחה מתנה זו לקנות, ואף על גב דאין עומד בצד השדה.

TRANSLATION AND COMMENTARY

himself with the transfer of ownership. For all practical purposes the tithes are ownerless until they are physically delivered into the possession of their lawful recipients. At that point they are acquired by the regular methods used to acquire ownerless objects — *meshikhah* ("pulling") or courtyard-acquisition. *Meshikhah* is out of the question here. Hence the correct interpretation of the Mishnah in *Ma'aser Sheni* must be that suggested by Rabbi Abba, namely, that Rabban Gamliel's tithes were delivered through courtyard-acquisition, even though Rabbi Yehoshua and Rabbi Akiva, who had leased the field, were on the ship at the time of the acquisition and not standing near the field.

וְלֹא הִיא [1]**But** the Gemara now rejects the argument advanced by Rava: **This is not so**. Rava's argument is incorrect. It was based on two false assumptions: (1) Rabban Gamliel could equally well have transferred ownership in the tithes by means of *ḥalifin*. (2) The fact that he did not do so shows that a transfer of ownership did not take place. In fact, says the Gemara, discretionary power may be the equivalent of true ownershp, and it may be possible to sell it by the normal modes of sale. But in the case of tithes this would not be proper, since the word **"giving" is stated** in the Biblical text **with regard to the gifts of priesthood**. [2]The Torah states (Deuteronomy 26:12) that tithes must be *given*, not sold, to their recipients, and since ***ḥalifin* is a form of sale**, it is improper to transfer tithes to their recipients by this method. On the other hand, **the transfer of movable property along with land is a most powerful method of "giving,"** and hence tithes are permitted to be given in this way. The Gemara has now demonstrated that Rabban Gamliel was unable to use the method of *ḥalifin* in distributing his tithes, but he may well have used the method of transferring them along with land, as suggested above. Thus no objection to Ulla can be raised from the Mishnah in *Ma'aser Sheni*.

רַב פַּפָּא אָמַר [3]**Rav Pappa** now returns to the original interpretation of the Mishnah in *Ma'aser Sheni*, according to which Rabban Gamliel distributed the tithes on board ship by means of courtyard-acquisition. He **said** that even if Rabbi Akiva and Rabbi Yehoshua acquired the tithes from Rabban Gamliel through courtyard-acquisition, the Mishnah would still not pose any difficulty to Ulla, who claimed that ownerless property can be acquired by means of a courtyard only if the owner of the courtyard is standing nearby. For where the **ownership** of property is **transferred by** the **willing consent** of the original owner to the new owner, the law **is different**. The Halakhah differentiates between (a) the acquisition of ownerless property by means of the finder's courtyard, and (b) the use of a courtyard in the acquisition of property which is actively transferred from one party to another (e.g., a gift, like the tithes in our case).

CONCEPTS

קִנְיַן אַגַּב Kinyan aggav. A mode of acquisition inferred from the Bible (II Chronicles 21:3), this is one way of transferring ownership of many movable items without resorting to the physical action of pulling them. According to the Halakhah, when a person transfers land to someone else, he can transfer movable goods together with it (אַגַּב = lit., "on its back"), wherever they may be. Since the transfer of property can take place even if the parties to the transaction are not present at the property (such as through a deed or the transfer of money), this means of transfer may also be used for many possessions for which there is no simple method of transfer.

SAGES

רַב פַּפָּא Rav Pappa. One of the leading Babylonian Amoraim of the fifth generation, Rav Pappa was a student of Abaye and of Rava, and was a colleague of Rav Huna the son of Rav Yehoshua. After Rava's death his yeshivah was divided: part went to Pumbedita with Rav Naḥman bar Yitzḥak, and the other part went to Neresh with Rav Pappa. Rav Pappa's yeshivah was famous and had many students, and among his disciples were Rav Ashi and Ravina. He served as head of his yeshivah for nineteen years.

NOTES

מִטַּלְטְלִין אַגַּב מְקַרְקַע נְתִינָה אַלִּימְתָּא הִיא The transfer of movable property along with land is a most powerful method of giving. Once Rabbi Akiva and Rabbi Yehoshua acquired Rabban Gamliel's land by paying him the rental fee, they acquired the tithes automatically along with the land by *kinyan aggav*. Thus, even though the land was leased to them in exchange for money, the tithes themselves were given to them as a gift (*Ritva*).

several places in Talmudic literature. *Shittah Mekubbetzet* points out, however, that even according to the opinion that, in general, the market value of discretionary power is a true monetary interest in the object itself, our case may be somewhat different, since the degree of true money value involved is not sufficient to enable the object to be transferred through *ḥalifin* and other symbolic acts of acquisition.

SAGES

רַבִּי יִרְמְיָה Rabbi Yirmeyah. Born in Babylonia, Rabbi Yirmeyah was one of the leading Amoraim of the third and fourth generations. Rabbi Yirmeyah studied in Babylonia in his youth but soon thereafter he immigrated to Eretz Israel and studied with the greatest Sages of the generation, the students of Rabbi Yoḥanan, and he became the student of Rabbi Zera and Rabbi Abbahu.

Rabbi Yirmeyah had a special dialectical method involving great acuity, and he used to ask provocative questions of his teachers and colleagues. As a result he was even punished and removed from the House of Study for a limited period.

Rabbi Yirmeyah's teachings are quoted extensively in both the Babylonian and the Jerusalem Talmuds, so much so that in Babylonia his teachings are often simply called, "They say in the West" (i.e., in Eretz Israel).

TRANSLATION AND COMMENTARY

וּמְנָא תֵּימְרָא [1]**And from what source**, says Rav Pappa, **do you infer** that such a distinction is valid? [2]He answers: **From what we have learned** in our Mishnah: "**If** the owner of a field **saw** people in his field **running after an ownerless object, etc.**" [3]We know that, in connection with this statement, **Rabbi Yirmeyah said in the name of Rabbi Yoḥanan: This** law, that the owner of a field can acquire ownerless objects moving through his field, **applies** only **where** the owner of the field **could run after** the ownerless objects **and reach them** while they are still in his field. Only if this condition is fulfilled does the field acquire the ownerless objects for him.

בָּעֵי רַבִּי יִרְמְיָה [4]Continuing the analysis of the principles involved in the statement he transmitted in the name of Rabbi Yoḥanan, **Rabbi Yirmeyah asked: In the case of a gift, how do we decide?** If a person's animals or birds were in another person's field and their owner gave them as a present to the owner of the field, would the latter have to be able to catch them within his field in order to acquire them by courtyard-acquisition, or is this not necessary? [5]We also know that **Rabbi Abba bar Kahana accepted the distinction** between the acquisition of an ownerless object and the acquisition of a gift inherent in Rabbi Yirmeyah's question and replied: [6]**Even if** the owner of the field **runs after** the objects or animals given to him **and cannot reach them, he** nevertheless **acquires them** by means of his field. [7]**What is the reason** for this distinction between the acquisition of a gift and the acquisition of ownerless objects by means of a courtyard? [8]**Is it not because** the law in a case where the **ownership** of property is **transferred by** the **willing consent** of the original owner to the new owner **is different** from the law in the case of ownerless property? Rabbi Yirmeyah's statement, then, seems to support Rav Pappa's view, that it is only with regard to the acquisition of ownerless objects that the owner of the field must be present for courtyard-acquisition to be effective, and that the owner's presence is not needed in the case of the acquisition of tithes.

אֲמַר לֵיהּ רַב שִׁימִי לְרַב פַּפָּא [9]**Rav Shimi said to Rav Pappa:** But **what about a bill of divorce, where the willing consent of another party** — the husband — **is needed** in order **to transfer it** to the wife?

[1]וּמְנָא תֵּימְרָא? [2]דִּתְנַן: "רָאָה אוֹתָן רָצִין אַחַר הַמְּצִיאָה כו׳". [3]וְאָמַר רַבִּי יִרְמְיָה אָמַר רַבִּי יוֹחָנָן: וְהוּא שֶׁרָץ אַחֲרֵיהֶן וּמַגִּיעָן.

[4]וּבָעֵי רַבִּי יִרְמְיָה: בְּמַתָּנָה הֵיאָךְ? [5]קִבְּלָהּ מִינֵּיהּ רַבִּי אַבָּא בַּר כָּהֲנָא: [6]אַף עַל פִּי שֶׁרָץ אַחֲרֵיהֶן וְאֵין מַגִּיעָן. [7]מַאי טַעְמָא? [8]לָאו מִשּׁוּם דְּדַעַת אַחֶרֶת מַקְנָה אוֹתָן שָׁאנֵי? [9]אֲמַר לֵיהּ רַב שִׁימִי לְרַב פַּפָּא: הֲרֵי גֵּט, דְּדַעַת אַחֶרֶת מַקְנָה אוֹתָהּ?

LITERAL TRANSLATION

[1]And from where do you say [this]? [2]As we have learned: "[If] one saw [people] running after a found object, etc." [3]And Rabbi Yirmeyah said in the name of Rabbi Yoḥanan: And that is where he could run after them and reach them.

[4]And Rabbi Yirmeyah asked: In [the case of a] gift, how [do we decide]? [5]Rabbi Abba bar Kahana accepted [the distinction] from him: [6]Even if he runs after them and cannot reach them [he acquires them]. [7]What is the reason? [8]Is it not because the will of another party transferring ownership of them is different?

[9]Rav Shimi said to Rav Pappa: What about (lit., "behold") a bill of divorce, where the will of another party is [needed in] transferring it?

RASHI

והוא שרץ אחריהן — הצבי מהלך והגוזלות מדדין. ומתניתין דקתני זכתה לו שדהו — כגון שהיה יכול לרוץ אחריהן, ומגיען קודם שיצאו משדהו. הכי גרסינן: **ובעי רבי ירמיה במתנת היאך** — אם היו צבי וגוזלות של אדם אחד, והם בתוך שדה חבירו, ונותנן בעליהן לבעל שדה במתנה — היאך הדין? מי בעינן והוא שרץ אחריהן ומגיען, ואי לא — לא קני. ומאי נותן למיהדר ביה, או לא? **קבלה מיניה רבי אבא** — להך בעיא מרבי ירמיה, דשפיר דק שיש חילוק בין מתנה להפקר. ובמתנה אף על פי כו׳.

NOTES

דַּעַת אַחֶרֶת מַקְנָה The will of another party transferring ownership. Most transactions have two parties, a seller and a buyer, or a donor and a recipient. The juridical essence of acquisition therefore requires two intentions, that of the giver and that of the receiver, and the transaction takes place by virtue of the mutual agreement between the two parties. However, when a person acquires lost or ownerless property, the act of acquisition is one-sided, and, since there is no partner on the other side, this manner of acquisition must be more comprehensive than that by mutual agreement.

HALAKHAH

קִנְיַן חָצֵר בְּמַתָּנָה Acquisition of gifts by means of one's courtyard. "If the owner of a field received as a gift an object or an animal rolling or moving through his property, the gift is valid and the field acquires the object for its owner, even if he is unable to reach it. But if the gift was a gazelle running normally (which a person obviously could never catch), the field does not acquire it for its owner, even though the animal was intended as a gift." (*Shulḥan Arukh, Ḥoshen Mishpat* 268:4.)

TRANSLATION AND COMMENTARY

וְאָמַר עוּלָּא [1]**And yet Ulla said** that the rule that a divorce thrown into the wife's house or courtyard is valid **applies only where she is** herself **standing next to her house or next to her courtyard** at the time!

שָׁאנֵי גֵּט [2]Rav Pappa answered: **A bill of divorce is different, because it is enforced** even when given **against** the wife's **will**. The husband has the power to give his wife a bill of divorce even against her will, and does not require her active consent to make its transfer effective.

מַתְקִיף לָהּ [3]**Rav Sheshet, the son of Rav Idi, objected** to this explanation: Can we **not** arrive at the opposite conclusion by means of the following ***kal vaḥomer*** argument? [4]**A bill of divorce is valid** even if given **against** the wife's **will**. Nevertheless, only **if** the wife **is standing next to her house or next to her courtyard** is the **delivery** of the divorce **considered valid, but if not**, it is **not** valid. [5]**How much more so** should the recipient in the case of **a gift, which can be** effectively **transferred** to him **only with his willing consent,** be required to stand near his courtyard or field in order to acquire it!

אֶלָּא אָמַר רַב אַשִׁי [6]The Gemara now accepts Rav Sheshet's objection and rejects the previously suggested distinction between bills of divorce and gifts based on the fact that a divorce can be effective without the wife's consent. **Rather, Rav Ashi** suggested a new distinction between bills of divorce and gifts and **said:** [12A] The difference between the power of a courtyard to acquire a bill of divorce for a wife and the power of a courtyard to acquire a gift on behalf of its recipient is not based on the fact that a bill of divorce may be given to a wife even against her will. The difference lies in the fundamental nature of acquisition by means of one's courtyard. We concluded earlier (10b-11a) that, at least regarding bills of divorce, **courtyard-acquisition is an extension of the principle of acquisition by means of one's hand. But** the notion that courtyard-acquisition is a form of agency was not rejected.

[1]וְאָמַר עוּלָּא: וְהוּא שֶׁעוֹמֶדֶת בְּצַד בֵּיתָהּ אוֹ בְּצַד חֲצֵרָהּ! [2]שָׁאנֵי גֵּט, דְּאִיתֵיהּ בְּעַל כָּרְחָהּ.

[3]מַתְקִיף לָהּ רַב שֵׁשֶׁת בְּרֵיהּ דְּרַב אִידִי: וְלָאו קַל וָחוֹמֶר הוּא: [4]וּמַה גֵּט דְּאִיתֵיהּ בְּעַל כָּרְחָהּ, אִי עוֹמֶדֶת בְּצַד בֵּיתָהּ וּבְצַד חֲצֵרָהּ, אִין, אִי לָא, לָא. [5]מַתָּנָה, דְּמִדַּעְתֵּיהּ, לֹא כָּל שֶׁכֵּן!

[6]אֶלָּא אֲמַר רַב אַשִׁי: [12A] חָצֵר אִיתְרַבַּאי מִשּׁוּם יָד,

LITERAL TRANSLATION

[1]And [yet] Ulla said: And that is [only] where she is standing by the side of her house or by the side of her courtyard!

[2]A bill of divorce is different, because it is [enforced] against her will.

[3]Rav Sheshet, the son of Rav Idi, objected: Is it not a *kal vaḥomer* argument: [4]If a bill of divorce, which is [valid] against her will, if she is standing by the side of her house or by the side of her courtyard, is [considered delivered], [but] if not, not, [5]a gift, which [can be transferred only] with [the recipient's] willing consent, how much more so!

[6]Rather, Rav Ashi said: [12A] Courtyard [acquisition] is an extension of the principle of [acquisition by means of one's] hand,

RASHI

ואמר עולא – במסכת גיטין (עז,ב) גבי הזורק גט לאשתו בתוך ביתה או בתוך חצרה. **שאני גט דאיתיה בעל כרחה** – שהוא נותנו לה ולא ניחא לה למגרשה. **ולאו קל וחומר הוא** – מן הטעם הזה יש לדון דכל שכן לקנין אחר. **מה גט** – דכי איתה בצד חצרה, ולא ניחא לה למקנייה – אפילו הכי קנייה לה חצרה, אמרינן דאי איתה – אין, אי לא – לא. **מתנה** – דליתה בעל כרחה, דאי אמרה לא בעינא – לא קניא. **לא כל שכן** – דכי אמרה בעינא – צריכה שתהא בצד חצרה. **אלא אמר רב אשי** – לא תתלי טעמא משום דאיתה בעל כרחה. אלא גבי מתנה היינו טעמא דלא בעינן עומד אצלה – דכיון דמ"ידה" אתרבאי לא גרעה משלוחה להיטיב לה. ואילו שלוחה שקיבל לה מתנה – מי לא קני לה, ואפילו אין עומדת בצדו, חצרה נמי, לא שנא. הלכך, גבי מתנה דזכות הוא לה – אנן סהדי דניחא לה שתהא שלוחה, וקנייא לה כשליח.

NOTES

וְלָאו קַל וָחוֹמֶר הוּא **Is it not a *kal vaḥomer* argument**. This *kal vaḥomer* inference is not necessarily sound. An argument can actually be made that involuntary receipt requires the recipient's presence even more than voluntary receipt. Nevertheless, for the purpose of refuting Rav Pappa's position, it is sufficient to show that a *kal vaḥomer* argument exists whereby a gift should require the recipient's presence at least as much as the delivery of a bill of divorce does (*Ri Aboab*).

HALAKHAH

גֵּט בְּחָצֵר **A bill of divorce in the wife's courtyard**. "If a husband throws a bill of divorce into his wife's courtyard, the divorce takes effect only if she is standing there and if the courtyard is 'guarded'; but if she is not standing there, even though the courtyard is 'guarded,' the divorce is invalid," following the Gemara. (Ibid., *Even HaEzer* 139:1.)

מַה גֵּט בְּעַל כָּרְחָהּ **Divorcing a wife against her will**. "According to Torah law, a wife may be divorced against her

וְלָא גָּרְעָה מִשְּׁלִיחוּת. [1]גַּבֵּי גֵּט, דְּחוֹב הוּא לָהּ, אֵין חָבִין לְאָדָם אֶלָּא בְּפָנָיו. [2]גַּבֵּי מַתָּנָה, דִּזְכוּת הוּא לוֹ, זָכִין לְאָדָם שֶׁלֹּא בְּפָנָיו.

LITERAL TRANSLATION

and is no worse than agency.

[1] [Hence], with regard to a bill of divorce, which is a disadvantage to her, one may not do something to a person's disadvantage unless [the person] is present. [2] With regard to a gift, which is an advantage to him, one may do something to a person's advantage [even] when he is not present.

TRANSLATION AND COMMENTARY

Hence courtyard-acquisition **is no worse than agency,** and in those circumstances where hand-acquisition is not effective but agency is effective, courtyard-acquisition can derive its validity from agency as well. In other words, the laws of courtyard-acquisition are an application of both the "hand" laws and the "agency" laws. Only when the owner of a courtyard is next to it, can it act as an extension of his hand, since one's hand is always close to one's body. But even when the owner of the courtyard is not present, it can still acquire for him as his agent.

גַּבֵּי גֵּט [1] Rav Ashi now proceeds to show why the law of courtyard-acquisition is different in the case of a bill of divorce from the case of a gift: **With regard to a bill of divorce**, an agent is unable to receive it on behalf of the wife unless the wife explicitly appointed him to do so, because the act of receiving the bill of divorce **is to her disadvantage**, and **one may not do something to a person's disadvantage unless the person is present** and expressly consents to the appointment of the agent to act on his or her behalf. Thus, the wife's courtyard cannot act as her agent to accept the bill of divorce on her behalf, and the efficacy of courtyard-acquisition in cases of divorce depends entirely on the principle that it is an extension of hand-acquisition. And hand-acquisition is applicable only when the wife is standing next to her courtyard. [2] By contrast, **with regard to a gift**, the acquisition of **which is to** the recipient's **advantage**, both the "hand" and the "agency" principles are applicable, for an agent can accept a gift on behalf of its recipient on his own initiative, even if the latter is not present and knows nothing about the matter, since **one may do something** that is **to a person's advantage even when** that person **is not present**. In the same way the recipient's courtyard can act as his agent to accept the gift

RASHI

אבל גבי גט, דחוב הוא לה — לא ניחא לה שתהא שלוחה. הלכך, כי עומדת בצדה — על כרחה ידה היא, וידה קניא גבי גט על כרחה. ואי לא — לאו ידה הוא, ולא שלוחה הוא. טעמא דיש חילוק בין גט למתנה, ואף על גב דתרווייהו דעת אחרת מקנה אותן, משום דהך חצר, אף על גב דאתרבאי משום יד, כדאמרן לעיל (י,ב), לא גרעה משליחות דאי נמי לא אתרבאי מ״ונתן בידה״ הוי נפקא לן חצר משליחות. וכי אצטריך לרבויי משום יד — משום קטן וקטנה, דליתנהו, בתורת שליחות אצטריך, וכל היכא דאיתיה לשליחות — איתיה לדין חצר. הלכך, גבי גט דחוב הוא לה — אין חבין כו׳. כלומר: אין אדם יכול לעשות שליח לחוב אדם שלא מדעתו, וחצרו נמי לאו בתורת שליחות מצית לאתויי דתתגרש שלא מדעתה. הלכך, בגט לא תרבייה אלא משום יד, ומה ידה דסמוכה לה — אף חצירה בסמוכה לה. **גבי מתנה דזכות הוא לו זכין לו לאדם שלא בפניו** — ושלא מדעתו, דאנן סהדי דניחא ליה שתהא שלוחו. הלכך, כי ליתיה בצד חצרו, דליכא לדמויי לידה דאינה סמוכה לה — תיפוק לה זכייתה משליחותה, כי היכי דשלוחו זוכה לו שלא בפניו חצרו נמי זוכה לו שלא בפניו. ומיהו, גבי מציאה כי ליתי גבה, דלא נפקא זכייתה משום יד — ליכא לרבויי משליחות. דגבי שליחות איכא דעת השולח או דעת שליח, אבל חצר — ליכא לא דעת שולח ולא דעת שליח. הלכך בעינן דעת אחרת מקנה אותו.

NOTES

וְלָא גָּרְעָה מִשְּׁלִיחוּת **And it is no worse than agency.** *Tosefot HaRosh* explains that this principle is arrived at through logic without the necessity of a specific verse from the Torah. We may assume that a person will certainly wish his courtyard to be his agent to acquire articles whose acquisition is to his advantage. In contrast, the fact that a person's courtyard is considered an extension of his person (his hand) does require a specific derivation since it is applied only where agency is ineffective, such as in the case of acquisition by a minor.

Ra'avad explains that a courtyard's effectiveness as an agent is derived by a *kal vaḥomer* argument: A person's courtyard is considered as an extension of his person and is effective in situations where the principle of agency is not effective. Therefore, we may assume that it will surely also be effective in all areas where an agent *is* effective.

גֵּט חוֹב הוּא לָהּ **A bill of divorce is a disadavantage to her.** This principle applies even in situations where in fact

HALAKHAH

will. But Rabbenu Gershom [960–1040 C.E.] pronounced a ban [ḥerem] upon anyone who divorces his wife without her consent." This prohibition became widely accepted with time, and is now followed by Jewish communities throughout the world. (*Shulḥan Arukh, Even HaEzer* 119:6.)

אֵין חָבִין לְאָדָם אֶלָּא בְּפָנָיו **One may not do something to a person's disadvantage unless the person is present.** "If a husband divorces his wife, the bill of divorce is only valid if it is delivered in her presence. Thus, if he left the bill of divorce in his wife's courtyard at a time when she was not present, the divorce is invalid. The reason for this is that the divorce is by its very nature considered to be to her disadvantage, and one may not do something on a person's behalf which is to that person's disadvantage unless the person is present." (*Rambam, Sefer Nashim, Hilkhot Gerushin* 5:2.)

זָכִין לְאָדָם שֶׁלֹּא בְּפָנָיו **One may do something to a person's advantage even when he is not present.** "Anything that is to a person's advantage may be done on his behalf even

LITERAL TRANSLATION

[1] We learnt above (lit., "the thing itself"): "[If] one saw [people] running after a found object, etc." [2] Rabbi Yirmeyah said in the name of Rabbi Yoḥanan: And that is where he could run after them and reach them. [3] [And] Rabbi Yirmeyah asked: In [the case of a] gift, how [do we decide]? [4] Rabbi Abba bar Kahana accepted [the distinction] from him: Even if he runs after them and cannot reach them [he acquires them]. [5] Rava asked: [If] he threw a purse through one doorway [of a house] and it flew out through another doorway, what is [the law]?

[1] גּוּפָא: ״רָאָה אוֹתָן רָצִין אַחַר הַמְּצִיאָה וכו׳״. [2] אָמַר רַבִּי יִרְמְיָה אָמַר רַבִּי יוֹחָנָן: וְהוּא שֶׁרָץ אַחֲרֵיהֶן וּמַגִּיעָן. [3] בָּעֵי רַבִּי יִרְמְיָה: בְּמַתָּנָה הֵיאָךְ? [4] קִבְּלָהּ מִינֵּיהּ רַבִּי אַבָּא בַּר כָּהֲנָא: אַף עַל פִּי שֶׁרָץ אַחֲרֵיהֶן וְאֵין מַגִּיעָן.

[5] בָּעֵי רָבָא: זָרַק אַרְנָקֵי בְּפֶתַח זֶה וְיָצָא בְּפֶתַח אַחֵר, מַהוּ?

RASHI

זרק ארנקי — והפקירו לכל הקודם.

TRANSLATION AND COMMENTARY

on his behalf, even if he is not present and knows nothing about the matter. Thus, it is possible to deliver a gift by means of courtyard-acquisition even in the recipient's absence, even without his knowledge, and even (according to Rabbi Yirmeyah) if the gift is an animal that cannot easily be caught. But the distinction made between a gift and an ownerless object still holds: It is not possible for a person's courtyard to act as his agent without his express appointment, unless the transfer is being carried out at the behest of the object's previous owner. Agency is only created if at least one of the parties to the transaction is actively involved. Hence, an ownerless object can be acquired only through the "hand" principle, with all the limitations involved in its use. This concludes the Gemara's discussion of Shmuel's distinction (above, 11a) between guarded and unguarded courtyards.

גּוּפָא [1] The Gemara now goes on to probe more deeply into one of the subjects mentioned earlier in the discussion, namely Rabbi Yirmeyah's attempt to apply our Mishnah to the case of a gift: **We learnt above**: Our Mishnah states, **"If** the owner of a field **saw people** in his field **running after an ownerless object, etc."** [2] In connection with this Mishnah, **Rabbi Yirmeyah said in the name of Rabbi Yoḥanan: This** law, that the owner of a field can acquire ownerless objects moving through his field, **applies** only **where** the owner of the field **could run after** the ownerless objects **and reach them** while they are still in his field. If he could not reach them, the field does not acquire them on his behalf. [3] **Rabbi Yirmeyah asked: In the case of** a gazelle, which can still outrun him and which was placed in his field as **a gift, how do we decide**? [4] **Rabbi Abba bar Kahana accepted the distinction** between the acquisition of an ownerless object and the acquisition of a gift inherent in Rabbi Yirmeyah's question and replied: **Even if** the owner of the field **runs after** the objects or animals given to him **and cannot reach them, he** nevertheless **acquires them** by means of his field.

בָּעֵי רָבָא [5] In connection with this earlier discussion, and based on Rabbi Abba bar Kahana's ruling that a gift moving through a field is acquired by the owner of the field, **Rava asked: What is the law if** a person relinquished ownership of **a purse** and **threw** it **through one doorway of** another's person **house and it flew out** of that person's house **through another doorway** without touching the floor inside the house? Does the owner of the house acquire it, because it has passed through the airspace of the house, or not?

NOTES

receiving the bill of divorce is to the woman's advantage, such as where she herself asks to be divorced. The reason for this assumption is that, technically, a bill of divorce is given without regard for the woman's wishes (*Geon Tzvi*).

זָרַק אַרְנָקֵי If he threw a purse. Rashi explains (in accordance with a number of variant readings) that the situation here is that the person who threw the purse declared it ownerless (הֶפְקֵר). *Tosafot* objects to *Rashi's* interpretation on the grounds that the entire passage is based on the principle of דַּעַת אַחֶרֶת מַקְנָה — that the active consent of the person transferring the object is needed. That consent is apparently lacking in the case of an ownerless article.

Ramban explains that a person who declares an object ownerless is, by his very declaration, actively consenting to the transfer of the object into the ownership of the person who finds it. *Rashba*, however, expresses doubt as to the correctness of *Ramban's* explanation. *Ramban's* thesis is

HALAKHAH

when he is not present himself. Thus, a person can accept a gift on behalf of another person even in the latter's absence, and the latter becomes its owner even before it reaches his hand. But if the recipient of the gift does not want it, he does not become its owner against his will." (*Rambam, Sefer Kinyan, Hilkhot Zekhiah U'Mattanah* 4:2.)

זָרַק אַרְנָק דֶּרֶךְ חֲלַל הַבַּיִת If a person threw a purse through the airspace within a house. "If a person wishes to give a purse to another person as a present and he throws it in through the doorway of the latter's house, and it flies straight out through another doorway without having touched the ground in the house, if the donor retracts the gift while it is in the homeowner's airspace, the homeowner does not acquire the purse. Because the discussion of this

[1]אֲוִיר, שֶׁאֵין סוֹפוֹ לָנוּחַ, כְּמוּנָּח דָּמֵי, אוֹ לֹא? [2]אֲמַר לֵיהּ רַב פַּפָּא לְרָבָא, וְאָמְרִי לָהּ: רַב אַדָּא בַּר מַתָּנָה לְרָבָא, וְאָמְרִי לָהּ: רָבִינָא לְרָבָא: [3]לָאו הַיְינוּ מַתְנִיתִין: ״רָאָה אוֹתָן רָצִין אַחַר הַמְּצִיאָה״. [4]וְאָמַר רַבִּי יִרְמְיָה אָמַר רַבִּי יוֹחָנָן: וְהוּא שֶׁרָץ אַחֲרֵיהֶן וּמַגִּיעָן. [5]וּבָעֵי רַבִּי יִרְמְיָה: בְּמַתָּנָה הֵיאָךְ? [6]וְקִבְּלָה מִינֵּיהּ רַבִּי אַבָּא בַּר כָּהֲנָא: בְּמַתָּנָה, אַף עַל פִּי שֶׁרָץ אַחֲרֵיהֶן וְאֵין מַגִּיעָן.

LITERAL TRANSLATION

[1]Is [an article traveling through] the airspace [of a house or courtyard, but] which will never come to rest [there], considered as if it came to rest [there] or not?

[2]Rav Pappa said to Rava, and others say: Rav Adda bar Mattanah said to Rava, and others say: Ravina said to Rava: [3]Is this not the same as our Mishnah: "[If] one saw [people] running after a found object." [4]And Rabbi Yirmeyah said in the name of Rabbi Yoḥanan: And that is where he could run after them and reach them. [5]And Rabbi Yirmeyah asked: In [the case of a] gift, how [do we decide]? [6]And Rabbi Abba bar Kahana accepted [the distinction] from him: In [the case of a] gift, even if he runs after them and cannot reach them [he acquires them].

TRANSLATION AND COMMENTARY

[1]In other words, **is an article which passes through the airspace of a house or a courtyard, but which does not eventually come to rest** inside the house, **considered as having come to rest there, or not**?

אֲמַר לֵיהּ רַב פַּפָּא לְרָבָא [2]In reply to this question, **Rav Pappa said to Rava** — **according to others** it was **Rav Adda bar Mattanah** who said **to Rava**; [3]**and according to others** it was **Ravina** who said **to Rava**: **Is not** the principle involved in your question **the same as** that involved in **our Mishnah**, which states: "**If** the owner of a field **saw** people in his field **running after an ownerless object**"? [4]**And** we know that in connection with this statement **Rabbi Yirmeyah said in the name of Rabbi Yoḥanan**: **This** law, that the owner of a field can acquire ownerless objects moving through his field, **applies** only **where** the owner of the field **could run after** the ownerless objects **and reach them** while they are still in his field. [5]**And Rabbi Yirmeyah asked**: **In the case of a gift, how do we decide?** [6]**And** we also know that **Rabbi Abba bar Kahana accepted the distinction** between the acquisition of an ownerless object and the acquisition of a gift inherent in Rabbi Yirmeyah's question and replied: **In the case of a gift, even if** the owner of the field **runs after** the objects or animals given to him **and cannot reach them**, he nevertheless

RASHI

שאין סופו לנוח — בתוך האויר. **כמונח דמי** — וקנאו בעל הבית הראשון, או לאו כמונח דמי. להכי בעי: אויר שאין סופו לנוח בתוך הבית, כמונח דמי. דאילו אויר שהיה סופו לנוח בתוך הבית — פשיטא לן דאפילו קדם איש אחר וקלטה בתוך האויר — לא קנה. דמשנכנס לאויר קנאו בעל הבית. דתנן במסכת גיטין (עט,א): היתה עומדת בראש הגג וזרק לה גט, כיון שנכנס לאויר הגג — הרי זו מגורשת. הוא למעלה והיא למטה, כיון שיצא מרשות הגג, נמחק או נשרף — הרי זו מגורשת. **ואינו מגיען** — אלמא: מתגלגלים ויוצאין הן, ואין סופן לנוח, וקאמר דקנה ליה שדהו.

LANGUAGE

אֲוִיר Air or space. The source of the word is the Greek word ἀήρ, a'ir, which has the same meaning.

TERMINOLOGY

לָאו הַיְינוּ מַתְנִיתִין Is this not the same as our Mishnah? This question is asked in two situations: (1) Sometimes it serves as a proposal to solve a problem raised by the Amoraim, and its meaning is: "Is there no possibility of resolving this question through the words of the Mishnah?" (2) Occasionally, it appears as a comment on a statement of an Amora, and in this case it expresses astonishment: "Why did the Amora have to say this, since it is already found in the Mishnah?" In neither case does this mean that the matter raised as a problem or stated as a fact by the Amora is stated explicitly in the Mishnah. But the Gemara tries to prove that it is *implied* by the Mishnah, and that there is no other way to understand the matter except this.

NOTES

further developed by *Ran*, who differentiates between the acquisition of an article whose owner has declared it ownerless and the acquisition of an article that had no owner at all. In the former case, it is as if the person who declares the article ownerless is giving his consent for anyone to acquire it. By contrast, in the latter case, there is no owner to give his consent.

אֲוִיר שֶׁאֵין סוֹפוֹ לָנוּחַ An article traveling through the airspace of a house but which will never come to rest there. The emphasis conveyed by this phrase is necessary here, because a person owns everything in the airspace over his courtyard, reaching up to the sky, and if an object were suspended in the air over a courtyard (for example, on a high branch), there would be no doubt that it belongs to the owner of the courtyard. Moreover, in the case of a guarded courtyard, like a house, when it is clear that an object is about to land in a courtyard, ownership of it takes effect as soon as it reaches the airspace over the coutryard, even before it lands. (Indeed, the Halakhah rules in this way regarding a bill of divorce thrown into such a courtyard.) Therefore the question here relates only to the special case of something that is not going to land in the courtyard.

This question is another form of the ancient philosophical question regarding the essence of motion through space: Should it be viewed as a series of tiny resting points or should it be viewed as a single continuous movement? We can thus understand the distinction made by Rava below between an object moving through the air and one rolling or running along the ground. When a gazelle runs through a courtyard it is clear that it comes to rest at every moment; but after being momentarily still, it moves on out of the domain. On the other hand, with regard to an object moving through the air, there is doubt as to whether it can be considered as being in any way partially at rest.

אֲוִיר שֶׁאֵין סוֹפוֹ לָנוּחַ An article traveling through the airspace of a house or a courtyard, but which will never

HALAKHAH

problem in the Gemara was inconclusive, the ownership of the purse remains with the donor. But if the original owner of the purse renounces his ownership of it before throwing it, and a third party picks it up after it has passed through the homeowner's airspace, it is restored to the possession of the homeowner, because his claim to it takes precedence over the claim of the third party." (*Shulḥan Arukh, Ḥoshen Mishpat* 243:24.)

LITERAL TRANSLATION

[1]He said to him: You are speaking about [something that is] moving (lit., "rolling") [along the ground]. Moving [along the ground] is different, as it is considered like resting [on the ground].

MISHNAH [2]An [ownerless] object found by one's minor son or daughter, an object found by his Canaanite male slave or female slave, an object found by his wife — these belong to him.

[1]אֲמַר לֵיהּ: מִתְגַּלְגֵּל קָאָמְרַתְּ. שָׁאנֵי מִתְגַּלְגֵּל, דִּכְמוּנָּח דָּמֵי.

מִשְׁנָה [2]מְצִיאַת בְּנוֹ וּבִתּוֹ הַקְּטַנִּים, מְצִיאַת עַבְדּוֹ וְשִׁפְחָתוֹ הַכְּנַעֲנִים, מְצִיאַת אִשְׁתּוֹ — הֲרֵי אֵלּוּ שֶׁלּוֹ.

RASHI

משנה מציאת בנו ובתו הקטנים כו׳ — בנו קטן בגמרא מפרש מאי טעמא. בתו הקטנה בכתובות (מו,ב) ילפינן לה מקראי, דקטנה ואף נערה כל שבח נעוריה לאביה. **מציאת עבדו ושפחתו הכנענים שלו** — שהרי גופו קנוי לו עולמית, כדכתיב (ויקרא כה) "והתנחלתם וכו׳". **מציאת אשתו** — רבנן תקינו ליה משום איבה.

TRANSLATION AND COMMENTARY

acquires them by means of his field. From this, says Rav Pappa, it is clear that an object that passes through a person's domain, even though it does not come to rest there, may be acquired by him. In the same way, in the case of the purse, since it is being given away, if it passes through a person's house or courtyard, even though it does not remain there, it should be considered to have been acquired by the owner of the house or courtyard!

אֲמַר לֵיהּ [1]Rava **said to him** in reply: In your reference to our Mishnah **you are talking about** animals **moving along the ground** but maintaining constant contact with it. **Moving along the ground is different** from flying through the air, **as it is considered** in some ways **like resting** in one place **on the ground.** An animal moving through a field cannot be compared to an object crossing the airspace within a building. Such an object does not come in contact with the ground at all, and may well not be governed by the same rules as apply to an object, stationary or moving, in a field. Therefore, says Rava, I do not accept that the problem I presented can be solved by reference to the circumstances described in our Mishnah. The problem thus remains unresolved.

MISHNAH מְצִיאַת בְּנוֹ וּבִתּוֹ הַקְּטַנִּים [2]**An ownerless object found by a man's son or daughter**, while they are **minors** (normally understood to refer to sons below the age of thirteen, and daughters below the age of twelve, but see below, 12b), or **an object found by a man's Canaanite** (non-Jewish) **male slave or female slave,** or **an object found by a man's wife — these belong to him** (the father, the slave-owner, and the husband, respectively).

NOTES

come to rest there. A similar question is raised (*Shabbat* 4a) with regard to the laws of the Sabbath. If a person throws an article through a domain on the Sabbath without it coming to rest there, is the article considered to have come to rest within the domain? (If it is, he would be liable for transgressing the prohibition of transferring objects from one domain to another on the Sabbath.)

Ritva, however, maintains that even those opinions that consider the thrower liable in that instance, may not consider in our case that it is as if the purse has come to rest within the homeowner's house or courtyard. The severity of the Sabbath laws forces us to adopt different criteria, which do not necessarily apply to other areas of Halakhah. (This explanation also solves a similar problem raised by *Rabbi Tzvi Ḥayyot*.)

מְצִיאַת בִּתּוֹ An object found by one's daughter, before she reaches majority. According to *Rashi* and *Rambam*, the right of a father to acquire ownership of objects found by his daughter is of Torah origin. Other commentators, however, maintain that this law is a Rabbinic decree, instituted by the Sages to prevent tension between a father and his daughter (*Rosh, Ran,* and others, based on the Gemara in *Ketubot* 46b).

עַבְדּוֹ וְשִׁפְחָתוֹ הַכְּנַעֲנִים His Canaanite male slave or female slave. The distinction between a Hebrew servant or maidservant and a Canaanite slave derives from the essential difference between their modes of acquisition. A Hebrew servant is not completely enslaved, as it is said in the Torah: "They are My servants... they shall not be sold as bondmen" (Leviticus 25:42). Torah law therefore restricts the scope of ownership of Hebrew servants, who never enter into a state of absolute bondage. In fact, they are viewed as hired workers contracted for a long period. All their obligations and rights as free people remain even while they are slaves. This situation is different regarding Canaanite slaves. Since the Torah does not accord them such a special status, they are like their master's other possessions. The master may sell them to other people, and they lose their

HALAKHAH

מְצִיאַת יְלָדִים קְטַנִּים Objects found by one's children while they are minors. "A male minor may keep the ownerless objects he finds, provided that he is not being supported financially by his father," following Rabbi Yoḥanan below (12b), against Shmuel. (*Shulḥan Arukh, Ḥoshen Mishpat* 270:2.)

מְצִיאַת בְּנֵי בֵּיתוֹ Objects found by the members of a man's household. "Objects found by a man's children belong to their father, provided that he is supporting them financially, even if the children have already reached the age of majority. Likewise, objects found by a man's wife belong to her husband," following the Mishnah and Rabbi Yoḥanan below (12b). (Ibid.)

מְצִיאַת עֲבָדִים Objects found by slaves." Jewish slaves who find lost objects may keep them, but the lost objects found by non-Jewish slaves belong to their masters." (Ibid.)

[1]מְצִיאַת בְּנוֹ וּבִתּוֹ הַגְּדוֹלִים, מְצִיאַת עַבְדּוֹ וְשִׁפְחָתוֹ הָעִבְרִים, מְצִיאַת אִשְׁתּוֹ שֶׁגֵּירְשָׁהּ, [2]אַף עַל פִּי שֶׁלֹּא נָתַן כְּתוּבָּה — הֲרֵי אֵלּוּ שֶׁלָּהֶן.

גמרא [3]אָמַר שְׁמוּאֵל: מִפְּנֵי מָה אָמְרוּ: ״מְצִיאַת קָטָן לְאָבִיו״? [4]שֶׁבְּשָׁעָה שֶׁמּוֹצְאָהּ, מְרִיצָהּ אֵצֶל אָבִיו, וְאֵינוֹ מְאַחֵר בְּיָדוֹ.

[5]לְמֵימְרָא דְּסָבַר שְׁמוּאֵל קָטָן לֵית לֵיהּ זְכִיָּה לְנַפְשֵׁיהּ מִדְּאוֹרַיְיתָא? [6]וְהָתַנְיָא: ״הַשּׂוֹכֵר אֶת הַפּוֹעֵל, יְלַקֵּט בְּנוֹ אַחֲרָיו; [7]לְמֶחֱצָה, לִשְׁלִישׁ, וְלִרְבִיעַ, לֹא יְלַקֵּט בְּנוֹ אַחֲרָיו.

LITERAL TRANSLATION

[1]An object found by one's adult son or daughter, an object found by his Jewish manservant or maidservant, an object found by his wife whom he has divorced, [2]even though he has not [yet] given [her her] ketubah — these belong to them.

GEMARA [3]Shmuel said: Why did [the Sages] say: "An [ownerless] object found by a man's minor son belongs to his father"? [4]Because when he finds it, he hurries [to bring] it to his father, and he does not delay it in his hand.

[5][Do you mean] to say that Shmuel maintains [that] a male minor cannot acquire [property] on his own behalf by Torah law? [6]Surely it was taught [in a Baraita]: "[If] one hires a worker, his son may glean behind him; [7][if he is hired] for half, [or] a third, [or] a quarter [of the produce], his son may not glean behind him.

TRANSLATION AND COMMENTARY

[1]But **an object found by a man's adult son or daughter**, or **an object found by a man's Jewish manservant or maidservant**, or **an object found by a man's ex-wife** after **he** has **divorced** her, [2]**even though he has not yet given her her ketubah** (the money due to her under her marriage settlement) — **these belong to them** (the finders).

GEMARA אָמַר שְׁמוּאֵל [3]**Shmuel said: Why did the Sages say** that **an object found by a male minor belongs to his father**? [4]**Because when** the child picks up the object he has found, he has no intention of acquiring it for himself. Rather, the moment **he finds it, he hurries to bring it to his father, and does not delay** holding **it in his hand.** Hence, even at the moment that he picked the object up, his intention was merely to act as an instrument to enable his father to acquire it.

לְמֵימְרָא דְּסָבַר שְׁמוּאֵל [5]The Gemara now proceeds to analyze Shmuel's statement and asks: **Do you mean to say that** we can infer from here that **Shmuel** in fact **maintains that a male minor cannot acquire property on his own behalf by Torah law?** [6]But **surely** this would be inconsistent with another statement Shmuel made regarding the following Baraita in which **it was taught**: "If a landowner **hires a worker** to harvest his field, the worker's **son may glean** the ears of corn left by the reapers during the harvesting (as may any other poor person; see Leviticus 19:9) **behind** his father. [7]But **if** the worker **was hired** as a tenant-farmer and receives **half, or a third or a quarter of the produce** as wages (rather than being paid on a daily basis), **his son may not glean behind him**. A tenant-farmer is considered as a part-owner of the field for the purposes of gleaning, and has the status of a wealthy person. Hence his son

RASHI

מציאת עבדו ושפחתו העברים – בגמרא פריך: לא יהא אלא פועל, דאמרינן לעיל (י,א) מציאתו לבעל הבית.

גמרא מפני מה אמרו מציאת קטן לאביו – בשלמא בתו ואשתו – טעמא מפרש להו במקומן בכתובות, אלא בנו טעמא מאי? **מריצה אצל אביו** – הלכך, כשמגביה לצורך אביו הגביהה. **ילקט בנו אחריו** – מותר לבנו של פועל, אם עני הוא, ללקוט אחר אביו את לקט הנשר. אבל אם קבל הפועל את השדה למחצה לשליש ולרביע – עשיר הוא, והרי הוא כבעל הבית בשדה זה, ולא ילקט בנו אחריו, לפי שלקט בנו לאביו.

NOTES

status as free people, for they are also deprived of the rights they had according to Torah law as non-Jews. Since they belong to their masters, they have no right of acquisition of their own, and everything they acquire belongs necessarily to their masters.

אַף עַל פִּי שֶׁלֹּא נָתַן כְּתוּבָּה **Even though he has not yet given her her ketubah**. Generally, the status of the wife is not affected by the fact that she has or has not received her ketubah. Since a woman severs all legal contact with her former husband upon being divorced, the ketubah becomes a promissory note which the former husband must pay her. Therefore, the Rabbis come to the conclusion (below, 12b) that in this case, despite the fact that she is divorced, her husband must continue to support her; and thus there is reason to believe that, since he has an obligation towards her, she too has a parallel financial obligation towards him.

מְצִיאַת קָטָן לְאָבִיו **An object found by a male minor belongs to his father**. The Gemara asks specifically about

HALAKHAH

מְצִיאַת אִשְׁתּוֹ גְּרוּשָׁה **Objects found by a man's divorced wife**. "Objects found by a man's ex-wife, even if the divorce was of doubtful validity and must be repeated, belong to her." (*Shulḥan Arukh, Ḥoshen Mishpat* 270:2.)

אִשְׁתּוֹ וּבָנָיו שֶׁל פּוֹעֵל **The wife and sons of a worker**. "The wife and sons of an agricultural worker may glean in the field where the husband (father) is working, even if he is entitled, according to the terms of his agreement, to a certain percentage of the harvest," following the opinion of Rabbi Yose, which is discussed extensively in the Gemara here. (*Rambam, Sefer Zeraim, Hilkhot Mattenot Aniyyim* 4:11.)

TRANSLATION AND COMMENTARY

is not permitted to glean after him. [1]**Rabbi Yose says: In both cases his son and his wife may glean behind him."** And in relation to this Baraita we know that **Shmuel said: The Halakhah is in accordance with** the opinion of **Rabbi Yose**, and the son may glean.

אִי אָמְרַתְּ בִּשְׁלָמָא [2]Now **there is no problem** in understanding Shmuel's point of view in relation to the Baraita **if you say that a male minor can acquire property on his own behalf**. For then, in the case of the tenant-farmer, **when the son gleans, he gleans for himself**. Since the son owns no property of his own, he is considered a poor person who is permitted to glean the fallen ears of corn, regardless of the tenant-farmer status of his father, and he acquires the gleanings for himself. He is then permitted to give the gleanings to his father as a present, and **his father** is allowed to **acquire** the gleanings **from him**. [3]**But if you say that a male minor cannot acquire property on his own behalf**, as would appear to be the case from Shmuel's explanation of our Mishnah, there is a problem. For then, **when the son gleans, he is gleaning** directly on behalf of **his father,** in accordance with the Rabbinic enactment described in our Mishnah! [4]But **his father is** considered **wealthy**, since he is a tenant-farmer, and hence he is not entitled to glean the fallen ears of corn. **Why, then, may his wife and his son glean behind him**? Thus, it would seem that Rabbi Yose, at least, must be of the opinion that a male minor is indeed able to acquire property on his own behalf. Hence, Shmuel's ruling in favor of Rabbi Yose appears to contradict his remark at the beginning of the discussion in the Gemara, that the Rabbis enacted that a male minor should acquire property on behalf of his father!

שְׁמוּאֵל טַעְמָא דְּתַנָּא דִּידָן [5]The Gemara answers: In fact, Shmuel, like Rabbi Yose, is of the opinion that a male minor *is* able to acquire property on his own behalf. But in his explanation of the ruling in our Mishnah, **Shmuel was** merely **explaining the reasoning of our Tanna** ("because when he finds it he hurries to bring it to his father"), but **he himself does not hold that opinion**.

וְסָבַר רַבִּי יוֹסֵי [6]The Gemara now raises a further difficulty and objects: **But does Rabbi Yose maintain**, as we have postulated until now, **that a male minor can acquire property** on his own behalf **by Torah law?** [7]**Surely, we**

[1]רַבִּי יוֹסֵי אוֹמֵר: בֵּין כָּךְ וּבֵין כָּךְ, יְלַקֵּט בְּנוֹ וְאִשְׁתּוֹ אַחֲרָיו". וְאָמַר שְׁמוּאֵל: הֲלָכָה כְּרַבִּי יוֹסֵי.

[2]אִי אָמְרַתְּ בִּשְׁלָמָא קָטָן אִית לֵיהּ זְכִיָּיה לְנַפְשֵׁיהּ. כִּי קָא מְלַקֵּט, לְנַפְשֵׁיהּ קָא מְלַקֵּט, וַאֲבוּהּ מִינֵּיהּ קָא זָכֵי. [3]אֶלָּא אִי אָמְרַתְּ קָטָן לֵית לֵיהּ זְכִיָּיה לְנַפְשֵׁיהּ, כִּי קָא מְלַקֵּט, לְאָבִיו קָא מְלַקֵּט! [4]אֲבוּהּ עָשִׁיר הוּא. אַמַּאי אִשְׁתּוֹ וּבְנוֹ מְלַקֵּט אַחֲרָיו? [5]שְׁמוּאֵל טַעְמָא דְּתַנָּא דִּידָן קָאָמַר, וְלֵיהּ לָא סְבִירָא לֵיהּ. [6]וְסָבַר רַבִּי יוֹסֵי קָטָן אִית לֵיהּ זְכִיָּיה מִדְּאוֹרַיְיתָא? [7]וְהָתְנַן:

LITERAL TRANSLATION

[1]Rabbi Yose says: In both cases (lit., 'between thus and between thus'), his son and his wife may glean behind him." And Shmuel said: The Halakhah is in accordance with Rabbi Yose.

[2]It is well if you say [that] a male minor can acquire [property] on his own behalf. When [the son] gleans, he gleans for himself, and his father acquires from him. [3]But if you say [that] a male minor cannot acquire [property] on his own behalf, when [the son] gleans, he gleans for his father! [4][But] his father is wealthy. Why [then] may his wife and his son glean behind him?

[5]Shmuel was stating the reason of our Tanna, but he himself does not hold [that opinion].

[6]But does Rabbi Yose maintain that a male minor can acquire [property] by Torah law? [7]Surely we have learned [in a Mishnah]:

RASHI

בין כך ובין כך כו' – דאם האב עשיר – הבן עני וזוכה לעצמו. **טעמא דתנא דידן קאמר** – מפני מה אמרו מציאת קטן לאביו. **וליה לא סבירא ליה** – דמציאת קטן לאביו.

NOTES

an object found by a male minor (קָטָן), since in general a father has no rights to income earned by his son (whereas he does have rights to income earned by his daughter). The Gemara's question, therefore, is: *How* does the father acquire an object found by his son?

אֲבוּהּ עָשִׁיר הוּא His father is considered wealthy. Some commentators explain that the produce of half a field (or even a third of a field) is presumed to be worth at least 200 zuz. And since anyone who owns at least 200 zuz is considered "wealthy" (see *Pe'ah* 8:8), the tenant-farmer is not entitled to glean the field (see *Ritva*). Others explain that, since the father *owns* part of the field, he is considered "wealthy" with regard to this particular Halakhah, because the Torah did not grant even a poor farmer the right to glean his own field (*Tosafot, Rosh*).

וְסָבַר רַבִּי יוֹסֵי קָטָן אִית לֵיהּ זְכִיָּיה מִדְּאוֹרַיְיתָא But does Rabbi Yose maintain that a male minor can acquire property by Torah law? The Rishonim ask: How does the Baraita concerning gleanings prove that Rabbi Yose is of the opinion that a male minor acquires by Torah law? Even if, as appears from the Mishnah in *Gittin*, this was merely a Rabbinic enactment, Rabbi Yose's position concerning

TRANSLATION AND COMMENTARY

have learned to the contrary in a Mishnah (*Gittin* 59b): "It is forbidden **to take away an object found by a deaf-mute, an imbecile, or a minor**. Even though they lack legal competence and are thus technically incapable of acquiring even ownerless objects, nevertheless the physical removal of such objects from their hands **has the character of a kind of robbery, and is prohibited because of the 'ways of peace,'** i.e., in order to prevent the social disorder that would result from the abuse of their legal status. [1]**Rabbi Yose says:** The taking away of an object found by these people is not only prohibited in the interests of peace, **it is outright robbery.**" **And** we know that **Rav Ḥisda** explained Rabbi Yose's statement and **said**: Rabbi Yose did not mean that a deaf-mute, an imbecile, and a minor can acquire ownerless objects by Torah law. What he meant was that such an act was declared **outright robbery by Rabbinic enactment**. Rabbi Yose agrees that it was the Rabbis who made the taking away of such objects from their finder an act of robbery, but he maintains that the enactment had a stricter character than that conveyed by the expression "the ways of peace."

נָפְקָא מִינָּהּ [2]The Gemara notes parenthetically: **The practical difference** between the two opinions mentioned in this Mishnah, "robbery prohibited in the interests of peace" (as maintained by the first Tanna), and "outright robbery prohibited by Rabbinic enactment" (as maintained by Rabbi Yose as explained by Rav Ḥisda), **is whether** we may **take the object** found by the deaf-mute, etc., **away** from the robber **by resort to** the decision of **judges**. "Outright robbery," even if it is prohibited only by Rabbinic enactment, can be recovered by resort to the judicial system, whereas "robbery prohibited in the interests of peace" cannot. At all events we can see from this Mishnah as explained authoritatively by Rav Ḥisda that Rabbi Yose does *not* maintain that a male minor can acquire property on his own behalf by Torah law! How, then, did Rabbi Yose, in the Baraita concerning gleaning, allow the son of the tenant-farmer to glean behind his father? Surely by this act he is robbing the poor!

אֶלָּא אָמַר אַבַּיֵי [3]The Gemara now accepts this objection and rejects the previous explanation, according to which Rabbi Yose disagreed with our Mishnah. In fact, even according to Rabbi Yose, a male minor cannot acquire property on his own behalf by Torah law, and Shmuel's explanation of our Mishnah, that a male minor

״מְצִיאַת חֵרֵשׁ, שׁוֹטֶה, וְקָטָן, יֵשׁ בָּהֶן מִשּׁוּם גֶּזֶל, מִפְּנֵי ׳דַּרְכֵי שָׁלוֹם׳. [1]רַבִּי יוֹסֵי אוֹמֵר: גֶּזֶל גָּמוּר״. וְאָמַר רַב חִסְדָּא: גֶּזֶל גָּמוּר מִדִּבְרֵיהֶן.
[2]נָפְקָא מִינָּהּ לְהוֹצִיאָהּ בְּדַיָּינִין.
[3]אֶלָּא אָמַר אַבַּיֵי: עֲשָׂאוּהָ כְּמִי שֶׁהָלְכוּ בָּהּ נְמוּשׁוֹת, דַּעֲנִיִּים גּוּפַיְיהוּ מַסְחִי דַּעְתַּיְיהוּ. סָבְרִי:

LITERAL TRANSLATION

"[To take away] an object found by a deaf-mute, an imbecile, or a minor, has [the character] of a kind of robbery, [and is prohibited] because of the 'ways of peace.' [1]Rabbi Yose says: [It is] outright robbery." And Rav Ḥisda said: [It is] outright robbery by Rabbinic enactment (lit., "from their words").

[2]The practical difference [between the two opinions] is [whether] to take [the object] away by [resort to] judges.

[3]Rather, Abaye said: They made it like [a field] through which the last of the gleaners have passed, for the poor themselves take their minds [off it]. [For] they think:

RASHI

מדבריהם — מפני דרכי שלום. **ונפקא מינה** — מדרבי יוסי, הא אתא לאשמועינן דהחמירו החכמים בתקנתן כגזל גמור להוציאו בדיינין. וכיון דמדאורייתא לית ליה זכייה — נמצא אביו גוזל את העניים. **אלא אמר אביי** — רבי יוסי נמי כתנא דידן סבירא ליה, דקטן לית ליה זכייה. וגבי קטן היינו טעם, דכיון דיש לו לפועל זה בנים ואשה — עניים עצמן מייאשי מלקט שלה, לפיכך עשאוה כשדה שהלכו בו הנמושות, דתנן (פאה פרק ח׳ משנה א׳): מאימתי כל אדם מותרין בלקט — משילכו בו הנמושות, לקוטי בתר לקוטי. דמההיא שעתא מסחו עניים דעתייהו מיניה, והנה נמי מסחו דעתייהו כו׳.

NOTES

גֶּזֶל גָּמוּר מִדִּבְרֵיהֶן **Outright robbery by Rabbinic enactment.** Rabbi Yose's statement has to be interpreted this way, since Rabbi Yose spoke of "outright robbery" from an imbecile, and such a person obviously has no ownership rights according to Torah law (*Torat Ḥayyim, Pnei Yehoshua*).

gleanings would still be in order. Some commentators answer: The Sages granted minors the power to acquire ownerless objects, in order to avoid quarrels. But the gleanings of fields, while technically ownerless, really belong to the poor, and the Sages would not themselves have instituted a law that might deprive the poor of their rights (*Tosafot, Rosh* and others).

HALAKHAH

מְצִיאַת חֵרֵשׁ, שׁוֹטֶה וְקָטָן **Objects found by a deaf-mute, an imbecile, or a minor.** "Objects found by a deaf-mute, an imbecile, or a minor do not belong to them by Torah law. But the Sages ordained that they may keep these objects, in the interests of peace, and one who takes by force lost objects found by a deaf-mute, an imbecile, or a minor violates a Rabbinic prohibition against robbery. But the object seized cannot be reclaimed in court," following the view of the first Tanna in the Mishnah in *Gittin*. (*Shulḥan Arukh, Ḥoshen Mishpat* 270:1.)

TRANSLATION AND COMMENTARY

can acquire property on his father's behalf, is consistent with his ruling in favor of Rabbi Yose's opinion in the Baraita about gleaning. Nevertheless, the objection to Rabbi Yose's own opinion about the laws of gleaning remains: How can Rabbi Yose rule that the son of a tenant-farmer is permitted to glean the field that his father is harvesting, when the son is not acquiring for himself but for his (disqualified) father? In reply to this question **Abaye said**: It is because this field **is treated like a field through which the last of the gleaners,** the elderly, slow gleaners who walk so slowly that they leave hardly anything behind, have already **passed**. Such a field may thereafter be gleaned by everybody, even by wealthy people, because the poor have lost interest in gleaning there. Similarly in the case of the tenant-farmer and his son, we may assume that **the poor themselves have dismissed** this field **from their minds** and lost interest in it. **For they** no doubt **think** to themselves: "**The sons of this tenant-farmer are going to glean** this field, and there will be nothing left for us to glean anyway." Therefore, since the poor have no intention of gleaning there, anyone, including the son of the tenant-farmer acting as his father's agent, can take the gleanings.

אָמַר לֵיהּ רַב אַדָּא בַּר מַתָּנָה [1]**Rav Adda bar Mattanah said to Abaye**: According to your argument, because the other poor people assume that the tenant-farmer's sons are gleaning in this field, they despair of gleaning there themselves the ears of corn to which they are entitled. But **is it permitted for a person to place a lion crouching** threateningly **in his field, so that poor people will see it and run away**? Here too the tenant-farmer is using his children as a threat, to frighten the poor from exercising their rights to the gleanings. But who gave the tenant-farmer's children exclusive rights to these gleanings at the expense of other poor people? Surely such a practice cannot be permitted!

אֶלָּא אָמַר רָבָא [2]**Rather, Rava said,** Abaye's explanation must be rejected and a different explanation given for Rabbi Yose's ruling: [12B] The minor son of an agricultural worker (and even of a tenant-farmer) may glean behind his father because the Sages **made** a special enactment here that **a person who does not** by right **acquire** gleanings — namely, the tenant-farmer's son — should in this case be treated **like a** person **who does** by right **acquire** the gleanings. [3]**What is the reason** that the Sages made this special enactment? [4]**It** is because this arrangement **is advantageous to the poor themselves, so that** they themselves will benefit **when others hire them** as agricultural workers, in that **their children will be able to glean after them**. This concludes the discussion of the objections to Shmuel's interpretation and Rabbi Yose's ruling.

"בְּרֵיהּ דְּהַיאַךְ מְלַקְטֵי לֵיהּ". [1]אֲמַר לֵיהּ רַב אַדָּא בַּר מַתָּנָה לְאַבַּיֵי: וְכִי מוּתָּר לְאָדָם לְהַרְבִּיץ אֲרִי בְּתוֹךְ שָׂדֵהוּ כְּדֵי שֶׁיִּרְאוּ עֲנִיִּים וְיִבְרְחוּ? [2]אֶלָּא אֲמַר רָבָא: [12B] עָשׂוּ שֶׁאֵינוֹ זוֹכֶה כְּזוֹכֶה. [3]מַאי טַעְמָא? [4]עֲנִיִּים גּוּפַיְיהוּ נִיחָא לְהוּ, כִּי הֵיכִי דְּכִי אָגְרוּ לְדִידְהוּ, נִלְקוֹט בְּנַיְיהוּ בַּתְרַיְיהוּ.

LITERAL TRANSLATION

"The sons of this [tenant-farmer] are gleaning it." [1]Rav Adda bar Mattanah said to Abaye: But is it permitted for a person to make a lion crouch in his field so that poor people will see [it] and run away?

[2]Rather, Rava said: [12B] They made [a person] who does not acquire like one who does acquire. [3]What is the reason? [4]It is advantageous to the poor themselves, so that when [others] hire them, their children will [be able to] glean after them.

RASHI

עשו את שאינו זוכה כזוכה — אף על פי שאין לקטן זכייה במקום אחר — כאן עשאוהו כזוכה. **מאי טעמא עניים גופייהו ניחא להו** — בהאי תקנתא, דכי אגרו להו לדידהו כו'.

NOTES

לְהַרְבִּיץ אֲרִי בְּתוֹךְ שָׂדֵהוּ To make a lion crouch in his field. If the owner of a field actively prevents the poor from gleaning there, he is violating both a positive and a negative Torah commandment. "Making a lion crouch in the field" is an indirect way of preventing the poor from gleaning. Although the property-owner does nothing directly, he creates a situation in which the poor cannot in fact glean in his field. Therefore, while he is not violating the negative commandment, he is nevertheless violating the positive commandment. (See *Minḥat Ḥinnukh*.)

עָשׂוּ אֶת שֶׁאֵינוֹ זוֹכֶה כְּזוֹכֶה They made a person who does not acquire like one who does acquire. The translation and explanation in the commentary here follows the interpretation of the text given by *Rashi*. Other commentators explain that the Sages decreed that poor people who have not yet acquired fallen gleanings should be considered as if they have already acquired them, and are in a position to give them away. They are then considered to have given them away willingly, so that on other occasions their children will be able to glean for them (*Tosefot HaRosh*).

עָשׂוּ אֶת שֶׁאֵינוֹ זוֹכֶה כְּזוֹכֶה They made a person who does not acquire like one who does acquire. In other words,

HALAKHAH

מַרְבִּיץ אֲרִי בְּשָׂדֵהוּ Causing a lion to crouch in one's field. "It is forbidden to place a lion crouching in one's field to frighten the poor away and thereby prevent them from gleaning those parts of the field to which they are entitled (e.g., *lekket, pe'ah*)." (*Rambam, Sefer Zeraim, Hilkhot Mattenot Aniyyim* 4:13.)

TRANSLATION AND COMMENTARY

וּפְלִיגָא דְּרַבִּי חִיָּיא בַּר אַבָּא [1]The Gemara now notes: **And this** interpretation of Shmuel's, that the reason why the Mishnah awards objects found by a minor to his father is because a minor cannot acquire property on his own behalf, **differs from the view of Rabbi Ḥiyya bar Abba. For Rabbi Ḥiyya bar Abba said in the name of Rabbi Yoḥanan**: [2]The expression "**adult**" mentioned in our Mishnah **does not** necessarily **mean a real adult**, who has reached majority, **and** the expression "**minor**" mentioned in our Mishnah **does not** necessarily **mean a real minor**, who has not reached majority. [3]**Rather,** the Mishnah should instead be interpreted as follows: **An adult child who is still supported financially by his father is** considered to be still **a minor** for the purpose of acquiring ownerless objects. Since his father supports him, the father is permitted to keep the lost objects found by his son so as to avoid ill-feeling between them. [4]But **a minor who is not supported financially by his father** and who has established his own financial independence, **is** considered to be **an adult**, in the context of this Mishnah, and hence he is permitted to keep whatever lost objects he finds.

[1]וּפְלִיגָא דְּרַבִּי חִיָּיא בַּר אַבָּא, דְּאָמַר רַבִּי חִיָּיא בַּר אַבָּא אָמַר רַבִּי יוֹחָנָן: [2]לֹא "גָּדוֹל" גָּדוֹל מַמָּשׁ, וְלֹא "קָטָן" קָטָן מַמָּשׁ. [3]אֶלָּא, גָּדוֹל וְסָמוּךְ עַל שֻׁלְחַן אָבִיו — זֶהוּ קָטָן; [4]קָטָן וְאֵינוֹ סָמוּךְ עַל שֻׁלְחַן אָבִיו — זֶהוּ גָּדוֹל.

[5]"מְצִיאַת עַבְדּוֹ וְשִׁפְחָתוֹ הָעִבְרִים — הֲרֵי הוּא שֶׁל עַצְמָן". [6]אַמַּאי? לֹא יְהֵא אֶלָּא פּוֹעֵל. [7]וְתַנְיָא: "מְצִיאַת פּוֹעֵל לְעַצְמוֹ. [8]בַּמֶּה דְּבָרִים אֲמוּרִים? בִּזְמַן שֶׁאָמַר לוֹ: [9]'נַכֵּשׁ עִמִּי הַיּוֹם', 'עֲדוֹר עִמִּי הַיּוֹם'.

LITERAL TRANSLATION

[1]And this differs from [the view of] Rabbi Ḥiyya bar Abba, for Rabbi Ḥiyya bar Abba said in the name of Rabbi Yoḥanan: [2]An "adult" is not really an adult, and a "minor" is not really a minor. [3]Rather, an adult who relies on his father's table — this is a minor; [4]a minor who does not rely on his father's table — this is an adult.

[5]"An object found by one's Jewish manservant or maidservant — these belong to them." [6]Why? Let him not be [considered] other than a [hired] worker. [7]And it has been taught: "Whatever is found by a worker is his. When do these words apply? [8]When [the employer] said to him: [9]'Weed for me today,' [or:] 'Hoe for me today.'

RASHI

ופליגא – דשמואל, דפירש טעמא דמתניתין משום דלית ליה זכייה. אדרבי חייא בר אבא – דאמר אף גדול שיש לו זכייה, אם סמוך הוא על שולחן אביו – מציאתו לאביו משום איבה. אבל אינו סמוך על שולחן אביו, אפילו הוא קטן – מציאתו שלו. לא יהא אלא פועל – לא יהא עבדו אלא שכיר בעלמא, תניא דמציאתו לבעל הבית בזמן שלא פירש לו לאיזו מלאכה שכרו. ועבד זה כשקנאו רבו – לסתם מלאכה קנאו.

מְצִיאַת עַבְדּוֹ [5]The Gemara now considers the next clause in the Mishnah: We have learned in our Mishnah: "**An object found by** a man's **Jewish manservant or maidservant — these belong to them**." [6]The Gemara asks: **Why** should this be so? **Ought not** the Jewish manservant to **be** considered as no different from **a** hired **worker,** and should not the employer still be entitled to the objects he finds? [7]**And it has been taught** in a Baraita (above, 10a): "**Whatever is found by a worker belongs to him**, and not to the employer for whom he is working at the time. [8]**When,** and under what circumstances, **does this** ruling **apply? When the employer said to** the worker: [9]'Perform a specific type of work for me' — for example, '**Weed for me today**,' or '**Hoe for**

NOTES

what we have here is a Rabbinic ordinance granting the capacity to acquire to someone who, legally speaking, does not have it, thus allowing him to acquire things and transfer them to others. In such a case, the Sages decide (according to various considerations of public utility) to regard someone without the power to acquire as though he did have that power in full. Since this is a specific, restricted regulation, no proof can be derived from it regarding the Halakhah in general on this subject.

לֹא גָּדוֹל מַמָּשׁ Not really an adult. Rabbi Yoḥanan did not interpret the word גָּדוֹל — "adult" — literally, because such an intepretation is open to the following objection: Why did the Mishnah need to teach us that lost objects found by adults belong to them? Was there any reason to think otherwise? How long could the law allow a father the right to acquire objects found by (and rightfully belonging to) his adult chldren? Instead, the Mishnah must have had something else in mind when it spoke of "adults," and hence Rabbi Yoḥanan's unusual interpretation of this word here (*Torat Ḥayyim*).

קָטָן וְאֵינוֹ סָמוּךְ A minor who does not rely. This refers only to a man's minor son; for a father is entitled by Torah law to keep objects which his minor daughters find, even if he is not supporting them (*Ramban, Ran*).

HALAKHAH

מְצִיאַת פּוֹעֵל An object found by a worker. "A worker who has been hired by an employer to work for him without the particular type of work having been specified by the employer (and certainly a worker who has been hired to perform a specific type of work) may keep the ownerless objects that he finds during his work period. But if he was hired specifically to collect ownerless objects on behalf of his employer, the objects he finds belong to his employer." (*Shulḥan Arukh, Ḥoshen Mishpat* 270:3.)

[1]אֲבָל אָמַר לוֹ: ׳עֲשֵׂה עִמִּי מְלָאכָה הַיּוֹם׳, מְצִיאָתוֹ לְבַעַל הַבַּיִת״!

[2]אָמַר רַבִּי חִיָּיא בַּר אַבָּא אָמַר רַבִּי יוֹחָנָן: הָכָא בְּעֶבֶד נוֹקֵב מַרְגָּלִיּוֹת עָסְקִינַן, [3]שֶׁאֵין רַבּוֹ רוֹצֶה לְשַׁנּוֹתוֹ לִמְלָאכָה אַחֶרֶת.

[4]רָבָא אָמַר: בְּמַגְבִּיהַּ מְצִיאָה עִם מְלַאכְתּוֹ עָסְקִינַן.

[5]רַב פַּפָּא אָמַר: כְּגוֹן שֶׁשְּׂכָרוֹ לְלַקֵּט מְצִיאוֹת.

[6]וְהֵיכִי דָּמֵי?

LITERAL TRANSLATION

[1]But if he said to him: Work for me today, whatever he finds [belongs] to the employer!"

[2]Rabbi Ḥiyya bar Abba said in the name of Rabbi Yoḥanan: Here we are dealing with a manservant who pierces holes in pearls, [3]so that his master does not want to change him over to another [type of] work.

[4]Rava said: We are dealing with [a manservant] who lifts up a found object in [the course of] his work.

[5]Rav Pappa said: For example, where he hired him to collect found objects.

[6]And how is this to be visualized (lit., "what is it like")?

TRANSLATION AND COMMENTARY

me today. In such a case an object found by the worker during the time he is employed belongs to the worker. [1]**But if** the employer did not hire the worker to perform a specific type of work, and instead **he said to him: 'Work for me today,'** without specifying what particular type of work was involved, **whatever** the worker **finds belongs to the employer!**" Now, since a manservant is required to do whatever work his master tells him to do, he should be considered in this respect no different from a worker hired to perform unspecified tasks all day. Why, then, is the master not entitled to keep the objects that the servant finds?

אָמַר רַבִּי חִיָּיא בַּר אַבָּא [2]The Gemara now offers three possible explanations: **Rabbi Ḥiyya bar Abba said in the name of Rabbi Yoḥanan: Here** in our Mishnah, which says that a Jewish manservant may keep objects that he finds, **we are dealing with a manservant** whose work for his master consists of **piercing pearls.** [3]Because his work is so highly skilled and profitable, **his master does not want to change him over to another type of work**. Such a manservant has the same status as a worker who was hired to perform a specific type of work. He is not, in fact, permitted to take the time to pick up ownerless objects, and he will have to recompense his master for the lost time. But if he does so, the object belongs to him and not to his master.

רָבָא אָמַר [4]**Rava** offered a second explanation of the circumstances in our Mishnah and **said: We are dealing** in our Mishnah **with a manservant who picked up a found object in the course of his work**. Since the manservant is able to continue working while he picks up the object and is not forced to interrupt his work in order to do so, his master incurs no loss thereby, and hence the manservant is permitted to keep the object as his own.

רַב פַּפָּא אָמַר [5]**Rav Pappa** provided a third explanation by redefining and severely limiting the circumstances in which the Baraita quoted above grants an employer the right to ownerless objects found by his hired worker. He **said** that an employer is permitted to keep ownerless objects found by his employee **where he hired** the worker specifically **to collect ownerless objects** on his behalf. In other situations, says Rav Pappa, the hired worker is entitled to keep objects that he finds while working for his employer.

וְהֵיכִי דָּמֵי [6]The Gemara asks: **How can we visualize a case** in which a worker would be hired specifically to collect ownerless objects?

RASHI

שאין רבו רוצה לשנותו – הלכך לא ניחא ליה שיגביה לו מציאה, דמציאה מעולה בדמיה משכר ביטול מלאכתו לא שכיחא. הלכך, אי אתרמי ואשכח – שלו הוא, וישלם לרבו שכר ביטולו. **עם מלאכתו** – שלא ביטל כלום, הלכך לעצמו. **רב פפא אמר** – הא דתניא פועל מציאתו לבעל הבית. **ששכרו ללקט מציאות** – הרבה. **והיכי דמי** – דאתרמי.

NOTES

בְּמַגְבִּיהַּ עִם מְלַאכְתּוֹ We are dealing with a manservant who lifts up a found object in the course of his work. Our commentary follows *Rashi,* who interprets this phrase as referring to our Mishnah. Other commentators interpret it as referring to the Baraita: An employer may keep ownerless objects found by his employee, if the objects were found while he was working, since picking them up interfered with his work. But if the worker was not actually working at the time, so that picking up the object caused him no loss of time, the worker may keep it. Thus, our Mishnah, which rules that a Jewish manservant may keep the objects he finds, must also be referring to a case where the servant was not actually working at the time he found the object.

BACKGROUND

דְּאַקְפֵי אַגְמָא בְּכְווֹרֵי **Where a field was flooded with fish.** This method of fishing was common in Babylonia. Since the country was very flat, the land was irrigated from early antiquity by large and small canals leading from the rivers. Since the rivers of Babylonia were full of fish, one way of catching them was to flood an area with river or lake water and then drain it, narrowing the outlets of the water so that the fish could not escape.

CONCEPTS

שְׁתֵּי שְׂעָרוֹת **Two pubic hairs.** According to the Halakhah, the transition from the status of minor to that of adult depends on sexual maturity. Upon reaching sexual maturity a boy or a girl is considered an adult in almost every respect. Naturally, the process of maturing is gradual, and the stages have various external signs. In most matters the Halakhah holds that a young person with two pubic hairs of a certain length is an adult. There is also an assumption that a girl who is twelve years and one day old and a boy who is thirteen years and one day old have reached physical maturity (hence the custom of celebrating a Bar or Bat Mitzvah when a child reaches this age). However, where a matter of Halakhic importance is involved, the child's body must be examined to determine whether these signs have appeared.

TERMINOLOGY

וְלָאו אִיתּוֹתַב רֵישׁ לָקִישׁ **But has not Resh Lakish already been refuted?** When a serious objection is made against the viewpoint of a Sage (תְּיוּבְתָּא) on a certain issue, and he cannot find a response, in almost every instance the approach taken by that Sage on that issue is removed entirely from the Halakhah. The question therefore arises here: since Resh Lakish's approach has already been rejected in tractate *Kiddushin*, where the main discussion of this subject is to

LITERAL TRANSLATION

[1]Where a field was flooded with fish.

[2]This [Jewish] maidservant — how is this to be visualized? [3]If she has grown two [pubic] hairs, what does she need with him? [4]And if she has not grown two [pubic] hairs — if the father is [alive, the found object] belongs to the father, [5]and if the father is not [alive], she should have gone [free] upon the death of the father! [6]For Resh Lakish said: A Jewish maidservant acquires herself from her master's possession upon the death of her father, [7]by means of a *kal vaḥomer* inference.

[8]But has not Resh Lakish [already] been refuted?

[9]Let us say that from this [Mishnah] too there can be an objection!

[1]דְּאַקְפֵי אַגְמָא בְּכְווֹרֵי.

[2]הַאי שִׁפְחָה — הֵיכִי דָּמֵי? [3]אִי דְּאַיְיתֵי שְׁתֵּי שְׂעָרוֹת, מַאי בָּעֲיָא גַּבֵּיהּ? [4]וְאִי דְּלָא אַיְיתֵי שְׁתֵּי שְׂעָרוֹת — אִי אִיתֵיהּ לְאָב, דַּאֲבוּהּ הָוְיָא. [5]וְאִי דְּלֵיתֵיהּ לְאָב, תֵּיפּוֹק בְּמִיתַת הָאָב! [6]דְּאָמַר רֵישׁ לָקִישׁ: אָמָה הָעִבְרִיָּה קוֹנָה עַצְמָהּ בְּמִיתַת הָאָב מֵרְשׁוּת הָאָדוֹן, [7]מִקַּל וָחוֹמֶר!

[8]וְלָאו אִיתּוֹתַב רֵישׁ לָקִישׁ?

[9]נֵימָא מֵהַאי נַמִי תֶּיהֱוֵי תְּיוּבְתָּא!

TRANSLATION AND COMMENTARY

דְּאַקְפֵי אַגְמָא בְּכְווֹרֵי [1]The Gemara answers: Such a situation could arise **where** an overflowing river or lake **flooded a field with fish**, and after the waters receded the owner of the field hired workers to collect the fish remaining in the field. Only under such circumstances is the owner of the field entitled to the fish collected by his workers.

הַאי שִׁפְחָה הֵיכִי דָּמֵי [2]The Gemara now considers another aspect of the same clause in the Mishnah: The Mishnah stated that a Jewish maidservant may keep the ownerless objects that she finds. Accordingly, the Gemara asks: **This** Jewish **maidservant** who was mentioned in the Mishnah — **how do we visualize such a case?** [3]**If she has grown two** pubic **hairs**, the accepted sign of physical maturity, at which point a girl is no longer considered a minor, **what is she doing** remaining **with** her master? For once a Jewish maidservant reaches puberty, she automatically goes free! [4]**And if**, on the other hand, **she has not** yet **grown two pubic hairs**, she is still a minor, and **if her father is** alive, any object found by her **belongs to her father**, since a father is entitled to any income earned by his daughters before they reach majority, [5]**and if the father is not** alive, **she should** already **have gone free upon the death of** her **father** while she was still a minor, in accordance with the following ruling of Resh Lakish! [6]**For Resh Lakish said: A Jewish maidservant** automatically **acquires her** freedom **from her master's possession on the death of her father**, regardless of her age or the number of years she has served, [7]and this ruling may be learned **by means of a *kal vaḥomer* inference**. Namely: If signs of puberty in a girl over the age of twelve, which do not release the girl from her father's authority, nevertheless do release her from her master's possession, then the death of her father, which *does* release her from her father's authority and that of his heirs, should certainly release her from her master's possession! Thus, if the girl's father is not alive, how can she still be a maidservant?

וְלָאו אִיתּוֹתַב רֵישׁ לָקִישׁ [8]The Gemara now objects: **But has not Resh Lakish**'s view **already been refuted** and rejected? We have surely proved elsewhere (*Kiddushin* 16b) that his argument is flawed?

נֵימָא מֵהַאי נַמִי תֶּיהֱוֵי תְּיוּבְתָּא [9]The Gemara continues: **Let us say** at all events **that from this Mishnah too an objection can be** brought against the opinion of Resh Lakish!

RASHI

דאקפי אגמא בכוורי — שצף הנהר חוץ לגדותיו, וצפו הדגים שם, וכשיבשו המים היוצאים נמצאו שם דגים הרבה. דאקפי — תרגום של הציף, כדמתרגמינן "ויצף הברזל" — "וקפא ברזלא" (מלכים ב, ו). **מאי בעיא גביה** — הא תניא: יוצאה בסימנין. **דאבוה הויא** — מציאתה, דהא קטנה היא. **ואי דליתיה לאב** — מאי בעיא גבי האדון? תיפוק מיניה במיתת האב! **מקל וחומר** — בפרק קמא דקדושין (טז,א): מה סימנין שאין מוציאין מרשות האב — מוציאין מרשות האדון, כדילפינן: "ויצאה חנם" — אלו ימי בגרות, "אין כסף" — אלו ימי נערות. מיתת האב, שמוציאה מרשות האב, שאינו מוריש לבניו מה שזכתה לו תורה בבתו שיהא מעשה ידיה לאחין, כדילפינן (כתובות מג,א) "והתנחלתם אותם לבניכם" ולא בנותיכם לבניכם — אינו דין שמוציאה מרשות האדון? **ולאו איתותב רבי שמעון בן לקיש** — בקדושין (שם).

HALAKHAH

אָמָה הָעִבְרִיָּה **A Jewish maidservant.** "When a Jewish maidservant develops signs of puberty, she goes free without having to pay her master any money." (*Rambam, Sefer Kinyan, Hilkhot Avadim* 4:5.)

TRANSLATION AND COMMENTARY

לֹא לְעוֹלָם דְּאִיתֵיהּ לָאָב [1]The Gemara answers: No! **Our Mishnah** cannot serve that purpose, because **in fact it can be** explained as referring to a **case where the** maidservant's **father is** alive, and ownerless objects that she finds do indeed belong to him.

וּמַאי [2]**And what** then **is** the meaning of the words in our Mishnah: **"These objects belong to them,"** which we have until now understood as meaning that the maidservant herself acquires ownerless objects that she finds, just like the manservant, the adult child, and the divorced wife? According to the interpretation just suggested, objects that the maidservant finds belong to her father, not to herself!

לְאַפּוּקֵי [3]The Gemara answers that this statement in our Mishnah comes **to exclude** the possibility that ownerless objects found by a maidservant belong to **her master**. The Mishnah's purpose is to say that Jewish servants do not automatically acquire for their masters. The Mishnah does not focus on who actually does acquire the ownerless objects. In most cases it would be the finder himself, but in the case of a Jewish maidservant, who is a minor, it would be her father. Hence this Mishnah poses no problem, even according to Resh Lakish.

מְצִיאַת אִשְׁתּוֹ [4]The Gemara proceeds to analyze the next clause of our Mishnah: **"An object found by** a man's **wife** after he has divorced her belongs to her." [5]Surely **if he has divorced her, it is obvious** that whatever she finds belongs to her; for once she is divorced, what authority does her husband have over her?

הָכָא בְּמַאי עָסְקִינַן [6]The Gemara answers: **With what** situation **are we dealing here?** [7]**With** a case of **a woman who is "divorced and yet not divorced,"** i.e., with a case where it is uncertain whether the woman's divorce was valid or not, and thus the divorce process is as yet incomplete. [8]**For Rabbi Zera said in the name of Shmuel: Wherever the Sages** have **said that a woman is "divorced and yet not divorced,"** as explained above, **her husband is still obligated to provide her food**. Our Mishnah, therefore, comes to teach us that even where it is uncertain whether the divorce is valid, and where she is still dependent financially on her ex-husband, nevertheless the previous arrangement whereby ownerless property found by the wife belongs to the husband as a counterpart to the husband's obligation to maintain her, is at an end.

טַעְמָא מַאי אֲמוּר רַבָּנַן [9]The Gemara now goes on to explain why this is so: Now, **what is the reason why**

[1]לָא! לְעוֹלָם דְּאִיתֵיהּ לָאָב.
[2]וּמַאי ״הֲרֵי הֵן שֶׁלָּהֶן״?
[3]לְאַפּוּקֵי דְּרַבָּה.
[4]״מְצִיאַת אִשְׁתּוֹ״. [5]גֵּירְשָׁהּ, פְּשִׁיטָא!
[6]הָכָא בְּמַאי עָסְקִינַן?
[7]בִּמְגוֹרֶשֶׁת וְאֵינָהּ מְגוֹרֶשֶׁת.
[8]דְּאָמַר רַבִּי זֵירָא אָמַר שְׁמוּאֵל: כָּל מָקוֹם שֶׁאָמְרוּ חֲכָמִים מְגוֹרֶשֶׁת וְאֵינָהּ מְגוֹרֶשֶׁת, בַּעְלָהּ חַיָּיב בִּמְזוֹנוֹתֶיהָ.
[9]טַעְמָא מַאי אֲמוּר רַבָּנַן

LITERAL TRANSLATION

[1]No! In fact [our Mishnah may be referring to a case] where the father is [alive].

[2]And what is [the meaning of:] "These [objects] belong to them"?

[3]To exclude her master.

[4]"An object found by his wife."

[5][If] he has divorced her, it is obvious!

[6]With what are we dealing here? [7]With a woman who is divorced and [yet] not divorced.

[8]For Rabbi Zera said in the name of Shmuel: Wherever the Sages have said that a woman is divorced and [yet] not divorced, her husband is [still] obligated [to provide] her food.

[9]What is the reason why the Rabbis said

RASHI

לאפוקי דרבה — לאפוקי שאינו של רבה אלא של אביה. וקרי ליה שלהן — משום דאב מינה קזכי. **במגורשת ואינה מגורשת** — כגון זרק לה גיטה, ספק קרוב לה ספק קרוב לו ברשות הרבים. **חייב במזונותיה** — ומשום הכי אצטריך לאשמועינן דמציאתה שלה. דטעמא מאי אמור רבנן מציאת האשה כו׳.

be found, what is the point of adding another objection to refute an approach that has been refuted?

In fact, such a situation does not usually prevent the posing of additional difficulties, justified by the phrase נֵימָא מֵהָאי נַמִי תֶּיהֱוֵי תְּיוּבְתָּא — "let us say that there can also be a refutation from this." There are both general and practical reasons for presenting additional proofs. In principle, since discussion in the Talmud is not primarily intended to reach Halakhic conclusions or to refute specific arguments, but rather to clarify the truth, any additional refutation does have meaning with regard to discovering the truth. It may also have a certain amount of practical significance. It is possible that Sages in later generations will find a weak point in the first refutation and reinstate the refuted argument. Therefore it is important that there be another refutation as well, despite the fact that the first one seems to be sufficient.

NOTES

לְאַפּוּקֵי דְּרַבָּה **To exclude her master**. Our translation of רַבָּה as "her master" follows *Rashi*'s commentary. Other commentators read the word as רָבָא and interpret the phrase to mean: "to the exclusion of Rava's view"; for Rava holds elsewhere (*Kiddushin* 16a) that a Jewish servant is considered the property of his or her master. But from our Mishnah it would seem that this is not the case, since it is the father of the maidservant, rather than her master, who keeps the ownerless objects she finds. (*Rabbenu Ḥananel* and others.)

מְגוֹרֶשֶׁת וְאֵינָהּ מְגוֹרֶשֶׁת **A woman who is divorced and yet not divorced**. The Jerusalem Talmud explains that even someone who has validly divorced his wife must still continue to maintain her until he finishes paying her ketubah, and describes our Mishnah as dealing with such a case. The Rishonim differ as to whether the Jerusalem Talmud's explanation conforms to the discussion here in the Babylonia Talmud.

HALAKHAH

מְגוֹרֶשֶׁת וְאֵינָהּ מְגוֹרֶשֶׁת **A woman who is divorced and yet not divorced**. "In any case where it is uncertain whether or not a divorce was valid, the husband must maintain his wife until a valid divorce between them has been effected." (*Shulḥan Arukh, Even HaEzer* 93:2.)

TRANSLATION AND COMMENTARY

the Rabbis said that an object found by a wife belongs to her husband? [1]**So that** her husband **may not show her hostility**. For if the wife were permitted to keep ownerless objects that she finds, her husband could object that he bears the burden of maintaining her, yet she may keep whatever she finds! For this reason, the Rabbis instituted that such property should belong to the husband. [2]But **here, let there be serious hostility** between them, so that the husband will completely sever his relationship with her and grant her a fully valid divorce. Thus, since we do not care if there is ill-feeling between husband and wife in this case, any objects found by the wife during the period after the doubtfully valid bill of divorce was given belong to her.

MISHNAH מָצָא שְׁטָרֵי חוֹב [3]If a person **finds promissory notes** [4]containing a clause mortgaging the borrower's landed **property as security for the loan,** i.e., if the borrower stipulates in the promissory note that his landed property may be used for collection of the debt, [5]the finder **should not return** such promissory notes to the lender, **because the court may enforce payment** against innocent third parties **by means of them**. The court may even authorize the lender to seize landed property sold by the borrower after the date of the loan, if the borrower has no other resources to repay the loan. Thus, the interests of a third party, the purchaser of the land, may be affected by the actions of the finder, and he may not, therefore, return the notes. [6]But **if the** promissory notes **do not contain a clause mortgaging the borrower's landed property as security for the loan,** [7]the finder **should return them** to the lender, **because the court cannot** use them to **enforce payment** from a third party who may have bought landed property from the debtor after the date of the loan, since the documents did not, in fact, establish a lien on the property. [8]These are **the words of Rabbi Meir**. [9]**But the Sages say: In both cases, he should not return** the notes to the lender, **because the court may enforce payment by means of them** from a third party, even in the second case, by virtue of an implied lien, as the Gemara will explain.

מְצִיאַת אִשָּׁה לְבַעְלָהּ? [1]כִּי הֵיכִי דְּלָא תֶּיהֱוֵי לָהּ אֵיבָה; [2]הָכָא, אִית לָהּ אֵיבָה וְאֵיבָה!

משנה [3]מָצָא שְׁטָרֵי חוֹב, [4]אִם יֵשׁ בָּהֶן אַחֲרָיוּת נְכָסִים, [5]לֹא יַחֲזִיר, שֶׁבֵּית דִּין נִפְרָעִין מֵהֶן. [6]אֵין בָּהֶן אַחֲרָיוּת נְכָסִים, [7]יַחֲזִיר, שֶׁאֵין בֵּית דִּין נִפְרָעִין מֵהֶן. [8]דִּבְרֵי רַבִּי מֵאִיר. [9]וַחֲכָמִים אוֹמְרִים: בֵּין כָּךְ וּבֵין כָּךְ לֹא יַחֲזִיר, מִפְּנֵי שֶׁבֵּית דִּין נִפְרָעִין מֵהֶן.

LITERAL TRANSLATION

that an object found by a wife [belongs] to her husband? [1]So that she will not have hostility; [2]here, let there be (lit., "she has") serious hostility (lit., "hostility and hostility")!

MISHNAH [3][If] one found promissory notes, [4]if they contain [a clause] mortgaging [the borrower's landed] property [as security for the loan], [5]he should not return [them], because the court will enforce payment from them. [6][If] they do not contain [a clause] mortgaging [the borrower's landed] property [as security for the loan], [7]he should return them, because the court will not enforce payment from them. [8][These are] the words of Rabbi Meir. [9]But the Sages say: In both cases (lit. "between thus and between thus") he should not return [them], because the court will enforce payment from them.

RASHI

משנה אחריות נכסים – שעבוד קרקעות, שיגבה מהן. יחזיר ולא יחזיר – טעמא בגמרא מפרש.

NOTES

דְּלָא תֶּיהֱוֵי לָהּ אֵיבָה **So that she will not have hostility.** The hostility that might result if a wife could keep what she found and not give it to her husband is explained in two ways. On the one hand, the Sages explain that the husband has undertaken a number of financial obligations toward his wife (such as to support her, to care of her when she is sick, to redeem her if she is kidnapped, etc.), and these obligations are weighted in favor of the wife. To prevent them from causing hostility, the Sages placed a number of financial obligations upon the wife, and these actually parallel those of the husband.

Another explanation of this particular Halakhah is that if the wife had the right to keep what she found, her husband would have no way of accounting for the money in her possession, for she could always claim she had found it. Such a situation could give rise to suspicion and animosity between husband and wife.

HALAKHAH

הַמּוֹצֵא שְׁטָרֵי חוֹב **If a person finds promissory notes.** "A person who finds a lost promissory note may not return it to the lender, even if it has been certified by the court as authentic and even if the borrower admits that he owes the money, because we suspect that there may be a conspiracy between the lender and the borrower to defraud an innocent third party who may have purchased from the borrower property that was mortgaged as security for the loan. Only if the promissory note states explicitly that it does not mortgage the borrower's property in repayment of the loan, and only if the borrower admits that the note is genuine, may the finder return it to the lender." (*Shulḥan Arukh, Ḥoshen Mishpat* 65:6.)

גמרא [1]בְּמַאי עָסְקִינַן? [2]אִילֵימָא: כְּשֶׁחַיָּיב מוֹדֶה, כִּי יֵשׁ בָּהֶן אַחֲרָיוּת נְכָסִים, אַמַּאי לֹא יַחֲזִיר? [3]הָא מוֹדֶה! [4]וְאִי כְּשֶׁאֵין חַיָּיב מוֹדֶה, כִּי אֵין בָּהֶן אַחֲרָיוּת נְכָסִים, [5]אַמַּאי יַחֲזִיר? [6]נְהִי דְּלָא גָּבֵי מִמְּשַׁעְבְּדֵי, מִבְּנֵי חָרֵי מִגְבָּא גָּבֵי!

[7]לְעוֹלָם, כְּשֶׁחַיָּיב מוֹדֶה, וְהָכָא הַיְינוּ טַעְמָא: [8]דְּחָיְישִׁינַן שֶׁמָּא כָּתַב לִלְוֹת בְּנִיסָן, וְלֹא לָוָה עַד תִּשְׁרֵי, [9]וְאָתֵי לְמִטְרַף לָקוֹחוֹת שֶׁלֹּא כַּדִּין.

LITERAL TRANSLATION

GEMARA [1]With what are we dealing? [2]If you say: Where the debtor admits [his debt], [then even] if [the notes] contain [a clause] mortgaging [the debtor's landed] property [as security for the loan], why should [the finder] not return [them]? [3]Surely [the debtor] admits [his debt]! [4]And if [we are dealing with a situation] where the debtor does not admit [his debt], [then even] if [the notes] do not contain [a clause] mortgaging [the debtor's landed] property [as security for the loan], [5]why should [the finder] return them? [6]Granted that [the creditor] cannot collect from mortgaged property, he can certainly collect from free property!

[7]In fact, [we are dealing with a case] where the debtor admits [his debt], and here this is the reason [why the document should not be returned]: [8]For we suspect that perhaps [the borrower] wrote to borrow in Nisan, but he did not borrow until Tishri, [9]and [so the lender] may come to seize [property from] the buyers unlawfully.

TRANSLATION AND COMMENTARY

GEMARA בְּמַאי עָסְקִינַן [1]The Gemara begins its analysis of the Mishnah and asks: **With what** circumstances **are we dealing** in this case? [2]**If you say** that the Mishnah is referring to a case **where the debtor admits** that he wrote this promissory note and that it has not yet been repaid, **then even if the note contains a clause mortgaging the debtor's landed property as security for the loan, why should the finder not return it** to the creditor? [3]**Surely the debtor admits** that he has not yet repaid his debt, and any lien attached to his property is appropriate, and payment should indeed be enforced! [4]**And if we are dealing with a situation where the debtor does not admit his debt**, maintaining that he has repaid the loan, received the promissory note back from the creditor, and subsequently lost it himself, **then even if the note does not contain a clause mortgaging the debtor's landed property as security for the loan,** [5]**why should** the finder **return it** to the creditor? [6]**Granted that the creditor cannot** use this note to **collect** his debt **from** the debtor's **mortgaged property**, i.e., landed property which the debtor has sold to another person after the date of the loan and which the creditor can seize on the basis of a mortgage, **he can certainly** use this note to **collect** his debt **from** the debtor's **free property**, i.e., property which is at present in the debtor's possession, and which the creditor can seize without a mortgage. But the debtor, who claims he owes nothing, may be telling the truth, and if so, returning the note to the creditor could cause the debtor an unjustified loss even if the debtor's property was not mortgaged as security for the loan!

לְעוֹלָם כְּשֶׁחַיָּיב מוֹדֶה [7]The Gemara answers: **In fact, we are dealing with a case where the debtor admits his debt, and here this is the reason why the** promissory **note should not be returned** to the creditor: [8]**We suspect that** the borrower **may** perhaps **have written** in the promissory note **that he was borrowing** the money **in Nisan, but did not** actually **borrow until Tishri**. And between Nisan and Tishri, before he actually borrowed the money and mortgaged his property, he may have sold his (unmortgaged) property to innocent third parties. [9]**And thus the lender,** relying on the date in Nisan written in the document, **may come to seize property from the buyers unlawfully**. Such a seizure would be unlawful, because the loan only took place in Tishri, after the borrower's property had already been sold.

RASHI

גמרא כשחייב מודה – שהלוה מודה שהשטר אינו פרוע. **אמאי לא יחזיר** – אם לטרוף לקוחות בא – בדין הוא טורפן. **ממשעבדי** – ממקרקעי שמכר אחר כן.

NOTES

חָיְישִׁינַן שֶׁמָּא כָּתַב **We suspect that the borrower may have written the note....** At this point in the discussion, the Gemara has not yet considered the possibility, raised later (13b), that the lender and the borrower are engaged in a conspiracy to defraud the buyers. Our concern at the moment is that the borrower may have forgotten the exact date of the loan, and there is a risk that as a result the buyers may have their property taken away from them unfairly, without there having been any intention of defrauding them (*Ran, Rashba*).

וְלֹא לָוָה עַד תִּשְׁרֵי **But he did not borrow until Tishri.** The mortgage created by a loan is, in a certain sense, a conditional transfer of the mortgaged property. For if the debtor does not pay his debt, the creditor will receive the property in payment. The question under discussion here and on the following page is: What is the moment at which that transfer takes effect? The first assumption is that this conditional acquisition takes place the moment the money changes hands. Even if the promissory note was written and signed earlier, the lien, which, according to this view, is a

SAGES

רַב אַסִי Rav Assi. A Babylonian Amora of the first generation, Rav Assi was one of the Sages of the city of Hutzal, near Neharde'a. When Rav arrived in Babylonia he met Rav Kahana and Rav Assi, who were already eminent scholars. On several occasions Rav Assi disagrees with Rav, and Rav takes heed of his words and acts accordingly. Rav Assi reports several teachings in the name of Rav. He was also a colleague of Shmuel. Once, Rav, Shmuel, and Rav Assi met at a festive banquet, and each deferred to the other at the entrance. Rav's and Shmuel's students, in particular Rav Yehudah and Rav Huna, were also students of Rav Assi and transmit teachings in his name. This Rav Assi is often confused with Rabbi Assi, who was one of the leaders of the third generation of Amoraim in Eretz Israel and a colleague of Rabbi Ami.

TRANSLATION AND COMMENTARY

אִי הָכִי [1]The Gemara objects: **If** we suspect that the date on a promissory note may be earlier than the actual date of the loan mentioned in it, **we should likewise suspect all documents that come before us** of having been dated earlier than the loans they mention!

כָּל שְׁטָרֵי לָא רִיעֵי [2]The Gemara answers: The authenticity of **all** other **documents has not been weakened**. Since promissory notes generally remain the possession of the creditor, there is no reason to question their authenticity. But the authenticity of **these** promissory notes mentioned in our Mishnah **has been weakened**, because they were lost. The fact that they were lost leads us to suspect that the date on them may also not be correct. In other words, if they had been genuine, the creditor would have been more careful in looking after them.

אֶלָּא הָא דִּתְנַן [3]Again the Gemara objects: **But** how do we reconcile what we have said above about predated documents with **what we have learned** elsewhere in the following Mishnah (*Bava Batra* 10:3, 167b): "**A promissory note may be written for the borrower even though the lender is not with him.**" Since it is the borrower who enters into the obligations contained in the promissory note, only his presence is necessary at the time it is written. [4]But **how could** we give permission for such a promissory note to **be written *ab initio?*** If we are concerned about a document being predated, if we allow the promissory note to be drawn up in the lender's absence, [5]**we should be concerned in case the borrower may write** in the promissory note **that he is borrowing** the money **in Nisan,** when the note is drawn up, **but does not** actually **borrow** the money **until Tishri.** [6]**And** thus **the lender may come to seize property from the buyers** who bought the borrower's property between Nisan and Tishri **unlawfully!**

אָמַר רַב אַסִי [7]**Rav Assi said** in reply: [13A] The objection is well taken, and generally it is indeed improper to draw up a promissory note in the lender's absence, as this can lead to problems of predating. However, **that Mishnah** in *Bava Batra* **is dealing with** a special case where there is no danger of predating, and no reason to require the lender's presence when the loan is drawn up. It is a case where the borrower is drawing up "**deeds of transfer,**" a special kind of promissory note in which the borrower explicitly mortgages his property to the lender, as security for a loan, from the date written in the document, irrespective of the actual date on which the loan took place — indeed, regardless of whether the loan takes place at all. Such documents cannot lead to the unjust penalizing of future buyers of the borrower's property, **because** the borrower **obligated himself**, mortgaging his property from the date written in the document. The lender has the right to enforce the document and, if necessary, to reclaim from a third party who bought property from the borrower after the date of the "deed of transfer."

אִי הָכִי [8]The Gemara objects: **If** it is the case that ordinary promissory notes, other than deeds of transfer,

[1]אִי הָכִי, כָּל שְׁטָרֵי דְּאָתוּ לְקַמָּן נֵיחוּשׁ לְהוּ הָכִי! [2]כָּל שְׁטָרֵי לָא רִיעֵי; הָנֵי רִיעֵי. [3]אֶלָּא הָא דִּתְנַן: "כּוֹתְבִין שְׁטָר לְלֹוֶה אַף עַל פִּי שֶׁאֵין מַלְוֶה עִמּוֹ". [4]לְכַתְּחִילָּה הֵיכִי כָּתְבִינְהוּ? [5]נֵיחוּשׁ שֶׁמָּא כָּתַב לִלְוֹת בְּנִיסָן, וְלֹא לָוָה עַד תִּשְׁרֵי, [6]וְאָתֵי לְמִטְרַף לָקוֹחוֹת שֶׁלֹּא כַּדִּין! [7]אָמַר רַב אַסִי: [13A] בְּשִׁטְרֵי הַקְנָאָה, דְּהָא שַׁעְבֵּיד נַפְשֵׁיהּ. [8]אִי הָכִי, מַתְנִיתִין דְּקָתָנֵי: "אִם

LITERAL TRANSLATION

[1]If so, we should likewise suspect all documents that come before us!

[2]All documents are not weakened; these are weakened.

[3]But [regarding] what we learned [in a Mishnah]: "A promissory note may be written for the borrower even though the lender is not with him." [4]How could it be written *ab initio?* [5]We should be concerned in case [the borrower] wrote to borrow in Nisan, but he did not borrow until Tishri, [6]and [the lender] may come to seize [property from] the buyers unlawfully!

[7]Rav Assi said: [13A] [That Mishnah is dealing] with deeds of transfer, because he obligated himself.

[8]If so, [what about] our Mishnah which teaches: "If

RASHI

הני ריעי – הואיל ונפל – אתרע, דיש לומר: אם היה כשר – היה נזהר בו. בשטרי הקנאה – שמקנה לו נכסיו מהיום, בין ילוה בין לא ילוה יגבה מהן לאותו זמן מהיום. אי הכי – דבשטרי דלאו הקנאה לא עבידי דכתבי, אלא אם כן ראו הלואת המעות מתניתין דקתני כו'.

NOTES

matter of inner agreement on the part of the person who mortgages his property, begins only at the moment the money is actually lent. Therefore any agreement to sell property made by the borrower between the date on which the promissory note was written and the date when the lien actually came into force is a fully effective transfer of ownership, for no true lien existed at the time. As we shall see below, the solution of this problem, which is proved in various ways, is that the lien is actually in force from the moment the document is signed.

TRANSLATION AND COMMENTARY

are only drawn up in the presence of both borrower and lender, there is a problem in understanding **our Mishnah, which teaches: "If the promissory notes contain a clause mortgaging the borrower's landed property, the finder should not return them** to the lender." [1]**We have** already **established that** our Mishnah **is referring to a situation where the debtor admits his debt, and** the reason why the promissory note is not returned to the lender **is because we suspect that the borrower may have written** in the promissory note that he was **borrowing** the money **in Nisan, but did not** actually **borrow** it **until Tishri. And** thus **the lender may come to seize property from the buyers unlawfully.** [2]Now, asks the Gemara, if Rav Assi's restrictive explanation of the Mishnah in *Bava Batra* is correct, **why** in our Mishnah **should the finder not return** the promissory notes to the lender? [3]**We** need only **consider** the following possibilities: **If** the documents **we are dealing with** are **deeds of transfer, surely** the borrower **has obligated himself** to repay the lender from the date appearing in the document, and predating can never present a problem. [4]**And if we are dealing with** promissory **notes which are not deeds of transfer, there is** also **no reason for concern,** [5]**because you,** Rav Assi, **have said that** the Mishnah in *Bava Batra* does not apply to such documents, and hence **if the lender is not** present **together with** the borrower, **we do not write such documents.** We may therefore presume that the document was written in the presence of both parties and that the loan was given at that time. In either case, therefore, the date on the document is correct and there seems to be no good reason not to return the document to the lender.

אָמַר לָךְ רַב אַסִי [6]**Rav Assi could say to you:** Your argument is not correct: **Even though we do not** normally **write** promissory **notes which are not deeds of transfer when the lender is not** present **together with** the borrower, [7]we are still concerned about predating in **our Mishnah**, since it is dealing with a promissory note that was lost and later found by a third party. **Once the document fell** and was lost, **its** authenticity **was weakened, and** as a result **we suspect that** the note may be irregular in other ways as well. [8]It may **perhaps** be that **someone happened to write it** in the absence of the lender, with an inaccurate date, in violation of the law.

יֵשׁ בָּהֶן אַחֲרָיוּת נְכָסִים, לֹא יַחֲזִיר״. [1]וְאוֹקִימְנָא כְּשֶׁחַיָּיב מוֹדֶה, וּמִשּׁוּם שֶׁמָּא כָּתַב לִלְוֹת בְּנִיסָן, וְלֹא לָוָה עַד תִּשְׁרֵי, וְאָתֵי לְמִטְרַף לָקוֹחוֹת שֶׁלֹּא כַּדִּין, [2]אַמַּאי לֹא יַחֲזִיר? [3]נֶחֱזֵי: אִי בִּשְׁטַר הַקְנָאָה, הָא שַׁעְבֵּיד לֵיהּ נַפְשֵׁיהּ; [4]אִי בִּשְׁטָר דְּלָא הַקְנָאָה, לֵיכָּא לְמֵיחַשׁ, [5]דְּהָא אָמְרַתְּ: כִּי לֵיכָּא מַלְוֶה בַּהֲדֵיהּ, לָא כָּתְבִינַן.

[6]אָמַר לָךְ רַב אַסִי: אַף עַל גַּב דִּשְׁטָרֵי דְּלָאו הַקְנָאָה כִּי לֵיכָּא מַלְוֶה בַּהֲדֵיהּ לָא כָּתְבִינַן, [7]מַתְנִיתִין, כֵּיוָן דְּנָפַל, אִתְרַע לֵיהּ, [8]וְחָיְישִׁינַן דִּלְמָא אִקְרִי וּכְתוּב.

LITERAL TRANSLATION

[the promissory notes] contain [a clause] mortgaging [the borrower's landed] property, [the finder] should not return [them]." [1]And we have established [that] it [refers to a situation] where the debtor admits [his debt], and [it is] because [we suspect that] perhaps [the borrower] wrote to borrow in Nisan, but he did not borrow until Tishri, and [the lender] may come to seize [property from] the buyers unlawfully. [2]Why should [the finder] not return [them]? [3]Let us see: If [we are dealing] with a deed of transfer, surely he has obligated himself to him; [4]if [we are dealing] with a note which is not a [deed of] transfer, there is no [reason] for concern, [5]because you said: If the lender is not together with him, we do not write [such a document].

[6]Rav Assi could say to you: Even though [it is true] that we do not write notes that are not [deeds of] transfer when the lender is not [present] together with him, [7][in] our Mishnah, once [the document] fell, it became weakened, [8]and we suspect [that] perhaps [someone] happened to write [it].

RASHI

כי ליכא מלוה בהדיה – ונותן מעות כפניהם, לא כתבינן.

NOTES

כֵּיוָן דְּנָפַל אִתְרַע לֵיהּ Once the document fell, it became weakened. If this note had remained in the lender's possession, as it should have done, it would have permitted him to collect his debt without any problem (unless one of the parties involved produced proof that there was some flaw or fraud in the matter). But the note was lost, is now in someone else's possession, and is now the subject of a court case. Therefore, its reliability has been weakened. There is another aspect to this question: the assumption that something important to its owner would be carefully kept by him. One is inclined to suspect that a note that was lost may not have been regarded as important by its owner, probably because it was flawed in some way.

LITERAL TRANSLATION

[1] Abaye said: The witnesses transfer [the right to property] to him by their signatures, [2] even [if they sign] notes that are not [deeds of] transfer.

[3] [Abaye gave this explanation] because he had [the following] objection [to Rav Assi's explanation]: [4] Since you say that in [the case of] notes that are not [deeds of] transfer, when the lender is not [present] together with [the borrower], we do not write [them], [5] there is no [reason] to suspect that [someone] happened to write [them].

[1] אַבַּיֵי אָמַר: עֵדָיו בַּחֲתוּמָיו זָכִין לוֹ, [2] וַאֲפִילוּ שְׁטָרֵי דְּלָאו הַקְנָאָה. [3] מִשּׁוּם דְּקַשְׁיָא לֵיהּ: [4] כֵּיוָן דְּאָמְרַתְּ בִּשְׁטָרֵי דְּלָאו הַקְנָאָה, כִּי לֵיתֵיהּ לְמַלְוֶה בַּהֲדֵיהּ, לָא כָּתְבִינַן, [5] לֵיכָּא לְמֵיחַשׁ דְּאִקְרֵי וּכְתוּב.

TRANSLATION AND COMMENTARY

אַבַּיֵי אָמַר [1] Abaye did not accept Rav Assi's explanation of the Mishnah in *Bava Batra*, that only deeds of transfer can be written in the absence of the lender. He **said**: There is no danger of predating in any promissory note, since **the witnesses** to any document **transfer the right to the property** mortgaged in that document **to** the lender **by** putting **their signatures** on the document! According to Abaye, the lien on the borrower's property created by any promissory note begins the moment the witnesses sign it, regardless of when the loan actually takes place. [2] Moreover, this applies to all documents, **even notes that are not deeds of transfer**. Thus, in Abaye's opinion, the Mishnah in *Bava Batra* permits the writing of even ordinary promissory notes for a borrower in the absence of the lender, because there is no danger of a potential buyer of the borrower's property being harmed thereby. The moment the witnesses sign the note, the mortgage takes effect, irrespective of the ultimate date of the loan.

מִשּׁוּם דְּקַשְׁיָא לֵיהּ [3] The Gemara goes on to explain: **Abaye gave this explanation because he had the following objection to the explanation of Rav Assi:** [4] **Since you**, Rav Assi, **say that** ordinary promissory **notes which are not deeds of transfer may not be written if the lender is not present together with the borrower,** [5] there is no **reason to suspect that** it may have occurred that **someone happened to write** such a document unlawfully in the absence of the lender.

RASHI

אביי אמר – הא דתנן כותבין שטר ללוה בלא מלוה – אפילו בשטר דלאו הקנאה נמי. ואי נמי אתי למיטרף מהאידנא; והוא לא לוה עד תשרי – לא שלא כדין הוא, דעדיו בחתומיו זכין לו, מיום שחתמוהו זכין לו השעבוד ואפילו לא הלוה המעות עד תשרי. ולהכי מוקי ליה אביי בהאי טעמא משום דקשיא ליה, כיון דאמרת כו׳. אבל השתא דתנן כותבין – חיישינן דלמא כתב ללות ולא לוה, ולקמיה פריך: אמאי לא יחזיר – הרי זכו ליה עדיו בחתומיו, ושפיר טריף.

TERMINOLOGY

מִשּׁוּם דְּקַשְׁיָא לֵיהּ **Because he had an objection.** This term explains why a Sage interprets a source differently from another Sage, or why he interprets it in a way that does not seem to follow the plain sense of the text. The Gemara explains, "Because he had an objection," because he found a certain difficulty in earlier explanations, either a linguistic or stylistic difficulty, or a difficulty of content (for example, where the interpretation offered appears to contradict another source). קַשְׁיָא לֵיהּ means that he has not found a difficulty so great as to contradict the previous interpretation completely, but that he views that interpretation as somewhat problematical, and for this reason he prefers another interpretation.

NOTES

מִשּׁוּם דְּקַשְׁיָא לֵיהּ **Because he had an objection....** According to a tradition cited by the Rishonim, this passage was not originally part of the Gemara, but was a later addition by Rav Yehudai Gaon. Indeed, the commentators have noted numerous difficulties posed by this passage. For example, Abaye's conclusion, that all documents are valid from the moment they are signed, which is primarily an interpretation of the Mishnah in *Bava Batra*, does not follow from the reasoning cited here, "because he had an objection to Rav Assi's interpretation." The objection raised by Abaye has no direct bearing at all on the Mishnah from *Bava Batra*. Even if Abaye were to interpret that Mishnah like Rav Assi, namely that ordinary promissory notes may not be drawn up if the lender is not present, he could still interpret our Mishnah the same way he does below, i.e., that the reason why the promissory note may not be returned to the lender is because of a possible conspiracy between the lender and the borrower to defraud people who bought property from the borrower. This interpretation by Abaye is possible even if we assume that regular documents are not yet valid the moment they are signed!

Some commentators, therefore, explain that the sentence, "because he had an objection...," was not meant as a justification of Abaye's interpretation of the Mishnah from *Bava Batra*, but rather as a parenthetical remark, explaining why Abaye disagrees with Rav Assi's interpretation of *our* Mishnah (*Tosafot*).

Others explain that the sentence, "because he had an objection...," by discrediting Rav Assi's interpretation of our Mishnah, removes the basis for Rav Assi's interpretation of the Mishnah from *Bava Batra*. It is clearly preferable to interpret the Mishnah from *Bava Batra* as referring to all documents, as Abaye does, rather than to just one unusual kind of document, as Rav Assi does. The only advantage of

HALAKHAH

כּוֹתְבִים שְׁטָר לְלֹוֶה **Writing a promissory note for the borrower when the lender is not present.** Many Halakhic authorities (including *Rif* and *Rambam*) rule (following Rav Assi) that a promissory note may be written for the borrower even if the lender is not present, provided that the note explicitly stipulates that the lien on the debtor's property takes effect as of the date appearing in the document. *Ri, Rosh,* and *Tur,* however, follow Abaye's view, ruling that a promissory note may be written for the borrower in the absence of the lender, even if the note does not state explicitly that the lien on the borrower's property takes effect immediately. (On the basis of *Shulḥan Arukh, Ḥoshen Mishpat* 39:13.)

LITERAL TRANSLATION

[1] But [what about] what we have learned [in another Mishnah]: "[If] one found bills of divorce of women or writs of emancipation of slaves, wills, [deeds of] gift, or receipts, [2] he should not return [them], in case they were written and he changed his mind about them, [deciding] not to give them"? [3] Now, even if he changed his mind about them, what [difference] is there? [4] Surely you said: The witnesses transfer [the right to property] to him by their signatures!

[5] This applies (lit., "these words") where they reached his hands, [6] but where they did not reach his hands, we do not say [this].

[7] But [what about] our Mishnah, which teaches: "[If] one finds promissory notes, if they contain [a clause] mortgaging [the borrower's landed] property [as security for the loan], he should not return [them]"?

[1] אֶלָּא הָא דִּתְנַן: ״מָצָא גִּיטֵּי נָשִׁים וְשִׁחְרוּרֵי עֲבָדִים, דְּיַיתִּיקִי, מַתָּנָה, וְשׁוֹבְרִים, [2] הֲרֵי זֶה לֹא יַחֲזִיר, שֶׁמָּא כְּתוּבִים הָיוּ וְנִמְלַךְ עֲלֵיהֶם שֶׁלֹּא לִיתְּנָם״. [3] וְכִי נִמְלַךְ עֲלֵיהֶם, מַאי הָוֵי? [4] וְהָא אָמְרַתְּ: עֵדָיו בַּחֲתוּמָיו זָכִין לוֹ!

[5] הָנֵי מִילֵּי הֵיכָא דְּקָא מָטוּ לִידֵיהּ, [6] אֲבָל הֵיכָא דְּלָא מָטוּ לִידֵיהּ, לָא אָמְרִינַן.

[7] אֶלָּא מַתְנִיתִין, דְּקָתָנֵי: ״מָצָא שִׁטְרֵי חוֹב, אִם יֵשׁ בָּהֶם אַחֲרָיוּת נְכָסִים, לֹא יַחֲזִיר״.

TRANSLATION AND COMMENTARY

אֶלָּא הָא דִּתְנַן [1] The Gemara now objects: **But** how do we reconcile Abaye's statement, that the witnesses to a document create a lien on the borrower's property by their signing it, with **what we have learned** in the following Mishnah (below, 18a): **"If someone finds bills of divorce or writs of emancipation of slaves, wills, deeds of gift, or receipts** of repayment of loans, [2] **he should not return them** to the people for whom they were written, **in case they were** originally **written**, and ready for use, and then the person who caused them to be written **changed his mind about them and decided not to hand them over**"? [3] Now, we may ask: **Even if** the person who caused them to be written **changed his mind about them** and cancelled them, **what difference** does it make? [4] **Surely you**, Abaye, **have said that the witnesses** to a document **transfer the right to property to** the recipient of the document **by** putting **their signatures** on the document, and this transfer is effective from the moment when they sign the document. Why, then, is someone who finds a deed of gift, for example, forbidden to return it to the recipient of the gift? Even if the deed was never delivered, surely the gift was effective from the moment the witnesses signed the deed!

הָנֵי מִילֵּי [5] The Gemara answers: **This** ruling of Abaye — that the witnesses transfer the right to property by their signatures and the critical date in a transaction is the date when the witnesses signed the document, not the date of its delivery — only **applies where** the documents eventually **did reach** the lender's **hands**; [6] **but where they did not reach his hands** at all, **we do not apply** Abaye's rule. Thus the date when the witnesses signed is only significant if the document was actually delivered. Even if the delivery took place long after the date on which they signed, the lender's lien on the borrower's property is reckoned retroactively from the date on which they signed. But as long as delivery has not taken place, the parties to the transaction can still change their minds, provided that the document was not a deed of transfer. Therefore, our Mishnah, which is dealing with ordinary documents, has reason to be concerned about the possibility of improper loss being caused to the buyers, because it is possible that the loan has already been repaid or perhaps never took place at all. The note should not, therefore, be used to collect payment from the buyers.

אֶלָּא מַתְנִיתִין [7] The Gemara now objects: **But what about our Mishnah, which states**: "If a person **finds promissory notes containing a clause mortgaging the borrower's landed property as security for the loan,** the finder

RASHI

דייתיקי = צואת שכיב מרע. ולשון דייתיקי — דא תיקו, זאת תיקום, דדברי שכיב מרע ככתובין וכמסורין דמי. **מתנה** — מתנת בריא. **ושוברין** — פרעון שטר. **הני מילי היכא דמטא שטר לידיה** — ואפילו לאחר זמן זכו לו חותמיו לגבות מזמן הכתוב בו. ואי קשיא הא דתנן (שביעית פרק י׳ משנה ה׳): שטרי חוב המוקדמין — פסולין, והמאוחרין — כשרין. במאי מוקי לה אביי? תריץ: במוקדמת כתיבתן לחתימתן, ולהכי פסולין, שבא לטרוף משעת כתיבה. אי נמי, שכתבו וחתמוהו בתשרי, והס כתבו בתוכו ניסן שהוא ראש השנה לשטרות.

LANGUAGE

דְּיַיתִּיקִי Will. This word is derived from the Greek διαθήκη, *diatheke*, which means "will." The Sages, however, suggested an Aramaic etymology for this term (see below, 19a), based on a play on words. Such punning etymologies are found in many places in the Talmud.

CONCEPTS

שִׁחְרוּרֵי עֲבָדִים Writs of emancipation for slaves. When a non-Jewish slave was freed he received a bill of emancipation stating that he had been freed from his master. The former slave needed such a bill not only as proof that he had been freed but also for Halakhic reasons, for a properly freed slave had the status of a convert, with all the obligations and privileges of a Jew. But until the slave had received his bill of emancipation, he did not yet have all the rights of a free person.

שׁוֹבְרִים Receipts. A שׁוֹבֵר is a receipt for repayment of a debt or fulfillment of some other obligation. There is a difference of opinion among the Sages as to whether a lender who has lost the original promissory note can collect his debt and give a receipt, or whether he must return the original promissory note so that the borrower can destroy it. Nevertheless, when the original obligation was not recorded in a written contract, but was a legal obligation imposed by a court (such as a marriage contract [כְּתוּבָּה] in those communities where the כְּתוּבָּה is not written down), all authorities agree that a receipt is sufficient.

NOTES

Rav Assi's interpretation is that it leads to a straightforward interpretation of *our* Mishnah, without needing to resort to the rather far-fetched "conspiracy theory." Now that Rav Assi's interpretation of our Mishnah has been weakened and we need to rely on the "conspiracy theory" to explain our Mishnah, Abaye's interpretation of the Mishnah from *Bava Batra* appears preferable to Rav Assi's (*Ramban*, *Rashba* and *Ran*).

LANGUAGE

קְנוּנְיָא **Conspiracy.** The source of this word is the Greek κοινωνία, *koinonia*, "a partnership," or "a partnership agreement." The Sages always used this word in a pejorative sense, meaning an agreement between two people to defraud someone or deprive him of his rights.

LITERAL TRANSLATION

[1]And we have established [that] it [refers to a situation] where the debtor admits [his debt], [2]and [it is] because [we suspect that] perhaps [the borrower] wrote to borrow in Nisan, but he did not borrow until Tishri. [3]Granted [according] to Rav Assi, who said [that the Mishnah in *Bava Batra* deals only] with deeds of transfer, he explains it [as referring] to notes that are not [deeds of] transfer, as we have said. [4]But [according] to Abaye, who said: The witnesses transfer [the right to property] to him by their signatures, what is there to say?

[5]Abaye could say to you: [In] our Mishnah, the reason is as follows: Because [the Tanna] suspects payment and conspiracy.

[6]But [according] to Shmuel, who said:

[1]וְאוֹקִימְנָא כְּשֶׁחַיָּיב מוֹדֶה, [2]וּמִשּׁוּם שֶׁמָּא כָּתַב לִלְווֹת בְּנִיסָן, וְלֹא לָוָה עַד תִּשְׁרֵי. [3]בִּשְׁלָמָא לְרַב אַסִּי, דְּאָמַר בִּשְׁטָרֵי אַקְנָיְיתָא, מוֹקֵי לַהּ בִּשְׁטָרֵי דְּלָאו אַקְנָיְיתָא, וְכִדְאָמְרִינַן. [4]אֶלָּא לְאַבָּיֵי, דְּאָמַר: עֵדָיו בַּחֲתוּמָיו זָכִין לוֹ, מַאי אִיכָּא לְמֵימַר?

[5]אָמַר לָךְ אַבָּיֵי: מַתְנִיתִין, הַיְינוּ טַעְמָא: דְּחָיֵישׁ לְפֵרָעוֹן וְלִקְנוּנְיָא.

[6]וְלִשְׁמוּאֵל, דְּאָמַר:

TRANSLATION AND COMMENTARY

should not return them to the lender"? [1]**We have** already **established that** our Mishnah **is referring to a situation where the borrower admits his debt,** [2]**and** the reason why the promissory note is not returned to the lender **is because we suspect that** the borrower **may have written** in the promissory note **that he was borrowing** the money **in Nisan, but did not** actually **borrow until Tishri.** [3]This Mishnah **does not pose a problem to** the viewpoint advocated by **Rav Assi, who said that the Mishnah in** *Bava Batra*, allowing a promissory note to be written for the borrower even if the lender is not present, **deals only with a deed of transfer. He can explain** our Mishnah, which forbids the return of promissory notes, **as referring** specifically **to** promissory **notes which are not deeds of transfer** and which may have been improperly predated, **as we have said.** [4]**But according to Abaye, who said that the witnesses** to a document **transfer the right to property to** the recipient of the document **by** putting **their signatures** to the document, **what is there to say?** The only possible danger to the buyers is if the loan has already been repaid or never took place, as explained above, and we have established that the Mishnah is referring to a situation where the debtor admits that he owes the money!

אָמַר לָךְ אַבָּיֵי [5]The Gemara answers: **Abaye could say to you: In our Mishnah, the reason** why the finder is forbidden to return the promissory note to the lender **is as follows: Because the Tanna suspects payment** by the borrower **and conspiracy** between the borrower and the lender. Abaye argues that even though the borrower admits his debt, we suspect that he and the lender may be in conspiracy to defraud other people. For even though the borrower maintains that the loan is still outstanding, he may already have repaid it, and he may be conspiring with the lender to fabricate a nonexistent debt. The lender will claim that he has not been repaid, as the borrower himself "admits," and the lender will then seize property which the borrower has sold to other people. Later the lender and the borrower will divide this stolen property between them! Because of this possible conspiracy, we cannot allow a lost promissory note to be returned to the lender, even when the borrower admits that he has not repaid the loan.

וְלִשְׁמוּאֵל [6]The Gemara now asks: **But according to Shmuel, who says** (below, 16a) that

RASHI

בשלמא לרב אסי – דמוקי להווא דכותבין בשטרי אקנייתא. **מוקי** – מתניתין בדלאו אקנייתא, ולהכי לא יחזיר. כדקאמר איתרע ליה, וחיישינן דלמא אקרי וכתב והוה ליה מוקדם ולכן הופקר להשליכו. **לפרעון ולקנוניא** – שמא פרעו, ומן הלוה כפל. והא דקא מודה "לא פרעתי" – עלה היא ביניהם של רמאות לטרוף את הלקוחות שלקחו ממנו קרקע שלא באחריות ויחלקו ביניהם. **ולשמואל דאמר** – לקמן.

NOTES

פֵּרָעוֹן וּקְנוּנְיָא **Payment and conspiracy**. From the wording of the Gemara here ("payment *and* conspiracy"), it would appear that there is no basis for concern about the possibility of "payment" alone (i.e., the possibility that the borrower retained the promissory note after he had repaid the loan, in order to take out another loan at a later date). The reason why the Gemara does not take into consideration the possibility of payment alone is that it is unlikely that the borrower would risk causing a major potential loss to the people who bought his property merely in order to save the cost of paying a scribe to write a new promissory note (*Tosafot*). *Rosh* notes that, according to *Rif*, "conspiracy" includes not only dating the promissory note earlier than the actual date of the loan, but also writing a fictitious promissory note for a loan that was never taken (see *Me'orot Natan*).

TRANSLATION AND COMMENTARY

[1]**we do not suspect** that there may have been **payment and conspiracy**, because he maintains that we always presume that as soon as a loan has been repaid, the borrower immediately tears up the promissory note, **what is there to say** — how can the ruling in our Mishnah forbidding the return of a lost promissory note to the lender be explained? [2]**This** ruling **presents no problem if** Shmuel **shares the viewpoint of Rav Assi, who says that the Mishnah in** *Bava Batra*, allowing a promissory note to be written for the borrower even if the lender is not present, **deals only with a deed of transfer**. Shmuel **can explain our Mishnah,** which forbids the return of promissory notes, **as referring** specifically **to** promissory **notes that are not deeds of transfer** and may have been improperly predated. [3]**But if he shares the viewpoint of Abaye, who said** that **the witnesses** to a document **transfer the right to property to** the recipient of the document **by** putting **their signatures** to the document, **what is there to say**? Why, from Shmuel's point of view, should a lost promissory note not be restored to the lender?

שְׁמוּאֵל מוֹקֵי לְמַתְנִיתִין [4]The Gemara answers: **Shmuel explains our Mishnah** differently from both Rav Assi and Abaye, **as referring** specifically **to a case where the debtor does not admit** that the loan was ever made. He claims that the promissory note is a forgery. The fact that it was lost tends to strengthen his claim, and this is why a person who finds the promissory note may not return it to the lender.

אִי הָכִי [5]The Gemara objects: But **if** our Mishnah is dealing with a case where the borrower does not admit his debt, then **when the** promissory **notes do not contain a clause mortgaging the borrower's landed property as security for the loan, why**, according to Rabbi Meir in our Mishnah, **should the finder return them** to the lender? [6]**Even though the lender cannot** use these notes to **collect** his debt **from** the borrower's **mortgaged property**, i.e., landed property which the borrower has sold to another person after the date of the loan, **he can certainly** use these notes to **collect** his debt **from** the borrower's **free property**, which is at present in the borrower's possession! But the borrower, who claims he owes nothing, may be telling the truth!

[1]לָא חָיְישִׁינַן לְפֵרָעוֹן וְלִקְנוּנְיָא, מַאי אִיכָּא לְמֵימַר? [2]הָנִיחָא, אִי סָבַר לָהּ כְּרַב אַסִי, דְּאָמַר בִּשְׁטָרֵי הַקְנָאָה, מוֹקֵי מַתְנִיתִין בִּשְׁטָרֵי דְּלָאו הַקְנָאָה. [3]אֶלָּא אִי סָבַר כְּאַבַּיֵי, דְּאָמַר: עֵדָיו בַּחֲתוּמָיו זָכִין לוֹ, מַאי אִיכָּא לְמֵימַר?

[4]שְׁמוּאֵל מוֹקֵי לְמַתְנִיתִין כְּשֶׁאֵין חַיָּיב מוֹדֶה.

[5]אִי הָכִי, כִּי אֵין בָּהֶן אַחֲרָיוּת נְכָסִים, אַמַּאי יַחֲזִיר? [6]נְהִי דְּלָא גָּבֵי מִן מְשַׁעְבְּדִי, מִבְּנֵי חָרֵי מִגְבֵּי גָּבֵי!

LITERAL TRANSLATION

[1]We do not suspect payment and conspiracy, what is there to say? [2]This is acceptable if he shares the viewpoint of (lit., "maintains on it like") Rav Assi, who says that [the Mishnah in *Bava Batra* deals only] with deeds of transfer. He can explain our Mishnah [as referring] to noters that are not [deeds of] transfer. [3]But if he shares the viewpoint of Abaye, who said: "The witnesses transfer [the right to property] to him by their signatures," what is there to say?

[4]Shmuel explains our Mishnah [as referring to a case] where the debtor does not admit [his debt].

[5]If so, when [the notes] do not contain [a clause] mortgaging [the borrower's landed] property [as security for the loan], why should [the finder] return them? [6]Even though [the lender] cannot collect from mortgaged property, he can certainly collect from free property!

RASHI

לא חיישינן לפרעון — בשטר הנמצא, ואפילו אין חייב מודה. דאם איתא דפריעה — מקרע הוה קרע ליה, דאמר שמואל לקמן (טז,ב): המוצא שטר הקנאה בשוק — יחזיר לבעלים וכל שכן כשחייב מודה מהאי טעמא גופיה דמיום פריעתו הוא קורעו. הלכך, ליכא למיחש לאחר זמן לקנוניא, מתניתין במאי מוקי לה. **הניחא כו'** — ואי קשיא, על כרחך לא סבירא ליה באביי דאי כאביי סבירא ליה מאי איריא שטר הקנאה? הא לאביי אין חילוק בין זה לזה דאפילו דלאו הקנאה נמי יחזיר, הואיל ושמואל לא חייש לפרעון — לאו פירכא הוא, דמודה אביי בדלא מטא שטרא לידיה, כדאמרן, הלכך איכא למימר כתב ללות ולא לוה לגמרי, ולא מטא לידיה מעולם. **בשאין חייב מודה** — בכתיבת השטר, שאומר לוה לא כתבתי, ומזויף הוא. ואם תאמר: יתקיים בחותמיו? כיון שנפל אתרע ליה, ואמרינן מפני שפסול היה לא נזהר, מהמנינן ליה להאי.

NOTES

לָא חָיְישִׁינַן לְפֵרָעוֹן וְלִקְנוּנְיָא **We do not suspect payment and conspiracy**. Shmuel believes that, because the note was found intact, there is no reason to suspect that it has already been paid, for one assumes that someone who has paid his debt and received his note in return would not wish to save it but would instead destroy it at once, to avoid possible complications. Thus the possibility exists that the borrower did not destroy the note because he was conspiring with the lender to defraud third parties (people who had bought property from the borrower). But Shmuel believes that such a suspicion is far-fetched, and we should not deprive the lender of his rights because we suspect, without any evidence, that he is conspiring with the borrower.

וְלִשְׁמוּאֵל... מַאי אִיכָּא לְמֵימַר **According to Shmuel, who**

TRANSLATION AND COMMENTARY

שְׁמוּאֵל לְטַעְמֵיהּ [1]The Gemara answers: **Shmuel** is consistent and **follows his own opinion, for Shmuel said: Rabbi Meir used to say:** [2]**In the case of a promissory note which does not contain a clause mortgaging** the **borrower's landed property as security for the loan, the lender may not collect payment** at all — **neither from mortgaged** (landed) **property**, as has been our assumption until now, **nor** even **from free property**, for reasons that will be explained later on in the Gemara. Hence, the promissory note may be returned to the lender without fear of its being misused.

וְכִי מֵאַחַר שֶׁאֵינוֹ גּוֹבֶה [3]The Gemara objects: **But since** the lender **cannot** use the note to **collect** his debt, **why should the finder** take the trouble to **return** it to him? It is of no use to anyone!

אָמַר רַבִּי נָתָן בַּר אוֹשַׁעְיָא [4]**Rabbi Natan son of Oshaya said** in reply: The document must be returned, because the paper on which it was written has a certain value, since it can be used **to stop up the lender's bottle**.

וְנַהַדְרֵיהּ [5]Again the Gemara objects: But why return it to the lender? **Let the finder return it to the borrower to stop up the borrower's bottle!** For if the promissory note cannot be used to collect the debt, why shouldn't it be returned to the borrower?

לֹוֶה הוּא [6]The Gemara answers: **It is the borrower** [13B] **who said**: The whole transaction **never happened**. Since he maintains that the promissory note is a forgery, he is clearly not entitled to the paper on which it was written.

[1]שְׁמוּאֵל לְטַעְמֵיהּ, דְּאָמַר שְׁמוּאֵל: אוֹמֵר הָיָה רַבִּי מֵאִיר: [2]שְׁטַר חוֹב שֶׁאֵין בּוֹ אַחֲרָיוּת נְכָסִים, אֵין גּוֹבֶה, לֹא מִמְּשַׁעְבְּדֵי וְלֹא מִבְּנֵי חֲרֵי. [3]וְכִי מֵאַחַר שֶׁאֵינוֹ גּוֹבֶה, אַמַּאי יַחֲזִיר? [4]אָמַר רַבִּי נָתָן בַּר אוֹשַׁעְיָא: לָצוּר עַל פִּי צְלוֹחִיתוֹ שֶׁל מַלְוֶה! [5]וְנַהַדְרֵיהּ לְהוּ לַלֹּוֶה לָצוּר עַל פִּי צְלוֹחִיתוֹ שֶׁל לֹוֶה! [6]לֹוֶה הוּא [13B] דְּאָמַר: ״לֹא הָיוּ דְּבָרִים מֵעוֹלָם״.

LITERAL TRANSLATION

[1]Shmuel [follows] his [own] opinion, for Shmuel said: Rabbi Meir used to say: [2][In the case of] a promissory note that does not contain [a clause] mortgaging [the borrower's landed] property [as security for the loan, the lender] may not collect, not from mortgaged property and not from free property.

[3]But since he does not collect, why should [the finder] return [the note]!

[4]Rabbi Natan bar Oshaya said: To stop up the lender's bottle.

[5]Then let [the finder] return it to the borrower to stop up the borrower's bottle!

[6]It is the borrower [13B] who said: "It never happened."

NOTES

says that we do not suspect that there may have been payment and conspiracy, what is there to say? Even though Shmuel could explain that our Mishnah follows those Tannaim who are concerned about the possibility of payment (see above, 7b), the Gemara nevertheless prefers to explain the Mishnah in accordance with the views of all the Tannaim (*Melo HaRo'im*).

שְׁטָר בְּלֹא אַחֲרָיוּת אֵינוֹ גּוֹבֶה **Payment cannot be collected from a promissory note that does not contain a clause mortgaging the borrower's landed property**. A number of different explanations of this view have been offered. Some commentators suggest that no one would ever lend money on the basis of such a note; therefore, even if the borrower had it drawn up in the hope of finding a compliant lender, we must assume he never actually used it to borrow money. Hence, it cannot be used as evidence of a loan (*Ra'avad*). Others explain that a note that lacks a clause mortgaging the borrower's landed property loses the legal status usually accorded to such a document; hence it is merely the equivalent of verbal testimony that a loan took place. Such verbal testimony is insufficient in order to seize as repayment of the loan property that the borrower sold to innocent buyers. It is also insufficient in order to seize the borrower's unencumbered property, if the borrower claims that he has paid back the loan. Furthermore, this defective "document" may not even be the equivalent of verbal testimony. Ordinarily, the Torah does not accept written testimony; witnesses must testify in person and be examined by the court. Exceptions to this rule are promissory notes or other properly drawn-up documents; these have the status of testimony that has already been thoroughly examined by the court. But a note that does not contain a clause mortgaging the borrower's landed property lacks the legal status of a document. (*Ramban* and others).

לָצוּר עַל פִּי צְלוֹחִית **To stop up the lender's bottle**. The Gemara has previously stated (7b; cf. the note there) that people do not ordinarily quarrel about the ownership of an invalid document whole sole worth is as a piece of paper. But in our case the issue at stake is not how we should rule in the unlikely instance of a dispute arising regarding such a piece of paper, but rather what to do if one was lost and found — should it be returned and to whom? (*Ein Yehosef.*)

LITERAL TRANSLATION

[1] Rabbi Elazar said: The difference of opinion [applies] in [a case] where the debtor does not admit [his debt]. [2] For Rabbi Meir maintains: [In the case of] a promissory note which does not contain [a clause] mortgaging [the borrower's landed] property [as security for the loan], [the lender] may not collect [at all]: not from mortgaged property and not from free property. [3] But the Sages maintain: It is from mortgaged property that he may not collect; from free property he may certainly collect. [4] But where the debtor admits [his debt], all agree (lit., "the words of all") [that the finder] should return [the promissory note], and we do not suspect payment and conspiracy.

[1] אָמַר רַבִּי אֶלְעָזָר: מַחֲלוֹקֶת בְּשֶׁאֵין חַיָּיב מוֹדֶה. [2] דְּרַבִּי מֵאִיר סָבַר: שְׁטָר שֶׁאֵין בּוֹ אַחֲרָיוּת נְכָסִים, אֵינוֹ גּוֹבֶה: לֹא מִמְּשַׁעְבְּדֵי וְלֹא מִבְּנֵי חָרֵי. [3] וְרַבָּנַן סָבְרִי: מִמְּשַׁעְבְּדֵי הוּא דְּלָא גָּבֵי; מִבְּנֵי חָרֵי מִגְבָּא גָּבֵי. [4] אֲבָל כְּשֶׁחַיָּיב מוֹדֶה, דִּבְרֵי הַכֹּל יַחֲזִיר, וְלָא חָיְישִׁינַן לְפֵרָעוֹן וְלִקְנוּנְיָא.

TRANSLATION AND COMMENTARY

אָמַר רַבִּי אֶלְעָזָר [1] **Rabbi Elazar said: The difference of opinion** in our Mishnah between Rabbi Meir and the Sages **applies** specifically **to a case where the debtor does not admit his debt.** [2] **For**, according to Rabbi Elazar, **Rabbi Meir maintains: In the case of a promissory note which does not contain a clause mortgaging the borrower's landed property as security for the loan, the lender may not collect at all, neither from** the borrower's **mortgaged property nor from his free property**. According to Rabbi Meir, a promissory note which does not contain a clause mortgaging the borrower's landed property is defective and is no more effective than an unwitnessed verbal loan. The only way the lender will receive his money back in such a case is if the borrower admits that he owes the money. [3] **But the Sages maintain: It is** only **from mortgaged property that** the lender **may not collect; from free property he may certainly collect**. According to the Sages, a promissory note which does not contain a clause mortgaging the borrower's landed property is to some degree defective, but it is no less effective than a witnessed verbal loan, and would ordinarily be strong enough to enable the lender to collect from the borrower's free property. In this case, since the note was lost and the borrower denies the loan, it may not be returned to the lender. [4] **But** in a case **where the debtor admits his debt, all agree that the finder should return the promissory note, and we do not suspect payment** by the borrower **and conspiracy** between the borrower and the lender. There is no reason to assume that the debt may have already been paid, and that the borrower and the lender are conspiring to defraud people who bought property from the borrower, because the note cannot be used for this purpose in any case.

RASHI

אינו גובה לא מנכסים משועבדים ולא מבני חורין – אם אין הלוה מודה, דשטרא דלא שעבד בה נכסים – לאו שטרא הוא, והוה כמלוה על פה, ושאין עליה עדים. **ורבנן סברי** – להא מיהא הוי שטרא, שתהא כמלוה על פה בעדים. הלכך גבי מבני חרי. ולהכי לא יחזיר, דכיון דנפל – אתרע ליה, ואמרינן מזויף הוא, כדקאמר לוה.

LANGUAGE

בְּנֵי חָרֵי **Free property**. The use of this term both in Aramaic and in Hebrew (בְּנֵי חוֹרִין) is analogous to the use of שִׁעְבּוּד — "bondage" — for mortgages. Hence, unmortgaged property which is owned without restriction is called נְכָסִים בְּנֵי חוֹרִין.

NOTES

מִמְּשַׁעְבְּדֵי הוּא דְּלָא גָּבֵי **It is only from mortgaged property that the lender may not collect**. These words appear to have been missing from ancient texts of the Gemara, which read: וְרַבָּנַן סָבְרִי מִגְבָּא גָּבֵי — "and the Sages maintain that he may certainly collect," presumably from both kinds of property. The version found in our text conforms to *Rashi's* interpretation, though it is not at all certain that in *Rashi's* own version these words appeared explicitly. At first glance, there is no obvious reason for Rabbi Elazar to make this distinction in the Sages' position; their ruling that documents lacking a clause mortgaging landed property should not be returned if the borrower denies his debt would be just as valid, if not more so, if they maintained that the lender could use them to collect from *mortgaged property* as well. In fact, several commentators (*Ramban*, *Rashba*, and others) object to *Rashi's* interpretation for several reasons, the main one being because of the Baraita cited later in the discussion to refute Rabbi Elazar's position. If Rabbi Elazar does in fact maintain that the Sages deny the lender's power to collect from *mortgaged property* using this document, he will find himself in conflict with the Baraita on a point not mentioned by the Gemara; for the Baraita clearly states that the Sages *do* allow the lender to collect from *mortgaged property* using a document that lacks a clause mortgaging landed property.

Ran defends *Rashi's* interpretation, saying that the Gemara did not mention this additional conflict between Rabbi Elazar and the Baraita because it is merely a matter of detail closely bound up with the other, known conflicts. He adds that *Rashi* felt that Rabbi Elazar prefers to explain

HALAKHAH

שְׁטָר שֶׁאֵין בּוֹ אַחֲרָיוּת **A promissory note without a clause mortgaging the borrower's landed property**. "The lender can collect from the borrower's mortgaged property even if the promissory note does not contain a clause specifically mortgaging the borrower's landed property as security for the loan," following the view of the Sages, as will be explained in detail later on in the discussion. (*Shulḥan Arukh, Ḥoshen Mishpat* 39:1.)

[1]וְרַבִּי יוֹחָנָן אָמַר: מַחֲלוֹקֶת כְּשֶׁחַיָּיב מוֹדֶה. [2]דְּרַבִּי מֵאִיר סָבַר: שְׁטָר שֶׁאֵין בּוֹ אַחֲרָיוּת נְכָסִים, מִמְּשַׁעְבְּדֵי הוּא דְּלָא גָּבֵי, אֲבָל מִבְּנֵי חָרֵי מִגְבָּא גָּבֵי. [3]וְרַבָּנַן סָבְרִי: מִמְּשַׁעְבְּדֵי נַמִי גָּבֵי. [4]אֲבָל כְּשֶׁאֵין חַיָּיב מוֹדֶה, דִּבְרֵי הַכֹּל לֹא יַחֲזִיר, דְּחָיְישִׁינַן לְפֵרָעוֹן.

[5]תַּנְיָא כְּוָותֵיהּ דְּרַבִּי יוֹחָנָן, וּתְיוּבְתָּא דְּרַבִּי אֶלְעָזָר בַּחֲדָא, וּתְיוּבְתָּא דִּשְׁמוּאֵל בִּתַרְתֵּי: [6]״מָצָא שִׁטְרֵי חוֹב וְיֵשׁ בָּהֶם אַחֲרָיוּת נְכָסִים, אַף עַל פִּי שֶׁשְּׁנֵיהֶם מוֹדִים, לֹא יַחֲזִיר, לֹא לָזֶה וְלֹא לָזֶה. [7]אֵין בָּהֶן

LITERAL TRANSLATION

[1]But Rabbi Yoḥanan said: The difference of opinion [applies] in [a case] where the debtor admits [his debt]. [2]For Rabbi Meir maintains: [In the case of] a promissory note which does not contain [a clause] mortgaging [the borrower's landed] property [as security for the loan], [the lender] may not collect from [the borrower's] mortgaged property, but he may certainly collect from [his] free property. [3]But the Sages maintain: He may also collect from [the borrower's] mortgaged property. [4]But where the debtor does not admit [his debt], all agree [that the finder] should not return [the document], because we suspect payment.

[5][A Baraita] was taught in accordance with Rabbi Yoḥanan, and [in] refutation of Rabbi Elazar in one [respect] and [in] refutation of Shmuel in two [respects]: [6]"[If] one finds promissory notes containing [a clause] mortgaging [the borrower's landed] property [as security for the loan], even though both of them admit [the debt], [the finder] should not return [the notes], not to this one and not to this one. [7][If] they

TRANSLATION AND COMMENTARY

וְרַבִּי יוֹחָנָן אָמַר [1]**But Rabbi Yoḥanan** disagreed with Rabbi Elazar and **said: The difference of opinion** in our Mishnah between Rabbi Meir and the Sages **applies** specifically **to a case where the debtor admits his debt.** [2]**For,** according to Rabbi Yoḥanan, **Rabbi Meir maintains: In the case of a promissory note which does not contain** a clause **mortgaging the borrower's landed property as security for the loan, the lender may not collect from the borrower's mortgaged property, but he may certainly collect from his free property.** According to Rabbi Yoḥanan, Rabbi Meir maintains that since the document does not contain a mortgage on the borrower's landed property, there is no danger in returning it to the lender. He can only collect from the borrower's free property and not from an innocent third party, and the borrower admits that he owes the money! [3]**But the Sages maintain**: In the case of a promissory note that does *not* contain a clause mortgaging the borrower's landed property, the lender **may also collect from the borrower's mortgaged property**. According to Rabbi Yoḥanan, as explained below, the Sages consider that every promissory note mortgages the borrower's landed property as security for the loan, irrespective of whether a clause to this effect appears on the document. Therefore the note, if lost, must not be returned to the lender, because we suspect a conspiracy between the lender and the borrower to defraud the buyer of the borrower's property. [4]**But** in a case **where the debtor does not admit** his debt, **all**, even Rabbi Meir, **agree that the finder should not return** the document, **because we suspect** that the borrower may be telling the truth when he claims that **payment** of the debt has been made.

תַּנְיָא כְּוָותֵיהּ דְּרַבִּי יוֹחָנָן [5]The Gemara now observes that there is **a Baraita** which **was taught in accordance with** the view of **Rabbi Yoḥanan, and** this Baraita is a **refutation of Rabbi Elazar in one respect and a refutation of Shmuel in two respects.** [6]The Baraita states: "**If someone finds promissory notes containing a clause mortgaging** the **borrower's landed property as security for the loan, even though both** borrower and lender **admit** that **the debt** is outstanding, **the finder should not return the** promissory **notes, neither to the one** party **nor to the other**, because we suspect conspiracy. [7]But **if** the notes **do not contain a clause mortgaging the borrower's landed**

RASHI

ממשעבדי נמי גבי — כדמפרש לקמן אחריות טעות סופר הוא, וחיישינן לפרעון ולקנוניא. **אבל כשאין חייב מודה** — ואפילו מודה שכתבו, אלא שאמר "פרעתיו". **דברי הכל לא יחזיר** — דחיישינן לפרעון כדקאמר. **אף על פי ששניהם מודים כו׳** — חיישינן לקנוניא.

NOTES

the Sages' view this way, in order to restrict the points of controversy between Rabbi Meir and the Sages to the barest minimum. Rabbi Elazar was presumably not aware of the Baraita, and since there is no internal argument forcing us to believe that the Sages hold that the creditor *can* collect from *mortgaged property* as well, it is natural to assume them to be in agreement with Rabbi Meir on this point.

תְּיוּבְתָּא דִּשְׁמוּאֵל בִּתַרְתֵּי The Baraita refutes Shmuel in two respects. At first glance, there seems to be no difference between Shmuel's position and that of Rabbi Elazar, and if Rabbi Elazar is refuted in only one respect, then so is Shmuel. Rashi explains (below, 14a) that Rabbi Elazar's two problems with the Baraita result from one premise — his decision to interpret the Mishnah as dealing with a case where the borrower denies his debt.

Some commentators explain that the numbers "one" and

TRANSLATION AND COMMENTARY

property as security for the loan, [1]then **as long as the borrower admits** his debt, **the finder should return the note** to the lender, as such a document poses no danger to the buyers. [2]But **if the borrower does not admit** his debt, **the finder should not return the** promissory **note, neither to the one** party **nor to the other**, because the borrower may be telling the truth. [3]**These are the words of Rabbi Meir.** [1]**For Rabbi Meir used to say: In the case of promissory notes which contain a clause mortgaging** the **borrower's landed property as security for the loan, the lender may collect from** the borrower's **mortgaged property,** [4]**and** even **in the case of notes which do not contain a clause mortgaging the borrower's landed property as security for the loan, the lender may** still **collect from** the borrower's **free property.** [5]**But the Sages say: In both cases,** irrespective of whether the promissory notes contain a clause mortgaging the borrower's landed property as security for the loan, **the lender may collect from the borrower's mortgaged property,**" and therefore the finder should not return the promissory note to the lender, even if both parties agree that the debt is still outstanding, because we suspect payment and conspiracy.

תְּיוּבְתָּא דְּרַבִּי אֶלְעָזָר בַּחֲדָא [6]Now, says the Gemara, **this** Baraita **is a refutation of Rabbi Elazar in one respect,**

אַחֲרָיוּת נְכָסִים, [1]בִּזְמַן שֶׁהַלֹּוֶה מוֹדֶה, יַחֲזִיר. [2]אֵין הַלֹּוֶה מוֹדֶה, לֹא יַחֲזִיר, לֹא לָזֶה וְלֹא לָזֶה. [3]דִּבְרֵי רַבִּי מֵאִיר. שֶׁהָיָה רַבִּי מֵאִיר אוֹמֵר: שְׁטָרֵי שֶׁיֵּשׁ בָּהֶם אַחֲרָיוּת נְכָסִים, גּוֹבֶה מִנְּכָסִים מְשׁוּעְבָּדִים, [4]וְשֶׁאֵין בָּהֶם אַחֲרָיוּת נְכָסִים, גּוֹבֶה מִנְּכָסִים בְּנֵי חוֹרִין. [5]וַחֲכָמִים אוֹמְרִים: אֶחָד זֶה וְאֶחָד זֶה גּוֹבֶה מִנְּכָסִים מְשׁוּעְבָּדִים״.

[6]תְּיוּבְתָּא דְּרַבִּי אֶלְעָזָר בַּחֲדָא,

LITERAL TRANSLATION

do not contain [a clause] mortgaging [the borrower's landed] property [as security for the loan], [1]as long as the borrower admits, [the finder] should return [the note]. [2][If] the borrower does not admit, [the finder] should not return [the note], not to this one and not to this one. [3][These are] the words of Rabbi Meir. For Rabbi Meir used to say: [In the case of] promissory notes which contain [a clause] mortgaging [the borrower's landed] property [as security for the loan], [the lender] collects from mortgaged property, [4]and [in the case of notes] which do not contain [a clause] mortgaging [the borrower's landed] property [as security for the loan], he collects from free property. [5]But the Sages say: In both cases (lit., 'one this and one this') [the lender] may collect from [the borrower's] mortgaged property."

[6][This is] a refutation of Rabbi Elazar in one [respect],

RASHI

בזמן שהלוה מודה – שהוא חייב לו. **יחזיר למלוה** – שאין כאן קנוניא, דלא גבי ממשעבדי. **גובה מנכסים משועבדים** – ולא יחזיר, ואפילו שניהם מודים, דחיישינן לקנוניא.

NOTES

"two" used by the Gemara do not refer to the number of points that are refuted by the Baraita, but rather to the number of separate statements made by Rabbi Elazar and Shmuel which conflict with the Baraita. It is only on this one occasion, in connection with the conspiracy theory, that Rabbi Elazar dismisses the danger of a lost note having been paid. Conceivably, under different circumstances he may entertain the possibility of payment. On the other hand, Shmuel, in addition to interpreting the difference of opinion between Rabbi Meir and the Sages in a manner like that of Rabbi Elazar, also stated on a different occasion that in all cases, even without a conspiracy theory, the possibility of a lost note having been paid can be rejected out of hand. *Two* of his statements are thus refuted by the Baraita (*Tosefot Sens*).

תְּיוּבְתָּא דְּרַבִּי אֶלְעָזָר בַּחֲדָא **The Baraita contradicts Rabbi Elazar in one respect.** There is a tradition cited by the Rishonim that the entire discussion revolving around this Baraita is not part of the original Gemara but is a later insertion from the Geonic period. Many commentators found this passage, and *Rashi*'s interpretation of it, to be full of difficulties, and they accordingly rejected it (*Ramban*, *Rashba*, and others). Others attempted to defend this passage, interpreting it slightly differently from *Rashi*: Rabbi Elazar never openly stated his position, that there is no reason to suspect payment and conspiracy. The Gemara merely deduced it from his position regarding the difference of opinion between Rabbi Meir and the Sages. Shmuel, on the other hand, openly stated his opposition to the payment and conspiracy theory (*Rabbenu Ḥananel*).

Ra'avad suggests that Rabbi Elazar may have been talking specifically about deeds of transfer. *Ra'avad*, unlike *Rashi*, holds that deeds of transfer are effective only if a loan actually takes place. Accordingly, if the borrower denies his debt, it is improper to return a lost deed of transfer if it includes a clause mortgaging the borrower's property, or even if it does not include one, according to the Sages who say that such a document is effective for seizing free property. But if the borrower admits his debt, there is no reason not to return the note, since we are not concerned about a possible conspiracy, and since the document is a deed of transfer. The Baraita, on the other hand, may be talking about ordinary promissory notes that are not deeds of transfer. These may not be returned because of the problem raised by Rav Assi that they may have been illicitly predated. There is, therefore, no proof from the Baraita that we suspect payment and conspiracy. Shmuel, on the other hand, is known to have supported Abaye's position — this is *Ra'avad*'s interpretation of the previous discussion — and therefore considers all promissory notes to be, in effect, deeds of transfer. (See *Ran* in *Shittah Mekubbetzet*.)

דְּאָמַר: לְרַבִּי מֵאִיר, שְׁטָר שֶׁאֵין בּוֹ אַחֲרָיוּת נְכָסִים, אֵינוֹ גּוֹבֶה מִנְּכָסִים מְשׁוּעְבָּדִים וְלֹא מִנְּכָסִים בְּנֵי חוֹרִין. [1]וְקָאָמַר: בֵּין לְרַבִּי מֵאִיר בֵּין לְרַבָּנַן, לָא חָיְישִׁינַן לִקְנוּנְיָא. [2]וּבָרַיְיתָא קָתָנֵי: שְׁטָר שֶׁאֵין בּוֹ אַחֲרָיוּת נְכָסִים, מִמְּשַׁעְבְּדֵי הוּא דְּלָא גָּבֵי, הָא מִבְּנֵי חוֹרִין מִגְבָּא גָּבֵי. [3]וְקָתָנֵי בֵּין לְרַבִּי מֵאִיר בֵּין לְרַבָּנַן, חָיְישִׁינַן לִקְנוּנְיָא. [4]דְּקָתָנֵי: ״אַף עַל פִּי שֶׁשְּׁנֵיהֶם מוֹדִים, לֹא יַחֲזִיר, לֹא לָזֶה וְלֹא לָזֶה״. [5]אַלְמָא, חָיְישִׁינַן לִקְנוּנְיָא.
[6]וְהָא הָנֵי תַּרְתֵּי הוּא!
[14A] [7]חֲדָא הוּא, דְּחַד טַעַם

LITERAL TRANSLATION

for he said: [According] to Rabbi Meir, [in the case of] a promissory note which does not contain [a clause] mortgaging [the borrower's landed] property [as security for the loan], [the lender] does not collect from mortgaged property and not from free property. [1]And he said: Both [according] to Rabbi Meir and [according] to the Sages, we do not suspect conspiracy. [2]But the Baraita teaches: [In the case of] a promissory note which does not contain [a clause] mortgaging [the borrower's landed] property [as security for the loan], it is from mortgaged property that he does not collect, but from free property he may certainly collect.

[3]And it [also] teaches [that] both [according] to Rabbi Meir and [according] to the Sages, we suspect conspiracy. [4]For it teaches: Even though both of them admit [the debt], [the finder] should not return [the note], not to this one and not to this one." [5]Thus, we do suspect conspiracy.

[6]But surely these are two [respects]!

[14A] [7]It is [considered] one [respect], for it is [based on] one reason.

TRANSLATION AND COMMENTARY

for Rabbi Elazar **said: According to Rabbi Meir, in the case of a promissory note which does not contain a clause mortgaging the borrower's landed property as security for the loan, the lender may not collect from** the borrower's **mortgaged property nor from his free property.** [1]**And** Rabbi Elazar further **said: Both according to Rabbi Meir and according to the Sages, we do not suspect conspiracy** between the borrower and lender, as explained above. [2]**But the Baraita teaches: In the case of a promissory note which does not contain a clause mortgaging the borrower's landed property as security for the loan, it is** only **from** the borrower's **mortgaged property** that the lender **may not collect, but from his free property he may certainly collect!**

וְקָתָנֵי בֵּין לְרַבִּי מֵאִיר [3]**And** the Baraita **also teaches** by implication that **both according to Rabbi Meir and according to the Sages, we** do indeed **suspect conspiracy** between the borrower and the lender, [4]**for it teaches** regarding promissory notes which contain a clause mortgaging the borrower's landed property as security for the loan: "**Even though both** parties **admit** that **the debt** is still outstanding, **the finder should not return the note, neither to the one** party **nor to the other.**" Now, there can be no reason not to return a promissory note which the borrower admits has not yet been paid, unless there is some sort of conspiracy to defraud the buyers. [5]**Thus,** by implication, it would appear that **we do suspect** the possibility of **conspiracy!** This concludes the Gemara's use of the Baraita as a refutation of Rabbi Elazar's statement.

וְהָא הָנֵי תַּרְתֵּי הוּא [6]The Gemara now objects: **But surely these** refutations raised from the Baraita **are two** separate **respects** in which the Baraita refutes Rabbi Elazar, one concerning Rabbi Meir's viewpoint on collecting a debt from free property, and the other concerning the question of conspiracy. Why, then, did the Gemara state previously that the Baraita refutes Rabbi Elazar in only one respect?

חֲדָא הוּא [14A] [7]The Gemara answers: The two difficulties posed by the Baraita to the viewpoint of Rabbi Elazar are really a refutation of him in only **one respect, for one reason underlies** both elements of Rabbi

RASHI

הני תרתי מילי הוי — ואת אמרת תיובתא דרבי אלעזר בחדא. **ומשני חדא הוא דחד טעמא הוא** — טעם אחד הזקיקו לרבי אלעזר לומר את שתיהן. דמשום דקאמר מחלוקת דמתניתין ״בשאין חייב מודה״, הוזקק לומר שאינו גובה אפילו מבני חורין. וכיון דהוצרך לסיים ״אבל כשחייב מודה דברי הכל יחזיר״, הוזקק לומר לא חיישינן לקנוניא.

NOTES

חָיְישִׁינַן לִקְנוּנְיָא **The Baraita implies that we do suspect conspiracy.** There is no conclusive evidence in the Baraita that it forbids returning the promissory note because it suspects conspiracy. It is possible to interpret its prohibition of returning a lost promissory note in a case where the borrower admits his debt, in accordance with the suspicion (mentioned by Rav Assi) that the borrower may have written the note in the absence of the lender and borrowed later, at a date different from the one in the document. At all events the refutation of Rabbi Elazar's position would be identical, according to either interpretation (*Tosafot*).

הוּא. דְּמִשּׁוּם דְּקָאָמַר רַבִּי אֶלְעָזָר מַחֲלוֹקֶת בְּשֶׁאֵין חַיָּיב מוֹדֶה, הוּא מְתָרֵץ הָכִי.
[1] תְּיוּבְתָּא דִּשְׁמוּאֵל בְּתַרְתֵּי: [2] חֲדָא כְּרַבִּי אֶלְעָזָר, דְּהָא מוֹקֵי מַתְנִיתִין בְּשֶׁאֵין חַיָּיב מוֹדֶה. [3] וַחֲדָא דַּאֲמַר שְׁמוּאֵל: מָצָא שְׁטַר הַקְנָאָה בַּשּׁוּק, יַחֲזִיר לַבְּעָלִים, וְלָא חָיְישִׁינַן לְפֵרָעוֹן. [4] תְּיוּבְתָּא, דְּקָתָנֵי הָכָא: ״אַף עַל פִּי שֶׁשְּׁנֵיהֶם מוֹדִים, לֹא יַחֲזִיר לֹא לָזֶה וְלֹא לָזֶה״. [5] אַלְמָא, חָיְישִׁינַן לְפֵרָעוֹן, וְכָל שֶׁכֵּן הָכָא, דְּלָא מוֹדֶה לֹוֶה, דְּחָיְישִׁינַן לְפֵרָעוֹן!

LITERAL TRANSLATION

For [it is] because Rabbi Elazar said that the difference of opinion [applies] when the debtor does not admit [his debt], [that] he explains [the difference of opinion] this way.

[1] [The Baraita is] a refutation of Shmuel in two [respects: The] [2] one is like [the refutation of] Rabbi Elazar, for [Shmuel also] explained the Mishnah [as referring to a case] where the debtor does not admit [his debt]. [3] And one [respect] is that Shmuel said: [If] one finds deeds of transfer in the marketplace, [the finder] should return [them] to the owner, and we do not suspect payment. [4] This is a refutation [of this statement of Shmuel], for [the Baraita] teaches here: "Even though both of them admit [the debt, the finder] should not return [the promissory note], not to this one and not to this one." [5] Thus, we do suspect payment, and how much more so here, where the borrower does not admit [the debt], should we suspect payment!

TRANSLATION AND COMMENTARY

opinion between Rabbi Meir and the Sages in **this way**. By assuming that the difference of opinion in the Mishnah applies when the borrower denies the debt, where it is possible that he is telling the truth, Rabbi Elazar is forced to say that, according to Rabbi Meir, the document is in any case of no value, because the lender cannot extract payment even from the borrower's free property with a document from which the mortgage clause is lacking. This leads him inevitably to the conclusion that, if the borrower admits the debt, both the Rabbis and Rabbi Meir agree that the document should be returned to the lender, and this in its turn shows that we do not suspect payment and conspiracy. Thus the two conclusions in which Rabbi Elazar finds himself in conflict with the Baraita are really derived from the same premise.

תְּיוּבְתָּא דִּשְׁמוּאֵל בְּתַרְתֵּי [1] The Gemara continues: Similarly, **the Baraita is a refutation of Shmuel in two respects:** [2] **The one** — the double objection mentioned above — **is like the refutation of Rabbi Elazar; for Shmuel also explained the Mishnah as referring to a case where the debtor does not admit his debt** and this led him, like Rabbi Elazar, to conclusions that are in conflict with the Baraita. [3] **And the other respect** in which Shmuel is in conflict with the Baraita **is that Shmuel said: If someone finds a deed of transfer in the marketplace** (i.e., a promissory note stating that the lien on the borrower's property takes effect from the date of the document, irrespective of whether the loan was given on that date or later or not at all), **the finder should return** the note **to the owner, and we do not suspect payment**, because Shmuel is of the opinion that a claim of payment is never credible, since once a debt has been repaid the borrower immediately destroys the promissory note. [4] Now, says the Gemara, the Baraita **is** also **a refutation of this statement of Shmuel, for the Baraita states here: "Even though both** borrower and lender **admit the debt, the finder should not return the promissory note, neither to the one** party **nor to the other."** [5] **Thus**, by implication, it would appear that **we do suspect** the possibility of **payment. How much more so here**, in the case of deeds of transfer, **where the borrower does not admit** that he owes money to the creditor, **should we suspect** the possibility of **payment**!

RASHI

שטר הקנאה — דליכא למימר כתב ללות ולא לוה, דהא אפילו לא לוה שעביד נפשיה. **ולא חיישינן לפרעון** — אפילו אין חייב מודה. דאם איתא דפרעיה — מקרע הוה קרע ליה. והכא קתני אף על פי ששניהם מודים כו׳. **וכל שכן בשאינו מודה** — והוא לא קשיא לרבי אלעזר, דהוא אמר בשאין חייב מודה לא יחזיר שום שטר הראוי לגבות, דהאי דקאמר רבי מאיר יחזיר משום דלאו בר גבייה הוא.

NOTES

תְּיוּבְתָּא דִּשְׁמוּאֵל **A refutation of Shmuel**. The commentators ask: Why is this Baraita considered to be a refutation of Shmuel? Shmuel may agree with those Tannaim (see above, 7b) who maintain that there is no reason to suspect that the loan may have been repaid! *Ḥokhmat Manoaḥ* therefore explains that it is not Shmuel's Halakhic ruling (i.e., that we do not suspect the possibility of payment) which is refuted here, but rather his interpretation of the dispute between Rabbi Meir and the Sages.

[1]אֲמַר שְׁמוּאֵל: מַאי טַעֲמַיְיהוּ דְּרַבָּנַן? סָבְרִי: אַחֲרָיוּת טָעוּת סוֹפֵר הוּא.
[2]אֲמַר לֵיהּ רָבָא בַּר אִיתַּי לְרַב אִידִי בַּר אָבִין: וּמִי אֲמַר שְׁמוּאֵל הָכִי? וְהָאֲמַר שְׁמוּאֵל: שֶׁבַח, שְׁפָר וְשִׁעְבּוּד צָרִיךְ

LITERAL TRANSLATION

[1] Shmuel said: What is the Sages' reason? They maintain: [Omission of a clause] mortgaging [the borrower's landed property as security for the loan] is an error of the scribe.

[2] Rava bar Ittai said to Rav Idi bar Avin: But did Shmuel say this? But surely Shmuel said: Appreciation [in value], best property, and mortgage need consultation!

TRANSLATION AND COMMENTARY

אֲמַר שְׁמוּאֵל [1] Having completed its discussion of Rabbi Meir's view, the Gemara now turns to consider the view of the Sages. Since they do not allow the finder to return any lost note, and they make no distinction between notes containing guarantee clauses and notes lacking such clauses, it is clear that they maintain that even notes laking such clauses generate a lien that could threaten the buyers. The Gemara now examines this position. **Shmuel said**: **What is the Sages' reason** for ruling that property sold by the borrower to a third party may be seized by the lender in repayment of his loan, even if the promissory note contains no clause mortgaging the borrower's landed property as security for the loan? The Sages **maintain: The omission of a clause** in the promissory note **mortgaging the borrower's landed property as security for the loan is an** accidental **error** on the part **of the scribe**. Since it is inconceivable that a man would lend money and receive a promissory note without asking for some sort of collateral, we must assume that the omission of a clause mortgaging the borrower's property was the result of an accidental error by the scribe who drew up the document, and the note must be treated as if it contains such a clause.

אֲמַר לֵיהּ רָבָא בַּר אִיתַּי [2] **Rava bar Ittai said to Rav Idi bar Avin**: **But did Shmuel** really **say** that the omission of a clause in the document mortgaging the borrower's landed property is merely an error by the scribe? **Surely Shmuel said**: (1) **Appreciation** in value, (2) **best property**, **and** (3) **mortgage need consultation**! When a scribe writes a deed of sale for a field, he must not simply assume that the seller wants to guarantee the

RASHI

מאי טעמייהו דרבנן — דאמרי כי אין בו אחריות נכסים גובה אף מן המשועבדים. **אחריות טעות סופר הוא.** — כשאינו כתוב בשטר — סופר הוא שטעה. אבל זה לא לוה לו מעותיו בלא אחריות נכסים, דלא שדי איניש זוזי בכדי. **שבח שפר ושעבוד צריך לימלך** — הסופר צריך לימלך במוכר שדה לחבירו, לישאל הימנו אם יקבל עליו לכתוב בשטר המכירה שהוא שיעבד לו נכסיו למכירה זו, שאם יבא בעל חובו ויטרפנה מן הלוקח שיגבה לוקח זה הקרן והשבח שהשביח בה לפני טירפא משפר = עידית שבנכסים. ואם לא נמלך בו — לא יכתוב. שיש מוכר שאין מקבל עליו אחריות, ואף אם קבל על הקרן — לא קבל על השבח. ואף אם קבל על שניהם — לא קבל להגבותו מן העידית, אלא מן הבינונית. אלמא: לאו טעות סופר הוא, דאיכא למימר אמליך ביה, ולא קבל עליה.

NOTES

מַאי טַעֲמַיְיהוּ דְּרַבָּנַן What is the Sages' reason? *Tosafot* ask: How does Shmuel know that the Sages consider a promissory note that lacks the usual clause mortgaging the borrower's property to be sufficient to seize the borrower's property sold to a third party? All we really know is that they forbid returning such a document to the lender if the borrower denies he owes any money. Perhaps they are not concerned about the buyers at all, but rather about the lender unjustly seizing *free property* from the borrower himself? It is true that the Baraita might have served as a source for Shmuel's interpretation of the Sages' view, but we know that the Baraita explicitly contradicts Shmuel himself. Hence, we must assume that Shmuel was not aware of the Baraita.

Some commentators explain that Shmuel was indeed aware of the Baraita, but that he consciously rejected it because he felt that it did not offer a convincing interpretation of our Mishnah. Accordingly, he rejected the Baraita's version of Rabbi Meir's position, as well as its implied opinion on the question of suspected payment. On the other hand, concerning the question of the Sages' views on documents lacking the mortgage clause, Shmuel saw no reason not to accept the Baraita's version as the definitive ruling (*Tosefot Sens*).

Other commentators suggest that after Shmuel became aware of the Baraita, he retracted his previous opinion, and then explained the reasoning of the Sages as described in the Baraita (*Talmid Rabbenu Peretz*).

אַחֲרָיוּת טָעוּת סוֹפֵר Omission of a clause mortgaging property is assumed to be the result of scribal error. Most commentators maintain that even if the omission was not literally caused by the scribe's carelessness, in other words, even if the lender and the borrower genuinely failed to mention anything about a clause mortgaging property when the scribe drew up the document, it was still necessary to include such a clause in the document. Therefore, a lien is still generated, even in such a case (*Rashba*, *Ran*, and others).

שֶׁבַח וּשְׁפָר Appreciation and best property. *Meiri* cites an opinion that the right of the buyer to compensation from

HALAKHAH

אַחֲרָיוּת טָעוּת סוֹפֵר Omission of a mortgage of landed property as security may be attributed to scribal error. "Any promissory note or deed of sale, even if it does not contain a clause mortaging property as security, is considered as if it does contain such a clause and generates a property lien accordingly, since omission of such a clause

CONCEPTS

סוֹפֵר Scribe. The main meaning of this word is "a professional scribe." But the term also became a title bestowed on various kinds of men. In Biblical Hebrew it is a special title, and it has various uses in Rabbinical Hebrew. In the language of the Sages, when used in the plural (סוֹפְרִים) it refers to the Sages in general, mainly to the Sages of the early generations; hence the term דִּבְרֵי סוֹפְרִים, meaning "Rabbinical decrees." In its more limited sense it refers to professional scribes who used to write documents for other people, in particular legal documents of various kinds, in the proper wording of which not everyone was expert. In the context here it is mentioned that, despite the fact that the scribe is a professional, he sometimes makes a mistake and omits a section of an official document. Many scribes were also schoolteachers, and occasionally the word has that specific meaning. There were also special scribes attached to a court, something like an official clerk to the court, and they would also write the formal decisions of the court.

SAGES

רַב אִידִי בַּר אָבִין Rav Idi bar Avin. Rav Idi bar Avin belonged to the third and fourth generations of Babylonian Amoraim. Of Rav Idi's father, Rav Avin Nagara ("the carpenter"), it is told that he was especially punctilious in the ceremony of lighting the Sabbath candles, and Rav Huna predicted that Rav Avin would be privileged to have sons who were eminent scholars. Indeed, his sons were Rav Ḥiyya bar Avin and Rav Idi bar Avin.

Rav Idi bar Avin was a student of Rav Ḥisda, but he also quotes other Sages of the second generation of Babylonian Amoraim. He was one of the greatest authorities of his generation, and many of his Halakhic discussions with Abaye are recorded in the Talmud. Rav Idi was the chief Rabbinic authority in his city, Shekanzib, where he apparently had a private yeshivah. Rav Idi lived to a great age, and the most

לִימָלֵךְ! [1] לֵימָא מַאן דַּאֲמַר הָא לָא אֲמַר הָא?

[2] לָא קַשְׁיָא. כָּאן בִּשְׁטַר הַלְוָאָה, דְּלָא יָהֵיב אֱינָשׁ זוּזֵי בִּכְדִי. [3] כָּאן בְּמִקָּח וּמִמְכָּר, דְּעָבֵיד אֱינָשׁ דְּזַבֵּין אַרְעָא לְיוֹמֵיהּ.

[4] כִּי הַהִיא, דַּאֲבוּהּ בַּר אִיהִי זַבֵּין עֲלִיתָא מֵאַחְתֵיהּ. אֲתָא בַּעַל חוֹב טָרְפָא מִינֵּיהּ. [5] אֲתָא לְקַמֵּיהּ דְּמָר שְׁמוּאֵל. אֲמַר לֵיהּ: ״כָּתְבָה לָךְ אַחֲרָיוּת?״

LITERAL TRANSLATION

[1] Must we say: The one who said this did not say this?

[2] There is no difficulty. Here [we are dealing with] a note for a loan, for a person does not give money for nothing. [3] [But] here [we are dealing] with buying and selling, for a person may buy land for a day.

[4] Like this [incident], where Avuh bar Ihi bought an attic from his sister. A creditor came [and] seized it from him. [5] He came before Mar Shmuel. [Shmuel] said to him: "Did she write a guarantee for you?"

RASHI

לימא מאן דאמר הא – משמיה דשמואל. **לא אמר הא** – ואמוראי נינהו אליבא דשמואל.

TRANSLATION AND COMMENTARY

sale absolutely, because not every seller is willing to give such a sweeping guarantee. Instead he must ask the seller whether he wants to include a guarantee that (1) in the event of the field being seized by a creditor of the seller, the seller will reimburse the buyer for any **appreciation in the value** of the field resulting from the buyer's efforts; (2) that such reimbursement will be made from the seller's **best property**; and (3) that the seller's remaining property will be **mortgaged** to the buyer as security in case a creditor comes and seizes the field as repayment for a previous loan. To protect the buyer in these three ways it is necessary for the scribe to consult with the parties and receive the seller's express permission! Thus, it would appear from this statement that Shmuel does not assume that all documents recording transactions automatically contain a clause mortgaging property as security for the transaction. [1] Accordingly, Rava asks: **Must we say** that the Sage **who transmitted the one** statement of Shmuel **did not transmit the other?** In other words, must we assume that there is a difference of opinion between Amoraim regarding Shmuel's view?

לָא קַשְׁיָא [2] The Gemara answers: **There is no difficulty. Here**, in connection with our Mishnah, where Shmuel said that the omission of a clause in a promissory note mortgaging the borrower's landed property as security for the loan is an error by the scribe, **we are dealing with a note** issued in connection **with a loan**, and the reason for Shmuel's statement is that **a person does not give** another person a loan of **money for nothing**, i.e., without providing himself with some sort of collateral to guarantee collection of the loan. [3] **But here**, in Shmuel's other statement, where he said that the scribe must obtain the seller's express permission before including any sort of guarantee in the document, **we are dealing** specifically **with** a deed issued in connection with **buying and selling**, and the reason for Shmuel's statement is that **a person may** be willing to **buy land for a day**. In other words, a person may be prepared to buy land, even if his investment is not guaranteed, because he expects to be able to benefit from the land in the short term, even if it is ultimately taken away from him.

כִּי הַהִיא דַּאֲבוּהּ בַּר אִיהִי [4] As proof of the correctness of this answer, the Gemara cites an actual case: Consider, it says, **the** following **incident, where Avuh bar Ihi bought an attic from his sister.** [5] **A creditor** of his sister **came and seized it from him. He came before Mar Shmuel** to file a claim against his sister, and **Shmuel said to him: "Did she write a guarantee for you**, indicating that she would reimburse you if the attic were seized by a creditor?"

eminent scholars of the next generation, Rav Pappa and Rav Huna the son of Rav Yehoshua, were his students. In his old age he called his students דַּרְדְּקֵי — "infants." We know little of his deeds or the story of his life, except that he had two sons who were Sages.

BACKGROUND

מָר שְׁמוּאֵל Mar Shmuel. The word מָר — "master" — is used as a form of respect in addressing an elder scholar. As a title it is used to denote scholars of the family of the Exilarch. The case of Shmuel is exceptional, because even though he did not receive formal ordination, and was not called Rabbi, he was one of the greatest scholars of his time. Hence the honorific title מָר is often added to his name.

NOTES

the best property of the seller is not under discussion here, and it is clear that such a right can be exercised only if it is mentioned explicitly in the document. Instead, the word שְׁפַר is to be translated as "improved" rather than "best." According to this interpretation, שְׁפַר is virtually synonymous with שְׁבַח, but שְׁבַח is identified with an appreciation in market value caused by independent factors, such as a general rise in land prices, while שְׁפַר refers to improvements brought about through the buyer's efforts.

מַאן דַּאֲמַר הָא The one who said this.... *Rashi* explains this passage as suggesting that different students of Shmuel may have cited conflicting traditions in Shmuel's name. Others explain that the Gemara is suggesting that one of Shmuel's statements is merely his interpretation of the Sages' view, with which he himself is not in agreement (*Ritva*, in the name of his teacher).

דְּזַבֵּין אַרְעָא לְיוֹמֵיהּ For a person may buy land for a day. In such a case there must be a significant difference in price between property that a person buys with the intention of keeping it permanently, and property whose acquisition involves substantial risk. Here Shmuel takes the approach that one cannot bring proof from the price paid, for occasionally a person needs something and is willing to pay far more than its normal price for it.

HALAKHAH

is assumed to have been the result of scribal error," in accordance with the view of Rava, who disagrees with Shmuel later in the discussion (below, 15b). (*Shulḥan Arukh, Ḥoshen Mishpat* 39:1 and 225:1.)

BACKGROUND

רְאוּבֵן **Reuven.** The Sages used the names of Jacob's sons as standard names, like John Doe, instead of using more general expressions like "a man," "another man," etc. In these cases the names stand for anyone and have no particular significance except convenience. But in some cases these names, as well as those of the Patriarchs and Matriarchs, are used to indicate people who are related to each other. For example, three brothers might be called Reuven, Shimon, and Levi, and the father might be called Jacob, etc.

TRANSLATION AND COMMENTARY

[1] **He said to** Shmuel: **"No."** [2] Shmuel **said to him**: **"If** this is the case, **go in peace**, for there is nothing I can do for you in the matter." [3] **Avuh** bar Ihi **said to** Shmuel: **"But you, Sir, are the one who said that** the **omission of a clause mortgaging property is an error of the scribe!"** The same principle should apply here, and Avuh's sister should be required to reimburse him! [4] Shmuel **said to him**: **"This** principle that I have stated **applies to notes** issued in connection **with loans, but not to deeds of purchase, for a person may buy land for a day."**

אָמַר אַבַּיֵי [5] **Abaye said**: If **Reuven sold a field to Shimon with a guarantee** mortgaging Reuven's other landed property in the event that a creditor of Reuven's should come and seize the field he sold to Shimon, **and Reuven's creditor came and** attempted to **seize it from** Shimon in payment for an outstanding debt of Reuven, [6] **the law is that Reuven can go and sue the creditor**, and file a counterclaim, in order to prevent the latter from taking possession of the field. [7] In such a situation the creditor **cannot say to** Reuven: "Since you have already sold the field to Shimon, **you have no legal standing** in my claim against Shimon to expropriate his field. He can sue you separately to recover the purchase price of the field, and you can sue me separately for any other claim you have against me. But you cannot prevent me from recovering my debt from Shimon's field." [8] Such an argument by Reuven's creditor is not accepted, **because Reuven can say to** the creditor: **"Whatever you take from** Shimon **comes back to me** for repayment. Since I sold the field to Shimon with a guarantee, I have to reimburse him for the loss of his property. Therefore I stand to lose if you seize his property, and hence I am entitled to make a counterclaim against you, to prevent you from seizing the field from Shimon. Your claim against Shimon and my claim against you are interconnected, and you cannot assert that they are separate."

[1] אֲמַר לֵיהּ: ״לָא״. [2] אֲמַר לֵיהּ: ״אִם כֵּן, זִיל לִשְׁלָמָא״. [3] אֲמַר לֵיהּ: ״וְהָא מָר הוּא דַּאֲמַר אַחֲרָיוּת טָעוּת סוֹפֵר הוּא!״ [4] אֲמַר לֵיהּ: ״הָנֵי מִילֵּי בִּשְׁטָרֵי הַלְוָאָה, אֲבָל בִּשְׁטָרֵי מִקָּח וּמִמְכָּר לָא, דְּעָבֵיד אֱינָשׁ דְּזַבֵּין אַרְעָא לְיוֹמֵיהּ״.

[5] אֲמַר אַבַּיֵי: רְאוּבֵן שֶׁמָּכַר שָׂדֶה לְשִׁמְעוֹן בְּאַחֲרָיוּת, וּבָא בַּעַל חוֹב דִּרְאוּבֵן וְקָא טָרֵיף לֵיהּ מִינֵּיהּ, [6] דִּינָא הוּא דְּאָזֵיל רְאוּבֵן וּמִשְׁתָּעֵי דִּינָא בַּהֲדֵיהּ, [7] וְלָא מָצֵי אֲמַר לֵיהּ: ״לָאו בַּעַל דְּבָרִים דִּידִי אַתְּ״. [8] דַּאֲמַר לֵיהּ: ״דְּמַפְּקַתְ מִינֵּיהּ עֲלַי דִּידִי הָדַר״.

LITERAL TRANSLATION

[1] He said to him: "No." [2] [Shmuel] said to him: "If so, go in peace." [3] [Avuh] said to him: "But [you], Sir, [are] the one who said that [omission of a clause] mortgaging [property] is an error of the scribe!"

[4] [Shmuel] said to him: "This applies (lit., "these words") to notes for a loan, but not to deeds of purchase, for a person may buy land for a day.

[5] Abaye said: Reuven who sold a field to Shimon with a guarantee, and Reuven's creditor came and seized it from him, [6] the law is that Reuven can go and sue him (lit., "talk justice with him") [the creditor], [7] and [the creditor] cannot say to him: "You have no legal standing (lit., 'you are not my master of words')." [8] For [Reuven] can say to him: "What you take from him comes back to me."

RASHI

בשטרי הלואה – טעות סופר הוא, כיון דלא אכיל פירות ולא מתהני מידי – לא שדי זוזי בכדי לאוזפיה בלא אחריות, וזה ימכור נכסיו, וכשיבא לגבות לא ימצא כלום. **עביד אינש דזבין ארעא ליומא** – לספק יום אחד, שמא לא יטרפוה ממנו. ואם יטרפוה – שמא לזמן מרובה, ואוכל בתוך כך פירות הרבה. **זיל לשלמא** – אין כאן עוד דין, שמחלת על הכל. **באחריות** – אם יטרפוה ממנו ישלם לו. **לאשתעויי דינא בהדיה** – דבעל חוב, ולסלקו מעל שמעון בכל טענה שיוכל לטעון, ולומר: פרעתיך כך וכך, או כך וכך יש לי עליך תביעה, ואני מעכב חוב זה תחתיו. **ולא מצי** – בעל חוב למימר ליה: לאו בעל דברים דידי את בדבר זה, קרקע שמעון אני נוטל, אם יש לך תביעה עלי העמידני בדין. **דמפקת מיניה עלי הדר** – מה שאתה מוציא משמעון יחזור עלי.

NOTES

דִּינָא הוּא דְּאָזֵיל רְאוּבֵן **The law is that Reuven may go and sue his creditor**. The commentators explain that Reuven is under no obligation to sue the creditor in order to help Shimon. Rather, he is permitted to do so, if he so desires (see *Ritva* and *Shittah Mekubbetzet*).

דְּאָזֵיל רְאוּבֵן וּמִשְׁתָּעֵי דִּינָא **Reuven may go and sue**. *Tosafot* asks: What difference does it make whether or not Reuven is entitled to sue? Any arguments that Reuven can present can just as well be presented by Shimon, and if Shimon does not offer them, the court will do so on his behalf, in accordance with standard procedure for the protection of innocent buyers threatened by the seller's creditors.

Tosafot suggests several advantages that Reuven may have over Shimon in rebutting the creditor's claim to the field, such as the possibility that the creditor may be less likely to perjure himself when faced with the actual borrower, rather than with a stranger.

In a similar vein, *Ḥokhmat Manoaḥ* suggests that Reuven may be intelligent enough to present arguments that the court has not thought of. Alternatively, he may explain that something very unusual happened in this case — a claim that cannot be advanced by the court, even to protect the interests of innocent buyers.

Others, following *Rashi*, explain that Reuven can claim

[1] אִיכָּא דְּאָמְרִי: אֲפִילּוּ שֶׁלֹּא בְּאַחֲרָיוּת נַמִי. דְּאָמַר לֵיהּ: ״לָא נִיחָא לִי דְּלֵיהֱוֵי לְשִׁמְעוֹן תַּרְעוֹמֶת עֲלַי״.

[2] וְאָמַר אַבַּיֵי: רְאוּבֵן שֶׁמָּכַר שָׂדֶה לְשִׁמְעוֹן שֶׁלֹּא בְּאַחֲרָיוּת, וְיָצְאוּ עָלֶיהָ עֲסִיקִין, עַד שֶׁלֹּא הֶחֱזִיק בָּהּ [14B] יָכוֹל לַחֲזוֹר בּוֹ; מִשֶּׁהֶחֱזִיק בָּהּ, אֵינוֹ יָכוֹל לַחֲזוֹר בּוֹ.

LITERAL TRANSLATION

[1] There are some who say: Even [if he sold] without a guarantee too. For [Reuven] can say to him: "I do not want Shimon to have complaints against me."

[2] Abaye also said: Reuben who sold a field to Shimon without a guarantee, and [people] came out protesting against it, as long as [Shimon] has not taken possession of it, [14B] he can go back on [the purchase]; once he has taken possession of it, he cannot go back on it.

RASHI

עסיקין = עוררין, כמו ״התעשקו עמו״ (בראשית כו). **יכול לחזור בו** — ובשלא נתן מעות. **אינו יכול לחזור בו** — ואפילו לא נתן מעות. שהקרקע נקנית בחזקה, והמעות על זה מלוה.

TRANSLATION AND COMMENTARY

אִיכָּא דְּאָמְרִי [1] **There are some who** have a different version of Abaye's ruling. They **say** that Abaye maintained that Reuven can make a counterclaim against the creditor **even if he sold** the field to Shimon **without a guarantee**. **For Reuven can say to** the creditor: **"I do not want Shimon to have complaints against me**, that I treated him unfairly in selling him property that he cannot keep."

וְאָמַר אַבַּיֵי [2] **Abaye also said** on a related topic: If **Reuven sold a field to Shimon without a guarantee, and people came out, protesting against** the sale and claiming that they were the owners of the field, **as long as Shimon has not** formally **taken possession of** the field, by performing a symbolic act making him the owner of the field (see below) [14B] **he can go back on the purchase**, but **once he has taken possession of it, he cannot go back on** the purchase.

NOTES

that the creditor actually owes him money in another, separate, transaction, and that the two loans thus cancel each other out. Obviously the court cannot advance such a claim on the buyers' behalf (*Rid* explaining *Rashi*).

Other commentators suggest that the field sold by Reuven to Shimon may not only have been mortgaged as security for the loan taken out earlier by Reuven but may actually have been designated as absolute collateral (אַפּוֹתִיקֵי מְפוֹרָשׁ) for that loan. When a field has been designated as absolute collateral, the creditor is entitled to refuse any substitute for the field, except for payment in cash directly from the borrower. Accordingly, Shimon cannot persuade Reuven's creditor to accept an alternative to the field. Only Reuven can divert the creditor from the field by offering a cash payment (*Rashba*).

מִשֶּׁהֶחֱזִיק בָּהּ Once he has taken possession of it. There is a difference of opinion among the commentators as to the exact meaning in the present context of the phrase "to take possession" (לְהַחֲזִיק). Usually, חֲזָקָה refers to a particular mode of acquiring landed property: As soon as the new owner symbolically demonstrates his ownership by making repairs to the fence, he acquires the field, even though he has not yet paid for it. *Rashi* explains that our passage is indeed referring to this form of acquisition when it says, "he takes possession." Accordingly he explains the phrase דָּיֵישׁ אַמְּצְרֵי (literally, "stepping upon the boundaries") as meaning, "repairing the boundary fence." According to *Rashi*, then, the Gemara is stating that once a valid transfer is effected, the buyer cannot change his mind.

Some commentators, however, explain that the case under discussion is where the buyer has already acquired the field using one of the accepted modes of acquisition, but has not yet paid for it before the seller's creditor appears and tries to seize it. Accordingly, the buyer now wants to hold on to the money and to give up the field to the seller (or to his creditor). The Gemara tells us that the buyer may do so, even though the transfer has already been effected, if he has not paid the money, so long as he has not yet "taken possession," in the special sense of walking around his field and viewing his new property (*Tosafot* and *Rosh*).

Others explain that the buyer may retract even if he has already paid for the field. Since he had not yet begun using it when he discovered that it would probably be taken away, the sale is considered to have taken place under false pretences and is therefore retroactively invalid. But if the buyer has already begun using the field, and only then does he learn that other people are contesting ownership of it, he has no right to invalidate the sale — although, of course, he may still enforce whatever guarantees the seller may have given him. The reason for this ruling is that a problem of ownership which arises at the time of acquisition can be viewed not merely as a matter for the seller to make good under his guarantee, but as a flaw in the field itself which the seller failed to mention. But after a certain point the buyer's problem can only be solved by invoking the seller's guarantee. The cutoff point is when the buyer begins to use the field (*Ran*).

Others point out that in our passage the Gemara uses the past tense to describe the buyer's taking possession (מִשֶּׁהֶחֱזִיק), rather than the future tense (מִשֶּׁיַּחֲזִיק). Accordingly, they explain that the Gemara does not mean to say that the moment of taking possession is the last point

HALAKHAH

מִי רַשַּׁאי לָדוּן בִּנְכָסִים שֶׁנִּטְרְפוּ Who is entitled to sue when property is seized? "If Reuven sold his field to Shimon, and then Levi came and attempted to seize the field from Shimon, Reuven may bring a counterclaim against Levi, and Levi cannot claim that Reuven has no further standing in Reuven sold the field to Shimon with a property guarantee, but even if he sold it without such a guarantee." This ruling follows the second version of Abaye's statement here, in keeping with the regular practice that the Halakhah ordinarily follows the second version of a statement. (*Shulḥan Arukh, Ḥoshen Mishpat*, 226:1.)

CONCEPTS

תַּרְעוֹמֶת Complaints, resentment. Resentment may have merely emotional significance, because a person does not want others to harbor resentment against him for having caused them problems. However, in the Halakhah resentment has a quasi-legal meaning. In cases where a person has behaved unfairly and has thus caused material or other damage to another, the latter has grounds for resentment. An ethical person who wishes to act not only in accordance with the letter of the law but also with its spirit must be sure to compensate the other person for his loss. Therefore the expression אֵין לוֹ תַּרְעוֹמֶת — he has no resentment — is used, meaning that in a certain case there is no moral reason even for resentment.

LANGUAGE

עֲסִיקִין Protesters. As *Tosafot* (ד״ה וְיָצְאוּ) demonstrates, this means that plaintiffs challenge the seller's right to the field, either arguing that they themselves have a prior claim, or that the seller is not the legal owner of the field. The basic meaning of the word is already found in the Bible, when the servants of Avimelekh claim ownership of Isaac's well. There, too, they use the same verb — כִּי הִתְעַשְּׂקוּ עִמּוֹ — "because they strove with him." (Genesis 26:20.)

BACKGROUND

אַחֲוֵי טָרְפָּךְ **Show me your deed of seizure.** A buyer whose field was seized in repayment of a debt incurred by the seller has the right to receive compensation from the seller. The buyer would go to the court and obtain a certificate (טִירְפָּא) from the judges that the field that he bought was taken from him legally. Now he can bring a complaint against the seller, and if the seller does not compensate him, he receives another note, an אַדְרַכְתָּא — "authorization" — giving him the right to seize the debtor's property wherever it may be.

TRANSLATION AND COMMENTARY

דְּאָמַר לֵיהּ [1]**For Reuven can say to him: You knowingly accepted a "bundle of knots"** (a colloquial expression meaning a very risky transaction). For you bought the field without insisting on a guarantee, and thereby took a risk that my title to the field might be contested.

מֵאֵימָתַי הָוְיָא חֲזָקָה [2]The Gemara now asks: **From when** in this case **is** the buyer considered to have taken **possession**?

מִכִּי דָּיֵישׁ אַמְצְרֵי [3]The Gemara answers: **From the time when the buyer walks around** and repairs **the boundaries** of the field.

וְאִיכָּא דְּאָמְרִי [4]**There are some who say** that the buyer of the field **also** cannot retract **even** if the field was sold **with a guarantee**. Even though the buyer will ultimately get redress from the seller in the form of damages, he cannot save himself trouble by simply going back on the original transaction as soon as the protesters appear, provided that the original transaction was carried out in a lawful manner. **For the seller can say to him**: "**Show** me **your deed of seizure** stating that the court has decided that the field you bought from me rightfully belongs to the person claiming it and that you are entitled to redress from me, **and** then **I will repay you**."

אִיתְּמַר [5]The Gemara now begins a discussion of a different but related matter: **It was said** (a term used to introduce an Amoraic discussion): A difference of opinion between Amoraim on the following subject has been recorded: If **someone sells a field to another person and it is discovered that it was not** the seller's to sell, as he had stolen it, and the rightful owner of the field comes and seizes it from the buyer, and now the buyer claims compensation from the seller, [6]**Rav said**: **The buyer has** a right to demand the return

[1]דְּאָמַר לֵיהּ: "חַיְיתָא דִּקְטְרֵי סָבְרַתְּ וְקַבֵּלְתְּ".
[2]מֵאֵימָתַי הָוְיָא חֲזָקָה?
[3]מִכִּי דָּיֵישׁ אַמְצְרֵי.
[4]וְאִיכָּא דְּאָמְרִי: אֲפִילּוּ בְּאַחֲרָיוּת נַמִי, דְּאָמַר לֵיהּ: "אַחֲוֵי טָרְפָּךְ וַאֲשַׁלֵּם לָךְ".
[5]אִיתְּמַר: הַמּוֹכֵר שָׂדֶה לַחֲבֵירוֹ וְנִמְצֵאת שֶׁאֵינָהּ שֶׁלּוֹ, [6]רַב

LITERAL TRANSLATION

[1]For [Reuven] can say to him: "You knew about and accepted a bundle of knots."

[2]From when is it [considered] possession?

[3]From [the time] when [the buyer] walks around its boundaries.

[4]And there are some who say: Even with a guarantee, also, for [the seller] can say to him: "Show [me] your [deed of] seizure and I will pay you."

[5]It was said: Someone who sells a field to his fellow and it is discovered that it is not his, [6]Rav

RASHI

חייתא = שק מלא קשרים. **מכי דייש אמצרי** — מתקן גבולי השדה ומגביהם. **איכא דאמרי אפילו באחריות נמי** — אף על גב דסוף סוף עליה הדר — אין יכול לחזור בו, שהמוכר מעכב עליו, ולא מצי אמר הוא הואיל וסופך לשלם לי מעותי השתא דבידי אעכבם. **דאמר ליה אחוי טרפך ואשלם לך** — כשיעמידוך ויזכו בדין, ויכתוב לך הדיין שטר טורף עלי, שבדין טרפוה ממך בשבילי — בא ואשלם לך. וכל כמה דלא עמדת בדין איכי ירא מהם. **שאינה שלו** — שלא היתה של מוכר, שהיתה גזולה בידו. והנגזל בא ומוציא מיד הלוקח.

NOTES

If the buyer refrains from taking possession until after he has thoroughly investigated the field's ownership, and if he promptly invalidates the sale on discovering the existence of another claimant to ownership of the field, the sale is invalidated; but if the buyer wastes no time in taking possession of the field, he is clearly unconcerned about the ownership question and cannot thereafter invalidate the sale. If the buyer, upon hearing about the other claimant, does not promptly declare his intention of invalidating the sale, the sale cannot subsequently be invalidated even if he has not yet taken possession (*Ra'avad*).

חַיְיתָא דִּקְטְרֵי **A bundle of knots**. The colloquial meaning of this phrase — a very risky transaction — is clear. But its literal meaning is not. Here, and in his commentary on *Ketubot* 93a, *Rashi* translates חַיְיתָא דִּקְטְרֵי as "a sack full of knots." In his commentary on *Bava Kamma* 9a, *Rashi* translates it as "a tied sack full of air." The Arukh explains that חַיְיתָא means a leather bottle. Some scholars think that this is an Aramaic form of the Persian *chai*, that has this meaning.

דָּיֵישׁ אַמְצְרֵי **Fixing the boundaries of the field**. *Rashi*'s interpretation has been followed here (see previous note: מִשֶּׁהֶחֱזִיק בָּהּ — "Once he has taken possession of it"). Others explain that he walks around the field to see what work needs to be done (*Rosh*). Still others interpret דָּיֵישׁ אַמְצְרֵי as meaning "trampling on the boundary." They explain that we are referring to a case where the buyer happened to own a field adjacent to the one in question. Therefore, he takes possession when he tears down the fence dividing the two fields (*Rif*).

HALAKHAH

חֲזָרָה בְּשָׂדֶה שֶׁיָּצְאוּ עָלֶיהָ עֲסִיקִין **Going back on the sale of a field whose ownership has been contested.** "If one person has sold a field to another using any of the standard modes of acquisition, and people begin to contest the ownership of the field, the buyer may retract, provided that he has not begun using the field, and the seller must return the purchase price to the buyer. But if the buyer has made even the most minimal use of the field ("fixing its boundaries"), he may no longer retract, and he must litigate with the people who are contesting ownership of the field. If they succeed in taking the field away from him by decision of the court, he may then seek reimbursement from the seller," following *Rambam*'s opinion. *Rosh* and *Tur*, however, maintain that if the original sale was effected by one of the standard modes of acquisition, the buyer cannot afterwards retract, and they explain the expression דָּיֵישׁ אַמְצְרֵי ("fixing its boundaries") differently. (*Shulḥan Arukh, Ḥoshen Mishpat* 226:5.)

LITERAL TRANSLATION

said: He [the buyer] has money and he has improvement. [1]And Shmuel said: Money he has; improvement he does not have.

[2]They asked Rav Huna: [If the seller] specified the improvement to him, what is [the law?]

[3]Is Shmuel's reason because [the seller] did not specify improvement; but here surely he specified it! [4]Or perhaps Shmuel's reason is: Since [the seller] does not have land, it appears like interest.

[5]He said to them: Yes and no, and he found it difficult to decide (lit., "it was unsteady in his hands").

[6]It was said: Rav Naḥman said in the name of Shmuel: Money he has; improvement

אָמַר: יֵשׁ לוֹ מָעוֹת וְיֵשׁ לוֹ שֶׁבַח. [1]וּשְׁמוּאֵל אָמַר: מָעוֹת יֵשׁ לוֹ, שֶׁבַח אֵין לוֹ.

[2]בָּעוּ מִינֵּיהּ מֵרַב הוּנָא: פֵּירֵשׁ לוֹ אֶת הַשֶּׁבַח מַהוּ?

[3]טַעְמָא דִשְׁמוּאֵל מִשּׁוּם דְּלָא פֵּירֵשׁ שִׁבְחָא; וְהָכָא הָא פֵּירֵשׁ לֵהּ! [4]אוֹ דִּלְמָא טַעְמֵיהּ דִּשְׁמוּאֵל: כֵּיוָן דְּלֵית לֵיהּ קַרְקַע, מֶחֱזֵי כְּרִיבִּית.

[5]אֲמַר לְהוּ: אִין וְלָאו, וְרַפְיָא בִּידֵיהּ.

[6]אִיתְּמַר: אָמַר רַב נַחְמָן אָמַר שְׁמוּאֵל: מָעוֹת יֵשׁ לוֹ, שֶׁבַח

RASHI

יש לו — ללוקח מן המוכר מעות. **ויש לו שבח** — אם זה השביח את הקרקע בזבל או בגדר, קודם שהוליא נגזל מידו — גובה לוקח מן המוכר שבח. ואם תאמר: הנגזל יתן השבח, שהרי השיבו קרקע משובחת, כגון שגזלה משובחת והכסיפה ביד הגזלן. **שבח אין לו** — לקמן מפרש טעמא. **פירש לו את השבח** — כשמכרה לו התנה: אם יטרפוה מידך — אשלם לך את השבח, מהו? **כיון דלית ליה קרקע** — הואיל ואין קרקע זו שלו, נמלא שאין כאן שום מכר, והמעות מלוה אללו, וכשמשלם יותר ממה שנטל — מחזי כרבית. **אין ולאו** — תחילה אמר אין, וחזר ואמר לאו, רפוי היה הדבר בידו שלא היה יודע טעמו של דבר יפה.

TRANSLATION AND COMMENTARY

of the **money** he paid when he bought the field, and he also **has** a right to demand compensation for the **improvement** he made in the field. According to Rav, the buyer is entitled to demand reimbursement from the seller of the money he paid when he bought the field from him and for any improvements he made in the field during the period in which he occupied it. [1]But **Shmuel said**: The buyer indeed **has** the right to demand the return of the **money** he paid when he bought the field, but **he has no** right to demand compensation for the **improvement** he made in the field. According to Shmuel, the buyer can demand reimbursement from the seller of the money he paid when he bought the field from him, but not for any improvements he may have made in the field during his period of possession. In the following discussion, the Gemara will assume that Shmuel's position has been accepted.

בָּעוּ מִינֵּיהּ מֵרַב הוּנָא [2]The Sages **asked Rav Huna**: **If the seller specified** that he would compensate the buyer for **the improvement**, **what** is the law? I.e., what is the law if the seller explicitly guaranteed in the deed of sale that if for any reason the field was lawfully seized from the buyer by a third party he would reimburse the buyer for any improvement he made in the field?

טַעְמָא דִשְׁמוּאֵל [3]The Gemara now clarifies the question: Is Shmuel's reason for ruling that the buyer is usually not entitled to reimbursement for improvements he made **the fact that the seller did not specify** in the deed of sale that he would reimburse the buyer for land **improvement**? If that was his reason, it would not apply in this case, because **here, surely**, the seller **did specify** that he would reimburse the buyer! [4]**Or is Shmuel's reason, perhaps**, different: **Since the seller did not own the land** he "sold" to the buyer, there really was no sale in the first place, and the money paid was, in effect, a kind of loan, albeit one obtained by fraudulent means. If this is so, the "reimbursement" is, in effect, merely the repayment of the original loan, and any additional money the "seller" now gives to the "buyer" as compensation for improvements **appears like interest** on the original loan, and the Torah prohibits the collecting of interest on loans (Leviticus 25:36).

אֲמַר לְהוּ [5]Rav Huna first **said to** his questioners: **Yes, and** then **no**, for **he found it difficult to decide**. Rav Huna was not certain about the law in this case. At first he replied in the affirmative, then he changed his mind, and ultimately he did not reach any firm conclusions about the matter.

אִיתְּמַר [6]The Gemara now introduces another related Amoraic statement: **It was said: Rav Naḥman said in the name of Shmuel**: In the case described above, where a person sells a field not owned by him, the buyer **has** the right to demand the return of his **money**; but **he has no** right to demand compensation

TERMINOLOGY

אִין וְלָאו וְרַפְיָא בִּידֵיהּ Yes and no and it was unsteady in his hand. Sometimes a scholar was not certain about the answer to a question; in such cases the Talmud may state that he gave hesitant or even contradictory answers to the question, because the issue was not clear to him.

NOTES

מֶחֱזֵי כְּרִיבִּית It appears like interest. Obviously there is no actual interest here, for there was no agreement between the two parties that the money would be returned together with an additional sum. Nevertheless, this is what has in fact taken place — someone has received more than he paid. This problem is by no means simple, for if such a situation had arisen in connection with a true sale that was later cancelled, it would not be regarded as a case of interest. But here, since the sale was not cancelled after a period of time but was considered void from the start, we find that there

אֵין לוֹ, אַף עַל פִּי שֶׁפֵּירַשׁ לוֹ אֶת הַשֶּׁבַח. [1]מַאי טַעְמָא? [2]כֵּיוָן דְּקַרְקַע אֵין לוֹ, שְׂכַר מָעוֹתָיו עוֹמֵד וְנוֹטֵל.

[3]אֵיתִיבֵיהּ רָבָא לְרַב נַחְמָן: ״אֵין מוֹצִיאִין לַאֲכִילַת פֵּירוֹת, וּלְשֶׁבַח קַרְקָעוֹת, וְלִמְזוֹן הָאִשָּׁה וְהַבָּנוֹת מִנְּכָסִים מְשׁוּעְבָּדִים, מִפְּנֵי תִּיקּוּן הָעוֹלָם״.

[4]מִמְּשַׁעְבְּדֵי הוּא דְּלָא מַפְּקִינַן,

LITERAL TRANSLATION

he does not have, even though he specified the improvement for him. [1]What is the reason? [2]Since [the seller] has no land, [the buyer] stands and takes payment for his money.

[3]Rava raised an objection to Rav Naḥman: "[Payment] may not be extracted for produce consumed, or for land improvement, or for food for the wife and the daughters from mortgaged property, for the public good (lit., 'for the correction of the world')."

[4]It is from mortgaged property that we may not extract [payment],

TRANSLATION AND COMMENTARY

for any **improvement** he made in the field, **even though** the seller **specified** in the deed of sale that he would pay **him** for his **land improvement**. [1]**What is the reason?** [2]**Since** the seller **did not own the land** he "sold" to the buyer, it is as if **the buyer is standing** there, **taking** additional **payment** from the seller, beyond the original loan, merely **for** leaving **his money** in the seller's possession, and this is considered like taking interest, as explained above.

אֵיתִיבֵיהּ רָבָא לְרַב נַחְמָן [3]**Rava raised an objection to Rav Naḥman** from a Mishnah in tractate *Gittin* (5:1, 48b): "**Payment may not be extracted from mortgaged property** as compensation **for produce consumed**, **nor for land improvement**, **nor for food for the** maintenance of a man's **widow and** orphaned **daughters** whom the estate of the deceased husband is obligated to support as part of the ketubah given by the husband to his wife when they married, even if these obligations preceded the sale of the mortgaged property and would ordinarily have established a lien. The overriding consideration is **the public good.**" The reason why these debts are exceptions is that, since almost all people have such obligations, and since their costs are very difficult to quantify in advance, the Sages ordained that claims based upon these obligations should not be collected from mortgaged property, in order to protect prospective buyers and thus not discourage them from entering into commercial dealings.

מִמְּשַׁעְבְּדֵי הוּא דְּלָא מַפְּקִינַן [4]The Gemara now makes the following inference from this Mishnah: **It is from mortgaged property that payment may not be extracted** for produce, improvements and maintenance. This

BACKGROUND

מְזוֹן הָאִשָּׁה וְהַבָּנוֹת **Food for the wife and for the daughters.** One of the standard conditions of a ketubah (which, by Rabbibical decree, are observed even if they were not explicitly written in the ketubah) is that a widow is entitled to continue receiving food and payment for her other needs from her deceased husband's property until she receives her marriage settlement or marries another man. Similarly, the daughters of the marriage have the right to maintenance until they grow up or marry. For male children there is no such explicit condition, since they are the heirs and benefit in full from the legacy.

RASHI

לאכילת פירות כו׳ – מפרש להו לקמן. **למזון האשה והבנות** – תנאי כתובה שמקבל עליו: את תהא יתבא בביתי ומיתזנא מנכסי. וכן הבנות: בנן נוקבן דיהוו ליכי מינאי אינון יהון יתבן בביתי ומיתזנן מנכסי עד דתלקחן לגוברין, אין מוציאין לאחד מכל אלו מנכסים משועבדים. **מפני תיקון העולם** – שאם אתה אומר יטרפו לקוחות על כך – אין לך אדם שלוקח שדה מחבירו, דהא אין לך אדם שאין חוב זה מוטל עליו, ודבר שאין לו קצבה היא. ואכילת פירות ושבח קרקעות נמי דבר שאינו ידוע הוא, ואין הלקוחות יודעין להזהר בכך.

NOTES

was no true contract of sale to begin with, and thus there are grounds for viewing the money paid as being a loan for an unspecified period.

תִּיקּוּן הָעוֹלָם **For the public good.** *Rashi* here cites two explanations of why this regulation was established. Both of these explanations are taken from the Gemara (*Gittin* 51a). (1) "Produce consumed" and "land improvement" are not matters of public record; there is no way a buyer could know about a potential claim against the seller based upon such a prior obligation. (2) The rights of the wife and daughters under the ketubah, while they are a matter of public record, do not have a fixed limit. They depend on the circumstances prevailing at the time of the husband's/father's death, and there is no way a buyer can know how extensive a potential claim against a seller may turn out to be. Accordingly, in both types of situation the buyer's interests must be protected if we want people to be able to sell their land.

HALAKHAH

הוֹצָאָה לַאֲכִילַת פֵּירוֹת מִנִּכְסֵי הַגַּזְלָן **Collecting payment from a robber as compensation for produce consumed.** "If a person has bought a field from a robber and has eaten the field's fruit, he must reimburse the field's rightful owner for the fruit he ate. The buyer may then sue the robber. If the buyer did not know that the field did not belong to the robber, he may collect reimbursement from the robber's free property, but if he did know that the field did not belong to the robber, he is not entitled to any compensation." (*Shulḥan Arukh, Ḥoshen Mishpat* 273:2.)

הוֹצָאָה לְשֶׁבַח מִנְּכָסִים מְשׁוּעְבָּדִים **Compensation for land improvement costs from mortgaged property.** "When a creditor seizes property which the debtor has sold to a third party, the buyer is entitled to collect reimbursement for the cost of the field from the seller's mortgaged property, but he may only collect compensation for land improvement costs from the seller's free property." (Ibid., 115:1.)

מְזוֹן הָאִשָּׁה וְהַבָּנוֹת **The maintenance of a man's widow and daughters.** "A man's widow and daughters may only be supported from free property, but not from mortgaged property of the deceased husband's/father's estate." (Ibid., *Even HaEzer* 93:20; 112:7.)

הָא מִבְּנֵי חוֹרִין מַפְּקִינַן. [1]וְקָתָנֵי מִיהָא: ״לְשֶׁבַח קַרְקָעוֹת״. מַאי לָאו בְּלוֹקֵחַ מִגַּזְלָן?
[2]לָא, בְּבַעַל חוֹב.
[3]אִי בְּבַעַל חוֹב, אֵימָא רֵישָׁא: ״אֵין מוֹצִיאִין לַאֲכִילַת פֵּירוֹת״. [4]וְאִי בְּבַעַל חוֹב, בַּעַל חוֹב מִי אִית לֵיהּ פֵּירֵי? [5]וְהָאָמַר שְׁמוּאֵל: בַּעַל חוֹב גּוֹבֶה אֶת הַשֶּׁבַח — שֶׁבַח, אִין, אֲבָל פֵּירוֹת, לָא!

LITERAL TRANSLATION

but from free property, we may extract [payment]. [1]And at all events [the Mishnah] teaches: "For land improvement." Is it not [referring] to someone who buys from a robber?
[2]No, [it refers] to a creditor.
[3]If [it is referring] to a creditor, consider the first clause: "[Payment] may not be extracted for produce consumed." [4]Now, if [it refers] to a creditor, does a creditor have [a right to] produce? [5]But surely Shmuel said: A creditor collects [land] improvement — [land] improvement, yes, but produce, no!

TRANSLATION AND COMMENTARY

implies that **from free property payment may be extracted**, even for these purposes. **At all events**, says the Gemara, **the Mishnah does teach** that payment may be collected **for land improvement**, albeit only from free, unmortgaged property. [1]**Is** the Mishnah **not referring to** a case where **someone buys** a field **from** a person who later turns out not to have been the rightful owner of the land he was selling, in other words a **robber?** And we may infer from this Mishnah that a robber must reimburse the buyer for improvements the latter makes in the field!

לָא בְּבַעַל חוֹב [2]The Gemara rejects this explanation: **No**, the Mishnah **is referring to** a legitimate sale of a field and to **a creditor** who later came and seized this field from the buyer in payment of a previous debt owed to him by the seller. In such a case, the sale can in no sense be considered a loan, and when the seller reimburses the buyer, he is paying for damage done, not repaying a loan. Hence he must also reimburse the buyer for the land improvements that he made in the field, and the Mishnah is informing us that such reimbursement can be collected by the buyer only from the seller's free property.

אִי בְּבַעַל חוֹב [3]The Gemara now asks: **If** you maintain that the Mishnah in Gittin **is referring to a creditor**, **consider the first clause** of the Mishnah, which seems to rule out such an explanation: **"Payment may not be extracted** as compensation **for produce consumed."** Until now we have understood this clause as referring to a case where the field was taken away from its present occupier before its produce was harvested, and the occupier is now attempting to collect reimbursement for the produce from the seller. [4]**Now, if** we interpret the Mishnah **as referring to a creditor**, who is collecting the debt owed to him by the seller of the field by seizing the field from the buyer, **does a creditor have the right to the produce** about to be harvested in the field he is seizing as repayment for a debt? [5]**But surely** the produce was grown by the buyer, not the debtor, and the lien does not apply to it, as **Shmuel said** in explaining the law in these borderline cases: **A creditor may collect** his debt even from **land improvement**. From this the Gemara infers: At most he may collect his debt from **land improvement**, which is to some extent related to the mortgage, **but not** from **produce** grown by the buyer!

RASHI

מאי לאו בלוקח שדה מגזלן — והשביחה, ובא נגזל וטרפה. חוזר לוקח וגובה קרן מן המוכר, אפילו מנכסים משועבדים שמכר אחר מכירה זו, דשטרו של זה קודם, שכתב בו אחריות. והשבח מנכסים בני חורין ולא ממשועבדים, מפני תיקון העולם. שהשבח לא היה קצוב בשעת מכירה כשקיבל עליו אחריות. אלמא: אית ליה ללוקח שבח מגזלן. **לא בבעל חוב** — שטרפה בעל חוב ממנו בשביל חובו, ולא גזולה היתה. דההיא ודאי אית ליה שבחא, דמכירה מעלייתא היא כל זמן שלא טרפה ממנו. שאם פרע המוכר מעותיו לבעל חוב — הרי הוא מסולק מן הלקוחות. הלכך, כי משלם ליה יותר ממה שקיבל — השתא הוא דהדר זבין מיניה קרקע המכורה לו, ולא מחזי כשכר מעותיו. לאכילת פירות — סלקא דעתך הא מיירי בשדה שטרפוה מליאה פירות מיד הלוקח, וחוזר לוקח לגבות מן המוכר. ואי בשטרפה בעל חוב — מי אית ליה לבעל חוב פירות גמורין המחוברין בקרקע ואינן צריכין לקרקע כלום, שיכול לטורפן? **גובה את השבח** — וכל הקרקע טורף מיד הלוקח כמו שהיא משובחת על ידי הלוקח.

NOTES

שֶׁבַח לְקוֹנֶה מִגַּזְלָן Compensation for land improvement for one who buys from a robber. The Rishonim ask: Since the rightful owner of the field is the one who ultimately benefits from the improvements, he, and not the robber, should be required to compensate the buyer for land improvement!

The Geonim answer that the owner of the field may argue that the buyer has no legal standing to demand compensation from him, as no legal relationship exists between the buyer and the rightful owner. Thus the buyer has no choice but to sue the robber. Subsequently, the robber can sue the owner to attempt to recover the money he paid to the buyer for land improvement.

Rashi avoids this difficulty by explaining that the Gemara is referring to a case where the robber himself damaged the field, and all the buyer's improvements merely served to restore it to its original value. Since the owner has derived no benefit from the buyer's actions, the buyer has no right to claim compensation from him.

Accordingly, some authorities maintain that the buyer is indeed entitled to compensation from the field's owner for any expenses he may have incurred in improving the field. However, appreciation in land value is normally greater than

TERMINOLOGY

מִידֵּי אִירְיָא? הָא כִּדְאִיתָא וְהָא כִּדְאִיתָא Are they in any way connected? This case is as it is, and this case is as it is! This expression is used when the Talmud rejects a proposed analogy between two cases occurring together in the same passage of a Mishnah: "Is this an argument [i.e., is the comparison between the two cases valid]? This case as it is, and this case as it is [i.e., the particulars of case A do not apply in case B, even though both cases are mentioned together in the same source]!"

[1]אֶלָּא, פְּשִׁיטָא בְּגוֹזֵל וְנִגְזָל, [2]וּמִדְּרֵישָׁא בְּגוֹזֵל וְנִגְזָל, סֵיפָא נַמִי בְּגוֹזֵל וְנִגְזָל! [3]מִידֵּי אִרְיָא?! הָא כִּדְאִיתָא וְהָא כִּדְאִיתָא. [4]וְהָא לָא תָּנֵי הָכִי: "לְשֶׁבַח קַרְקָעוֹת, כֵּיצַד? הֲרֵי שֶׁגָּזַל שָׂדֶה מֵחֲבֵירוֹ, וַהֲרֵי הִיא יוֹצְאָה מִתַּחַת יָדוֹ, כְּשֶׁהוּא גּוֹבֶה, גּוֹבֶה אֶת הַקֶּרֶן מִנְּכָסִים מְשׁוּעְבָּדִים, וְשֶׁבַח גּוֹבֶה מִנְּכָסִים בְּנֵי חוֹרִין". [5]הֵיכִי דָּמֵי? [6]אִילֵימָא: כִּדְקָתָנֵי, גַּזְלָן מִמַּאן גָּבֵי? [7]אֶלָּא לָאו כְּגוֹן שֶׁגָּזַל שָׂדֶה

LITERAL TRANSLATION

[1]Rather, it is obvious [that the Mishnah is referring] to a robber and someone who has been robbed, [2]and since the first clause [refers] to a robber and someone who has been robbed, the latter clause also [must refer] to a robber and someone who has been robbed!

[3]Are they in any way connected?! This is as it is, and this is as it is.

[4]But surely [there is a Baraita, which] does not teach this way: "For land improvement, how so? When someone has robbed his fellow of his field, and it leaves his possession, when he collects, he collects the capital value [of the field] from mortgaged property, and the [land] improvement he collects from free property." [5]How is it to be visualized (lit., "how is it like")? [6]If we say: As it teaches, from whom does a robber collect? [7]Rather, is it not [referring to a case] where, for example, [someone] robbed his fellow of his field,

TRANSLATION AND COMMENTARY

אֶלָּא פְּשִׁיטָא [1]**Rather, it is obvious**, says the Gemara, **that the Mishnah** here **is referring to a robber** who robbed someone of his field and then sold it, **and someone who was robbed**, who is taking the field back from the buyer. A person who has been robbed is certainly entitled to the produce of his own field, and at most he owes the buyer his expenses for his land improvement (see note). [2]**And since the first clause** of the Mishnah **refers to a robber and someone who has been robbed, the latter clause**, which mentions that reimbursement is made for land improvement, **must also be referring to a robber and someone who has been robbed**! Thus, Rava's objection to Rav Naḥman and Shmuel remains unsolved!

מִידֵּי אִרְיָא [3]But the Gemara rejects this line of reasoning: Is this an argument? **Are** the two clauses necessarily **in any way connected?** Perhaps the first clause **is** to be left **as it is**, dealing with a case of a robber, **and** the second clause **is** to be left **as it is**, dealing with a case of a creditor. Perhaps it is inappropriate to demand that the various examples given in the Mishnah refer to a single set of circumstances!

וְהָא לָא תָּנֵי הָכִי [4]But again the Gemara objects: **But surely there is a Baraita** explaining this Mishnah which **does not support this way** of understanding the Mishnah: "**How** does a person collect compensation **for land improvement?** If **someone has robbed another person of his field, and it leaves his possession** when the court compels the robber to return it to its rightful owner, then **when he collects, he collects the capital value of the field from mortgaged property, and he collects the land improvement from free property**." [5]The Gemara now attempts to clarify the meaning of this Baraita: **How do we visualize the case** described by the Baraita? [6]**If we say** that the Baraita should be interpreted **literally**, that the subject of the whole sentence in the Baraita is the robber, and that it is the robber who is collecting compensation, **from whom does a robber collect**? A robber is surely not entitled to compensation for anything! [7]**Rather, is it not referring to a case where**, **for example, someone robbed another person of his field, and** then the robber **sold** the field **to someone else, and this buyer** then **improved it**? And

RASHI

בגוזל ונגזל — וכגון שגזלה עם פירותיה, ומכרה. אי נמי, גזלה בלא פירות, ומכרה לאחר ועשה בה פירות. וטוען נגזל: ארעאי אשבח. ומיהו, היציאה שהוציא הלוקח — ישלם לו הנגזל, שהרי מתוך כך הושבחה יותר. ואם אין השבח יותר אלא היציאה יתירה — נותן לו יציאה שיעור שבח, ודיו. **הא כדאיתא כו׳** — רישא בנגזל וסיפא בבעל חוב. ולקמיה מותיב לה מרישא. **והא לא תני הכי** — בברייתא, עלה דהך מתניתין דאין מוציאין, דתוקמה בבעל חוב. **והרי היא יוצאה מתחת ידו** — שבית דין מוציאין אותה מידו. **כשהוא גובה** — לקמיה מפרש לה. **אילימא כדקתני** — שלא מכרה גזלן, ומידו היא יוצאה בדין. **גזלן ממאן גבי** — ממאן יש לו לגבות, וכי מה נתן בה?

NOTES

the expenses involved in achieving it, and the buyer has no right to demand the difference from the owner (*Rosh* and *Tosafot*).

Other commentators differentiate between *artificial* appreciation resulting from improvements introduced by the buyer, and *natural* appreciation resulting from a general rise in land value. The buyer has the right to demand compensation compensation from the rightful owner for the former, but the latter he must claim from the robber. The reason for this is that, according to the Halakhah, land cannot be stolen, and thus stolen land is considered as if it never left the possession of its rightful owner. Hence, the natural appreciation in value occurred while the field was in the possession of its owner (*Rashba*).

מֵחֲבֵירוֹ, וּמְכָרָהּ לְאַחֵר וְהִשְׁבִּיחָהּ.

[1]אֲמַר לָךְ: לָאו תָּרוּצֵי קָא מְתָרְצַתְּ? תְּרֵיץ נַמִי בְּבַעַל חוֹב.

[2]תָּא שְׁמַע: ״לַאֲכִילַת פֵּירוֹת, כֵּיצַד? [3]הֲרֵי שֶׁגָּזַל שָׂדֶה מֵחֲבֵירוֹ, וַהֲרֵי הִיא יוֹצְאָה מִתַּחַת יָדוֹ, [4]כְּשֶׁהוּא גּוֹבֶה, גּוֹבֶה אֶת הַקֶּרֶן מִנְּכָסִים מְשׁוּעְבָּדִים, וּפֵירוֹת גּוֹבֶה מִנְּכָסִים בְּנֵי חוֹרִין״.

[5]הֵיכִי דָּמֵי? [6]אִילֵימָא: כִּדְקָתָנֵי, גַּזְלָן מִמַּאן גָּבֵי? [7]אֶלָּא לָאו כְּגוֹן שֶׁגָּזַל שָׂדֶה מֵחֲבֵירוֹ וּמְכָרָהּ לְאַחֵר, וְהִשְׁבִּיחָהּ.

LITERAL TRANSLATION

and he sold it to someone else and [the buyer] improved it?

[1]He can say to you: Did you not explain this? Explain [it] also [as referring] to a creditor.

[2]Come and hear: "[Compensation] for produce consumed, how so? [3]When someone has robbed his fellow of his field, and it leaves his possession, [4]when he collects, he collects the capital value [of the field] from mortgaged property, and the produce [consumed] he collects from free property." [5]How is it to be visualized? [6]If we say: As it teaches, from whom does a robber collect? [7]Rather, is it not [referring to a case] where, for example, someone robbed his fellow of his field and sold it to someone else, and [the buyer] improved it?

TRANSLATION AND COMMENTARY

now, when the court restores the field to its rightful owner, it is the buyer who is suffering the loss, and he is entitled to claim compensation for the improvements he has made in the field from the person who sold it to him — the robber. Understood in this way, the Baraita, and the Mishnah which it is explaining, must mean that compensation for land improvement *is* collected, albeit only from the robber's free property, in contradiction to the point of view of Rav Naḥman and Shmuel!

אֲמַר לָךְ [1]The Gemara answers: Rav Naḥman and Shmuel **can say to you**: **Have you not** already been forced to **explain** the Baraita as referring to a robber who sold the field to someone else? Have you not already explained that the Baraita cannot be interpreted literally? Just as the Baraita can be explained as referring to the case of a robber who sold the field to someone else, **you can also explain** the Baraita **as referring to** the case of **a creditor** who seized a field after it had been improved by the buyer. You can amend the Baraita to read: "If a person *sold* (instead of *robbed*)," etc. In this way, the original answer to Rava's objection may still be maintained.

תָּא שְׁמַע [2]The Gemara now brings another objection to Shmuel's ruling that a person who bought a field from a robber is not entitled to compensation for anything beyond the original purchase price, because of the prohibition against the taking of interest. **Come and hear** what has been taught in another Baraita, clarifying the first clause of the Mishnah in *Gittin*: "**How** does a person collect compensation **for produce consumed**? [3]If **someone has robbed another person of his field, and it leaves his possession** when the court compels the robber to return it to its rightful owner, [4]**when he collects, he collects the capital value of the field from mortgaged property, and he collects** compensation for **the produce consumed from free property**."

הֵיכִי דָּמֵי [5]The Gemara now attempts to clarify the meaning of this Baraita: **How do we visualize the case** described by the Baraita? [6]**If we say** that the Baraita should be interpreted **literally**, that the subject of the whole sentence in the Baraita is the robber, and that it is the robber who is collecting compensation, **from whom does a robber collect**? A robber is surely not entitled to compensation for anything! [7]**Rather, is it not referring to a case where someone robbed another person of his field**, **and** then the robber **sold** the field **to someone**

RASHI

והשביחה — והרי היא בדין יוצאה מתחת ידו של לוקח. אלמא: אית ליה שבחא ללוקח מגזלן. **שגזל שדה מחבירו ומכרה לאחר והשביח** — ונעשה פירות גמורין, ונגזל לוקחה עם פירותיה, ואינו נותן אלא יציאה דקאמר: ארעאי אשבח. וקתני דלוקח חוזר וגובה מגזלן מן המחוררין.

NOTES

אִילֵימָא כִּדְקָתָנֵי... תְּרֵיץ נַמִי בְּבַעַל חוֹב **If we say that the Baraita should be interpreted literally... explain it as referring to a creditor**. At first glance, it would appear unnecessary to engage in a radical emendation that eliminates the robber from the Baraita altogether. Even according to Shmuel's view, that the buyer cannot claim

HALAKHAH

הַחְזָרַת גְּזֵלָה שֶׁהִשְׁבִּיחָה **Restoration by a robber of a field whose value has increased**. "If someone robs another of a field and improves it, and its increase in value is greater than his expenses, when the owner of the field reclaims it, he only

TRANSLATION AND COMMENTARY

else, and this buyer improved it? Thus we see that compensation for produce, and presumably also compensation for land improvement, is collected from the robber, and this contradicts Rav Naḥman's and Shmuel's view that a robber does not reimburse the buyer for anything beyond the original purchase price.

אָמַר רָבָא [1]The Gemara now gives three answers to this objection. (1): **Rava said**: **What are we dealing with here**? [2]With a case, **for example, where, someone robbed another person of his field, which was full of fruit** at the time, **and** the robber did not sell it at all, but **ate the fruit** himself. The original owner now has a claim against the robber for recovery of his field and compensation for his produce. But the Baraita does not mention recovery of the field but rather compensation for the value of the field. Since we are no longer dealing with the case of a buyer, but rather with the owner of the field himself, this seems difficult to understand. Hence Rava explains that the robber damaged the field by **digging pits, ditches, or caves in it**. According to Rava, then, the Baraita is not referring to compensating the person who bought the field from the robber, but to making the robber compensate the field's original owner for produce consumed and damage caused. [3]Thus, **when the one who was robbed comes to collect the** original **capital value** of the now worthless field, **he may collect** even **from the robber's mortgaged property**, [4]but when **the one who was robbed comes to collect compensation** from the robber **for the produce** consumed, **he collects** only **from** the robber's **free property**.

רַבָּה בַּר רַב הוּנָא אָמַר [5](2) **Rabbah bar Rav Huna said**: The Baraita refers to a situation **where, for example**, the robber did not sell the field, but rather **non-Jewish bandits**, as a result of their dealings with

[1]אָמַר רָבָא: הָכָא בְּמַאי עָסְקִינַן? [2]כְּגוֹן שֶׁגָּזַל שָׂדֶה מֵחֲבֵירוֹ מְלֵאָה פֵּירוֹת, וְאָכַל אֶת הַפֵּירוֹת, וְחָפַר בָּהּ בּוֹרוֹת, שִׁיחִין, וּמְעָרוֹת. [3]בָּא נִגְזָל לִגְבּוֹת קֶרֶן, גּוֹבֶה מִנְּכָסִים מְשׁוּעְבָּדִים; [4]בָּא נִגְזָל לִגְבּוֹת פֵּירוֹת, גּוֹבֶה מִנְּכָסִים בְּנֵי חוֹרִין.

[5]רַבָּה בַּר רַב הוּנָא אָמַר: כְּגוֹן

LITERAL TRANSLATION

[1]Rava said: With what are we dealing here? [2]Where, for example, he robbed his fellow of a field full of fruit, and he ate the fruit, and dug pits, ditches, or caves in it. [3][When] the one who was robbed comes to collect the capital value, he collects from [the robber's] mortgaged property; [4][when] the one who was robbed comes to collect [compensation for] the produce, he collects from [the robber's] free property.

[5]Rabbah bar Rav Huna said: Where, for example,

RASHI

אמר רבא כו׳ — האי כשהוא גובה לאו בלוקח קאמר, דבשלא מכרה עסקינן, ו״גובה את הקרן״ דקאמר — בנגזל. ואם תאמר: קרן אמאי גובה מנכסים משועבדים? הרי קרקע לפניו! כגון שחפר בה בורות, דאפחתה משוייה.

NOTES

compensation for land improvement from the robber, it is still possible to interpret the Baraita as referring to a case where a robber sold the property he had expropriated, provided we explain the Baraita לִצְדָדִין — "disjunctively" — along the lines Rav Ashi uses later on in the passage (15a). The Baraita would then read as follows: If a person robbed another person of a field and sold it to a third party, if the rightful owner then took it back and the buyer claimed compensation from the robber, the buyer can collect the principal *from the robber*, even from *mortgaged property*, whereas the land improvement he collects *only from the owner*, and only from his *free property* (see previous note on "Compensation for land improvement," which deals with the question of claiming land improvement from the owner).

But the Gemara is not willing to consider the possibility of such a "disjunctive" interpretation, because throughout the passage it is clear that the Gemara understands that payment in the Baraita is being demanded from *only one person*. It is true that Rav Ashi later explains the Baraita "disjunctively" as referring to the claims against one person, the robber, of two different people, the owner and the buyer. But even he would not accept an interpretation of the Baraita in which one person, the buyer, has a claim against two people, the owner and the robber (*Ritva*).

HALAKHAH

compensates the robber for his expenses. If the expenses were greater than the increase in value, the owner of the field only compensates him for the increase in value." (*Shulḥan Arukh, Ḥoshen Mishpat* 372:1.)

גַּזְלָן שֶׁהִפְסִיד הַשָּׂדֶה שֶׁגָּזַל A robber who damaged the field which he robbed. "If a person robbed another of his land and damaged it (e.g., by digging holes in it), or consumed the produce which had grown in the field, the person who was robbed is entitled to compensation from the robber's free property, but not from his mortgaged property." (Ibid., 372:1.)

[15A] שֶׁנְּטָלוּהָ מַסִּיקִין. [1]בָּא נִגְזָל לִגְבּוֹת קֶרֶן, גּוֹבֶה מִנְּכָסִים מְשׁוּעְבָּדִים; [2]בָּא נִגְזָל לִגְבּוֹת פֵּירוֹת, גּוֹבֶה מִנְּכָסִים בְּנֵי חוֹרִין.

[3]רָבָא לָא אָמַר כְּרַבָּה בַּר רַב הוּנָא: "הֲרֵי הִיא יוֹצְאָה מִתַּחַת יָדוֹ" "בְּדִינָא" מַשְׁמַע.

[4]וְרַבָּה בַּר רַב הוּנָא לָא אָמַר כְּרָבָא: "הֲרֵי הִיא יוֹצְאָה מִתַּחַת יָדוֹ" "בְּעֵינָא" מַשְׁמַע.

LITERAL TRANSLATION

[15A] [non-Jewish] bandits took it away. [1][When] the one who was robbed comes to collect the capital value, he collects from mortgaged property; [2][but when] the one who was robbed comes to collect the produce, he collects from free property.

[3]Rava did not say like Rabbah bar Rav Huna: [The expression] "when it leaves his possession" means: "Through a court [ruling.]"

[4]And Rabbah bar Rav Huna did not say like Rava: [The expression] "when it leaves his possession" means: "In its original condition."

TRANSLATION AND COMMENTARY

the robber (see note), [15A] forcibly **took** the field **away** from him, thus preventing him from returning the field itself to its rightful owner. [1]However, **the person who was robbed** is still entitled to compensation from the robber, and **when he comes to collect the** original **capital value of the field** from the robber, **he collects** even **from mortgaged property**. [2]But **when the person who was robbed comes to collect** compensation for **the produce** consumed, to which he is also entitled, **he collects** only **from** the robber's **free property**.

רָבָא לָא אָמַר [3]The Gemara now explains the basis of the dispute between Rava and Rabbah bar Rav Huna. According to both of them, the Baraita reads well and does not need emendation. However, **Rava did not explain** the Baraita **like Rabbah bar Rav Huna**, because he understood that **the expression** in the Baraita — **"when it leaves his possession"** — means "it leaves the possession of the robber **through a court ruling**," and returns to the possession of its rightful owner. It does not mean that it is forcibly seized by one robber from another.

וְרַבָּה בַּר רַב הוּנָא [4]**And Rabbah bar Rav Huna did not explain** the Baraita **like Rava**, because he understood that the expression in the Baraita — **"when it leaves his possession"** — **means** "it leaves **in its original condition**," and not damaged by the robber. Thus any attempt to explain that it is not the buyer but rather the owner of the field himself who is suing for financial compensation because he cannot physically recover the field itself, is not supported by the language of the Baraita.

RASHI

שנטלוה מסיקין – אנסים נכרים נטלוה מן הגזלן ומתחתו. ותנן בבבא קמא (קטז,ב): הגוזל שדה מחבירו ונטלוה מסיקין, אם מחמת הגזלן – חייב להעמיד לו שדה אחר. ו"הרי היא יוצאה מתחת ידו" דקתני, בנטילת מסיקין הוא. **בדינא משמע** – הלכך בהוצאת נגזל קאמר, ו"גובה את הקרן" דקאמר – כשחפר בו בורות. **בעינא משמע** – כמו שהיתה, ולא שחפר בה בורות.

BACKGROUND

מַסִּיקִין Officials, collectors, oppressors. From other sources it would appear that this expression refers to soldiers discharged from the Roman army. These soldiers were allocated land by the Roman government, which they were permitted to appropriate from the property of the subject nation's farmers. Sometimes, such property was appropriated on the basis of an imperial edict, but often it was confiscated on a totally arbitrary basis.

NOTES

שֶׁנְּטָלוּהָ מַסִּיקִין Where non-Jewish bandits took the field away. The Mishnah in *Bava Kamma* (10:5;116b) states that if non-Jewish bandits (an epithet for the government) were seizing fields in the area and happened to seize a field from a robber who had stolen it from someone else, the robber is not required to repay the original owner, because he can claim that the field would have been seized anyway. But if the seizure was in any way the robber's own fault, such that if he himself had not taken the field, it would not have been seized (the examples given in the Gemara are: (a) if the bandits took only the robber's fields, or (b) if the robber advised them which fields to take), then the robber must repay the original owner.

Accordingly *Rashi* notes that our Gemara must be referring to a case where the bandits insisted on taking this particular field, presumably because it was in the robber's possession. But if the bandits were also seizing other people's fields, the owner could not sue the robber for compensation.

Other commentators go further: If the bandits took no other fields, or if the only other fields they took were fields belonging to the robber, we may assume that the robber was at fault. But if, for example, along with this field the bandits seized all the other fields that were still in the possession of the owner, he would not be entitled to compensation from the robber, since presumably he, and not the robber, was their intended target. (*Talmid Rabbenu Peretz.*)

HALAKHAH

גְּבִיַּית קֶרֶן וּפֵירוֹת Collecting the capital value and the produce. "If a person robbed another of a field and damaged it, or ate the produce, the capital value of the field is collected from the robber's mortgaged property, and the value of the produce is collected from the robber's free property. If the robber was himself robbed of the field by oppressive officials who had previous dealings with the robber, he is liable to provide the owner with another field." (*Shulḥan Arukh, Ḥoshen Mishpat* 372:1-2).

TRANSLATION AND COMMENTARY

רַב אַשִׁי אָמַר (3) [1]**Rav Ashi said** that the Baraita **is to be read disjunctively** (i.e., the two parts of the Baraita deal with different cases and with two claimants): **Where, for example, someone robbed another person of his field** when it was **full of produce, and he ate the produce** himself **and then sold the** now empty **field** to a third party. The original owner then sued the buyer and recovered his field, and sued the robber to recover the produce. The buyer, in turn, also sued the robber to recover the purchase price of the field. Hence the robber faces two lawsuits from two separate claimants. [2]**When the buyer comes to collect the capital value** of the field, **he may collect** the capital value even **from** the robber's **mortgaged property**. But **when the person who was robbed comes to collect the** value of the **produce, he may collect** only **from** the robber's **free property**. According to Rav Ashi, the expression in the Baraita, "it leaves his possession," means: It leaves the possession of the *buyer* through a court ruling and in its original state. In this way Rav Ashi avoids the difficulties inherent in the explanations of Rava and Rabbah bar Rav Huna.

בֵּין לְרָבָא [3]The Gemara asks: **Whether** we interpret the Baraita **according to Rava or according to Rabbah bar Rav Huna**, the obligation of the robber to repay the person he has robbed has the status of **a verbal loan**, since it was created by an act of robbery, and it is different from his obligation to compensate a buyer, which is supported by a written deed of sale. [4]**And a verbal loan does not** give the creditor (in this case the person who was robbed) the right to **collect from** the robber's own **mortgaged property**, which he legally sold to a third party. Since the contents of a verbal agreement are not ordinarily public knowledge, prospective buyers have no way of knowing that property they are planning to buy is liable to be seized by someone with a prior claim! Thus, in the case of the robber, buyers of property legally sold by the robber cannot be expected to know that claims are going to be made against their seller based on another piece of property of which he has robbed other people.

[1]רַב אַשִׁי אָמַר: לִצְדָדִין קָתָנֵי: ״כְּגוֹן שֶׁגָּזַל שָׂדֶה מֵחֲבֵירוֹ מְלֵאָה פֵּירוֹת, וְאָכַל אֶת הַפֵּירוֹת וּמָכַר אֶת הַשָּׂדֶה. [2]בָּא לוֹקֵחַ לִגְבּוֹת קֶרֶן, גּוֹבֶה מִנְּכָסִים מְשׁוּעְבָּדִים; בָּא נִגְזָל לִגְבּוֹת פֵּירוֹת, גּוֹבֶה מִנְּכָסִים בְּנֵי חוֹרִין״.
[3]בֵּין לְרָבָא בֵּין לְרַבָּה בַּר רַב הוּנָא, מִלְוֶה עַל פֶּה הוּא, [4]וּמִלְוֶה עַל פֶּה אֵינוֹ גּוֹבֶה מִנְּכָסִים מְשׁוּעְבָּדִים!

LITERAL TRANSLATION

[1]Rav Ashi said: [The Baraita] is to be read (lit., "taught") disjunctively: "Where, for example, he robbed his fellow of a field full of produce, and he ate the produce and [then] sold the field. [2][When] the buyer comes to collect the capital value, he collects from mortgaged property; [when] the one who was robbed comes to collect the produce, he collects from free property."
[3]Both [according] to Rava and [according] to Rabbah bar Rav Huna, it is a verbal loan, [4]and a verbal loan does not collect from mortgaged property!

RASHI

ומכר את השדה — והרי היא יוצאה מתחת ידו של לוקח בדינא ובעינא. **בין לרבא בין לרבה** — דמוקמי גביית קרן מן הגזלן בנגזל, הא מלוה על פה הוא, ולא טרפא ממשעבדי.

NOTES

רַב אַשִׁי אָמַר לִצְדָדִין Rav Ashi explained the Baraita disjunctively. Rav Ashi did not accept the interpretations of this Baraita suggested by Rava and Rabbah bar Rav Huna, because both of these interpretations are open to criticism, as the Gemara has already noted. On the other hand, Rava and Rabbah bar Rav Huna did not accept Rav Ashi's explanation, because they found his "disjunctive" interpretation of the Baraita forced.

כְּשֶׁעָמַד בַּדִּין Where the robber stood trial. The Gemara appears to be saying that a hearing in court is equivalent to a signed document. But the Gemara will later (16b-17a) discuss the question of whether a defendant who claims to have repaid the plaintiff in accordance with a court ruling is believed. We know that a borrower is generally not believed when he claims to have repaid a lender, if the lender is still in possession of a promissory note. Hence, we see that a court ruling does not have the same power as a signed document.

Some commentators, including *Rif*, answer that in our Gemara there is no question of the robber having compensated the owner of the field in accordance with the court ruling; on the contrary, the robber is a criminal who has no intention of obeying the court if he can avoid doing so. Only in such cases does the court ruling have the status of a signed document. But if two law-abiding citizens are judged, and the defendant announces his intention of

HALAKHAH

מִלְוֶה עַל פֶּה A verbal loan. "Payment for a loan which was not recorded in writing can only be collected from the borrower's free property, but not from his mortgaged property." (*Shulḥan Arukh, Ḥoshen Mishpat* 39:1; 111:1.)

כְּשֶׁעָמַד בַּדִּין Where the robber stood trial. "If the robber stood trial and was convicted, the person who was robbed is entitled to collect compensation even from the robber's mortgaged property for the principal, produce, or both, provided that the court sentenced the robber to pay these expenses." (Ibid., 372:1.)

[1]הָכָא בְּמַאי עָסְקִינַן? כְּשֶׁעָמַד בַּדִּין וַהֲדַר זַבֵּין. [2]אִי הָכִי, פֵּירוֹת נַמִי! [3]כְּשֶׁעָמַד בַּדִּין עַל הַקֶּרֶן, וְלֹא עָמַד בַּדִּין עַל הַפֵּירוֹת. [4]וּמַאי פָּסְקָא? [5]סְתָמָא דְמִילְּתָא, כִּי תָּבַע אִינִישׁ, קַרְנָא תָּבַע בְּרֵישָׁא. [6]וְסָבַר שְׁמוּאֵל לוֹקֵחַ מִגַּזְלָן לֵית לֵיהּ שְׁבָחָא? [7]וְהָא אֲמַר לֵיהּ שְׁמוּאֵל לְרַב חִינָּנָא בַּר שֵׁילַת: "אִמְלִיךְ וּכְתוֹב: שׁוּפְרָא, שְׁבָחָא, וּפֵירִי". [8]בְּמַאי? אִי בְּבַעַל חוֹב, מִי

LITERAL TRANSLATION

[1]With what are we dealing here? Where [the robber] stood trial and later sold.

[2]If so, [the same should apply to] produce too!

[3]Where [the robber] has stood trial for the capital value, but he has not stood trial for the produce.

[4]But what is [the basis for] the distinction?

[5][In] an ordinary case, when a man sues, he first claims the capital value.

[6]But does Shmuel maintain that one who buys from a robber does not have [the right to compensation for land] improvement? [7]Surely Shmuel said to Rav Ḥinnana bar Shelat: "Consult and write: Best property, [land] improvement, and produce."

[8]In what [case]? If in [the case of] a creditor,

TRANSLATION AND COMMENTARY

הָכָא בְּמַאי עָסְקִינַן [1]The Gemara answers: **With what are we dealing here**? With a case **where the robber stood trial** for the robbery he committed **and later sold** a different piece of his own property to someone else. Since the robber has been tried for robbery, it is public knowledge that his own property is liable to be seized by the person he robbed, and any potential buyer of the robber's property should be aware of the situation. Thus there is no reason why the person who was robbed should not collect payment from the robber's own mortgaged property sold by him to others.

אִי הָכִי [2]But the Gemara objects: **If so**, if the robber has already stood trial, **the same should apply to produce too**! Following this reasoning, the person who was robbed should also be allowed to collect compensation for the produce of his field from the robber's mortgaged property!

כְּשֶׁעָמַד בַּדִּין [3]The Gemara answers: We are dealing with a case **where the robber has stood trial for the capital value** of the field, **but has not** yet **stood trial for the produce**.

וּמַאי פָּסְקָא [4]The Gemara objects: **But what is the basis for** such an arbitrary **distinction**, asserting that the Baraita is specifically referring to a case where the robber stood trial only for the land, but not for the produce?

סְתָמָא דְמִילְּתָא [5]The Gemara answers: The distinction is not arbitrary. **In any ordinary case, when a man sues, he first claims the capital value**, and only later does he sue for other things, like produce.

וְסָבַר שְׁמוּאֵל [6]The Gemara now proceeds to question the basis of the teaching quoted above (14b) by Rav Naḥman in Shmuel's name: **But does Shmuel** in fact **maintain that a person who buys** land **from a robber does not have the right to** demand **compensation for the improvement** he made in the field because it resembles interest on a loan? And does Shmuel maintain this even if the seller stipulated that the buyer should indeed have such a right? [7]**But surely Shmuel said to Rav Ḥinnana bar Shelat**, who was a scribe: "When you write a deed of sale, **consult** the seller **and**, if he agrees, **write** that the buyer is entitled to reimbursement from the seller's **best property**, for **land improvement, and** for **produce**," a standard formula in deeds of sale.

בְּמַאי [8]The Gemara now attempts to clarify this statement: **In** anticipation of **what case** was this clause inserted? **If** we are concerned **in case a creditor** seizes the property, **does** a creditor **have the right to produce**

RASHI

כשעמד בדין – קודם שמכר נכסיו. וכיון דחייבוהו בית דין – אית ליה קלא, והוה ליה כמלוה בשטר. **מאי פסקא** – בתמיה: פסקא תנא למלתיה דהעומד בדין אינו עומד על הפירות? **רב חיננא בר שילת** – סופר היה. **אמליך** – כשאתה כותב שטר המלך במוכר, אם יקבל עליו להגבות ללוקח משפר נכסיו, קרנא ושבחא ופרי – אם יטרפוה ממנו.

NOTES

obeying the court, and leaves the courtroom with the plaintiff with the express purpose of paying his debt, he is believed when he returns and says that he has, in fact, paid it, and the court's ruling does not have the status of a signed document.

Other commentators suggest that when our Gemara says that the owner of the field has already sued the robber, it means that the court has actually issued him a document confirming his right to compensation. Accordingly, the point of our Gemara is to say that such a document has the same validity as a document signed by the robber himself. In its discussion below (17a), by contrast, the Gemara is specifically dealing with the powers of a verbal ruling of the court, which has not been delivered in written form (*Rabbenu Hananel* and *Rabbenu Efraim*).

Other commentators distinguish between the power of a document to enable a plaintiff to seize *mortgaged property*, and the fact that a document in the hands of a lender is compelling evidence that a loan is still outstanding. The former quality is shared by a court ruling, but the latter is inherent in the nature of written evidence, and does not apply to an oral ruling (*Ran*).

SAGES

רַב חִינָּנָא בַּר שֵׁילַת Rav Ḥinnana bar Shelat. A Babylonian Amora of the first generation. This Sage was such a close friend of the great Amora, Rav, that Rav said he knew that Rav Ḥinnana loved him as a father loves his son. (It has been suggested that he was Rav's cousin.) We do not know much about his life and activities, but it seems he was one of the Sages close to the house of the Exilarch and was highly regarded by the Exilarch. Perhaps it was by virtue of his functions in the house of the Exilarch (as a court scribe or the like) that Shmuel gave him the instruction recorded in the Gemara here. We also find Shmuel teaching him the Halakhah, but Shmuel, too, relates to him as a close friend.

TRANSLATION AND COMMENTARY

about to be harvested in a field he is seizing as repayment for a debt? [1]**Surely Shmuel said: A creditor collects his debt from land improvement**, from which we can infer: It is from **land improvement** that he collects his debt, **but** he does **not** collect his debt from **produce**! [2]**Rather, are we not dealing with a person who** suspects that he may have **bought** property **from a robber**, and wants to protect his interests by the inclusion of this clause?! From this it seems that, according to Shmuel, a person who buys property from a robber is indeed entitled to compensation for land improvement expenses, if he so stipulated, in contradiction to the opinion ascribed to Shmuel earlier!

אִית לֵיהּ פֵּירֵי? [1]וְהָאָמַר שְׁמוּאֵל: בַּעַל חוֹב גּוֹבֶה אֶת הַשֶּׁבַח. שֶׁבַח, אִין, אֲבָל פֵּירוֹת, לָא! [2]אֶלָּא לָאו בְּלוֹקֵחַ מִגַּזְלָן! [3]אָמַר רַב יוֹסֵף: הָכָא בְּמַאי עָסְקִינַן? כְּגוֹן שֶׁיֵּשׁ לוֹ קַרְקַע. [4]אָמַר לֵיהּ אַבָּיֵי: וְכִי מוּתָּר לִלְוֹת סְאָה בִּסְאָה בְּמָקוֹם שֶׁיֵּשׁ לוֹ קַרְקַע?

LITERAL TRANSLATION

does he have [the right to] produce? [1]But surely Shmuel said: A creditor collects [his debt from land] improvement. Land improvement, yes, but produce, no! [2]Rather, are we not [dealing] with one who bought from a robber!

[3]Rav Yosef said: With what are we dealing here? For example, where [the robber] has land.

[4]Abaye said to him: But is it permissible to borrow a *se'ah* for a *se'ah* in a place where [the borrower] has land?

RASHI

כגון שיש לו קרקע — לגזלן זה, שמגבהו ללוקח קרקע ולא מעות, דהשתא לא מחזי כרבית. אסור ללות סאה בסאה — שמא יוקרו חטין.

אָמַר רַב יוֹסֵף [3]**Rav Yosef said** in reply: **With what are we dealing here**? **For example**, with a case **where the robber has** other **land**. As explained above, Shmuel ruled that it is not permitted for a buyer to receive compensation from a robber for improvements made by the buyer while the field was in his possession, because this resembles taking interest. But if the robber reimburses the buyer with another piece of property, rather than with money, this does not give the impression that the buyer is receiving interest, and hence it is permitted.

אָמַר לֵיהּ אַבָּיֵי [4]**Abaye said to** Rav Yosef: **But is it permissible to borrow a *se'ah*** — a certain measure of produce — **for a *se'ah* in a place where the borrower has land**? The Rabbis forbade lending produce in return for an equal quantity of produce, because this, too, resembles taking interest. For if the cost of the produce increases, the same quantity of produce is now worth more than it was when the loan was originally taken, and thus returning an equal quantity of produce appears like interest. Here, too, in the case of the robber, the buyer is receiving land worth more than the land he originally bought, and this is also interest!

NOTES

שֶׁיֵּשׁ לוֹ קַרְקַע וכו׳ Where the robber has other land. The Torah prohibits the taking of interest on a loan of money, land, fruit, or any other commodity. For example, if someone lends a bag of fruit, he does not normally expect to be repaid with the original bag, but with a similar bag of equal value. In this case, therefore, we are dealing with a הַלְוָאָה, and it is strictly forbidden to demand the return of, say, two bags. It is, of course, permitted to lend commodities as a הַלְוָאָה, provided that no more is returned than was originally lent. But there is a Rabbinic prohibition against lending commodities by volume or weight rather than by value. Since market prices fluctuate, the lender may be repaid with a bag of fruit that is more expensive than the one he lent, and this is forbidden as a form of interest. This Rabbinic prohibition only applies to an actual commodity loan (הַלְוָאָה), since the added value of the returned commodity resembles interest. It does not apply to a *bona fide* sale, even if the object sold was seized by the seller's creditor after it had increased in value in the possession of the buyer, and the buyer was reimbursed by the seller at the higher price. But if the object sold had in fact been stolen by the seller, and was therefore seized from the buyer, not by a creditor, but by its rightful owner, then a sale never really took place and the "buyer" was really a lender who had been defrauded by the "seller" into lending him money. Therefore, the Rabbinic prohibition applies and the robber may not return to the "buyer" more than was originally "lent" to him (*Rashi*).

The Gemara here is telling us that if the robber has other landed property that was mortgaged as security for the "sale," or if, at the time of the original "sale," the robber and the buyer performed a symbolic act of acquisition, by exchanging a kerchief, then the Rabbinic prohibition no longer applies. The reason for this distinction is that in our case the "lender" never intended to lend at all; he was, in fact, defrauded into buying property from a robber. Since the laws of interest apply only to a הַלְוָאָה, they ought not to apply here at all, even at the Rabbinic level. The reason why the buyer cannot sue the robber for appreciation in land value is because the sale resembles a הַלְוָאָה, since no object was in fact sold. But if there were other fields which were mortgaged as security for the sale, or if the sale was guaranteed by the symbolic kerchief-exchange, it becomes unmistakably a sale and is no longer subject to the prohibition against interest (*Ritva*).

It can in fact be argued that, since the seller knew all

TRANSLATION AND COMMENTARY

אֲמַר לֵיהּ [1]Rav Yosef **said to** Abaye: The cases are different: **There**, where a person lends one *se'ah* in return for another, it **is a** legitimate **loan**, and hence anything which even resembles taking interest is prohibited. **But here**, the sale of stolen property, though it is in a sense a kind of loan, still takes the form of **a sale**, and since the robber originally sold the stolen property to the buyer, the substitution of one piece of property — even if it is worth more — for another does not resemble interest.

אִיכָּא דְּאָמְרִי [2]**There are some who say** that a different exchange took place between Rav Yosef and Abaye, and report it as follows: **Rav Yosef said: With what are we dealing here**? **For example**, with a case **where the seller** did not merely stipulate in the deed of sale that he would reimburse the buyer under all circumstances for land improvement expenses, but actually **obligated himself**, by a formal act of acquisition using a kerchief, to make this reimbursement. The formal act of acquisition converts the value of future land improvement into an immediate obligation and not a future one which might resemble interest.

[1]אֲמַר לֵיהּ: הָתָם, הַלְוָאָה; הָכָא, זְבִינֵי.
[2]אִיכָּא דְּאָמְרִי: אֲמַר רַב יוֹסֵף: הָכָא בְּמַאי עָסְקִינַן? כְּגוֹן שֶׁקָּנוּ מִיָּדוֹ.
[3]אֲמַר לֵיהּ אַבַּיֵי: וְכִי מוּתָּר לִלְוֹת סְאָה בִּסְאָה בְּמָקוֹם שֶׁקָּנוּ מִיָּדוֹ?
[4]אֲמַר לֵיהּ: הָתָם, הַלְוָאָה; וְהָכָא, זְבִינֵי.
[5]גּוּפָא: ״אָמַר שְׁמוּאֵל: בַּעַל חוֹב גּוֹבֶה אֶת הַשֶּׁבַח״. [6]אָמַר רָבָא: תֵּדַע, שֶׁכָּךְ כּוֹתֵב לוֹ מוֹכֵר לַלּוֹקֵחַ: [7]״אֲנָא אֵיקוּם, וַאֲשַׁפֵּי, וַאֲדַכֵּי וַאֲמָרֵיק זְבִינֵי אִילֵּין —

LITERAL TRANSLATION

[1]He said to him: There, it is a loan; here, it is a sale.

[2]There are some who say: Rav Yosef said: With what are we dealing here? For example, where [the seller] obligated himself (lit., "when they acquired from his hand").

[3]Abaye said to him: But is it permitted to borrow a *se'ah* for a *se'ah* in a place where [the borrower] obligated himself?

[4]He said to him: There, it is a loan; but here, it is a sale.

[5]Returning to the statement quoted above (lit., "the thing itself"): "Shmuel said: A creditor collects [his debt from land] improvement." [6]Rava said: Know [that this is so], for the seller writes as follows to the buyer: [7]"I shall confirm, and satisfy, and clear and cleanse these sales —

RASHI

בהלואה – שייך רבית טפי ממכר. **שקנו מידו** – על השבח, דהוה ליה מחויב משעת המכר קודם שיש שכר המתנת מעות. **תדע** – דגובה, ולא מצי לוקח למימר "אנא אשבחי". **שכך כותב לו מוכר ללוקח** – באחריות שטר המכר. **ואשפי** = אשקיט. ודומה לו "על הר נשפה" דמתרגם: על טורא שליוא (ישעיה יג). **ואדכי** = אטהר מכל ערעור.

אֲמַר לֵיהּ אַבַּיֵי [3]**Abaye said to him: But is it permitted to borrow a *se'ah* for a *se'ah* where the borrower obligated himself** by a formal act of acquisition at the time of the loan to repay the exact quantity of the produce lent, even if the produce increased in price meanwhile? Surely this resembles taking interest, as explained above, and an act of acquisition makes no difference!

אֲמַר לֵיהּ [4]Rav Yosef **said to** Abaye in reply: **There**, where one borrows one measure of produce for another, **it is a loan**, and because it resembles interest it is forbidden. **Here**, where a person buys from a robber, **it is a sale**, and the return of one more valuable piece of property for another less valuable one does not resemble taking interest, as explained above.

גּוּפָא [5]The Gemara now **returns to** study more closely **the statement** of Shmuel **quoted above**: **"Shmuel said: A creditor may collect his debt from land improvement."** In other words, when a creditor seizes mortgaged property from a buyer, he may take it as it is, without regard to any change in land values since the creation of the lien. Thus, if through the buyer's efforts the land has doubled in value, the creditor can seize it as payment for twice as much of the debt as was originally visualized, and the buyer's only recourse is to sue the debtor who sold him the field. [6]Commenting on Shmuel's statement, **Rava said: Know that this is** indeed **so, for the following** is the formula of guarantee which **the seller writes to the buyer** in a standard deed of sale: [7]**"I shall confirm, and satisfy, and clear and cleanse this sale** (i.e., I shall ensure that the sale is carried out properly,

NOTES

along that the field he was selling was not his, he was, from the very beginning, really selling *the other*, so-called "mortgaged," field. Accordingly, we are dealing with a *bona fide* sale, and the difference in value between the original field and the "mortgaged" one amounts to no more than a perfectly permissible discount on the sale price (*Ra'avad*).

וַאֲמָרֵיק **And I shall cleanse**. Some commentators suggest that the word וַאֲמָרֵיק should be translated, "I shall complete, finish," in the sense of: "I will see to it that the sale is carried out in full." The word is used in this sense in the Mishnah (*Yoma* 3:4). (*Melo HaRo'im*.)

TRANSLATION AND COMMENTARY

and solve any difficulties that may arise in connection with it) — [1]the purchase **itself, and the labor** invested **in it, and the improvement** resulting **from it, and I shall set** their value **before you. And this buyer agreed to this and acceptd it upon himself.**" (The formal, stilted Aramaic used in this phraseology is standard in Talmudic legal documents.) Now, since the seller need only compensate the buyer for property lawfully seized by someone with a prior claim to the land, it is clear that the items listed in the standard formula, including land improvement, are subject to seizure by the seller's creditor, in accordance with Shmuel's ruling. The buyer cannot prevent such seizure; rather he must seek redress from the seller in accordance with the deed of sale drawn up between them.

[1]אִינּוּן, וַעֲמָלֵיהוֹן, וּשְׁבָחֵיהוֹן, וְאֵיקוּם קֳדָמָךְ. וְצָבֵי זְבִינָא דְּנַן וְקַבֵּיל עֲלוֹהִי״.

[2]אֲמַר לֵיהּ רַב חִיָּיא בַּר אָבִין לְרָבָא: אֶלָּא מֵעַתָּה, מַתָּנָה, דְּלָא כְּתִיב לֵיהּ הָכִי, הָכִי נַמִי דְּלָא טָרֵיף שְׁבָחָא?

[3]אֲמַר לֵיהּ: אִין.

[4]וְכִי יָפֶה כֹּחַ מַתָּנָה מִמֶּכֶר?

LITERAL TRANSLATION

[1]them, and their labor [expenses], and their improvement [value], and I shall set them before you. And this buyer agreed to [this] and accepted [it] upon himself."

[2]Rav Ḥiyya bar Avin said to Rava: But if this is the case (lit., "but from now"), a gift, where [the donor] does not write this for him, may [a creditor] really not seize [land] improvement?

[3][Rava] said to him: Yes.

[4]But is the power of a gift more effective (lit., "beautiful") than [that of] a sale?

RASHI

אינון ועמליהון ושבחיהון — וכיון דעל מוכר הדר גבי שבחא בעל חוב מלוקח וחוזר הלוקח על המוכר. **מתנה דלא כתיב ביה הכי** — שאין אדם מקבל עליו אחריות מה שהוא נותן. **הכי נמי** — דאם נותן נכסיו במתנה לא גבי בעל חוב שבחא, הואיל ולא הדר על הנותן. **וכי יפה כח מתנה כו׳** — בתמיה.

אֲמַר לֵיהּ רַב חִיָּיא בַּר אָבִין [2]The only reason why the creditor's claim is favored over the buyer's, and we allow the creditor to collect his debt at the expense of the buyer's improvement efforts, is because the buyer can still sue the seller for compensation, in accordance with the clause cited by Rava from the deed of sale. **Rav Ḥiyya bar Avin said to Rava: But if this is the case,** then in the case of **a gift, where** the donor **does not** customarily **write this** formula of guarantee **for** the recipient, as gifts are not usually guaranteed, would we favor the recipient's claim over that of the creditor? **Is a creditor really not** entitled in this case to **seize** all the property that was mortgaged as security for his claim, including **land improvement,** as he would be entitled to do in the case of a sale, merely because the land was given away and not sold?

אֲמַר לֵיהּ אִין [3]Rava **said** in reply **to** Rav Ḥiyya bar Avin: **Yes,** it is true that the creditor may *not* seize the improvement, and he may take only that part of the field that is equivalent in value to the entire field at the time it was given to the recipient.

וְכִי יָפֶה כֹּחַ מַתָּנָה מִמֶּכֶר [4]Rav Ḥiyya bar Avin then asked, **But is a gift more effective than a sale** in this respect? The creditor's claim is based on his lien. It overrides the claim of any subsequent buyer. Why should the fact that someone received the field as a gift rather than paid for it affect the superior status of the creditor's lien? Why should a buyer be required to hand over his land improvement to his seller's creditor, while the recipient of a gift is not?

NOTES

וְצָבֵי זְבִינָא **And this buyer agrees.** The simple meaning of this phrase is that it refers to *the seller.* But there are some difficulties with this interpretation, e.g., the Gemara will rule later in the discussion that in those documents that do not include this phraseology, the buyer's rights are *greater.* Therefore some commentators interpret the phrase as referring to the buyer — the terms "buyer" and "seller" are quite similar in Aramaic. According to this interpretation, followed here in the translation, the buyer agrees to limit any future claims he may have to the agreed procedure (*Tosefot Sens* quoting *Rabbenu Ḥananel,* probably also *Rambam*; see also *Ran* and *Ritva*).

HALAKHAH

שֶׁבַח מִמַּתָּנָה **Land improvement in the case of a gift.** "A creditor who collects his debt from property that had been given by the debtor to someone else as a gift is not entitled to land improvement. Thus, if the recipient improved the land, the creditor is only entitled to reimbursement for the land's value at the time of the gift. But if the land's value increased in the normal course of events, and not because of any effort on the part of the person who received it, the creditor may collect the increase." Some authorities rule that even in this case he may not collect land improvement (*Rema* in the name of *Tur, Rosh,* and *Razah.*) (*Shulḥan Arukh, Ḥoshen Mishpat* 372:3.)

TRANSLATION AND COMMENTARY

אֲמַר לֵיהּ אִין [1]Rava **said** in reply to Rav Ḥiyya bar Avin: **Yes**. A gift **is indeed more effective** in this respect. Since the recipient of a gift cannot expect to be reimbursed by the donor, he will suffer a severe loss if he yields to the creditor's claims. Hence, the claim to the field itself is honored, in accordance with the lien. But improvements in the land made by the recipient are considered to belong to him, and the creditor is not entitled to seize them from him.

אֲמַר רַב נַחְמָן [2]**Rav Naḥman said, The following Baraita supports Mar Shmuel** in his opinion that a creditor collects payment from land improvement, **but our colleague, Huna, explains it as referring to another matter**, and according to him it does not support Shmuel. [3]**For it has been taught** in a Baraita: "If **someone sells a field to another person, and it** subsequently **leaves** the buyer's **possession** because it had previously been mortgaged by the seller as security for a loan, [4]then **when** the buyer **collects** reimbursement from the seller, **he collects the capital value of the field from** the seller's **mortgaged property, and he collects the land improvement from** the seller's **free property**." Now, since the buyer is entitled to claim compensation for land improvement from the seller, we may assume that the creditor had previously seized from the buyer the land improvement made by him. Thus, the Baraita supports Shmuel's view that a creditor is entitled to collect land improvement.

וְהוּנָא חַבְרִין מוּקִים [5]**But our colleague Huna explains** the Baraita **as referring to other matters, namely, to someone who buys a field from a robber**. For no one would dispute that the owner of a field that was stolen and sold to a third party is entitled to have his entire field restored to him, including any improvements that may have been made to it by the "buyer," since the latter has no right at all to the field, and can only sue the robber. But, in Rav Huna's view, and contrary to the opinion of Shmuel, the case of a creditor is different, because the sale of the field to the buyer was legal, and until the moment that the creditor came to seize the field in repayment of his loan, the buyer was fully entitled to make improvements in his own property. Hence the Baraita cannot be used to support Shmuel.

[1]אֲמַר לֵיהּ: אִין, יָפֶה וְיָפֶה. [2]אֲמַר רַב נַחְמָן: הָא מַתְנִיתָא מְסַיְּיעַ לֵיהּ לְמָר שְׁמוּאֵל, וְהוּנָא חַבְרִין מוּקִים לַהּ בְּמִילֵּי אַחֲרִינֵי. [3]דְּתַנְיָא: ״הַמּוֹכֵר שָׂדֶה לַחֲבֵירוֹ, וַהֲרֵי הִיא יוֹצְאָה מִתַּחַת יָדוֹ, [4]כְּשֶׁהוּא גּוֹבֶה, גּוֹבֶה אֶת הַקֶּרֶן מִנְּכָסִים מְשׁוּעְבָּדִים, וְשֶׁבַח גּוֹבֶה מִנְּכָסִים בְּנֵי חוֹרִין״.

[5]וְהוּנָא חַבְרִין מוּקִים לַהּ בְּמִילֵּי אַחֲרִינֵי — בְּלוֹקֵחַ מִגַּזְלָן.

LITERAL TRANSLATION

[1][Rava] said to him: Yes, it is indeed more effective (lit., "beautiful and beautiful").

[2]Rav Naḥman said: The following Baraita supports Mar Shmuel, but our colleague Huna explains it [as referring] to other matters. [3]For it has been taught: "One who sells a field to his fellow, and it leaves his [the buyer's] possession, [4]when he collects, he collects the capital value [of the field] from mortgaged property, and he collects the [land] improvement from free property."

[5]But our colleague Huna explains it [as referring] to other matters — [namely,] to one who buys [a field] from a robber.

RASHI

יפה ויפה — בדבר זה. דכיון דלא הדר גבי ליה — לא מפסיד ליה בנדידי דלא אפסדיה לבעל חוב, דבשלמא גופה של קרקע אמר לו: אמאי זכנתיה; מאין אגבה חובי? אבל שבחא — אמר לו: מאי אפסדתיך? **מסייע ליה למר שמואל** — דבעל חוב גובה את השבח. **כשהוא גובה** — כשלוקח חוזר וגובה מן המוכר. **במילי אחריני** = בדבר אחר. **בלוקח מגזלן** — דנגזל ודאי טריף שבחא, דאמר ליה: ארעאי אשבח. אבל בעל חוב, כל כמה דלא טרפה לה — לאו דידיה הוא, וברשותא דלוקח אשבח.

BACKGROUND

הוּנָא חַבְרִין Our colleague Huna. Rav Huna was considered the greatest Sage of his generation, and all the other Sages bowed to his opinion in most matters, whereas Rav Naḥman was much younger than he. Nevertheless, because Rav Naḥman had married into the house of the Exilarch and was the chief judge of his city, he allowed himself to call Rav Huna "our comrade," though he did not refer to him in this way to his face.

NOTES

יָפֶה וְיָפֶה It is indeed more effective. The natural inference to be drawn from this double language (יָפֶה וְיָפֶה) is that the power of a deed of gift is greater in other ways, apart from the one mentioned here. Accordingly, the commentators looked for other advantages a deed of gift might have over a deed of sale. One commentator points out that a sale of land to a third party can be invalidated if a neighbor of the seller, whose land lies next to that being sold, was denied the opportunity to buy at the same price, whereas a *gift* of land to a third party is not subject to this restriction (*Talmidei Rabbenu Yonah*). Another commentator points out that, ordinarily, a sale of a field is assumed *not* to include its wells and pits, whereas a gift is assumed to be inclusive (*Ra'avad*).

וְהוּנָא חַבְרִין מוּקִים לַהּ But our colleague, Huna, explains it as referring to another matter. The commentators ask: Since Rav Naḥman knew that there was an alternative way of interpreting the Baraita, how could he use it as evidence

HALAKHAH

גְּבִיַּית קֶרֶן וְשֶׁבַח Collecting capital value and land improvement. "When a creditor collects his debt from property which the debtor had sold to someone else, he collects both the capital value and the improvement. The

TRANSLATION AND COMMENTARY

תַּנְיָא אִידָךְ [1]Another Baraita was taught: "If someone sold a field to another person and the buyer improved it, and a creditor subsequently came and seized the field in repayment of a loan he had given to the seller, [2]when the buyer collects reimbursement for his expenses, he collects the capital value of the field from the seller. As for compensation for land improvement, however, the procedure is based on the law applicable when a workman improves another person's property without being requested to do: If the value — to the owner of the land — of the improvement is greater than the expenses incurred by the buyer to improve it, the buyer receives the net improvement from the owner of the land, i.e., the seller, who guaranteed the buyer against loss. And the buyer receives the expenses he incurred in making the improvements from the creditor, who must pay this amount for the improvements he will be enjoying. [3]But if the expenses incurred by the buyer are greater than the value to the creditor of the improvement, i.e., the buyer spent more money improving the field than the improvements are worth, then the buyer cannot recover this loss. He only has the right to demand that the creditor, who will be enjoying the improvements, reimburse him for his expenses up to an amount equal in measure to the value of the improvement and no more."

וְהָא שְׁמוּאֵל בְּמַאי מוֹקִים לַהּ [4]The Gemara now asks: Now, to what circumstances can Shmuel explain this second Baraita as referring? [5]If he were to explain it as referring to someone who buys a field from a robber, the first clause, which states that the buyer collects land improvement value, beyond his expenses, from the seller, would be difficult; [6]for Shmuel said above: Someone who buys a field from a robber does not have the right to claim compensation for land improvement from the seller, as this resembles interest! [7]And if he explains the Baraita as referring to a creditor, both the first clause and the second clause, which state that the creditor must reimburse the buyer for the value of the improvements or for the expenses, whichever is less,

[1]תַּנְיָא אִידָךְ: "הַמּוֹכֵר שָׂדֶה לַחֲבֵירוֹ וְהִשְׁבִּיחָהּ, וּבָא בַּעַל חוֹב וּטְרָפָהּ, [2]כְּשֶׁהוּא גּוֹבֶה: אִם הַשֶּׁבַח יוֹתֵר עַל הַיְּצִיאָה נוֹטֵל אֶת הַשֶּׁבַח מִבַּעַל הַקַּרְקַע, וְהַיְּצִיאָה מִבַּעַל חוֹב. [3]וְאִם הַיְּצִיאָה יְתֵירָה עַל הַשֶּׁבַח, אֵין לוֹ אֶלָּא הוֹצָאָה שִׁיעוּר שֶׁבַח מִבַּעַל חוֹב".

[4]וְהָא, שְׁמוּאֵל בְּמַאי מוֹקִים לַהּ? [5]אִי בְּלוֹקֵחַ מִגַּזְלָן, קַשְׁיָא רֵישָׁא, [6]דְּאָמַר שְׁמוּאֵל: לוֹקֵחַ מִגַּזְלָן לֵית לֵיהּ שְׁבָחָא. [7]אִי בְּבַעַל חוֹב, קַשְׁיָא רֵישָׁא וְסֵיפָא,

LITERAL TRANSLATION

[1]Another [Baraita] was taught: "One who sells a field to his fellow and he improved it, and a creditor came and seized it, [2]when he collects, [the procedure is as follows:] If the improvement is greater than the expenses, [the buyer] receives the improvement from the owner of the land, and the expenses from the creditor. [3]But if the expenses are greater than the improvement, he only has expenses [equal in] measure to the improvement from the creditor."

[4]Now, this [Baraita], to what can Shmuel explain it [as referring?] [5]If [it refers] to one who buys [a field] from a robber, the first clause is difficult, [6]for Shmuel said: One who buys from a robber does not have [land] improvement. [7]If [it refers] to a creditor, the first clause and last clause are difficult,

RASHI

על הוצאה — שהוציא הלוקח בשבחה. **נוטל** — הלוקח. **את השבח מבעל הקרקע** — מה שעודף על היציאה, דאמר ליה: פרעתי את חובך. **אין לו** — ללוקח, אלא מן היציאה שהוציא בה פורע לו שיעור שבח, והשאר מפסיד. **אי בלוקח מגזלן** — האי בעל חוב היינו נגזל. **קשיא רישא** — דקתני נוטל את השבח מבעל הקרקע. **קשיא רישא וסיפא** — דקתני בעל חוב נותן את היציאה. ולשמואל בעל חוב גובה השבח ואינו נותן כלום.

NOTES

to support Shmuel's position? Furthermore, why did Rav Naḥman bring a proof from a Baraita rather than from the Mishnah from tractate *Gittin* quoted above (14b)? The inference that the Gemara draws there is virtually identical with the one Rav Naḥman draws from the Baraita.

They answer that the Mishnah on 14b can be explained as referring to a robber, as it mentions "fruits." But the Baraita, quoted by Rav Naḥman, which does not mention fruits, may be explained more easily as referring to a creditor. Even though Rav Huna was prepared to interpret this Baraita as referring to a robber, Rav Naḥman felt sufficiently confident of his own interpretation to use the Baraita as evidence to support Shmuel (see *Tumim, Ma'ayan HaḤokhmah*).

HALAKHAH

buyer of the property from the debtor can then claim compensation from the seller. He collects the principal even from the seller's mortgaged property, but the improvement he collects only from the seller's free property." (*Shulḥan Arukh, Ḥoshen Mishpat* 115:1.)

TRANSLATION AND COMMENTARY

are difficult, [1]for Shmuel said: A creditor collects land improvement together with the capital value, and the buyer has no recourse but to sue the seller!

אִיבָּעֵית אֵימָא [2]The Gemara answers that the Baraita can be reconciled to Shmuel's viewpoint in two ways: (1) If you wish, you can say that the Baraita is referring to a case of someone who bought a field from a robber, but the ruling is limited to the two exceptions to Shmuel's ruling, discussed above. For example, where (a) the robber has other land; and even according to Shmuel, the buyer can collect land improvement from him in a way that does not give the appearance of taking interest; [3]or alternatively (b) where the seller obligated himself from the moment of the original transaction to repay the buyer, and the money for the improvements was an obligation from the time of the sale and does not come under the category of interest, even according to Shmuel.

אִיבָּעֵית אֵימָא (2) [4]If you wish, you can say that the Baraita is referring to a creditor, and yet there is no difficulty in reconciling it with Shmuel's viewpoint: [5]Here in the Baraita, which rules that the creditor must compensate the buyer, it is referring only to improvement [15B] that has reached the point of being carried away on the shoulders of the porters, produce which has grown to the point where it is almost ready to be handed over to the porters for shipment. Although such produce is still not quite ready for harvest, it is so close to being ready that it is considered as if it has already been harvested. It is thus in an intermediate category, between land improvements, which the creditor can seize without payment, and harvested produce which the creditor cannot seize at all. Therefore, the creditor must reimburse the buyer of the field for his expenses in growing the crop. [6]But here, in his ruling that a creditor may collect land improvement without compensation, Shmuel is referring to improvement that has not reached the point of being carried away on the shoulders of the porters — produce which is not fully grown. Such produce is considered still to be an integral part of the field, the creditor may collect his debt from it, and the buyer's sole recourse is to sue the seller.

[1]דְּאָמַר שְׁמוּאֵל: בַּעַל חוֹב גּוֹבֶה אֶת הַשֶּׁבַח! [2]אִיבָּעֵית אֵימָא: בְּלוֹקֵחַ מִגַּזְלָן, כְּגוֹן שֶׁיֵּשׁ לוֹ קַרְקַע. [3]אִי נַמִּי בְּשֶׁקְּנוֹ מִיָּדוֹ. [4]אִיבָּעֵית אֵימָא: בְּבַעַל חוֹב, וְלָא קַשְׁיָא: [5]כָּאן בְּשֶׁבַח [15B] הַמַּגִּיעַ לִכְתֵפַיִם; [6]כָּאן בְּשֶׁבַח שֶׁאֵינוֹ מַגִּיעַ לִכְתֵפַיִם.

LITERAL TRANSLATION

[1]for Shmuel said: A creditor collects [land] improvement!

[2]If you wish, say: [It is referring] to one who buys [a field] from a robber, for example, where he [the robber] has land. [3]Or alternatively where he obligated himself.

[4]If you wish, say: [It is referring] to a creditor, and there is no difficulty: [5]Here [it is referring] to improvement [15B] which has reached the shoulders [of the porters]; [6]here [Shmuel is referring] to improvement that has not reached the shoulders [of the porters].

RASHI

המגיע לכתפים – קרוב ליקצר, אלא שעדיין צריכין לקרקע – הוי להו כפירות גמורין, ואין בעל חוב גובה אותו בלא יציאה.

NOTES

שֶׁבַח הַמַּגִּיעַ לִכְתֵפַיִם Improvement that has reached the shoulders. Most commentators explain that this refers to fully grown produce that is ready to be taken away on the harvesters' shoulders (*Rif, Rabbenu Ḥananel* and others). According to *Rashi*, it refers to produce which is nearly ready to harvest, but which still needs a little more growing time.

Others explain that this phrase refers to produce in general, and to any kind of "land improvement" whose connection to the land is temporary, in that it will eventually be taken away on the harvesters' shoulders. By contrast, שֶׁבַח שֶׁאֵינוֹ מַגִּיעַ לִכְתֵפַיִם refers to actual improvement in the land itself, such as improved soil quality, or tree growth (*Tosafot* on *Bava Kamma* 95b, *Rabbenu Tam* in *Sefer Hayashar*).

Still other commentators explain that the word "shoulders" refers to physical labor. Accordingly, שֶׁבַח הַמַּגִּיעַ לִכְתֵפַיִם refers to land improvement brought about by human effort, as opposed to land which appreciated of its own accord (*Tosafot* in the name of *Rabbenu Tam* on *Bava Kamma* 95b, *Ra'avad* in the name of *Rav Hai Gaon*).

שֶׁבַח אֵין לוֹ He does not receive compensation for land improvement. On 14b, Rav and Shmuel disagreed as to whether a fraudulent sale of stolen property should be treated as an invalidated sale or as a kind of loan, and thus subject to the law prohibiting interest. Rav's opinion there was that land improvement by the buyer in such a case should not be treated like interest, and that the buyer should therefore be able to claim compensation for land improvement. But in the present case on 15b, Rav agrees that the so-called "sale" by the robber to the buyer, who knew he was receiving stolen property, was actually not a sale at all, but merely a kind of deposit.

On this point the Rishonim note that the money is not really a deposit (פִּקָּדוֹן) but rather a loan (הַלְוָאָה), since the "buyer" of the field is not interested in the return of the actual coins he "deposited" with the seller, but in the return of their value (*Rosh, Ritva*). Thus the question of interest raised on 14b arises again here, and Rav would agree that in this case compensation for land improvement would be nothing more than a legal fiction to hide the collection of illegal interest, and the buyer is therefore not entitled to it (*Geonim*).

[1]וְהָא מַעֲשִׂים בְּכָל יוֹם וְקָא מַגְבֵּי שְׁמוּאֵל אֲפִילּוּ בְּשֶׁבַח הַמַּגִּיעַ לִכְתֵפַיִם!
[2]לָא קַשְׁיָא: הָא דְּמָסֵיק בֵּיהּ כְּשִׁיעוּר אַרְעָא וְשִׁבְחָא; [3]הָא דְּלָא מַסֵּיק בֵּיהּ אֶלָּא כְּשִׁיעוּר אַרְעָא, [4]דְּיָהֵיב לֵיהּ שְׁבָחֵיהּ וּמְסַלֵּיק לֵיהּ.
[5]הָנִיחָא לְמַאן דַּאֲמַר: אִי אִית לֵיהּ זוּזֵי לְלוֹקֵחַ, לָא מָצֵי מְסַלֵּיק לֵיהּ לְבַעַל חוֹב. שַׁפִּיר. [6]אֶלָּא לְמַאן דַּאֲמַר: כִּי אִית לֵיהּ זוּזֵי לְלוֹקֵחַ, מָצֵי מְסַלֵּיק לֵיהּ לְבַעַל חוֹב, [7]נֵימָא לֵיהּ:

LITERAL TRANSLATION

[1]But surely incidents [took place] every day [in which] Shmuel permitted [creditors] to collect even from improvement that has reached the shoulders [of the porters]!

[2]There is no difficulty: This [ruling applies] where he is owed the value of the land and the improvement; [3]this [other ruling applies] where he is only owed the value of the land, [4]so [the creditor] gives him the improvement and gets rid of him.

[5]This is satisfactory according to the one who says: [Even] if the buyer has money, he cannot get rid of the creditor. Well and good. [6]But [according] to the one who says: Where the buyer has money, he can get rid of the creditor, [7]let [the buyer] say to him:

TRANSLATION AND COMMENTARY

וְהָא מַעֲשִׂים בְּכָל יוֹם [1]The Gemara objects: **But surely incidents took place every day in which Shmuel permitted creditors to collect** their debts from buyers, **even from improvement that has reached** the point of being carried away on **the shoulders of the porters!** How, then, can the Gemara explain that according to Shmuel a creditor may only collect his debt without compensation from produce which is not fully grown?

לָא קַשְׁיָא [2]The Gemara answers: **There is no difficulty. This ruling**, that creditors may collect their debts from even fully grown produce, **applies where** the creditor **is owed the value of the land together with the** land **improvement**. Accordingly, the creditor collects both the land and the land improvement as payment for the original loan from the buyer without compensation. [3]But **this other ruling**, that the creditor is required to reimburse the buyer of the land for his expenses in growing the crop, **applies where** the creditor **is only owed the** original unimproved **value of the land**. The creditor now has two options. He can either take a portion of the field equal in value to the loan, or he can take the entire field and reimburse the buyer for his expenses, in accordance with the law applied when a workman improves property without having been requested to do so. [4]Throughout the following discussion, the Gemara assumes that the buyer favors the first option and the creditor favors the second. The Baraita informs us that it is **the creditor** whose claim is preferred, and it is his prerogative to **give** the buyer all his land **improvement** expenses **and** thus **get rid of him** by forcing him to sell his rights. The buyer will thus have no further claims on the land.

הָנִיחָא לְמַאן דַּאֲמַר [5]The Gemara objects: **This** explanation **is satisfactory according to the** opinion of the authority **who says**: In cases like this, we always favor the creditor and allow him to choose the option he prefers. Thus, if a creditor wishes to seize land in accordance with a mortgage, the buyer cannot stop him, and **even if the buyer has money** with which to repay the seller's debt, **he cannot get rid of the creditor** by forcing him to sell his rights and accept repayment of his loan in cash. The creditor can insist on receiving the land in repayment of his loan, because his claim precedes the sale of the field to the buyer. Thus, if we were to follow this opinion consistently, the explanation of the Baraita would be **well and good**. [6]However, this opinion is disputed **according to the** opinion of the authority **who says**: In cases like this, we always favor the buyer and allow him to choose the option he prefers. And **where the buyer has money** to repay the seller's debt, **he can get rid of the creditor** by forcing him to abandon his rights, and can repay the debt in cash (later the buyer will claim reimbursement from the seller). [7]Thus in the case discussed in the Baraita we should

RASHI

והא מעשים בכל יום — דייני טורפי מקח באין לפני שמואל, ומגבי לבעל חוב כל השבח עם הקרקע ואפילו מגיע לכתפים, כל זמן שצריכין לקרקע. **הא** — דקתני נוטל יציאה מבעל חוב — דלא מסיק ביה בעל חוב במוכר שיעור ארעא ושבחא, הלכך יהיב בעל חוב ללוקח שבחיה, ומסליק ליה. והאי דנקט למלתיה בלשון יציאה ולא תנא: נוטל כנגד החוב מבעל הקרקע, והמותר מבעל חוב — לאשמועינן היא גופא אתא, דהיכא דיציאה יתירה על השבח — אין לו אלא יציאה שיעור שבח. **הניחא למאן דאמר כו׳** — פלוגתא היא בכתובות (צא, ב). **אי אית ליה זוזי ללוקח** — לפרוע החוב. **לא מצי מסלק ליה לבעל חוב** — מן ארעא, דבעל חוב קדים. **שפיר** — דמצי למימר דהיכא דיש קרקע מותר על החוב עם השבח מסלק ליה ללוקח בזוזי על כרחו דלוקח, ולא מצי אמר לוקח: הב לי מן ארעא שיעור שבחי. דאמר: כוליה דידי, ואת ירדת בה שלא ברשות.

HALAKHAH

סִילּוּק בַּעַל חוֹב בְּמָמוֹן Getting rid of a creditor by paying him cash. "If a creditor seeks to collect a debt by seizing a field which the debtor had sold to a third party, the person who bought the field can pay the creditor cash, rather than

TRANSLATION AND COMMENTARY

favor the buyer and **let the buyer say to** the creditor: [1]**"If I had money** to repay the debt owed to you by the seller, **I would get rid of you** and force you to sell your rights to **all the land.** [2]**Now that I do not have money,** and I cannot keep you away from the field entirely, at least **give me a piece of ground in the land equivalent in measure to the** land **improvement** costs I incurred, rather than take away the entire piece of property and reimburse me the money you owe me for the land improvement!"

הָכָא בְּמַאי עָסְקִינַן [3]The Gemara answers: **With what are we dealing here** in the Baraita, where the creditor is allowed to take possession of the field and the improvement, and can force the buyer to accept cash? [4]**For example**, with a case **where the debtor made that particular piece of land a hypothec** for the loan, specifying that the debt was to be collected either by direct cash payment from the debtor or from this field alone (אַפּוֹתֵיקִי מְפוֹרָשׁ). **For he said to** the creditor: "**You will receive payment only from this piece of land**, and need accept no other form of payment." Hence the buyer cannot force the creditor to sell his rights to any part of the field, and the creditor is entitled to receive the entire piece of land in repayment of the loan. He need only reimburse the buyer for his expenses, in accordance with the law applied when a workman improves property without having been requested to do so.

הִכִּיר בָּהּ שֶׁאֵינָהּ שֶׁלּוֹ [5]**If the buyer realized that the land was not** the seller's, because he knew that the seller had robbed someone else of it, **and he** nevertheless **bought it**, [6]**Rav said**: The buyer **has** the right to repayment by the seller of the **money** he paid for the field. But **he does not have** the right to receive **compensation for land improvement**, for he knew from the outset that the field did not belong to the seller. [7]**Shmuel said: He does not even have** the right to repayment of the **money** he paid, for he knew from the outset that the field did not belong to the seller.

בְּמַאי קָמִיפַּלְגִי [8]The Gemara asks: **Regarding what do** Rav and Shmuel **disagree**? What is the basis of their difference of opinion?

רַב סָבַר [9]The Gemara answers: **Rav maintains** that the buyer **knows that he has no right to the land**, since he knows that the seller robbed the rightful owner of it, **and** it is inconceivable that he would imagine that the buying of stolen property has any legal effect. [10]Hence, the entire sale is considered to have been a fiction, and we assume that the "buyer" **made up his mind to give** the money to the seller **as a deposit**. Hence, the "buyer" is entitled to a refund of his deposit and no more.

---

[1]״אִילּוּ הֲוָה לִי זוּזֵי, הֲוָה מְסַלְּקִינָךְ מִכּוּלָּהּ אַרְעָא. [2]הָשְׁתָּא דְּלֵית לִי זוּזֵי, הַב לִי גַּרְבָּא דְּאַרְעָא בְּאַרְעָא שִׁיעוּר שִׁבְחַאי!״

[3]הָכָא בְּמַאי עָסְקִינַן? [4]כְּגוֹן שֶׁעֲשָׂאוֹ אַפּוֹתֵיקִי, דַּאֲמַר לֵיהּ: ״לֹא יְהֵא לְךָ פֵּרָעוֹן אֶלָּא מִזּוֹ״.

[5]הִכִּיר בָּהּ שֶׁאֵינָהּ שֶׁלּוֹ וּלְקָחָהּ, [6]אָמַר רַב: מָעוֹת יֵשׁ לוֹ; שֶׁבַח אֵין לוֹ. [7]וּשְׁמוּאֵל אָמַר: אֲפִילּוּ מָעוֹת אֵין לוֹ.

[8]בְּמַאי קָמִיפַּלְגִי?

[9]רַב סָבַר: אָדָם יוֹדֵעַ שֶׁקַּרְקַע אֵין לוֹ, [10]וְגָמַר וְנָתַן לְשׁוּם פִּקָּדוֹן.

LITERAL TRANSLATION

[1]"If I had money, I would get rid of you from all the land. [2]Now that I do not have money, give me a piece of ground in the land [equal in] measure to my improvement!"

[3]With what are we dealing here? [4]For example, where [the debtor] made [that particular piece of land] a hypothec, as he said to him: "You may have payment only from this [piece of land]."

[5][If the buyer] realized that [the land] was not his and he bought it, [6]Rav said: He has money; he does not have [compensation for land] improvement. [7]But Shmuel said: He does not even have money.

[8]Regarding what do they disagree?

[9]Rav maintains: A person knows that he does not have [a right to the] land, [10]and he made up his mind and he gave [the money] as a deposit.

RASHI

דשוויא נהליה – לוה לבעל חוב אפותיקי להא ארעא, והכל מודים בזו דאי הוה ליה זוזי ללוקח – לא הוה מצי מסלק ליה. **הכא במאי עסקינן** – האי ברייתא דלעיל. **הכיר בה** – לוקח בקרקע זו. **שאינה שלו** – של מוכר, שגזולה היתה אצלו ולקחה. **מעות יש לו** – מן המוכר, לכשיוציאנה נגזל מידו. **שבח אין לו** – שקרקע זה אינו קנוי לו.

LANGUAGE

אַפּוֹתֵיקִי This word is derived from the Greek ὑποθήκη, *hypotheke*, meaning "mortgage, security." As used by the Sages, this word has special meaning — a hypothec applying to a specific piece of property (unlike אַחֲרָיוּת — responsibility, a generalized mortgage against all the borrower's property). The Sages also interpreted it as a compound of Aramaic words: אַפּוֹ תְּהֵי קָאֵי, meaning, "on this let it stand." If a specific piece of property has been mortgaged to guarantee a loan or another obligation, the creditor has no right to claim other property owned by the debtor; nor may he demand an additional sum if the value of the property has fallen.

BACKGROUND

הַב לִי גַּרְבָּא Give me a piece of ground. In Talmudic times most Jews were farmers, and only a few of them dealt in commerce. Moreover, there was a shortage of available land, particularly land that Jews were permitted to purchase. Consequently, everyone wanted land, which was regarded as a more secure investment than cash. Hence the use of the term סִילּוּק — "to get rid of" — in describing the removal of a person from land even when he is given money. On the other hand, the discussion also illustrates how everyone wished to obtain a piece of land.

HALAKHAH

give him the field. But if this field had been explicitly mortgaged to the creditor for payment of the debt, the buyer cannot pay the creditor cash but must allow him to take possession of the field." (*Shulḥan Arukh, Ḥoshen Mishpat* 115:1.)

הִכִּיר בָּהּ שֶׁאֵינָהּ שֶׁלּוֹ If the buyer realized that the field did not belong to the seller. "If a person buys a field, realizing at the time of the sale that it was stolen, he is repaid the amount he paid for the field by the robber when the field returns to its rightful owner. In addition, the rightful

CONCEPTS

הַמְקַדֵּשׁ אֶת אֲחוֹתוֹ One who betroths his sister. Although a marriage may sometimes be valid even when the man in question was forbidden to marry the woman in question, this is not true with regard to violations of the severe prohibitions against incest, which are punishable by a courtimposed death sentence or by excision, and totally lack the legal status and meaning of marriage. Someone who betroths his sister, a woman forbidden to him by the prohibitions against incest, has carried out an act with no legal meaning. But since he has given her money for the purpose of betrothal, the question arises as to what must be done with that money.

TRANSLATION AND COMMENTARY

וְנֵימָא לֵיהּ לְשׁוּם פִּקָּדוֹן [1]The Gemara objects: **But let the buyer** explicitly **say to** the seller that **he is giving him the money as a deposit**! Why the fictitious sale?

סָבַר לָא מְקַבֵּל [2]The Gemara answers: The buyer **thinks** that **the seller will not** be willing to **accept** the money as a deposit. Therefore the buyer uses the device of the sale to ensure that the seller takes care of the purchase price for him for a limited period.

וּשְׁמוּאֵל סָבַר [3]**But Shmuel maintains** a position slightly different from that of Rav: The buyer **knows that he has no right to the land**, just as Rav argued, and the sale is a fiction. [4]**But**, according to Shmuel, the "buyer" **made up his mind to give** the money to the seller **as a gift** rather than as a deposit. Hence the "buyer" is entitled to nothing.

וְנֵימָא לֵיהּ לְשׁוּם מַתָּנָה [5]The Gemara objects: **But let** the buyer explicitly **say to** the seller that he is giving him **the money as a gift**! Why the fictitious sale?

כְּסִיפָא לֵיהּ מִילְּתָא [6]The Gemara answers: **It would be an embarrassment for** the seller to accept a gift. Therefore, the buyer does not explicitly state that the money is a gift, but instead he uses the device of the sale as a means of enabling the seller to receive the money.

וְהָא פְּלִיגֵי בֵּיהּ [7]The Gemara now objects: **But surely** Rav and Shmuel have already **had a difference of opinion about this** matter **on a previous occasion, for it was said:** If **someone betroths his sister** by giving her money for the purpose of betrothal, [8]**Rav says: The** betrothal **money is returned** to the brother. It is his property and the sister may not keep it. [9]**But Shmuel says: The money is a gift.**

[1]וְנֵימָא לֵיהּ: ״לְשׁוּם פִּקָּדוֹן״! [2]סָבַר: ״לָא מְקַבֵּל״. [3]וּשְׁמוּאֵל סָבַר: אָדָם יוֹדֵעַ שֶׁקַּרְקַע אֵין לוֹ, [4]וְגָמַר וְנָתַן לְשׁוּם מַתָּנָה. [5]וְנֵימָא לֵיהּ: ״לְשׁוּם מַתָּנָה״! [6]כְּסִיפָא לֵיהּ מִילְּתָא. [7]וְהָא פְּלִיגֵי בֵּיהּ חֲדָא זִימְנָא, דְּאִיתְּמַר: הַמְקַדֵּשׁ אֶת אֲחוֹתוֹ, [8]רַב אָמַר: מָעוֹת חוֹזְרִין, [9]וּשְׁמוּאֵל אָמַר: מָעוֹת מַתָּנָה.

LITERAL TRANSLATION

[1]But let [the buyer] say to him: "[This money is given] as a deposit"!

[2]He thinks: "[The seller] will not accept [it]."

[3]But Shmuel maintains: A person knows that he does not have [a right to the] land, [4]and he made up his mind and he gave [the money] as a gift.

[5]But let [the buyer] say to him: "[The money is] a gift"!

[6]The thing embarrasses him.

[7]But surely they disagreed about this once [before], for it was said: One who betroths his sister, [8]Rav says: The money returns, [9]but Shmuel says: The money is a gift.

RASHI

לא מקבל – לשמור. **מעות חוזרין** – הקדושין חוזרין לו.

NOTES

וְהָא פְּלִיגֵי בֵּיהּ חֲדָא זִימְנָא But surely they disagreed about this once before. The Gemara always assumes that two Sages never disagree about the same fundamental issue in two different forms, since such repetition would suggest that they themselves were unaware of the issues at stake. When, as here, a difference of opinion on a particular issue is reported in two forms, the repetition must be intended to teach us something more.

Some commentators ask: Rav and Shmuel may both have felt that their rulings on the subject of the buyer of a field from a robber could not be inferred from their rulings on the subject of the betrothal of a sister, because of the question raised by the Gemara later on in the passage, when it asks how the buyer could have taken possession of the field and improved it when he knew that it had not belonged to the seller in the first place. Although it is obvious that a man who attempts to betroth his sister is not acting with serious intent, a man who knowingly buys stolen property may think that the sale has some sort of legal validity. As the Gemara asks, if the buyer really intended that the money he gave to the seller was to be a gift or a deposit, why did he bother working the field and eating its produce? What purpose could he have had in mind in doing so? Even though the Gemara does give an answer below, Rav and Shmuel might have preferred to anticipate the question by unambiguously stating their opinions in the context of the purchase of stolen property.

These commentators reply: If that had been their intention, Rav, at least, need not have mentioned the right of the buyer to repayment of the purchase price. The fact that the buyer gets his "deposit" back according to Rav is a simple application of the "sister" case. Rav needed only to have said that a person who knowingly buys stolen property is not entitled to compensation for land improvement (*Shittah Mekubbetzet*).

HALAKHAH

owner must reimburse the buyer for his expenses in improving the property, or for the increase in the value of the land, whichever is lower. Some authorities maintain that the buyer is not entitled to any compensation for the expenses he incurred." (*Rema* in the name of *Rosh* and *Tur*.) (*Shulḥan Arukh, Ḥoshen Mishpat* 373:1.)

מְקַדֵּשׁ אֲחוֹתוֹ A man who betrothes his sister. "Since a man who betroths his sister knows full well that the betrothal has no validity, the betrothal money he gave her is considered to have been a gift," following Shmuel. (Ibid., *Even HaEzer* 50:2.)

TRANSLATION AND COMMENTARY

רַב אָמַר [1]The Gemara now explains their disagreement: **Rav said** that **the money is returned**, because we assume that the brother **knows that his betrothal of his sister has no validity**, [2]**and** we interpret the "betrothal" as a fiction. We assume that the brother in fact **made up his mind to give the money** to his sister **as a deposit**, just as in the case of the stolen field.

וְנֵימָא לַהּ לְשׁוּם פִּקָּדוֹן [3]The Gemara objects: **But let** the brother explicitly **say to her** that he is **giving** her **the money as a deposit**! Why the fictitious betrothal?

סָבַר לָא מְקַבְּלָה מִינֵּיהּ [4]The Gemara answers: The brother **thinks that** his sister **will not** be willing to **accept a deposit from him**. Therefore, he uses the device of a betrothal to ensure that his sister will take care of the betrothal money for him.

וּשְׁמוּאֵל אָמַר מָעוֹת מַתָּנָה [5]**But Shmuel said** that **the money is a gift**, because **a person knows that his betrothal of his sister has no validity**, [6]**and he made up his mind to give the money** to his sister **as a gift**, just as in the case of the stolen field.

וְנֵימָא לַהּ לְשׁוּם מַתָּנָה [7]The Gemara objects: **Then let** the brother explicitly **say to her** that he **is giving** her **the money as a gift**! Why the fictitious betrothal?

כְּסִיפָא לַהּ מִילְּתָא [8]The Gemara answers: **It would be an embarrassment for her** to take a gift from her brother, and therefore he does not state outright that he is giving her the money as a gift, but instead uses the device of betrothal as a means of giving her the money.

צְרִיכָא [9]The Gemara now explains that, while the two recorded statements of Rav and Shmuel are indeed identical in their reasoning, **it was necessary to report both differences of opinion between Rav and Shmuel,** because their respective opinions in one case cannot be inferred from their opinions in the other. [10]**For if the difference of opinion** between Rav and Shmuel **had been recorded** only **in** connection with **this former case**, where a person buys a stolen field, I might have thought that **Rav said** that the money is returned only **in this case, because people do not ordinarily give gifts to a stranger**, and therefore the money must have been given as a deposit. [11]**But** in the case of the betrothal money, which **concerns his sister**, I might **say that Rav would agree with Shmuel** that the money was intended as a gift. Therefore, Rav had to state his opinion in the betrothal case. [12]Similarly, **if the difference of opinion** between Rav and Shmuel **had been recorded** only **in** connection with **this latter case**, where a man betroths his sister, I might have thought that **Shmuel said** that the money is a gift only **in this case.** [13]**But in the other case**, where a person buys a stolen field from a stranger, I might **say that** Shmuel **would agree with Rav** that the money was given as a deposit. Therefore, Shmuel had to state his opinion in the case of the stolen field. [14]**Therefore, it was necessary** for both Rav and Shmuel **to state** their opinions in **both cases**.

[1]רַב אָמַר: מָעוֹת חוֹזְרִין. אָדָם יוֹדֵעַ שֶׁאֵין קִידּוּשִׁין תּוֹפְסִין בַּאֲחוֹתוֹ, [2]וְגָמַר וְנָתַן לְשׁוּם פִּקָּדוֹן.
[3]וְנֵימָא לַהּ: "לְשׁוּם פִּקָּדוֹן"!
[4]סָבַר לָא מְקַבְּלָה מִינֵּיהּ.
[5]וּשְׁמוּאֵל אָמַר: מָעוֹת מַתָּנָה. אָדָם יוֹדֵעַ שֶׁאֵין קִידּוּשִׁין תּוֹפְסִין בַּאֲחוֹתוֹ, [6]וְגָמַר וְנָתַן לְשׁוּם מַתָּנָה.
[7]וְנֵימָא לַהּ: "לְשׁוּם מַתָּנָה"!
[8]כְּסִיפָא לַהּ מִילְּתָא.
[9]צְרִיכָא. [10]דְּאִי אִיתְּמַר בְּהָא, בְּהָא קָאָמַר רַב, דְּלָא עָבְדִי אֱינָשֵׁי דְּיָהֲבִי מַתָּנוֹת לְנוּכְרָאָה. [11]אֲבָל גַּבֵּי אֲחוֹתוֹ, אֵימָא: מוֹדֶה לֵיהּ לִשְׁמוּאֵל. [12]וְאִי אִיתְּמַר בְּהַךְ, בְּהַךְ קָאָמַר שְׁמוּאֵל. [13]אֲבָל בְּהָא, אֵימָא: מוֹדֶה לֵיהּ לְרַב. [14]צְרִיכָא.

LITERAL TRANSLATION

[1]Rav said: The money returns. A person knows that his betrothal of [his] sister has no validity, [2]and he made up his mind and he gave [the money] as a deposit.

[3]But let him say to her: "[The money is given] as a deposit"!

[4]He thinks [that] she will not accept [a deposit] from him.

[5]But Shmuel said: The money is a gift. A person knows that his betrothal of his sister has no validity, [6]and he made up his mind and he gave [the money] as a gift.

[7]But let him say to her: "[I am giving the money] as a gift"!

[8]The thing embarrasses her.

[9]It was necessary [for both differences of opinion between Rav and Shmuel to have been reported]. [10]For if it had been said [that they disagreed] in this [former case], in this [case] Rav said [his ruling], because people do not ordinarily give gifts to a stranger. [11]But concerning his sister, say: [Rav] would agree with Shmuel. [12]And if it had been said [that they disagreed] in this [latter case], in this [case] Shmuel said [his ruling]. [13]But in the other [case], say: He would agree with Rav. [14][Therefore] it is necessary [to state both cases].

[1] בֵּין לְרַב, דְּאָמַר פִּקָּדוֹן, בֵּין לִשְׁמוּאֵל, דְּאָמַר מַתָּנָה, [2] הַאי לְאַרְעָא בְּמַאי קָא נָחֵית, וּפֵירוֹת הֵיכִי אָכֵיל?
[3] סָבַר: "אֲנָא אֵיחוֹת לְאַרְעָא, וְאִיעֲבִיד וְאֵיכוֹל בְּגַוַּיהּ, כִּי הֵיכִי דַּהֲוָה קָא עָבֵיד אִיהוּ. [4] לְכִי אָתֵי מָרֵיהּ דְּאַרְעָא, זוּזַאי נֶהֱווּ, [5] לְרַב, דְּאָמַר פִּקָּדוֹן, פִּקָּדוֹן, [6] לִשְׁמוּאֵל, דְּאָמַר מַתָּנָה, מַתָּנָה".
[7] אָמַר רָבָא: הִלְכְתָא: יֵשׁ לוֹ מָעוֹת וְיֵשׁ לוֹ שֶׁבַח, וְאַף עַל פִּי שֶׁלֹּא פֵּירַשׁ לוֹ אֶת הַשֶּׁבַח.

LITERAL TRANSLATION

[1] Both [according] to Rav, who says [that the money is a] deposit, and [according] to Shmuel, who says [that the money is a] gift, [2] by what [right] does this [buyer] go down to the land, and how does he eat the produce?

[3] He thinks: "I shall go down to the land, and I shall work it and eat [what is] in it, just as he would have done. [4] When the owner of the land comes, my money will be a deposit, [5] [according] to Rav, who said [that the money is a] deposit, [6] [or] a gift, [according] to Shmuel, who said [that it is] a gift."

[7] Rava said: The Halakhah is: [The buyer] has money and he has improvement, even though [the seller] did not specify improvement for him.

TRANSLATION AND COMMENTARY

בֵּין לְרַב דְּאָמַר פִּקָּדוֹן [1] The Gemara now asks: **Both according to Rav, who says that the money** paid for the stolen field **is** considered to be **a deposit, and according to Shmuel, who says that the money is** considered to be **a gift**, in both situations the "sale" was surely never meant seriously, and the "buyer" did not expect actually to take possession of the land. But in fact the "buyer" *did* take the land until the owner came and seized it from him. [2] But if Rav or Shmuel were correct, **by what** right **does the buyer go down to** work **the land, and how is he** allowed to **eat** its **produce**? Since he knows that the field did not belong to the seller, why does he benefit from the land? Surely he *must* believe that the sale to him *was* valid, and the reasons for Rav's and Shmuel's rulings must be different from those given above!

סָבַר [3] The Gemara answers: The buyer knows that the sale was not valid. But he **thinks** to himself: "Until the owner comes to reclaim his field, why should the robber enjoy the use of it? Rather, **I shall go down to the land, and I shall work it and eat the** produce **that is in it, just as** the robber who sold me the field **would have done** if I had not 'bought' it. The owner loses nothing by this arrangement. [4] **When the owner of the land comes**, he will take the field and **my money will be** considered to have been **a deposit** and will be returned to me by the robber, [5] **according to Rav, who said that the money is** considered to be a **deposit, or a** non-returnable **gift**, [6] **according to Shmuel, who said that it is** considered to be **a gift**."

אָמַר רָבָא הִלְכְתָא [7] The Gemara now presents a summary of the views accepted as authoritative in the differences of opinion raised in the previous discussions: **Rava said, The Halakhah** follows the viewpoint of Rav (above, 14b) **that a person who bought** a field which was later seized by a creditor in payment of a loan he had given to the seller **has** the right to demand the return of his **money, and he** also **has** the right to demand compensation for the **improvement** he made in the field, **even though the seller did not specify** in the deed of sale that he would compensate the buyer for any **improvement** he made in the field.

RASHI

בין לרב דאמר כו׳ — כלומר: היכי מלינן לומר טעמא דרב משום דגמר ונתן לשום פקדון, וטעמא דשמואל משום דגמר ונתן לשום מתנה. ואי הוה דעתיה לחד מהנך, היכי הוה נחית להאי ארעא לעובדה ולאכול פירותיה? על כרחיה סבור היה שיהא המכר קיים, ולא היה בקי בדין. וטעמא דפלוגתא דרב ושמואל — טעם אחרינא הוא. **דהוה עביד** — הגזלן. **לרב דאמר פקדון פקדון** — כלומר: אליבא דרב מפרשינן דהאי מימר אמר: זוזי נהוו פקדון. ולשמואל מפרשינן דהאי אמר: זוזי נהוו מתנה. **הלכתא** — בפלוגתא קמייתא יש לו מעות ויש לו שבח. ואף על פי דלא פירש — ולית לן דשמואל, דאמר שבח צריך לימלך.

NOTES

אֲנָא אֵיחוֹת לְאַרְעָא וכו׳ **I shall go down to the land, etc.** *Ritva* suggests that the buyer benefited from the sale in that he enjoyed the produce of the field until the rightful owner came. Initially *Ritva* felt that the buyer was not even required to compensate the rightful owner for the produce he ate. But *Ritva* ultimately decided that the rightful owner is entitled to the produce, and the buyer is entitled only to his expenses, up to the value of the produce. Nevertheless, the buyer has nothing to lose by buying the stolen field and "borrowing" the produce, since in any case he will get back the money he originally paid from the robber, and his expenses from the owner.

אָמַר רָבָא הִלְכְתָא וכו׳ **Rava said: The Halakhah is....** In his first two rulings, Rava decides in favour of Rav in his differences of opinion with Shmuel. Therefore, it would seem that Rava could have formulated this ruling more concisely, by simply stating that the Halakhah follows Rav's view in both cases. *Ramban* points out that Rav did not give a ruling at all on the third question, that of notes lacking a property guarantee. Hence, Rava could not simply state that the Halakhah follows Rav in all the cases discussed here.

Rashba and *Rosh* suggest that Rava was concerned about the possibility of confusion over the question of compensation for land improvement. If he simply ruled in favour

TRANSLATION AND COMMENTARY

[1]It also follows the viewpoint of Rav (above, 15b) that **if the buyer realized that the land was not** the seller's **and he** nevertheless **bought it, he has** the right to repayment by the seller of the **money** he paid for the field, **but he does not have** the right to receive compensation for **land improvement**. Moreover, the Halakhah does not accept the distinction made in Shmuel's name (above, 14a) between promissory notes and deeds of sale. [2]Rather, **the omission** in any legal document **of a clause mortgaging property is an error of the scribe, both in promissory notes and in deeds of buying and selling**, unless the contrary is explicitly stated. We therefore treat the seller's or the debtor's property as if it was mortgaged as security for the sale/loan, even though this was not stipulated in the document.

בְּעָא מִינֵּיהּ שְׁמוּאֵל מֵרַב [3]**Shmuel asked Rav** the following question: If the robber **returned** after he had sold to a third party the field he had stolen **and bought the field from the original owner**, **what** is the law? May the robber go and, on the basis of a valid deed of sale, claim the field from the buyer, since he has now bought it from the rightful owner, as would be the case if anyone else had bought it? Or does the buyer's transaction with the robber give him some rights in the field vis-à-vis the robber himself?

אֲמַר לֵיהּ [4]Rav **said to** Shmuel in reply: **What did the first one** — the robber — **sell to the second** — the buyer — at the time of their original transaction? Surely the robber, like any other seller, sold him **every right that he** himself **might subsequently acquire**. All of the robber's present and future rights to the field are included in the original sale to the buyer. Thus, when the robber rectifies the original situation and legally acquires the field, ownership of it is automatically transferred to the buyer, and the robber cannot take it away from him.

LITERAL TRANSLATION

[1][If the buyer] realized that [the land] was not his and he bought it, he has money, [but] he does not have [land] improvement. [2][The omission of a clause] mortgaging [property] is a scribal error, both in promissory notes and in deeds of buying and selling.

[3]Shmuel asked Rav: [If the robber] returned and bought [the field] from the original owner, what is [the law]?

[4]He said to him: What did the first one sell to the second one? Every right that he might subsequently acquire (lit., "that will come to his hand").

[1]הִכִּיר בָּהּ שֶׁאֵינָהּ שֶׁלּוֹ וּלְקָחָהּ, מָעוֹת יֵשׁ לוֹ, שֶׁבַח אֵין לוֹ. [2]אַחֲרָיוּת טָעוּת סוֹפֵר הוּא, בֵּין בִּשְׁטָרֵי הַלְוָאָה בֵּין בִּשְׁטָרֵי מִקָּח וּמִמְכָּר.

[3]בְּעָא מִינֵּיהּ שְׁמוּאֵל מֵרַב: חָזַר וּלְקָחָהּ מִבְּעָלִים הָרִאשׁוֹנִים, מַהוּ?

[4]אֲמַר לֵיהּ: מַה מָּכַר לוֹ רִאשׁוֹן לַשֵּׁנִי? כָּל זְכוּת שֶׁתָּבֹא לְיָדוֹ.

RASHI

ואחריות טעות סופר הוא – ולית לן דשמואל דאמר שעבוד צריך לימלך. **חזר** – גזלן ולקחה מבעלים הראשונים לאחר שמכר ללוקח. **מהו** – להיות במקום בעלים, כאילו לקחה אחר, ויוציאה מיד הלוקח. **אמר ליה** – לא מצי לאפוקה. שכשמכר מכר לו כל זכות שתבא לידו, וכשלקחה לא לקחה אלא כדי שתהא מקוים ביד הלוקח.

SAGES

בְּעָא מִינֵּיהּ שְׁמוּאֵל מֵרַב **Shmuel asked Rav**. Rav and Shmuel were indeed colleagues, and there are many recorded differences of opinion between them regarding the Halakhah. Nevertheless, Shmuel was younger than Rav, and not only had Rav been ordained officially by Rabbi Yehudah HaNasi, but he had also received a large number of traditions from the various Rabbis with whom he had studied in Eretz Israel. Therefore we occasionally find that Shmuel asks Rav questions about Halakhic matters.

NOTES

of Rav, we might have thought that such compensation is conditional upon the presence of a specific clause mentioning it in the deed of sale. Therefore, Rava spelled out his ruling in detail.

חָזַר וּלְקָחָהּ מִבְּעָלִים **If the robber returned and bought the field from the original owner**. Most commentators explain that the Gemara here is referring back to the original case of a buyer who is defrauded into buying a stolen field. It is only concerning such a buyer that we need to consider the possibility that the robber might wish to save his reputation (*Rabbenu Ḥananel, Rif, Rashba*).

But other commentators say that the Gemara's question applies even to the case where the buyer knew that the field was stolen (*Ritva* and *Meiri*; some commentators maintain that *Rashi*, on 16a ד״ה בְּמַאֲמִינוֹ, also interpreted the Gemara in this way).

מַה מָּכַר לוֹ רִאשׁוֹן לַשֵּׁנִי **What did the first one sell to the second?** *Rabbenu Yehonatan*, whose view is followed in the commentary here, understands the phrase, "the first one," to refer to the robber, and "the second one" to refer to the buyer. In other words, already at the time of the original sale, the robber sold to the buyer any rights to the field he might acquire in the future.

But most commentators have reservations about the legal validity of a robber selling future rights in a field he does not yet own. Therefore, they understand the transfer of the robber's rights to the buyer as taking place at the time of the subsequent purchase of the field by the robber from the owner. In other words, the robber is in effect buying the field from the owner as the agent of the buyer.

HALAKHAH

אַחֲרָיוּת טָעוּת סוֹפֵר **Omission of a clause mortgaging landed property as security is a scribal error**. "Any promissory note or deed of sale, even if it does not contain a clause mortgaging property as security, is considered as if it does contain such a clause, and generates a property lien accordingly. Omission of such a clause is assumed to be a scribal error, unless the document explicitly states that the signer's property was *not* mortgaged as security for the obligation recorded in the document." (*Shulḥan Arukh, Ḥoshen Mishpat* 39:1; 111:1; 225:1.)

חָזַר הַגַּזְלָן וּלְקָחָהּ **A robber who bought the field he had previously stolen**. "If a person robbed another of a field and

LITERAL TRANSLATION

[1] What is the reason?

[2] Mar Zutra said: He prefers that [the buyer] not call him a robber. [3] Rav Ashi said: He prefers that he maintain his [reputation for] trustworthiness.

[4] What is [the difference] between them?

[5] There is [a difference] between them where the buyer died. [6] [According to] the one who says: He prefers that [the buyer] not call him a robber, [16A] surely he died! [7] But [according to] the one who says [that] he prefers that he maintain his [reputation for] trustworthiness, he prefers that he maintain his [reputation for] trustworthiness with the sons too!

[1] מַאי טַעְמָא? [2] מַר זוּטְרָא אֲמַר: נִיחָא לֵיהּ דְּלָא נִקְרְיֵיהּ גַּזְלָנָא. [3] רַב אַשִׁי אֲמַר: נִיחָא לֵיהּ דְּלֵיקוּ בְּהֵימָנוּתֵיהּ.

[4] מַאי בֵּינַיְיהוּ?

[5] אִיכָּא בֵּינַיְיהוּ דְּמִית לוֹקֵחַ. [6] מַאן דַּאֲמַר: נִיחָא לֵיהּ דְּלָא לִקְרְיֵיהּ גַּזְלָנָא, [16A] הָא מִית לֵיהּ! [7] וּמַאן דַּאֲמַר נִיחָא לֵיהּ דְּלֵיקוּם בְּהֵימָנוּתֵיהּ, בַּהֲדֵי בְּנֵי נַמִּי נִיחָא לֵיהּ דְּלֵיקוּם בְּהֵימָנוּתֵיהּ!

TRANSLATION AND COMMENTARY

מַאי טַעְמָא [1] The Gemara now asks: If the robber may not now reclaim the field from the buyer, **for what reason** did he buy it from the rightful owner?

מַר זוּטְרָא אֲמַר [2] The Gemara now gives two answers to this question: (1) **Mar Zutra said**: The robber **prefers** the buyer **not to call him a robber**. (2) [3] **Rav Ashi said**: The robber **prefers to maintain his reputation for trustworthiness**. He does not want people to refrain from buying possibly stolen property from him for fear of losing it later.

מַאי בֵּינַיְיהוּ [4] The Gemara asks: **What** practical **difference is there between** the answers given by Mar Zutra and Rav Ashi?

אִיכָּא בֵּינַיְיהוּ דְּמִית לוֹקֵחַ [5] The Gemara answers: **There is a difference between them where the person who bought** the field from the robber **died**. [6] **According to** Mar Zutra, **who says** that the robber **prefers the buyer not to call him a robber**, [16A] **surely**, since the buyer has already **died**, the robber no longer has any reason to be concerned about him, and this was not the reason why the robber bought the field. [7] **But according to** Rav Ashi, **who says that** the robber **prefers to maintain his reputation for trustworthiness, he prefers to maintain his reputation for trustworthiness with the sons** of the buyer **too**! Therefore, Rav Ashi's reason why the robber bought the field *does* apply in such a case!

RASHI

דלא ליקרייה גזלנא – שלא יחרפנו לוקח זה כשיוציאנה נגזל מידו ויקראנו גזלן, לכך חוזר להעמיד ממכרו. **דמית לוקח** – לאחר שלקחה גזלן מן הבעלים, והגזלן בא להוציאה מבניו. **למאן דאמר** – לא חזר להעמיד ממכרו אלא דלא ליקרייה לוקח גזלן. **הא מית** – לוקח, ומי יחרפנו עוד? הלכך, לא נתכוון לזה, אלא להעמידה בידו בחייו ולא לאחר מותו. **מאן דאמר כו׳.**

NOTES

מַאי טַעְמָא מַר זוּטְרָא וכו׳ What is the reason? Mar Zutra said.... At first glance, Mar Zutra's and Rav Ashi's explanations seem unnecessary, since Rav, the author of this ruling, has already explained that "the first one [the robber] sells the second [the buyer] whatever rights he [the robber] may subsequently acquire." Some authorities point out that in several places in the Talmud there is a difference of opinion over whether a person can sell future rights in an object he does not yet own. Rav is of the opinion that such a sale is valid, but the final ruling of the Gemara is that it is invalid. Perhaps, then, the first reason, which was given by Rav himself, was acceptable only according to Rav's own opinion. Accordingly, Mar Zutra and Rav Ashi felt that they had to give additional reasons for supporting this ruling, which would be valid even according to the accepted Halakhah (*Rashba*).

Other commentators suggest that Mar Zutra's reasoning is built upon Rav's. Even if the robber originally intended to sell the buyer all his future rights, the sale would not be valid, at least according to the accepted Halakhah and possibly even according to Rav, if the robber were to change his mind. Mar Zutra is merely arguing that we have reason to believe that the robber has not changed his mind and that Rav's reasoning continues to apply (*Ritva*).

Other commentators point out that the reason given earlier, "the first one sells the second...," could be understood as meaning that *the person who was robbed sold the robber* any future rights to the land, and thus the robber would be permitted to take the land away from the buyer. The Gemara, therefore, teaches us here that *it is the robber who transfers the field to the buyer*, in order to maintain his own reputation for trustworthiness (*Rosh*).

דְּלֵיקוּ בְּהֵימָנוּתֵיהּ To maintain his reputation for trustworthiness. The difference between the two reasons is not only the difference between a negative and a positive definition. A man who fears to be known as a robber is afraid of the social stigma and the practical inconvenience of having a person constantly accuse him of being a robber

HALAKHAH

sold it to another person (or gave it to him as a gift), and then bought it from the original owner, the person who bought the field from the robber may keep it, since we assume that the robber bought the field from its rightful owner in order to maintain his reputation for trustworthiness." (*Shulḥan Arukh, Ḥoshen Mishpat*, 374:1.)

TRANSLATION AND COMMENTARY

סוֹף סוֹף קָרוּ לֵיהּ [1]The Gemara now objects: This distinction is surely unrealistic! **Ultimately**, when the field is taken away by the rightful owner, **the sons of the buyer will** also **call him a robber**. Thus, even Mar Zutra would agree that if the buyer has died, the robber may still have a good reason for wishing to buy the field from the rightful owner!

אֶלָּא [2]**Rather**, we must give a different example of the situation where Rav Ashi and Mar Zutra would disagree: **There is a difference between them where the robber** himself **died**. **According to** Mar Zutra **who says** that **a person prefers** people **not to call him a robber, surely** since the robber **has died**, this reason no longer applies and his heirs should be able to take the field for themselves. [3]But **according to** Rav Ashi, **who says** that the robber **prefers to maintain his reputation for trustworthiness, here, too, even though he has** now **died, he** also **prefers to maintain his reputation for trustworthiness** even **after his death**.

סוֹף סוֹף, קָרוּ לְבָנֵיהּ [4]The Gemara again objects: This distinction, too, between the reasons given by Mar Zutra and Rav Ashi cannot be maintained! **Ultimately** the cheated buyer **will call** the robber's **sons "the sons of a robber"**! Thus, even according to Mar Zutra, the robber's reason for wishing to rectify the situation should apply even after his death!

אֶלָּא [5]**Rather**, explains the Gemara, **there is a** situation where the **difference** of opinion **between** Rav Ashi and Mar Zutra becomes apparent, and this is **where the robber gave the field as a gift** to another person and did not sell it at all. [6]**According to** Rav Ashi, **who says** that the robber **prefers to maintain his reputation for trustworthiness**, here, **too, in the case of a gift, he prefers to maintain his reputation for trustworthiness**.

[1]סוֹף סוֹף, קָרוּ לֵיהּ בְּנֵי לוֹקֵחַ ״גַּזְלָנָא״!
[2]אֶלָּא אִיכָּא בֵּינַיְיהוּ דְּמִית גַּזְלָן. מַאן דַּאֲמַר: נִיחָא לֵיהּ לְאִינִישׁ דְּלָא לִקְרִיוּהוּ גַּזְלָן, הָא מִית לֵיהּ. [3]לְמַאן דַּאֲמַר: נִיחָא לֵיהּ דְּלֵיקוּם בְּהֵימָנוּתֵיהּ, הָכִי נַמִי, אַף עַל גַּב דְּמִית, נִיחָא לֵיהּ דְּלֵיקוּם בְּהֵימָנוּתֵיהּ.
[4]סוֹף סוֹף, קָרוּ לְבָנֵיהּ ״בְּנֵי גַּזְלָנָא״!
[5]אֶלָּא, אִיכָּא בֵּינַיְיהוּ דְּיָהֲבָהּ בְּמַתָּנָה. [6]מַאן דַּאֲמַר: נִיחָא לֵיהּ דְּלֵיקוּם בְּהֵימָנוּתֵיהּ, מַתָּנָה נַמִי נִיחָא לֵיהּ דְּלֵיקוּם

LITERAL TRANSLATION

[1]Ultimately, the sons of the buyer will [also] call him a robber!

[2]Rather, there is a [difference] between them where the robber died. [According to] the one who says: A person prefers that [people] not call him a robber, surely he died. [3][According] to the one who says: He prefers that he maintain his [reputation for] trustworthiness, here too, even though he has died, he prefers that he maintain his [reputation for] trustworthiness [after his death].

[4]Ultimately, they will call his sons "the sons of a robber"!

[5]Rather, there is a [difference] between them where [the robber] gave [the field] as a gift. [6][According to] the one who says: He prefers that he maintain his [reputation for] trustworthiness, [in the case of] a gift, too, he prefers that he maintain his [reputation for]

RASHI

דמית גזלן – לאחר שלקחה, והכניס בכיס להוציא מיד הלוקח. **הא מית ליה** – ולא נתכוון להעמיד ממכרו אלא בימי חייו, שלא יחרפוהו. **אף על גב דמית ניחא ליה** – מעיקרא. **דליקו בהימנותיה** – אפילו לאחר מיתה. **סוף סוף קרו לבניה בני גזלנא** – נמצא שאף לאחר מיתה מחרפין אותו.

NOTES

and a cheat. In contrast, a person who wants to be considered trustworthy wishes to strengthen his social status and be considered reliable, someone who keeps his word in every transaction into which he enters.

דְּמִית גַּזְלָן Where the robber died. *Rashi* explains that the Gemara is referring to a case where the robber bought the field, presumably to enable the buyer to keep it, and only then died. But *Tosafot* and others object, noting that if the robber bought the field with that intention, the buyer would immediately acquire ownership of it, and neither the robber nor his heirs could subsequently change their minds. *Tosafot* therefore suggest that the Gemara is referring to a case where the robber bought the property while he was on his deathbed. On the one hand, he may still be trying to save his reputation in the eyes of the buyer, but, on the other hand, he may no longer care about his reputation since he is about to die anyway.

Other commentators explain that the Gemara is referring to a case where the robber died without buying the field from the person he had robbed, and subsequently his heirs bought it. The question would then be to what extent were the heirs concerned about their father's reputation (*Rabbi Avraham Av Bet Din*).

HALAKHAH

מַתְּנַת גַּזְלָן The gift of a robber. "If a person robbed someone of a field, gave it to another person as a gift, and then bought it from its rightful owner, we assume that the purpose of the robber is that the field should legally belong to the recipient, because he wishes to maintain his reputation for trustworthiness." (*Shulḥan Arukh, Ḥoshen Mishpat* 374:1.)

TRANSLATION AND COMMENTARY

[1]But **according to** Mar Zutra, **who says that** a person **prefers people not to call him a robber**, the robber **may say to the recipient** of the gift after the field has been taken away from him by the rightful owner: **"Of what did I rob you**? For even if the gift is taken away from you, you have not lost anything, since you did not spend any money on it in the first place."

פְּשִׁיטָא [2]The Gemara continues to discuss the case of someone who stole a field, sold it, and then bought it from its rightful owner: **It is obvious** that **if**, after selling the field to one person, **the robber** later **sold it** to another person, **or bequeathed it** to his heirs, **or gave it** away **as a gift**, and then bought it from its rightful owner, **his purpose** in buying the field **was not** in order **to place it** in the legal possession of **the** first **buyer**. By his action in selling, bequeathing, or giving the field to a second person, after having sold it the first time, the robber shows that whatever his motive is in subsequently buying the field from the rightful owner, it is *not* to protect and help the first buyer. The field now legally belongs to the second buyer/heir/recipient, and the first buyer can sue the robber for his money.

נָפְלָה לֵיהּ בִּירוּשָּׁה [3]Similarly, it is obvious that **if** the field **fell to** the robber **as an inheritance** from the rightful owner, after the robber had sold it to another person, **the inheritance takes effect of its own accord, and it was not** the robber **who took trouble over it** as he did in the case where he bought the field. Hence, we have no reason to assume that the robber wants to ensure that the field remain in the possession of the person to whom he sold it. Rather, he can now, as its legal owner, claim it back from the buyer, and the latter upon receipt of compensation must give it up to the robber.

גָּבֵי אִיהוּ בְּחוֹבוֹ [4]On the other hand, **if the robber**, after selling the field to another person, **himself collected it in payment of a debt** owed to him by the rightful owner, **we examine** the possible motives of the robber: **If the field's** rightful **owner has other land** from which the robber could have collected the debt, **and the robber said: "I want this** particular field," we assume that the robber **wanted to place** the field in **the buyer's** legal possession, and this is why he insisted on this particular piece of land in repayment of his loan.

בְּהֶימָנוּתֵיהּ. [1]מַאן דַּאֲמַר: נִיחָא לֵיהּ דְּלָא נִקְרִיוּהוּ גַּזְלָנָא, אֲמַר לֵיהּ: ״מַאי גְּזַלֵינָא מִינָּךְ?״

[2]פְּשִׁיטָא: זַבְּנָהּ, אוֹרְתָהּ, וְיָהֲבָהּ בְּמַתָּנָה, לָאו לְאוֹקְמָהּ קַמֵּי לוֹקֵחַ קָא בָּעֵי.

[3]נָפְלָה לֵיהּ בִּירוּשָּׁה, יְרוּשָּׁה מִמֵּילָא הִיא, וְלָאו אִיהוּ קָא טָרַח אַבַּתְרָהּ.

[4]גָּבֵי אִיהוּ בְּחוֹבוֹ, חָזֵינָא: אִי אִית לֵיהּ אַרְעָא אַחֲרִיתֵי, וַאֲמַר: ״הַאי בָּעֵינָא״, לְאוֹקְמָהּ

LITERAL TRANSLATION

trustworthiness. [1][According to] the one who says: He prefers that [people] not call him a robber, he may say to [the recipient]: "What did I rob from you?"

[2]It is obvious: [If the robber] sold it [the field], [or] bequeathed it, or gave it as a gift, his purpose was not to place it before the buyer.

[3]If it fell to him as an inheritance, an inheritance [takes effect] of its own accord, and it was not he who took trouble over it.

[4][If the robber] himself collected [the field in payment] of his debt, we see: If [the field's owner] has other land, and [the robber] said: "I want this," he

RASHI

זבנה אורתה — אם קודם שלקח מן הבעלים חזר ומכרה לאיש אחר לבד מן הראשון, או הורישה לאחד מבניו, או יהבה במתנה, ואחר כך לקחה — האי ודאי איגלי דעתיה דלאו לאוקמי קמיה לוקח ראשון בעי, ולא ניחא ליה דליקום בהימנותיה, שהרי מכרה לשני. **נפלה ליה** — לגזלן בירושה, שמתחילה גזלה לאחד ממורישיו ומת הנגזל. **ירושה ממילא הויא** — והא ליכא למימר ניחא ליה דליקו בהימנותיה, דהא לא טרח אבתרה, דנימא גלי דעתיה דניחא ליה דליקו. הלכך, הוי כיורש דעלמא, וחוזר ותובעה, ונותן מעות ללוקח. **גבייה בחובו** — לאחר שגזלה ומכר לו, ובא לו אצל נגזל, ואמר לו: הגבה לי בחובי קרקע שגזלתיך. **אי אית ליה ארעא אחריתי** — לנגזל, שיכול לגבות חובו ממנה, ואמר ליה: בזו שגזלתי אני חפץ — הא טרח אבתרה. ואמרינן: לאוקמה קמיה לוקח בעי.

HALAKHAH

זַבְּנָהּ, אוֹרְתָהּ וְיָהֲבָהּ בְּמַתָּנָה. נָפְלָה לֵיהּ בִּירוּשָּׁה **If the robber sold the field, or bequeathed it, or gave it away as a gift.... If it fell to him as an inheritance.** "If a person stole a field, sold it to another person, bought it from the rightful owner, and sold, or bequeathed, or gave the field to another person, his actions in trasferring the field to a second person show that he does not want the field to remain in the possession of the original purchaser. Similarly, if the robber inherited the field, it is not thereby established as the legal property of the buyer. However, some authorities disagree, and maintain that where the robber sold the field to another person *after* having bought it from the rightful owner, the original buyer may keep the field, but where the robber sold the field to another person *before* buying it from the rightful owner, the original buyer has not acquired the field." (*Shulḥan Arukh, Ḥoshen Mishpat* 374:2.)

גָּבֵי גַּזְלָן בְּחוֹבוֹ **Debt collection by a robber.** "If a person stole a field and sold it, and later the field's rightful owner gave it to him in payment of a debt, the buyer may keep the field, as long as the rightful owner owns other fields (in this case, we assume that the robber by collecting his debt from this field wanted to establish the field in the buyer's

קַמֵּיהּ לוֹקֵחַ קָא בָּעֵי. [1]וְאִי לָא, זוּזֵי הוּא דְּבָעֵי אִפָּרוּעֵי.
[2]יָהֲבָהּ נִהֲלֵיהּ בְּמַתָּנָה, פְּלִיגִי בָּהּ רַב אַחָא וְרָבִינָא. [3]חַד אֲמַר: מַתָּנָה כִּירוּשָּׁה, דְּהָא מִמֵּילָא. [4]וְחַד אֲמַר: מַתָּנָה כְּמֶכֶר, דְּאִי לָאו דְּטָרַח וְאַרְצֵי קַמֵּיהּ, לָא הָוֵי יָהֵיב לֵיהּ מַתָּנָה. [5]לְהָכִי טָרַח וְאַרְצֵי קַמֵּיהּ, כִּי הֵיכִי דְּלֵיקוּם בְּהֵימָנוּתֵיהּ.
[6]וְעַד אֵימַת נִיחָא לֵיהּ דְּלֵיקוּם בְּהֵימָנוּתֵיהּ?

TRANSLATION AND COMMENTARY

[1]**But if** the field's rightful owner does **not** have other land, or if it was the owner and not the robber who insisted on paying with this particular field, we assume that the robber merely **wanted to be paid his money**, and there is no reason to assume that he had any intention of securing the field for the buyer.

יָהֲבָהּ נִהֲלֵיהּ בְּמַתָּנָה [2]**If the owner gave** the field **to the** robber **as a gift**, after the robber had sold it to another person, **Rav Aḥa and Ravina disagree.** [3]**One says: A gift is like an inheritance, because it becomes** the recipient's property **of its own accord**, and its acquisition by the robber cannot be interpreted as a positive effort on his part to ensure that the field will remain in the buyer's legal possession. [4]**And the other says: A gift is like a sale, because if the robber had not taken the trouble to ingratiate himself** with the field's rightful owner, the latter **would not have given him the gift.** [5]And **this is the reason** why **the robber took the trouble to ingratiate himself** with the rightful owner, in order **to maintain his reputation for trustworthiness** and ensure that the buyer could keep the field.

וְעַד אֵימַת נִיחָא לֵיהּ [6]The Gemara now asks: **But until what point does** the robber's action in buying the field from its rightful owner show that he **prefers to maintain his reputation for trustworthiness**, and to legitimize his earlier sale of the field to the buyer? Surely at some point we can no longer assume that the robber is interested in rectifying a transaction completed long before!

LITERAL TRANSLATION

wants to place it before the buyer. [1]But if not, he wants to be paid money.
[2][If the owner] gave it to him as a gift, Rav Aḥa and Ravina disagree about this. [3]One says: A gift is like an inheritance, because it [comes] of its own accord. [4]And the other says: A gift is like a sale, because if [the robber] did not take trouble and ingratiate [himself] before him, he would not have given him the gift. [5]For this [reason the robber] takes trouble and ingratiates [himself] before him, so that he may maintain his [reputation for] trustworthiness.
[6]But until when does he prefer to maintain his [reputation for] trustworthiness?

RASHI

יהביה ניהליה במתנה — נגזל לגזלן.
ועד אימת — יקנה מבעלים הראשונים, דאמרינן דמשום דניחא ליה דליקו בהימנותיה, לקחה.

NOTES

מַתָּנָה כְּמֶכֶר **A gift is like a sale.** Despite the many Halakhic differences between selling and giving, the general conclusion reached is that the legal act of giving to some extent resembles the legal act of selling. In other words, a gift is not an entirely arbitrary donation: something is received in return for it, whether it be money or some other benefit or satisfaction which the giver at one time received from the recipient. Nevertheless, in a sale there must be a clear balance between the amount paid and the value of the object sold, whereas in the case of a gift there need not be any relation between the satisfaction derived by the donor and the value of his gift.

HALAKHAH

legal possession). But if the rightful owner of the field owned only this field, we assume that the robber wanted this field as payment for his debt, and the buyer does not acquire the field." (Ibid., 374:3.)

קִבְּלָה הַגַּזְלָן בְּמַתָּנָה **If the robber received the field as a gift.** "If a person stole a field and sold it to another person, and then the rightful owner of the field gave it to the robber as a gift, the buyer has thereby acquired the field (the same law applies here as if the rightful owner of the field had sold it to the robber)." According to the *Gra*, since the Gemara renders no clear-cut decision regarding the law in this case, we follow the general principle governing unresolved property disputes, namely, that the person at present in possession of the disputed item (in this case, the person who bought the field from the robber) is permitted to keep it. *Rema*, however, disagrees, maintaining that the buyer may not keep the field unless he brings conclusive proof that the robber intended that he (the buyer) should acquire the field. According to *Rema*, the buyer is not considered to be in possession of the field. And since the Halakhah regarding this case is not clear, the robber is entitled to the field. (Ibid., 374:4.)

עַד מָתַי נוֹחַ לוֹ לַעֲמוֹד בְּנֶאֱמָנוּתוֹ **How long is he concerned about maintaining his reputation for trustworthiness.** "The robber is assumed to be concerned about maintaining his reputation for trustworthiness if he buys the field he has stolen and sold, before the court announces that his property is up for sale as compensation to the buyer for the illicit sale. But if, after this time, he buys the field he has stolen and sold, there is no reason to assume that he did so in order to establish it in the buyer's legal possession." (Ibid., 374:1.)

¹אָמַר רַב הוּנָא: עַד שְׁעַת הָעֲמָדָה בְּדִין. ²חִיָּיא בַּר רַב אָמַר: עַד דְּמָטָא אַדְרַכְתָּא לִידֵיהּ. ³רַב פַּפָּא אָמַר: עַד דְּמַתְחֲלָן יוֹמֵי אַכְרַזְתָּא. ⁴מַתְקִיף לָהּ רָמִי בַּר חָמָא: מִכְּדִי, הַאי לוֹקֵחַ, בְּמַאי קָנֵי לְהַאי אַרְעָא? בְּהַאי שְׁטָרָא. הַאי שְׁטָרָא חַסְפָּא בְּעָלְמָא הוּא!

LITERAL TRANSLATION

[1] Rav Huna said: Until the time of his appearance in court.

[2] Hiyya bar Rav said: Until the writ authorizing seizure reaches his [the buyer's] hands.

[3] Rav Pappa said: Until the days of announcement begin.

[4] Rami Bar Ḥama strongly objected: Now, this buyer, with what did he buy this field? With that deed. That deed is a mere potsherd!

TRANSLATION AND COMMENTARY

אָמַר רַב הוּנָא [1] Three answers are given by the Gemara to this question: (1) **Rav Huna said: Until the time** when the field is seized from the buyer by the rightful owner, and the buyer sues the robber for compensation and makes him **appear in court**. Once the buyer has started legal proceedings against the robber, the latter is presumably no longer concerned about his reputation, since the buyer has indicated through his actions that he does not trust him.

חִיָּיא בַּר רַב (2) [2] **Ḥiyya bar Rav** gave a later date and **said: Until the writ authorizing seizure reaches** the buyer's **hands**. If the court has ruled that the robber must reimburse the buyer, and if after a period he has still failed to comply, the court issues the buyer a "writ authorizing seizure," granting him the right to collect his compensation from the robber's property, wherever it may be. Once this writ is issued, we assume that the robber is no longer concerned about maintaining his reputation.

רַב פַּפָּא אָמַר (3) [3] **Rav Pappa** gave an even later date and **said**: The robber is concerned about his reputation **until the days of announcing** the public sale of the robber's property **begin**, i.e., until the court begins announcing publicly that the robber's property is up for sale in order to provide reimbursement for the buyer.

מַתְקִיף לָהּ רָמִי בַּר חָמָא [4] The next passage in the Gemara goes back to a further discussion of Rav's ruling (above, 15b), that if the robber buys the stolen field from its rightful owner after he has sold it to someone else, it becomes the legal property of the buyer, because the robber wanted him to keep it. **Rami Bar Ḥama strongly objected** to the fundamental basis of Rav's view: **Now** let us consider the following point: **This buyer — by what means did he buy the field** which the robber sold him? Was it not **by means of the deed** of sale which the robber gave him? But surely **this deed is a mere potsherd**! It has no legal value, since the robber did not own the property at the time he sold it, and a person cannot convey ownership to someone else of something that he does not himself own. Hence the original sale was not valid, and no other formal act of acquisition took place!

RASHI

עד שעת העמדה בדין — עד שיטרפוה מן הלוקח ויעמידהו בדין. אבל משעמד ברשעו עד שעת העמדה בדין — גלי אדעתיה דלא מהימן הוא, ואם לקחה אחרי כן — לאו לאוקמיה קמיה לוקח בעי. **עד דמטא אדרכתא לידיה** — עד שיחייבוהו בית דין לפרוע ללוקח מעותיו, ועמד במרדו עד שכתבו פסק דין ונתנו ללוקח על נכסיו של גזלן, שבכל מקום שימצאם יחזיק בהן. והיינו תשעים יום לאחר שעמד בדין, כדאמרינן ב״הגוזל [בתרא״] (בבא קמא קיב, ב). **עד דמתחלן יומא דאכרזתא** — לאחר שמצא זה קרקע משל גזלן, ובא לבית דין והן מכריזין שכל מי שרוצה לקנות קרקע יבא ויקחנה, כדאמרינן בערכין (כא, ב): שום היתומין שלשים יום. **מתקיף ליה רמי בר חמא** — אהא מה מכר ראשון לשני כו׳.

NOTES

עַד שְׁעַת הָעֲמָדָה בְּדִין **Until the time of his appearance in court.** Some commentators interpret this phrase as referring to the moment when the *rightful owner* sues the *buyer* to recover his stolen property. But most commentators interpret it as meaning: Until the *buyer* sues the *robber* for selling him stolen property. Since the buyer offended the robber by suing him, we may assume that the robber is no longer concerned about the buyer's good will towards him (*Rabbenu Yehonatan* and others; this view is followed in the commentary here).

אַדְרַכְתָּא **A writ authorizing seizure.** When a court rules that one person must pay another, he is given ninety days to pay. If at the end of that period he has not yet paid, whether because of intransigence or because of lack of liquid assets, the court can issue a writ authorizing seizure, permitting the plaintiff to search for any property that belongs to the defendant and to seize it.

הַאי לוֹקֵחַ בְּמַאי קָנֵי **With what did this buyer acquire this field?** The Rishonim object that this question appears to be superfluous. It challenges Rav's ruling that the robber acquires the land only as an agent of the buyer. But Rav has already explained his reasoning, declaring that the robber at the time he sold the field transferred all his future rights to the buyer. Mar Zutra and Rav Ashi then developed the idea further, saying that the robber had an ongoing interest in defending his reputation. What, then, was lacking in these explanations that prompted Rami bar Hama to ask the same question again?

Some commentators suggest that Rami bar Hama objects to Rav's ruling only in the case where the robber collected the field from the rightful owner in payment of a debt. Here, it is difficult to explain that the robber is acting as the buyer's agent and that the rightful owner is transferring the property directly to him, since the robber is not actually

BACKGROUND

אַכְרַזְתָּא **Announcement.** When property was offered for sale as the result of a court order, this sale would be announced over a period of thirty days so as to attract the best possible offer. In certain cases (with consecrated property), this period was extended to sixty days. Conversely, in times of urgent need (for the payment of living expenses which the claimants needed immediately) or for other reasons (such as the sale of slaves who might run away), the sale was made with no prior announcement. But it was customary to wait until the announcement period was over before concluding the sale.

CONCEPTS

אַדְרַכְתָּא **An authorization.** A legal document written by the court, authorizing a creditor to seek out and take possession of any property belonging to his debtor in order to recover the debt.

TERMINOLOGY

מַתְקִיף לָהּ **He strongly objects to it.** This term is used when an Amora objects to a statement of another Amora on logical grounds rather than on the authority of a literary source (e.g., a Mishnah or a Baraita).

TRANSLATION AND COMMENTARY

אֲמַר לֵיהּ רָבָא [1]**Rava said** in reply **to** Rami bar Hama: In fact, a second act of acquisition did take place between the buyer and the robber. When a person agrees to do something for someone else and receives some form of consideration, this too is considered to be an act of acquisition. In our case, we can explain Rav's ruling **as applying where the buyer trusts** the seller, and tells him that he is relying on him to ensure that the sale takes full legal effect. **Because of the satisfaction that the robber feels, that** the buyer **did not say anything to him** indicating that he had doubts about the validity of the sale, **but relies on him** completely, **the robber** agrees to **make the effort to transfer the field to** the buyer. Hence the robber is now obligated, in exchange for the satisfaction he received, to act as the buyer's agent and to purchase the field for him. When he buys the field from its rightful owner, he makes up his mind to transfer legal ownership of it to the buyer, in accordance with his agreement. The transfer then takes place immediately, **and** by buying the field from its rightful owner **he conveys legal ownership of it to** the buyer. In return for the buyer's trust at the time of the original sale, the robber resolved to transfer the field to him by buying it himself, even though the original sale was not valid.

מְתִיב רַב שֵׁשֶׁת [2]To this **Rav Sheshet objected**, quoting a Tosefta (*Nedarim* 6): "**If a person said, 'What I shall inherit from my father is** hereby **sold to you,'** or '**What my** hunting or fishing **net will bring up is** hereby **sold to you,' he has said nothing**. The sale is not valid, because a person cannot sell something which does not yet exist as his property. [3]But **if he said, 'What I shall inherit from my father today is** hereby **sold to you,'**

[1]אֲמַר לֵיהּ רָבָא: תְּהֵא בְּמַאֲמִינוֹ! בְּהַהוּא הֲנָאָה דְּלָא קָאָמַר לֵיהּ מִידֵי, וְקָא סָמֵיךְ עֲלֵיהּ, טָרַח וּמַיְיתֵי לֵיהּ, גָּמַר וּמַקְנֵי לֵיהּ.

[2]מְתִיב רַב שֵׁשֶׁת: "׳מַה שֶּׁאִירַשׁ מֵאַבָּא מָכוּר לָךְ׳ ׳מַה שֶּׁתַּעֲלֶה מְצוּדָתִי מָכוּר לָךְ׳, לֹא אָמַר כְּלוּם. [3]׳מַה שֶּׁאִירַשׁ מִן אַבָּא הַיּוֹם מָכוּר לָךְ׳,

LITERAL TRANSLATION

[1]Rava said to him: Let it [apply] where [the buyer] trusts him! Because of that satisfaction [that the robber feels], that [the buyer] does not say anything to him and relies on him, [the robber] makes the effort and brings [the field] to him, [and] he makes up his mind to transfer [it] to him.

[2]Rav Sheshet objected: "[If a person said,] 'What I shall inherit from [my] father is sold to you,' 'What my net will bring up is sold to you,' he has said nothing. [3][If he said,] 'What I shall inherit from [my] father today is sold to you,'

RASHI

תהא – הא דרב. **במאמינו** – שאמר לו: אני סומך עליך שתתקנה בידי. **גמר ומקני** – כשלקחה מבעלים הראשונים. **מצודתי** – של חיות ועופות ושל דגים.

NOTES

buying the field and the owner is not actually selling it, but rather the robber is receiving it automatically as payment of a debt (*Rashba*).

Others explain that Rami bar Hama's objection is that even if the robber does want to transfer the land to the buyer, in accordance with the reasoning of Rav, Mar Zutra, or Rav Ashi, mere intention cannot consummate a transfer of ownership, unless it is accompanied by a valid act of acquisition. Rava answers, however, that the satisfaction that the robber derives from the buyer's confidence in him is worth money, and since receipt of something of value — even if it is intangible — is a valid mode of acquisition, the transfer of ownership is valid, and the field is acquired by the buyer. (*Ran, Ritzbash*)

טָרַח וּמַיְיתֵי גָּמַר וּמַקְנֵי **The robber makes the effort to transfer the field to the buyer**. Some commentators question the implications of our Gemara where the thief acts, as it were, as the agent of the buyer, without informing the owner at all. But Rava's answer satisfies this objection as well, since the rightful owner, seeing the extraordinary efforts of the robber to pay him off and to establish a legal transfer of the field he stole, assumes that the robber is trying to salvage his reputation in the eyes of the buyer and agrees to transfer the property to him (*Rosh*).

מַה שֶּׁאִירַשׁ מֵאַבָּא הַיּוֹם **What I shall inherit from my father today**. The major principle adopted by most of the Sages is that no transaction or other legal action can take place with regard to something which does not at present exist (לֹא בָּא לָעוֹלָם), especially with regard to an object about which there is doubt as to whether it will actually come into being within the specified period of time. The Halakhic issue here is whether such a legal action has significance or whether it

HALAKHAH

מְכִירַת דָּבָר שֶׁאֵינוֹ בִּרְשׁוּתוֹ **Selling something that has not yet entered one's possession**. "A person cannot sell an object which he does not yet own, just as a person cannot sell an object which does not yet exist. For example, a person cannot sell a field now which he is due to inherit later, or fish which he intends to catch later, or an item which he intends to buy later." According to *Rema*, however, the seller may stipulate that he is selling *a specific item* which he is due to inherit later, and in such a case the sale is valid. (*Shulḥan Arukh, Ḥoshen Mishpat* 211:1.)

מַה שֶּׁאִירַשׁ מֵאַבָּא הַיּוֹם **What I shall inherit from my father today**. "If a person's father was close to death, and the son needed money to pay for the burial expenses (and the only way for him to obtain this money was by selling part of the

[1]שֶׁתַּעֲלֶה מְצוּדָתִי הַיּוֹם מָכוּר לְךָ׳, דְּבָרָיו קַיָּימִין״.
[2]אֲמַר רָמִי בַּר חָמָא: הָא גַּבְרָא וְהָא תְּיוּבְתָּא!
[3]אֲמַר רָבָא: גַּבְרָא קָא חָזֵינָא, וּתְיוּבְתָּא לָא קָא חָזֵינָא. הָכָא סָמְכָא דַּעְתֵּיהּ, וְהָכָא לָא סָמְכָא דַּעְתֵּיהּ. [4]הָכָא סָמְכָא דַּעְתֵּיהּ, דְּאָזֵיל טָרַח וּמַיְיתֵי לֵיהּ, כִּי הֵיכִי דְּלָא נִקְרְיֵיהּ גַּזְלָנָא; הָכָא, לָא סָמְכָא דַּעְתֵּיהּ.
[5]שְׁלָחוּהָ לְקַמֵּיהּ דְּרַבִּי אַבָּא בַּר זַבְדָּא. אֲמַר לְהוּ: זוֹ אֵינָהּ צְרִיכָה לִפְנִים. [6]אֲמַר רָבָא: זוֹ

LITERAL TRANSLATION

[1]'What my net will bring up today is sold to you,' his words are valid."

[2]Rami bar Ḥama said: Here is a man and here is a refutation!

[3]Rava said: I see the man, but I do not see the refutation. [4]Here he relies [on him], but here he does not rely [on him]. Here he relies on [the seller] to go [and] make the effort and bring [the field] to him, so that he will not call him a robber; here, he does not rely [on him]. [5]They sent it [this objection] to Rabbi Abba bar Zavda. He said to them: This [objection] does not need [to be brought] inside [the Academy for discussion]. [6]Rava said: It

TRANSLATION AND COMMENTARY

or [1]'**What my net will bring up today is** hereby **sold to you,' his words are valid,"** and the sale takes effect (the basis of this ruling is explained below). Thus, from this statement we see that if at the time of the sale the property was not yet owned by the seller, the sale is not valid, even though the seller may later come to be in a position to sell the property. The same, says Rav Sheshet, should apply to a stolen field, which the robber later bought from its rightful owner, in contradiction to the ruling of Rav above.

אֲמַר רָמִי בַּר חָמָא [2]**Rami bar Hama said: Here is a** great **man** — Rav Sheshet — **and here is a** convincing **refutation**! Rav Sheshet's objection is a conclusive refutation of Rav's view!

אֲמַר רָבָא [3]**Rava said: I see the** greatness of the **man, but I do not see the** cogency of the **refutation**. Rav Sheshet's objection is not a conclusive refutation. [4]Rava goes on to explain: **Here**, in the case of the stolen field, the buyer **relies** on the seller, **but here**, in the case of the man selling his future inheritance, the buyer **does not rely** on the seller. **Here**, in the case of the stolen field, the buyer **relied** on the fact **that the seller would go and make the effort to transfer the field to him** legally, **so that** the buyer **should not call him a robber**, and it is this reliance which is the consideration creating the obligation to act as the buyer's agent. But **here**, in the case of the man selling his future inheritance, the buyer **did not rely** on the seller to see to it that the sale would take effect. It was not in the seller's power to guarantee that he would inherit his father's property, because his father could decide to dispose of his property differently. Thus, in the case of the inheritance no effective act of acquisition took place.

שְׁלָחוּהָ לְקַמֵּיהּ דְּרַבִּי אַבָּא בַּר זַבְדָּא [5]The Gemara now relates that the Sages **sent** Rav Sheshet's objection **to Rabbi Abba bar Zavda**, to find out if he considered it valid. **He said to them: This objection does not need to be brought inside the Academy for** additional **discussion**, as it is a conclusive refutation of Rav. [6]**Rava**, however,

RASHI

דבריו קיימין — לקמן פריך: מאי שנא רישא כו׳? **הא גברא והא תיובתא** — הרי אדם גדול. וכמוהו תשובתו. דקתני ״לא אמר כלום״, ולכשיירש לא קנה לוקח, כיון דההיא שעתא לאו דידיה הוו נכסי אביו, ולא אמרינן מה מכר לו ראשון לשני — כל זכות שתבא לידו. **לא סמכא דעתיה** — דלוקח, דקאמר: מי יימר שירש מאביו כלום? שמא ימכור אביו נכסיו בחייו. **שלחוה** — להא תיובתא דרב ששת דאותיב אדרב. **אינה צריכה לפנים** — אינה צריכה כדי לתרצה להכניסה לפני בני הישיבה, שאין בהן יודע לפרקה. ותשובת הגאונים פורשין לגנאי: דליכא קושיא מעליא, אלא תעלוה לגיו.

NOTES

should be considered merely as a random remark (דְּבָרִים בְּעָלְמָא) obligating neither party. The Sages decreed that in certain cases, for special reasons, such a transaction should be regarded as valid, for otherwise people would not trust the son's promise, and they would not give him the money needed for his father's burial.

הָכָא סָמְכָא דַּעְתֵּיהּ Here he relies. At first sight, it would appear that a simpler distinction can be drawn between the case of a robber who sells a stolen field and the case of someone who says, "What I will inherit is sold to you." Since the stolen field is already in the possession of the buyer at the time the robber buys it from the rightful owner, the sale is valid; by contrast, a person cannot sell an inheritance which he has not yet received. Nevetheless, the Gemara does not suggest this distinction, because land is always treated as if it is in the possession of its rightful owner (קַרְקַע אֵינָהּ נִגְזֶלֶת — "land cannot be stolen"), and the fact that it is now in the physical possession of the buyer is Halakhically insignificant (*Melo HaRo'im*).

אֵינָהּ צְרִיכָה לִפְנִים Bringing a question inside and bringing

HALAKHAH

father's property), the Sages permitted him to sell a small portion of the inheritance. Similarly, a poor fisherman who has no food may sell what he is due to catch that day, and the sale is valid." (*Shulḥan Arukh, Ḥoshen Mishpat* 211:2)

CONCEPTS

מַה שֶּׁתַּעֲלֶה מְצוּדָתִי What my net will bring up. The term appears to mean a fishing net, and the fisherman is offering to sell whatever he succeeds in catching in the course of the day. In Mishnaic times there were many Jewish fishermen on the banks of the Sea of Galilee. Halakhically, there is of course no difference between a fishing net and any other kind of animal trap; but there were far fewer trappers, because the land was densely populated.

אֵינָהּ צְרִיכָה לִפְנִים It does not need to be brought inside. The background to the standard interpretations of this concept is that the בֵּית הַמִּדְרָשׁ — House of Study — was the place where joint consultations involving all the Sages were held. A problem raised in the House of Study was thus examined from every angle, and everyone present was able to contribute an argument or tradition he had learned. Therefore we also find that important Sages came to the House of Study to find solutions to problems which they themselves could not solve. Talmudic discussions naturally also took place outside the House of Study, either in small groups gathered around an important teacher, or among Sages or students of the same level. Less important problems were usually solved outside the House of Study, and only the most serious problems were brought into the House of Study — those demanding the active participation of all the Sages.

SAGES

רַבִּי אַבָּא בַּר זַבְדָּא Rabbi Abba bar Zavda. A Palestinian Amora of the second and third generations. He went to Babylonia, became a disciple of Rav, and transmitted teachings in his name. He also studied with Rav Huna. He later returned to Eretz Israel and studied with Rabbi Elazar. After Rabbi Elazar's death he was considered the most important Sage in Eretz Israel.

TRANSLATION AND COMMENTARY

in accordance with his view cited above, **said**: Rav Sheshet's objection **does need to be brought inside, and even to the innermost area** of the Academy for thorough reexamination by the leading scholars. Rava maintains that Rav Sheshet's objection is not valid: **Here**, in the case of the stolen field, the buyer **relies** on the seller; but **here**, in the case of the inheritance, **he does not rely** on him, as explained above.

הֲוָה עוּבְדָא בְּפוּמְבְּדִיתָא [1]The Gemara goes on to relate: **There was an incident in Pumbedita** where the court ruled in accordance with Rav's opinion, **and** Rav Sheshet's **objection** cited above **was raised by the Sages. Rav Yosef said to them: This objection does not need to be brought inside the Academy for** additional **discussion**, as it is a conclusive refutation of Rav. [2]**But Abaye said to him**: This objection **does need to be brought inside, and even to the innermost area** of the Academy for thorough reexamination by the leading scholars, as it is not a valid objection: **Here**, in the case of the stolen field, the buyer **relies** on the seller; **but here**, in the case of the inheritance, **he does not rely** on him.

וּמַאי שְׁנָא רֵישָׁא [3]Since the Tosefta dealing with the question whether it is possible to transfer ownership of something not yet in existence, or not yet in the possession of the seller, was quoted in the previous discussion, the Gemara now asks: **And what is the difference between the first clause** of the Tosefta **and the last clause**? Why can someone sell an inheritance that he will receive later today, as stated in the second clause of the Baraita, but not an inheritance that he will receive at some unspecified date in the future, as stated in the first clause of the Baraita? Surely in both cases the person is attempting to sell property that he does not yet own and the same principle should apply in both cases!

אֲמַר רַבִּי יוֹחָנָן [4]**Rabbi Yoḥanan said** in reply: There is a major difference between the two clauses. **The last clause**, which states, **"What I will inherit from** my **father today," is** an exceptional arrangement made by the Sages, **because of** a son's **respect for his father**. The seller thinks that his father, who is very seriously ill, will

צְרִיכָה לִפְנִים, וְלִפְנֵי לִפְנִים: הָכָא סָמְכָא דַּעְתֵּיהּ, וְהָכָא לָא סָמְכָא דַּעְתֵּיהּ.

[1]הֲוָה עוּבְדָא בְּפוּמְבְּדִיתָא וְאוֹתְבֵיהּ. אֲמַר לְהוּ רַב יוֹסֵף: זוֹ אֵינָהּ צְרִיכָה לִפְנִים. [2]וַאֲמַר לֵיהּ אַבַּיֵי: צְרִיכָה לִפְנִים, וְלִפְנֵי לִפְנִים: הָכָא סָמְכָא דַּעְתֵּיהּ, הָכָא לָא סָמְכָא דַּעְתֵּיהּ.

[3]וּמַאי שְׁנָא רֵישָׁא וּמַאי שְׁנָא סֵיפָא?

[4]אֲמַר רַבִּי יוֹחָנָן: סֵיפָא — "מַה שֶּׁאִירַשׁ מֵאַבָּא הַיּוֹם" — מִשּׁוּם כְּבוֹד אָבִיו.

LITERAL TRANSLATION

does need [to be brought] inside, and [even] to the innermost [area]: Here he relies, but here he does not rely.

[1]There was [such] an incident in Pumbedita and they [the Sages] raised this objection. Rav Yosef said to them: This [objection] does not need [to be brought] inside [the academy for discussion]. [2]But Abaye said to him: It does need [to be brought] inside, and [even] to the innermost [area]: Here he relies, but here he does not rely.

[3]And what is the difference between the first clause and the last clause?

[4]Rabbi Yoḥanan said: The last clause — "What I will inherit from [my] father today" — is because of respect for his father.

RASHI

הוה עובדא בפומבדיתא — שדנו דין כרב. ואותבינן מהא מתניתין, ואמר רב יוסף כו׳. משום כבוד אביו — כשהיה אביו גוסס, וצריך מעות לקבורתו ולתכריכין, מוזהר לכבוד אביו שלא לשהותו בבזיון.

NOTES

it to the innermost area (לִפְנִים וְלִפְנֵי לִפְנִים). Numerous explanations of this expression have been suggested. *Rashi* suggests that a question that should not be "brought inside" is very strong and could not be answered even by the Talmudic experts in the Academy. Alternatively, the question is very weak and need not be examined by serious scholars.

According to some commentators, a question that need not be "brought inside" need not be brought to the attention of the leading scholars, as it can be readily handled by ordinary Talmudic students, while a question that must be "brought to the innermost area" must be brought to the attention of the most senior scholars to do it justice (*Ritva*).

Others understand the word "inside" to refer to the *underlying idea* behind the question. A matter that does not need an "inside" needs only superficial attention; a matter that needs an "innermost" requires real depth to grasp its implications fully (*Geonim*).

Still others understand the word "inside" as being opposed to "outside," in other words, sheltered from publicity. A question that does not need "inside" should be published as an apparent obvious refutation, in the hope that someone somewhere will be able to answer it, while a question that needs "innermost" should be abandoned, as the question itself is obviously incorrect (*Tosefot Sens*).

The *Arukh* has a different version of our Gemara in which Rabbi Abba says: "This does not need to be brought inside or even in front of the inside" (the word לִפְנֵי can mean either "inside" or "in front of"). According to this view, Rabbi Abba is saying that the question does not deserve serious consideration — neither inside the Academy, nor even in the corridor of the Academy, where the level of scholarly expertise is lower.

[1]״מַה שֶׁתַּעֲלֶה מְצוּדָתִי הַיּוֹם״ [16B] מִשּׁוּם כְּדֵי חַיָּיו.
[2]אָמַר רַב הוּנָא אָמַר רַב: הָאוֹמֵר לַחֲבֵרוֹ: ״שָׂדֶה שֶׁאֲנִי לוֹקֵחַ, לִכְשֶׁאֶקָּחֶנָּה קְנוּיָה לְךָ מֵעַכְשָׁיו״, קָנָה.
[3]אָמַר רָבָא: מִסְתַּבְּרָא מִלְּתָא דְּרַב בְּ״שָׂדֶה״ סְתָם, אֲבָל בְּ״שָׂדֶה זוֹ״ לָא, [4]מִי יֵימַר דְּמְזַבֵּין לָהּ נִיהֲלֵיהּ?

LITERAL TRANSLATION

"What my net brings up today" [16B] is because of his livelihood.

[2]Rav Huna said in the name of Rav: Someone who says to his fellow, "The field that I am buying — after I buy it, it is sold to you as of now," [the buyer] acquires it.

[3]Rava said: Rav's statement is reasonable in [the case of] an unspecified field, but not in [the case of] "this field," [4][for] who says that [the owner] will sell it to him?

TRANSLATION AND COMMENTARY

die today and he knows that he will need money from his father's estate for the burial expenses. The Sages did not want the burial to be delayed while the son raised the money. Therefore, when he sells the inheritance, the Sages have enacted that in such a situation the act of transfer of ownership is effective. Likewise, in the case of "**What my net brings up today**," [16B] [1]the Sages validated the sale **because** they wanted to ensure the fisherman's immediate **livelihood**, so that he would not be left without food to eat that day. Thus in both these cases there are special reasons why the Sages enacted that the sale is valid. But where these reasons do not apply, as in the cases mentioned in the first clause, it is not possible to sell property that one does not yet own.

אָמַר רַב הוּנָא [2]The Gemara now continues to analyze the laws governing the transfer of property which has not yet entered the seller's/donor's possession. **Rav Huna said in the name of Rav**: If **someone says to another person**, "**The field that I am** about to **buy is sold** (or given) **to you** retroactively **as of now, after I have bought it**," **the buyer acquires it**. The moment the seller acquires the field, it passes retroactively into the ownership of the buyer.

אָמַר רָבָא [3]The sale described by Rav is an example of דָּבָר שֶׁלֹּא בָּא לָעוֹלָם — a sale of an object that does not yet exist, or, in other words, the sale of a future right. There is a dispute among the Sages as to whether such sales are valid. The Halakhah is that they are not valid, but Rav was known to follow the contrary opinion, identified with the Tanna, Rabbi Meir, that they are valid. **Rava said**: Even on the assumption that we are following Rabbi Meir's opinion, **Rav's statement is reasonable**, and the transfer of ownership is valid, only **in a case** where **the field is not specified**, where the seller (or donor) did not indicate which field he was planning to sell to the buyer, as he will certainly be able to find a field to buy, and will thereby fulfill his commitment to the buyer. **But** Rav's ruling **does not** apply **in a case where** the seller said, "**This field**," specifying which particular field he was planning to sell, [4]**for who can say that the owner** of that particular field **will** agree to **sell it to** the seller? Since it is not certain that the seller will be able to acquire the field, he cannot transfer his future ownership of it to another person, even according to the opinion that future rights can ordinarily be sold.

RASHI

משום כדי חייו — ״מה שתעלה מצודתי היום״ תקנו חכמים שיהיו דבריו קיימין, שמא צריך הוא למלונות דבר מועט. אבל ״מה שתעלה מצודתי כל חדש״ או ״כל שנה״ — אין שם משום כדי חייו. **קנויה לך מעכשיו** — שכשאקחנה לא אוכל לחזור בו. **קנה** — אם יקחנה, ואין יכול לחזור כשלקחה. **בשדה סתם** — ״שדה שאני לוקח״, ולא אמר ״זו״. דסמכא דעתיה דמקבל מתנה לסמוך עליו שיקח שדה ויתננה לו, שהרבה שדות מצויות ליקח. אבל אמר לו ״שדה זו״ — לא סמכא דעתיה דמקבל מתנה, ולא האמינו, דנימא: ניחא ליה דליקו בהימנותיה. ולא מסתבר כוותיה דרב בהא.

NOTES

כְּדֵי חַיָּיו **To ensure his immediate livelihood**. *Rav Hai Gaon* ruled that this law applies only when the quantity involved is sufficient for at most one day's sustenance, but not when it is greater.

Other commentators, however, point out that there is a similar law regarding the sale of a movable object in which one of the parties is a child. Even though a minor does not normally have the legal capacity to transfer ownership, such sales involving minors were made valid by the Rabbis in order to provide the child with elementary sustenance. In that case, all sales of movable objects involving minors were validated, not merely ones involving small sums of money. Similarly, in our case, any sale of future rights involving objects that will be acquired today should be valid, regardless of the quantity involved (the full discussion is found in *Ramban* and *Ran*).

HALAKHAH

שָׂדֶה שֶׁאֲנִי לוֹקֵחַ **The field that I am buying**. "If someone sells a field that he does not yet own (but which he intends to buy later) to another person, the sale is not valid, and both sides may retract." Rav's opinion, which follows Rabbi Meir's view, is not accepted. (*Shulḥan Arukh, Ḥoshen Mishpat* 209:5; 211:1.)

[1]וְהָאֱלֹהִים, אֲמַר רַב אֲפִילּוּ "בְּשָׂדֶה זוֹ". [2]מִכְּדִי, רַב כְּמַאן אֲמָרָהּ לִשְׁמָעֲתֵיהּ? [3]כְּרַבִּי מֵאִיר, דְּאָמַר: אָדָם מַקְנֶה דָּבָר שֶׁלֹּא בָּא לָעוֹלָם, דְּתַנְיָא: [4]"הָאוֹמֵר לְאִשָּׁה: הִתְקַדְּשִׁי לִי לְאַחַר שֶׁאֶתְגַּיֵּיר, לְאַחַר שֶׁתִּתְגַּיְּירִי, לְאַחַר שֶׁאֶשְׁתַּחְרֵר, לְאַחַר שֶׁתִּשְׁתַּחְרְרִי, לְאַחַר שֶׁיָּמוּת בַּעֲלֵיךְ, לְאַחַר שֶׁיַּחֲלוֹץ לָךְ יְבָמֵיךְ, לְאַחַר שֶׁתָּמוּת אֲחוֹתֵיךְ, אֵינָהּ מְקוּדֶּשֶׁת. [5]רַבִּי מֵאִיר אוֹמֵר: מְקוּדֶּשֶׁת". [6]וְהָא אִשָּׁה כְּ"שָׂדֶה זוֹ" דָּמְיָא, וְאָמַר רַבִּי מֵאִיר מְקוּדֶּשֶׁת!

LITERAL TRANSLATION

[1]But, by God, Rav said [his statement] even in [the case of] "this field"! [2]Now, according to whom did Rav make his statement? [3]According to Rabbi Meir, who said: A person can transfer ownership of something that has not [yet] come into the world, as it has been taught: [4]"One who says to a woman: Be betrothed to me after I become a proselyte, after you become a proselyte, after I am freed, after you are freed, after your husband dies, after your brother-in-law performs *halitzah* with you, after your sister dies, she is not betrothed. [5]Rabbi Meir says: She is betrothed." [6]But surely [the case of the] woman is like [the case of] "this field," and Rabbi Meir said [that] she *is* betrothed!

RASHI

והאלהים — בשבועה. רב אמרה אפילו "בשדה זו", דמכדי רב כמאן אמר לשמעתיה — כרבי מאיר כו'. **והא אשה בשדה זו דמיא** — דיש באלו שאין בידו להביא עצמו לכלל קדושין כאשר אין ביד זה לכוף את בעל השדה למוכרה לו, דעבד ושפחה אין בידם לשחרר עצמם, ואין ביד אשה להמית את בעלה או אחותה. ואמר רבי מאיר: דלכשיבאו לכלל קדושין — מקודשת היא למפרע.

TRANSLATION AND COMMENTARY

וְהָאֱלֹהִים [1]Rava now exclaims: **But, by God,** it is well known that **Rav made his statement even in the case of "this field,"** where the seller indicated explicitly which field he was planning to sell to the buyer. According to the opinion that future rights can be sold, it is unimportant whether the future right is certain or doubtful. Moreover, we can prove that the distinction is immaterial. [2]**Now,** let us consider: **In accordance with whose** opinion **did Rav make his statement?** [3]**In accordance with** the opinion of **Rabbi Meir, who said** that, as a general principle, **a person can transfer ownership of something that has not** yet **come into existence** or something that has not yet entered his possession, **as it has been taught** in the following Baraita: [4]"If a man **says to a woman: Be betrothed to me after I become a proselyte,** or **after you become a proselyte, after I am freed** from slavery, or **after you are freed** from slavery, even though non-Jews and slaves, whether male or female, cannot perform the act of betrothal (קִידּוּשִׁין), **after your husband dies,** or **after your brother-in-law performs *halitzah* with you,** thereby enabling you to remarry, or **after your sister** who is at present married to me **dies,** and I will then be permitted to marry you, the woman **is not betrothed.** In all these cases, since betrothal cannot take effect now, it does not take effect later either, even if the impediment to betrothal has been removed, since this would be a case of the transfer of future rights. [5]**Rabbi Meir,** however, **says:** The woman **is betrothed** after the impediment to betrothal has been removed." According to Rabbi Meir, it is possible to perform a transaction that will take effect later on, even if such a transaction would not be valid if performed now. Similarly Rabbi Meir would maintain that a person can transfer ownership of property now even if he does not at present own it, as long as he acquires it later. [6]**But surely** some of **the cases of the women** mentioned in the Baraita **are like the case of "this field."** In the same way as the seller of the field is unable to ensure that the field he wishes to sell will become his property, so in the case of the betrothal of a married woman, for example, the woman is unable to ensure that her husband will die before she does, leaving her free to remarry. **And** yet **Rabbi Meir said that** the woman **is betrothed!** Accordingly, we see that Rabbi Meir, whose opinion is accepted by Rav, makes no distinction between "a field" and "this particular field." He maintains that a person *can* transfer ownership of something that does not yet exist (or that has not yet entered his possession), even if he specifies a particular object whose attainment by him he is unable to guarantee.

BACKGROUND

וְהָאֱלֹהִים By God. This expression is used like an oath. It is not a true oath but rather an emphatic expression to reinforce or confirm a statement. We find that certain Sages had their own characteristic ways of expressing themselves, using expressions similar to oaths, and each one was used to give clearer emphasis to a certain idea.

NOTES

אֲמַר רַב אֲפִילּוּ בְּשָׂדֶה זוֹ Rav made his statement even in the case of "this field." The commentators ask: How do we know that Rav made his statement even with regard to a specific field? They answer that since Rav holds the same viewpoint as Rabbi Meir (as we know from other sources; see, for example, *Yevamot* 93a), and Rabbi Meir's opinion applies even in the case of a specific object (see below in the Gemara), Rav's statement must also apply even where a particular field was specified (see *Shittah Mekubbetzet*).

לְאַחַר שֶׁיַּחֲלוֹץ לָךְ יְבָמֵיךְ After your brother-in-law performs *halitzah* with you. Ordinarily, betrothal is invalid where the union is punishable by death or excision,

HALAKHAH

הִתְקַדְּשִׁי לִי לְאַחַר שֶׁאֶתְגַּיֵּיר Be betrothed to me after I become a proselyte. "If a man requests a woman to become betrothed to him after he (or she) becomes a proselyte, or under any other circumstances under which

TRANSLATION AND COMMENTARY

אָמַר שְׁמוּאֵל [1]**Shmuel said**: If **someone finds a deed of transfer** (see above, 14a) **in the marketplace, he should return it to its owner**, as all the concerns that normally apply to lost documents do not apply to deeds of transfer. [2]**For if we are concerned about the possibility that the borrower may have written** the deed in order **to borrow** money **but** in fact lost the deed and **did not borrow, surely he obligated himself** to pay the money in any case! In a deed of transfer the borrower agrees to repay irrespective of whether a loan takes place, and a lien is established from the moment the document is drawn up. [3]**And if we are concerned because of** the possibility that the loan may already have been **repaid**, this is also not a serious concern, because **we do not suspect payment** of an outstanding document. [4]**For if it were true that** the borrower **had repaid** the lender, **he would** certainly **have torn up** the promissory note. Hence, in the case of the deed of transfer found in the marketplace, since the note was not torn up, the loan was presumably not repaid.

אָמַר רַב נַחְמָן [5]The first of Shmuel's arguments, that a deed of transfer is valid even if a loan never took place, is accepted by the Gemara. The subject of the ensuing discussion is the second argument, that we need never suspect that a lost document has been repaid: **Rav Naḥman said**: My **father was one of Mar Shmuel's judges' scribes, and I was then about six or seven years old, and I remember that the courts used to make announcements, saying**: [6]**"Deeds of transfer that are found in the marketplace should be returned to their owners,"** in accordance with Shmuel's ruling.

אָמַר רַב עַמְרָם [7]**Rav Amram said**: **We have also learned** the same thing in the following Mishnah (below, 20a): **"Any decision of the court** that is lost and later found **shall be returned."** Rav Amram understands the expression "decision of the court" as referring to a promissory note whose authenticity was certified in court. Such a court-certified document is similar to a deed of transfer. There is no possibility that it was lost by the borrower before he borrowed the money, as the court certification is always given at the lender's request. But we might have suspected that the note was repaid and subsequently lost by the borrower. [8]**Hence**, it is clear from this Mishnah that **we do not suspect the possibility of repayment**.

[1]אָמַר שְׁמוּאֵל: הַמּוֹצֵא שְׁטַר הַקְנָאָה בַּשּׁוּק, יַחֲזִירוֹ לַבְּעָלִים. [2]דְּאִי מִשּׁוּם דְּכָתַב לִלְוֹת וְלֹא לָוָה, הָא שַׁעְבֵּד נַפְשֵׁיהּ! [3]וְאִי מִשּׁוּם פֵּרָעוֹן — לָא חָיְישִׁינַן לְפֵרָעוֹן, [4]דְּאִם אִיתָא דְּפָרְעֵיהּ — מִקְרַע הֲוָה קָרַע לֵיהּ.

[5]אֲמַר רַב נַחְמָן: אַבָּא מִן סָפְרֵי דַּיָּינֵי דְּמָר שְׁמוּאֵל הֲוָה, וְהָוֵינָא כְּבַר שִׁיתָּא כְּבַר שְׁבַע, וּדְכַרְנָא דַּהֲווּ מַכְרְזֵי וְאָמְרִי: [6]הָנֵי שְׁטָרֵי אַקְנָיָיתָא דְּמִשְׁתַּכְּחִי בְּשׁוּקָא — נְהַדְרִינְהוּ לְמָרַיְיהוּ.

[7]אֲמַר רַב עַמְרָם: אַף אֲנַן תְּנֵינָא: "כָּל מַעֲשֵׂה בֵּית דִּין הֲרֵי זֶה יַחֲזִיר". [8]אַלְמָא, לָא חָיְישִׁינַן לְפֵרָעוֹן.

LITERAL TRANSLATION

[1]Shmuel said: One who finds a deed of transfer in the marketplace should return it to the owner. [2]For if [we are concerned] because of [the possibility that the borrower] wrote to borrow but did not borrow, surely he obligated himself! [3]And if [we are concerned] because of payment, we do not suspect payment, [4]for if it was [true] that [the borrower] had repaid it, he would certainly have torn it up.

[5]Rav Naḥman said: Father was one of Mar Shmuel's judges' scribes, and I was [then] about six or seven years old, and I remember that [the courts] used to make announcements, saying: [6]Those deeds of transfer that are found in the marketplace — return them to their owners.

[7]Rav Amram said: We have also learned [a Mishnah]: "Any decision of the court shall be returned." [8]Hence, we do not suspect [the possibility of] repayment.

RASHI

שטר הקנאה — שקנו ממנו, שאפילו לא ילוה המעות — שיעבד עצמו לשלם. כל מעשה בית דין — קא סלקא דעתך שטר שכתב בו הנפק, שנתקיים בבית דין. אלמא: כיון דליכא למיחש לשמא לא לוה, שהרי אין מקיימין את השטר אלא בפני בעל דין, כדאמרינן ב"הגוזל" (בבא קמא קיב, ב) לפרעון לא חיישינן.

NOTES

but not invalid where the union carries a lesser punishment (as in the case of the betrothal of a childless widow who has not yet received *ḥalitzah*). The Sages in the Baraita quoted here seem to be of the opinion (cf. *Yevamot* 92b) that betrothal of a childless widow does not take effect because of a special Torah decree (*Rashba*).

כְּבַר שִׁיתָּא **I was about six or seven years old**. In other words, between six and seven years old. Ordinarily, childhood recollections are not Halakhically acceptable as proofs. But here Rav Nahman's statement merely corroborates a known fact, that Shmuel maintained that lost deeds of transfer may be returned to their owners (*Rabbi Ya'akov Emden*).

HALAKHAH

betrothal cannot *now* take effect, the betrothal is invalid, even if the impediment to betrothal is later removed," following the opinion of the Sages in the Baraita. (*Shulḥan Arukh, Even HaEzer* 40:5.)

TRANSLATION AND COMMENTARY

אֲמַר לֵיהּ רַבִּי זֵירָא [1]**Rabbi Zera said to him**: No proof may be drawn from this Mishnah, since **the Mishnah may be referring**, not to ordinary court-certified documents, but specifically **to deeds of adjudication**, documents issued by the court granting the bearer title to property seized from a recalcitrant debtor, **and** to deeds of **authorization**, documents issued by the court giving the bearer authority to search for and to seize property from a recalcitrant debtor. For these documents are not promissory notes; they are essentially title deeds, **which are not subject to repayment**.

אֲמַר רָבָא [2]**Rava** objected to the statement of Rabbi Zera and **said**: **But are these** documents **not subject to repayment**? Even after the court has assessed the debtor's property and has assigned it to the creditor, the debtor can still repay the original loan and redeem his property. In fact, there is an established principle permitting him to redeem it even after the creditor has taken possession of it! [3]**Surely the scholars of Neharde'a say**: **A valuation** made by the court **of** a debtor's **property**, forcing him to hand it over to his creditor in repayment of a loan, **returns** to the debtor. i.e., can be redeemed upon repayment of the original loan, **until** the end of a **twelve-month period** after the creditor has taken possession of the property. [4]Moreover, **Amemar said**: **I am from Neharde'a, and** nevertheless **I maintain that a property valuation returns for ever**! According to Amemar, property assessed by the court and seized from the debtor can be redeemed as long as the debtor wishes. Accordingly, even deeds of adjudication and authorization are subject to repayment, since the debtor may have already redeemed the land which was assigned by the court to the creditor, and then lost the deed. If we return such a document to the creditor, we may be allowing him to seize the debtor's property for a second time! Thus, even if we accept Rabbi Zera's interpretation of the Mishnah, it would still support Shmuel's ruling that we do not suspect that a lost document has already been repaid.

[1]אֲמַר לֵיהּ רַבִּי זֵירָא: מַתְנִיתִין בְּשְׁטָרֵי חַלְטָאתָא וְאַדְרַכְתָּא, דְּלָאו בְּנֵי פֵּרָעוֹן נִינְהוּ. [2]אֲמַר רָבָא: וְהָנֵי לָאו בְּנֵי פֵּרָעוֹן נִינְהוּ? [3]וְהָא אָמְרִי נְהַרְדְּעֵי: שׁוּמָא הָדַר עַד תְּרֵיסַר יַרְחֵי שַׁתָּא. [4]וַאֲמַר אַמֵימָר: אֲנָא מִנְּהַרְדְּעָא אֲנָא, וּסְבִירָא לִי דְּשׁוּמָא הָדַר לְעוֹלָם!

LITERAL TRANSLATION

[1]Rabbi Zera said to him: This Mishnah [refers] to deeds of adjudication and authorization, which are not subject to repayment.

[2]Rava said: But are these not subject to repayment? [3]But surely the Nehardeans say: A [property] valuation returns until [the end of] the twelve months of the year. [4]And [concerning this] Amemar said: I am from Neharde'a, and I maintain that a [property] valuation returns for ever!

RASHI

בשטרי חלטאתא — שטר שכתבו בית דין למוציא שטר על חבירו וחייבוהו לשלם ולא שילם, וירדו לנכסיו ושמו לבעל חוב אחד מהם, ונתנו לו שטר שעל פי בית דין באה לו. **אדרכתא** — שלא מצאו לו עכשיו נכסים, וכתבו לו שירדוף לחזור על נכסיו ואם ימצא יגבה. **אדרכתא** — לשון רודף ומשיג. כמו: פרסה בחלא ולא אדרכיה (כתובות ס, ב). ולשון המקרא "כתרו את בנימין הרדיפוהו מנוחה הדריכוהו" (שופטים כ). **שומא** — ששמו בית דין לבעל חוב קרקע הלוה. **הדר** — אם יפרע לו מעות, עד שנה.

NOTES

חַלְטָאתָא וְאַדְרַכְתָּא Deeds of adjudication and authorization. The commentary here follows *Rashi*, who explains that חַלְטָא is a deed given to a creditor by the court when it assigns to him property of the debtor, while אַדְרַכְתָּא is an authorization for the creditor to seek out property belonging to the debtor.

Some commentators question this explanation, because the order in our Gemara, חַלְטָאתָא before אַדְרַכְתָּא, is the reverse of the natural order in which such documents would be issued. Accordingly, they explain that חַלְטָאתָא in our Gemara is not חַלְטָאתָא in *Rashi's* sense, which comes after the אַדְרַכְתָּא, but is a special deed issued by the court when the ownership of a field which has been made absolute collateral for the loan is transferred from the debtor to the creditor. In such a case, an אַדְרַכְתָּא is not required (*Rashba*).

Other commentators emend the text to exclude the word אַדְרַכְתָּא, as it is still possible for the debtor to pay off his debt after an אַדְרַכְתָּא has been issued, until the issuing of a final חַלְטָא (*Rid* and others).

HALAKHAH

שׁוּמָא הָדַר לְעוֹלָם Redemption at any time of property valued by the court. "If the court has assessed the debtor's property and assigned it to the creditor, and later the debtor or his heirs obtain funds to repay the debt, the debtor or his heirs may redeem the land from the creditor, even if the property has been in the creditor's possession for many years. This is permissible because the Torah requires us to "do what is right and just" (and not to follow the letter of the law strictly), provided that neither of the parties involved incurs a loss. Some authorities maintain that only the debtor or his heirs are entitled to redeem property from the creditor, but if a person bought land that was later seized by a creditor in payment of a debt incurred by the seller, the buyer cannot redeem it after the creditor has taken possession of it (*Rema*). Only land can be redeemed in this manner, but not movable property." (Ibid., *Hoshen Mishpat* 103:9.)

CONCEPTS

שְׁטָרֵי חַלְטָאתָא Deeds of adjudication. This term is derived from the root חלט, meaning "finished, agreed upon." A שְׁטַר חַלְטָאתָא is a deed that transfers some of the debtor's property to the plaintiff once and for all. The deed is given that name because, in contrast to other deeds, such as שְׁטַר טִירְפָּא (a deed giving right of seizure) or שְׁטַר אַדְרַכְתָּא (a deed of authorization), which are intermediary documents and only accomplish part of the legal process, a שְׁטַר חַלְטָאתָא concludes the judicial proceedings and conclusively transfers the property to the plaintiff.

SAGES

אָמְרִי נְהַרְדְּעֵי The Nehardeans say. Although this expression is a general one and refers to the Sages of the city of Neharde'a, nevertheless the Sages in the Talmud (*Sanhedrin* 17b) attribute this expression to one particular Sage, Rav Ḥama, who was one of the most important Rabbis of that city. Occasionally this expression is used because the opinion expressed is not only Rav Ḥama's personal view but reflects the approach taken by all the Sages of Neharde'a.

SAGES

אַמֵימָר Amemar. One of the greatest Babylonian Amoraim of the fifth and sixth generations, Amemar was born in Neharde'a and was one of its chief Sages. He studied under Rav Zevid and Rav Dimi of Neharde'a, and he also studied with the elders of Pumbedita. He cites the teachings of Rava, Rav Pappa, and others. He was the head of the yeshivah in his city. On several occasions he is found in the company of Mar Zutra and Rav Ashi. Rav Aḥa bar Rava and Rav Gamda were among his most prominent students. He also had a son who was a Sage, known as Mar.

TRANSLATION AND COMMENTARY

אֶלָּא אֲמַר רָבָא [1]**Rather, Rava said: There**, the Mishnah is indeed referring only to deeds of adjudication and authorization written by the court, and it does not provide support for Shmuel's view. But **the reason** why we rule that the document is to be returned to its owner is not because such deeds are not redeemable, but rather **it is** because **we say** that if the debtor had redeemed such a deed and then lost it, **it would be** the debtor **himself who caused himself the loss** by not destroying the document. [2]**For at the time when** the debtor **paid** the creditor to redeem the land, **he should have torn up the deed** issued by the court, authorizing the creditor to keep the land. **Or alternatively**, if the creditor claimed that the deed was lost, he should have arranged for the creditor **to write another deed for** the land, indicating that the land now belonged to the debtor.

דְּמִדִּינָא אַרְעָא לָא בָּעֲיָא [3]The Gemara now explains why a new deed should have been written confirming the debtor's ownership of the land: **For according to the** letter of the **law, the land need not be returned** at all to the debtor, even if he wants to redeem it. [4]It is only **because of** the Biblical injunction, **"You shall do that which is right and good in the eyes of the Lord"** (Deuteronomy 6:18), that **the Sages said that** the debtor's land **should be returned** to him. [5]**Hence we consider the debtor as if he is** now **buying** the property **for the first time. And he should have** arranged for the creditor to **write a deed of sale** for the property being returned to the debtor, and the debtor should have looked after that deed of sale to protect his rights. But this argument applies only to deeds of adjudication and authorization, not to ordinary promissory notes or even deeds of transfer, as the Gemara will explain.

גַּבֵּי שְׁטַר חוֹב [6]The Gemara now asks: **In the case of an** ordinary **promissory note** or a deed of transfer, **what is there to say** to allay our suspicion that the debt may have been repaid and the note lost? [7]Only **that if it were true that the borrower had paid** the lender, **he should have torn up the promissory note!**

אֵימוֹר [8]The Gemara answers that in this case we can **say**: **The lender** may have retained the note even though the debt has already been paid, because **he is being evasive. For he may have said to** the borrower: **"Tomorrow I will give** the note **to you, for I have not got it with me now." Or alternatively he may have retained**

[1]אֶלָּא אֲמַר רָבָא: הָתָם, הַיְינוּ טַעְמָא דְּאָמְרִי: אִיהוּ הוּא דְּאַפְסִיד אַנַּפְשֵׁיהּ, [2]דִּבְעִידָּנָא דִּפְרָעֵיהּ, אִבָּעֵי לֵיהּ לְמִקְרְעֵיהּ לִשְׁטָרֵיהּ, אִי נַמִי לְמִכְתַּב שְׁטָרָא אַחֲרִינָא עִילָּוֵיהּ. [3]דְּמִדִּינָא, אַרְעָא לָא בָּעֲיָא לְמִיהֲדַר, [4]וּמִשּׁוּם "וְעָשִׂיתָ הַיָּשָׁר וְהַטּוֹב בְּעֵינֵי ה׳" הוּא דַּאֲמוּר רַבָּנַן תִּהֲדַר. [5]הִלְכָּךְ מֵרֵישָׁא הוּא דְּקָא זָבֵין, אִיבָּעֵי לֵיהּ לְמִכְתַּב שְׁטַר זְבִינֵי.

[6]גַּבֵּי שְׁטַר חוֹב, מַאי אִיכָּא לְמֵימַר — [7]אִם אִיתָא דִּפְרָעֵיהּ, אִיבָּעֵי לֵיהּ לְמִיקְרְעֵיהּ לִשְׁטָרֵיהּ?

[8]אֵימוּר: אִשְׁתַּמּוּטֵי קָא מִשְׁתַּמֵּיט לֵיהּ, דַּאֲמַר לֵיהּ: "לְמָחָר יָהֲבְנָא לָךְ, דְּהָשְׁתָּא

LITERAL TRANSLATION

[1]Rather, Rava said: There, the reason is that we say: It was he himself who caused himself the loss, [2]for at the time when he paid it, he should have torn up his deed, or alternatively have written another deed for it.

[3]For according to the law, land need not be returned, [4]but because of "You shall do that which is right and good in the eyes of the Lord," the Sages said that it should be returned. [5]Hence [we consider the debtor as if] he is buying for the first time, [and] he should have written a deed of sale.

[6][But] in the case of a promissory note, what is there to say — [7][that] if it is [true] that [the borrower] has paid it, he should have torn up his promissory note?

[8]Say: [The lender] is being evasive, for he says to him: "Tomorrow I will give it to you, for now

RASHI

אפסיד אנפשיה — אם פרע ולא קרע השטר. ואם דחהו לומר "אבד" — היה לו לומר: כתוב לי שטר מיד שאתה חוזר ומוכרה לי. **דמדינא ארעא לא בעי למיהדר** — טעם נותן לדבריו שראוי לכתוב שטר מכירה עליה שקנויה לו לחלוטין, ומדינא לא בעי למיהדר בפדיון, אם לא מדעתו. **מרישא דקא זבין** — כלומר: אין זה פדיון אלא תחילת קניין כאילו שלו היתה. לפיכך, הכותב שטר מכירה עליה — אינו טועה, והיה לו לזה לתבוע שטר מכירה, הואיל ודחהו מלהחזיר לו שטר של בית דין.

NOTES

וּמִשּׁוּם "וְעָשִׂיתָ הַיָּשָׁר וְהַטּוֹב **Because of "You shall do that which is right and good in the eyes of the Lord."** By Torah law, this obligation is not merely a moral admonition. The verse requires us to act in a morally exemplary fashion, even if such conduct is not specifically required by the letter of the law (cf. the precept "you shall be holy" [Leviticus. 19:2], and *Ramban's* commentary on this verse). The Sages instituted many decrees to ensure that people would act in an exemplary fashion, and in certain cases they even authorized the Rabbinical courts to use force, if necessary, to ensure the observance of these decrees (see *Rabbi Zvi Ḥayyot*).

TRANSLATION AND COMMENTARY

it because of the scribe's fee, which is normally paid by the borrower, but which the borrower has not yet paid. Thus, the debt described in the promissory note may have been paid by the borrower, even though the note has not been torn up, and the borrower cannot demand a new deed for the land mortgaged under the original loan, as the land is not yet the creditor's to sell. Hence, in cases other than deeds of adjudication and authorization, we should suspect repayment, and a lost note should not be returned to the lender.

אָמַר רַבִּי אַבָּהוּ [1]**Rabbi Abbahu said in the name of Rabbi Yoḥanan**: If **someone finds a promissory note in the marketplace, even if a court endorsement is written on it, he should not return it to the owner.** [2]The Gemara goes on to explain: **There is no need to state this** ruling in a case **where no court endorsement was written on** the note, [3]**for it is possible to say** that **the borrower wrote** the promissory note **for the purpose of borrowing, but did not** in fact **borrow** the money. In such a case it is obvious that the note should not be returned to the lender. [4]**But even if a court endorsement is written on it, and that means** that the document **has been** officially **certified** by the court, [5]**the finder should not return it, as we suspect the possibility of repayment** and do not accept Shmuel's argument presented above.

אֵיתִיבֵיהּ רַבִּי יִרְמְיָה [6]**Rabbi Yirmeyah raised an objection to** the statement of **Rabbi Abbahu** from the Mishnah cited previously. His objection is identical to the comment of Rav Amram, above: "**Any** document containing a **decision of the court shall be returned** to its owner!" Surely an endorsed promissory note comes into this category!

אֲמַר לֵיהּ [7]Rabbi Abbahu **said to him**: "**Yirmeyah, my son, not all** documents containing **court decisions are equal. Rather, the Mishnah's** ruling that the document should be returned refers only to a special case. [8]It may **refer, for example, to a case where the borrower** named in the promissory note **has been confirmed as being a liar.** Since he has been proved to be a liar, he is not now believed if he claims that he has repaid the loan. Hence, the promissory note may be returned to the lender. But if he were not a confirmed liar, we would suspect payment, in accordance with the viewpoint of Rabbi Abbahu and contrary to the viewpoint of Shmuel.

לֵיתֵיהּ גַּבַּאי״. אִי נַמִי אַפְּשִׁיטֵי דְסָפְרָא זָיֵיר לֵיהּ.

[1]אָמַר רַבִּי אַבָּהוּ אָמַר רַבִּי יוֹחָנָן: הַמּוֹצֵא שְׁטַר חוֹב בַּשּׁוּק, אַף עַל פִּי שֶׁכָּתוּב בּוֹ הֶנְפֵּק, לֹא יַחֲזִירוּ לַבְּעָלִים. [2]לָא מִיבַּעְיָא הֵיכָא דְּלָא כָּתוּב בּוֹ הֶנְפֵּק, [3]דְּאִיכָּא לְמֵימַר: כָּתַב לִלְווֹת וְלֹא לָוָה. [4]אֶלָּא אֲפִילּוּ כָּתוּב בּוֹ הֶנְפֵּק — וּמַאי נִיהוּ? [5]דִּמְקוּיָּם — לֹא יַחֲזִיר, דְּחָיְישִׁינַן לְפֵרָעוֹן.

[6]אֵיתִיבֵיהּ רַבִּי יִרְמְיָה לְרַבִּי אַבָּהוּ: ״כָּל מַעֲשֵׂה בֵּית דִּין הֲרֵי זֶה יַחֲזִיר!״

[7]אֲמַר לֵיהּ: יִרְמְיָה בְּרִי, לֹא כָּל מַעֲשֵׂה בֵּית דִּין שָׁוִים. [8]אֶלָּא, כְּגוֹן שֶׁהוּחְזַק כַּפְרָן.

LITERAL TRANSLATION

it is not with me." Or alternatively he is retaining it because of the scribe's fee.

[1]Rabbi Abbahu said in the name of Rabbi Yoḥanan: One who finds a promissory note in the marketplace, even if a court endorsement is written on it, he should not return it to the owner. [2]There is no need [to state this] where no court endorsement was written on it, [3]for it is [possible] to say: [The borrower] wrote to borrow, but did not borrow. [4]But even if there was a court endorsement written on it — and what [does] that [mean]? [5]That it is certified — [the finder] should not return [it], as we suspect [the possibility] of repayment.

[6]Rabbi Yirmeyah raised an objection to Rabbi Abbahu: "Any decision of the court shall be returned"!

[7][Rabbi Abbahu] said to him: "Yirmeyah, my son, not all court decisions are equal. [8]Rather, [the Mishnah refers to a case], for example, where [the borrower] has been confirmed [as being] a liar.

RASHI

אי נמי אפשיטי דספרא זייר ליה — שעל הלוה ליתן שכר הסופר, ופעמים שאין לו מעות ללוה בשעת הלואה, והמלוה נותן שכר לכתיבת השטר. **וכשפרעו** — מעכב השטר בידו עד שיפרע השכר. **זייר** — לשון עוצר, כמו מעצרתא זיירא (עבודה זרה ס,א). ובלשון המקרא ״ויזר את הגזה״ (שופטים ו). **כל מעשה בית דין** — והאי נמי מעשה בית דין הוא. **ירמיה ברי** גרסינן. **שהוחזק** — לוה זה כפרן פעם אחרת, לפיכך אין נאמן לומר ״פרעתי״, ובההיא תנן ״יחזיר״.

LANGUAGE

פְּשִׁיטֵי Fee. This word apparently derives from the Persian *pashez*, meaning a small coin. This word was used for many generations to describe the smallest coins in circulation in many countries. Here, however, it does not refer to a specific coin or sum, but, in general, to small coins given to a scribe in payment.

CONCEPT

הוּחְזַק כַּפְרָן A confirmed liar. According to the Halakhah, if a person has made a false claim to the court, this does not completely disqualify him or cause him to be considered a wrongdoer. (The same is not true of a witness, and a witness found guilty of perjury is no longer eligible to appear in court as a witness.) Nevertheless, when it becomes clear that a person has made a false claim, he is no longer considered trustworthy, at least in that matter. The reason for this is that a person may occasionally evade a certain responsibility or may mistakenly deny the truth of a claim, and may then be led into telling lies in order to support his initial false claim.

NOTES

הוּחְזַק כַּפְרָן A confirmed liar. Some commentators explain that the Gemara is referring to someone who has been proven to be a liar in another unconnected matter. Hence, according to Rabbi Abbahu, he is suspect with regard to this document as well (*Ra'avad*).

Others explain that Rabbi Abbahu understands the Mishnah as referring to a case where the debtor has been proven to be a liar with regard to *this document*, and this is why the document may be returned to the lender. Rava, on the other hand, maintains that even in such a case his claims are not automatically rejected, because, since the document was lost, it is considered flawed (*Rashba* and *Tosafot*).

TERMINOLOGY

הוֹאִיל וַאֲתָא לְיָדָן, נֵימָא בֵּיהּ מִלְּתָא Since it has come into our hand, let us say something about it. Sometimes, after a topic is mentioned in passing during a Talmudic discussion, one of the scholars suggests: "Since this matter has come to our attention [i.e., incidentally], let us discuss it further...".

[1]אֲמַר רָבָא: וּמִשּׁוּם דְּהוּחְזַק כַּפְּרָן חֲדָא זִמְנָא, תּוּ לָא פָּרַע כְּלָל?
[2]אֶלָּא אֲמַר רָבָא: מַתְנִיתִין בִּשְׁטַר חַלְטָאתָא וְאַדְרַכְתָּא, וְכִדְרַבִּי זֵירָא.
[3]וְכַפְּרָן, הוֹאִיל וַאֲתָא לְיָדָן, נֵימָא בֵּיהּ מִלְּתָא. [4]דְּאָמַר רַב יוֹסֵף בַּר מַנְיוּמֵי אָמַר רַב נַחְמָן: אָמְרוּ לוֹ, ״צֵא תֵּן לוֹ״, [17A] וְאָמַר: ״פָּרַעְתִּי״, נֶאֱמָן. [5]בָּא מַלְוֶה לִכְתּוֹב, אֵין כּוֹתְבִין וְנוֹתְנִין לוֹ. [6]״חַיָּיב אַתָּה לִיתֵּן לוֹ״, וְאָמַר: ״פָּרַעְתִּי״, אֵינוֹ נֶאֱמָן. [7]בָּא מַלְוֶה לִכְתּוֹב, כּוֹתְבִין וְנוֹתְנִין לוֹ.

LITERAL TRANSLATION

[1]Rava said: And because he has been confirmed as being a liar once, he will never pay again? [2]Rather, Rava said: Our Mishnah [refers] to deeds of adjudication and authorization, and in accordance with Rabbi Zera. [3]And [with regard to] a liar, since [the subject] has come to our hand, let us say something [more] about it. [4]For Rav Yosef bar Manyumi said in the name of Rav Naḥman: [If the court] said to him, "Go, give him [what you owe him]," [17A] and he said: "I have paid," he is believed. [5][If] the lender came [before the court] to write [a deed of authorization], we do not write [it] and give [it] to him. [6][If the court said:] "You are obliged to give him," and he said: "I have paid," he is not believed. [7][If] the lender came [before the court] to write [a deed of authorization], we write [it] and give [it] to him.

TRANSLATION AND COMMENTARY

אֲמַר רָבָא [1]**Rava**, commenting on this, **said: And because** a person **has been confirmed as being a liar once**, must we assume that **he will never again pay** any other debt? Surely not!

אֶלָּא אֲמַר רָבָא [2]**Rather, Rava said: The Mishnah is referring** specifically **to deeds of adjudication and authorization, in accordance with Rabbi Zera's** view, and Rabbi Zera and Rava have given explanations above of why such documents *are* to be returned to their owners.

וְכַפְּרָן [3]The Gemara further notes: **Since the subject of a liar has come to hand** in the previous discussion, **let us say something more about it.** [4]**For Rav Yosef bar Manyumi said in the name of Rav Naḥman: If the court** issued a formal order and **said to** the litigant whom they had found liable to pay, **"Go and give** the other claimant **what you owe him,"** using this decisive language, [17A] **and** later the creditor demanded his money and the debtor **said** in response, **"I have** already **paid,** as the court ruled," the debtor is **believed**, provided that he takes the standard oath supporting his claim (שְׁבוּעַת הֶיסֵּת). [5]For the same reason, if **the lender came before the court** at any time after the verdict was delivered, and asked them **to write a deed authorizing** him to collect the loan, **we do not write it and give it to him** without first checking with the borrower, as it is possible that the debt has already been repaid. [6]But **if the court stated: "You are obliged to give** the other claimant his money," and issued a theoretical ruling but did not explicitly *order* him to pay, **and** afterwards, when the lender demanded his money, the borrower **said** in reply: **"I have** already **paid** as the court ruled," the borrower **is not believed**, since it is presumed that he would not pay immediately after the court ruled that he ought to do so, but would wait until the court issued an order compelling him to do so. Since he is suspected of making a false declaration, he is not believed even if he takes an oath in support of his claim. Instead, the other claimant takes an oath that he has not been paid (שְׁבוּעַת הַנּוֹטְלִין), and then he may collect the money due him. [7]For the same reason, **if the lender came before the court** at any time after the verdict was delivered and asked them **to write** a deed of authorization, **we write it for him and give it to him**, regardless of the claims of the borrower, as we presume that the debt has not been repaid.

RASHI

ותו לא פרע כלל – בתמיה, ולי חיישינן לפרעון – זה שלא נזהר לשמור שטרו יפסיד. **צא תן לו** – שפסקו לו דינו בבית דין, שליוו עליו לתת לו. **ואמר** – לאחר זמן. **פרעתי** – על פי בית דין. **נאמן** – ובשבועת היסת. **בא מלוה** – לפנינו, לכתוב לו אדרכתא עליו – אין כותבין ונותנין לו. **אינו נאמן** – לישבע, אלא שכנגדו נשבע ונוטל. דכיון דתחילתו הולרך לתובעו לדין – אין דרכו למהר לפרוע עד שיפסקו דינו פסק גמור.

NOTES

צֵא תֵּן...חַיָּיב אַתָּה... Go and give it to him... You are obliged to give it to him.... In fact, both of these rulings have equal force (see *Tosafot*, ד״ה חַיָּיב). But the defendant is liable to misinterpret a verdict of "You are obliged to give him" as being subject to additional deliberation, whereas "Go and give him" is accepted by him as being final (*Ritva*).

HALAKHAH

מוֹדֶה בְּהַלְוָאָה שֶׁטּוֹעֵן שֶׁפָּרַע One who admits taking a loan, but claims that he has already repaid it. "If two litigants appear in court, and one admits that he owes the other money, after which the court tells him, 'You are obliged to pay the plaintiff,' or 'Go and give him what you owe him,' he is believed if he later says, 'I have already paid'

[1]רַב זְבִיד מִשְּׁמֵיהּ דְּרַב נַחְמָן אָמַר: בֵּין "צֵא, תֵּן לוֹ", בֵּין "חַיָּיב אַתָּה לִיתֵּן לוֹ", וְאָמַר: "פָּרַעְתִּי", נֶאֱמָן. [2]בָּא מַלְוֶה לִכְתּוֹב, אֵין כּוֹתְבִין וְנוֹתְנִין לוֹ. [3]אֶלָּא אִי אִיכָּא לְפְלוּגֵי, הָכִי הוּא דְּאִיכָּא לְפְלוּגֵי: [4]אָמְרוּ לוֹ: "צֵא, תֵּן לוֹ", וְאָמַר: "פָּרַעְתִּי", [5]וְהָעֵדִים מְעִידִין אוֹתוֹ שֶׁלֹּא פְּרָעוֹ, וְחָזַר וְאָמַר: "פָּרַעְתִּי", הוּחְזַק כַּפְרָן לְאוֹתוֹ מָמוֹן. [6]"חַיָּיב אַתָּה לִיתֵּן לוֹ", וְאָמַר: "פָּרַעְתִּי", [7]וְהָעֵדִים מְעִידִין אוֹתוֹ שֶׁלֹּא פָּרַע, וְחָזַר וְאָמַר: "פָּרַעְתִּי", לֹא הוּחְזַק כַּפְרָן לְאוֹתוֹ מָמוֹן.

TRANSLATION AND COMMENTARY

רַב זְבִיד מִשְּׁמֵיהּ דְּרַב נַחְמָן אָמַר [1]**Rav Zevid** transmitted Rav Naḥman's statement, reported above by Rav Yosef bar Manyumi, in a different way. He **said in the name of Rav Naḥman**: Ordinarily, it is immaterial which language the court used. **Whether they said**: "Go and **give him**," or: "**You are obliged to give him**," if the debtor later **said**: "**I have paid**," **he is believed.** [2]Hence, **if the lender came before the court**, asking it **to write a deed of authorization, we do not write it** for him **and give it to him** without first checking with the borrower. [3]But if there is an instance where we *do* **make a distinction** between the two possible expressions that the court can use in delivering the verdict, **the following** is the instance when **we do make this distinction**: [4]**If** the court **said to** one of the litigants: "**Go** and **give** the other litigant what you owe him," using decisive language, **and he said** later: "**I have paid** as the court ruled," [5]**and witnesses testify that** the creditor demanded payment in their presence and the debtor **did not pay, and** later **he again said**: "**I have** now **paid** him what I was ordered, but I did not do so in the presence of witnesses," he is not believed and he is not permitted to take an oath in support of his claim, because **he is** already **established as being a liar with regard to that money**. His only recourse is to pay the money in the presence of witnesses. [6]But **if the court said**: "**You are obliged** in principle **to give** the other litigant his money," but the court did not actually order him to pay the money, **and he said** later: "**I have paid,**" [7]**and witnesses testify that** the other litigant demanded payment in their presence and **he did not pay, and** later **he again said**: "**I have paid,**" he may take an oath in support of his claim, and if he does so he is believed, because **he is not established as being a liar with regard to that money**.

LITERAL TRANSLATION

[1]Rav Zevid said in the name of Rav Nahman: Whether [they said: "Go, give him," or: "You are obliged to give him," and he said: "I have paid," he is believed. [2][If] the lender came [before the court] to write [a deed of authorization], we do not write [it] and give [it] to him. [3]But if there is [room] to distinguish, we may distinguish as follows: [4][If] they said to him: "Go, give him," and he said: "I have paid," [5]and witnesses testify [about] him that he did not pay it, and he again said: "I have paid," he is established as being a liar regarding that money. [6][If the court said:] "You are obliged to give him," and he said: "I have paid," [7]and witnesses testified [about] him that he did not pay, and he again said: "I have paid," he is not established as being a liar regarding that money.

RASHI

ואמר פרעתי – לאחר זמן, על פי בית דין. **והעדים מעידים אותו שלא פרע** – בפנינו תבעו לפרוע לו על פי בית דין ולא פרעו. הואיל ובפניהם העיז לעבור על פי בית דין – אינו נאמן שוב לומר "פרעתיו שלא בעדים". **הוחזק כפרן לאותו ממון** – שאין נאמן עוד עליו לומר "החזרתי ופרעתי", עד שיפרע בעדים. **לא הוחזק כפרן** – ונשבע שפרעו. ואף על פי שלא פרעו מיד כשתבעו בפני עדים. ואין זה מעיז בבית דין, דכיון דלא פסקו לו פסק גמור – נשמט ממנו, סבר כו׳.

SAGES

רַב זְבִיד Rav Zevid. A Babylonian Amora of the fifth generation, Rav Zevid studied under Abaye and Rava and quotes many statements in their names. We find him involved in discussions with the greatest Amoraim of his generation. He seems to have been expert in the Baraitot of the School of Rabbi Oshaya, many of which he transmitted. (Other opinions ascribe these quotations to another Rav Zevid of the third generation.) After Rava's death, his yeshivah was divided, and Rav Zevid served as the head of the yeshivah of Pumbedita for ten years.

NOTES

וְהָעֵדִים מְעִידִין אוֹתוֹ שֶׁלֹּא פְּרָעוֹ And witnesses testify that he did not pay it. How do the witnesses know that the defendant never paid? According to *Rashi*, the Gemara means that the witnesses testify that the plaintiff at least once demanded payment from the defendant and encountered a refusal. Accordingly, we no longer find credible a plea of change of heart on the part of the defendant and the burden of proof falls on him to prove that he did, in fact, pay.

Most of the Rishonim, however, explain that the witnesses were in the company of the defendant (and/or the plaintiff) from the moment they left the courtroom, and saw that no payment was made (*Ramban*, *Rashba*, *Ran* and others). *Tosafot* and *Ritva* suggest that the defendant may have stated the occasion on which he claims to have paid. In that case, it would be sufficient for the witnesses to testify that no payment was made at that time.

הוּחְזַק כַּפְרָן He has been established as being a liar.

HALAKHAH

(provided that he takes an oath supporting his claim). Therefore, if the plaintiff requests the court to provide him with written documentation of the borrower's admission, they do not do so, since the borrower may have already paid," following the Gemara. (*Shulḥan Arukh, Ḥoshen Mishpat* 39:9, 79:12.)

עֵדִים הַמַּכְחִישִׁים אֶת הַפֵּרָעוֹן If witnesses deny that the borrower has paid. "If two litigants appear in court, and the court orders one of them, 'Go and pay the other,' and he later says, 'I have paid,' after which witnesses testify that he has not paid (e.g., if they have been with him the whole time), the borrower is confirmed as being a liar with regard

LITERAL TRANSLATION

[1] What is the reason?

[2] He is attempting to avoid him. [3] [For] he thinks: "[I will postpone repaying him] until the Rabbis examine my case."

[4] Rabbah bar Bar Ḥanah said in the name of Rabbi Yoḥanan: [If a person said:] "You owe me a maneh" (lit., "I have a maneh in your hand"), and the other [person] says: "I owe you nothing," [5] and witnesses testify that he does owe, and again he said: "I have paid," he is established as being a liar with regard to that money.

[6] [This] is like [the case] where Shabbetai, the son of Rabbi Marinus, wrote for his daughter-in-law in her ketubah [that he would give her] a cloak of fine wool, and accepted [responsibility] upon himself. [7] Her ketubah was lost. [8] [Shabbetai] said [to her]: "It never happened" (lit., "there were never such things"). [9] Witnesses came and said: "Yes, he did write [this] for her." Subsequently he said to them: "I have paid it." [10] [The case] came before Rabbi Ḥiyya, [and] he said to [Shabbetai]:

[1] מַאי טַעְמָא? [2] אִשְׁתַּמּוּטֵי הוּא קָא מִשְׁתַּמֵּיט מִינֵּיהּ. [3] סָבַר: ״עַד דְּמְעַיְּינוּ בֵּי רַבָּנַן בְּדִינַי״.

[4] אָמַר רַבָּה בַּר בַּר חָנָה אָמַר רַבִּי יוֹחָנָן: ״מָנֶה לִי בְּיָדְךָ״, וְהַלָּה אוֹמֵר: ״אֵין לְךָ בְּיָדִי כְּלוּם״, [5] וְהָעֵדִים מְעִידִים אוֹתוֹ שֶׁיֵּשׁ לוֹ, וְחָזַר וְאָמַר: ״פְּרַעְתִּי״, הוּחְזַק כַּפְרָן לְאוֹתוֹ מָמוֹן.

[6] כִּי הָא דְּשַׁבְּתַאי בְּרֵיהּ דְּרַבִּי מָרִינוּס כְּתַב לַהּ לְכַלָּתֵיהּ אִיצְטְלָא דְּמִילְתָא בִּכְתוּבָּתָהּ, וְקַבְּלָהּ עֲלֵיהּ. [7] אִירְכַּס כְּתוּבָּתָהּ. [8] אֲמַר [לַהּ]: ״לֹא הָיוּ דְּבָרִים מֵעוֹלָם״. [9] אָתוּ סָהֲדֵי וְאָמְרִי: ״אִין, כְּתַב לַהּ״. לְסוֹף אֲמַר לְהוּ: ״פְּרַעְתִּיהָ״. [10] אֲתָא לְקַמֵּיהּ דְּרַבִּי חִיָּיא, אֲמַר לֵיהּ:

RASHI

אצטלא = לבוש.

TRANSLATION AND COMMENTARY

מַאי טַעְמָא [1] The Gemara asks: **What is the reason** that he is not considered a liar in this case?

אִשְׁתַּמּוּטֵי הוּא קָא מִשְׁתַּמֵּיט מִינֵּיהּ [2] The Gemara answers: When he first claimed that he had paid, **he may have been** merely **attempting to avoid** the lender, and to delay payment for as long as possible. [3] **For he may have thought**: **"I will postpone repaying him until the Rabbis** in the court **examine my case** more carefully and give a final decision, which may be in my favour."

אָמַר רַבָּה בַּר בַּר חָנָה [4] **Rabbah bar Bar Ḥanah said in the name of Rabbi Yoḥanan: If one person says** to another: **"You owe me a maneh," and the other person says**: **"I owe you nothing,"** [5] **and witnesses testify that he does owe** the plaintiff money, **and** the borrower **again says**: **"I have paid," he is established as being a liar with regard to that money.** The borrower is not believed, and he is not permitted to take an oath in support of his claim.

כִּי הָא דְּשַׁבְּתַאי בְּרֵיהּ דְּרַבִּי מָרִינוּס [6] The Gemara now provides support for Rabbi Yoḥanan's ruling by citing an actual case: **This is like the case where Shabbetai, the son of Rabbi Marinus, wrote for his daughter-in-law in her ketubah that he would give her a cloak of fine wool**, in the event that she became widowed or divorced, **and he accepted responsibility** for this obligation on behalf of his son. [7] **The** daughter-in-law's **ketubah got lost**, and a dispute arose between the two sides as to what was written in it. [8] **Shabbetai said to** his daughter-in-law: **"It never happened**. I completely deny that I ever promised you the cloak." [9] **Witnesses came and said**: **"Yes, he did write her** the guarantee that he would give her the cloak." **Subsequently he said to them**: **"I have** now **paid it to her**, in accordance with the court's ruling." [10] **The case came before Rabbi Ḥiyya,**

LANGUAGE

אִיצְטְלָא Cloak. This word may be derived from the Greek στολίς, *stolis*, which means "garment" or "robe."

מִילְתָא Fine wool. Some authorities explain that מִילְתָא means "fine wool of high quality," and was so called after the city of Μίλητος, Miletus, in Asia Minor, where such wool was manufactured. Others explain that it is derived from the Greek μηλωτή, *melote*, which means "wool."

מָרִינוּס Marinus. This word is derived from the Latin *marinus*, meaning "associated with the sea," "a sailor."

SAGES

רַבִּי מָרִינוּס Rabbi Marinus. Rabbi Marinus was a Tanna of the generation of Rabbi Yehudah HaNasi, and his teachings appear in Baraitot. The Jerusalem Talmud discusses, with a slight change, the incident related here, describing Rabbi Marinus as the guarantor to his daughter-in-law. In the description found there, the case was brought before Rabbi Ḥanina and Rabbi Hoshaya, and they asked Rabbi Ḥiyya how they should relate to the second claim — that the debt had already been paid.

NOTES

According to some authorities, since the defendant has been proved to be a liar, from now on he must pay the plaintiff in the presence of witnesses, so that he will not be accused of further deception in this matter (*Rashba*). *R. Elḥanan Wasserman* explains that since the defendant has been proven to be a liar, he can no longer present other claims in support of his position.

כְּתַב לַהּ אִיצְטְלָא He wrote for his daughter-in-law a cloak of fine wool. Some commentators explain that he did not promise her a fine woolen cloak, but it was stated in the ketubah that his daughter-in-law's dowry included such a cloak, and that he was responsible for giving it to her. Therefore, if the marriage were to be dissolved later, Shabbetai would be required to return the cloak to his daughter-in-law as stated in the ketubah (*Rid*).

HALAKHAH

כָּפַר בְּחוֹב כְּנֶגֶד עֵדִים וְטָעַן פָּרַעְתִּי One who denied a debt against the evidence of witnesses and later claimed to have paid. "If one litigant denies that he borrowed from another, and witnesses testify that he does owe the money, after which he claims that he has paid, he is confirmed as

to this transaction. But if the court says, 'You are obliged to pay,' and he later says, 'I have paid,' even if witnesses testify that he has not paid, he is not confirmed as being a liar with regard to this transaction," following the Gemara. (*Shulḥan Arukh, Ḥoshen Mishpat* 79:13)

TRANSLATION AND COMMENTARY

and **he said to Shabbetai: "You have been established as being a liar with regard to that cloak**, and even if you take an oath that you gave your daughter-in-law the cloak, we will not believe you."

אָמַר רַבִּי אָבִין [1]**Rabbi Avin said in the name of Rabbi Il'a, who said in the name of Rabbi Yoḥanan: If someone was obliged to take an oath to rebut** the claim of **another person, and he said: "I have taken the oath,"** [2]**but witnesses testify that he did not take the oath, and later he again said: "I have taken the oath," he is established as being a liar with regard to that oath.** The other litigant is given the opportunity to take an oath, after which he may collect the money due him, in accordance with the standard procedure for litigants who are not permitted to take an oath.

אֲמָרוּהָ [3]It is related that **the Sages quoted this** ruling **before Rabbi Abbahu.** [4]**He said to them: Rabbi Avin's statement is reasonable** in a case **where** the litigant **was required to take an oath in court** as a result of a court hearing, and then lied and said that he had taken an oath when in fact he had not done so. [5]**But if he** merely **obligated himself** to the other litigant **to take an oath** without having been ordered to do so by the court, **he is believed** when he says, for the second time, that he has taken the oath, despite the fact that the first time he made this statement he was contradicted by witnesses. [6]**For a person may happen to speak this way**. Since the litigant undertook voluntarily to take an oath, he might simply have regretted giving the undertaking, and instead of saying that he had changed his mind, he preferred to say that he had already taken the oath. Hence, the fact that his first claim was contradicted by witnesses does not prove that he is a confirmed liar even regarding this oath.

אַהַדְרוּהָ קַמֵּיהּ דְּרַבִּי אָבִין [7]**The Sages sent Rabbi Abbahu's comment back to Rabbi Avin.**

"הוּחְזַקְתָּ כַּפְרָן לְאוֹתָהּ אִיצְטְלָא".

[1]אָמַר רַבִּי אָבִין אָמַר רַבִּי אִלְעָא אָמַר רַבִּי יוֹחָנָן: הָיָה חַיָּיב לַחֲבֵירוֹ שְׁבוּעָה, וְאָמַר: "נִשְׁבַּעְתִּי", [2]וְהָעֵדִים מְעִידִין אוֹתוֹ שֶׁלֹּא נִשְׁבַּע, וְחָזַר וְאָמַר: "נִשְׁבַּעְתִּי", הוּחֲזַק כַּפְרָן לְאוֹתָהּ שְׁבוּעָה.

[3]אֲמָרוּהָ קַמֵּיהּ דְּרַבִּי אַבָּהוּ. [4]אֲמַר לְהוּ: מִסְתַּבְּרָא מִלְּתָא דְּרַבִּי אָבִין שֶׁנִּתְחַיֵּיב שְׁבוּעָה בְּבֵית דִּין, [5]אֲבָל חִיֵּיב עַצְמוֹ שְׁבוּעָה, [נֶאֱמָן], [6]עָבֵיד אִינִישׁ דְּמִקְרֵי וְאָמַר.

[7]אַהַדְרוּהָ קַמֵּיהּ דְּרַבִּי אָבִין.

LITERAL TRANSLATION

"You have been established as being a liar with regard to that cloak."

[1]Rabbi Avin said in the name of Rabbi Il'a, [who] said in the name of Rabbi Yoḥanan: If someone was obliged [to take] an oath to [rebut] another person, and he said: "I have taken the oath," [2]but witnesses testify that he did not take the oath, and again he said: "I have taken the oath," he is established as being a liar with regard to that oath.

[3][The Sages] said this before Rabbi Abbahu. [4]He said to them: Rabbi Avin's statement is reasonable [where] he was required [to take] an oath in court, [5]but if he obligated himself [to take] an oath, he is believed, [6][for] a person may happen to speak [this way].

[7]The [Sages] sent [Rabbi Abbahu's comment] back to Rabbi Avin.

RASHI

הוחזק כפרן לאותה אצטלא — עד שיפרע. **הוחזק כפרן לאותה שבועה** — לומר "נשבעתי", עד שישבע בפנינו. **כשנתחייב שבועה בבית דין** — דכיון דתבעו בעדים לקיים דברי בית דין, ולא אבה — אינו נאמן לומר עוד "קיימתי אחרי כן". **אבל חייב עצמו שבועה** — שאמר לו "אשבע לך", ותבעו בעדים ולא אבה, ואחר כך אמר "נשבעתי" — נאמן. ואף על גב דקמי עדים דחייה. **עביד איניש דמקרי ואמר** — "לא אעשה מה שלא חייבוני בית דין, אלא אני בעצמי". ואין זו סרבנות ותרטה, אלא דחייה בעלמא.

NOTES

מִקְרֵי וְאָמַר A person may happen to speak this way. Some commentators explain that the defendant is not considered a confirmed liar in this case because we can apply the Halakhic principle of *miggo*: Since the defendant had it in his power to cancel his obligation to take this oath (for he obligated himself to do so), there is no reason to regard him as a confirmed liar (*Meiri*). Others explain the expression "happened to say" as meaning that the defendant made a statement which could be construed as an offer to take an oath, but this may not have been his true intention (*Ge'onim*).

HALAKHAH

being a liar with regard to this transaction, and must pay the lender," following Rabbi Yoḥanan. (Ibid., 79:5.)

הַטּוֹעֵן נִשְׁבַּעְתִּי וְעֵדִים מַכְחִישִׁים One who claims to have taken an oath, but witnesses deny this. "If the court required a person to take an oath to rebut the claim of another person, and he later claimed to have done so, then if witnesses testify that he has not taken an oath, he is proven to be a liar with regard to that oath. But if a person voluntarily undertook to take an oath, without having been required to do so by the court, and later claimed to have done so, even if witnesses deny his claim, he is not proven to be a liar with regard to this oath," following the Gemara's conclusion. (Ibid., 87:27.)

SAGES

רַבִּי אָבִין Rabbi Avin. An Amora of the third and fourth generations, he was apparently born in Babylonia and studied Torah in Eretz Israel. In most cases where his name appears in the Babylonian Talmud, it is abbreviated to Ravin. He returned to Babylonia several times, bringing with him the teachings of the Sages of Eretz Israel. He was one of the most important of the נְחוּתֵי דְּמַעַרְבָא (the Sages who traveled from Eretz Israel to Babylonia). His son was also named Rabbi Avin, and it is difficult to know which teachings to attribute to the one and which to the other. In Eretz Israel he was a disciple of the Sages of the third generation: Rabbi Abbahu, Rabbi Zera, and Rabbi Il'a, from whom he learned many teachings of Rabbi Yoḥanan. Rabbi Avin's teachings were transmitted by the Sages of the fourth generation: Rava, Rabbi Yudan, and others. Rabbi Avin's son was one of the greatest Palestinian Amoraim of the fifth generation. According to tradition, the day Rav Adda bar Ahavah died, Rabbi Avin was born, and the day Rabbi Avin died, his son Rabbi Avin was born. The younger Rabbi Avin was the head of the yeshivah of Tiberias. His colleague was Rabbi Mana, the head of the yeshivah of Tzipori, and he transmitted the teachings of the Sages of the fourth generation: Rabbi Aḥa, Rabbi Berekhia, Rabbi Pineḥas, and Rabbi Shammai.

TERMINOLOGY

אַהַדְרוּהָ קַמֵּיהּ They sent it back to him. This expression is used when one Sage comes to a conclusion or expresses an opinion, and another Sage, who lives elsewhere, voices a different opinion or expresses a reservation. In these cases we are sometimes told that the problem was sent back (and sometimes this happens several times) from one Sage to the other to receive a proper response.

TRANSLATION AND COMMENTARY

[1]**He said to them: I, too, stated my ruling** only **in the case of** an oath imposed by **a court**, and there is no difference of opinion between me and Rabbi Abbahu.

אִיתְּמַר נַמִי [2]**It was similarly stated: Rabbi Avin said in the name of Rabbi Il'a, who said in the name of Rabbi Yoḥanan: If someone was obliged to take an oath to rebut** the claim of **another person in court, and he said: "I have taken the oath," [3]but witnesses testify that he did not take the oath, and again he said: "I have taken the oath," he is established as being a liar with regard to that oath.** This version of Rabbi Avin's ruling explicitly states that it applies only in the case of a court-imposed oath, and corresponds exactly to the viewpoint of Rabbi Abbahu.

אָמַר רַבִּי אַסִי [4]**Rabbi Assi said in the name of Rabbi Yoḥanan:** If **someone finds a promissory note in the marketplace and there is a court endorsement written on it, and the date written on it** shows that it was written **on the** very **same day** on which it was found, the finder **shall return it to its owner.** [5]**For** the two arguments against returning it do not apply in such a case: (1) **If we are concerned because the borrower may have written** the promissory note **for** the purpose of **borrowing, but did not borrow** the money, this cannot be so here, because **surely there is a court endorsement written on it!** [6]And (2), **if** we are concerned **because we suspect** that the note may already have been **repaid, we do not suspect** that **repayment** was made **the same day**, for people do not ordinarily take out loans with the intention of repaying them the same day that they borrowed the money.

אָמַר לֵיהּ רַבִּי זֵירָא לְרַבִּי אַסִי [7]**Rabbi Zera said to Rabbi Assi: Did Rabbi Yoḥanan** really **say so?**

[1]אָמַר לְהוּ: אֲנָא נַמִי בְּבֵית דִּין אָמְרִי.

[2]אִיתְּמַר נַמִי: אָמַר רַבִּי אָבִין אָמַר רַבִּי אִלְעָא אָמַר רַבִּי יוֹחָנָן: הָיָה חַיָּיב לַחֲבֵירוֹ שְׁבוּעָה בְּבֵית דִּין, וְאָמַר: ״נִשְׁבַּעְתִּי״, [3]וְהָעֵדִים מְעִידִין אוֹתוֹ שֶׁלֹּא נִשְׁבַּע, וְחָזַר וְאָמַר: ״נִשְׁבַּעְתִּי״, הוּחְזַק כַּפְרָן לְאוֹתָהּ שְׁבוּעָה.

[4]אָמַר רַבִּי אַסִי אָמַר רַבִּי יוֹחָנָן: הַמּוֹצֵא שְׁטַר חוֹב בַּשּׁוּק וְכָתוּב בּוֹ הֶנְפֵּק, וְכָתוּב בּוֹ זְמַנּוֹ — בּוֹ בַּיּוֹם — יַחֲזִירוֹ לַבְּעָלִים. [5]אִי מִשּׁוּם כָּתַב לִלְוֹת וְלֹא לָוָה, הָא כָּתוּב בּוֹ הֶנְפֵּק! [6]אִי מִשּׁוּם פֵּרָעוֹן, לְפְרִיעָה בַּת יוֹמָא לָא חָיְישִׁינַן. [7]אָמַר לֵיהּ רַבִּי זֵירָא לְרַבִּי אַסִי: מִי אָמַר רַבִּי יוֹחָנָן הָכִי?

LITERAL TRANSLATION

[1]He said to them: I too said [my statement] in [the case of] a court.

[2]It was similarly stated: Rabbi Avin said in the name of Rabbi Il'a, [who] said in the name of Rabbi Yoḥanan: [If] someone was obliged [to take] an oath to [rebut] another person in court, and he said: "I have taken the oath," [3]and witnesses testify that he did not take the oath, and again he said: "I have taken the oath," he is established [as being] a liar with regard to that oath.

[4]Rabbi Assi said in the name of Rabbi Yoḥanan: One who finds a promissory note in the marketplace and there is a court endorsement written on it, and its date is written on it — the same day — he shall return it to its owner. [5][For] if [we are concerned] because [the borrower] wrote to borrow but did not borrow, surely there is a court endorsement written on it! [6][And] if because [we suspect the possibility of] repayment, we do not suspect repayment the same day.

[7]Rabbi Zera said to Rabbi Assi: Did Rabbi Yoḥanan say so?

RASHI

וכתוב בו זמנו בו ביום — שביום שנמלא נכתב.

NOTES

אָמַר נִשְׁבַּעְתִּי **He said: "I have taken the oath."** He is not required to take a Rabbinical oath (שְׁבוּעַת הֶיסֵּת) in support of his claim, since Rabbinical oaths are not administered to confirm claims made by a person that he has already taken an oath (*Rosh*). *Rav Hai Gaon* distinguishes between a claim made by a person that he has taken an oath required by Torah law, which must be confirmed by a Rabbinical oath, and a claim made by a person that he has taken an oath of Rabbinical origin, which need not be confirmed by another oath of Rabbinical origin (since one Rabbinic decree is not ordinarily imposed on another).

HALAKHAH

שְׁטָר שֶׁזְּמַנּוֹ בְּאוֹתוֹ יוֹם **A promissory note which was found the same day it was written.** "If a promissory note endorsed by the court was found the same day it was written, and the borrower admits that he has not repaid the loan, it may be returned to the lender." Some Aḥaronim (*Shakh*, *Gra*) follow the opinion of Rav Kahana and maintain that, even if the note has not been endorsed by the court, it may be returned, as long as the borrower admits that he has not repaid the loan. Other authorities uphold the view of the *Shulḥan Arukh* (see *Ketzot HaḤoshen*, *Netivot HaMishpat*). (Ibid., *Ḥoshen Mishpat* 65:7.)

[1]הָא אַתְּ הוּא דְּאָמְרַתְּ מִשְּׁמֵיהּ דְּרַבִּי יוֹחָנָן: שְׁטָר שֶׁלָּוָה בּוֹ וּפְרָעוֹ, אֵינוֹ חוֹזֵר וְלֹוֶה בּוֹ, שֶׁכְּבָר נִמְחַל שִׁיעְבּוּדוֹ. [2]אֵימַת? אִילֵימָא: לְמָחָר וּלְיוֹמָא חֲרָא, מַאי אִרְיָא שֶׁכְּבָר נִמְחַל שִׁעְבּוּדוֹ? [3]תֵּיפּוֹק לֵיהּ דַּהֲוָה לֵיהּ מוּקְדָּם, וּתְנַן: "שִׁטְרֵי חוֹב הַמּוּקְדָּמִין פְּסוּלִין". [4]אֶלָּא לָאו בְּיוֹמֵיהּ. אַלְמָא: פָּרְעִי אֱינָשֵׁי בְּיוֹמֵיהּ! [5]אֲמַר לֵיהּ: מִי קָא אָמִינָא דְּלָא

LITERAL TRANSLATION

[1]Surely you yourself said in the name of Rabbi Yoḥanan: [Regarding] a promissory note with which one has borrowed and [later] repaid, one may not borrow again with it, since the lien [it generated] has already been canceled! [2]When? If we say: Tomorrow or the day after, what is the relevance of its lien having already been canceled? [3]Let him derive [this] from [the fact that] it was antedated, and we have learned [in a Mishnah]: "Antedated promissory notes are invalid"! [4]Rather, is it not [the case that the note was to be used again] on the same day. Hence: People do repay on the same day!

[5][Rabbi Assi] said to [Rabbi Zera:] Did I say that [people]

TRANSLATION AND COMMENTARY

[1]**Surely you yourself said in the name of Rabbi Yoḥanan: A promissory note which has been used to borrow** money **and which has later been repaid may not be used to borrow** money **again, since the lien** that **it generated** on the borrower's estate **has already been canceled** by the repayment of the loan! A promissory note is nothing other than a record of an obligation. In this case, once the loan has been repaid, the obligation is at an end, and the promissory note is now without value. If, therefore, the borrower takes out a new loan without writing a new promissory note, the new loan has the status of a verbal obligation which does not generate a lien on his estate.

אֵימַת [2]The Gemara now analyzes Rabbi Yoḥanan's statement here, in order to clarify the basis of Rabbi Zera's objection: **When** was the promissory note repaid, and when did the borrower take out the second loan? **If we say** that the second loan was not to take place on the date when the note was originally written, but **on the next day or the day after, what is the relevance of** the reason Rabbi Yoḥanan mentioned for disqualifying the note, that **its lien had already been canceled?** [3]**Let him** instead **derive this** same law, that the promissory note is invalid, **from the fact that it was antedated** — the date on the note is earlier than the actual date of the transaction — **as we have learned in a Mishnah** (*Shevi'it* 10:5): **"Antedated promissory notes are invalid"!** [4]**Rather, is it not the case that** Rabbi Yoḥanan was referring to a situation where **the note was to be used** a second time **on the same day** on which it was originally written and repaid. Hence we see that **people do pay** back loans **on the same day** as they borrow, in contradiction to the ruling by Rabbi Assi in the name of Rabbi Yoḥanan at the beginning of our discussion!

אֲמַר לֵיהּ [5]Rabbi Assi **said** in reply **to** Rabbi Zera: **Did I say that people *never* repay** a loan **on the same day**

RASHI

שכבר נמחל שעבודו – משפרע מלוה ראשונה, ועל האחרונה לא נכתב. והויא לה מלוה על פה, וטורף לקוחות שלא כדין, דאין מלוה על פה גובה מן הלקוחות. **אימת** – דפרעיה אימתי, וחזר ולוה אימתי? אי נימא **למחר** – ולא ביום שנכתב. **וליומא חרא** – שתי תיבות הן: וליום אחריו. וקיצור סופרים הוא. **תיפוק ליה** – דאפילו נכתב על מלוה זו אחרונה, וכתוב בו יום מוקדם כזה – הוה ליה השטר מוקדם.

NOTES

הַמּוּקְדָּמִין פְּסוּלִין Antedated promissory notes are invalid. The Jerusalem Talmud cites a dispute between Rabbi Yoḥanan and Resh Lakish as to whether such notes are totally invalid, or whether they generate a lien on the borrower's property beginning from the time when the document was signed by witnesses and the loan actually took place.

HALAKHAH

שְׁטָר שֶׁלָּוָה בּוֹ וּפְרָעוֹ A promissory note with which a person has borrowed but which was later repaid. "If the loan recorded in a promissory note was repaid, the note may not be used for another loan, even if both loans take place on the same day (so that there is no problem of an antedated note), since the lien generated by the first loan was canceled when it was repaid. *Rema* writes in the name of *Mordekhai* that if a symbolic act of acquisition was performed by the parties in relation to the second loan (or, according to others, if the borrower returned the promissory note to the lender in the presence of witnesses), he may take another loan with the note." (*Shulḥan Arukh, Ḥoshen Mishpat* 48:1.)

שְׁטָר חוֹב מוּקְדָּם Antedated promissory notes. "A promissory note dated before the loan actually took place is invalid. The Sages ruled that debts may be collected with such a document only from the borrower's free property. According to *Rema*, such a promissory note is completely worthless (although the lender may collect the debt if the debtor admits his obligation)." (Ibid., 43:7.)

TRANSLATION AND COMMENTARY

they take it out? [1]**I said that people do not *usually* repay** a loan **on the same day**. Accordingly, since it is rare, though not unknown, for people to repay loans on the same day that they borrow, a promissory note endorsed by the court may be returned to the lender if it was found on the same day that it was written.

רַב כָּהֲנָא אָמַר [2]**Rav Kahana said** in reply: Loans are often repaid on the same day they are taken out. But Rabbi Yoḥanan's statement, that a lost promissory note endorsed by the court is to be returned to its owner, **applies** only **when the debtor admits** that he has not yet repaid **his debt**.

אִי הָכִי מַאי לְמֵימְרָא [3]The Gemara objects: **If so, what is there to say?** If the borrower admits that he has not yet repaid his debt, it is surely obvious that the finder should return the note to the lender!

מַהוּ דְתֵימָא [4]The Gemara replies: The statement of Rabbi Yoḥanan *was* necessary, for **you might have said: The borrower has indeed repaid** the lender, [5]**and** the reason **why he says, "I have not repaid it," is because he wants to return and borrow with** the same promissory note **another time,** because **he is concerned about** saving **the scribe's fee**. The borrower does not want to have to pay for the preparation of a new promissory note, and this is the reason why he wants it to be returned to the lender. [6]**Therefore, Rabbi Yoḥanan's** statement **informs us that** we do not argue in this way; for **if this were** really **so, the lender himself would not permit** the promissory note to be used a second time. [7]**For the lender thinks**: "If I use the same promissory note twice, **the Rabbis will hear about me and**, realizing that I have been lending money with an invalid promissory note, they will **cause me to lose** all the money I might collect from the borrower's estate with such a note."

מַאי שְׁנָא מֵהָא [8]The Gemara now asks: **What is the difference between this** case and **what we have learned in** the following **Mishnah** (above, 12b): "**If someone finds promissory notes containing a clause mortgaging the borrower's landed property as security for the loan, he should not return them**"? [9]**And concerning this we explained** there **that this** Mishnah **refers to a case where the debtor admits his debt**.

פָּרְעֵי כְּלָל? [1]דְּלָא שְׁכִיחִי אֱינָשֵׁי דְּפָרְעִי בְּיוֹמֵיהּ קָא אָמֵינָא.

[2]רַב כָּהֲנָא אָמַר: כְּשֶׁחַיָּיב מוֹדֶה.

[3]אִי הָכִי, מַאי לְמֵימְרָא? [4]מַהוּ דְתֵימָא: הַאי מִפְרַע פְּרָעֵיהּ, [5]וְהַאי דְּקָא אָמַר, "לָא פְּרַעְתִּיהָ", מִשּׁוּם דְּקָבָעֵי מֶהֱדַר לְמִזְפָּא בֵּיהּ זִמְנָא אַחֲרִיתֵי, וְלִפְשִׁיטֵי דְסָפְרָא חָיֵישׁ. [6]קָא מַשְׁמַע לָן דְּאִם כֵּן, מַלְוֶה גּוּפֵיהּ לָא שָׁבֵק. [7]סָבַר: "שָׁמְעִי בֵּי רַבָּנַן וּמַפְסְדִי לִי".

[8]מַאי שְׁנָא מֵהָא דִּתְנַן: "מָצָא שִׁטְרֵי חוֹב, אִם יֵשׁ בָּהֶן אַחֲרָיוּת נְכָסִים, לֹא יַחֲזִיר", [9]וְאוֹקִימְנָא כְּשֶׁחַיָּיב מוֹדֶה.

LITERAL TRANSLATION

never repay [on the same day]? [1]I said that people do not *usually* pay on the same day.

[2]Rav Kahana said, [Rabbi Yoḥanan's statement applies] when the debtor admits [his debt].

[3]If so, what is there to say?

[4]You might have said: This [borrower] has indeed repaid it, [5]and what he says, "I have not repaid it," is because he wants to return to borrow with it another time, and he is concerned about the scribe's fee. [6][Therefore R. Yoḥanan] informs us that if [this were] so, the lender himself would not permit [this. [7]For the lender] thinks: "The Rabbis will hear about me and cause me to lose."

[8]What is the difference [between this and] what we have learned [in a Mishnah]: "[If] one found promissory notes, if they contain [a clause] mortgaging [the borrower's landed] property [as security for the loan], he should not return [them]"? [9]And [concerning this] we explained [that it refers to a case] where the debtor admits [his debt].

RASHI

דלא שכיחי [אינשי] דפרעי [ביומיה] קאמינא – הלכך לא חיישינן למידי דלא שכיח, ואי אתרמי – הוצרכו לומר דאין חוזר ולוה בו. **רב כהנא אמר** – הא דאמר רבי יוחנן יחזיר לבעלים. **כשחייב מודה** – שלא פרע.

NOTES

כְּשֶׁחַיָּיב מוֹדֶה **When the debtor admits that he has not yet repaid his debt**. According to *Rif* and *Rambam*, even if the borrower admits his debt, the promissory note may only be returned if it bears the endorsement of the court. Other commentators disagree, ruling that the promissory note may be returned even if it has no court endorsement (*Tosafot*, *Rashba*, *Ran*). The Aḥaronim discuss the matter at great length (see *Shakh* and others).

כְּשֶׁחַיָּיב מוֹדֶה **When the debtor admits**.... There is no concern about the possibility of conspiracy in this case (see above, 12b), since it is unlikely that the lender and borrower would conspire together to defraud people who bought property from the borrower on precisely that day (*Talmid Rabbenu Peretz*).

Others explain that since the hour of the loan does not appear in the promissory note, there is a much easier way

[1]וּמִשּׁוּם שֶׁמָּא כָּתַב לִלְוֹת בְּנִיסָן וְלֹא לָוָה עַד תִּשְׁרֵי, [2]וְאָתֵי לְמִטְרַף לָקוֹחוֹת מִנִּיסָן וְעַד תִּשְׁרֵי שֶׁלֹּא כַּדִּין. [3]וְלָא אָמְרִינַן דְּאִם כֵּן מַלְוֶה גּוּפֵיהּ לָא שָׁבֵיק, דְּאָמַר לֵיהּ: [4]״כְּתוֹב שְׁטָרָא אַחֲרִינָא בְּתִשְׁרֵי, דְּדִלְמָא שָׁמְעִי רַבָּנַן וּמַפְסְדִי לִי״.

[5]אָמְרִי: הָתָם, מִשּׁוּם דְּאִית לֵיהּ רַוְחָא. [6]דְּקָא טָרֵיף לָקוֹחוֹת מִנִּיסָן וְעַד תִּשְׁרֵי, מֵינָח נִיחָא לֵיהּ, וְלָא אָמַר וְלָא מִידֵּי. [7]הָכָא, כֵּיוָן דְּלֵית לֵיהּ רַוְחָא, דְּסוֹף שְׁטָרָא הָאִידָּנָא כְּתִיב, [8]מַאי אִיכָּא דְּקָטָרֵיף לָקוֹחוֹת? [9]בִּשְׁטָר שֶׁנִּמְחַל שִׁיעְבּוּדוֹ, לָא שָׁבֵיק.

LITERAL TRANSLATION

[1]And [such notes are not returned] because [we suspect that] perhaps [the borrower] wrote to borrow in Nisan, but he did not borrow until Tishri, [2]and [so the lender] may come to seize [property] from the buyers from Nisan until Tishri unlawfully. [3]And we do not say that, if so, the lender himself would not permit [this], for he would say to him: [4]"Write another promissory note in Tishri, because perhaps the Rabbis will hear and they will cause me to lose!" [5][The Sages] say: There [it is different], because he has profit. [6]Since he seizes [property from] the buyers from Nisan until Tishri, he would certainly be pleased, and he would not say anything. [7]Here, since he does not have profit, for after all the promissory note is written now, [8]what "seizure from buyers" is there? [9]In [the case of] a note whose lien was canceled, he will not let it [be used].

TRANSLATION AND COMMENTARY

[1]**And** we said that the reason **such notes are not returned** is **because we suspect that the borrower may perhaps have written** in the promissory note **that he was borrowing** the money **in Nisan**, **but did not** actually **borrow until Tishri**, [2]**and so the lender may come to seize property unlawfully from buyers** who purchased property from the borrower **from Nisan until Tishri**, before the loan took place and before the borrower's property was in fact mortgaged as security for the loan. [3]**And we did not say** there **that if** this was **so the lender himself would not permit** the borrower to use **this** invalid promissory note. Rather, **he would say to** the borrower: [4]"**Write** me **another promissory note** in Tishri, stating that the loan took place **in Tishri**, **because** otherwise **the Rabbis will perhaps hear** that this note is invalid, **and they will cause me to lose** any money I might collect with it!" Thus we see that people are not afraid to lend money with invalid promissory notes! Why, then, does Rabbi Yoḥanan permit the return of the promissory note in our case?

אָמְרִי [5]The Gemara answers: **The Sages** can **say** in reply: **There**, in the Mishnah dealing with promissory notes containing a clause mortgaging the borrower's landed property, the situation **is different**, since the lender might be willing to risk retaining the antedated notes, **because he has** potential **profit**. [6]**Since** on the basis of such a note **he** can illegally **seize property from buyers** who bought land from the borrower **from Nisan until Tishri**, **he would certainly be pleased** to retain the notes, even though there is a danger that he may be caught. Accordingly, **he would** accept the note and **say nothing**. [7]But **here**, in the case of a promissory note with today's date on it, **since** the creditor **does not have** any **profit**, **for after all the promissory note has** only **been written now**, [8]**what** possible **seizure from buyers is there** on the basis of the old note, which will not exist if a new promissory note is written? Both documents will bear today's date! The only point of using the invalid note is to do the borrower a favor and save him the scribe's fee! [9]We can, therefore, assume that **in the case of a** promissory **note whose lien was canceled** when the loan was repaid, the lender **will not let** the borrower **use** this invalid promissory note again, since he gains nothing thereby, and he stands to lose everything. The note can thus be safely returned to the lender.

BACKGROUND

מִנִּיסָן וְעַד תִּשְׁרֵי From Nisan until Tishri. This discussion assumes that the month of Nisan (in the spring) is before Tishri (in the autumn). But the Jewish year begins in Tishri! The reason that Nisan precedes Tishri here is that promissory notes were dated not by the calendar year but by the years of the king's reign. These years begin officially in Nisan.

RASHI

שמעי בי רבנן — שנמחל שעבודו. **ומפסדי לי** — למטרף לקוחות, משום דשטרי חוב המוקדמין פסולין. דכיון דהאי דאוקמא הכי לית ליה עדיו בחתומיו זכין לו — אף זה מן המוקדמין. **מינח ניחא ליה** — ברמאות, ותלי נפשיה בספיקא. ואמר: דלמא לא שמעי, ואיכא רווחא. **מאי איכא דטריף לקוחות** — מה טרפא יש בזה שלא יהא בשטר שיחזור ויכתוב לו? והלא שניהם ביום אחד! הלכך, בשטר שנמחל שעבודו לא שביק.

NOTES

of defrauding the buyers than resorting to borrowing, repaying and then borrowing again on the same day. All the borrower and lender would need to do is to write a promissory note any time the same day, after the borrower has sold his property. (*Rashba*, *Ran*).

שְׁטָר שֶׁנִּמְחַל שִׁיעְבּוּדוֹ A note whose lien was canceled. The deed recording a transaction is a means, a way of acquisition, or a proof of acquisition. But the essence of a business transaction is the inner agreement on the part of the seller and buyer to transfer the property. It is this that brings about the acquisition, and as a result of this there is a monetary and personal responsibility by the parties to carry out the appropriate action. With the acceptance of a loan a lien is created, an obligation by the borrower to repay

¹אָמַר רַבִּי חִיָּיא בַּר אַבָּא אָמַר רַבִּי יוֹחָנָן: הַטּוֹעֵן אַחַר מַעֲשֵׂה בֵּית דִּין [17B] לֹא אָמַר כְּלוּם. ²מַאי טַעְמָא? ³כָּל מַעֲשֵׂה בֵּית דִּין כְּמַאן דְּנָקֵיט שְׁטָרָא בִּידֵיהּ דָּמֵי.

⁴אֲמַר לֵיהּ רַבִּי חִיָּיא בַּר אַבָּא לְרַבִּי יוֹחָנָן: וְלָא מִשְׁנָתֵינוּ הִיא זוֹ: ⁵"הוֹצִיאָה גֵּט וְאֵין עִמּוֹ כְּתוּבָּה, גּוֹבָה כְּתוּבָּתָהּ"!

⁶אֲמַר לֵיהּ: אִי לָאו דִּדְלַאי לָךְ חַסְפָּא, לָא מַשְׁכַּחַתְּ מַרְגָּנִיתָא תּוּתָהּ.

LITERAL TRANSLATION

[1] Rabbi Ḥiyya bar Abba said in the name of Rabbi Yoḥanan: One who claims [to have paid] after a court decision [17B] has not said anything.

[2] What is the reason? [3] Every court decision is considered as if [the claimant] is holding a promissory note in his hand.

[4] Rabbi Ḥiyya bar Abba said to Rabbi Yoḥanan: Is this not [the same as] our Mishnah: [5] "[If a woman] produced a bill of divorce and there was no ketubah with it, she collects her ketubah"!

[6] [Rabbi Yoḥanan] said to him: If I had not lifted up the potsherd for you, you would not have found the pearl underneath it.

TRANSLATION AND COMMENTARY

אָמַר רַבִּי חִיָּיא בַּר אַבָּא [1] **Rabbi Ḥiyya bar Abba said in the name of Rabbi Yoḥanan**: If **someone claims to have paid after a court decision**, i.e., if someone has a responsibility imposed by the court to pay a certain sum of money, such as a husband's obligation to pay his divorced wife her ketubah, whose authority derives not from a voluntary undertaking but from a permanent Halakhic enactment, and he claims that he has already fulfilled his obligation and paid, but he has no witnesses to the truth of his claim, [17B] **his words are of no effect**. Unless he can produce witnesses to support his claim, he is not believed.

מַאי טַעְמָא [2] **What is the reason?** [3] **Every "court decision,"** as defined above, **is considered** just as effective **as if** the claimant **were holding a promissory note in his hand.** Just as no one can shrug off an obligation supported by a document by making an unsupported claim that he has paid, similarly an unsupported claim to have paid a "court decision" is not accepted.

אֲמַר לֵיהּ רַבִּי חִיָּיא בַּר אַבָּא [4] **Rabbi Ḥiyya bar Abba said to Rabbi Yoḥanan**: **Is this** ruling of yours **not** contained in the following **Mishnah** (*Ketubot* 88b/89a): [5] **"If a woman produced a bill of divorce but there was no ketubah with it**, presumably because it had been lost, **she** nevertheless **collects** the money due to her in **her ketubah**"! We thus see that a woman may collect her ketubah even without producing the document itself, and the husband cannot simply say, "I have already paid." Presumably, this is because the obligation on the husband to pay a ketubah is considered a "court decision," and he cannot deny such an obligation without proof.

אֲמַר לֵיהּ [6] Rabbi Yoḥanan **said to** Rabbi Ḥiyya: The deduction you make from that Mishnah is convincing, but **if I had not lifted up the potsherd for you, you would not have found the pearl underneath it**. It was only after you heard my statement that you were able to make this deduction (the "pearl") from the Mishnah.

RASHI

הטוען אחר מעשה בית דין — דבר שהוא תנאי בית דין, כגון כתובה ומזון האשה והבנות, הטוען ואמר "פרעתי שלא בעדים" — לא אמר כלום.

REALIA

חַסְפָּא וּמַרְגָּנִיתָא Potsherds and pearls. Rabbi Yoḥanan's remark ("If I had not lifted up the potsherd, you would not have found the pearl") can be interpreted literally, as describing the contrast between a cover of no value and the precious item under it. *Tosafot*, however, argues that there must be a closer connection between these two items, and suggests that the expression for potsherd (חַסְפָּא) refers to the shell surrounding the pearl (this meaning of חַסְפָּא is indeed found in Aramaic). Thus Rabbi Yoḥanan meant that one who does not notice the plain-looking shell, which resembles a potsherd, will not find the pearl inside it either.

NOTES

the debt to the lender. But when the borrower returns the money, the lien is cancelled and נִמְחַל (forgiven). The note testifying to receipt of the first loan is also testimony to the first lien. But if a person wants to borrow again, the lien resulting from the earlier agreement and obligation is no longer in force, and the parties must create a new lien. Therefore, since the note that has been redeemed represents a lien that has expired, it has no value in itself. Now, it may happen that the parties to the loan wish to use the old note again, to save the trouble and expense of having a new note written. But the old note is already null and void, because the obligation in it was a one-time obligation, and it cannot be renewed.

מַעֲשֵׂה בֵּית דִּין **Court decisions** . These include standard legal documents whose formulation was fixed by the Rabbis, such as bills of divorce, marriage contracts, and the like, as well as the endorsements given by the court and attached to personal documents that have been presented to it for certification (see *Ramban*).

מַעֲשֵׂה בֵּית דִּין כִּשְׁטָר **A court decision is considered like a written document.** Ordinarily, a written document is valid only when it is written with the consent of the party who stands to lose (e.g., the debtor in the case of a promissory note). The Gemara teaches us here that, even if this party is not present (or does not consent to writing a promissory note), a court-imposed obligation is binding and cannot be canceled by unsupported claims of payment (see *Ra'avad*, *Ran*, and others).

אִי לָאו דִּדְלַאי לָךְ חַסְפָּא **If I had not lifted up the potsherd for you.** According to Rabbi Yoḥanan, Rabbi Ḥiyya might

HALAKHAH

הוֹצִיאָה גֵּט בְּלֹא כְּתוּבָּה **A woman who produced a bill of divorce without a ketubah.** "If a woman produces a bill of divorce without her ketubah, and she demands payment of her ketubah from her former husband, she may collect the statutory sum contained in her ketubah by means of her bill of divorce, if the local custom is not to write a ketubah. But if it *is* customary in this place to write a ketubah, the woman may not collect even the statutory sum contained in the

LITERAL TRANSLATION

[1] Abaye said: What pearl? Perhaps we are dealing with a place where [people] do not write a ketubah, so that the [woman's] bill of divorce is her ketubah! [2] But in a place where [people] write a ketubah, if she is holding [her] ketubah, she collects; if not, she may not collect.

[3] Later Abaye said: What I said was [worth] nothing. For if you imagine that we are dealing with a place where [people] do not write a ketubah, [4] but that in a place where [people] do write a ketubah, if [the woman] is holding [her] ketubah, she collects, [but] if not, she does not collect — [5] with what can a widow from betrothal collect? [6] With witnesses [who testify] to the husband's death? Let [the husband's heir] claim and say:

[1] אֲמַר אַבַּיֵי: מַאי מַרְגָּנִיתָא? דִּלְמָא בְּמָקוֹם שֶׁאֵין כּוֹתְבִין כְּתוּבָּה עָסְקִינַן, דְּגֵט הַיְינוּ כְּתוּבָּתָהּ. [2] אֲבָל בְּמָקוֹם שֶׁכּוֹתְבִין כְּתוּבָּה, אִי נְקִיטָא כְּתוּבָּה, גָּבְיָא; אִי לָא, לָא גָּבְיָא.

[3] הֲדַר אֲמַר אַבַּיֵי: לָאו מִלְּתָא הִיא דַּאֲמַרִי. דְּאִי סָלְקָא דַעְתָּךְ בְּמָקוֹם שֶׁאֵין כּוֹתְבִין כְּתוּבָּה עָסְקִינַן, [4] אֲבָל בְּמָקוֹם שֶׁכּוֹתְבִין כְּתוּבָּה, אִי נְקִיטָא כְּתוּבָּה, גָּבְיָא, אִי לָא, לָא גָּבְיָא — [5] אַלְמָנָה מִן הָאֵירוּסִין בְּמַאי גָּבְיָא? [6] בְּעֵדֵי מִיתַת בַּעַל? לִטְעוֹן וְלֵימָא:

RASHI

במקום שאין כותבין כתובה — אלא סומכין על תנאי בית דין, ותגבה לעולם עד שיוציא הבעל שובר. דגט שמעיד שגירשה הוא מוכיח שחייב הוא לה כתובה. **אי לא** — נקיט לה. **לא גביא** — אי משום דחיישינן דלמא הדרא ומפקא כתובה וגביא זימנא אחריתי, אי נמי: משום דאי בעי אמר "פרעתיה". **לאו מלתא היא דאמרי** — דבמקום שכותבין שטר כתובה יכול לטעון "פרעתי", דאם כן אלמנה מן האירוסין, דאף במקום שכותבין אין כותבין מן האירוסין. **במאי גביא** — כתובה? על כרחך בעדי מיתת בעל. **לטעון** — יורש, ולומר "פרעתיה".

TRANSLATION AND COMMENTARY

אֲמַר אַבַּיֵי [1] When this incident was related in Babylonia, **Abaye said**: **What pearl** did Rabbi Ḥiyya find? Does Rabbi Ḥiyya's conclusion necessarily follow from this Mishnah? The Mishnah does not say that the reason why the woman failed to produce the ketubah was because she had lost it. **Perhaps we are dealing** in this Mishnah **with a place where people do not** ordinarily **write a ketubah**, and that is why she had no ketubah. But never having had a ketubah is not the same as losing one. Perhaps the rule is **that** in such circumstances **the woman's bill of divorce is** considered to be **her ketubah**! Thus, the woman collects in such a case because her bill of divorce is the only documentary proof that she ever required, and it is still in her hands. [2] **But** if she were to lack the requisite documentary proof, if, for example, she were to fail to produce her ketubah **in a place where people** do ordinarily **write a ketubah**, her husband could claim that he had already paid, and his claim would be believed. Only **if she is** still **holding her ketubah**, may she **collect**, but **if not, she may not collect**. Accordingly, no proof can be brought from this Mishnah that an unsubstantiated claim that one has already paid a court-imposed obligation is unacceptable.

הֲדַר אֲמַר אַבַּיֵי [3] **Later, Abaye said**: **What I said was worth nothing**. It was incorrect. **For if you were to imagine that we are dealing** in this Mishnah **with a place where people do not** ordinarily **write a ketubah**, [4] **but that in a place where people** ordinarily **do write a ketubah**, **if** the woman **is holding her ketubah**, **she collects, but if not, she does not collect**, [5] **with what** documentary proof **can a widow** whose husband died **after** their **betrothal** (אֵירוּסִין), but before he actually married her (נִישּׂוּאִין), **collect** payment at all, if not on the basis of an undocumented "court decision"? Even in places where the ketubah is customarily written down, this is only done at the time of the marriage, not at the time of the betrothal. Moreover, a widow does not have a bill of divorce to use as a substitute for a ketubah. Thus, a widow after betrothal must rely on an undocumented "court decision" to collect payment. [6] If you say that she can collect payment of her ketubah **by** producing **witnesses who testify to the husband's death**, surely **the husband's heir can claim** that he is exempt from payment

CONCEPTS

אֵירוּסִין **Betrothal.** The first stage of the marriage process. The bond created by אֵירוּסִין is so strong that, after betrothal, a woman requires a divorce before she can marry another man. Similarly, sexual relations with other men are considered adulterous and are punishable by death. At this stage the betrothed couple may not yet live together as man and wife, and most of the couple's mutual obligations do not yet apply.

NOTES

not have found "the pearl," because this Mishnah can be interpreted differently. The Mishnah's ruling might apply only to marriage contracts and bills of divorce, which are governed by special regulations (e.g., since the Jews were forbidden to write ketubot during the Roman persecution, the Sages decreed that a woman could collect her ketubah by merely presenting her bill of divorce). Thus, this Mishnah does not necessarily prove that claims to have paid a "court decision" are invalid (see *Ḥokhmat Manoaḥ*).

בְּמָקוֹם שֶׁאֵין כּוֹתְבִין כְּתוּבָּה **A place where people do not write a ketubah**. As indicated by its name, a ketubah (marriage contract) is essentially a written deed (from the

HALAKHAH

ketubah, provided that her former husband takes an oath in support of his claim (שְׁבוּעַת הֶיסֵּת, ordained by the Rabbis)." (*Shulḥan Arukh, Even HaEzer* 100:12.)

SAGES

מָר קְשִׁישָׁא בְּרֵיהּ דְּרַב חִסְדָּא **Mar Keshisha the son of Rav Ḥisda**. The great Amora Rav Ḥisda (or, according to other opinions, another later scholar of the same name) had two sons. To distinguish between them the elder was called קְשִׁישָׁא — "the old one," — and the younger was called יָנוֹקָא — "the young one," though some authorities believe that the latter was actually the elder and received his name because he was born in Rav Ḥisda's youth. Both of these Sages discussed Halakhic matters with Rav Ashi, but Mar Keshisha is much more frequently cited than his brother.

LITERAL TRANSLATION

"I paid her"! [1] And if you say [that this is] indeed so, if so, what did the Sages achieve through their decree?

[2] Mar Keshisha the son of Rav Ḥisda said to Rav Ashi: [3] And from where [do we know] that a widow after betrothal has [the right to receive] a ketubah?

"פְּרַעְתִּיהָ". [1] וְכִי תֵּימָא הָכִי נַמִי, אִם כֵּן, מַה הוֹעִילוּ חֲכָמִים בְּתַקָּנָתָן? [2] אֲמַר לֵיהּ מָר קְשִׁישָׁא בְּרֵיהּ דְּרַב חִסְדָּא לְרַב אַשִׁי: [3] וְאַלְמָנָה מִן הָאֵירוּסִין דְּאִית לַהּ כְּתוּבָּה מְנָא לַן?

RASHI

בתקנתן – שתקנו כתובה לארוסה, והלא הכל יטענו "פרעתי".

TRANSLATION AND COMMENTARY

by saying: "I paid her"! What proof does she have to rebut such a claim? [1] **And if you say that this is indeed so**, that the heir *can* claim that he paid her — **what did the Sages achieve through their decree** entitling a woman to her ketubah even if her husband died after their betrothal but before their marriage? If the husband's heir can exempt himself from payment in this way, what point was there in ordaining that a widow after betrothal can collect her ketubah? The heir will simply claim that he has paid, and the wife will never be able to collect her ketubah! Rather, Rabbi Ḥiyya must have been right, and a claim of payment of a court decision is *not* accepted without proof, even if the court decision itself is not supported by any documentation at all.

אֲמַר לֵיהּ מָר קְשִׁישָׁא בְּרֵיהּ דְּרַב חִסְדָּא [2] **Mar Keshisha the son of Rav Ḥisda said to Rav Ashi**: Abaye's assumption that a widow after betrothal is entitled to her ketubah is questionable. [3] **From where do we know that a widow after betrothal has the right to receive a ketubah**? Maybe it is only after marriage that a woman is entitled to her ketubah, and not after betrothal?

NOTES

Hebrew root כתב — "to write"). But there were places where the authorities passed anti-Jewish decrees and forbade them from observing the commandments of their religion. In such places ketubot were not written, and the Rabbis made do with the fact that most of the obligations appearing in the ketubah did not depend on mutual agreement between the parties but followed a standard procedure laid down by the court. Under these circumstances, Jews used to pay the obligations stipulated in the ketubah and carry out the other conditions of matrimony as though a ketubah had in fact been written. These payments were, of course, the minimum sums set by the Sages, for only a written contract can contain additional conditions and sums.

מַה הוֹעִילוּ חֲכָמִים בְּתַקָּנָתָן **What did the Sages achieve through their decree**. This question is asked when a Rabbinical ordinance is mentioned, and there is also a simple way to circumvent it, or it is possible to limit its application, so that it is clear that the ordinance cannot achieve its goal. In such cases one asks, "If so, then what good did the Sages do with their ordinance?" In fact, they rectified nothing by introducing it.

כְּתוּבַּת אַלְמָנָה מִן הָאֵירוּסִין **The right of a widow after betrothal to a ketubah**. Under Torah law, a woman is considered legally married from the time of "betrothal" (אֵירוּסִין or קִידּוּשִׁין), but she does not live with her husband until after the second ceremony of "marriage" (נִישּׂוּאִין). Accordingly, there is no doubt that a bill of divorce is required in order to undo a betrothal, but it is less certain that a betrothed woman has the right to a ketubah if her betrothal is dissolved. This is the background to the Gemara's question about the ketubah rights of a woman who is widowed after her betrothal.

From other passages in the Gemara it seems clear that it was well known that such a widow may indeed collect a ketubah. Therefore the Rishonim have difficulty in explaining the Gemara's question here. *Tosafot* suggests that the Gemara is specifically looking for a Tannaitic source for this practice. Alternatively, the Gemara may know that such a widow is *theoretically* entitled to a ketubah, but may be questioning her ability to obtain it in the event of its being contested. If her ketubah was given the status of a court decision, the Rabbis did make some provision to enable her to collect it, since an unproven claim of payment made against a court decision is not acceptable. But if the ketubah merely has the status of a universal custom, it may not be possible for her to collect if the heirs claim to have paid (*Tosafot* and *Ritva*).

Other commentators claim that there is no evidence, other than that cited in our Gemara, that a widow after betrothal is in fact entitled to a ketubah. All the other proof-texts demonstrate that a *divorcee* after betrothal is entitled, but they prove nothing about a widow (*Ran*).

HALAKHAH

אִם יֵשׁ כְּתוּבָּה לַאֲרוּסָה **The right to a ketubah after betrothal**. "If a man betrothed a woman but did not write a ketubah for her, and then he died or divorced her, she is not entitled to a ketubah (*Rambam*). Others, however, maintain that in such a case, she is entitled to a ketubah (*Rosh*, *Ran*, and *Tur*). The accepted practice is that in such a case a woman is not entitled to a ketubah (*Rema*)." (*Shulḥan Arukh, Even HaEzer* 55:6.)

כְּתוּבַּת אֲרוּסָה **A ketubah that was written at the time of betrothal**. "If a man wrote a ketubah for his wife when he betrothed her, and he died or divorced her after the betrothal but before the marriage, she is entitled to the standard, fixed ketubah payment from the husband's free property. But she is not entitled to any additional sum which the husband may have undertaken to pay her in the ketubah," following the view of Rabbi Elazar ben Azaryah. (Ibid., 55:6.)

TRANSLATION AND COMMENTARY

אִילֵימָא מֵהָא דִּתְנַן [1]**If you say** that we can derive it **from what we have learned** in the following Mishnah (*Ketubot* 5:1,54b): "**If a woman was widowed or divorced, whether after betrothal or after marriage, she collects everything** that was written in the ketubah, both the standard, fixed ketubah payment (100 or 200 zuz, depending on whether the woman had been married previously), and any addition to the basic sum which the husband had undertaken to pay in the ketubah (תּוֹסֶפֶת כְּתוּבָּה)," this Mishnah does not prove the general principle that a widow after betrothal is entitled to her ketubah. [2]For **perhaps** the Mishnah **refers to a case where the husband wrote a ketubah for** his wife at the time of their betrothal, even though this is not customary. But other widows, whose husbands did not write a ketubah, would not collect anything.

וְכִי תֵּימָא [3]**And if you say**: If this Mishnah is referring only to a case where the husband had written a ketubah for his wife, **what** need is there **to say** that he must pay her whatever was stipulated in the ketubah! It is obvious that his heirs must honor the late husband's written obligation! [4]The answer is that even so, the statement in the Mishnah **was necessary**, in order **to exclude** (i.e., to reject) the view **of Rabbi Elazar ben Azaryah, who said** that a widow after betrothal does not collect the entire ketubah, but only the basic 100 or 200 zuz, even if the late husband gave her a written ketubah containing a larger sum, because the husband **only wrote the** additional sum recorded in the **ketubah for her on condition that he would marry her**. But since the husband did not marry her, Rabbi Elazar ben Azaryah would maintain that she does not collect the additional sum which the husband undertook to pay her in the ketubah. Therefore, the Mishnah had to teach us that Rabbi Elazar ben Azaryah's view is not accepted, and the widow is entitled to collect everything written in the ketubah. But we cannot prove from this Mishnah that a widow after betrothal is entitled to her ketubah even if a formal document was not written.

דַּיְקָא נַמִי [5]The Gemara now provides additional support for this interpretation of the Mishnah: **There is** linguistic **evidence, too**, from the choice of words in the Mishnah itself, that it is dealing specifically with a case where the husband departed from custom and wrote the ketubah at the time of their betrothal. **For the Mishnah teaches: "She collects everything."** [6]**Granted, if you say that** the Mishnah refers to a case where **the husband wrote a ketubah for** his wife, then we can understand **why the Mishnah teaches: "She collects**

[1]אִילֵימָא מֵהָא דִּתְנַן: "נִתְאַרְמְלָה אוֹ נִתְגָּרְשָׁה, בֵּין מִן הָאֵירוּסִין וּבֵין מִן הַנִּישּׂוּאִין", [2]גּוֹבָה אֶת הַכֹּל — דִּלְמָא הֵיכָא דִּכְתַב לַהּ. [3]וְכִי תֵּימָא: מַאי לְמֵימְרָא? [4]לְאַפּוּקֵי מִדְּרַבִּי אֶלְעָזָר בֶּן עֲזַרְיָה, דְּאָמַר: שֶׁלֹּא כָּתַב לָהּ אֶלָּא עַל מְנָת לְכוֹנְסָהּ אִצְטְרִיכָא לֵיהּ. [5]דַּיְקָא נַמִי, דְּקָתָנֵי: "גּוֹבָה אֶת הַכֹּל". [6]אִי אָמְרַתְּ בִּשְׁלָמָא דִּכְתַב לַהּ, הַיְינוּ דְּקָא תָּנֵי:

LITERAL TRANSLATION

[1]If you say: From what we have learned [in the following Mishnah]: "[If a woman] was widowed or divorced, whether after betrothal or after marriage, [2]she collects everything" — perhaps [this refers to a case] where [the husband] wrote [a ketubah] for her. [3]And if you say: What [does it mean] to say? [4]It was necessary to exclude [the view] of Rabbi Elazar ben Azaryah, who said: He only wrote [the ketubah] for her on condition that he would marry her. [5]There is evidence, too (lit., "it is also precise"), for [the Mishnah] teaches: "She collects everything." [6]Granted, if you say that [the husband] wrote [a ketubah] for her, this is why [the Mishnah] teaches:

RASHI

גובה את הכל — בין כתובה של תנאי בית דין, דהיינו מנה לאלמנה ומאתיים לבתולה, בין תוספת. **שלא כתב לה** — את התוספת. **דיקא נמי** — דכתב לה מיירי.

SAGES

רַבִּי אֶלְעָזָר בֶּן עֲזַרְיָה Rabbi Elazar ben Azaryah. One of the most important Tannaim of the generation following the destruction of the Second Temple, Rabbi Elazar ben Azaryah came from a highly learned family, of distinguished lineage and wealthy. His father Azaryah was also a scholar and a very wealthy man, who supported his brother, the Sage Shimon, known for that reason as "Shimon the brother of Azaryah." Rabbi Elazar ben Azaryah's family was a priestly one, descended from Ezra the Scribe, and the story is told that there was a physical resemblance between them.

Rabbi Elazar ben Azaryah took part in the great dispute in which Rabban Gamliel II was dismissed from his position as president of the Sanhedrin. Rabbi Elazar was very young (only sixteen or eighteen) at the time, and he was declared the most worthy candidate for the post because of the virtues the Sages found in him, and because he maintained good relations with everyone. Even after he became a kind of deputy president he remained very active in community affairs and traveled to Rome at the head of a delegation of Jewish sages, as a representative of his people.

Despite his youth, the greatest Sages of his generation regarded him as an equal, and he expressed his opinions about them with vigor. Nevertheless he refrained from implementing his own decision when he disagreed with his colleagues, and he fasted for a long period to atone for having misled his neighbors into committing a transgression (even though he himself believed that the act in question was permitted).

Rabbi Elazar ben Azaryah was one of the greatest preachers of his generation, and even Rabbi Yehoshua marvelled at his talent, saying: "No generation is orphaned if Rabbi Elazar ben Azaryah is one of its members."

NOTES

גּוֹבָה אֶת הַכֹּל She collects everything. A ketubah may contain various monetary obligations undertaken by a husband towards his wife. If she brings her own property into the marriage (נִכְסֵי מְלוֹג), this property must be listed, so that the husband will return it if he divorces her. Usually the woman also brings a dowry from her father's home, either possessions or money, and the husband gives her similar sums of his own as a present, and these too (known as נִכְסֵי צֹאן בַּרְזֶל) are paid to the woman if the marriage is dissolved. The transfer of property, whether נִכְסֵי מְלוֹג or נִכְסֵי צֹאן בַּרְזֶל, takes place at the time of the marriage; hence it does not concern a betrothed woman. But apart from these sums, there is עִיקַּר הַכְּתוּבָּה — the basic ketubah, the minimum sum that a man must include in the document (200 zuz if the woman is a virgin, and 100 zuz if she is not). There is also the תּוֹסֶפֶת כְּתוּבָּה — an additional sum which the husband promises his wife beyond the minimum amount required by law. The difference of opinion between Rabbi Elazar ben Azaryah and the Sages is with regard to this bonus. Rabbi Elazar Ben Azaryah is of the opinion that the husband's promise of the bonus only applies if the marriage in fact takes place. In the generations after the Talmud was completed, various communities in Spain and

CONCEPTS

אוֹנֵן A mourner during the period of acute mourning on the day of the death of a close relative. The אוֹנֵן is exempt from all positive commandments from the time of the death of the close relative until after the burial. At that point the mourner's status changes from that of an אוֹנֵן to that of an אָבֵל. In Temple times an אוֹנֵן was forbidden to eat מַעֲשֵׂר שֵׁנִי (the second tithe), בִּיכּוּרִים (the first-fruit offerings), and קָדָשִׁים (sacrificial food). If he was a priest he could not take part in the Temple service; this prohibition did not, however, apply to the High Priest.

"גּוֹבָה אֶת הַכֹּל". [1]אֶלָּא אִי אָמְרַתְּ דְּלָא כָּתַב לָהּ, [18A] [2]מַאי "גּוֹבָה אֶת הַכֹּל"? מָנֶה וּמָאתַיִם הוּא דְּאִית לָהּ! [3]וְאֶלָּא מִדְּתָנֵי רַב חִיָּיא בַּר אַמִּי: "אִשְׁתּוֹ אֲרוּסָה, לֹא אוֹנֵן, וְלֹא מְטַמֵּא לָהּ, [4]וְכֵן הִיא לֹא אוֹנֶנֶת, וְלֹא מְטַמְּאָה לוֹ. [5]מֵתָה,

LITERAL TRANSLATION

"She collects everything." [1]But if you say that he did not write for her, [18A] [2]what [is the meaning of] "she collects everything"? What she has is a maneh or 200 [zuz]!

[3]Rather, then, from [the Baraita that] Rav Ḥiyya bar Ammi taught: "[If] one's betrothed wife [died], he does not observe *aninut* for her, nor does he become ritually impure for her, [4]and similarly [if he died] she does not observe *aninut* for him, and she does not become ritually impure for him. [5]If she died,

TRANSLATION AND COMMENTARY

everything." The Mishnah, by using this expression, emphasizes that the widow collects not only the 100 or 200 zuz to which she is entitled by Rabbinic decree, but also whatever additional sum the husband undertook to pay her, because we reject the viewpoint of Rabbi Elazar ben Azaryah. [1]**But if you say that** the case dealt with in the Mishnah is one where **he did not write** a ketubah **for her** at all, [18A] [2]**what is the meaning of "she collects everything"?** Surely **she is** only entitled to **a maneh or 200 zuz**, and no more, since this was the extent of the Rabbinic enactment. Therefore, since we have proved that this Mishnah is referring to a case where the husband departed from established custom and wrote a ketubah for his wife at the time of their betrothal, it cannot be used to decide the basic question of whether a widow after betrothal is entitled to a ketubah by law, even if it is not formally written down.

אֶלָּא [3]The Gemara now suggests another source from which we may be able to prove that a widow after betrothal is entitled to a ketubah: **Rather, then,** let us deduce that a widow after betrothal is entitled to a ketubah **from the Baraita transmitted by Rav Ḥiyya bar Ammi**: **"If one's betrothed wife died, he does not observe *aninut*** (the laws of mourning observed on the day of death) **for her, nor does he become ritually impure for her**, if he is a priest, since she is not considered to have been fully his wife with regard to these laws. A priest is ordinarily forbidden to become ritually impure by coming into contact with dead bodies, except for those of certain close relatives, such as his wife. But the Baraita tells us that a priest is not permitted to become ritually impure for a woman who had been betrothed to him but not married. [4]**Similarly,** if her husband **dies, she does not observe *aninut* for him, and she does not** have to **become ritually impure for him**. In this case, she is not forbidden to become ritually impure, even if she is the daughter or the wife of a priest, but she need not do so unless she so desires (see notes). [5]**If she dies,**

RASHI

מאי גובה את הכל — מאחר שלא התנה עמה כלום, מהו התוספת? **לא אונן** — אין אנינות חל עליו, לאיסור אכילת קדשים. **ולא מטמא לה** — אם כהן הוא, דכתיב (ויקרא כא) "כי אם לשארו" והיינו אשתו. והאי לאו שארו הוא, דלא באו עדיין לידי קירוב בשר. **ולא מטמאה לו** — לאו משום כהונה קאמר, דאין כהנות מוזהרות על הטומאה, דכתיב (שם) "בני אהרן", אלא אינה זקוקה לטמא לו, לא כהנת ולא ישראלית. שמצוה להתעסק בשבעה מתי מצוה האמורים בפרשה, דכתיב "לה יטמא". ותניא: "לה יטמא" — מצוה, ואם לא רצה — מטמאין אותו על כרחו, ומעשה ביוסף הכהן כו', בתורת הכהנים.

NOTES

Germany passed ordinances stipulating what was to be done regarding dowries and additions to ketubot in a situation where a marriage only lasted a very short time (see Takkanot Toledo, Takkanot Shum).

לֹא מְטַמֵּא לָהּ A priest may not become ritually impure for his betrothed wife. *Rashi* (in *Yevamot*) explains that the priest may not become ritually impure on account of his betrothed wife because the Torah states that a priest may only become ritually impure "for his relative who is *near* him" (לִשְׁאֵרוֹ הַקָּרוֹב אֵלָיו, Leviticus 21:2). A woman who was betrothed is not considered to be "near" her husband, even though she is considered his relative. A similar explanation is found in the Jerusalem Talmud. Elsewhere, however, *Rashi* states that the betrothed wife is not only not "near," she is also not "a relative" (see *Rashi* here, ד״ה וְלֹא מְטַמֵּא לָהּ).

לֹא מְטַמְּאָה לוֹ She does not become ritually impure for him. The Rishonim (and the Ge'onim before them) note that this expression cannot be interpreted literally, since a female member of a priestly family by birth or marriage is not forbidden to come into contact with dead bodies. They explain that the wording of this clause was influenced by that of the previous clause (i.e., "*he* may not become ritually impure for *her*").

Rashi, however, explains (*Yevamot* 29b) that the Baraita

HALAKHAH

אַלְמָנוֹת מִן הָאֵירוּסִין A widow after betrothal. "If a woman dies after she has been betrothed, her husband does not inherit her property, nor is he obliged to arrange her burial. If he is a priest, he may not become ritually impure on her account. Similarly, if the husband dies, his betrothed wife is not required to become ritually impure on his account," following the ruling of the Baraita. (*Shulḥan Arukh, Even HaEzer* 55:5.)

TRANSLATION AND COMMENTARY

he does not inherit her property. If he dies, she collects her ketubah."

דִּלְמָא [1]This statement would seem to prove that a widow after betrothal *is* entitled to a ketubah, but again the Gemara rejects the proof: **Perhaps this** Baraita **applies** specifically **where** the husband **wrote a ketubah for her!** [2]**And if you say: If he wrote a ketubah for her, what** need **is there to say** it at all? Surely it is obvious that the woman collects her ketubah in such a case! [3]I can reply, says the Gemara, that Rav Ḥiyya bar Ammi's Baraita **was necessary** in order **to teach us** what is stated in the previous clause, namely: **"If she dies, he does not inherit her property."** Because this ruling needed to be stated, the point about the ketubah was also included, even though it is obvious. Thus this statement cannot be used to prove that a widow after betrothal is entitled to a ketubah.

אֶלָּא [4]The Gemara now presents another explanation of why Abaye retracted: **Rather,** we must say that the reason why **Abaye retracted** and concluded that the Mishnah must be referring to a place where people ordinarily do write a ketubah, and that the Mishnah is telling us that even if she loses her ketubah she can still collect upon proof of divorce, **was because of** an argument based on **the Mishnah itself,** and not because of the argument from the case of the betrothed widow. [5]**For if you** were to **imagine that** the Mishnah **is dealing with a place where people do not** ordinarily **write a ketubah, and that** the woman's **bill of divorce** *is* **her ketubah,** and *this* is the reason why she is entitled to a ketubah, rather than because of the authority of a Rabbinically ordained "court decision," **does a bill of divorce have a maneh or 200 zuz written in it?** You cannot argue that the bill of divorce is the means whereby the obligation to pay the wife's ketubah is expressed. A document obliging payment must contain the specific amount to be paid, and a bill of divorce does not contain any such thing!

וְכִי תֵּימָא [6]**And if you say: Since the Sages have ordained that she should collect** her ketubah in this way, her bill of divorce **is** considered **as if it had** the specific amounts of **a maneh or 200 zuz written in it,** [7]**let the husband** or his heirs **claim, and say: "I have** already **paid"!** The husband (or his heir) should be able to claim that he has paid, since there is nothing to disprove his claim.

אֵינוֹ יוֹרְשָׁהּ; מֵת הוּא, גּוֹבָה כְּתוּבָּתָהּ".

[1]דִּלְמָא דְּכָתַב לָהּ! [2]וְכִי תֵּימָא: דְּכָתַב לָהּ, מַאי לְמֵימְרָא? [3]"מֵתָה אֵינוֹ יוֹרְשָׁהּ" אִיצְטְרִיכָא לֵיהּ.

[4]אֶלָּא, אַבַּיֵי מִגּוּפָהּ דְּמַתְנִיתִין קָא הֲדַר בֵּיהּ. [5]דְּאִי סָלְקָא דַּעְתָּךְ בְּמָקוֹם שֶׁאֵין כּוֹתְבִין כְּתוּבָּה עָסְקִינַן, דְּגֵט הַיְינוּ כְּתוּבָּתָהּ, אַטּוּ גֵּט מָנֶה מָאתַיִם כְּתִיב בֵּיהּ?

[6]וְכִי תֵּימָא: כֵּיוָן דְּתַקִּינוּ רַבָּנַן לְמִגְבָּא לָהּ, כְּמַאן דִּכְתִיב בֵּיהּ דָּמֵי, [7]לִטְעוֹן וְלֵימָא: "פָּרַעְתִּי"!

LITERAL TRANSLATION

he does not inherit her [property]; if he died, she collects her ketubah."

[1]Perhaps [this applies] where he wrote a ketubah for her! [2]And if you say: If he wrote [a ketubah for her, what is there to say? [3]It was necessary to [teach us that] "if she died he does not inherit her [property]."

[4]Rather, Abaye retracted because of the Mishnah itself. [5]For if you imagine that we are dealing with a place where [people] do not write a ketubah, for [her] bill of divorce *is* her ketubah, does a bill of divorce [have] a maneh or 200 [zuz] written in it?

[6]And if you say: Since the Sages ordained that she should collect, it is like something that [had a maneh or 200 zuz] written in it, [7]let [the husband] claim and say: "I paid"!

TERMINOLOGY

מַאי לְמֵימְרָא **What does it mean to say?** An expression used by the Gemara following a seemingly superfluous statement (usually in a Mishnah or a Baraita): "Why was this statement made, since it is obvious?"

RASHI

מתה אינו יורשה – דירושת הבעל נפקא לן מ"שארו הקרוב אליו ממשפחתו וירש אותה וגו'" בבבא בתרא (קיא, ב), והא לאו שארו הוא. **אלא אביי** – דאמר לעיל לאו מילתא היא דאמרי, מגופה דמתניתין דהוציאה גט, משום דהיא גופא קשיא ליה הדר ביה. **דאי סלקא דעתך** – דטעמא לאו משום דאין טוענין אחר מעשה בית דין הוא, אלא משום דגט היינו כתובה. **אטו גט מנה מאתים כתיב ביה** – דנימא הוא מוכיח על החוב. **כמו דכתיב ביה דמי** – דהא פסיקא לן מילתא דכתובה מנה מאתים.

NOTES

here is referring to the period of the year of the Pilgrim Festivals, when all Jews (even those who are not priests) are forbidden to come into contact with dead bodies (unless they are attending the funeral of a close relative), so as to be ritually pure for the approaching Festival.

מֵתָה אֵינוֹ יוֹרְשָׁהּ אִיצְטְרִיכָא לֵיהּ **Rav Ḥiyya bar Ammi's Baraita was necessary to teach us that "if she died, he does not inherit her."** Otherwise, we might have thought that, since the husband does not inherit the betrothed wife's property if she dies, she does not receive her ketubah if he dies (cf. *Ketubot* 89a). Therefore, the Baraita was necessary in order to teach us that the betrothed wife's right to collect her ketubah is not contingent on the husband's right to her property.

TRANSLATION AND COMMENTARY

וְכִי תֵּימָא [1]**And if you say**: The bill of divorce is indeed treated as if it were a ketubah, but the husband cannot claim that he has paid, **because we** (the court) can **say to him**: "**If you have** in fact **paid her, you should have torn** the bill of divorce" — [2]**he can say to us** in reply: "**She would not let me** tear it! **For she said**: 'Do not tear the bill of divorce, because **I want to use it to get married** again, and if you tear it I will not be able to remarry, because the bill of divorce is the only proof I have that I have been divorced!'"

וְכִי תֵּימָא [3]**And if you say**: It is true that the bill of divorce is treated as if it were a ketubah, but we do not accept the husband's claim that he has paid it, because **we say to him**: "**If you** really **did pay** the ketubah, **you should have made a tear** in the bill of divorce **and written on the back of it** the formula used in such circumstances by the court: '**This bill of divorce, in which we have made a tear**, has been

אַטּוּ כָּל דְּמַגְבֵּי בְּבֵי דִינָא מַגְבֵּי [5]Against this argument, says the Gemara, I can answer: **Does everyone who pays** a debt **pay it in court**?! Only a court would write such a statement on a bill of divorce, but not a private person. Thus, the fact that the woman can produce her bill of divorce does not necessarily prove that the husband did *not* pay her ketubah. Yet it is clear that the husband cannot claim that he has paid without himself bringing proof! Accordingly, we can infer that the reason why the wife's claim is favored is because a ketubah is a "court decision," and claims to have paid a Rabbinically ordained "court decision" are *not* accepted, as such ordinances have the status of written promissory notes, even when they are not actually supported by any written documentation.

MISHNAH מָצָא גִּיטֵּי נָשִׁים [6]**If someone finds bills of divorce or writs of emancipation of slaves, wills, deeds**

[1]וְכִי תֵּימָא: דְּאָמְרִינַן לֵיהּ: "אִי פְּרַעְתָּהּ, אִיבָּעֵי לָךְ לְמִיקְרְעֵיהּ", [2]אָמַר לָן: "לָא שְׁבַקְתַּן. אָמְרָה: 'בָּעֵינָא לְאִנְסוּבֵי בֵּיהּ'"! [3]וְכִי תֵּימָא: אָמְרִינַן לֵיהּ: "אִיבָּעֵי לָךְ לְמִיקְרְעֵיהּ וּמִכְתַּב אַגַּבֵּיהּ, 'גִּיטָּא דְּנַן דְּקָרַעֲנוּהוּ, [4]לָא מִשּׁוּם דְּגִיטָּא פְּסוּלָה הוּא. אֶלָּא כִּי הֵיכִי דְּלָא תִּגְבֵּי בֵּיהּ זִמְנָא אַחֲרִיתֵי'". [5]אַטּוּ כָּל דְּמַגְבֵּי בְּבֵי דִינָא מַגְבֵּי?

משנה [6]מָצָא גִּיטֵּי נָשִׁים וְשִׁחְרוּרֵי עֲבָדִים, דְּיַיתִּיקִי,

LITERAL TRANSLATION

[1]And if you say: For we say to him: "If you paid her, you should have torn it," [2]he can say to us, "She would not let me. [For] she said: 'I want to get married [again] with it'"!

[3]And if you say: We say to him: "You should have torn it and written on the back of it, 'This bill of divorce that we have torn, [4]it is not because it is an invalid bill of divorce. Rather it is in order that she will not collect with it another time.'" [5]Does everyone who pays pay in court?

MISHNAH [6][If] one found bills of divorce of women or writs of emancipation of slaves, wills, [deeds of]

RASHI

אטו כל דמגבי בבי דינא מגבי לה – וכי כל הפורע חוב בא לבית דין? במקום שפרע לה לא היו בית דין שיכתבו לו כן.

NOTES

איבעי לך למיקרעיה You should have torn it. The reason why the bill of divorce must be torn, instead of merely writing a note on it that the ketubah has been paid, is that the divorced wife might erase the court's note and attempt to use the bill of divorce to collect her ketubah again (*Hokhmat Manoah, Maharam Schiff*).

גיטי נשים Bills of divorce. The commentators ask: Why does the Mishnah state that a bill of divorce should not be returned to the woman because the husband may have changed his mind? Even if he has not changed his mind, a divorce is only valid if the husband explicitly gives instructions that it be given! *Pnei Yehoshua* explains that the Mishnah is referring to a case where the woman claims that she has already been divorced, and she wants the bill of divorce as proof of her claim. Theoretically her contention seems reasonable, since a woman is more likely to be careless about a bill of divorce which she has already received than her husband would be about a bill of divorce which he has not yet given. Nevertheless, the Mishnah rules that the bill of divorce may not be returned to the woman, because there is a possibility that the husband may have lost it. Even if he originally wanted to give it to his wife, he may have changed his mind later.

מצא דייתיקי If a person finds a will. The Mishnah tells us that we are concerned with the possibility that the writer of the will may have changed his mind and not delivered the will. Therefore, if we were to give it to its designated recipient, he might attempt to collect with it unlawfully.

Meiri asks: Even if the dying man did change his mind, no harm would be done by delivering the will, since a dying man can always change or cancel his will, even after delivery. He answers that we are concerned with the possibility that the dying man may in fact die in the meantime, before he even hears about the discovery of his lost will, and thus not have an opportunity to cancel it. Therefore, the only safe thing for the finder to do is to keep the will until it can be determined who in fact lost it.

TRANSLATION AND COMMENTARY

of gift, or receipts of repayment of loans, [1]**he should not return them** to the people for whom they were written — to the wife, the slave, the recipient, or the debtor — without checking first with the documents' authors. **For**, despite the fact that the authenticity of the documents is not in doubt, the finder should **say**: It is possible that **they were** indeed **written**, and ready for use, **and** then **the person who** caused them to be **written changed his mind about them** and decided **not to give them** to the people for whom they were written. Hence, these documents may not be returned to the recipients specified in them, unless they can prove that they had previously received the documents.

GEMARA טַעְמָא דְּנִמְלַךְ [2]In examining the Mishnah, the Gemara suggests the following inference: **The reason** given in the Mishnah why these documents may not be returned **is that** we suspect that the person who arranged for them to be written may have **changed his mind and decided not to give them**. [3]**Thus** the implication of this is that **if** the finder checked with the author of the document and **he said** to the finder: **"Give them** to the recipient," **we do give** them to the recipient, **even if a long period of time** has elapsed since the documents were lost.

וּרְמִינְהוּ [4]In connection with this inference **a contradiction was raised** from another Mishnah (*Gittin* 3:3,27a): **"If** the husband's agent **was bringing a bill of divorce** to his wife **and** the agent **lost it, if he found it immediately, it is valid; if not, it is invalid,"** since it may not, in fact, be the same document that he lost. Thus, from this Mishnah it would appear that a lost bill of divorce may only be delivered if it was found *immediately* after it was lost, whereas our Mishnah implies that a lost bill of divorce may be returned even if it was found *long after* it was lost, as long as the husband consents!

אָמַר רַבָּה [5]**Rabbah said, There is no** difficulty. **There, the Mishnah** from *Gittin* just cited, which states that a bill of divorce may only be delivered if it was found immediately after it was lost, **refers to a place where caravans pass frequently**. Since large numbers of people ordinarily pass through such an area, the bill of divorce which was found may have been written by another husband with the same name for his wife with the same name (and such a divorce would be invalid if given by the wrong husband). [6]But **here, our Mishnah**, which implies that a lost bill of divorce may be returned after a long period of time (if the husband approves), **is referring to a place where caravans do not pass frequently**. Therefore, there is no reason to assume that the lost bill of divorce may have been written by another person.

מַתָּנָה, וְשׁוֹבְרִין, [1]הֲרֵי זֶה לֹא יַחֲזִיר, שֶׁאֲנִי אוֹמֵר: כְּתוּבִין הָיוּ, וְנִמְלַךְ עֲלֵיהֶן, שֶׁלֹּא לִתְּנָן.
גמרא [2]טַעְמָא דְּנִמְלַךְ שֶׁלֹּא לִתְּנָן. [3]הָא אָמַר: ׳תְּנוּ׳, נוֹתְנִין, וַאֲפִילּוּ לִזְמַן מְרוּבֶּה.
[4]וּרְמִינְהוּ: ״הַמֵּבִיא גֵּט וְאָבַד הֵימֶנּוּ, מְצָאוֹ לְאַלְתַּר, כָּשֵׁר; אִם לָאו, פָּסוּל.
[5]אָמַר רַבָּה: לָא קַשְׁיָא: כָּאן, בְּמָקוֹם שֶׁהַשַּׁיָּירוֹת מְצוּיוֹת; [6]כָּאן, בְּמָקוֹם שֶׁאֵין הַשַּׁיָּירוֹת מְצוּיוֹת.

LITERAL TRANSLATION

gift, or receipts, [1]he should not return [them], for I may say: They were written, and [the person who wrote them] changed his mind about them, [deciding] not to give them.

GEMARA [2]The reason [is] that he [may have] changed his mind [and decided] not to give them. [3]Thus [if] he said: "Give [them]," we give [them], and even after a long [period of] time.

[4]A contradiction was raised: "[If] someone was bringing a bill of divorce and he lost it, [if] he found it immediately, it is valid; if not, it is invalid."

[5]Rabbah said: There is no difficulty: Here, [the Mishnah is referring] to a place where caravans pass frequently; [6]here, [the Mishnah is referring] to a place where caravans do not pass frequently.

RASHI

הא אמר תנו — עכשיו. **נותנין** — ואפילו נמלא לזמן מרובה משנפל, ולא חיישינן שמא גט אחר הוא ששמותיהן שוין, ומאדם אחר נפל.
מצאו לאלתר — התם (גיטין כז,ג) מפרש: כדי שתעבור שיירא ותשרה, ובתוך כך ליכא למימר משיירא שעברה שם נפל, שהרי לא שהה שיעור שתחנה.

LANGUAGE

לְאַלְתַּר Immediately. This word means "immediately," and it is used by the Tannaim although it is an abbreviation of two Aramaic words, עַל אֲתַר, meaning "on the spot." By extension it came to mean something done at once, and the modern Hebrew verb לְאַלְתֵּר — "to improvise" — is taken from it.

NOTES

הָא אָמַר תְּנוּ נוֹתְנִין **If he said, "Give them," we do give them**. *Tosafot* objects, noting that this inference does not necessarily follow from the Mishnah. Even though the Mishnah explains that a lost bill of divorce may not be returned because "the person who wrote it may have changed his mind," the Mishnah may mean the following: Since the husband may have changed his mind, he did not take proper care of the bill of divorce, and lost it; hence, it may not be returned, because it may not be the bill of divorce written by the husband. It may have been written by a person other than the present husband!

Some commentators answer that the Gemara's inference is based upon the Baraita cited below (18b), which explicitly rules that if the husband says, "Give my wife the bill of divorce," we may do so (*Rashba*). Others answer that since the Mishnah mentions other types of documents, where the problem mentioned above does not apply, we may infer that the Mishnah's sole concern is whether or not the owner of the lost document wants it to be returned, as the Gemara inferred here (*Torat Ḥayyim*).

BACKGROUND

חָיְישִׁינַן לִשְׁנֵי שְׁוִירֵי **We are concerned about two Sheviris.** Many countries have more than one city with the same name, and occasionally they are not even very far from each other, so that both of them may actually be on the same river. This is especially true where towns are named after people or are given standard names.

TERMINOLOGY

פּוֹק עַיֵּין בָּהּ **Go out and consider it.** In a courtroom or a House of Study all the Sages assembled and dealt with the subject being considered by the Sage or judge. When one of the Sages present needed to examine or verify something or to review something he had studied, he would have to leave the House of Study and do so by himself.

דִּלְאוּרְתָּא בָּעֵי מִינָּךְ רַב הוּנָא **This evening Rav Huna will ask you about it.** Rav Ḥisda, who was privileged to have been a student of the Amora Rav, was nevertheless a student and colleague of Rav's disciple Rav Huna. Rabbah was much younger than Rav Ḥisda, and was also a student of Rav Huna. Since Rav Ḥisda reckoned that the Halakhah stated here by Rav Huna would be a subject of discussion in the House of Study that evening after the court session, and because Rabbah was a young but exceptionally gifted scholar, Rav Ḥisda assumed that Rav Huna would choose to ask Rabbah whether there was any source for or contradiction to his earlier decision.

LITERAL TRANSLATION

[1]And even in a place where caravans pass frequently, this [applies] where two [people named] Yosef ben Shimon were known [to be living] in one city. [2]For if you do not say this, there will be a difficulty between [one teaching of] Rabbah and [another teaching of] Rabbah. [3]For [with regard to] that bill of divorce which was found in Rav Huna's courtroom, in which it was written: "In the city of Sheviri, on the Rakhis River," [4]Rav Huna said: [18B] We are concerned about two Sheviris. [5]And Rav Ḥisda said to Rabbah: "Go out, consider it, for this evening Rav Huna will ask you [about it]."

[1]וַאֲפִילּוּ בְּמָקוֹם שֶׁהַשַּׁיָּירוֹת מְצוּיוֹת, וְהוּא שֶׁהוּחְזְקוּ שְׁנֵי יוֹסֵף בֶּן שִׁמְעוֹן בְּעִיר אַחַת. [2]דְּאִי לָא תֵּימָא הָכִי, קַשְׁיָא דְּרַבָּה אַדְּרַבָּה. [3]דְּהַהוּא גִּיטָּא דְּאִשְׁתַּכַּח בֵּי דִּינָא דְּרַב הוּנָא, דַּהֲוָה כָּתוּב בֵּיהּ: "בְּשְׁוִירֵי מָתָא, דְּעַל רָכִיס נַהֲרָא," [4]אָמַר רַב הוּנָא: [18B] חָיְישִׁינַן לִשְׁנֵי שְׁוִירֵי. [5]וַאֲמַר לֵיהּ רַב חִסְדָּא לְרַבָּה: "פּוֹק, עַיֵּין בָּהּ, דִּלְאוּרְתָּא בָּעֵי מִינָּךְ רַב הוּנָא".

RASHI

ואפילו במקום כו׳ — לאו רבה קא מסיק, אלא גמרא הוא דקאמר לן, דכי אמר רבה במקום שהשיירות מצויות — לא אמר אלא כשהוחזקו בעיר אחת שנכתב בה הגט שנים ששמותיהן שוין, ושמות נשותיהן שוות. דאי לא תימא הכי — דרבה תרתי בעי, קשיא דרבה אדרבה. בי דינא דרב הונא — במקום שהוא יושב ודן. ומתוך שהכל רגילין אצלו לדון הוי ליה מקום שהשיירות מצויות שם. חיישינן לשני שוירי — אף על פי שבא אחד לפנינו ואמר "ממני נפל, ופלוני היה משלחו לאשתו", ויודעין אנו שאין שם בשוירי שני אנשים ששמותיהן שוין — חיישינן שמא שוירי אחרת יש, ויש בה יוסף בן שמעון אחר. ואמר ליה רב חסדא לרבה — גרסינן.

TRANSLATION AND COMMENTARY

וַאֲפִילּוּ בְּמָקוֹם שֶׁהַשַּׁיָּירוֹת מְצוּיוֹת [1]The Gemara notes: **Even in a place where caravans pass frequently**, it is forbidden to return a lost bill of divorce only **where two people** with the same name — e.g., **Yosef ben Shimon — are known to be living in the city** mentioned in the bill of divorce. Only if there are two men in the city where the bill of divorce was written whose names and whose fathers' names correspond to the names on the bill of divorce and whose wives' names are also the same, do we forbid the bill of divorce from being returned. For only in such a case are there grounds for assuming that the lost bill of divorce may have been written by the other husband with the same name. [2]**For if you do not say this**, but instead assume that wherever caravans pass frequently, a lost bill of divorce may not be returned unless it was found immediately, **a difficulty will arise between one teaching of Rabbah and another teaching of Rabbah.** [3]**For** the following incident was related **regarding a bill of divorce which was found in Rav Huna's courtroom, on which it was written**: "This bill of divorce was written **in the city of Sheviri**, which is **on the Rakhis River.**" The bill of divorce was identified by the husband's agent, who had lost it sometime previously and wished to proceed with the divorce. The question arose as to whether there was any reason to suspect that another husband of the same name had lost a similar bill of divorce in Rav Huna's courtroom. [4]**Rav Huna said**: [18B] **We are concerned about** the possibility that there may be **two** cities named **Sheviri**. According to Rav Huna, even if the agent states that he brought the bill of divorce on behalf of the husband in Sheviri and we know that no one else of the same name as the husband lives in Sheviri, the divorce may not be delivered, because it may belong to another husband bearing the same name who lives in some other city named Sheviri. [5]**And Rav Ḥisda** then **said to Rabbah**, who was a pupil of Rav Huna: "**Go**, and **consider** the matter further, **for this evening Rav Huna will ask you** to explain the basis of this law, in order to test you."

NOTES

וְהוּא שֶׁהוּחְזְקוּ **This applies where two people named Yosef ben Shimon were known to be living in one city.** But if caravans do not pass frequently through this area, the bill of divorce may be returned to the woman, even if two people with the same name were living in the city. Accordingly, the Rishonim ask: Why may the bill of divorce be returned? Perhaps it belongs to the other Yosef ben Shimon? *Tosafot* and *Rosh* answer that in this case we know which "Yosef ben Shimon" lost the bill of divorce, so it is most unlikely that the other Yosef ben Shimon also lost a bill of divorce at the same time.

חָיְישִׁינַן **We are concerned that there may be two Sheviris.** Many commentators read Rav Huna's remark as a question, namely: "Should we be concerned that there may be two Sheviris?" As proof of this interpretation, these commentators note that in the Gemara's discussion below, mention is only made of a dispute between Rabbah and Rabbi Zera, but not of a dispute between Rabbah and Rav Huna (*Shittah Mekubbetzet* and others). Others explain that Rav Huna made this statement in order to test his students, of whom Rabbah was one, to see if they could prove that it was incorrect (ibid.). According to *Gra*, however, this was indeed Rav Huna's opinion.

חָיְישִׁינַן לִשְׁנֵי שְׁוִירֵי **We are concerned that there may be two Sheviris.** Some commentators explain: There may be another place named Sheviri, in which another husband with the same name lives (see *Rabbenu Ḥananel, Tosafot*).

1נְפַק, דַּק, וְאַשְׁכַּח. דִּתְנַן: ״כָּל מַעֲשֵׂה בֵּין דִּין הֲרֵי זֶה יַחֲזִיר״. 2וְהָא בֵּי דִּינָא דְּרַב הוּנָא דְּכִי מָקוֹם שֶׁהַשַּׁיָּירוֹת מְצוּיוֹת דָּמֵי, וְקָא פָּשֵׁיט רַבָּה דְּיַחֲזִיר. 3אַלְמָא: אִי הוּחְזְקוּ שְׁנֵי יוֹסֵף בֶּן שִׁמְעוֹן, אִין; אִי לָא, לָא! 4עֲבַד רַבָּה עוּבְדָא בְּהַהוּא גִּיטָּא דְּאִשְׁתַּכַּח בֵּי כִּיתָּנָא דְּפוּמְבְּדִיתָא כִּשְׁמַעֲתֵיהּ. 5אִיכָּא דְּאָמְרִי: הֵיכָא דְּמְזַבְּנֵי כִּיתָּנָא, וְהוּא שֶׁלֹּא הוּחְזְקוּ, אַף עַל גַּב דִּשְׁכִיחִין שַׁיָּירָתָא. 6וְאִיכָּא

LITERAL TRANSLATION

1He went out, examined [the matter], and found [a source]. For we have learned [in a Mishnah]: "Any decision of a court shall be returned."

2But surely Rav Huna's court is considered like a place where caravans pass frequently, and Rabbah decided that [the finder] should return [the bill of divorce]. 3Hence: If two [people named] Yosef ben Shimon were known [to be living in one city], yes; if not, no!

4Rabbah decided a case involving a certain bill of divorce which was found in the linen-house of Pumbedita in accordance with his teaching. 5There are some who say: Where they sell linen, and where [two people of the same name] were not known [to be living in the place], even though caravans passed by frequently. 6And there are

TRANSLATION AND COMMENTARY

1Rabbah **went out** of the study hall, **examined the matter** carefully, **and found a source** dealing with this matter. **For we have learned in the** following **Mishnah** (below, 20a): "**Any decision of a court**, i.e., any court-certified document which is lost and later found, including a bill of divorce bearing court-certification, such as the one found in Rav Huna's court, **shall be returned**." Rabbah's conclusion was, therefore, that the bill of divorce should be returned.

וְהָא בֵּי דִּינָא דְּרַב הוּנָא 2**But surely**, continues the Gemara, **Rav Huna's court is considered like a place where caravans pass frequently**, since many people from many different places frequented his court, **and** nevertheless **Rabbah decided that the finder should return the bill of divorce**, as explained above, even though he ruled elsewhere (above, 18a) that a lost bill of divorce may not be returned where caravans pass frequently! 3**Hence** we may infer that, according to Rabbah, only **if two people named Yosef ben Shimon were known to be living in the city** where the bill of divorce was written, is there room for concern, and the bill of divorce may not be returned, even if caravans pass frequently. But **if** two people with the same name were **not** known to be living in the place where the bill of divorce was written, there is **no** reason not to return the lost bill of divorce. In other words, Rabbah required *two* conditions to be fulfilled for the bill of divorce *not* to be returned: (1) It had to be lost in a place frequented by many people, and (2) the husband and wife had to live in a place where at least one other couple bore the same names as they — "two men called Yosef ben Shimon."

עֲבַד רַבָּה עוּבְדָא 4**Rabbah decided a case involving a bill of divorce which was found in the linen-house of Pumbedita in accordance with his teaching**, and he ordered that the bill of divorce be returned. 5Regarding the exact details of this case, **there are some who say**: The bill of divorce was found in a place **where** people **sell linen, and** it was a situation **where two people of the same name were not known to be living in the place** where the bill of divorce was written, **even though caravans passed by frequently** there, since many people came to buy linen in the linen-house. 6**And there are some who say**: The bill of divorce was found in a place **where** people

RASHI

כל מעשה בית דין הרי זה יחזיר – כל מילתא דאתא לבית דין לקיים דליכא למיחש לנמלך עליהן שלא ליתנן – הרי זה יחזיר, וזה מקוים בבית דין היה, ולכך הוצא שם. **כשמעתיה** – דבעינן תרתי. והכא חדא הוא דהואי, ואכשריה. **היכא דמזבני כיתנא** – דשיירות מצויות שם לבא ולקנות, ואהדריה משום דלא הוחזקו שני יוסף בן שמעון בעיר שנכתב בה, ולא חיישינן לומר יש עיר אחרת ששמה כזו.

NOTES

כָּל מַעֲשֵׂה בֵּין דִּין **Any decision of the court**. Some commentators ask: Ordinarily, laws regarding ritual matters (e.g., the validity of a bill of divorce) cannot be deduced from laws governing monetary matters. How, then, did Rabbah conclude from the Mishnah (20a) which states that "any decision of the court may be returned" that a lost bill of divorce is valid? *Talmid Rabbenu Peretz* answers that, since the Mishnah there also speaks of *ḥalitzah* documents, bills of divorce are presumably governed by the same principle.

בֵּי דִּינָא דְּרַב הוּנָא **Rav Huna's court**. Some commentators explain that the reference to Rav Huna's court is not to be taken literally. The same ruling would apply to any court, since, even though other courts are not frequented quite as much as Rav Huna's, they are still open to the public. The proof of this position is that Rabbah based his argument on the fact that the Mishnah speaks of "any decision of a court." It is also possible that "the court of Rav Huna" was mentioned simply because the bill of divorce in question was in fact found there (*Shittah Mekubbetzet, Ma'ayan HaḤokhmah*).

BACKGROUND

דְּתָרוּ כִּיתָּנָא **Where they steep flax**. One of the processes in preparing stalks of flax to make linen thread is to soak them in water for a long time so that the wooden part of the stalks will rot, and then one can easily remove the fibers from them. This process creates a most unpleasant odor, and this would explain why few people would spend time in the vicinity.

TERMINOLOGY

רָמֵי **Raises a contradiction** (lit., "casts"). I.e., he raises a contradiction between two sources of equal authority — for example, two Mishnayot, a Mishnah and a Baraita, two Baraitot, or two Biblical verses — or between two statements made by the same authority.

TRANSLATION AND COMMENTARY

steep flax, and even though two people of the same name were known to be living in the place where the bill of divorce was written, Rabbah nevertheless ruled that the bill of divorce was to be returned, **because caravans did not pass by** there **frequently**, for few people would frequent such a linen-house. According to each of these versions, only one of the two conditions required by Rabbah for not returning the bill of divorce was present, and Rabbah ordered the bill of divorce to be returned.

רַבִּי זֵירָא [1]**Rabbi Zera** made a similar distinction to that made by Rabbah by **raising a contradiction between the Mishnah** in *Gittin* **and a Baraita and by resolving it**: [2]**We have learned in the Mishnah** in *Gittin* quoted above (18a): "**If the** husband's agent **was bringing a bill of divorce** to his wife **and** the agent **lost it, if he found it immediately, it is valid; and if not, it is invalid**," since it may have been lost by another husband of the same name. [3]**A contradiction can be raised** against this Mishnah from the following Baraita: "**If someone found a woman's bill of divorce in the marketplace, when the husband admits** that he ordered it to be written, **the finder may return it to the woman.** [4]**If the husband does not admit** that he ordered it to be written, **the finder may not return it either**

דְּאָמְרִי: הֵיכָא דְּתָרוּ כִּיתָּנָא, וְאַף עַל גַּב דְּהוּחְזְקוּ, דְּלָא שְׁכִיחָא שַׁיָּירוֹת.

[1]רַבִּי זֵירָא רָמֵי מַתְנִיתִין אַבָּרַיְיתָא וּמְשַׁנֵּי: [2]תְּנַן: "הַמֵּבִיא גֵּט וְאָבַד הֵימֶנּוּ, מְצָאוֹ לְאַלְתַּר, כָּשֵׁר; וְאִם לָאו, פָּסוּל". [3]וּרְמִינְהִי: "מָצָא גֵּט אִשָּׁה בַּשּׁוּק, בִּזְמַן שֶׁהַבַּעַל מוֹדֶה, יַחֲזִיר לָאִשָּׁה. [4]אֵין הַבַּעַל מוֹדֶה, לֹא יַחֲזִיר לֹא לָזֶה

LITERAL TRANSLATION

some who say: Where they steep flax, and even though [two people of the same name] were known [to be living in the place], for caravans did not pass by frequently.

[1]Rabbi Zera raised a contradiction between a Mishnah and a Baraita and resolved it. [2]We have learned [in a Mishnah]: "[If] someone was bringing a bill of divorce and he lost it, [if] he found it immediately, it is valid; and if not, it is invalid." [3]A contradiction can be raised: "[If] one found a woman's bill of divorce in the marketplace, when the husband admits [that he wrote it], [the finder] may return it to the woman. [4][If] the husband does not admit [that he wrote it, the finder] may not return it, neither to this one

RASHI

ואיכא דאמרי היכא דתרו כיתנא — במי המשרה, שם נמלא הגט. **ומאי כשמעתיה** — שהוחזקו שני יוסף בן שמעון באותה עיר שנכתב בה ולאכשריה, דבמקום שנמלא בו לא היו שיירות מלויות.

NOTES

הֵיכָא דְּתָרוּ כִּיתָּנָא **Where people steep flax**. This explanation was necessary in order to teach us that there may be parts of a city where caravans pass frequently, and other parts where caravans do not pass, and these different parts of the city are governed by different rules if a bill of divorce is found there. Thus, if caravans do not pass frequently through part of the city, a lost bill of divorce found there may be returned, even though caravans pass frequently through other parts of the city. (*Ritva*.)

רָמֵי מַתְנִיתִין אַבָּרַיְיתָא **Rabbi Zera raised a contradiction between the Mishnah and a Baraita**. Even though a similar contradiction could have been raised on the basis of another Mishnah (below, 20a), Rabbi Zera preferred to raise a contradiction from the Baraita, since it explicitly mentions bills of divorce.

לֹא יַחֲזִיר לֹא לָזֶה וְלֹא לָזֶה **The finder may not return the bill of divorce either to the husband or to the wife.** The bill of divorce may not be returned to the wife, because it might

HALAKHAH

אָבַד גֵּט וְנִמְצָא לְאַלְתַּר **A bill of divorce that was lost, and found immediately afterwards.** "If someone lost a bill of divorce in a place where caravans pass frequently, the bill of divorce may only be returned if it was found immediately after it was lost, or if it bears an identifying mark. Similarly, if caravans do not frequently pass through the area where the bill of divorce was lost, but it was written in a city where another husband with the same name lives (and his wife has the same name as the first husband's wife), the bill of divorce may only be returned if it was found immediately after it was lost, or if it bears an identifying mark. However, if two husbands with the same name do not live in the place where the bill of divorce was written, and caravans do not frequently pass through the area where the bill of divorce was lost, it may be returned, even if it was not found immediately after it was lost (*Rif* and *Rosh*, following Rabbi Zera, against Rabbah). Others rule that if the bill of divorce was lost in an area through which caravans do not pass frequently, it may be returned, even if another man with the same name as the first husband was known to be living in the place where the bill of divorce was written. In an area where caravans pass frequently, the bill of divorce may only be returned if it was found immediately after it was lost, or if it bears an identifying mark," according to *Rambam*, who follows Rabbi Zera's view, but interprets his opinion differently. (*Shulḥan Arukh, Even HaEzer* 132:4.)

מָצָא גֵּט וְהַבַּעַל מוֹדֶה **If a person found a bill of divorce and the husband admits that he wrote it**. "If a woman's bill of divorce was found in the marketplace, even if it has no identifying marks, it may be returned to the woman in order to divorce her, provided that the husband admits that he ordered it to be written; otherwise, it may not be returned either to the husband or to the wife," following the Baraita. (Ibid., 153:1.)

TRANSLATION AND COMMENTARY

to the husband or to the wife." [1]**At all events the Baraita teaches: "When the husband admits, the finder may return it to the woman," and** this implies that he should do so **even** if it was found **after a long time** had elapsed! Hence we do not suspect that it may have been written by another husband.

וּמְשַׁנֵּי [2]**And** Rabbi Zera **resolved** the contradiction as follows: **There,** in **the Mishnah,** which states that the lost bill of divorce may only be returned if it was found immediately after it was lost, it **is referring to a place where caravans pass frequently.** [3]**But here,** in **the Baraita,** which states that the bill of divorce may be returned, it **is referring to a place where caravans do not pass frequently.**

אִיכָּא דְּאָמְרִי [4]**There are some who say:** According to Rabbi Zera, **it is only** (1) **where two people of the same name are known to be living in the place** where the bill of divorce was written and (2) where the bill of divorce was found in a place where caravans pass frequently **that the finder may not return the lost bill of divorce.** [5]**And** according to **this** interpretation, Rabbi Zera's view **is the same as Rabbah's.** [6]But **there are some who say:** According to Rabbi Zera, **even though two people of the same name are not known to be living in the place** where the bill of divorce was written, **the finder may not return the lost bill of divorce,** if it was found in a place where caravans pass frequently, [7]**and this** interpretation of Rabbi Zera's view **disagrees with** that of **Rabbah.**

בִּשְׁלָמָא [8]The Gemara now examines the reasons why Rabbi Zera and Rabbah used different Tannaitic sources to draw their respective conclusions as to the meaning of our Mishnah and the Mishnah in *Gittin* quoted above: **I can understand why Rabbah,** who arrived at his opinion by reconciling our Mishnah with the Mishnah in *Gittin,* **did not use the same argument as Rabbi Zera,** who arrived at his opinion by reconciling the Mishnah in *Gittin* with a Baraita from that tractate, because **the Mishnah is a better source for raising difficulties** and resolving them. Rabbah preferred to base his view on the reconciliation of a contradiction between two

וְלֹא לָזֶה״. [1]קָתָנֵי מִיהַת: ״בִּזְמַן שֶׁהַבַּעַל מוֹדֶה, יַחֲזִיר לָאִשָּׁה״, וַאֲפִילּוּ לִזְמַן מְרוּבֶּה!

[2]וּמְשַׁנֵּי: כָּאן, בְּמָקוֹם שֶׁהַשַּׁיָּירוֹת מְצוּיוֹת. [3]וְכָאן, בְּמָקוֹם שֶׁאֵין הַשַּׁיָּירוֹת מְצוּיוֹת.

[4]אִיכָּא דְּאָמְרִי: וְהוּא שֶׁהוּחְזְקוּ דְּלָא נְהֲדַר, [5]וְהַיְינוּ דְּרַבָּה. [6]אִיכָּא דְּאָמְרִי: אַף עַל גַּב דְּלָא הוּחְזְקוּ, לָא נְהֲדַר, [7]וּפְלִיגָא דְּרַבָּה.

[8]בִּשְׁלָמָא רַבָּה לָא אֲמַר כְּרַבִּי זֵירָא: מַתְנִיתִין אַלִּימָא לֵיהּ

LITERAL TRANSLATION

nor to this one." [1]At all events [the Baraita] teaches: "When the husband admits, [the finder] may return it to the woman," and even after a long time!

[2]And he resolved [it]: Here, [the Mishnah refers] to a place where caravans pass frequently. [3]But here, [the Baraita refers] to a place where caravans do not pass frequently.

[4]There are some who say: It is [only] where [two people of the same name] are known [to be living in the place] that [the finder] may not return [the lost bill of divorce], [5]and this is the same as Rabbah's [view]. [6]There are some who say: Even though [two people of the same name] are not known [to be living in the place, the finder] may not return [the lost bill of divorce], [7]and this disagrees with Rabbah.

[8]Granted that Rabbah did not say like Rabbi Zera: The Mishnah is better (lit., "stronger")

RASHI

בשלמא רבה – דאמר שינויא ארומיא דמתניתין דגיטין אמתניתין דנזיקין. **לא אמר כרבי זירא** – דרמא מתניתין אברייתא. **דמתניתין אלימא ליה לאקשויי** – משום דהיא עיקר, ויש תימה כשסותרות זו את זו, וצריך לחזור שיתיישבו. דאילו ברייתא – יש לומר אינה עיקר, רבי לא שנאה רבי חייא מניין לו.

TERMINOLOGY

מַתְנִיתִין אַלִּימָא לֵיהּ **The Mishnah is better for raising a difficulty.** Although Baraitot, Tannaitic teachings not included in the Mishnah, are authoritative (so that there is good reason for pointing out contradictions between Mishnayot and Baraitot), nevertheless a Mishnah is a preferred source in every respect. This is because its wording was carefully verified. Baraitot, on the other hand, did not always come from an edited collection of teachings and were occasionally transmitted inaccurately. Another reason for using a Mishnah as a preferred source was because the Mishnah was accepted as Halakhically authoritative, and evidence taken from it was stronger.

NOTES

not have been given to her, and she might never have been divorced with it. Nor may it be returned to the husband, because the wife may have been divorced with it, and when she comes to claim her ketubah, the husband will produce the bill of divorce to attempt to prove that he has already paid her (*Rashi, Gittin* 27a). Others explain that the bill of divorce may not be returned to the husband because it may be invalid, and the husband may use it to divorce his wife at a later date (*Rashba*; cf. Jerusalem Talmud).

HALAKHAH

הַחֲזָרַת גֵּט לְאַחַר זְמַן **Returning a bill of divorce that was found long after it was lost.** "If the person delivering a bill of divorce lost it in an area where caravans pass frequently, or if two husbands with the same name lived in the city where the bill of divorce was written, the bill of divorce may be returned, provided that it bears a distinctive identifying mark (or if the owner recognizes it), even if it was found long after it was lost. Similarly, the bill of divorce may be returned if the witnesses who signed it testify that this was the only divorce they ever signed containing the names of the husband and wife appearing therein," following Rav Ashi and Rabbi Yirmeyah. (*Shulḥan Arukh, Even HaEzer* 132:4.)

לְאַקְשׁוּיֵי.

[1] אֶלָּא רַבִּי זֵירָא, מַאי טַעְמָא לֹא אָמַר כְּרַבָּה?

[2] אָמַר לָךְ: מִי קָא תָּנֵי: ״הָא אֲמַר ׳תְּנוּ׳, נוֹתְנִין, וַאֲפִילּוּ לִזְמַן מְרוּבֶּה״? [3] דִּלְמָא: ״הָא אָמַר ׳תְּנוּ׳, נוֹתְנִין״ — וּלְעוֹלָם כִּדְקַיְימָא לָן, לְאַלְתַּר!

[4] לְמַאן דַּאֲמַר לְרַבִּי זֵירָא בְּמָקוֹם שֶׁהַשַּׁיָּירוֹת מְצוּיוֹת, וְאַף עַל גַּב שֶׁלֹּא הוּחְזְקוּ שְׁנֵי יוֹסֵף בֶּן שִׁמְעוֹן, [5] וּפְלִיגָא דְּרַבָּה, בְּמַאי קָא מִיפַּלְגִי?

[6] רַבָּה סָבַר: דְּקָתָנֵי ״כָּל מַעֲשֵׂה בֵּית דִּין הֲרֵי זֶה יַחֲזִיר״ — דְּאִשְׁתַּכַּח בְּבֵית דִּין עָסְקִינַן, וּבֵית דִּין כְּמָקוֹם שֶׁהַשַּׁיָּירוֹת מְצוּיוֹת. [7] וְהוּא שֶׁהוּחְזְקוּ, לֹא יַחֲזִיר. [8] לֹא הוּחְזְקוּ, יַחֲזִיר.

LITERAL TRANSLATION

for raising a difficulty.

[1] But Rabbi Zera, what is the reason that he did not say like Rabbah?

[2] He can say to you: Does [the Mishnah] teach: "But if he said: 'Give,' we give, and even after a long time"? [3] Perhaps [it means]: "But if he said: 'Give,' we give" — but in fact, immediately, according to [the view] accepted by us!

[4] [According] to the one who says [that] in Rabbi Zera's [opinion a lost bill of divorce may not be returned] in a place where caravans pass frequently, and even though two [people named] Yosef ben Shimon were not known [to be living in the place], [5] and [that Rabbi Zera] disagrees with Rabbah, regarding what do they disagree? [6] Rabbah maintains that [when the Mishnah] teaches: "Any decision of a court shall be returned," we are dealing with [a case] where [the bill of divorce] was found in a courtroom, and a courtroom is [considered] like a place where caravans pass frequently. [7] And it is [only in a case] where [two people of the same name] were known [to be living in the place where the bill of divorce was written] that [the finder] may not return [it]. [8] [But if two people of the same name] were not known [to be living there, the finder] may return it.

TRANSLATION AND COMMENTARY

Mishnayot, since Baraitot are not always fully reliable as Halakhic source texts.

אֶלָּא רַבִּי זֵירָא [1] **But why did Rabbi Zera not use the same argument as Rabbah**? Why did Rabbi Zera prefer to base his opinion on the reconciliation of a contradiction between the Mishnah in *Gittin* and the Baraita there, rather than on the reconciliation of a contradiction between two Mishnayot, which were edited by the same person, Rabbi Yehudah HaNasi?

אָמַר לָךְ [2] The Gemara answers: Rabbi Zera **can say to you**: **Does our Mishnah** cited by Rabbah explicitly **teach**: **"But if** the husband **said** to the finder of the bill of divorce: '**Give** the bill of divorce to my wife,' **we give** it?" If the Mishnah had said this, you would be justified in deducing that there is no distinction made between a bill of divorce found immediately and one that was found **even a long time** after it was lost. But in fact our Mishnah says nothing about when the bill of divorce should be returned. It only lays down when it should *not* be returned. [3] **Perhaps** the Mishnah **means**: **"But if** the husband **said**, '**Give** the bill of divorce to my wife,' **we give** it" — **but in fact** we give it to the wife only if it was found **immediately** after it was lost, **following the accepted** view in the Mishnah in *Gittin*! Thus Rabbi Zera preferred to base his view on his reconciliation of the contradiction between the Mishnah in *Gittin* and the Baraita, because the Baraita explicitly refers to the circumstances under which the bill of divorce is to be returned.

לְמַאן דַּאֲמַר [4] The Gemara now asks: **According to** the authority **who says that, in Rabbi Zera's opinion, a lost bill of divorce may not be returned in a place where caravans pass frequently, even though two people named Yosef ben Shimon were not known to be living in the place** where the bill of divorce was written, [5] **and that Rabbi Zera disagrees with Rabbah**, **regarding what do** Rabbah and Rabbi Zera **disagree**? What is the basis of their difference of opinion?

רַבָּה סָבַר [6] The Gemara answers: **Rabbah maintains that when the Mishnah teaches**: **"Any decision of a court** (i.e., any court-certified document that is lost and later found, including a court-certified bill of divorce) **shall be returned," it is dealing with a bill of divorce that was found in a courtroom, and a courtroom is considered like a place where caravans pass frequently**. But what about our concern that someone else may have lost the document? Evidently it does not apply here. [7] From this Rabbah inferred that **it is only in a case where two people of the same name were known to be living in the place where the bill of divorce was written that the finder may not return** the bill of divorce. [8] **But if two people of the same name were not known to be living** in the place where the bill of divorce was written, **the finder may return** the bill of divorce, even though caravans pass by frequently.

RASHI

ולעולם כדקיימא לן כשנמצא לאלתר — ואם לאו פסול, שמא אינו של זה. **אבל ברייתא** — ליכא לשנויי הכי, דכיון דתנא בהדיא "יחזיר לאשה" — הוה ליה לפלוגי בין לאלתר בין לזמן מרובה. דלא דמיא למתניתין דהתם לא יחזיר תנא, ומדוקיא הוה דייק יחזיר היכא דאמר "תנו", וכיון דלא תנא "יחזיר" — לא הוה ליה לפלוגי.

TRANSLATION AND COMMENTARY

וְרַבִּי זֵירָא [1]The Gemara asks: **And Rabbi Zera**? How does he explain the reference in the Mishnah to the court?

אָמַר לָךְ [2]The Gemara answers: **Rabbi Zera can say to you**: **Does the Mishnah teach**: "Any decision of a court **found in a court** shall be returned"? **It** merely **teaches**: "**Any decision of a court shall be returned**"! [3]**And in fact** Rabbi Zera would explain that **the Mishnah refers to a bill of divorce**, or any other court-decision, **that was found outside the court**, in a place where caravans do not pass frequently. Accordingly, Rabbi Zera ruled that if the bill of divorce were found in a courtroom or anywhere where caravans pass frequently, the bill of divorce may not be returned, even if it is certain that no other person with the same name as the husband lives in the place where the bill of divorce was written.

רַבִּי יִרְמְיָה אָמַר [4]**Rabbi Yirmeyah** gave a different explanation of the circumstances dealt with in the Baraita and **said**: **The Baraita**, which states that where the husband admits the authenticity of the lost bill of divorce it may be returned, **refers to a case where, for example, the witnesses said**: "**We have only ever signed one bill of divorce** bearing the name **of Yosef ben Shimon**." Only in such a case, where there is no basis for assuming that the lost bill of divorce may have been written by another husband, is the bill of divorce to be returned.

אִי הָכִי [5]The Gemara objects: **If so**, if this is the situation referred to by the Baraita, **what** need **is there to say** that the bill of divorce is to be returned? Surely it is obvious that the bill of divorce may be returned in such a case!

מַהוּ דְּתֵימָא [6]The Gemara answers: **You might have said that we should be concerned in case there was a possibility that there might be another person with** the same **name as this husband's name, and** another pair of **witnesses with the same names as his witnesses**. Perhaps the lost bill of divorce was written by a different husband with the same name as the present husband for a wife with the same name as the present wife, and signed by different witnesses with the same names as the present witnesses, and hence it should not be returned! [7]Therefore, the Baraita **teaches us** that we need not be concerned about such a remote possibility, and the lost bill of divorce may safely be returned.

רַב אַשִׁי [8]**Rav Ashi** gave a different explanation of the circumstances dealt with in the Baraita and **said**: **The Baraita**, which states that where the husband admits the authenticity of the lost bill of divorce it may be returned, **refers to a case where, for example**, the husband or the agent **said**: "**There is** a clear identifying mark

[1]וְרַבִּי זֵירָא? [2]אָמַר לָךְ: מִי קָתָנֵי ״כָּל מַעֲשֵׂה בֵּית דִּין שֶׁנִּמְצְאוּ בְּבֵית דִּין״? ״כָּל מַעֲשֵׂה בֵּית דִּין יַחֲזִיר״ קָתָנֵי, [3]וּלְעוֹלָם דְּאִשְׁתַּכַּח אַבְּרַאי.
[4]רַבִּי יִרְמְיָה אָמַר: כְּגוֹן דְּקָא אָמְרִי עֵדִים: ״מֵעוֹלָם לֹא חָתַמְנוּ אֶלָּא עַל גֵּט אֶחָד שֶׁל יוֹסֵף בֶּן שִׁמְעוֹן״.
[5]אִי הָכִי, מַאי לְמֵימְרָא?
[6]מַהוּ דְּתֵימָא: לֵיחוּשׁ דִּלְמָא אִתְרַמִי שְׁמָא כִּשְׁמָא, וְעֵדִים כְּעֵדִים. [7]קָא מַשְׁמַע לָן.
[8]רַב אַשִׁי אָמַר: כְּגוֹן דְּקָא אָמַר: ״נֶקֶב יֵשׁ בּוֹ בְּצַד אוֹת

LITERAL TRANSLATION

[1]And Rabbi Zera?

[2]He can say to you: Does [the Mishnah] teach: "Any decision of a court found in a court"? It teaches: "Any decision of a court shall be returned," [3]and in fact [the Mishnah refers to a case] where [the bill of divorce] was found outside [the court].

[4]Rabbi Yirmeyah said: [The Baraita refers to a case] where, for example, witnesses say: "We only ever signed one bill of divorce of Yosef ben Shimon."

[5]If so, what is there to say?

[6]You might have said: Let us be concerned that perhaps there chanced to be [another person with] a name like [this husband's] name, and witnesses [with the same names] as his witnesses. [7][Therefore, the Baraita] teaches us [that we are not concerned about this].

[8]Rav Ashi said: [The Baraita refers to a case] where, for example, he said: "There is a hole in it, next to a certain

RASHI

דאשתכח אבראי – שאין השיירות מצויות. **רבי ירמיה אמר** – הא דקתני ״יחזיר״ – כגון דאמרי עדים החתומין בו ״מעולם לא חתמנו״ כו׳.

BACKGROUND

שְׁמָא כִּשְׁמָא With a name like this name. In every large population center there is a good chance of finding people (even couples) who have the same names. If we also bear in mind the fact that Jews did not use family names (but were called by their fathers' names), and that some names (as seen from lists of the Talmudic Sages) were very common, we see that the chances of such a case occurring are remote but not impossible.

NOTES

שְׁמָא כִּשְׁמָא וְעֵדִים כְּעֵדִים Perhaps the husbands and the witnesses had the same names. The Rishonim reject the possibility that we would go even further and assume that the two pairs of witnesses had the same handwriting. Such a possibility, of course, is exceedingly remote (see *Shittah Mekubbetzet*).

דְּקָאָמַר נֶקֶב Where he said (דְּקָאָמַר): "**There is a hole.**" Others read: "Where **they** said (דְּקָאָמְרִי): There is a hole," i.e., where the witnesses said that there was a hole. Witnesses are believed even if they testify *after* they have seen the lost bill of divorce that they recognize it by a hole in it, whereas the husband, or someone else who brings the bill of divorce to

פְּלוֹנִית״. [1]וְדַוְקָא בְּצַד אוֹת פְּלוֹנִית, אֲבָל נֶקֶב בְּעָלְמָא, לָא.

[2]רַב אַשִׁי מִסַּפְּקָא לֵיהּ סִימָנִים, אִי דְּאוֹרָיְיתָא אִי דְּרַבָּנַן.

[3]רַבָּה בַּר בַּר חָנָה [19A] אִירְכַּס לֵיהּ גִּיטָּא בֵּי מִדְרָשָׁא. [4]אֲמַר: ״אִי סִימָנָא, אִית לִי

LITERAL TRANSLATION

letter." [1]And only [if he says] next to a certain letter, but just a hole, no.

[2]Rav Ashi was in doubt [whether] identifying marks [are valid according] to Torah law or [according] to Rabbinic law.

[3]Rabbah bar Bar Ḥanah [19A] lost a bill of divorce in the House of Study. [4]He said: "If [you prefer] an identifying mark, I have one on it.

TRANSLATION AND COMMENTARY

that I can name, for example, **a hole next to a certain letter**, in the bill of divorce." [1]The Gemara adds: **Only** if the husband **says** that the hole appears **next to a certain letter** may the bill of divorce be returned, since such precise identification is judged conclusive. **But** if the husband **just** says that there is **a hole** somewhere on the bill of divorce, without indicating precisely where it is to be found, even though this would ordinarily be sufficient identification in property cases, it does **not** constitute conclusive identification for a bill of divorce, and the bill of divorce may not be returned.

רַב אַשִׁי מִסַּפְּקָא לֵיהּ [2]The Gemara explains: **Rav Ashi was in doubt** as to whether a claim for the return of lost property based on ordinary, non-specific **identifying marks is valid according to Torah law or Rabbinic law**. Rav Ashi was not certain whether the law stating that lost objects may be returned to their rightful owner on the basis of identifying marks applies according to the Torah or only by Rabbinical decree. Since a bill of divorce affects the woman's marital status (unlike other lost objects, where the interest of the owner is monetary only), Rav Ashi ruled that it may only be returned if it bears clear and definite identification marks, which are certainly valid by Torah law.

רַבָּה בַּר בַּר חָנָה [3]**Rabbah bar Bar Ḥanah** [19A] **lost a bill of divorce**, which he was delivering for someone else, **in the House of Study**, and it was later found. [4]**He said** to the people who found it: **"If you prefer an** ordinary, non-specific **identifying mark** in order to return the bill of divorce to me, **I** know of such a mark

RASHI

ודוקא בצד אות פלונית — דהוה ליה סימן מובהק. ואפילו אם תימצי לומר גבי חזרת אבידה בסימנין, דאיבעיא לן לקמן (כז,א): דאורייתא או דרבנן — אפילו פשטת סימנין דרבנן, יש לסמוך על סימן מובהק כזה למשרי אשת איש דאורייתא. **מספקא ליה לרב אשי סימנין** — שמחזירין בהן אבידה, אי דאורייתא היא, ואפילו באיסור דאורייתא סמכינן אסימן כל דהוא. **אי דרבנן** — ודוקא באבידה, שהפקר בית דין הפקר. אבל במידי דאיסורא — לא סמכינן. ואי קשיא: נימא הכי קסבר סימנין דרבנן, ונפשוט בעיין דלקמן! לאו פירכא הוא. דמנלן דפשיטא ליה? אי נמי מספקא ליה אית עליה למיסר מספיקא. **אירכס ליה גיטא** — שהיה שליח להביא, ואירכס ליה, ואשכחוהו. **אמר אי סימנא** — חשיבא לכו, אית לי בגויה סימנא.

SAGES

רַבָּה בַּר בַּר חָנָה Rabbah bar Bar Ḥanah. An Amora of the third generation, he was a student of Rabbi Yoḥanan. He was apparently born in Babylonia, emigrated to study Torah in Eretz Israel, and wandered in many lands. He transmitted teachings in the name of Rabbi Yoḥanan, his teacher, as well as in the name of Rabbi Yehoshua ben Levi, Resh Lakish, and Rabbi Elazar; he was also a student of Rabbi Yoshiah of Usha. One of his sons, Rabbi Yitzḥak, was a Sage. Rabbah bar Bar Ḥanah tells many stories of the wonders he saw in his travels.

NOTES

the wife, is believed only if he testifies to the identifying mark *before* he sees the lost bill of divorce (*Talmid Rabbenu Peretz* and others).

סִימָנִים Identifying marks. When a person finds a lost object, he is directed to return it to its owner (Deuteronomy 22:1-3). In ascertaining ownership, three methods are acceptable. (1) The claimant cites an ordinary distinguishing mark, like shape or color, or states that the document has a hole in it. (2) The claimant cites a conclusive distinguishing mark, such as a hole next to a particular letter. (3) The claimant looks at the object and recognizes it. The second method is valid by Torah law, and can be used even in cases bearing on marital status. The third method is also valid by Torah law, subject to a determination that the claimant is not lying. The first method is valid by Rabbinic law, but it may not be sufficient by Torah law, and thus it may not be acceptable in cases bearing on marital status.

סִימָנִים דְּרַבָּנַן Rav Ashi was in doubt whether identifying marks are valid only according to Rabbinic law. *Rashi* and most of the Rishonim explain that Rabbinically valid evidence is accepted regarding lost objects, because we have a general principle that the Rabbis were authorized by the Torah to transfer property from one person to another as they saw fit (הֶפְקֵר בֵּית דִּין הֶפְקֵר). Based on this principle, the Rabbis could override the laws of the Torah in monetary matters. However, the primary purpose of a bill of divorce is to change the woman's marital status. Hence, the returning of a lost bill of divorce is essentially a ritual, not a monetary matter, and only evidence that is acceptable according to Torah law may be used.

Some of the later commentators question whether, according to Torah law, there is any need to concern ourselves with the possiblity that the lost bill of divorce may belong to a different husband with the same name. Hence we may ask: Even if ordinary identifying marks are valid only according to Rabbinic law, they should suffice to warrant returning the bill in such a case, since it was the Rabbis and not the Torah who forbade returning it in the first place!

Some commentators answer that we have a general rule that Rabbinical decrees are modelled after Torah law and are usually subject to the same regulations. Therefore, only evidence that is acceptable according to Torah law may be used (*Ḥokhmat Manoaḥ*). Others point out that while our particular concern here is merely Rabbinic, bills of divorce are a Torah concept, and we frequently find that Rabbinic details of Torah laws are dealt with in accordance with the strict Torah law (*Pnei Yehoshua* on *Gittin* 27a, *Yeshuot Ya'akov*).

TRANSLATION AND COMMENTARY

on this bill of divorce. [1]**If you prefer recognition by sight** in order to return the bill of divorce to me, **I** do recognize it by sight." [2]The Rabbis **returned it to him.** [3]**He said: I do not know whether they returned it to me because of the** non-specific **identifying mark** I gave, **and they maintain that** ordinary **identifying marks** enable lost property to be returned to its claimant even **according to Torah law,** [4]**or whether they returned it to me** only **because I recognized it by sight.** [5]If the latter was the reason, it would apply **only** because I happen to be **a Rabbinical scholar** and I am trusted not to lie, [6]**but an ordinary person,** who cannot necessarily be trusted, would **not** have been able to recover the bill of divorce unless he brought witnesses or cited a conclusive identifying mark, such as a hole next to a particular letter, in support of his claim.

גּוּפָא [7]**Returning to the subject** cited above (18b): "**If someone found a woman's bill of divorce in the marketplace, when the husband admits that he** ordered it to be **written, the finder may return it to the woman.** [8]**If the husband does not admit that he** ordered it to be **written, the finder may not return** the bill of divorce **either to the** husband **or to the** wife." [9]**At all events,** says the Gemara, **when the husband admits** the authenticity of the bill of divorce, **the finder may return it to the woman.**

בְּגַוֵּיהּ. [1]אִי טְבִיעוּת עֵינָא, אִית לִי בְּגַוֵּיהּ". [2]אַהַדְרוּהּ נִיהֲלֵיהּ. [3]אֲמַר: לָא יָדַעְנָא אִי מִשּׁוּם סִימָנָא אַהַדְרוּהּ נִיהֲלִי, וְקָא סָבְרִי: סִימָנִין דְּאוֹרַיְיתָא, [4]אִי מִשּׁוּם טְבִיעוּת עֵינָא אַהַדְרוּהּ נִיהֲלִי, [5]וְדַוְקָא צוּרְבָא מִדְּרַבָּנַן, [6]אֲבָל אִינִישׁ דְּעָלְמָא, לָא.

[7]גּוּפָא: "מָצָא גֵּט אִשָּׁה בַּשּׁוּק, בִּזְמַן שֶׁהַבַּעַל מוֹדֶה, יַחֲזִיר לָאִשָּׁה. [8]אֵין הַבַּעַל מוֹדֶה, לֹא יַחֲזִיר לֹא לָזֶה וְלֹא לָזֶה". [9]בִּזְמַן שֶׁהַבַּעַל מוֹדֶה, מִיהָא, יַחֲזִיר לָאִשָּׁה.

LITERAL TRANSLATION

[1]If [you prefer] recognition by sight, I have one on it." [2]They returned it to him. [3]He said: I do not know whether they returned it to me because of the identifying mark, and they maintain: Identifying marks [are valid according] to Torah law, [4]or whether they returned it to me because of recognition by sight, [5]and only [from] a Rabbinical scholar (lit., "a firebrand of the Rabbis") [would they accept it], [6]but [from] an ordinary person, no.

[7]Returning to the subject (lit., "the thing itself"): "[If] one found a woman's bill of divorce in the marketplace, when the husband admits [that he wrote it, the finder] may return it to the woman. [8][If] the husband does not admit [that he wrote it, the finder] may not return it, neither to this one nor to this one." [9]When the husband admits, at all events, [the finder] may return [it] to the woman.

RASHI

ואי טביעות עין — חשיבא לכו, אית לי בגויה טביעות עינא. מכירו אני בכתב ידי הסופר והעדים, מדת ארכו ורחבו, כאדם המכיר את חבירו בטביעת עין שטבע בו ואין בו סימן. **וקסברי** — רבנן סימנין דאורייתא, שלא אמרתי סימן מובהק, והחזירוהו לי. **ודוקא לצורבא מדרבנן** — דמוחזק לן ביה דלא משני בדיבוריה.

LANGUAGE

צוּרְבָא דְּרַבָּנַן A Rabbinical scholar. This is a common term for a scholar (usually a young scholar) in the Talmud, though its source and precise significance are not clear. Some suggest that it derives from the root צרב, something hot, burning with the fire of Torah. Others suggest that it is derived from the Arabic word, meaning hard, strong, for indeed a צוּרְבָא דְּרַבָּנַן has a sharp and powerful mind (*Rav Hai Gaon*).

CONCEPTS

טְבִיעוּת עֵינָא Recognizing something by sight. The ability to recognize or identify something even though it does not have any distinguishing marks (i.e., the ability to recognize an article or a person by its or his general appearance). Literally טְבִיעוּת עֵינָא means the "imprinting of the eye," i.e., the ability to recognize things imprinted on the memory by sight.

NOTES

טְבִיעוּת עֵינָא Recognition by sight. The commentators explain that recognition is actually more reliable as a means of identification than an identifying mark. However, since it is impossible to prove that one recognizes an object by sight, such claims are accepted only when advanced by Torah scholars. This is not because the Torah scholar has greater powers of identification, but because he can be trusted not to lie (*Rashi*, *Tosafot*, and others).

Recognition by sight is, however, relied on to decide ordinary ritual questions, because these are private matters in which the court is not asked to intervene and determine who is telling the truth. In the same way, if the husband finds the bill of divorce and recognizes it, he may use it to divorce his wife. It is only in a case such as ours, where a third party found the bill and brought it to the court, that we refuse to accept a claim of recognition by sight from anyone but a Torah scholar (*Ritva*).

HALAKHAH

הַחֲזָרַת גֵּט בִּטְבִיעוּת עַיִן Returning a lost bill of divorce on the basis of recognition by sight. "If a bill of divorce carried by a Torah scholar is lost by him and later found, if he recognizes it as the bill of divorce that he had been carrying (or if he recognizes the container in which the bill of divorce was kept), it may be returned to him. (*Maggid Mishneh* maintains that this law does not appy to the Torah scholars living in our day.) But if the bill of divorce was found by the person carrying it immediately after it was lost, he is believed (irrespective of whether he is a Torah scholar or not) if he claims that he recognizes it by sight, because he could have made a better claim [מִגּוֹ], namely, that he never lost the bill of divorce in the first place (*Baḥ* in the name of *Tosafot*)." (*Shulḥan Arukh, Even HaEzer* 132:4.)

CONCEPTS

פֵּירוֹת Produce. Here the word is used in both its literal sense and in the extended sense of profits from a wife's personal property (נִכְסֵי מְלוֹג). The principal remains the wife's, even during the marriage, but the husband manages it and takes care of it, and he is entitled to enjoy the fruits and profits accruing from it.

[1] וְלֵיחוּשׁ שֶׁמָּא כָּתַב לִיתֵּן בְּנִיסָן, וְלֹא נָתַן לָהּ עַד תִּשְׁרֵי, [2] וְאָזַל בַּעַל זַבֵּין פֵּירֵי מִנִּיסָן וְעַד תִּשְׁרֵי. [3] וּמַפְּקָא לְגִיטָּא דִּכְתַב בְּנִיסָן, וְאָתְיָא לְמִטְרַף לָקוֹחוֹת שֶׁלֹּא כַּדִּין! [4] הָנִיחָא לְמַאן דְּאָמַר: כֵּיוָן שֶׁנָּתַן עֵינָיו לְגָרְשָׁהּ, שׁוּב אֵין לַבַּעַל פֵּירוֹת. שַׁפִּיר. [5] אֶלָּא לְמַאן דְּאָמַר: יֵשׁ לַבַּעַל פֵּירוֹת עַד שְׁעַת נְתִינָה, [6] מַאי אִיכָּא לְמֵימַר? [7] כִּי אָתְיָא לְמִטְרַף, אָמְרִינַן לָהּ: ״אַיְיתִי רְאָיָה אֵימַת מְטָא גִּיטָּא לִידָךְ״. [8] וּמַאי שְׁנָא מִשְּׁטָרֵי חוֹב?

LITERAL TRANSLATION

[1] But let us be concerned [that] perhaps [the husband] wrote [the bill of divorce] to give [it] in Nisan, but he did not give it to her until Tishri, [2] and [meanwhile] the husband went and sold the produce [of the wife's property] from Nisan until Tishri. [3] And [later] she will produce the bill of divorce that he wrote in Nisan, and she will come to seize [property from the] buyers unlawfully!

[4] This is acceptable [according] to the one who says: Once he has decided (lit., "given his eyes") to divorce her, the husband no longer has [the right to the] produce [of his wife's property]. It is well.

[5] But [according] to the one who says: A husband has [the right to the] produce [of his wife's property] until the time [when the bill of divorce is] given, [6] what is there to say?

[7] When she comes to seize [property from the buyers,] we say to her: "Bring proof [of] when the bill of divorce reached your hand."

[8] But why is this different from [the law regarding] promissory notes?

TRANSLATION AND COMMENTARY

וְלֵיחוּשׁ [1] **But**, the Gemara asks, **let us be concerned** about the possibility **that the husband may perhaps have written the bill of divorce with the intention of giving it in Nisan**, and the bill of divorce bears that date, **but he did not**, in fact, **give it to** his wife **until Tishri**. [2] **Meanwhile, the husband went and sold the produce of his wife's property**, produce that belongs to him as long as he is married to her, **between Nisan and Tishri**. [3] Later, **she will produce her bill of divorce, which** the husband **wrote in Nisan, and she will come to seize property unlawfully from the people who bought** the produce from the husband betwen Nisan and Tishri. She will claim that she was divorced in Nisan, as stated in the bill of divorce, and that she is entitled to any produce of her property sold by the husband after this date!

הָנִיחָא לְמַאן דְּאָמַר [4] The Gemara notes: **This** ruling of the Baraita **is acceptable according to the** authority **who maintains** that **once** a husband **has decided to divorce** his wife, **he no longer has the right to the produce of his wife's property**. According to this authority, the Baraita reads **well**, and the previous objection could not arise; for since the husband decided in Nisan to divorce his wife (as stated in the bill of divorce), he may not benefit from the produce of his wife's property from Nisan. The wife may, therefore, lawfully demand reimbursement from anyone who bought the produce of her property from her husband after that date.

אֶלָּא לְמַאן דְּאָמַר [5] **But according to the** authority **who says that a husband has the right to the produce of his wife's property until the time when the bill of divorce is** actually **given**, [6] **what is there to say**? How, by returning the bill of divorce to the wife, can we allow a situation to arise where she may unlawfully seize property from people who bought the produce of her property from her husband?

כִּי אָתְיָא לְמִטְרַף [7] The Gemara answers: **When** the woman **comes to seize** property in reimbursement for the produce of her property sold by her husband, **we say to her**: "**Bring proof** of **when the bill of divorce** actually **reached your hand**." And only after she proves that the bill of divorce was given on the date appearing in it may she seize the buyers' property.

וּמַאי שְׁנָא [8] The Gemara now asks: **But why is this** law **different from the law regarding promissory notes**?

RASHI

ולא נתן עד תשרי — וכל זמן שלא נתן היה לו לאכול ולמכור פירי נכסי מלוג שלה, שתקנו חכמים לבעל לאכול פירות של נכסי מלוג אשתו שנפלו לה לירושה. **וזבין פירי** — כמשפטו. **שפיר** — יש לה לטרוף כל מה שמכר משעות כתיבה. והא פלוגתא במסכת גיטין בפרק שני (יז,ב). **אימת מטא גיטא לידך** — מיד בעליך.

NOTES

כֵּיוָן שֶׁנָּתַן עֵינָיו לְגָרְשָׁהּ Once he has decided to divorce his wife. The Rabbinical ordinance, decreeing that the profits from a wife's personal property belong to her husband, does not derive from any actual right of the husband to his wife's property, but rather it is one of the ordinances implemented by the Sages whose purpose is to balance the mutual obligations between husband and wife, so as not to cause animosity between them. Therefore, it can plausibly be argued that once the husband has decided to divorce his wife, and there is already hostility between them, the husband's right to benefit from his wife's property is cancelled.

TRANSLATION AND COMMENTARY

[1]**For we have learned** in a Mishnah (above, 12b): **"If someone finds promissory notes containing a clause mortgaging the borrower's landed property as security for the loan, the finder should not return them."** [2]**And we explained that this refers to a case where the debtor admits his debt. And** the reason why we do not return the promissory note to the lender **is because we suspect that the borrower may perhaps have written** in the promissory note **that he was borrowing** the money **in Nisan, but he did not** actually **borrow until Tishri.** [3]**And** thus **the lender may come to seize property unlawfully from the buyers** who bought property from the borrower between Nisan and Tishri. [4]Now, following the same line of reasoning just suggested with regard to lost bills of divorce, why do we not say **there too** that **the finder should return the promissory note** to the lender? **And when the lender comes to seize property,** [5]**we can say to him: "Bring proof** of **when the promissory note** actually **reached your hand."** Why should we allow bills of divorce to be returned and not promissory notes?

אָמְרִי [6]The Gemara answers: **We** can **say** in reply: The two cases are different. **Here, in the case of a woman's bill of divorce, the buyer will come and demand proof from her** of the date when she actually received the bill of divorce. He realizes that the divorce may have been given after the date appearing in it, and he can therefore be expected to demand proof that she was actually divorced on that date. [7]For **he says** to himself: **"The reason why the Rabbis returned the** lost **bill of divorce to her was in order that she should not remain** permanently **unable to remarry.** But they were not concerned about the monetary implications of this ruling, and did not specify the exact date when the wife has the right to keep the produce of her property. [8]**Now that she is coming to seize property** from me on the basis of her bill of divorce, **let her go and bring proof of when the bill of divorce** actually **reached her hand."**

הָכָא, גַּבֵּי שְׁטַר חוֹב [9]But **here, in the case of a promissory note, the buyer will not come and demand proof** of when the note was written, for he will have no reason to suspect that such proof is necessary. [10]**For** he will make the following assumption: **"Since the Rabbis returned the** lost **promissory note to** the lender, **it is obvious what their purpose was when they returned it to him.** It was in order **to allow** the lender **to seize**

[1]דִּתְנַן: ״מָצָא שְׁטָרֵי חוֹב, אִם יֵשׁ בָּהֶן אַחֲרָיוּת נְכָסִים, לֹא יַחֲזִיר״, [2]וְאוֹקִימְנָא כְּשֶׁחַיָּיב מוֹדֶה, וּמִשּׁוּם שֶׁמָּא כָּתַב לִלְווֹת בְּנִיסָן, וְלֹא לָוָה עַד תִּשְׁרֵי, [3]וְקָא טָרֵיף לָקוֹחוֹת שֶׁלֹּא כְּדִין. [4]הָתָם נַמִי לִיהֲדַר, וְכִי אָתֵי לְמִטְרַף, [5]נֵימָא לֵיהּ: ״אַיְיתֵי רְאָיָה אֵימַת מְטָא שְׁטַר חוֹב לִידָךְ״.

[6]אָמְרִי: הָכָא, גַּבֵּי גֵּט אִשָּׁה, אָתֵי לוֹקֵחַ וּתְבָעָהּ. [7]אָמַר: ״הַאי דְּהַדְרוּהּ נִיהֲלָהּ רַבָּנַן לְגִיטָּא מִשּׁוּם דְּלָא תַּעֲגִין וְתֵיתִיב. [8]הַשְׁתָּא דְּקָא אָתְיָא לְמִטְרַף, תֵּיזִיל וְתֵיתֵי רְאָיָה אֵימַת מְטָא גִּיטָּהּ לְיָדָהּ״.

[9]הָכָא, גַּבֵּי שְׁטַר חוֹב, לָא אָתֵי לוֹקֵחַ וְתָבַע. [10]״מִדְּאַהַדְרוּהּ נִיהֲלֵיהּ רַבָּנַן לִשְׁטַר חוֹב, פְּשִׁיטָא לְמַאי הִלְכְתָא אַהַדְרוּהּ

LITERAL TRANSLATION

[1]For we have learned [above, in a Mishnah]: "[If] one finds promissory notes, if they contain [a clause] mortgaging [the borrower's landed] property [as security for the loan], [the finder] should not return [them]," [2]and we explained [that] this [refers to a case] where the debtor admits [his debt], and it is because [we suspect that] perhaps [the borrower] wrote to borrow in Nisan, but he did not borrow until Tishri, [3]and [the lender] may come to seize [property from the] buyers unlawfully. [4]There, too, let [the finder] return [the promissory note], and when [the lender] comes to seize [property], [5]let us say to him: "Bring proof [of] when the promissory note reached your hand."

[6]We say: Here, in the case of a woman's bill of divorce, the buyer comes and demands [proof] from her. [7]He says: "The [reason] why the Rabbis returned the bill of divorce to her is in order that she should not remain unable to remarry. [8]Now that she is coming to seize [property], let her go and bring proof [of] when the bill of divorce reached her hand."

[9]Here, in the case of a promissory note, the buyer will not come and demand [proof]. [10][For he will say:] "Since the Rabbis returned the promissory note to him [the lender], it is obvious for what purpose they

RASHI

אימת מטא שטרא לידך — מיד הלוה מתחלה. **אתי לוקח ותבע** — אי אתיא למיטרף מסיק אדעתיה לתבוע: אייתי ראיה אימת מטא גיטא לידך בזמנא קמא.

NOTES

לְמַאי הִלְכְתָא אַהַדְרוּהּ נִיהֲלֵיהּ לְמִטְרַף הוּא It is obvious why they returned it to him — to seize property. I.e., property that had been sold to others by the borrower after the date written in the note. The Aharonim ask: Even if the date on

TRANSLATION AND COMMENTARY

property from the buyer. [1]Accordingly, I can **deduce from this that the Rabbis verified the matter** before they returned the promissory note to the lender, **and the promissory note** originally **reached** the lender's **hand before the borrower sold me the property**, as indicated by the date on the note." Therefore, the Sages ruled that a lost promissory note may not be returned to the lender, unless there is proof that the loan was indeed given on the date appearing in the note.

שִׁחְרוּרֵי עֲבָדִים וכו׳ [2]The Mishnah stated above: "**Writs of emancipation of slaves, etc.,**" may not be returned. [3]**Our Rabbis taught the following Baraita**, which elaborates on our Mishnah: "**If someone found a writ of emancipation in the marketplace, when the master admits that he gave it the finder may return it to the slave.** [4]But **if the master does not admit that he gave it, the finder may not return it either to** the master **or to the** slave." [5]**At all events**, says the Gemara, the Baraita teaches that **when the master admits** the authenticity of the writ of emancipation, the finder **may return** it **to the slave**.

וְאַמַּאי [6]The Gemara now asks: **But why** should the writ be returned to the slave? **Let us be concerned** about the possibility **that** the master **may perhaps have written the writ of emancipation with the intention of giving it to him in Nisan**, and it bears that date, **but he did not** in fact **give it to him until Tishri.** [7]**And meanwhile the slave went and bought property between Nisan and Tishri**, and since he remained a slave until Tishri any property that he acquired between Nisan and Tishri

נִיהֲלֵיהּ — לְמִטְרַף הוּא. [1]שְׁמַע מִינָּהּ קָמוּ רַבָּנַן בְּמִילְּתָא, וּמִקַּמֵּי דִּידִי מְטָא שְׁטָרָא לִידֵיהּ״.

[2]״שִׁחְרוּרֵי עֲבָדִים וכו׳״. [3]תָּנוּ רַבָּנַן: ״מָצָא שְׁטַר שִׁחְרוּר בַּשּׁוּק, בִּזְמַן שֶׁהָרַב מוֹדֶה, יַחֲזִיר לָעֶבֶד. [4]אֵין הָרַב מוֹדֶה, לֹא יַחֲזִיר, לֹא לָזֶה וְלֹא לָזֶה״. [5]בִּזְמַן שֶׁהָרַב מוֹדֶה, מִיהָא, יַחֲזִיר לָעֶבֶד.

[6]וְאַמַּאי? נֵיחוּשׁ שֶׁמָּא כָּתַב לִיתֵּן לוֹ בְּנִיסָן, וְלֹא נָתַן לוֹ עַד תִּשְׁרֵי, [7]וַאֲזַל עַבְדָּא וְקָנָה נְכָסִין מִנִּיסָן וְעַד תִּשְׁרֵי.

LITERAL TRANSLATION

returned it to him — so that he could seize [property]. [1]Deduce from this that the Rabbis verified the matter, and the [promissory] note reached his hand before [the borrower sold] me [the property]."

[2]"Writs of emancipation of slaves, etc." [3]Our Rabbis taught [the following Baraita]: "[If] one found a writ of emancipation in the marketplace, when the master admits [that he gave it, the finder] may return it to the slave. [4][If] the master does not admit [that he gave it, the finder] may not return it, neither to this one nor to this one." [5]When the master admits, at all events, [the finder] may return [it] to the slave.

[6]But why? Let us be concerned [that] perhaps [the master] wrote [the writ of emancipation] to give [it] to him in Nisan, but he did not give [it] to him until Tishri, [7]and [meanwhile] the slave went and bought property between Nisan and Tishri.

RASHI

מקמי דידי — מקודם שמכר לי הלוה נכסיו מטא שטר מיד לוה למלוה כראשונה.

NOTES

the note is incorrect, the borrower certainly owes the lender money today. Perhaps the court returned the note to the lender to enable him to collect his debt directly from the debtor? They answer: If this were the case, and there was a doubt about the correctness of the date written in the note, the court would have torn it up and written a new one with today's date. The old note would not have been returned if the date had not been verified (*Torat Ḥayyim* and others).

וַאֲזַל עַבְדָּא וְקָנָה נְכָסִין **And the slave went and bought property**. The commentators ask: Why did the Gemara not raise a simpler objection? Perhaps the slave's master sold him to another master between Nisan and Tishri. Thus, when the writ of emancipation was delivered by the original master, in Tishri, it should have had no effect since the slave had already been sold. But since the date in the writ reads Nisan, the slave could fraudulently claim to have been freed before the sale.

Rashba answers: This objection is essentially the same as the one actually raised by the Gemara, since it is based on the possibility of unjust monetary loss caused by a delay

HALAKHAH

מָצָא שְׁטַר שִׁחְרוּר בַּשּׁוּק **If a person found a writ of emancipation in the marketplace.** "If a person found a writ of emancipation in the marketplace, and the person who wrote it claims that he never gave it to his slave, the finder may not return it either to the slave or his master. But if the master admits that he gave it to the slave, it may be returned to the slave. Nevertheless, the slave may not seize property which he bought after the date appearing in the writ of emancipation, and which the master thereafter sold, unless he can prove that he was set free on that date." (*Rema* notes that certain communities follow Abaye's ruling that "witnesses transfer rights by their signatures"; in these

[1]וְאָזֵיל הָרַב וְזַבְּנִינְהוּ, [2]וּמַפֵּיק לֵיהּ לְשִׁחְרוּר דִּכְתַב בְּנִיסָן, וְקָא טָרֵיף לָקוֹחוֹת שֶׁלֹּא כַּדִּין! [3]הָנִיחָא לְמַאן דַּאֲמַר: זְכוּת הוּא לָעֶבֶד שֶׁיּוֹצֵא מִתַּחַת רַבּוֹ לְחֵירוּת, [4]וּכְאַבַּיֵי דַּאֲמַר: עֵדָיו בַּחֲתוּמָיו זָכִין לֵיהּ. [5]שַׁפִּיר. [6]אֶלָּא לְמַאן דַּאֲמַר: חוֹב הוּא לָעֶבֶד שֶׁיּוֹצֵא מִתַּחַת רַבּוֹ לְחֵירוּת, מַאי אִיכָּא לְמֵימַר?

LITERAL TRANSLATION

[1]Then the master went and sold it, [2]and [later the slave] will produce the writ of emancipation which [the master] wrote in Nisan, and he will seize [property from the] buyers unlawfully!

[3]This is acceptable [according] to the one who says: It is a privilege for a slave that he goes out from under [the authority of] his master to freedom, [4]and in accordance with Abaye, who says: [A beneficiary's] witnesses acquire for him by their signatures. [5]It is well.

[6]But according to the one who says: It is a disadvantage for a slave that he goes out from under [the authority of] his master to freedom, what is there to say?

TRANSLATION AND COMMENTARY

automatically became the property of his master. [1]**Then the master went**, during the period before Tishri, **and sold** this property, since it belonged to him. [2]**Later the slave will produce the writ of emancipation which the master wrote in Nisan**, and will claim that the property was his and not his master's, because he had already been set free, **and he will seize property from the buyers unlawfully**, since in fact he only received the writ of emancipation in Tishri, and his master was fully entitled to sell the property, because it belonged to him!

הָנִיחָא לְמַאן דַּאֲמַר [3]The Gemara notes: **This** ruling of the Baraita **is acceptable** provided we make two assumptions: (1) That we rule **in accordance with the** authority **who says** that **it is a privilege for a slave to leave his master and attain freedom**, and (2) [4]that we rule **in accordance with** the viewpoint of **Abaye, who says**: **The witnesses** to a document **acquire the rights** granted in the document **for** the recipient **by** putting **their signatures** on the document. According to Abaye, once the witnesses sign the writ of emancipation, the slave at once gains his freedom, since a legal document takes effect immediately after the witnesses sign it, and the change in his status does not have to wait until the writ of emancipation reaches his hand. This law would, of course, apply only to a document that confers benefits on its recipient, for example, a writ of emancipation, according to the view that freedom is considered a benefit for the slave. In such a case, we apply the principle that "benefit may be conferred on another person even if he is not present" (זָכִין לְאָדָם שֶׁלֹּא בְּפָנָיו). Thus, according to this argument, the writ of emancipation frees the slave even if he was not present when it was written, and there is no reason not to return the lost writ of emancipation to the ex-slave. [5]The Baraita thus reads **well**.

אֶלָּא לְמַאן דַּאֲמַר [6]**But according to the** authority **who says** that **it is a disadvantage for a slave to leave his master and attain freedom, what is there to say**? According to this authority, the writ of emancipation only takes effect when it reaches the slave's hand, because a legal transaction which is to the disadvantage of one of the parties cannot be effected if that person is not present, and the signature of the witnesses did not bring about his change of status. Accordingly, the slave might not actually have gained his freedom until long after the writ of emancipation was written and signed, and hence he may come to seize property unlawfully, as explained above!

RASHI

הניחא למאן דאמר כו' – פלוגתא בפרק קמא דגיטין (יב, ב). **זכות הוא לעבד** – טובה היא אצלו שמתירו בקהל, וכיון דזכות הוא – איכא לתרוצי דמשמע שנכתב זוכה בשחרור, דלכי מטא שטר גט לידיה נעשה בן חורין למפרע, משעת חתימה. **חוב הוא לעבד** – חובתו הוא שיוצא מתחת רבו. כלומר: הפסד הוא לו, שאם עבד כהן הוא – פוסלו מן התרומה, ואם של ישראל – אוסרו בשפחה כנענית, דזילא ליה, ושכיחא ליה, ופריצא ליה. **מאי איכא למימר** – דהשתא ליכא למימר עדיו בחתומיו זכין לו, דאין זכין לאדם שלא בפניו.

NOTES

between writing and delivery. But the Gemara preferred to phrase the question as referring to buyers of property, because of the parallel with the question about bills of divorce in the previous passage.

The Aharonim added other arguments to show that the case of the buyers was the better case to use to illustrate the problem (*Ḥiddushei HaRim*, *Me'il Shmuel*, *Rashash*).

חוֹב הוּא לָעֶבֶד שֶׁיּוֹצֵא לְחֵירוּת **It is a disadvantage for a slave to go free.** Indeed, the Talmud states that there were many people, particularly elderly people, who sold

HALAKHAH

communities, the slave may seize property that he bought after the date appearing in the writ of emancipation, and which the master thereafter sold, even if he does not bring proof that he was freed on that date.) (Ibid., *Shulḥan Arukh, Ḥoshen Mishpat* 65:13.)

זְכוּת הוּא לָעֶבֶד שֶׁיּוֹצְאוּ לְחֵירוּת **It is a privilege for a slave to go free.** This view is the accepted Halakhah. (*Rambam, Sefer Kinyan, Hilkhot Avadim* 6:1 and *Kesef Mishneh* ad loc.)

TRANSLATION AND COMMENTARY

דְּכִי אָתֵי לְמִטְרַף [1]The Gemara answers: **When** the slave **comes to seize** property which he claims to have bought as a free man after the date appearing on his writ of emancipation, **we say to him**: **"Bring proof** of **when the writ of emancipation** actually **reached your hand,"** just as in the case of the bill of divorce. Only after he proves that the writ of emancipation was given on the date appearing in it may he seize the property bought by him and later sold by his master.

דְּיַיתִּיקֵי מַתָּנָה וכו׳ [2]The Mishnah stated above: **"Wills, deeds of gift, etc.,"** may not be returned. [3]**Our Rabbis taught the following Baraita**: **"What is a will** (דְּיַיתִּיקֵי)? [4]A document that states: **'This shall be to stand and be.'"** The term דְּיַיתִּיקֵי is taken here, in a play on words, as an abbreviation for דָּא תְּהֵא לְמֵיקַם וְלִהְיוֹת — "this shall be to stand and be," i.e., this will is a valid deed of transfer — **"so that if the author of the will dies, his property will go to** the person designated in the will."

מַתָּנָה [5]The Baraita continues: "What is **'a deed of gift'**? — **Any deed that has** the words **'From today but after death' written in it**." The recipient acquires the property immediately — "from today" — but he may not benefit from its use until after the donor's death.

אַלְמָא [6]The Gemara now asks: Do we, **therefore**, infer that **only if** the words **"From today but after death" are written in the deed** of gift **does the recipient acquire the property**, [7]**but if not**, if the deed does not specify "after death," the recipient **does not acquire** the property at all?! Is a deed of gift only effective if it specifies that the recipient will only benefit from it after the donor's death? Surely deeds of gift prepared by healthy people take effect at once!

אָמַר אַבַּיֵי [8]**Abaye said** in reply: **This is what the Baraita is saying**: Ordinary gifts take effect

[1]דְּכִי אָתֵי לְמִטְרַף, אָמְרִינַן לֵיהּ: ״אַיְיתֵי רְאָיָה אֵימַת מְטָא שִׁחְרוּר לִידָךְ״.

[2]״דְּיַיתִּיקֵי מַתָּנָה וכו׳״. [3]תָּנוּ רַבָּנַן: ״אֵיזוֹ הִיא דְּיַיתִּיקֵי? [4]דָּא תְּהֵא לְמֵיקַם וְלִהְיוֹת, שֶׁאִם מֵת, נְכָסָיו לִפְלוֹנִי״.

[5]״מַתָּנָה כָּל שֶׁכָּתוּב בּוֹ ׳מֵהַיּוֹם וּלְאַחַר מִיתָה׳״.

[6]אַלְמָא, אִי כְּתִיבָא ״מֵהַיּוֹם וּלְאַחַר מִיתָה״ הוּא דְּקָנֵי, [7]וְאִי לָא, לָא קָנֵי?!

[8]אָמַר אַבַּיֵי: הָכִי קָאָמַר:

LITERAL TRANSLATION

[1]When he comes to seize [property], we say to him: "Bring proof [of] when the writ of emancipation reached your hand."

[2]"Wills, [deeds of] gift, etc." [3]Our Rabbis taught [the following Baraita]: "What is a will? [4]This shall be to stand and be, so that if [the author of the will] dies, his property [will go] to So-and-so."

[5]"A [deed of] gift is any [deed] [that has] 'From today but after death' written in it."

[6]Therefore, [only] if "From today but after death" is written [in the deed] does [the recipient] acquire [the property], [7]but if not, he does not acquire [it]?!

[8]Abaye said: This is what [the Baraita] is saying:

RASHI

מאי איכא למימר — דלאשתא ליכא למימר עדיו בחתומיו חבין לו, דאין חבין לאדם שלא בפניו. **דא תהא למיקם** — שטר זה יהיה לקום ולהיות בכל הכתוב בו, דדברי שכיב מרע ככתובין וכמסורין דמי. **מתנה** — מתנת בריא איזו היא, כל שכתוב בו כו׳. **מהיום ולאחר מיתה** — גוף הקרקע קנוי לו מן היום, ואין לו עוד רשות למוכרה וליתנה ולהורישה. והפירות אינו אוכל כל ימי חייו אלא לאחר מיתה. **ואי לא לא קני** — בתמיה: כל שכן דאם יהיב ליה גוף ופירות במעכשיו, דקני טפי. סתם מתנת שכיב מרע לא קניא לו אלא לאחר מיתה, דמתנת מיתה הוא מלווה.

LANGUAGE

דָּא תְּהֵא לְמֵיקַם וְלִהְיוֹת This shall be to stand and be. These words and others like them can be written in a will, but their use here is a kind of play on words connected with the Greek word διαθήκη, *diatheke*, dividing it into syllables as if it were a sentence in Aramaic.

NOTES

themselves into slavery, in order to ensure themselves a steady source of support; for although a master was not necessarily obligated to support his slaves for life, it was certainly normal practice for him to do so. However, the Tosefta (*Gittin* 1:10) clearly indicates that the advantages of slavery are experienced specifically by the slave of a priest, who is entitled to collect and eat the priestly tithe, even in the absence of his master, so long as he remains a slave.

There are also other reasons why it was said that it is a disadvantage for a slave to go free. A freed slave has the legal status of a Jew and must fulfill all the commandments, both positive and negative, like a Jew, whereas until he is freed he has merely to avoid transgressing negative commandments. An additional factor is that while he was a slave he was permitted to have sexual relations with non-Jewish maidservants, which led to licentiousness.

אַיְיתֵי רְאָיָה אֵימַת מְטָא שִׁחְרוּר לִידָךְ **Bring proof of when the bill of divorce actually reached your hand.** A bill of divorce can be delivered long after it was written, because the date in the bill refers only to the day of writing. The Gemara here appears to assume that it is only in a case of a *lost bill* that the people to whom the husband sold the produce of the wife's fields can demand proof of the date of delivery. *Rashi* on *Gittin* 17b suggests that the only way any divorced woman may collect reimbursement for produce is by bringing witnesses to testify to the date of the delivery of the bill of divorce. But most commentators reject this position. They maintain that a bill of divorce is always assumed to have been delivered on the day it was written, and only special circumstances, such as the bill being lost, can account for its being delayed. But an unusual occurrence tends to become public knowledge. Therefore, when a woman is divorced with a predated bill, people will become aware of the fact. Accordingly, the buyers will be forewarned to demand proof of the date of delivery (*Ramban* and others).

TRANSLATION AND COMMENTARY

immediately. [1]**But what gift of a healthy person is treated like the gift of a dying person, in that the recipient does not acquire the gift until after the donor's death?** [2]**Any deed** of gift **that has** the words **"From today but after death" written in it.**

טַעְמָא דְּלָא אֲמַר תְּנוּ [3]The Gemara now returns to the text of the Mishnah and asks: **Is the reason why** lost wills and deeds of gift **may not be returned** to the recipient **because the donor did not say: "Give** them to the recipient"? [4]**But if he did say "give,"** does it not follow by implication that **we** do **give them to the recipient.**

וּרְמִינְהוּ [5]If this inference is correct, continues the Gemara, **a contradiction can be raised** from the following Baraita: **"If someone found wills, hypothecs** stating that a particular piece of property was mortgaged as absolute collateral for a loan, **or deeds of gift,** [6]**even though both parties agree** that the lost document is genuine and has already been given to the recipient, **the finder should not return them to either of them"!** This seems to contradict our Mishnah, which implies that if the donor verifies the genuineness of the lost document it may be returned to the recipient!

אָמַר רַבִּי אַבָּא בַּר מֶמֶל [7]**Rabbi Abba bar Memel said** in reply: **There is no difficulty** in reconciling these

[1]אֵיזוֹ הִיא מַתְּנַת בָּרִיא שֶׁהִיא כְּמַתְּנַת שְׁכִיב מְרַע, דְּלָא קָנֵי אֶלָּא לְאַחַר מִיתָה? [2]כָּל שֶׁכָּתוּב בָּהּ ״מֵהַיּוֹם וּלְאַחַר מִיתָה״.

[3]טַעְמָא דְּלָא אֲמַר ״תְּנוּ״, [4]הָא אֲמַר ״תְּנוּ״, נוֹתְנִין.

[5]וּרְמִינְהוּ: ״מָצָא דַּיְיתִּקָאוֹת, אַפּוֹתִיקָאוֹת, וּמַתָּנוֹת, [6]אַף עַל פִּי שֶׁשְּׁנֵיהֶם מוֹדִין, לֹא יַחֲזִיר, לֹא לָזֶה וְלֹא לָזֶה״!

[7]אָמַר רַבִּי אַבָּא בַּר מֶמֶל: לָא קַשְׁיָא.

LITERAL TRANSLATION

[1]What gift of a healthy person is [treated] like the gift of a dying person, in that [the recipient] does not acquire [the gift] until after [the donor's] death? [2]Any [deed] that has written in it: "From today but after death."

[3]The reason [why these documents may not be returned] is because [the donor] did not say: "Give," [4]but if he said: "Give," we give [them to the recipient].

[5]A contradiction was raised: "[If] one found wills, hypothecs, or [deeds of] gifts, [6]even though both [parties] agree, [the finder] should not return [them], neither to this one nor to this one"!

[7]Rabbi Abba bar Memel said: There is no difficulty.

RASHI

הא אמר תנו נותנין – אמתניתין פריך, דאלי טעמא דשאני אומר נמלך עליהם שלא לתתן. **אפותיקאות** – שעשה לו שדהאפותיקי למלוה על פה, שהיתה לו עליו מלוה ישנה. **לא יחזיר** – שמא כתבה לזה ולא מסר לו, ולא זכה בקרקע. וחזר וכתב לאחר ומסר לו השטר, וזכה בו. ובא לחזור בו מן השני, ורוצה לתת לראשון, ותפך שימסרו לו שטר זה שיוליאנה בבית דין, ונמלא זמן שטר של זה קודם לשטרו של שני, ויוליאנה מידו בדין.

SAGES

רַבִּי אַבָּא בַּר מֶמֶל **Rabbi Abba bar Memel.** A Palestinian Amora of the second and third generation, Rabbi Abba bar Memel studied in the yeshivah of Rabbi Oshaya in Caesarea. Rabbi Elazar ben Pedat calls him his teacher. He is found in Talmudic sources in discussion with Rabbi Ami, Rabbi Assi, Rabbi Zera, and others.

CONCEPTS

מַתְּנַת שְׁכִיב מְרַע **A gift of a person on his deathbed.** By Rabbinic decree, gifts given by a person on his deathbed differ in several ways from those given in other circumstances. For example, the gift of a person on his deathbed is valid even if no act of acquisition (קִנְיָן) was performed, as long as the donor expressed his intention in words. Likewise, a mortally ill person may retract his gift as many times as he wishes, provided that he is of sound mind when doing so. All gifts given by a person on his deathbed are invalidated if he recovers.

NOTES

מַתְּנַת בָּרִיא שֶׁהִיא כְּמַתְּנַת שְׁכִיב מְרַע **A gift of a healthy person that is treated like the gift of a dying person.** The commentators differ as to the exact status of such a deed. Clearly, some right is being transferred immediately, and some other right is being retained by the donor. Some commentators interpret this passage in the light of a parallel passage in *Bava Batra* (136a), where this phrase is interpreted to mean that the theoretical ownership of the field is transferred immediately, and the donor loses the right to change his mind and sell it or give it to someone else, but he retains a life interest, so that the practical use of the field, including the consumption of its crops, remains his prerogative for as long as he lives (*Rashi*, *Ramban*, and others).

Other commentators, however, while not disputing the meaning imparted to this phrase in the passage in *Bava Batra*, insist that we must interpret it differently here, since the point of our Gemara is to describe a form of transfer which is similar to the gift of a dying man, and the key feature of the gift of a dying man is his ability to change his mind. Accordingly, these commentators maintain that the donor transfers all practical ownership rights immediately, but retains the prerogative to retract his gift as long as he lives (*Rabbenu Tam*, *Rashba*, and *Ran*).

Still other commentators suggest that both kinds of transfer are possible, depending on the precise wording of the deed issued by the donor (*Ritva*).

HALAKHAH

מַתְּנַת בָּרִיא שֶׁהִיא כְּמַתְּנַת שְׁכִיב מְרַע **The gift of a healthy person which is treated like the gift of a dying person.** "If a healthy person writes a deed of gift, stating that he is giving his property "from today but after death" (and he performed a formal act of acquisition [e.g., transfer of a handkerchief] to confirm the gift — *Sma*), the gift takes effect after the donor's death, and even though the donor cannot retract, the recipient may not make use of the gift (e.g., eat the produce of the field) in the donor's lifetime." (*Shulḥan Arukh, Ḥoshen Mishpat* 257:6.)

TRANSLATION AND COMMENTARY

statements. [19B] The Baraita **refers to** a deed of gift drawn up by **a healthy person**, [1]**and** the Mishnah **refers to** a deed of gift drawn up by **a dying person**.

מַתְנִיתִין [2]The Gemara now explains in greater detail: **The Mishnah, which** by inference, as explained above, **teaches that if** the donor **says,** "**Give** the lost deed to the recipient," **we** do **give** it, **is referring to** the gift of **a dying person, who has the right to retract**. According to the Halakhah, a dying person may retract any gift which he stipulated should take effect after his death, and may write another deed giving it to someone else. Hence, if the gift of a dying person was lost, it may be returned, provided the dying donor acquiesces. [3]**For we say: What is there to say** against returning the lost deed? [4]**That** the donor **may perhaps have originally written** the lost deed of gift **for one** person (A), **and may have changed his mind and not given it to him,** [5]**and may later have written** another deed of gift **for another person** (B) **and given it to him**; and **now he has** decided to **retract his gift** to **the second person** (B) **to whom he gave it**, and to give it instead to A?! [6]This would not be a valid reason not to return the lost deed of gift to A, for **if** the donor **gave** the second deed **to** B **as the gift of a healthy person**, B **suffers no loss** in the return of the lost deed to A, [7]**for when** the **two** deeds of gift **are produced, the later** deed, bearing the later date, **confers ownership** of the gift on B, **since the donor** clearly **retracted the first** gift to A, as he was entitled to do.

[19B] הָא בְּבָרִיא, [1]וְהָא בִּשְׁכִיב מְרַע.

[2]מַתְנִיתִין, דְּקָתָנֵי הָא אֲמַר ״תְּנוּ״, נוֹתְנִין, בִּשְׁכִיב מְרַע, דָּבָר מְהַדַּר הוּא. [3]דְּאָמְרִינַן: מַאי אִיכָּא לְמֵימַר? [4]דִּלְמָא כְּתָבָהּ מֵעִיקָּרָא לְהַאי, וְאִמְלִיךְ וְלָא יְהָבָהּ נִיהֲלֵיהּ, [5]וַהֲדַר כְּתָבָהּ לְאִינִישׁ אַחֲרִינָא וִיהָבֵיהּ נִיהֲלֵיהּ, הַשְׁתָּא קָא הָדַר בֵּיהּ מֵהַהוּא דִּיהָבָהּ נִיהֲלֵיהּ? [6]אִי בְּמַתְּנַת בָּרִיא יְהָבָהּ לֵיהּ, לֵית לֵיהּ פְּסֵידָא, [7]דְּכִי נָפְקָא תַּרְתֵּי, בַּתְרַיְיתָא זָכֵי, דְּהָא הָדַר בֵּיהּ מִקַּמַּיְיתָא.

LITERAL TRANSLATION

[19B] This [refers] to a healthy person; [1]and this [refers] to a dying person.

[2]The Mishnah, which teaches that [if] he said: "Give," we give, [refers] to a dying person, who has the right to retract. [3]For we say: What is there to say? [4][That] perhaps he originally wrote it for this one, and he changed his mind and did not give it to him, [5]and later he wrote it for another person and gave it to him, [and] now he has retracted [his gift] from the [second] one to whom he gave it? [6]If he gave it to him as the gift of a healthy person, he has no loss, [7]for when [the] two [deeds of gift] are produced, the later [deed] confers ownership, since [the donor] retracted the first [gift].

RASHI

הא בבריא – שהיה שטר מתנת בריא, דלא כתיב ביה ״כדקאיר ורמי בערסיה״ כדין שכותבין בשטרי מתנות שכיב מרע.
דבר מהדר הוא – שיכול לחזור במתנתו. אם כתב שני שטרות השני זוכה, שהרי חזר בו מראשון. אי במתנת בריא יהבה ניהליה – להאוא בתרא. לית ליה פסידא – בהאי שטרא דמהדרא ליה להאי.

NOTES

הָא בְּבָרִיא **The Baraita is referring to the gift of a healthy person**. *Ran* asks: How can Rabbi Abba bar Memel make such a suggestion? The Baraita refers specifically to the kind of will called דְּיָיתִיקִי which can only be issued by a dying man! It is true that later on Rav Zevid will raise this very objection, but it is inconceivable that Rabbi Abba bar Memel entirely overlooked this point!

Ran answers: Rabbi Abba bar Memel accepts that the Baraita is referring to a דְּיָיתִיקִי issued by a dying man, but he holds that included in this particular דְּיָיתִיקִי was a clause that the gift was to be confirmed by a formal act of transfer (קִנְיָן). Such language is included in all ordinary deeds of gift, but not in a דְּיָיתִיקִי. Thus Rabbi Abba bar Memel understands the Baraita as saying that this particular dying man had, in effect, issued an ordinary healthy person's gift. Rav Zevid, on the other hand, rejected this interpretation because a gift written in such a manner should not be called a דְּיָיתִיקִי at all, regardless of the state of health of its author.

דָּבָר מְהַדַּר הוּא **The Mishnah applies to the gift of a dying person who has the right to retract**. By contrast, the Baraita refers either to a healthy person, or to the heir of the donor, neither of whom has the right to retract. *Ramban* asks: The Gemara arrived at this interpretation of the Baraita specifically in order to avoid a contradiction with our Mishnah. But there is an internal problem in the Baraita independent of the contradiction with the Mishnah: The Baraita rules that a lost will may not be returned to its beneficiary, even with the concurrence of its author. Now if the Baraita is talking about a person who is allowed to retract his gifts, why should the lost will not be returned?

HALAKHAH

מְצִיאַת שְׁטַר מַתָּנָה **Returning a lost deed of gift**. "A person who finds a lost deed of gift may not return it to the recipient, even if the donor admits that he gave it to him, unless the deed explicitly states that the donor may retract the gift whenever he pleases, or the deed of gift was a "deed of transfer," stating that the recipient was to acquire the property immediately after the deed was signed. If a deed of gift made by a dying person is found, it may be returned

TRANSLATION AND COMMENTARY

אִי בְּמַתְּנַת שְׁכִיב מְרַע [1]And on the other hand **even if** the donor **gave** the second deed **to** B **as the gift of a dying person**, B still **suffers no loss** in the return of the lost deed to A; [2]**for** when the two deeds of gift are produced, **the later deed**, bearing the later date, **confers ownership** of the gift on B, **since the donor retracted the first gift** to A.

כִּי קָתָנֵי בְּבָרַיְיתָא [3]But by contrast, **when the Baraita teaches: "Even though both parties agree** that the lost document is genuine, [4]**the finder should not return it to either of them,"** [5]**this refers to** the gift of **a healthy person, who does not have the right to retract** gifts he has given. [6]**For we say: The donor may perhaps have originally written** the lost deed of gift **for one** person (A), **and may have changed his mind and not given it to him** at all, [7]**and may later have written** another deed of gift for the same property **for another person** (B) **and given it to him, and now he** has decided unlawfully to **retract his gift** to **the second person** (B), **to whom he has** already **given it**, and to give it instead to A. But he does not simply write a new deed. Instead, he takes out the old one and announces that he has already delivered it. [8]**For he thinks** as follows: **"I cannot retract** the gift to B, because I have already given it, and the gift of a healthy person is irrevocable. **So I will say to** the judges **that I gave** the lost deed of gift **to the first person** (A), which is not true, [9]**and they will return the deed to him, so that when** A **produces his deed, which came first, he will acquire the gift."**

אֶלָּא, אָמְרִינַן לֵיהּ אֲנַן [10]**Rather, we,** the judges, **say to** the donor: **"We will not give this document to the**

[1]אִי בְּמַתְּנַת שְׁכִיב מְרַע נַמִּי יָהֲבָהּ נִיהֲלֵיהּ, לֵית בָּהּ פְּסֵידָא; [2]דְּבַתְרַיְיתָא זָכֵי, דְּקָא הָדַר בֵּיהּ מִקַּמַּיְיתָא.

[3]כִּי קָתָנֵי בְּבָרַיְיתָא: ״אַף עַל פִּי שֶׁשְּׁנֵיהֶם מוֹדִים, [4]לֹא יַחֲזִיר לֹא לָזֶה וְלֹא לָזֶה״, [5]בְּבָרִיא, דְּלָאו בַּר מִהֲדַר הוּא, [6]דְּאָמְרִינַן: דִּלְמָא כְּתָבָהּ לְהַאי מֵעִיקָּרָא, וְאִמְּלִיךְ וְלָא יְהָבָהּ לֵיהּ, [7]וַהֲדַר כְּתָבָהּ לְאִינִישׁ אַחֲרִינָא וִיהָבָהּ לֵיהּ, הָשְׁתָּא קָא הָדַר בֵּיהּ מֵהַהוּא דִּיהָבָהּ לֵיהּ. [8]וְסָבַר: ״מִהֲדַר לָא מָצֵינָא הָדַרְנָא בִּי, אֵימַר לְהוּ דַּאֲנָא לְהַאי יְהַבְתָּא, [9]וְנִיהַדְרוּ נִיהֲלֵיהּ כְּתָבָא, כִּי הֵיכִי דְּכִי מַפֵּיק הַאי כְּתָבָא, דְּקָדֵים, זָכָה בֵּיהּ הוּא״. [10]אֶלָּא, אָמְרִינַן לֵיהּ אֲנַן: ״הַאי כְּתָבָא לָא יָהֲבִינַן לֵיהּ לְהַאי.

LITERAL TRANSLATION

[1]Even if he gave it to him as the gift of a dying person, he has no loss; [2]for the later [deed] confers ownership, since [the donor] retracted the first [gift].

[3]When the Baraita teaches: "Even though both [parties] agree, [4][the finder] should not return it, neither to this one nor to this one," [5][this refers] to a healthy person, who does not have the right to retract. [6]For we say: Perhaps [the donor] originally wrote it for this one, and he changed his mind and did not give it to him, [7]and later he wrote it for another person and gave it to him, [and] now he has retracted [his gift] from the [second] one to whom he gave it. [8]For he thinks: "I cannot retract, [so] I will say to them that I gave it to this one, [9]and they will return the deed to him, so that when this one produces his deed, which came first, he will acquire [the gift]." [10]Rather, we say to [the donor]: "This document we are not giving to this one.

RASHI

דאי יהבתיה לאיניש אחרינא לית ליה פסידא — בשטרא דכתבת השתא, דמאן דקדים שטריה זכה.

BACKGROUND

מַתְּנַת בָּרִיא וּמַתְּנַת שְׁכִיב מְרַע The gift of a healthy person and the gift of a dying person. The main difference between these two types of gift in this context concerns the validity of deeds of gift of different dates. In general, the gift of a healthy person takes effect the moment the deed is written and transferred, and the recipient acquires it immediately. Therefore the deed of gift bearing the earliest date is the valid one. In contrast, a person who is ill may change his mind, since his gift is not acquired until after his death, and while he is still alive the gift does not take effect. Therefore, in the case of a will, the document bearing the latest date is the valid one.

NOTES

Ramban replies: The Gemara could have proved its point using this reasoning, but it preferred to use the seeming contradiction between the Mishnah and the Baraita to bring out the difference in the cases more clearly.

דְּאָמְרִינַן...דְּאָמְרִינַן For we say.... For we say... There is a tradition that these four long explanatory passages beginning with the words "for we say" are not an integral part of the Talmud, but are later glosses added by *Rav Yehudai Gaon* (eighth century C.E.) after the Talmud was completed. Hence they are not considered authoritative, and *Ramban*, in fact, disagrees with some of their implications.

A later commentator explains that the length of these passages was necessary in order to teach us that the court must explain in full to the donor and the beneficiary why the lost deed may not be returned, even with the concurrence of both parties. This rule applies whenever a litigant asks for an explanation of a verdict; but such a demand is to be expected almost as a matter of course in a ruling as subtle as this one (*Ḥokhmat Manoaḥ*).

HALAKHAH

to the recipient, provided that the donor is alive and agrees that the deed should be given to the recipient. But if the donor has died, even if his heirs consent to having the deed returned to the recipient, it may not be returned, unless it was a deed of transfer," in accordance with the Gemara's conclusion here. (*Shulḥan Arukh, Ḥoshen Mishpat* 65:14.)

[1]דִּלְמָא מִכְתַּב כְּתַבְתְּ, מִיהַב לָא יְהַבְתְּ נִיהֲלֵיהּ, וִיהַבְתָּהּ לְאִינִישׁ אַחֲרִינָא וְקָא הָדְרַתְּ בֵּיהּ. [2]אִי לָא יְהַבְתָּהּ לְאִינִישׁ אַחֲרִינָא, וְקָא בָּעֵית דְּתִתְבָהּ לְהַאי, [3]כְּתִיב לֵיהּ הָשְׁתָּא כְּתָבָא אַחֲרִינָא וִיהָבֵיהּ נִיהֲלֵיהּ, [4]דְּאִי יְהַבְתְּ לְאִינִישׁ אַחֲרִינָא, לֵית בָּהּ פְּסֵידָא, דְּקָדֵים זָכֵי.

[5]מַתְקִיף לָהּ רַב זְבִיד: וְהָא אִידִי וְאִידִי ״דְּיַיתִּקָאוֹת״ קָא תָּנֵי!

[6]אֶלָּא אֲמַר רַב זְבִיד: הָא וְהָא בִּשְׁכִיב מְרַע, וְלָא קַשְׁיָא. [7]הָא בֵּיהּ, וְהָא בִּבְרֵיהּ.

[8]מַתְנִיתִין: ״דְּקָא אֲמַר ׳תְּנוּ׳, נוֹתְנִין״, בְּדִידֵיהּ, [9]דְּבַר מִהֲדַר הוּא. [10]דְּאָמְרִינַן: אִי נַמִי יְהָבָהּ לְאִינִישׁ אַחֲרִינָא, לֵית בָּהּ פְּסֵידָא, [11]דְּקַמָּא וּבַתְרָא, בַּתְרָא זָכֵי, [12]דְּהָא הֲדַר בֵּיהּ מִקַּמָּא.

[13]כִּי קָא תָּנֵי בְּבָרַיְיתָא: ״אַף עַל פִּי שֶׁשְּׁנֵיהֶם מוֹדִים, לֹא יַחֲזִיר, לֹא לָזֶה וְלֹא לָזֶה״, [14]בִּבְרֵיהּ. [15]דְּאָמְרִינַן: דִּלְמָא כָּתַב אֲבוּהּ

LITERAL TRANSLATION

[1]Perhaps you did write it, [but] you did not give it to him, and you gave it to another person and [then] you retracted. [2]If you did not give it to another person, and you wish to give it to this one, [3]write another document for him now, and give it to him, [4]because if you [previously] gave [this property] to another person, he will have no loss, for the earlier one acquires."

[5]Rav Zevid strongly objected: Surely both this [Mishnah] and this [Baraita] teach "wills"!

[6]Rather, Rav Zevid said: This [Mishnah] and that [Baraita refer] to [a will drawn up by] a dying person, and there is no difficulty. [7]This [Mishnah refers] to him, and this [Baraita refers] to his son.

[8]The Mishnah, which [states]: "[If] he said: 'Give,' we give," [refers] to him, [9]since he has the right to retract. [10]For we say: Even if he gave it to another person, [the other person] has no loss, [11]for [in a confrontation between] the first [deed] and the second [deed], the second [deed] confers ownership, [12]since [the donor] retracted the first [deed].

[13]When the Baraita teaches: "Even though both [parties] agree, [the finder] should not return [the will], neither to this one nor to this one," [14][this refers] to his son. [15]For we say: Perhaps his father wrote [the lost will]

TRANSLATION AND COMMENTARY

first person (A), [1]because **you may perhaps have written it but you may not have given it to him, and you** may have written another deed and **given it to another person** (B) **and you may** then **have retracted** and decided that you do not want B to have it. [2]**If** in fact **you did not give it to another person** (B), **and you** now **wish to give it to** the first **person** (A), [3]**write another document for him now, and give it to him,** [4]**because if you did previously give this property to another person** (B), B **will suffer no loss** from the fact that you are now drawing up another deed of gift for the same property you gave B. **For the** person with the **deed** dated **earlier will acquire** the gift."

מַתְקִיף לָהּ רַב זְבִיד [5]**Rav Zevid strongly objected** to this suggested resolution of the contradiction between the Mishnah and the Baraita: **Surely both the Mishnah and the Baraita refer to "wills,"** and not only to "deeds of gift"! But wills are issued by dying people. How, then, can we explain that the Baraita is referring specifically to a healthy person?

אֶלָּא אֲמַר רַב זְבִיד [6]**Rather, Rav Zevid said** that the contradiction may be resolved as follows: **Both the Mishnah and the Baraita refer to a will drawn up by a dying person, and there is no difficulty** in reconciling the rulings in the two sources. [7]**The Mishnah refers to** a case where the donor **himself** admitted before he died that the lost deed was authentic, **and the Baraita refers to** a case where **his son** authenticates the deed after the father, the donor, has died.

מַתְנִיתִין [8]The Gemara now explains in greater detail: **The Mishnah, which** by inference **states:** "**If** the donor **says, 'Give** the lost deed to the recipient,' **we do give** it," **refers** to the donor **himself,** [9]**since he has the right to retract** his gift if he wishes. [10]**For we say: Even if** the donor **gave** another deed, willing this property **to another person** (B), **that other person suffers no loss** by the returning of the lost deed to A, [11]**for in a confrontation between the first deed and the second deed, the second deed confers ownership** of the gift, [12]**since the donor retracted the first deed**. Thus, if we return the lost deed to A, no loss is suffered by B — if he exists!

כִּי קָא תָּנֵי בְּבָרַיְיתָא [13]But by contrast, **when the Baraita teaches:** "**Even though both parties agree** that the lost will is genuine, **the finder should not return** it **to either one,**" [14]**this refers to** returning the will after the death of the original donor, with the acquiescence of the donor's **son**. [15]**For we say: His father may perhaps have**

RASHI

ביה — שעדיין הוא קיים, ואמר "תנו לזה". **הא בבריה** — שמת מאליו, וזה בנו אומר "החזירהו". **דבר מהדר הוא** — ממתנה זו. אם חזר בו לאחר שיצאו שני שטרות בבית דין — יזכה האחרון. **אי נמי יהבה** — שוב לאיניש אחרינא במתנת בריא. **לית ליה פסידא** — להוא בתרא בהאי שטרא דמהדרינא ליה להאי.

TRANSLATION AND COMMENTARY

written the lost will for one person (A), the person named in the lost will, **and may have changed his mind and not given it to him** at all, [1]**and after the father died**, the son **may have written a deed of gift** for the same property **for another person** (B), **and may have given it to him.** [2]**But now the son wishes to retract his gift** to **that person** (B) and give it instead to A. But he does not simply write a new deed. Instead he takes out the old one and announces that his father had already delivered it. [3]**For he thinks** as follows: "**I cannot retract** my gift to B, since I am healthy, and a healthy person cannot withdraw his gift. [4]**So I will say to the** judges **that my father gave the** lost **will to the first person** (A), **and they will give him his deed.** [5]Then **we will go and take** the property **away from** B, **who was the one who really acquired it, and we will divide it between us.**"

הִלְכָּךְ אָמְרִינַן לֵיהּ אֲנַן [6]**Therefore**, in order to prevent this possible conspiracy from taking place, **we say to** the son: "**We will not give this** lost **document to the first recipient** (A), whose name appears on it, [7]**because your father may perhaps have written it, but he may not have given it to him,** [8]**and you may have** written a deed of gift after your father died and **given it to another person** (B), **and you may** then **have retracted** and decided that you do not want B to have it. [9]**But if your statement that your father gave** the lost will **to A is true,** [10]**go now yourself, and write another deed** of gift, **for** A, [11]**so that even if your father did not give it to him, and you wrote a deed of gift** transferring the same property **to another person** (B), B will **suffer no loss** from the fact that you are now drawing up another deed of gift for the same property and giving it to A.

לְהַאי, וְאִמְלִיךְ וְלָא יְהָבֵיהּ נִיהֲלֵיהּ, [1]וּבָתַר אֲבוּהּ, כָּתַב אִיהוּ לְאִינִישׁ אַחֲרִינָא, וִיהָבָהּ לֵיהּ. [2]וְהָשְׁתָּא קָא הָדַר בֵּיהּ מֵהַהוּא. [3]סָבַר: "מֶהְדַּר לָא מָצֵינָא הָדַרְנָא בִּי, [4]אֵימַר לְהוּ דְּאַבָּא יְהָבָהּ לֵיהּ לְהַאי, וְנִתְבוּ לֵיהּ כְּתָבֵיהּ; [5]וְנֵיזִיל וְנַפֵּיק מִינֵּהּ, דְּהוּא זָכֵי, וְנִפְלוֹג בַּהֲדֵיהּ".

[6]הִלְכָּךְ אָמְרִינַן לֵיהּ אֲנַן: "הַאי כְּתָבָא לָא יָהֲבִינַן לֵיהּ לְהַאי, [7]דְּדִלְמָא מִכְתַּב כְּתָבֵיהּ אֲבוּהּ, מֵיהַב לָא יְהָבָהּ לֵיהּ, [8]וִיהַבְתֵּיהּ אַתְּ לְאִינִישׁ אַחֲרִינָא וְקָא הָדְרַתְּ בֵּיהּ. [9]אֶלָּא אִי קוּשְׁטָא קָא אָמְרַתְּ, דִּיהַב לֵיהּ אֲבוּךְ, [10]זִיל אַתְּ הָשְׁתָּא, כְּתִיב לֵיהּ שְׁטָרָא אַחֲרִינָא, [11]דְּאִי נַמִי לָא יְהָבָהּ לֵיהּ אֲבוּהּ, וּכְתַבְתֵּיהּ אַתְּ לְאִינִישׁ אַחֲרִינָא, לֵית בָּהּ

LITERAL TRANSLATION

for this one, and he changed his mind and did not give it to him, [1]and after the father [died], he wrote [a deed of gift] for another person, and he gave it to him. [2]But now [the son wishes] to retract [his gift] from that one. [3][For] he thinks: "I cannot retract, [4][so] I will say to them that my father gave [the will] to this one, and they will give him his deed; [5]and we will go and take [the property] away from [the second person], who was the one who [really] acquired [it], and we will divide it together."

[6]Therefore, we say to him: "This document we do not give to this one, [7]for perhaps your father wrote it [but] he did not give it to him, [8]and you gave it to another person and you retracted. [9]But if [what] you said [is] the truth, that your father gave it to him, [10]go now yourself, [and] write for him another deed, [11]so that even if your father did not give it to him, and you wrote [a deed of gift] for another person, [the other person] has no

RASHI

כתבה איהו – הבן. **דהוא קדים** – שיהא שטרו קודם, דכיון דמת אביו מאליו זכה משנתנה לו. **ונפלוג בהדיה** – אחלוק עמו בקנויה זו.

NOTES

וְנִפְלוֹג בַּהֲדֵיהּ **And we will divide it.** Why was it Rav Zevid who expressed concern at the possibility of conspiracy, in explaining the Baraita as referring to the son of the donor, but not Rabbi Abba, who explained the Baraita as referring to a healthy man? After all, the healthy man could also conspire with the first recipient to take the gift away from the second recipient and then divide it!

The Rishonim point out that the authenticity of the deed is not in doubt, but merely whether it was delivered; and irrespective of whether the deed was delivered, the beneficiary was clearly friendly enough with the donor for him to consider giving him a gift. Accordingly, there is no reason to imagine that the donor is engaging in a conspiracy to recover the gift *for himself*. On the other hand, the son would not perjure himself in order to transfer his father's gift from one of his father's friends to another. If the son is lying, it can only be to benefit himself (*Talmid Rabbenu Peretz, Ritva*).

A later commentator adds that a man who has already given something away — perhaps twice — is clearly not interested in owning it himself and would not perjure himself in order to recover it (*Ḥokhmat Manoaḥ*).

TRANSLATION AND COMMENTARY

[1]**For in a confrontation between the first deed**, previously given to B, **and the second**, now being written for A, **the first deed**, whose date is earlier, **will confer ownership** of the property. Thus in this case the lost document is *not* returned, and there is no contradiction between our Mishnah and the Baraita quoted above.

תָּנוּ רַבָּנַן [2]**Our Rabbis taught in the following Baraita**: "If **someone found a receipt** for a ketubah, in a case **where the woman admits** that the receipt is genuine, that she has received the value of her ketubah, and that she has given him the receipt, the finder **should return it to the husband**. [3]**If the woman does not admit** that the receipt is genuine, **the finder should not return** the receipt **either to the** husband **or to the** wife."

בִּזְמַן שֶׁהָאִשָּׁה מוֹדָה [4]**At all events**, says the Gemara, **when the woman admits** the authenticity of the receipt, **the finder should return it to the husband**. [5]**But**, suggests the Gemara, **let us be concerned** about the possibility **that she may perhaps have written the receipt with the intention of giving it** to her husband **in Nisan**, and the receipt bears that date, **but** in fact **she did not give it** to him **until Tishri**, when he actually paid her the value of her ketubah. [6]Meanwhile, **she went and sold her** rights to collect the **ketubah** to another person **between Nisan and Tishri**, **for its potential value**. The term טוֹבַת הֲנָאָה here refers to a drastically discounted value. The buyer of the wife's future rights to her ketubah would not place a high value upon it, because he will only collect it in the event of the husband dying before his wife or divorcing her. In the event of the wife dying before her husband, the latter will be her heir and the buyer of the ketubah will receive nothing. But if the wife was in need of ready money, she might have sold the ketubah for a small sum. If she sold it between Nisan and Tishri, the sale is valid, as the ketubah had not yet been paid.

פְּסֵידָא, [1]דְּקַמָּא וּבַתְרָא, קַמָּא זָכֵי".

[2]תָּנוּ רַבָּנַן: "מָצָא שׁוֹבֵר, בִּזְמַן שֶׁהָאִשָּׁה מוֹדָה, יַחֲזִיר לַבַּעַל. [3]אֵין הָאִשָּׁה מוֹדָה, לֹא יַחֲזִיר, לֹא לָזֶה וְלֹא לָזֶה".

[4]בִּזְמַן שֶׁהָאִשָּׁה מוֹדָה, מִיהַת, יַחֲזִיר לַבַּעַל. [5]וְלִיחוּשׁ דִּלְמָא כְּתָבָה לִיתֵּן בְּנִיסָן, וְלֹא נְתָנָה עַד תִּשְׁרֵי. [6]וְאָזְלָה זַבִּנְתָּה לִכְתוּבָּה בְּטוֹבַת הֲנָאָה מִנִּיסָן

LITERAL TRANSLATION

[1]loss, for [in a confrontation between] the first [deed] and the second [deed], the first [deed] confers ownership.

[2]Our Rabbis taught [in the following Baraita]: "[If] one found a receipt, when the woman admits, he should return it to the husband. [3][If] the woman does not admit, [the finder] should not return it, neither to this one nor to this one."

[4]When the woman admits, at all events, [the finder] should return it to the husband. [5]But let us be concerned that perhaps she wrote [the receipt] to give it in Nisan, but she did not give [it] until Tishri. [6]And she went [and] sold her ketubah between Nisan and Tishri for its potential value (lit., "the good of benefit"),

RASHI

קמא זכה – מאחר ששני השטרות יצאו משמך, הקודם זכה, שמתנת בריא הם. והשתא דאוקימנא טעמא דלא יחזיר משום דלמא כתבה להאי, ואמליך ולא יהבה ליה, והדר כתבה לאיניש אחרינא – ליכא למרמי אמתנות. ולא תידוק מתניתין גבי מתנות הא אמר "תנו" נותנין, דכי נמי אמר "תנו" – שייך למימר טעמא דלא יחזיר, משום שאני אומר כתובין היו ונמלך עליהן שלא לתנן, והדר כתבה לאיניש אחרינא. וגבי דייתקאות, על כרחך אם אמר "תנו" – נותנין אם הוא קיים, דהא תלה תנא דידן טעמא משום שאני אומר נמלך עליהן שלא לתנן, ואי נמי הכי הוה דנמלך השתא, אם אמר "תנו" – נותנין דליכא למיחש למידי, והכי קאמר: מצא דייתיקי או מתנה לא יחזיר, שאני אומר כו'. והיכא דאמר "תנו", [אי] שייך למימר לא יחזיר, משום טעמא דשאני אומר, כגון מתנת בריא או בשכיב מרע ומת ובריה קאמר "תנו" – שמעינן ממתניתין דלא יחזיר, ולא דייקינן האמר "תנו" נותנין. והיכא דלא שייך למימר "שאני אומר", כגון בשכיב מרע שלא מת מחליו – דייקינן האמר "תנו", דבטל "שאני אומר", הלכך נותנין. **מצא שובר** – שכתבה אשה לבעלה "התקבלתי כתובתי", ועודה תחתיו. **ולא נתנה עד תשרי** – והוא לא פרע עד תשרי. **ואזלה** – איהי בעודה תחתיו, בין ניסן לתשרי. **וזבנתה לכתובה** – לאחר. **בטובת הנאה** – כלומר; בזול, לפי שנותן מעותיו בספק. שאם תמות היא – יירשנה בעלה, ויפסיד מי שלקחה. ואם ימות בעלה או יגרשנה – יהיה לוקח במקומה, ויגבה כתובתה. ושוב לא היה לבעלה לפרוע לה הכתובה אלא ללוקח. ושובר שנכתב בשמה אינו כלום.

NOTES

דִּלְמָא אָזְלָה זַבִּנְתָּה **Perhaps she went and sold**. The commentators ask: If we are to concern ourselves with the possibility that the ketubah may have been sold to another person after the date recorded on the receipt, then it should not be permitted to return any lost object to a person who presents identifying marks! That person may indeed have been the object's original owner, but he may, in the meantime, have sold it to someone else, and, remembering

HALAKHAH

מְצִיאַת שׁוֹבֵר כְּתוּבָּה **Returning a lost ketubah receipt**. "A person who finds a receipt stating that a woman has been paid her ketubah may return it to the husband, provided that the woman confirms that she has received her ketubah payment. But if she does not admit this, the receipt may not be returned either to the woman or her husband," following the Gemara. (*Shulḥan Arukh Even HaEzer* 110:2.)

BACKGROUND

זַבִּנְתָּה לִכְתוּבָּה בְּטוֹבַת הֲנָאָה **She sold her ketubah for its potential value**. As long as a woman is married, her ketubah is of no actual value, for it merely attests to the husband's obligation to pay his wife a certain sum when the marriage is dissolved. Moreover, unlike other promissory notes, which may be transferred in various ways, a ketubah, although it is guaranteed by the husband's property, is no more than a conditional obligation, for if the wife should die during her husband's lifetime, the obligation to her is cancelled. Therefore, someone who buys a ketubah does not pay an amount anywhere near the full sum indicated in it, but merely an estimate of its "potential value," for it is very doubtful whether he will ever receive anything in return for it.

עַד תִּשְׁרֵי, [1]וּמַפֵּיק לֵיהּ לַשּׁוֹבֵר דִּכְתִיב בְּנִיסָן, וַאֲתָא לְמִטְרַף לָקוֹחוֹת שֶׁלֹּא כַּדִּין!
[2]אֲמַר רָבָא: [20A] שְׁמַע מִינָּהּ אִיתָא לִדְשְׁמוּאֵל. [3]דְּאָמַר שְׁמוּאֵל: הַמּוֹכֵר שְׁטַר חוֹב לַחֲבֵירוֹ וּמְחָלוֹ, מָחוּל, [4]וַאֲפִילּוּ יוֹרֵשׁ מוֹחֵל.

LITERAL TRANSLATION

[1]and [the husband] will produce the receipt which was written in Nisan, and he will come to seize [property from the] buyers unlawfully!
[2]Rava said: [20A] Deduce from this that Shmuel's [view] is [accepted]. [3]For Shmuel said: One who sells a promissory note to another person and later renounces [repayment], [the debt] is renounced, [4]and even the heir may renounce [repayment].

TRANSLATION AND COMMENTARY

[1]But since the receipt was antedated, the husband **can produce the receipt which was written in Nisan, and seize unlawfully property** which had been designated for payment of the wife's ketubah **from the buyer** who purchased the rights to the ketubah. For the husband will claim — falsely — that the ketubah was already paid in Nisan, before the woman sold it, and accordingly he, rather than the buyers, is entitled to keep the property.

אֲמַר רָבָא [2]**Rava said** in reply: [20A] Since the Baraita is not concerned about the possibility of a predated receipt, we may **deduce from this that Shmuel's viewpoint is accepted**, [3]**for Shmuel said**: If **someone sells a promissory note to another person and later renounces repayment** of the loan, **the debt is renounced**, and the buyer of the promissory note cannot collect with it (although he may sue the seller for causing him a loss). [4]**And even the heir** of the person who sold the promissory note **may renounce repayment** of the loan, thereby preventing the buyer from collecting with the promissory note. Similarly, since a ketubah is a promissory note written by the husband for the wife, the wife may renounce payment of her ketubah at any time before it is due to be paid, and thus deprive the buyer of the ketubah of his right to collect payment, thus leaving the property in the husband's possession. Hence the date on the receipt is immaterial. Even if it was dated later than the date on which the ketubah was sold, it would still cancel the sale of the ketubah.

RASHI

ומפיק לשובר — שכתוב בניסן, ויקדוס לשטרו של לוקח, ויחזיק הבעל בקרקע המיוחדת לכתובתה שלא כדין. **שמע מינה** — מדלא חיישינן להכי, דאי נמי הוה הכי — שפיר זכי בעל בשובר שנכתב לשמה. **איתא לדשמואל** — דאמר: המוכר שטר חוב לחבירו, וחזר המוכר הזו ומחלו — מחול הוא אצל הלוה. הלכך, אם מכרה זו כתובתה באייר, דהיינו שטר חוב, וחזרה ומחלתה לבעל בתשרי — מחול, ושפיר טריף בעל.

NOTES

what it looked like, may have come forward now to identify it and claim it for himself!

The commentators answer that a finder of a lost object ordinarily announces his discovery publicly. Therefore, there is nothing to prevent the present owner from stepping forward and identifying the object himself. But in a case like ours, where there was no need for a public announcement because there was no doubt that the husband was the owner of the receipt, we must suspect the possibility of sale (*Ritva*).

מְחִילַת שְׁטַר חוֹב **Renouncing repayment of a promissory note**. The Rishonim found Shmuel's ruling problematic. If the sale of the promissory note was valid, the original creditor's rights were transferred to the buyer, and the former should no longer have the power to renounce repayment of the debt. And if the sale was invalid, then the buyer should not be able to collect at all, even if the debt was not renounced.

Numerous explanations have been suggested. According to some commentators the sale of a promissory note is valid only by Rabbinic decree; by Torah law the debt is still owed to the original creditor and hence can be renounced by him (*Rambam, Hilkhot Mekhirah* 6:12, *Ri* and *Rabbenu Tam* as cited by *Tosafot, Ketubot* 85b).

According to another view, the obligation to repay a loan is personal, and the lien generated by a promissory note is in effect a form of guarantee of repayment. A creditor can sell his rights to the lien on the borrower's property, but the borrower's personal obligation to repay the debt to the creditor cannot be sold. Hence, the creditor can cancel the borrower's personal obligation after the sale, and since the lien on the borrower's property is merely a guarantee, the cancellation of the personal obligation automatically nullifies the lien (alternative version of *Rabbenu Tam* quoted by *Tosefot HaRosh, Ketubot* 85b).

Still another view distinguishes between the creditor's right to collect and the debtor's obligation to pay. While it is possible for the creditor to transfer his right, only the debtor himself can transfer his obligation. Therefore, the debtor has no direct obligation to the buyer, even after the sale, and the creditor can still renounce the debt. According to this view, if the promissory note states explicitly that the borrower is obligated directly to the creditor or to anyone else to whom the creditor may transfer his rights, the debt cannot be renounced (*Ra'avad* on the above *Rambam*).

The *Sefer HaHashlamah* extends this idea, declaring that, even when the debt is not renounced, the buyer has no right to demand payment from the debtor; he must, instead, ask the creditor to claim the money for him.

הַמּוֹכֵר שְׁטַר חוֹב וּמְחָלוֹ **One who renounced repayment**

HALAKHAH

הַמּוֹכֵר שְׁטַר חוֹב וּמְחָלוֹ **If one sells a promissory note and renounces the debt**. "If a person sold a promissory note and then renounced repayment of the borrower's debt, the debt is cancelled. Even the creditor's heir may renounce repayment of the debt," following Shmuel's view. (*Shulḥan Arukh, Ḥoshen Mishpat* 66:23.)

[1]אַבַּיֵי אֲמַר: אֲפִילּוּ תֵּימָא לֵיתֵיהּ לִדְשְׁמוּאֵל. [2]הָכָא בְּמַאי עָסְקִינַן? [3]בְּשֶׁשְּׁטַר כְּתוּבָּה יוֹצֵא מִתַּחַת יָדָהּ.

[4]וְרָבָא אֲמַר: אִי מִשּׁוּם שְׁטַר כְּתוּבָּה, חָיְישִׁינַן לִשְׁתֵּי כְּתוּבּוֹת.

[5]וְאַבַּיֵי אֲמַר: חֲדָא, לִשְׁתֵּי כְּתוּבּוֹת לָא חָיְישִׁינַן; [6]וְעוֹד, שׁוֹבֵר בִּזְמַנּוֹ טָרֵיף.

[7]אַבַּיֵי לְטַעְמֵיהּ, דַּאֲמַר: עֵדָיו בַּחֲתוּמָיו זָכִין לוֹ.

TRANSLATION AND COMMENTARY

אַבַּיֵי אֲמַר [1]**Abaye** disagreed and **said: You may even say that Shmuel's view is not accepted**, because the Baraita can be interpreted differently: [2]**With what are we dealing here**, and why, according to the Baraita, may the receipt be returned to the husband? [3]We are dealing with a case **where a ketubah document is in the wife's possession** and she produces it. Since the woman produces the ketubah, it is obvious that she has not sold it to anyone else, and the whole theory suggested above by the Gemara is unfounded.

וְרָבָא אֲמַר [4]**But Rava said** in reply to this argument: **If** you argue that the receipt may be returned to the husband and **the husband may collect because** a **ketubah document is in the woman's possession**, this argument is not acceptable, because **we should be concerned about** the possibility of the wife having **two ketubot**. It is possible that the husband gave his wife two ketubot for some reason. The first ketubah was sold by the wife and later renounced by her in favor of her husband, and the other she kept for herself and is now producing!

וְאַבַּיֵי אֲמַר [5]**But Abaye said** in reply to this argument that Rava's reasoning is incorrect for two reasons: **First, we are not concerned about** the possibility that she may have **two ketubot**, as the likelihood that a husband has written two ketubot for his wife is very remote; [6]**and furthermore, a receipt enables its owner to seize property** from the buyers **from the date appearing on it**, irrespective of when the debt was actually repaid. Thus, the husband is entitled to keep the land designated for payment of the ketubah even if the receipt had been drawn up before he paid the ketubah. Even if the husband received the receipt in Tishri, the fact that it was dated in Nisan means that any disposal made by the wife of the potential value of her ketubah from after the date on the receipt has no validity. Thus the Baraita offers no support for Shmuel's viewpoint.

אַבַּיֵי לְטַעְמֵיהּ [7]The Gemara adds: **Abaye**'s statement here **is in accordance with his own view** expressed elsewhere, **for he said** (above, 13a): **The witnesses** to a document **confer ownership on** the beneficiary of the document **by** putting **their signatures** on it, and thus any legal document takes effect from the date appearing on it, even if it was actually delivered later.

LITERAL TRANSLATION

[1]Abaye said: You may even say that Shmuel's [view] is not [accepted]. [2]With what are we dealing here? [3]With a ketubah document that is in [the woman's] hand.

[4]But Rava says: If [the husband may collect] because of [the woman's] ketubah document, we are concerned about two ketubot.

[5]But Abaye says: First, we are not concerned about two ketubot; [6]and furthermore, a receipt [enables its owner] to seize [property] from the date [appearing] on it.

[7]Abaye [is in accordance] with his [own] view, for he said: His witnesses confer ownership on him by their signatures.

RASHI

בששטר כתובה יוצא מתחת ידה – שמביאה לפנינו, דליכא למיחש לשמא מכרה בטובת הנאה, שאילו מכרתה היתה מוסרת הכתובה ביד הלוקח. **לשתי כתובות** – שמא שני שטרי כתובה היו לה, [ויש] לחוש שמא מסרה אחד ללוקח, ובאה לחזור בה ולמחול אצל בעלה. ומוסרת לו שובר המוקדם לשטרו של לוקח. אלא ודאי איתא לדשמואל, ומתוך שבידו למחול שטר כתובה לבעלה עכשיו, לא חיישינן לשמא כתבה ליתן בניסן כו׳. **ואביי אמר** – מהכא לא תסייע לשמואל. **חדא דלשתי כתובות לא חיישינן** – הלכך ליכא למיחש לדלמא זבנתה בטובת הנאה. **ועוד** – אי נמי זבנתה בטובת הנאה לית לן למיחש לשמא כתבה לשובר בניסן ולא קבלה עד תשרי. דאי נמי הכי הוא, כי מטא שובר לידיה בתשרי – זוכה למפרע בו מזמן חתימתו, ולא הוה ממכרה שבנתיים כלום, ושובר בזמן הכתוב בו טורף. ואביי לטעמיה כו׳.

NOTES

of a sold promissory note. The Gemara (*Ketubot* 86a) concludes that a creditor who renounces repayment of a debt must reimburse the person who bought the note from him for his losses. But there is a difference of opinion among the Rishonim as to whether he must pay the entire sum of money stipulated in the promissory note (*Rashi*, *Ketubot* 86a), or whether he only need refund what the buyer actually paid him (*Tosafot*, *Bava Batra* 147b), and the discussion in *Tosafot* largely revolves around the passage in our Gemara.

בְּשֶׁשְּׁטַר כְּתוּבָּה יוֹצֵא מִתַּחַת יָדָהּ When the ketubah is in the wife's possession. Some commentators argue on the basis of this discussion that transfer of ownership of a document does not take effect unless the document is physically transferred to the buyer's possession (otherwise, the woman might have sold the ketubah to another person without actually giving it to him; see *Ittur*).

Others, however, maintain that in this particular case the buyer would not rely on the woman unless she actually gave him the ketubah (*Ramban* and others).

חָיְישִׁינַן לִשְׁתֵּי כְּתוּבּוֹת We are concerned that there might be two ketubot. This concern would apply only if the receipt were written in a general way, without specifically identifying the ketubah it was cancelling. In such a case, the receipt would effectively cancel both ketubot (*Ritva*).

TRANSLATION AND COMMENTARY

MISHNAH מָצָא אִיגְּרוֹת שׁוּם [1]**If someone found letters of assessment**, i.e., documents stating that the court had appraised a borrower's property and assigned it to the lender in repayment of an outstanding debt, **or letters of maintenance**, i.e., documents in which the court records a husband's undertaking to support his wife's daughter from a previous husband, **deeds of** ***ḥalitzah***, certifying that a woman had received *ḥalitzah* (see above, 16b), **or** ***me'un***, certifying that a fatherless girl below the age of majority, whose mother or brothers had arranged her marriage, had dissolved this marriage (without a divorce; see note), **or deeds of** ***berurin*** (as explained by the Gemara below), **or any** other **court decision** attested in a document, **he should return them**. In all these cases the deeds may be returned to their owners, because they are official court documents, which would not have been drawn up if the transactions recorded in them had not been completed.

מָצָא בַּחֲפִיסָה אוֹ בִּדְלוּסְקְמָא [2]**If a person found** lost documents of any kind **in a small bag or a case, or if he found a roll of documents or a bundle of documents, he should return them**. In all these cases the place or the situation in which the documents were found constitutes a means of identifying them. [3]**How many documents** constitute **"a bundle of documents"**?

משנה [1]מָצָא אִיגְּרוֹת שׁוּם וְאִיגְּרוֹת מָזוֹן, שִׁטְרֵי חֲלִיצָה וּמֵיאוּנִין, וְשִׁטְרֵי בֵּירוּרִין, וְכָל מַעֲשֵׂה בֵּית דִּין, הֲרֵי זֶה יַחֲזִיר. [2]מָצָא בַּחֲפִיסָה אוֹ בִּדְלוּסְקְמָא, תַּכְרִיךְ שֶׁל שְׁטָרוֹת אוֹ אֲגוּדָּה שֶׁל שְׁטָרוֹת, הֲרֵי זֶה יַחֲזִיר. [3]וְכַמָּה אֲגוּדָּה שֶׁל שְׁטָרוֹת?

LITERAL TRANSLATION

MISHNAH [1][If] one found letters of assessment or letters of maintenance, deeds of *ḥalitzah* or *me'un*, or deeds of *berurin*, or any court-decision, he should return [them].

[2][If] he found [documents] in a small bag or a case, [or if he found] a roll of documents or a bundle of documents, he should return [them]. [3]And how many [documents] are a bundle of documents?

RASHI

משנה איגרות שום — ששמו בית דין נכסי לוה למלוה בחובו. **ואיגרות מזון** — שקיבל עליו לזון את בת אשתו. **מיאונין** — קטנה יתומה שהשיאוה אמה ואחיה לדעתה, יוצאה ממנו במיאון, ואינה צריכה גט, אלא אומרת בפני שלשה: אי אפשי בפלוני בעלי. וכותבין לה בית דין שטר שמיאנה בפניהם, להיות לה עדות שמותרת לינשא. **שטרי ברורין** — בגמרא מפרש. **הרי זה יחזיר** — דליכא למיחש לשמא נמלך, דהא בית דין לא כתבוס אלא בדבר מקויים. ולפרעון נמי ליכא למיחש, דהני שטרות לא שייך בהו פרעון, כדאמרינן לעיל (טז,ב). ואפילו למאן דאמר שומא הדר — איהו דאפסיד אנפשיה. **מצא בחפיסה או בדלוסקמא** — שום שטר. **או שמצא תכריך של שטרות** — בכרך או באגודה. ובגמרא מפרש מאי חפיסה ודלוסקמא ותכריך ואגודה. **הרי זה יחזיר** — דדבר שיש בו סימן הוא, כדמפרש בגמרא שהכלי סימן, כשאמרו הבעלים בכלי כך וכך מצאת אותם. וכן תכריך ואגודה — הרי זה יחזיר, דדבר שיש בו סימן הוא, כדמפרש בגמרא.

NOTES

אִיגְּרוֹת שׁוּם וְאִיגְּרוֹת מָזוֹן Letters of assessment and letters of maintenance. *Rashi's* interpretation, followed also by the commentary here, is that a letter of assessment is issued when the court has appraised the debtor's property and assigns it to the creditor, and a letter of maintenance is issued when a man undertakes to support his wife's daughter from a previous husband. Accordingly, since these are court-issued documents, we need not suspect that they have not been delivered, and we may safely return them to their designated recipients.

Some commentators, however, ask: How do we know that these debts have not already been repaid? *Rashi* answers by referring us to 16b. There, the Gemara explained that our Mishnah is referring only to final, court-ordered transfers of land that can no longer be cancelled by simply paying the debt; instead, the debtor must buy the land back from the creditor.

Other commentators understand the Gemara on 16b to be referring only to the "any court decision" clause, and not to the rest of the Mishnah. Accordingly, they offer other interpretations of "letters of assessment" and "letters of maintenance" which do not refer to simple debts that can be repaid. One explanation is that these documents may not be deeds at all, but rather letters which the court is sending to another court asking for assistance in carrying out its decisions. Support for this explanation can be found in the fact that the Mishnah uses the word "letter" — אִגֶּרֶת — rather than "deed" — שְׁטָר (*Ritva*).

שִׁטְרֵי מֵיאוּנִין Deeds of ***me'un***. A girl who has not yet reached the age of majority can be married off by her father, even without her consent. The marriage is valid by Torah law and can be dissolved only by a bill of divorce. On the other hand, a girl whose father has died cannot be married by Torah law until she reaches the age of twelve. She can marry, however, by Rabbinic decree, upon her own consent and after consultation with her mother or older brothers, and the marriage attains Torah status on the girl's twelfth birthday. Until that time, the marriage is Rabbinic, and it can be dissolved by the girl unilaterally, by telling the court that she wishes to leave her husband. This procedure is called *me'un*, literally, "refusal." The court then issues the girl a deed attesting to the fact of the *me'un*.

HALAKHAH

מָצָא שְׁטָרוֹת מַעֲשֵׂה בֵּית דִּין If one found documents of court decisions. "If one found letters of assessment, letters of maintenance, deeds of *ḥalitzah*, *me'un*, documents recording litigants' selection of arbitration judges, or any other documents certified by the court, he may return them to their owners, for the court would not have written such

LANGUAGE

דְּלוּסְקְמָא Case. This word is probably derived from the Greek γλωσσόκομον, *glossokomon*, which means "box" or "case" (indeed, some texts of the Gemara here read: גְּלוּסְקְמָא).

CONCEPTS

שִׁטְרֵי חֲלִיצָה Deeds of ***ḥalitzah***. When a man dies without leaving children, his widow must either marry his brother (יִבּוּם) or free herself of that obligation by the ceremony of חֲלִיצָה — "taking off his shoe." This ceremony is performed in a Rabbinical Court, and afterwards the court gives the widow a certificate attesting that *ḥalitzah* has taken place and that she is free to marry anyone (except a priest). Unlike a bill of divorce, which is given by the husband, a deed of *ḥalitzah* is an official court document (מַעֲשֵׂה בֵּית דִּין).

שִׁטְרֵי מֵיאוּנִין Deeds of ***me'un***. The Sages ordained that the mother and brothers of a female minor whose father has died may marry her off. The validity of a marriage of this type does not derive from the Torah. Therefore, if the girl, while she is still a minor, shows in any way that she does not desire this marriage, it is thereby annulled, and she is regarded as if she has never been married. Although such a refusal does not need to be made in court, it was ordained that the court should issue a certificate attesting that the refusal has taken place and that the marriage has been annulled.

LITERAL TRANSLATION

Three tied together. [1]Rabban Shimon ben Gamliel says: One [borrower] who borrowed from three [lenders, the finder] should return [the documents] to the borrower; [2]three [borrowers] who borrowed from one [lender], [the finder] should return [the documents] to the lender.

[3][If] one found a document among one's documents and does not know what its nature is, it should remain [with him] until Elijah comes.

[4]If there are notes of cancellation among them, he must do what is [written] in the notes of cancellation.

GEMARA [5]What are "deeds of *berurin*"?

[6]Here [the Rabbis] explained: Deeds of arguments.

שְׁלֹשָׁה קְשׁוּרִין זֶה בָּזֶה. [1]רַבָּן שִׁמְעוֹן בֶּן גַּמְלִיאֵל אוֹמֵר: אֶחָד הַלֹּוֶה מִשְּׁלֹשָׁה, יַחֲזִיר לַלֹּוֶה; [2]שְׁלֹשָׁה הַלּוֹוִין מִן הָאֶחָד, יַחֲזִיר לַמַּלְוֶה.

[3]מָצָא שְׁטָר בֵּין שְׁטָרוֹתָיו וְאֵינוֹ יוֹדֵעַ מַה טִּיבוֹ, יְהֵא מוּנָּח עַד שֶׁיָּבוֹא אֵלִיָּהוּ.

[4]אִם יֵשׁ עִמָּהֶן סִמְפּוֹנוֹת, יַעֲשֶׂה מַה שֶּׁבַּסִּמְפּוֹנוֹת.

גמרא [5]מַאי "שְׁטָרֵי בֵירוּרִין"? [6]הָכָא תַּרְגְּמוּ: שְׁטָרֵי טַעֲנָתָא.

TRANSLATION AND COMMENTARY

Three tied together. [1]**Rabban Shimon ben Gamliel says** that the application of this law will also vary, depending on circumstances: **If** the lost documents were promissory notes recording loans that **one borrower borrowed from three** separate **lenders, the finder should return the documents to the borrower**, since it is reasonable to assume that it was he who lost them. [2]Conversely, if the lost documents record loans that **three** separate **borrowers borrowed from one lender, the finder should return the documents to the lender**, since it is reasonable to assume that it was he who lost them.

מָצָא שְׁטָר בֵּין שְׁטָרוֹתָיו [3]**If someone found among his documents a document** that someone else had placed in his care, **and he does not know what its nature is**, i.e., which party gave it to him and whether it has been paid in full or in part or not at all, **it should remain with him until Elijah comes**, for according to tradition the Prophet Elijah will resolve all unsolved legal questions.

אִם יֵשׁ עִמָּהֶן סִמְפּוֹנוֹת [4]If a creditor finds **among** his own documents **notes of cancellation** or receipts for repaid loans, **he must act** in accordance with **what is written in the notes of cancellation**. For we may assume that the notes of cancellation were written for the recipients specified in the documents, to indicate that the loans had been repaid. The creditor must assume that by chance he failed to pass on the receipt to the borrower and that the relevant loan has been repaid.

GEMARA מַאי שְׁטָרֵי בֵירוּרִין [5]The Gemara begins by clarifying the meaning of certain words in the Mishnah and asks: **What are "deeds of *berurin*"?**

הָכָא תַּרְגְּמוּ [6]The Gemara gives two explanations: (1): **Here**, in Babylonia, **the Rabbis explained**: They are **deeds containing arguments**, in which the claims of the litigants are recorded and are set forth.

RASHI

אחד הלוה משלשה – אם שלשה שטרות של לוה אחד הן, שלוה משלשה בני אדם. **יחזירם** – מוצאם. **ללוה** – דודאי פרעם והחזירם לו, ומידו נפלו. שאם מידם נפלו – מי קבצם למקום אחד? **ואם שלשה לוים הם** – שלוו מאדם אחד. **יחזירם** – המוצאם. **למלוה** – שהדבר ידוע שממנו נפלו. **מצא שטר בין שטרותיו ואין יודע מה טיבו** – אצלו, אם הלוה הפקידו אצלו או המלוה, או שמא מקצתו פרוע ומסרוהו לו להיות שליש ביניהם, ושכח. **יהא מונח** – בידו, ולא יחזיר לא לזה ולא לזה. **ואם יש עמהן סמפון** – מילי מילי קתני, המוצא בין שטריו שובר שנכתב על אחד משטרותיו. **יעשה מה שבסמפון** – והשטר בחזקת פרוע. ואף על פי שהיה לשובר הזה להיות מונח ביד הלוה, אמרינן: האמינו הלוה, ואומר: מחר תנה לי, ושכח.

CONCEPTS

סִמְפּוֹן **Note of cancellation, receipt**. This word is apparently derived from the Greek σύμφωνον, *symphonon*, which among its many other meanings also means "agreement," "written agreement." In Rabbinic Hebrew this word refers (1) to the cancellation of any kind of agreement, because of a flaw in the article being sold, as a result of which the sale is voided, or (2) to the payment of a debt, wholly or in part, which nullifies the promissory note, or (3) to a clause in a contract which invalidates it under certain circumstances.

TERMINOLOGY

הָכָא תַּרְגְּמוּ **Here they explained**. The Talmud sometimes uses this phrase when a Babylonian interpretation of a Mishnaic expression is cited as differing from an interpretation deriving from Eretz Israel, in this case the interpretation of Rabbi Yirmeyah.

NOTES

מָצָא שְׁטָר בֵּין שְׁטָרוֹתָיו **If one found a document among one's documents**. The commentary follows the opinion of most Rishonim, who explain that the Mishnah is referring to a third party to whom other people's documents were entrusted. Some of the Geonim ruled, however, that the same law applies to a creditor who finds a promissory note and cannot remember whether the debt is still outstanding, or whether it has already been repaid; he too is forbidden to collect until he is certain.

שְׁטָרֵי טַעֲנָתָא **Deeds recording arguments**. These are court records which are written to prevent the litigants from altering depositions they have already made (*Rashbam* on *Bava Batra* 168a).

HALAKHAH

documents unless they had fully clarified and decided the issue at hand (*Sma*)," following the ruling of our Mishnah. (*Shulḥan Arukh Ḥoshen Mishpat* 65:12.)

מָצָא שְׁטָר בֵּין שְׁטָרוֹתָיו **If one found a document among one's documents.** "If a person found among his documents a document of unknown origin, i.e., he did not know whether it had been deposited with him by the creditor or the debtor, or perhaps by both of them (as in the case of a promissory note which had been paid in part), he should retain the document until Elijah comes." (Ibid., 65:1.)

¹רַבִּי יִרְמְיָה אָמַר: זֶה בּוֹרֵר לוֹ אֶחָד, וְזֶה בּוֹרֵר לוֹ אֶחָד.
²״וְכָל מַעֲשֵׂה בֵּית דִּין, הֲרֵי זֶה יַחֲזִיר״. ³הַהוּא גִּיטָּא דְּאִשְׁתַּכַּח בֵּי דִינָא דְּרַב הוּנָא, דַּהֲוָה כְּתִיב בֵּיהּ: ״בְּשְׁוִירִי מָתָא, דְּעַל רָכִיס נַהֲרָא״. ⁴אָמַר רַב הוּנָא: [20B] חָיְישִׁינַן לִשְׁנֵי שְׁוִירִי. ⁵אֲמַר לֵיהּ רַב חִסְדָּא לְרַבָּה: ״פּוֹק, עַיֵּין, דִּלְאוֹרְתָא בָּעֵי לָהּ רַב הוּנָא מִינָּךְ״. ⁶נָפַק, דַּק, וְאַשְׁכַּח. ⁷דִּתְנַן: ״כָּל מַעֲשֵׂה בֵּית דִּין, הֲרֵי זֶה יַחֲזִיר״.
⁸אֲמַר לֵיהּ רַב עַמְרָם לְרַבָּה: ״הֵיכִי פָּשֵׁיט מָר אִיסּוּרָא מִמָּמוֹנָא?״
⁹אֲמַר לֵיהּ: ״תְּרָדָא! ׳שִׁטְרֵי חֲלִיצָה וּמֵיאוּנִין׳ תְּנַן״!

LITERAL TRANSLATION

¹Rabbi Yirmeyah said: This one chooses (*borer*) one for himself, and that one chooses (*borer*) one for himself.

²"Or any court decision, [the finder] should return."

³That bill of divorce that was found in Rav Huna's courtroom, in which it was written: "In the city of Sheviri, on the Rakhis River." ⁴Rav Huna said: [20B] We are concerned about two Sheviris. ⁵Rav Ḥisda said to Rabbah: "Go out, consider [it], for this evening Rav Huna will ask you about it." ⁶He went out, examined [the matter], and found [a source]. ⁷For we have learned [in our Mishnah]: "Any decision of a court shall be returned."

⁸Rav Amram said to Rabbah: "How can you, Sir, derive [a ruling regarding] ritual law from [a law governing] monetary matters?"

⁹He said to him: "Fool! We have learned [in our Mishnah]: 'Deeds of *halitzah* or *me'un*'"!

TRANSLATION AND COMMENTARY

(2): ¹**Rabbi Yirmeyah**, who lived in Eretz Israel, **said**: Deeds of *berurin* are deeds stating that **one** party **chooses** (בּוֹרֵר, *borer*) **one** judge as arbitrator **for himself, and the other** party **chooses** (בּוֹרֵר, *borer*) **one** judge as arbitrator **for himself.** In an arbitration tribunal each of the litigants is permitted to select one of the three judges who will arbitrate his dispute, and the two judges so chosen select the third judge.

וְכָל מַעֲשֵׂה בֵּית דִּין ²The Mishnah stated: **"Any court decision the finder should return."** ³The following incident was related concerning **a bill of divorce that was found in Rav Huna's courtroom, in which it was written**: "This bill of divorce was written **in the city of Sheviri,** which is **on the Rakhis River.**" ⁴**Rav Huna said**: [20B] **We are concerned about** the possibility that there may be **two Sheviris.** According to Rav Huna, the divorce may not be delivered, because it may belong to a couple with the same names from some other Sheviri. ⁵**Rav Ḥisda** then **said to Rabbah**, who was a pupil of Rav Huna: **"Go out,** and **consider** the matter further, **for this evening Rav Huna will ask you** for your opinion **about it."** ⁶Rabbah **went out** of the study hall, **examined the matter** carefully, **and found a source** dealing with this matter. ⁷**For we have learned in our Mishnah**: **"Any decision of a court shall be returned."** And this implies that we are not concerned about the possibility that there may be another city with the same name as that mentioned in the bill of divorce (in which there is an identically named couple, unless it is proven that such a city exists. Rabbah's conclusion was, therefore, that the bill of divorce, like any other lost court-certified document, should be returned. (This incident is discussed in detail on 18b, above.)

אֲמַר לֵיהּ רַב עַמְרָם לְרַבָּה ⁸**Rav Amram said to Rabbah**: **"How can you, Sir, derive a ruling regarding ritual law** and the validity of a divorce — **from a law governing monetary matters?"** The Mishnah speaks only of business documents, whereas the question of a bill of divorce's validity is a ritual matter of great stringency!

אֲמַר לֵיהּ תְּרָדָא ⁹Rabbah **said to him**: **"Fool!** Surely **we have learned in this** very **Mishnah**: **'Deeds of *ḥalitzah* or *me'un*** may be returned,' and these documents, like bills of divorce, also affect marital status!"

RASHI

גמרא זה בורר לו אחד — כשבוררין להן דיינין כותבין להן "זה בירר לו את פלוני, וזה בירר לו את פלוני", שלא יוכלו לחזור בהן. **דאשתכח בי דינא** — מקויים בהנפק, והשליח המביאו אומר ממנו נפל. **חיישינן לשני שוורי** — אף על פי שבשוורי הידוע לנו אין בה שני יוסף בן שמעון, שמא יש שוורי אחרת שיש שם יוסף בן שמעון, ושם נכתב, ומשליח אחר נפל. **הרי זה יחזיר** — דכיון דלא הוחזקו שני יוסף בן שמעון בעיר אחת, לעיר אחרת שאינה ידועה לנו לא חיישינן. **תרדא** = משועמם.

BACKGROUND

זֶה בּוֹרֵר לוֹ אֶחָד This one chooses one for himself. When a permanent Rabbinical Court sits in a city, litigants usually bring their disputes before it. Sometimes, however, a court was appointed to judge a specific case, and in order to ensure that the two parties would accept the court's decision, it was customary for each to choose one of the judges (and the two judges would choose the third). Similarly, the parties sometimes did not wish to go to court but preferred that their dispute be settled by arbitration. They would choose the arbitrators, and in order to prevent either of the parties from changing his mind after an adverse decision was issued, their choice of the arbitrator(s) was registered in writing.

LANGUAGE

תְּרָדָא Fool. Some authorities have suggested possible derivations for this word, such as the Latin *tardus*, meaning slow or backward. Some suggest that it comes from the Hebrew תֶּרֶד, a vegetable, as a pejorative term for a fool. Other languages provide analogies for this possibility.

NOTES

כָּל מַעֲשֵׂה בֵּית דִּין Any decision of a court shall be returned. Apparently, when Rabbah cited this clause, he was quoting the final clause of the Mishnah and had the entire Mishnah in mind, whereas Rav Amram thought that he was referring specifically to this clause (*Ḥayyim Shenayim Yeshallem*).

אִיסּוּרָא מִמָּמוֹנָא Deriving a ruling regarding ritual law from a law governing monetary matters. There are several differences between the Halakhic principles governing civil law and those regarding ritual law. Generally, civil law is more flexible, for two main reasons. First, as has been noted above, on 6a, money can be returned, and if a mistake has been made in a court decision, it can be rectified. A ritual transgression, on the other hand, cannot be undone. Moreover, in accordance with the important principle of הֶפְקֵר בֵּית דִּין הֶפְקֵר, (property can be declared ownerless by

[1] פָּקַע אַרְזָא דְּבֵי רַב. [2] מָר אֲמַר: מִשּׁוּם לְתַאי דִּידִי פָּקַע, וּמָר אֲמַר: מִשּׁוּם לְתַאי דִּידִי פָּקַע.

[3] "מָצָא בַּחֲפִיסָה אוֹ בִּדְלוּסְקְמָא". [4] מַאי חֲפִיסָה?

[5] אָמַר רַבָּה בַּר בַּר חָנָה: חֵמֶת קְטַנָּה.

[6] מַאי דְּלוּסְקְמָא?

[7] אֲמַר רַבָּה בַּר שְׁמוּאֵל: טְלִיקָא דְּסָבֵי.

[8] "תַּכְרִיךְ שֶׁל שְׁטָרוֹת אוֹ אֲגוּדָּה שֶׁל שְׁטָרוֹת וכו׳". [9] תָּנוּ רַבָּנַן: "כַּמָּה הוּא 'תַּכְרִיךְ שֶׁל שְׁטָרוֹת'? שְׁלֹשָׁה כְּרוּכִין זֶה בָּזֶה. [10] וְכַמָּה הִיא 'אֲגוּדָּה שֶׁל שְׁטָרוֹת'? שְׁלֹשָׁה קְשׁוּרִין זֶה בָּזֶה"!

LITERAL TRANSLATION

[1] The cedar [column supporting] the study-house cracked. [2] [One] Sage said: It cracked in my honor (lit., "because of my luck"), and [the other] Sage said: It cracked in my honor.

[3] "[If] he found [them] in a small bag or a case." [4] What is חֲפִיסָה?

[5] Rabbah bar Bar Ḥanah said: A small leather bag.

[6] What is דְּלוּסְקְמָא?

[7] Rabbah bar Shmuel said: A case [carried] by old people.

[8] "A roll of documents or a bundle of documents." [9] Our Rabbis taught [in a Baraita]: "How many are a 'roll of documents'? Three rolled together. [10] And how many are a 'bundle of documents'? Three tied together."

TRANSLATION AND COMMENTARY

פָּקַע אַרְזָא דְּבֵי רַב [1] At this **the cedar column supporting the study-house**, where this difference of opinion between Rav Amram and Rabbah took place, **cracked** in two. [2] **One Sage**, Rav Amram, **said**: **"It cracked in my honor**, because you insulted me." **And the other Sage**, Rabbah, **said**: **"It cracked in my honor**, because you insulted me by formulating your objection in a humiliating way."

מָצָא בַּחֲפִיסָה אוֹ בִּדְלוּסְקְמָא [3] The Mishnah states: **"If he found** lost documents **in a small bag or a case."** [4] The Gemara asks: **What is** the meaning of the word חֲפִיסָה?

אָמַר רַבָּה בַּר בַּר חָנָה [5] **Rabbah bar Bar Ḥanah said** in reply: It means **a small leather bag** in which various items are kept.

מַאי דְּלוּסְקְמָא [6] The Gemara asks: **What is** the meaning of the word דְּלוּסְקְמָא?

אֲמַר רַבָּה בַּר שְׁמוּאֵל [7] **Rabbah bar Shmuel said** in reply: It means **a case carried by old people**, where they keep their belongings.

תַּכְרִיךְ שֶׁל שְׁטָרוֹת [8] The Mishnah spoke of **"a roll of documents or a bundle of documents."** [9] **Our Rabbis taught in** the following **Baraita**: **"How many** documents **are there in a 'roll of documents'? Three rolled together**. The fact that they are rolled together constitutes a means of identifying them. [10] **How many** documents **are there in a 'bundle of documents'? Three tied together**." The fact that they are tied together constitutes a means of identifying them.

RASHI

פקע ארזא דבי רב – נשבר העמוד שבית המדרש נשען עליו. מר אמר משום לתאי דידי פקע – בשביל מזלי, שקינא על שגדפתני. ומר אמר משום לתאי דידי פקע – שהשבת על דברי לביישני בבית המדרש. חמת – של עור, שנותנין בו יין. טליקא דסבי – *טסקא שהזקנים מצניעים בה כלי תשמישן, שלא יצטרכו לחפש אחריהם. כרוכין זה בזה – וזהו סימן שהבעלים נותנים בהם. זה יכריז מציאה: שטרות מצאתי, וזה יאמר: שלי הם, ושלשה הן, כרוכין הן זה בזה.

BACKGROUND

אַרְזָא דְּבֵי רַב The cedar column supporting the study-house. The term בֵּי רַב has various meanings, and here it apparently refers to the building that the Sage Rav built for his House of Study in Sura, for even after Rav's death his students and their students used it and studied Torah there.

מַאי חֲפִיסָה What is חֲפִיסָה? Various terms in the Mishnah, including those referring to objects used in daily life or those taken from foreign languages, were not familiar to all the Sages. Hence they had to ask the meaning of these terms, and they received answers from a man like Rabbah bar Bar Ḥanah, who lived in Eretz Israel, or from Rabbah bar Shmuel, who was known to be an expert on the subject of Baraitot.

LANGUAGE

לַתָא Several origins from various languages, such as Persian and Latin, have been suggested for this word. All of them are connected with the idea of luck or fate. It has also been suggested that it is an abbreviation of עִילְּתָא, meaning a "cause." In other words, each Sage said that *he* was the cause of the occurrence.

טְלִיקָא Case. This word is possibly derived from the Greek θύλακος, *thulakos*, meaning "sack" or "bag".

LANGUAGE (RASHI)

טסקא* Tasche. From the Old French, meaning "bag."

NOTES

the court), the Sages are able to enact regulations, even if they entail confiscating property from its owner.

Conversely, it must be recalled that civil law cannot always be derived from ritual law because civil law involves a factor absent in ritual law: there are two parties to a civil suit, and therefore there can be no absolute stringencies or leniencies, for what is a leniency for one side is a stringency for his opponent. For these reasons, civil law and ritual law are viewed as separate bodies of Halakhah, and although they derive from the same source the considerations applicable to each cannot always be compared.

שְׁלֹשָׁה כְּרוּכִין Three documents rolled together. Rabbi Ḥiyya is not emending the text of the Baraita, but rather he is explaining that the word קָשׁוּר — "tied" — need not be taken in a strict sense, since it is often used in a general sense — for example in putting on tefillin — to mean simply "attached" (*Rosh*).

HALAKHAH

מָצָא בַּחֲפִיסָה If a person found documents in a bag. "If a person announces that he has found a document in a container, and the putative owner correctly describes the container in which the document was found, it may be returned to him. If the finder announces: 'I have found a document,' without specifying that the document was found in a container, and the claimant maintains that the document was lost in the type of container in which it was in fact found, this is considered valid identification, provided that such containers are not usually used to store documents." (*Shulḥan Arukh, Ḥoshen Mishpat* 65:9.)

מָצָא תַּכְרִיךְ שְׁטָרוֹת If a person found documents rolled together. "If a person found three or more documents rolled together, and announced that he had found 'documents,' they may be returned to the putative owner if he correctly states how many documents were lost. He need not describe how the documents were bound together," following the Gemara's conclusion. (*Shulḥan Arukh, Ḥoshen Mishpat* 65:10.)

¹שָׁמְעַתְּ מִינָּהּ: קֶשֶׁר סִימָן. ²הָא תָּנֵי רַבִּי חִיָּיא: ״שְׁלֹשָׁה כְּרוּכִין זֶה בָּזֶה״! אִי הָכִי, הַיְינוּ תַּכְרִיךְ! ³תַּכְרִיךְ, כָּל חַד וְחַד בְּרֹאשָׁהּ דְּחַבְרֵיהּ; ⁴אֲגוּדָּה, דְּרָמוּ אַהֲדָדֵי וּכְרוּכוֹת. ⁵מַאי מַכְרִיז? ⁶מִנְיָן. ⁷מַאי אִרְיָא תְּלָתָא? אֲפִילּוּ תְּרֵין נַמִי! ⁸אֶלָּא כְּדַאֲמַר רָבִינָא: ״טִבְעָא״ מַכְרִיז. ⁹הָכָא נַמִי, ״שְׁטָרֵי״ מַכְרִיז. ¹⁰״רַבָּן שִׁמְעוֹן בֶּן גַּמְלִיאֵל

LITERAL TRANSLATION

¹You may infer from this: A knot is an identification mark.

²[But] surely Rabbi Ḥiyya taught [a Baraita]: "Three rolled together"! If so, this is [the same as] a roll!

³[In the case of] a roll, each one is [folded] into the beginning of the next one; ⁴[in the case of] a bundle, [the documents] lie on top of one another and are [then] rolled up.

⁵What does [the finder] announce?

⁶The number.

⁷[Then] why does the [Mishnah] speak of three? Even two also!

⁸Rather, as Ravina said: [The finder] announces: "Coins." ⁹Here too, [the finder] announces: "Documents."

¹⁰"Rabban Shimon ben Gamliel

TRANSLATION AND COMMENTARY

שָׁמְעַתְּ מִינָּהּ ¹The Gemara notes: **From this** interpretation of the word "bundle," it would seem that **you may infer** the solution to a question asked elsewhere and say that **a knot is** considered a valid **identification mark**. According to this interpretation, a lost bundle of documents is to be returned to its putative owner, provided that he describes the knot holding them together.

הָא תָּנֵי רַבִּי חִיָּיא ²The Gemara rejects this inference: **Surely** this cannot be so, for **Rabbi Ḥiyya quoted a Baraita** giving a different version, in which it is stated that a "bundle" is also **"three** documents ***rolled*** **together"** with no knot to serve as an identification mark! But, objects the Gemara, **if** Rabbi Ḥiyya's definition is correct, a "bundle" **would be the same as a "roll."** What difference would there be between them?

תַּכְרִיךְ ³The Gemara answers that there is a difference: **In the case of a roll, each** document **is folded into the beginning of the next one**; ⁴**in the case of a bundle**, the documents **lie on top of one another and are then rolled up**. Thus the Mishnah uses two terms to describe them, even though they are essentially the same.

מַאי ⁵The Gemara asks: Since there is no knot, **what does the finder announce** when advertising that he has found the bundle or roll, so that the claimant will know what identifying mark to cite?

מִנְיָן ⁶The Gemara answers: The finder indicates **the number** of documents that have been found, so that the person who has lost them can identify the way they were rolled.

מַאי אִרְיָא תְּלָתָא ⁷But, objects the Gemara, if the claimant does not have to mention the number of documents that were lost, but merely the way in which they were fastened, or bound, or rolled together, **why does the Mishnah speak** specifically **of "three"** documents as a "bundle"? The same law should **also** apply **even** to **two**! Even if the finder announces that he found two documents, the claimant should be able to identify the documents as his by the way they were bound or rolled together!

אֶלָּא כְּדַאֲמַר רָבִינָא ⁸The Gemara answers: **Rather**, it is **as Ravina said** in another context: **The finder announces**: "I found **coins.**" ⁹**Here, too, the finder announces**: "I found **documents**," without specifying the number. Thus, if only two documents were found, and the putative owner claims that he lost two documents, this is not in itself valid identification, for as long as the finder announces that he found "documents" (plural), this implies that at least two documents were found. Hence, only if the claimant maintains that he lost the specific number of documents found, and that they were bound or rolled in a specific way, is his identification considered valid.

רַבָּן שִׁמְעוֹן בֶּן גַּמְלִיאֵל ¹⁰We learned in the Mishnah: "**Rabban Shimon ben Gamliel says** that a distinction is to be made between different cases where a number of documents were found together:

BACKGROUND

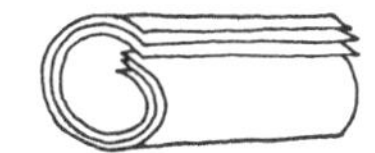

A "roll" of documents

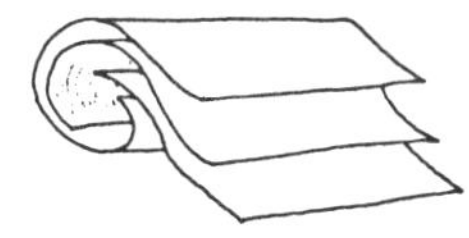

A "bundle" of documents

RASHI

שמע מינה קשר סימן – שיש קשרים שאינן דומים זה לזה, ויאמר: כך וכך הוא עשוי. דאי לא תימא הכי מאי סימנא איכא הכא? ותפשוט מינה בעלמא דקשר סימן, ובעיא בעלמא היא. ומשני: מהכא, לא תפשוט, דתני רבי חייא: שלשה כרוכין זה בזה הוא אגודה, דכרך הוי סימן, דכולי עלמא כרכי שטרא שטרא לעצמו וקושרין אותן יחד, וזה כרך שלשתן יחד. **דרמו אהדדי** – השכיבן זה על זה, אורכו על אורכו של חבירו. **מאי מכריז** – המוצא מאי מכריז. **מנין** – שלשה שטרות. וזה בא ונותן סימן שכרוכין היו יחד. **אפילו תרי נמי** – הואיל ואין צריך לבעלים לתת סימן אלא כריכתן. **כדאמר רבינא** – ב"אלו מציאות" (כה,א). **שטרי מכריז** – שטרות מצאתי, וזה צריך שיאמר: כך וכך היו, וכרוכין היו. הלכך דוקא תלתא, אבל תרי – מידע ידיע דמיעוט שטרות שתים, ואין מנין סימן.

אוֹמֵר: אֶחָד הַלֹּוֶה מִשְּׁלֹשָׁה, יַחֲזִיר לַלֹּוֶה וכו׳". [1]דְּאִי סָלְקָא דַּעְתָּךְ דְּמַלְוִין נִינְהוּ, מַאי בָּעוּ גַּבֵּי הֲדָדֵי?
[2]דִּלְמָא לְקִיּוּמִינְהוּ אָזְלִי?
[3]דִּמְקַיְּימֵי.
[4]דִּלְמָא מִידָא דְּסָפְרָא נָפֵיל?
[5]לָא מַשְׁהֵי אִינִישׁ קִיּוּמֵיהּ בִּידָא דְּסָפְרָא.
[6]"שְׁלֹשָׁה שֶׁלָּווּ מֵאֶחָד, יַחֲזִיר לַמַּלְוֶה וכו׳". [7]דְּאִי סָלְקָא דַּעְתָּךְ דְּלֹוִין נִינְהוּ, מַאי בָּעוּ גַּבֵּי הֲדָדֵי?
[8]דִּלְמָא לְמִכְתְּבִנְהוּ אָזְלִי?
[9]דִּכְתִיבִי בִּתְלָת יְדֵי סָפְרֵי.

LITERAL TRANSLATION

says: One [borrower] who borrowed from three [lenders, the finder] should return [the documents] to the borrower, etc." [1]For if you were to imagine that [the documents] are the lenders', what are they doing together?
[2]Perhaps they went to certify them?
[3]Where they had [already] been certified.
[4]Perhaps they fell from the scribe's hand?
[5]A person does not leave his [court-]certified [promissory note] in the scribe's hands.
[6]"Three [borrowers] who borrowed from one [lender], [the finder] should return [the documents], etc." [7]For if you were to imagine that they are the borrowers', what are they doing together?
[8]Perhaps they went [to the same scribe] to write them?
[9]Where [the promissory notes] were written in three hands.

TRANSLATION AND COMMENTARY

If one borrower borrowed from three lenders, the finder should return the documents to the borrower, etc." [1]The Gemara explains: **For if you were to imagine that the documents belong to the lenders, what are they doing together?** It is too much of a coincidence that all three lenders should have lost their promissory notes in the same place!

דִּלְמָא לְקִיּוּמִינְהוּ [2]The Gemara objects: **Perhaps** the lenders **went** together **to certify** the promissory notes, and lost the notes on the way!

דִּמְקַיְּימֵי [3]The Gemara replies: The Mishnah is referring to a case **where** the promissory notes **had already been certified**.

דִּלְמָא מִידָא דְּסָפְרָא נָפֵיל [4]Again the Gemara objects: **Perhaps the** promissory notes **fell from the hands of the** court **scribe** and got lost after he had certified them?

לָא מַשְׁהֵי אִינִישׁ [5]The Gemara replies: **A person does not leave his certified promissory note in the scribe's hands**. Hence it is clear that these three lost promissory notes all belong to the borrower.

שְׁלֹשָׁה שֶׁלָּווּ מֵאֶחָד [6]Similarly, the Mishnah states: "If **three borrowers borrowed from one lender, the promissory notes should be returned to the lender**." [7]The Gemara explains: **For if you were to imagine that** the promissory notes **belong to the borrowers, what are they doing together**? Surely it is too much of a coincidence to assume that all three borrowers lost their promissory notes in the same place!

דִּלְמָא לְמִכְתְּבִנְהוּ אָזְלִי [8]The Gemara objects: **Perhaps** the borrowers all **went to the same scribe to write** the promissory notes, and it was he who lost them!

דִּכְתִיבִי בִּתְלָת יְדֵי סָפְרֵי [9]The Gemara replies: The Mishnah is referring to a case **where the promissory notes were written in three** different **hands** by three scribes.

RASHI

ודלמא לקיומינהו אזלי – אצל סופר הדיינין, הכותב הנפק לכל השטרות. **דלווין היו** – שפרעום והוחזרו להם. **למכתבנהו אזלי** – ומן הסופר נפל, ומעולם לא לוו.

NOTES

דִּלְמָא לְקִיּוּמִינְהוּ אָזְלִי Perhaps they went together to certify them. The Gemara is not suggesting that the three lenders coincidentally all lost their notes on the way to the court. Rather, the concern is that the notes may have been lost by the court scribe before they were certified (*R. Ovadiah of Bertinoro, Maharam Schiff*). Alternatively, one of the lenders may have taken the others' notes to the court as a favor (*Ritva* in *Shittah Mekubbetzet*).

אֶחָד הַלֹּוֶה מִשְּׁלֹשָׁה וכו׳ If one person borrowed from three lenders.... Some commentators explain that this law applies even if the notes were not rolled together; the very fact that three notes found on the same spot all mention a single borrower proves that the documents belong to him (*Meiri*). Later commentators, however, rule that the documents may not be returned unless they are found rolled together (*Sma*). Further discussion of this matter can be found in *Hiddushei HaRim* and other Aharonim.

HALAKHAH

אֶחָד הַלֹּוֶה מִשְּׁלֹשָׁה If one person borrowed from three people. "If a person found three court-certified promissory notes issued by three different lenders who had lent money to one borrower, the documents may be returned to the borrower, even if he does not give an identifying mark. By contrast, they may not be returned to the individual lenders, even if they do give an identifying mark. But if the documents were not certified by the court, they may only be returned to the party who gives an identifying mark. If a person found three promissory notes of three borrowers written by three scribes for one lender, they may be returned to the lender, even if he does not give an identifying mark. If all three documents had been written by one scribe, they may be returned to whichever party gives an identifying mark," following the accepted opinion of Rabban Shimon ben Gamliel in our Mishnah. (*Shulhan Arukh, Hoshen Mishpat* 65:11.)

TRANSLATION AND COMMENTARY

וְדִלְמָא לְקִיּוּמִינְהוּ [1]The Gemara objects again: **But perhaps** the borrowers **went to certify** the promissory notes in court, and they were lost on the way?

מַלְוֶה מְקַיֵּים שְׁטָרֵיהּ [2]The Gemara answers that this is not likely, for it stands to reason that **the lender certifies his promissory notes** in court, so that he can use them to collect his debts, but **the borrower does not certify his promissory notes,** as he has no reason to do so. Hence, there is no reason to assume that the documents were lost under such circumstances.

אִם יֵשׁ עִמָּהֶן סִמְפּוֹנוֹת [3]The Mishnah states: "**If there are among** a person's documents **notes of cancellation** of loans, **he should act in accordance with what is written in the notes of cancellation.**" [4]**Rav Yirmeyah bar Abba said in the name of Rav:** If **a note of cancellation is found in the possession of the lender,** [5]**even though it is written in his** own **handwriting** and thus there is no reason to assume that it might be a forgery, **it is treated** as if the lender were playing **a trick, and** the note **is invalid.** It cannot be relied upon and does not cancel the debt.

לָא מִבָּעֲיָא [6]The Gemara observes: **There is no need to state this** ruling **where** the note of cancellation **was written in a scribe's handwriting,** in which case **it is possible to say that the scribe happened to be** with the lender **and wrote** the note so that there should be a receipt ready for the borrower when he came to repay the loan; [7]**but even where** the note **was written in the lender's own handwriting, it is invalid,** and the debt is not canceled. [8]**For the lender may have** written this note because he **thought:** "**The borrower may perhaps come on Friday at dusk, and pay me.** [9]**Now, if I do not give him a note of cancellation** immediately, **he will not give me the money,** [10]**so I will write a receipt** in advance **now, so that when he brings me the money, I will** be able to **give him** the receipt immediately."

[1]וְדִלְמָא לְקִיּוּמִינְהוּ אֲזַלִי? [2]מַלְוֶה מְקַיֵּים שְׁטָרֵיהּ, לֹוֶה לָא מְקַיֵּים שְׁטָרֵיהּ.

[3]"אִם יֵשׁ עִמָּהֶן סִמְפּוֹנוֹת, יַעֲשֶׂה מַה שֶּׁבַּסִּמְפּוֹנוֹת". [4]אָמַר רַב יִרְמְיָה בַּר אַבָּא אָמַר רַב: סִמְפּוֹן הַיּוֹצֵא מִתַּחַת יְדֵי מַלְוֶה, [5]אַף עַל פִּי שֶׁכָּתוּב בִּכְתַב יָדוֹ, אֵינוֹ אֶלָּא כִּמְשַׂחֵק, וּפָסוּל.

[6]לָא מִבָּעֲיָא כָּתוּב בִּכְתַב יַד סוֹפֵר, דְּאִיכָּא לְמֵימַר סָפְרָא אִתְרְמֵי לֵיהּ וְכָתַב, [7]אֶלָּא אֲפִילּוּ כָּתוּב בִּכְתַב יָדוֹ, פָּסוּל. [8]סָבַר: "דִּלְמָא מִתְרְמֵי וְאָתֵי בֵּין הַשְּׁמָשׁוֹת, וְקָא פָּרַע לִי, [9]דְּאִי לָא יָהֵיבְנָא לֵיהּ, לָא יָהֵיב לִי זוּזֵי; [10]אֶכְתּוֹב אֲנָא, דְּכִי אַיְיתֵי לִי זוּזֵי, אֶתֵּן לֵיהּ".

LITERAL TRANSLATION

[1]But perhaps they went to certify them?

[2]The lender certifies his [promissory] note, [but] the debtor does not certify his [promissory] note.

[3]"If there are notes of cancellation among them, he should do what is [written] in the notes of cancellation." [4]Rav Yirmeyah bar Abba said in the name of Rav: A note of cancellation that is found in the possession of (lit., "goes out from under the hands of") the lender, [5]even though it is written in his handwriting, is [treated as if it were] nothing but a trick, and is invalid.

[6]There is no need [to state this] where it was written in a scribe's handwriting, where it is possible to say that the scribe happened [to be there] and wrote it, [7]but even where it was written in [the lender's] own handwriting, it is invalid. [8][For the lender] thinks: "Perhaps [the borrower] will come by chance [on Friday] at dusk, and pay me. [9]For if I do not give him [a note of cancellation], he will not give me the money; [10][so] I will write [the receipt now], so that when he brings me the money, I will give him [the note].

RASHI

סמפון — שובר המבטל שטר. וכל דבר המבטל דבר קרי סמפון, כדאמר גבי קדושי אשה ומכירת עבד שהמום קרוי סמפון, מפני שמבטל את המקח. **היוצא מתחת ידי מלוה** — שהוא מונח בידו, ולא ביד הלוה. **ספרא אתרמי ליה** — וסבר: אם יבא בעל חובי לפרעני, ואני אין שטרי עכשיו בידי, ואם לא יהא שובר מוכן לי — לא יפרע כלום. **אפילו כתוב בכתב ידו** — שיש לומר: אם לא שנפרע למה ליה למהר ולכתוב לפני פרעון? הואיל ויודע לכתוב.

SAGES

רַב יִרְמְיָה בַּר אַבָּא **Rav Yirmeyah bar Abba.** A Babylonian Amora of the first and second generation, Rav Yirmeyah bar Abba was one of the first Sages who came to study under Rav when the latter arrived in Babylonia. Rav Yirmeyah bar Abba reports a large number of rulings in Rav's name, and many Sages from both Babylonia and Eretz Israel studied with him. His son, Rav Huna, was a Sage, as was his son-in-law, Rav Huna bar Ḥiyya, and his daughter's son, Levi ben Rav Huna bar Ḥiyya.

NOTES

אֵינוֹ אֶלָּא כִּמְשַׂחֵק **It is treated as if it were nothing but a trick.** The Jerusalem Talmud has a variant of this phrase, מִתְעַסֵּק בִּשְׁטָרוֹתָיו הָיָה, which means "he was occupying himself with his notes"; in other words, the lender wrote the receipt for his own purposes, for his own records and not as a cancellation of the debt, and this is the reason why he can continue to claim repayment of his loan, based on his promissory note.

HALAKHAH

סִמְפּוֹן בְּיַד הַמַּלְוֶה **A note of cancellation in the possession of the lender.** "If a receipt is found in the lender's possession stating that one of his promissory notes has been repaid, it is invalid, and hence does not cancel the promissory note. But if the promissory note referred to by the note of cancellation is found among torn promissory notes, even if it is not torn itself, it is invalid, as stated by the receipt." (Ibid., 65:18.)

[1] תְּנַן: ״אִם יֵשׁ עִמָּהֶן סִמְפּוֹנוֹת, יַעֲשֶׂה מַה שֶּׁבַּסִּמְפּוֹנוֹת״!
[2] כְּדַאֲמַר רַב סָפְרָא: שֶׁנִּמְצָא בֵּין שְׁטָרוֹת קְרוּעִין. [3] הָכָא נַמִי, שֶׁמְּצָאוֹ בֵּין שְׁטָרוֹת קְרוּעִין.
[4] תָּא שְׁמַע: ״נִמְצָא לְאֶחָד בֵּין שְׁטָרוֹתָיו שְׁטָרוֹ שֶׁל יוֹסֵף בֶּן שִׁמְעוֹן פָּרוּעַ, [5] שְׁטָרוֹת שְׁנֵיהֶם פְּרוּעִין״!
[6] כְּדַאֲמַר רַב סָפְרָא: שֶׁנִּמְצָא בֵּין שְׁטָרוֹת קְרוּעִין. [7] הָכָא נַמִי, שֶׁנִּמְצָא בֵּין שְׁטָרוֹת קְרוּעִין.

LITERAL TRANSLATION

[1] We have learned [in the Mishnah]: "If there are notes of cancellation among them, he should do what is [written] in the notes of cancellation"! [2] As Rav Safra said: Where it was found among torn notes. [3] Here, too, where he found it among torn notes.
[4] Come [and] hear: "[If a note] is found [by a lender] among his documents [stating that] Yosef ben Shimon's promissory note has been repaid, [5] both of their promissory notes are [considered to have been] repaid"!
[6] As Rav Safra said: Where it was found among torn notes. [7] Here, too, where it was found among torn notes.

TRANSLATION AND COMMENTARY

תְּנַן [1] The Gemara objects: Surely **we have learned in the Mishnah: "If there are among** a person's documents **notes of cancellation, he should act in accordance with what is written in the notes of cancellation,"** and this ostensibly applies specifically where the notes of cancellation were produced by the lender!

כְּדַאֲמַר רַב סָפְרָא [2] The Gemara replies: We may answer this objection **as Rav Safra said** in another context below: The ruling applies only **where** the note of cancellation **was found among torn documents.** [3] **Here, too,** the Mishnah is referring only to a case **where the lender found** the note of cancellation **among torn** promissory **notes.** Thus, even though the receipt that was found referred to a note that was not torn, nevertheless since the other notes **were** torn we may presume that this one was also paid. Only in such circumstances, says the Gemara, is a note of cancellation found in the possession of a lender deemed to be valid. In other circumstances the ruling of Rav Yirmeyah bar Abba applies — that a note of cancellation found in the possession of a lender is invalid.

תָּא שְׁמַע [4] The Gemara objects again, citing another Mishnah (*Bava Batra* 172a): **Come and hear: "If a note is found by a lender among his documents, stating that Yosef ben Shimon's promissory note has been repaid,** and this lender has lent money to two borrowers named Yosef ben Shimon, [5] **both of their promissory notes are considered to have been repaid,** since each borrower claims that he has repaid his debt and that the note refers to *his* debt. Accordingly, says the Gemara, we may infer from this Mishnah that the instructions in a "note of cancellation" found in the possession of a lender *are* binding and must be followed!

כְּדַאֲמַר רַב סָפְרָא [6] The Gemara answers: We may answer this objection **as Rav Safra said** in another context below: The ruling applies only **where** the note of cancellation **was found among torn** promissory **notes.** [7] **Here, too,** the Mishnah in *Bava Batra* is referring to a case **where it was found among torn** promissory **notes,** and this is why the note is deemed to be valid, as explained above.

RASHI

ואם יש עמהן סמפון — והכא במלוה עסקינן, דקתני: מצא שטר בין שטרותיו כו׳. **כדאמר רב ספרא** — לקמן בשמעתין. **שנמצא לו** — השטר שהשובר יוצא עליו. **בין שטרותיו קרועים** — והוא אינו קרוע, לפיכך סומכין על השובר. שמקום השטר מוכיח על השובר שהוא אמת, שאם לא נפרע לא היה נותן השטר אלא השטרות קרועין, כך שמעתי. ולי נראה: שנמצא השובר בין השטרות קרועין, הלכך איכא למימר שנתקבל החוב, והשובר הזה אין צריך למלוה הזה אלא ללוה, והלוה שכח ביד זה, לפיכך נתנו זה עם השטרות שאין צריכין לו. דאי סלקא דעתך מלוה כתבו להיות מוכן לו כשירצה לוה לפרעו — לא נתנו עם שטרות שאין צריכין לו. **נמצא בין שטרותיו** — מתניתין היא ב״גט פשוט״ (בבא בתרא קעב,א): שני יוסף בן שמעון בעיר אחת, ונמצא שובר לאדם אחד בין שטרותיו, וכתוב בו ״שטרו של יוסף בן שמעון שבידי פרוע הוא״, והיה לו שני שטרות על שניהם. **שטרות שניהם פרועין** — שכל אחד יכול לומר: על שלי נכתב שובר. ובבבא בתרא פרכינן: בלא שובר נמי, הא תנן: אין אחד יכול להוציא שטר חוב עליהם! ומוקמינן ליה במשולשין בשטר, ואין משולשין בשובר. והא הכא דיוצא מתחת יד מלוה הוא. **שנמצא** — השטר בין השטרות פרוען, וכל אחד אמר ״זהו שטר שלי״.

SAGES

רַב סָפְרָא Rav Safra. A Babylonian Amora of the third and fourth generations. He is found in Halakhic discussions as a student and colleague of the greatest Sages of the third generation, such as Rabbah, Rav Yosef, and others. He remained active during the generation of their students, Abaye and Rava. Rav Safra was apparently a merchant, and frequently visited Eretz Israel, where he held discussions with Sages such as Rabbi Abba and Rabbi Abbahu. He was a particular expert in Halakhah and is not quoted so frequently in Aggadic passages. Rav Safra was famous for his personal qualities, in particular for his punctiliousness in avoiding the slightest deviation from the truth. Since Rav Safra traveled widely, he did not have his own yeshivah, nor was he often found in the House of Study.

HALAKHAH

שְׁטָרוֹ שֶׁל יוֹסֵף בֶּן שִׁמְעוֹן Two promissory notes of Yosef ben Shimon. "If a lender has lent money to two people with the same names and each one has written a promissory note clearly identifying the borrower, and later the lender finds a court-certified receipt for one of the debts among his documents (but not indicating which of the loans has been repaid), he may not collect either of them, if both promissory notes were found among torn documents (or partially ripped ones, according to *Rashal*)," following the Gemara's conclusion. *Shakh* and *Gra* rule that neither debt may be collected even if only one of the conditions specified above — that the receipt was court-certified, or that the promissory notes were found among torn documents — is satisfied. (*Shulḥan Arukh, Ḥoshen Mishpat* 49:9.)

TRANSLATION AND COMMENTARY

תָּא שְׁמַע [1]**Come and hear** another objection based on a Mishnah (*Shevuot* 45a): "When orphans seek to collect a debt originally owed to their father from other orphans, the heirs of the original debtor, they must take the following oath: **'We declare on oath that our father did not instruct us** on his deathbed **and that our father did not tell us** at any earlier time that this debt had been repaid, [2]**and that we did not find a note among our father's documents stating that this promissory note was repaid.'"** From this Mishnah we see that if there had been a note of cancellation among the father's promissory notes, it would have been considered valid and would have canceled the debt!

אָמַר רַב סַפְרָא [3]The Gemara answers: **Rav Safra said**: This Mishnah refers to a case **where** the note of cancellation **was found among torn** promissory **notes**, as explained above.

תָּא שְׁמַע [4]The Gemara raises another objection from a Baraita: **Come and hear**: **"A note of cancellation which has the signatures of witnesses on it, should be authenticated by the signatures on it,"** even if it is produced by the lender. From this statement it would appear that a note of cancellation produced by the lender *is* valid, as long as the signatures of the witnesses are found to be genuine!

אֵימָא יִתְקַיֵּים מֵחוֹתְמָיו [5]The Gemara answers: **Say** as follows, i.e., emend the text of the Baraita as follows: The note of cancellation **should be authenticated by those who signed it**. [21A] Specifically, **we ask the witnesses whether or not** the debt **has been repaid**, and we act in accordance with their evidence.

תָּא שְׁמַע [6]Another objection to the statement of Rav Yirmeyah bar Abba in the name of Rav is raised: **Come and hear** another Baraita: **"A note of cancellation that has witnesses on it is valid."** Since this Baraita does not specify that the note of cancellation is valid only if it is *not* produced by the lender, it would seem that it does not matter who produces it!

[1]תָּא שְׁמַע: ״״שְׁבוּעָה שֶׁלֹּא פְקָדָנוּ אַבָּא, וְשֶׁלֹּא אָמַר לָנוּ אַבָּא, [2]וְשֶׁלֹּא מָצָאנוּ בֵּין שְׁטָרוֹתָיו שֶׁל אַבָּא שֶׁשְּׁטָר זֶה פָּרוּעַ״״.

[3]אָמַר רַב סַפְרָא: שֶׁנִּמְצָא בֵּין שְׁטָרוֹת קְרוּעִין.

[4]תָּא שְׁמַע: ״סִמְפּוֹן שֶׁיֵּשׁ עָלָיו עֵדִים, יִתְקַיֵּים בְּחוֹתְמָיו״!

[5]אֵימָא: יִתְקַיֵּים מֵחוֹתְמָיו, [21A] דְּשָׁיְילִינַן לְהוּ לְסָהֲדֵי אִי פָּרוּעַ, אִי לָא פָּרוּעַ.

[6]תָּא שְׁמַע: ״סִמְפּוֹן שֶׁיֵּשׁ עָלָיו עֵדִים כָּשֵׁר״.

LITERAL TRANSLATION

[1]Come [and] hear: ["We declare on] oath that father did not instruct us, and that father did not tell us, [2]and that we did not find [a note] among father's documents [stating] that this [promissory] note was repaid.'"

[3]Rav Safra said: Where it was found among torn notes.

[4]Come [and] hear: "A note of cancellation which has [the signatures of] witnesses on it, should be authenticated by the signatures on it."

[5]Say: It should be authenticated by those who signed it. [21A] For we ask the witnesses if it has been repaid, [or] if it has not been repaid.

[6]Come [and] hear: "A note of cancellation that has witnesses on it is valid."

RASHI

שבועה שלא פקדנו אבא – משנה היא בשבועות (מה,א): יתומין מן היתומין לא יפרעו אלא בשבועה. ומהו שבועתן – שבועה שלא יפקדנו אבא בצואת מיתה, ושלא יאמר לנו קודם לכן, ושלא מצינו שובר בין שטרותיו של אבא על שטר זה שהיה פרוע. הא אם מצאו – סמכינן עליה. **יתקיים בחותמיו** – קא סלקא דעתך אם אמר מלוה ״לא נפרעתי, ותדע, שהרי לא מסרתי לידך״ – יתקיים בחותמיו. על פי חותמיו יתקיים, אם החותמיו מעידין שחתמוהו – אין המלוה נאמן, אבל כל כמה דלא מקיים – מהימן. דמאן מפיק ליה – מלוה, ומלוה הא אמר פסול הוא. **דשיילינן להו** – אם ראו הפרעון. ואם לאו – נאמן המלוה לומר שלא נכתב אלא להיות מוכן לכשיפרע.

NOTES

שֶׁלֹּא פְּקָדָנוּ אַבָּא וְלֹא אָמַר לָנוּ **Our father did not instruct us and did not tell us.** What is the difference between "instructing" and "telling"? The commentary here follows *Rashi*, who said: Our father did not instruct us on his deathbed, nor did he tell us on an earlier occasion. *Meiri* offers an alternative explanation: He did not charge us through an intermediary and did not tell us himself. Others explain: He did not instruct us to return this note and did not tell us that the debt had been paid (*Talmid Rabbenu Peretz*).

דְּשָׁיְילִינַן לְהוּ לְסָהֲדֵי **For we ask the witnesses.** As a general rule witnesses do not simply sign a document: they testify that an act has taken place (although they are not responsible for the accuracy of details that are not essential to the document). The fact that the witnesses have signed the document is testimony that an act has taken place, and they may not retract or change that testimony. But if doubt arises, one can always ask the witnesses in order to clarify just what took place.

HALAKHAH

שֶׁלֹּא פְּקָדָנוּ אַבָּא **Our father did not instruct us.** "If a lender's heirs seek to collect the debt due him, and the borrower maintains that he has already repaid the father (and the orphans do not know whether or not this is true), the borrower must pay. If the borrower insists on having the orphans take an oath, they must swear that their father never told them that the debt had been repaid, and that they did not find any receipt among his promissory notes, etc." (Ibid., 108:5.)

TRANSLATION AND COMMENTARY

מַאי עֵדִים [1]The Gemara answers: **What is** the meaning of the word **"witnesses"** here? **Witnesses** to the fact **that** the note of cancellation **was certified** in court. Clearly the court would not certify the note unless they were sure that the debt had been repaid.

הָכִי נַמִי מִסְתַּבְּרָא [2]**Indeed,** notes the Gemara, **this** interpretation of the Baraita just cited **stands to reason**, because it has independent support from the language of the Baraita itself. **For the last clause** of the Baraita **teaches** as follows: **"But** a note of cancellation **that has no witnesses on it is invalid."** [3]Now, **what is** the meaning of the words: "A note of cancellation **that has no witnesses on it"**? [4]**If you say that** it means: **"It has no witnesses on it at all," is it necessary** for the Baraita **to say that it is invalid**? It is obvious that a document without witnesses is worthless, since no one attests to its authenticity!

אֶלָּא לָאו [5]**Rather, was not** the intention of the Baraita to teach that the note is invalid because it has no **witnesses** to the fact **that it was certified** in court?! The statement of Rav Yirmeyah bar Abba in the name of Rav thus remains unrefuted, and is, in fact, supported by this Baraita.

גּוּפָא [6]**Returning to the subject** discussed in an earlier Baraita: **"A note of cancellation that has** the signatures of **witnesses on it should be authenticated by the signatures on it.** [7]Likewise, a note of cancellation **that does not have the signatures of witnesses on it, but was produced by a third party**, to whom it was entrusted by lender and borrower, **or** a note of cancellation **that appears** on the promissory note itself **below the signatures on the document, is valid**." [8]The Gemara now explains that **"one that is produced by a third party"** is valid,

[1]מַאי ״עֵדִים״? עֵדֵי קִיּוּם. [2]הָכִי נַמִי מִסְתַּבְּרָא, מִדְּקָתָנֵי סֵיפָא: ״וְשֶׁאֵין עָלָיו עֵדִים פָּסוּל״. [3]מַאי ״אֵין עָלָיו עֵדִים״? [4]אִילֵימָא דְּלֵיכָּא עֲלָוֵיהּ עֵדִים כְּלָל, צְרִיכָא לְמֵימַר דְּפָסוּל? [5]אֶלָּא לָאו עֵדֵי קִיּוּם. [6]גּוּפָא: ״סִמְפּוֹן שֶׁיֵּשׁ עָלָיו עֵדִים יִתְקַיֵּים בְּחוֹתְמָיו. [7]אֵין עָלָיו עֵדִים, וְיוֹצֵא מִתַּחַת יְדֵי שָׁלִישׁ, אוֹ שֶׁיּוֹצֵא לְאַחַר חִיתּוּם שְׁטָרוֹת, כָּשֵׁר״. [8]״יוֹצֵא מִתַּחַת

LITERAL TRANSLATION

[1]What are "witnesses"? Witnesses [that it was] certified.

[2]Indeed, this stands to reason, for the last clause teaches: "But [one] that has no witnesses on it is invalid." [3]What is "one that has no witnesses on it"? [4]If you say that there are no witnesses on it at all, is it necessary to say that it is invalid?

[5]Rather, is it not [referring to] witnesses [that it was] certified.

[6]Returning to the subject (lit., "the thing itself"): "A note of cancellation that has [the signatures of] witnesses on it should be authenticated by the signatures on it. [7]One that does not have [the signatures of] witnesses on it and is produced by a third party, or one that appears below (lit., 'after') the document's signatures, is valid."

[8]"One that is produced

RASHI

עדי קיום – שכתבו הנפק, דבי דינא לא מקיימי ליה אלא אם כן פרע. סמפון שיש עליו עדים – בעדי קיום מוקמינן לה. יתקיים בחותמיו – ואפילו יוצא מתחת יד מלוה – כשר. אין עליו עדי קיום – אבל עדים חתומין עליו. ויוצא מתחת ידי שליש – שאין הלוה מוליאו ולא המלוה, אלא שליש שביניהם – נאמן. או שיוצא אחר חיתום שטרות – שיצא לפנינו כשהוא כתוב בשטר חוב אחר החתימה – כשר.

LANGUAGE

שָׁלִישׁ **A third party.** In the Bible the meaning of this word is a commander, an army officer. There, too, the root of the word is שלש (three), meaning the third man in the hierarchy, the third man on a chariot, etc. In Rabbinic Hebrew a שָׁלִישׁ is a third person to whom the two parties to a dispute entrust the documents in their possession, or someone who acts as a liaison between the two parties. Here, too, the word means someone appointed, for the third man has been appointed by at least one of the other two.

NOTES

שְׁטָר הַיּוֹצֵא מִתַּחַת יַד שָׁלִישׁ **A note of cancellation produced by a third party is valid**. Numerous interpretations of this ruling have been offered. Some authorities maintain that the promissory note must also be in the possession of the third party; otherwise, we cannot believe the third party when he says that it was the borrower who entrusted the receipt to him (*Rabbenu Tam, Ra'avad, Meiri*). Other commentators object: The point of entrusting a promissory note to a third party is for him to determine when the debtor has repaid. Hence, if the third party had the promissory note itself, the Baraita would not need to tell us that we believe him about the receipt; he

HALAKHAH

סִמְפּוֹן שֶׁיֵּשׁ עָלָיו עֵדִים **A note of cancellation signed by witnesses**. "If the lender produces a receipt signed by witnesses, and the witnesses confirm (orally) that the loan has been repaid, they are believed. If they do not know whether the loan was repaid, of if they are not available to be asked, the receipt is not valid, unless it has been certified by the court," following the Gemara. (*Shulḥan Arukh, Ḥoshen Mishpat* 65:18.)

סִמְפּוֹן יוֹצֵא מִתַּחַת יְדֵי שָׁלִישׁ **A note of cancellation produced by a third party**. "If both the note of cancellation and the promissory note which it purports to cancel were in the possession of a third party, who claims that the debt was repaid, the note is valid even if the court had previously seen that it was in his possession, and even if the receipt was not signed by witnesses, and even after the third party has died.

But if the third party possessed only the note of cancellation, but not the promissory note, the note is not valid, unless it was signed by witnesses and their signatures were authenticated in court," following the view of *Rabbenu Tam* (see notes). (Ibid., 65:19.)

TRANSLATION AND COMMENTARY

because the lender trusted the third party, as shown by the fact that he entrusted the note of cancellation to him; hence, the third party is believed when he claims that the debt was repaid. [1]"A note of cancellation **that appears below the signatures on the document"** is valid too, [2]**because if the debt had not been repaid, the lender would not have invalidated his own promissory note** by writing a note of cancellation on the promissory note itself.

יְדֵי שָׁלִישׁ", דְּהָא הֵימְנֵיהּ מַלְוֶה לְשָׁלִישׁ. [1]"יוֹצֵא לְאַחַר חִיתּוּם שְׁטָרוֹת" נַמִי, [2]דְּאִי לָאו דְּפְרִיעַ, לָא הֲוָה מֵרַע לֵיהּ לִשְׁטָרֵיהּ.

הדרן עלך שנים אוחזין

LITERAL TRANSLATION

by a third party" [is valid], because the lender trusted the third party. [1]"One that appears below the document's signatures" [is valid] too, [2]because if [the debt] had not been repaid, [the lender] would not have invalidated his [own promissory] note.

RASHI

דהא הימניה מלוה לשליש – דעל כרחך אין כותב שובר אלא מלוה, והוא מסרו ליד השליש.

הדרן עלך שנים אוחזין

NOTES

would be believed even without a receipt! Rather, the Baraita must be telling us that a third party in possession of a properly drawn up and witnessed receipt is believed when he claims to have been given it by the borrower, even though he is not in possession of the note itself (*Rashba*).

Moreover, the Rishonim point out: It is also obvious that if a third party were to come forward of his own volition and announce that he had a previously unknown receipt, he would be believed, since if he were attempting to defraud the lender he could have given the receipt to the borrower instead of making an announcement. Therefore, the Baraita must refer to a case where the court already knew that the receipt was in the third party's possession before he made his announcement (*Rosh* and *Ran*).

HALAKHAH

סִמְפּוֹן עַל הַשְּׁטָר A note of cancellation written on the promissory note itself. "A note of cancellation appearing on the promissory note itself is valid, even if it was produced by the lender and even if it was not signed." (Ibid., 65:20.)

Conclusion to Chapter One

One of the basic conclusions of the chapter was the determination, contrary to the opinion of Summakhos, that when the ownership of property is in doubt, the burden of proof rests on the person seeking to extract it from whoever is in possession of it (הַמּוֹצִיא מֵחֲבֵירוֹ עָלָיו הָרְאָיָה). For this reason, a significant number of discussions in the chapter deal with cases where it is not clear which claimant is in possession and which is seeking to take possession. Essentially, it was concluded that physical possession of an object, of which prior proof of ownership is lacking, in itself confers at least a claim to ownership. The validity and extent of this claim are determined according to the nature of the possession — in quantitative terms (how much of the body of the object is actually held by the claimant) and, no less important, how the object is being held. Seeing an object and proclaiming ownership of it constitute ineffective means of acquisition. By contrast, physical possession of the object, if combined with the intention of acquiring it, does confer ownership, as long as the act of acquisition is performed properly (for example, pulling and driving an animal confer ownership more effectively than riding or holding it).

We also learned that a person's field (and, by extension, the four cubits around him) confer ownership in certain cases, though this method has a number of limitations: the person must positively intend to acquire the object, and the act of acquisition is only valid if no one else had a prior claim to it, etc.

Another principle underlying the discussion in this chapter is the Halakhic assumption that both sides in a dispute are, at least in their own view, telling the truth, as long as this assumption is not contradicted by the facts. Moreover, even if we suspect that a litigant's claim is false, this in itself is not necessarily proof that he is an inveterate liar and entirely untrustworthy; rather, we consider his claim as an attempt at evasion, a view which receives additional support from the general principle that a person suspect in monetary matters is not necessarily suspected of perjury. For this reason the court administers an oath as a means of ultimately determining the validity of the claims.

Another subject discussed in this chapter was the protection of a third party's rights when only two claimants appear in court. Wherever there are reasons to suspect that damage may be caused to a third party who is not represented in court, the current situation is frozen, unless there is some way of ensuring that no one else will be harmed by a division of property or compromise between the two claimants. This only applies when the two claims are of equal weight, for a court may sometimes determine (on the basis of logic or experience) which of the two claims is the more convincing, and in such a case, even though complete proof is lacking, it may award full rights of ownership to one of the claimants.

These discussions form a basic introduction to the subjects to be considered in the next chapter — the laws of the restoration of lost property.

List of Sources

Agudah, Halakhic work by Rabbi Alexander Zuslin HaKohen, Germany (d. 1349).

Aḥaronim, lit., "the last," meaning Rabbinical authorities from the time of the publication of Rabbi Yosef Caro's code of Halakhah, the *Shulḥan Arukh* (1555).

Arukh HaShalem, Aramaic dictionary edited by Alexander Kohut (1894) on the basis of the *Arukh* by Rabbi Natan of Rome (11th century).

Baḥ (Bayit Ḥadash), commentary on the *Arba'ah Turim* by Rabbi Yoel Sirkes, Poland (1561-1640).

Ba'al HaMa'or, Rabbi Zeraḥyah ben Yitzḥak HaLevi, Spain, 12th century. *HaMa'or*, Halakhic commentary on *Hilkhot HaRif*.

Bertinoro, Ovadyah 15th century Italian commentator on the Mishnah.

Bet Yosef, a Halakhic commentary on the *Arba'ah Turim* by Rabbi Yosef Caro (1488-1575), which is the basis of his authoritative Halakhic code, the *Shulḥan Arukh*.

Ein Yehosef, novellae on *Bava Metzia* by Rabbi Yosef Ḥazan, Turkey (c. 1615-1700).

Even HaEzer, the section of the *Shulḥan Arukh* dealing with marriage, divorce, and related topics.

Geon Tzvi, novellae on *Bava Metzia* by Rabbi Tzvi bar Rabbi Yehudah. Poland, 18th-19th century.

Geonim, the heads of the academies of Sura and Pumbedita in Babylonia from the late 6th century to the mid-11th century.

Gra, Rabbi Eliyahu ben Shlomo Zalman (1720-1797), the Gaon of Vilna. Novellae on the Talmud and *Shulḥan Arukh*.

Hagahot Maimoniyot, commentary on the *Mishneh Torah* by Rabbi Meir HaKohen, Germany, 14th century.

Ḥavvat Da'at, novellae on *Shulḥan Arukh*, *Yoreh De'ah*, by Rabbi Ya'akov Lorberboim of Lissa, Poland (1760-1832).

Ḥayyim Shenayim Yeshallem, novellae on Bava Metzia by Rabbi Shmuel Vital.

Ḥiddushei HaRim, novellae on the Talmud and the *Shulḥan Arukh*, by Rabbi Meir (Rothenberg) Alter, Poland (1789-1866).

Ḥokhmat Manoaḥ, commentary on the Talmud by Rabbi Manoaḥ ben Shemaryah, Poland, 16th century.

Ḥoshen Mishpat, section of the *Shulḥan Arukh* dealing with civil and criminal law.

Imrei Binah, commentary on the *Shulḥan Arukh* by Rabbi Meir Auerbach, b. Poland, active in Jerusalem (1815-1878).

Ittur, Halakhic work by Rabbi Yitzḥak Abba Mari, Provence (1122-1193).

Kehillot Ya'akov, novellae on *Bava Metzia* by Rabbi Ya'akov Kaneyevsky, Lithuania-Eretz Israel (1899-1985).

Kesef Mishneh, commentary on the *Mishneh Torah* by Rabbi Yosef Caro, author of the *Shulḥan Arukh*.

Ketzot HaḤoshen, novellae on *Shulḥan Arukh*, *Ḥoshen Mishpat* by Rabbi Arieh Leib Heller, Galicia (1754?-1813).

Levush, abbreviation of *Levush Mordekhai*, Halakhic code by Rabbi Mordekhai Yafe, Poland (1530-1612).

Ma'ayan HaḤokhmah, novellae on the Talmud by Rabbi Yosef Moshe of Zolishtik, Poland, 17th-18th century.

Maggid Mishneh, commentary on *Mishneh Torah* by Rabbi Vidal de Tolosa, Spain 14th century.

MaHaram Schiff, novellae on the Talmud by Rabbi Meir ben Ya'akov HaKohen Schiff (1605-1641), Frankfurt, Germany.

Mahari ben Lev, summary of responsa and commentary by Rabbi Yosef ben Lev, Turkey (c. 1500-1580).

Me'il Shmuel, novellae on the Talmud by Rabbi Shmuel Shapira, Lithuania, 19th century.

Meiri, commentary on the Talmud (called *Bet HaBeḥirah*) by Rabbi Menaḥem ben Shlomo, Provence (1249-1316).

Melo HaRo'im, commentary on the Talmud by Rabbi Ya'akov Tzvi Yolles, Poland (c. 1778-1825).

Minḥat Ḥinnukh, commentary on *Sefer HaḤinnukh* by Rabbi Yosef Babad, Poland (1800-1874/5).

Mordekhai, compendium of Halakhic decisions by Rabbi Mordekhai ben Hillel HaKohen, Germany (1240?-1298).

Naḥalat Yisrael, novellae on *Bava Metzia*, by Rabbi Yisrael Heller, Poland, 19th century.

Netivot, short title of *Netivot Hamishpat*, commentary on *Shulḥan Arukh*, *Ḥoshen Mishpat*, by Rabbi Ya'akov Lorberboim of Lissa, Poland (1760-1832).

Nimmukei Yosef, commentary on *Hilkhot HaRif* by Rabbi Yosef Ḥaviva, Spain, early 15th century.

Otzar HaGeonim, 13 vol. collection of commentaries on the Talmud compiled from the Geonic literature by Dr. Binyamin Menashe Lewin, b. Russia (1879-1944).

Pnei Yehoshua, novellae on the Talmud by Rabbi Ya'akov Yehoshua Falk, Poland-Germany (1680-1756).

Ra'avad, Rabbi Avraham ben David, commentator and Halakhic authority. Wrote comments on the *Mishneh Torah*. Provence (c. 1125-1198?).

Rabbenu Efraim, Efraim Ibn Avi Alragan, Halakhist, North Africa, late 11th-early 12th century.

Rabbenu Hananel (ben Ḥushiel), commentator on Talmud, North Africa (990-1055).

Rabbenu Peretz, Peretz ben Eliyahu of Corbeil, France (died c. 1295).

Rabbenu Tam, commentator on Talmud, Tosafist, France (1100-1171).

Rabbenu Yehonatan, Yehonatan ben David HaKohen of Lunel, Provence, Talmudic Scholar (c. 1135-after 1210).

Rabbi Akiva Eger, Talmudist and Halakhic authority, Posen, Germany (1761-1837).

Rabbi Avraham Av Bet Din, Rabbi Avraham ben Yitzḥak, author of the Halakhic work *HaEshkol*. Provence (c. 1080-1158).

Rabbi Elhanan Wasserman, Lithuanian Talmud scholar and Halakhic authority (1875-1941).

Rabbi Ya'akov Emden, Talmudist and Halakhic authority, Germany (1697-1776).

Rabbi Zvi Ḥayyot (Chajes), Galician Rabbi, 19th century.

Rambam, Rabbi Moshe ben Maimon, Rabbi and philosopher, known also as Maimonides. Author of *Mishneh Torah*, Spain-Egypt (1135-1204).

Ramban, Rabbi Moshe ben Nahman, Rabbi and Biblical commentator, known also as Nahmanides, Spain-Eretz Israel (1194-1270).

Ran, Rabbi Nissim ben Reuven Gerondi, Spanish Talmudist (1310?-1375?).

Rash, Rabbi Shimshon ben Avraham, Tosafist, commentator on the Mishnah, Sens (late 12th-early 13th century).

Rashal, Rabbi Shlomo Luria, Talmudist, Poland (c. 1510-1573).

Rashash, Rabbi Shmuel ben Yosef Shtrashun, Lithuanian Talmud scholar (1794-1872).

Rashba, Rabbi Shlomo ben Avraham Adret, Spanish Rabbi famous for his commentaries on the Talmud and his responsa (c. 1235-c. 1314).

Rashbam, Rabbi Shmuel ben Meir, commentator of the Talmud (1085-1158).

Rashbatz, Rabbi Shimon ben Tzemaḥ Duran, known for his book of responsa, *Tashbetz*, b. Spain (1361-1444).

Rashi, Rabbi Shlomo b. Yitzḥak, the paramount commentator on the Bible and the Talmud, France (1040-1105).

Rav Hai Gaon, Babylonian Rabbi, head of Pumbedita Yeshivah, 10th century.

Rav Yehudai Gaon, Gaon of Sura, 8th century.

Razah, Rabbi Zeraḥyah HaLevi, see *Ba'al HaMa'or*.

Rema, Rabbi Moshe ben Yisrael Isserles, Halakhic authority, Poland (1525 or 1530-1572).

Remah, novellae on the Talmud by Rabbi Meir HaLevi Abulafya, Spain (c. 1170-1244).

Ri, Rabbi Yitzhak ben Shmuel of Dampierre, Tosafist, France (died c. 1185).

Ri Aboab, Rabbi Yitzḥak Aboab, Spain (the younger: 15th century).

Ri Migash, Rabbi Yosef ben Migash, commentator of the Talmud, Spain (1077-1141).

Rid, see *Tosefot Rid*.

Rif, Rabbi Yitzḥak Alfasi, Halakhist, author of *Hilkhot HaRif*, North Africa (1013-1103).

Rishonim, lit., "the first," meaning Rabbinical authorities active between the end of the Geonic period (mid-11th century) and the publication of the *Shulḥan Arukh* (1555).

Ritva, novellae and commentary on the Talmud by Rabbi Yom Tov ben Avraham Ishbili, Spain (c. 1250-1330).

Ritzbash, novellae of Rabbi Yitzhak bar Sheshet, Derfet, Spain (1326-1408).

Rivan, Rabbi Yehudah ben Natan, French Tosafist, 11th-12th centuries.

Rosh, Rabbi Asher ben Yeḥiel, also known as *Asheri*, commentator and Halakhist, Germany-Spain (c. 1250-1327).

Sefer HaHashlamah, supplement to *Hilkhot HaRif*, by Rabbi Meshullam ben Moshe, Provence, early 13th century.

Sefer HaTerumot, Halakhic work by Rabbi Shmuel ben Yitzḥak Sardi, Spain (1185/90-1255/56).

Sefer HaYashar, novellae on the Talmud by Rabbenu Tam. France (c. 1100-1171).

Shakh (Sifte Kohen), commentary on *Shulḥan Arukh* by Rabbi Shabbetai ben Meir HaKohen, Lithuania (1621-1662).

Shittah Mekubbetzet, a collection of commentaries on the Talmud by Rabbi Betzalel ben Avraham Ashkenazi of Safed (c. 1520-1591).

Shulḥan Arukh, the code of Halakhah by Rabbi Yosef Caro, b. Spain, active in Eretz Israel (1488-1575).

Sma (Sefer Meirat Einaim), commentary on *Shulḥan Arukh Ḥoshen Mishpat*, by Rabbi Yehoshua Falk Katz, Poland (c. 1550-1614).

Talmid Rabbenu Peretz, commentary on *Bava Metzia* by the school of the Tosafist Rabbi Peretz of Corbeil, France (13th century).

Talmidei Rabbenu Yonah, commentary on *Hilkhot HaRif*, by the school of Rabbi Yonah of Gerondi, Spain (c. 1190-1263).

Torat Ḥayyim, novellae on the Talmud by Rabbi Avraham Ḥayyim Shor, Galicia (d. 1632).

Tosafot, a collection of commentaries and novellae on the Talmud, expanding on Rashi's commentary, by the French-German Tosafists (12th-13th centuries).

Tosefot HaRosh, an edition based on *Tosefot Sens* by the *Rosh*, Rabbi Asher ben Yeḥiel, Germany-Spain (c. 1250-1327).

Tosefot Rid, commentary on the Talmud by Rabbi Yeshayahu ben Mali di Trani, Italian Halakhist (c. 1200-before 1260).

Tosefot Sens, the first important collection of Tosafot, by Rabbi Shimshon of Sens (late 12th-early 13th century).

Tosefot Yom Tov, commentary on the Mishnah by Rabbi Yom Tov Lipman HaLevi Heller, Prague and Poland (1579-1654).

Tummim, abbreviation of *Urim VeTummim*, commentary on *Shulḥan Arukh, Ḥoshen Mishpat*, by Rabbi Yehonatan Eibeschuetz, Poland-Germany (c. 1690-1764).

Tur, abbreviation of *Arba'ah Turim*, Halakhic code by Rabbi Ya'akov ben Asher, b. Germany, active in Spain (c.1270-1343).

Tzafnat Pa'aneaḥ, novellae and commentaries by Rabbi Yosef Rozin, Lithuania (1858-1936).

Yeshuot Ya'akov, novellae on Shulḥan Arukh, by Rabbi Ya'akov Orenstein, Poland (1775-1839).

Yoreh De'ah, section of *Shulḥan Arukh* dealing with dietary laws, interest, ritual purity, and mourning.